# Wiersbe's

# Expository

# Outlines

## on the

# Old Testament

# WIERSBE'S EXPOSITORY OUTLINES ON THE OLD TESTAMENT

## WARREN W. WIERSBE

VICTOR BOOKS

A DIVISION OF SCRIPTURE PRESS PUBLICATIONS INC.
USA CANADA ENGLAND

Copyediting: Miriam Mindeman, Robert N. Hosack
Cover Design: Scott Rattray

---

### Library of Congress Cataloging-in-Publication Data

Wiersbe, Warren W.
     [Expository outlines on the Old Testament]
     Wiersbe's expository outlines on the Old Testament / by Warren W. Wiersbe.
          p.   cm.
     Includes index.
     ISBN 0-89693-847-6
     1. Bible   O.T.—Commentaries.   2. Bible. O.T.—Outlines, syllabi, etc.   3. Bible. O.T.—Homiletical use.   I. Title.   II. Title: Expository outlines on the Old Testament.
     BS491.2.W5   1993
     221.7—dc20                                                      92-40776
                                                                          CIP

---

1   2   3   4   5   6   7   8   9   10   Printing/Year   97   96   95   94   93

# CONTENTS

DEDICATED WITH GRATEFUL APPRECIATION
TO THE MEMORY OF DR. D.B. EASTEP (1900–1962),
A LOVING AND FAITHFUL PASTOR,
A GIFTED EXPOSITOR OF THE WORD,
A GODLY MENTOR TO ALL PASTORS.

# PREFACE

The purpose of this book is to take you through the Old Testament and give you the opportunity to study each book and.its strategic chapters to learn how they fit into the total revelation God has given us of Christ and His redemptive work. The studies are concise and practical and are especially suitable for Sunday School classes and Bible study groups that want to examine God's Word in a systematic manner.

These studies grew out of the lessons I prepared for the Calvary Baptist Church, Covington, Kentucky, when I ministered there from 1961 to 1971. My godly predecessor, Dr. D.B. Eastep, had devised "The Whole Bible Study Course" which took the student through the Bible in seven years, three years in the Old Testament and four years in the New Testament. The lessons were duplicated and distributed week by week to the Bible School students. When requests began to come from other churches that wanted to follow the same study schedule, eventually the lessons were assembled in notebook form and published by the Calvary Book Room, the literature ministry of the church. Thousands of sets of these outlines have been distributed throughout the world, and the Lord has seen fit to bless them in a singular way.

When I decided it was time to publish the studies in a more permanent form, I approached Mark Sweeney at Victor Books; and he was more than glad to work with me on the project. I have revised and updated the material and added a section on 1 and 2 Chronicles which was not in the original studies; but there has been no change in the theological position or the basic interpretations.

If you have used any of the volumes in my *BE* series, you will recognize a similar approach in these studies. However, there is material in this volume that is not found in the *BE* series; and it focuses on strategic chapters rather than a verse-by-verse approach. Even if you have my *Bible Exposition Commentary*, you will find this new volume helpful in your studies.

I want to record my deep appreciation to Mrs. D.B. Eastep, for many years manager of the Calvary Book Room, who supervised the publishing and distributing of the original *Expository Outlines on the Old Testament*. She and her staff accepted this difficult task as a ministry of love for which the Lord will abundantly reward them. I can't begin to name individually all the dear people at Calvary

Baptist Church who have had a part in producing the original lesson sheets and then the notebooks, but they know who they are and that I love them and appreciate their sacrificial ministries. Some of them are in heaven and know firsthand how God has used these simple studies around the world to win the lost and build His church.

My editor at Victor Books, Robert Hosack, deserves special thanks for his patience and encouragement, particularly when I was struggling to get the computer program working right so I could edit the material quickly.

Finally, my wife Betty is surely being measured for a special crown to reward her for all the hours she gave me for Bible study and writing while these studies were in preparation. It wasn't easy for the pastor of a large and growing church, and the father of four active children, to carve out time to write these lessons; but Betty was always there to keep the household running smoothly, handle the phone calls and interruptions, and encourage me to practice Paul's philosophy of "this one thing I do."

My prayer is that this new edition of *Wiersbe's Expository Outlines on the Old Testament* will have a wide and fruitful ministry to the glory of God.

Warren W. Wiersbe

# *Introductory Notes to the Old Testament*

## I. Name

The word "testament" means "covenant," referring to an agreement between men or between God and men. As far as the Bible is concerned, the Old Testament is the record of the old covenant, the covenant God made with the Jews at Mt. Sinai; and the New Testament is the record of the new covenant that Christ made through His blood. From a literary standpoint, the OT begins with Genesis and ends with Malachi, while the NT begins with Matthew and ends with Revelation. However, from a doctrinal and dispensational point of view, this is not the case; for the old covenant really began in Ex. 20 and was set aside at the cross (Col. 2:14). The new covenant began with the death of Christ and will continue with God's people forever. In a broad sense, we might say that the OT is the record of God's dealings with His earthly people under law, and the NT is the record of God's dealings with His heavenly people (the church) under grace. The dividing line is the cross, not the blank page between Malachi and Matthew!

## II. Purpose

Too many Christians avoid the OT, thinking that it has no message for them or that it is too difficult to understand. But please realize that the OT was the only Bible that Christ, the apostles, and the early church possessed. When Paul referred to "Scripture," he was thinking of the OT books. Practically every book in the OT is quoted or referred to in the NT writings. Consider the fourfold purpose of the OT writings:

### A. Foundation.

We would have no information concerning the origin of the universe, the origin of man, the beginnings of sin, the birth of the Hebrew nation, or the purposes of God for the world, were it not for the OT record. Every NT doctrine can be traced back to OT history. An understanding of the OT record is necessary if we are to interpret the NT correctly.

### B. Preparation.

The OT reveals God's preparation for the coming of His Son into the world. In Genesis we see the need for a Savior and the promise that He will come through the woman, through the Jewish nation, and through the tribe of Judah. The rest of the OT amplifies these basic facts and shows how Satan tried to destroy the Jewish nation to prevent the birth of Christ. Genesis 3:15 indicates that there are two "seeds" in conflict in the world, the seed of Satan and the seed of Christ, and we see this conflict from Genesis 4 onward.

## C. *Illustration.*

The OT is God's picture gallery, in which He often shows His truth in types and symbols. Each NT doctrine has an OT illustration. The Passover Lamb of Ex. 12 is a picture of Christ (John 1:29; 1 Cor. 5:7). The OT tabernacle illustrates the resurrection; the anointing oil pictures the Holy Spirit; etc. As you study the OT, be sure to use the light of the NT to dispel the shadows (Col. 1:17), and be sure to look for the Person and work of Christ.

## D. *Demonstration.*

The OT is a practical book, showing the failures and successes of the people of God. We see God demonstrating His power in the lives of people, but we also see what sin and unbelief will do to people. God recorded these sins and successes for our benefit (1 Cor. 10:11). As we see men like Abraham, Moses, and David overcoming their problems by faith, we have encouragement and hope (Rom. 15:4). The prayers of the Psalms and the practical counsels of Proverbs can help us in our daily lives if we will "trust and obey."

Dr. Griffith-Thomas in his excellent book *Methods of Bible Study* suggests that the OT is a book of: (1) unfulfilled prophecies, (2) unexplained ceremonies, and (3) unsatisfied longings. In the NT we have the fulfillment of these prophecies, the explanation of these ceremonies, and the satisfying of these longings; and, of course, all of this was accomplished through the birth, life, death, and resurrection of Jesus Christ.

## III. Analysis

In each division of the Bible, you find historical events, personal experience, and prophetic expectation. The OT gives us the history of God's earthly people, Israel, as they prepared the way for Christ's birth, and the NT gives us the history of the church as

God's people live for Christ and look forward to His coming again. You may outline the main messages of the OT as follows:

*Foundation* — Genesis–Deuteronomy: the foundation for the rest of the Bible record.

*Demonstration* — Joshua–Esther: God at work in individual lives and in the nation.

*Aspiration* — Job–Song of Solomon: the longings of God's people for personal experience with their Lord.

*Expectation* — Isaiah–Malachi: prophecies of the coming Christ and the righteous kingdom of God.

## IV. Principles of Study

### A. Progressive revelation.

In the OT divine truths are revealed gradually, and we do not come into the full light of God's truth until we come to the NT. Therefore, beware of building doctrines on isolated OT verses, especially from Ecclesiastes and Psalms, and ignoring the clear teachings of the NT. Remember the old adage: "The New is in the Old concealed; the Old is by the New revealed." God's principles do not change, but His dispensations do.

### B. Christ.

Our Lord Jesus Christ is the key to the Bible, and it is impossible to understand the OT apart from Him. As Graham Scroggie aptly puts it, "Christ is predicted in the OT, present in the Gospels, proclaimed in the Acts, possessed in the Epistles, and predominant in the Revelation." The experiences of the Jewish nation in the OT are links in the chain that leads to His birth at Bethlehem. Every type and symbol is a picture of Him. Look for Christ and the OT will become a new book to you!

### C. Cross references.

Follow your OT cross references straight to the NT. The American Standard Version has one of the best systems of cross references available, and the New International Version is also very good. You may want to purchase R.A. Torrey's classic work *The Treasury of Scripture Knowledge,* a book of half-a-million cross references covering nearly every verse in the Bible. Be sure that you study each OT person, event, or doctrine in the light of the NT revelation. This will add a whole new dimension to your study.

### D. Obedience.

It is not enough to study the OT and find wonderful truths about Christ and His salvation. We must learn the practical lessons and put them to work in our lives! "All Scripture . . . is profitable for . . . instruction in righteousness . . ." (2 Tim. 3:16-17), and this includes the OT. It is wonderful to understand historical truth, doctrinal truth, and dispensational truth, but if our study fails to lead to practical truth—godly living—it is in vain.

# GENESIS

## *A Suggested Outline of Genesis*

I. History of Humanity in General (1–11)

  A. Creation of the heavens and earth (1–2)

  B. Adam and his family (3–5)
     The Fall of man (3)

  C. Noah and his family (6–11)
     The Flood (6–10)
     The Babel rebellion (11)

II. History of Israel in Particular (12–50)

  A. Abraham—The father who gave his son (12:1–25:18)

  B. Isaac—The son who took a bride (25:19–26:35)

  C. Jacob—The flesh vs. the Spirit (27:1–36:43)

  D. Joseph—The providence of God (37:1–50:26)

# *Introductory Notes to Genesis*

## I. Name

"Genesis" is from a Greek word meaning "beginning" or "generation." The word "genesis" is translated "generation" in Matt. 1:1. Genesis is the book of generations, or beginnings. There are ten generations noted in the book: the heavens and earth (2:4); Adam (5:1); Noah (6:9); Shem (11:10); Terah (11:27); Ishmael (25:12); Isaac (25:19); Esau (36:1); and Jacob (37:2). As the seed-plot for the entire Bible, Genesis records for us the momentous beginning of the universe, human history, civilization, sin, salvation, sacrifice, marriage, and the family.

## II. Author

It is generally agreed that Moses is the author of the first five books of the Bible, called "the Pentateuch" (from the Gk., *penta*, "five" and *teuchos*, "the case books were kept in"). Of course, Moses was not alive when the events in Genesis occurred, but the Spirit directed him in his writing (2 Peter 1:20-21). Christ believed that Moses wrote the books assigned to him (see John 5:45-47), and that is good enough authority for us.

## III. Purpose

As you read Genesis, you cannot help but note that the first eleven chapters are general and without extensive detail; while the rest of the book, starting with chapter 12, gives the lives of four men in great detail: Abraham, Isaac, Jacob, and Joseph. As you will note in our suggested outline of Genesis, the first section (1–11) deals with humankind in general and explains the origin of man and sin, while the last section (12–50) deals with Israel in particular. This suggests that the purpose of the book is to explain the beginnings of man and his sin and Israel and God's plan of salvation. In fact, one of the key themes in Genesis is divine election.

We begin with "the heavens and the earth," but then God chooses to deal with the earth, not the heavens; the theme from then on is God's program on earth. Having chosen the earth, God now bypasses the angels (fallen angels included) and elects to deal with man. From Adam's many sons, God chooses Seth (4:25). Of

Seth's many descendants (Gen. 5), God chooses Noah (6:8), and from Noah's family, He chooses Shem (11:10), Terah (11:27), and finally Abraham (12:1). Abraham has many children, but Isaac is the chosen seed (21:12). Isaac has two sons, Jacob and Esau, and God chooses Jacob to be the recipient of His blessing.

All of this reveals God's gracious divine election. Not one of those people chosen deserved the honor; as is true for all believers, their election resulted fully from God's grace. Along with the electing grace of God, Genesis illustrates the wonderful power and providence of God. Men would disobey and doubt Him, yet He would rule and overrule to accomplish His purposes. Had His program failed in Genesis, there could have been no Messiah born in Bethlehem centuries later.

## IV. Genesis and Revelation

The beginnings recorded in Genesis have their fulfillment in Revelation. God created the heaven and the earth (Gen. 1:1) and will one day create a new heaven and new earth (Rev. 21:1). Satan first attacked man (Gen. 3) yet will be defeated in his last attack (Rev. 20:7-10). God made darkness and light (Gen. 1:5), but one day there will no longer be night (Rev. 21:23; 22:5). There will be no more sea (Gen. 1:10; Rev. 21:1), and the curse will be lifted from creation (Gen. 3:14-17; Rev. 22:3). God drove man out of the garden (Gen. 3:24), but God's people will be welcomed into the heavenly paradise (Rev. 22:1ff), and the tree of life will be restored to man (Rev. 22:14). Babylon will be destroyed (Gen. 10:8-10; Rev. 17-19) and the promised judgment of Satan fulfilled (Gen. 3:15; Rev. 20:10).

## V. Christ in Genesis

According to Luke 24:27, 44-45 Christ is found in "all the Scriptures." Following are but a few of the references to Christ in Genesis.
1. The creative Word—Gen. 1:3; John 1:1-5; 2 Cor. 4:3-7
2. The Last Adam—Rom. 5; 1 Cor. 15:45
3. The Seed of the woman—Gen. 3:15; Gal. 3:19; 4:4
4. Abel—Gen. 4; Heb. 11:4; 12:24
5. Noah and the flood—Gen. 6-10; 1 Peter 3:18-22
6. Melchizedek—Gen. 14; Heb. 7-10
7. Isaac, the child of promise—Gen. 17; Gal. 4:21-31 (Isaac pic-

tures Christ in his miraculous birth, his willingness to die, his "resurrection" [Heb. 11:19], and his taking of a bride. Of course, Jesus actually died and arose from the dead. In Isaac, these events were only symbolic.)

8. The Lamb—Gen. 22:7-8; John 1:29

9. Jacob's ladder—Gen. 28:12ff; John 1:51

10. Joseph—Gen. 37–50 (Rejected by His brothers; beloved of the Father; made to suffer unjustly; exalted to reign. Joseph's brothers did not recognize him the first time they saw him, but they did recognize him the second time. So with Israel is their recognition of their Messiah.)

# GENESIS 1

We will confine ourselves to some major truths found in this important passage.

## I. The Creator

No scientist or historian can improve upon, "In the beginning God...." This simple statement refutes the atheist, who says there is no God; the agnostic, who claims we cannot know God; the polytheist who worships many gods; the pantheist, who says that "all nature is God"; the materialist, who claims that matter is eternal and not created; and the fatalist, who teaches that there is no divine plan behind creation and history. God's personality is seen in this chapter, for He speaks, sees, names, and blesses. The scientist may claim that matter just "came into being," that life "happened," and that all complex forms of life "gradually evolved" from lower forms, but he cannot prove his claim. That there are changes within species (such as the development of the horse or the house cat) we admit, but that there are changes from one kind of creature into another, we will not accept. Why did God create the universe? Certainly not to add anything to Himself, since He needs nothing. Actually, creation limits God, since the Eternal must now confine Himself to work in time and human history. The Word makes it clear that Christ is the Author, Sustainer, and Goal of creation (Col. 1:15-17; Rev. 4:11). Christ, the Living Word, reveals God in the written Word and in the book of nature (John 1:1-5; also see Ps. 19).

What does creation reveal about God? Creation reveals: (1) His wisdom and power (Job 28:23-27; Prov. 3:19); (2) His glory (Ps. 19:1; (3) His power and Godhead (Rom. 1:18-21); (4) His love for insignificant man (Ps. 8:3-9); (5) His providential care (Isa. 40:12ff). Our Lord, when on earth, saw the gracious hand of the Father even in the flowers and fowl (Matt. 6:25ff).

The Hebrew name for God in Gen. 1 is *Elohim*—the name of God that links Him with creation. The basic root of the name is *El* which means "mighty, strong, prominent." In 2:4 we have "LORD God" which is *Jehovah Elohim. Jehovah* is the covenant name of God and links Him to His people. This is the name He gave when He spoke to Moses: "I AM WHO I AM" (Ex. 3:14-15, NKJV). It means that He is the self-existing, unchanging God.

## II. The Creation

The existence of the angels and the fall of Satan antedated the Creation, for the angels ("sons of God") sang at Creation (Job 38:7). Lucifer was the highest of God's created beings in this original Creation (see Ezek. 28:11-19) and wanted to take the place of God (Isa. 14:12-17). We find Satan already on the scene in Gen. 3, so that his fall must have taken place earlier.

The earth was formless, so on the first three days, God formed what He wanted. The earth was empty, so God filled up what He had formed. He made the expanse of the heavens ("firmament") and filled it with stars and planets. He made the land and filled it with plants and animals. He made the seas and filled them with fish and water mammals. God brought light into being before He placed the lights into the heavens. Note the principle of separation illustrated in Creation; for God divided light from darkness and seas from land (see 2 Cor. 6:14-18). Note too that each living thing was to reproduce "after its kind"; there is no suggestion here of gradual evolution. We may breed different kinds of cattle, but we cannot breed a cow into a reindeer!

Man is the crown of Creation. There is a "divine conference" among the members of the Godhead before man is created, something not seen at any other step of the Creation. Some of the angels had already rebelled against God, and He certainly knew what man would do. Yet, in His love and grace, He molded the first man "in His image," referring to man's personality—mind, will, emotions, freedom—rather than his physical appearance. (See Eph. 4:24; Col. 3:10.) Man was given the place of dominion over the earth, the highest position in Creation. This explains the attack of Satan; for Satan (Lucifer) had once held this position and had wanted an even higher one! If Lucifer could not have the place of God in the universe, then he would try to take the place of God in human's lives. And he succeeded! Man lost his dominion through sin (Ps. 8 and Heb. 2:5-18), but this dominion has been regained for us by Christ, the Last Adam (see Rom. 5). When on earth, Jesus proved that He had dominion over the fish (Luke 5; Matt. 17:24ff), the fowl (Matt. 26:74-75), and the beasts (Matt. 21:1-7).

Man's diet was originally vegetarian, but this was changed in Gen. 9:3-4. The Jews were given dietary restrictions (Lev. 11), but there are no such restrictions today (Mark 7:17-23; Acts 10:9-16; 1 Tim. 4:1-5).

## III. The New Creation

Second Corinthians 4:3-6 and 5:17 make it clear that, in Christ, God has a new creation. Paul uses imagery from the Genesis creation account to illustrate this new creation. Man was created perfect but was ruined through sin. He is born a sinner, "without form and void"; his life is purposeless and empty and dark.

The Holy Spirit begins His work of conviction "moving" in men's hearts (Gen. 1:2). Indeed, salvation always begins with the Lord (Jonah 2:9); it is of His grace that any sinner is ever saved. The Spirit uses the Word to bring light (Ps. 119:130), for there can be no salvation apart from the Word of God (John 5:24). And Heb. 4:12 says that the Word has the power to "divide," calling to mind God's earlier dividing of light and darkness, waters and land.

Like the created beings in Genesis, believers have the responsibility of being fruitful and multiplying "after their kind." In a parallel to Adam's position of dominion, the believer is part of royalty under God's rule and can "reign in life" through Christ (Rom. 5:17ff).

Just as Adam was the head of the old creation, so Christ is the Head of the new creation; He is the Last Adam (1 Cor. 15:45-49). The OT is the "book of the generations of Adam" (Gen. 5:1), and it ends speaking of a curse (Mal. 4:6). The NT is the "book of the generation of Jesus Christ" (Matt. 1:1), and it ends with "no more curse" (Rev. 22:3).

# GENESIS 2

## I. The First Sabbath (2:1-3)

The word "Sabbath" simply means "to cease." God did not "rest" because He was weary, since God does not become weary (Ps. 121:4). Rather, He ceased from His creative works; the task was now finished. He had blessed the creatures (1:22) and man (1:28). Now He blessed the Sabbath by setting it apart as a special day. There is no commandment here for people to observe the Sabbath. In fact, since Adam was created on the sixth day, the Sabbath Day was actually the first day for him.

The Sabbath does not appear again in the OT until Ex. 20:8-11, where God gave the Sabbath to Israel as His special covenant sign (Ex. 31:12-17). There is no evidence in Scripture that God ever told the Gentiles to observe the Sabbath; in fact, Ps. 147:19-20 makes it clear that the OT Mosaic Law was given only to Israel. One reason why Israel went into captivity was that the people profaned the Sabbath (Neh. 13:15-22). While on earth, Christ observed the Sabbath since He lived under the dispensation of law. Of course, He did not follow the man-made rules of the Pharisees (Mark 2:23-28).

In the early years of the church, Christians did meet on the Sabbath in the synagogues, until Jewish believers were persecuted and driven out. However, the first day of the week (Sunday, the Lord's Day) was their special day for fellowship and worship (Acts 20:7; 1 Cor. 16:1-3; Rev. 1:10). The first day commemorates Christ's resurrection (Matt. 28:1; John 20:1), the completion of His work in bringing about the new creation. See 2 Cor. 5:17. These two special days—the Sabbath and the Lord's Day—commemorate different things and must not be confused. The Sabbath Day relates to the old creation and was given expressly to Israel. The Lord's Day relates to the new creation and belongs especially to the church. The Sabbath speaks of law as six days of labor which are followed by rest, but the Lord's Day speaks of grace, for we begin the week with rest that is followed by works.

Hebrews 4 indicates that the OT Sabbath is a type of the future kingdom of rest, as well as the spiritual rest we have through faith in Christ. Colossians 2:13-17 makes it clear that the Sabbath belongs to the "shadows" of law and not the full light of grace. If people want to worship on the Sabbath, they certainly may, but they must not judge or condemn believers who do not join them (Col. 2:16-17). Galatians 4:9-11 indicates that the legalistic keeping of Sabbaths is a return to bondage. Romans 14:4-13 suggests that Sabbath-keeping can be the mark of an immature Christian who has a weak conscience. Certainly various groups of professing Christians may worship on Saturday if they prefer, but they must not condemn those who give special emphasis to worship on Sunday, resurrection day.

## II. The First Garden (2:4-14)

Bible history can be summarized with four gardens: (1) Eden, where sin entered; (2) Gethsemane, where Christ yielded to death; (3) Calvary, where He died and was buried (see John 19:41-42); and (4) the heavenly "paradise garden" (Rev. 21:1ff). Moses describes the first home God gave to the first couple. Further details given here are not included in the creation account of chap. 1; these are complementary, not contradictory. Verse 5 indicates that God needed man to help till the ground. Man was "formed" as the potter forms the clay (same word in Jer. 18:1ff). Man was responsible to dress the garden (tend it) and keep it (guard it, suggesting the presence of an enemy). God gave Adam and Eve all they needed for life and happiness, all that was good and pleasant, and He allowed them to enjoy it in abundance.

The two trees are important. The text in 3:22 suggests that the tree of life sustained life for humankind (see also Rev. 22:2). Had Adam eaten of the tree of life after he sinned, he could not have died, and then death would not have passed upon all men (Rom. 5:12ff) and Christ could not have died to redeem men. The tree of knowledge symbolized the authority of God; to eat of that tree meant to disobey God and incur the penalty of death. We do not know what these trees were, yet it is certain that Adam and Eve understood their importance.

## III. The First Law (2:15-17)

Adam was a perfect creature, one having never sinned, but he had the ability to sin. God made Adam a king with dominion (1:26ff). But a ruler can only rule others if he can rule himself, so it was necessary for Adam to be tempted. God has always wanted His creatures to love and obey Him of their own free will and not out of compulsion or because of reward.

This test was perfectly fair and just. Adam and Eve enjoyed liberty and abundant provision in the Garden and did not need the fruit from the tree of the knowledge of good and evil.

## IV. The First Marriage (2:18-25)

Everything in Creation was "very good" (1:31) except the loneliness of Adam. "It is not good for man to be alone" points to the basis for marriage: (1) to provide companionship; (2) to carry on the race; (3) to help one another and bring out the best. The word "helpmeet" (v. 18) refers to helper: one that meets his needs. This companion was not found anywhere in animal creation, thus showing the great gulf that is fixed between brute creatures and human beings made in the image of God. God made the first woman out of the flesh and bone of the first man, and He "closed up the flesh in its place" (v. 21, NKJV). The verb "made" in v. 22 is actually the word "built," as one would build a temple. The fact that Eve was made from Adam shows the unity of the human race and the dignity of woman. It has been remarked that Eve was made, not from the man's feet to be trampled by him, or from his head to rule over him, but from his side, to be near his heart and loved by him.

Adam had named all the animals that God had brought him (v. 19), thus showing that the first man had intelligence, language, and speech. Now he names his bride "woman" (in the Heb. *ishshah* which is related to *ish* meaning "man"). Thus, in name and nature, man and woman belong to each other. How wonderful it would be if every wedding were performed by God. Then every home would be a paradise on earth.

Of course, this event is a beautiful picture of Christ and the church (Eph. 5:21-33). Christ, the Last Adam, gave birth to the church as He slept in death on the cross and men opened His side (John 19:31-37). He partook of our human nature that we might be partakers of His divine nature. Eve was the object of Adam's love and concern, just as the church receives Christ's love and his ministry. First Timothy 2:11-15 points out that Adam willingly ate of the forbidden fruit and was not deceived as was Eve. He was willing to become a sinner that he might stay with his bride! So Christ was willing to be made sin for us that we might be with Him forever. What love and grace! Note too that Eve was formed before sin came on the scene, just as we have been chosen in Christ "before the foundation of the world" (Eph. 1:4).

If we look closely, we can see three pictures of the church in these verses, just as the church is pictured in Ephesians. Eve was the bride (Eph. 5:21-33); she was also part of Adam's body (Gen. 2:23; Eph. 5:29-30); and she was made or "built," which suggests the church as a temple of God (Eph. 2:19-22).

# GENESIS 3

## I. Temptation (3:1-6)

### A. The tempter.

God is not the author of sin, nor does He tempt people to sin; this is the work of the devil (James 1:13). We have already seen that Satan fell into sin prior to the work of Gen. 1:3ff. He was a beautiful angel originally, rejoicing at God's Creation (Job 38:4-7), but he sinned and was judged by God (Isa. 14:12-17; Ezek. 28:11-19). Note that Satan came to Eve in the guise of a serpent, for he is a masquerader and appears to people in his true character. In Gen. 3, Satan is the serpent who deceives (2 Cor. 11:3); in Gen. 4, he is the liar that murders (John 8:44). We must take care to avoid his deceptive ways.

## B. The target.

Satan aimed at Eve's mind (2 Cor. 11:1-3; 1 Tim. 2:9-15) and succeeded in deceiving her. Man's mind is a part of his being created in God's image (Col. 3:9-10), so Satan attacks God when he attacks the human mind. Satan uses lies. He is a liar himself and the father of lies (John 8:44).

## C. The tactic.

As long as the mind holds to God's truth, Satan cannot win; but once the mind doubts God's Word, there is room for the devil's lies to move in. Satan questioned God's Word (v. 1), denied God's Word (v. 4), and then substituted his own lies (v. 5). Note that Satan seeks to undermine our faith in the goodness of God—he suggested to Eve that God was "holding out on them" by keeping them from the tree of the knowledge of good and evil. When we question God's goodness and doubt His love, we are playing right into the hands of Satan. Satan made the temptation sound wonderful by making an offer: "You will be like God!" Satan himself had wanted to be "like the Most High" (Isa. 14:14), and centuries later he offered Christ "all the kingdoms of the world" if He would worship him (Matt. 4:8).

## D. The tragedy.

Eve should not have "given place to the devil" (Eph. 4:27); she should have held to God's Word and resisted him. We wonder where Adam was during this conversation. At any rate, Eve took away from God's Word by omitting "freely" (v. 2); she added to the Word by adding "touch it" (v. 3); and she changed the Word by making God's "you shall surely die" into "lest you die" (v. 3, NKJV). In v. 6 (NKJV) we see the tragic operation of the lust of the flesh ("good for food"), the lust of the eyes ("pleasant to the eyes"), and the pride of life ("desirable to make one wise")—see 1 John 2:15-17. It is difficult to sin alone. Something in us makes us want to share the sin with others. Adam deliberately sinned and plunged the world into judgment (1 Tim. 2:14).

## II. Condemnation (3:7-19)

### A. Internal (vv. 7-13).

Immediately there came a loss of innocence and glory and a sense of guilt. They tried to cover their nakedness with their own works, garments that God did not accept (v. 21). Further, we see a loss of desire for fellowship with God. When they heard God approaching, they hid! Guilt, fear, and shame broke the fellowship with God that they had enjoyed before their disobedience. Note too that there was a growing attitude of self-defense: the man blamed the woman and the woman blamed the serpent. We see here the tragic internal effects of sin.

### B. External (vv. 14-19).

It is likely that the serpent that Satan used was not the crawling creature that we know today. The name suggests brightness and glory, but because the creature yielded to Satan and shared in the temptation, it was judged and condemned to a lowly life in the dust. The woman's judgment involved multiple conception and pain in childbirth. She was made subject to her husband. Note that Paul suggests that Christian women who marry unsaved men may have special dangers in bearing children (1 Tim. 2:8-15). The judgment on man involved his work: paradise would be replaced by wilderness, and the joy of ministry in the garden by the sweat and toil in the field. It is not work that is God's penalty, because work is not sinful (2:15). It is the sweat and toil of work and the obstacles of nature that remind us of the fall of man. All creation is cursed and in bondage because of sin (Rom. 8:15-25).

### C. Eternal (v. 15).

This is the first Gospel declared in the Bible: the good news that the woman's seed (Christ) would ultimately defeat Satan and his seed (Gal. 4:4-5). It is from this point on that the stream divides: Satan and his family (seed) oppose God and His family. God Himself put the enmity (hostility) between them, and God will climax the war when Satan is cast into hell (Rev. 20:10). Review the Parable of the Tares in Matt. 13, and note that Satan has children just as God does. In Gen. 4, Cain kills Abel, and 1 John 3:12

informs us that Cain was "of that wicked one"—a child of the devil. The OT is the record of the two seeds in conflict; the NT is the record of the birth of Christ and His victory over Satan through the cross.

## III. Salvation (3:20-24)

The only Gospel Adam heard was what God said in 3:15, yet he believed it and was saved. How do we know he believed it? Because he called his wife's name "Eve" which means "life" or "lifegiver." God had said that Adam and Eve would die, and Adam did die physically after 930 years. But he also died spiritually, in that he was separated from God because of sin. God promised the birth of a Savior through the woman, and Adam believed this promise and was saved. God did not change the physical consequences of sin, but he did remit the eternal consequences—hell.

The coats of skins in v. 21 are pictures of the salvation we have in Christ. There must be the shedding of blood, the offering of innocent life for the guilty. Adam and Eve had tried to cover their sin and shame with leaves (3:7), but these good works were not accepted by God. Nor does He accept such works today!

Garments in the Bible are often a picture of salvation. See Isa. 61:10 and Zech. 3. The prodigal son was clothed afresh when he came home (Luke 15:22). The garments of self-righteousness and good works are but filthy rags in God's sight (Isa. 64:6). Note that God wanted Adam and Eve to be covered; He approved their sense of shame. It is always a sign of degeneration when a people reverse this and go back to nakedness. "Modest apparel" is always God's standard (1 Tim. 2:9).

Verses 22-24 show a strange action of the grace of God: He drove the man and woman out of the garden! They had forfeited their right to the tree of life by disobeying God. If they had eaten of that tree, they would have lived forever in their sinful state. This would mean that the Savior, the Second Adam, could not come to die to deliver humans from sin. Thus, in driving Adam and Eve out of paradise, God was showing His grace and mercy to the whole human race. The sword that God placed at the garden barred the way. It is possible to translate this "a swordlike flame"—the fire of God that speaks of His holiness (Heb. 12:29).

Romans 5 and 1 Cor. 15:42-49 explain the contrasts between the first Adam and the Last Adam, Christ. Adam was made from the earth, but Christ came down from heaven. Adam was tempted in a perfect garden, while Christ was tempted in a terrible wilderness. Adam deliberately disobeyed and plunged the human race into sin and death, but Christ obeyed God and brought righteousness. As a thief, Adam was cast out of paradise. Speaking to a thief, Jesus said, "Today you will be with Me in Paradise" (Luke 23:43, NKJV).

Note that in Romans 5 we have several "much more" statements (9, 15, 17, 20), indicating that the death of Christ did not simply put us back to where Adam was. It gave us much more than Adam ever had. We are kings and priests unto God and will reign with Christ forever!

# GENESIS 4

Cain is the chief actor in this chapter, and his character and conduct are revealed in four different aspects.

## I. The Worshiper (4:1-5)

God's promise in 3:15 and Adam's faith in 3:20 are both seen in 4:1. Eve brought new life into the world, and she thought her child was the promised Seed. "I have gotten a man—the Lord!" is a possible translation. "Cain" means "acquired"—the baby boy was looked upon as a gift from God. Abel means "vanity, vapor"—it suggests the futility of life apart from God, or perhaps Eve's disappointment that Cain was not the promised Seed. From the very beginning, we see a division of work: as Cain is identified with the ground, Abel with the flock. God had already cursed the ground (3:17), so Cain is identified with that curse.

This earliest family must have known a definite place for worship, for both sons brought offerings to the Lord. It may be that the glory of God tabernacled at the tree of life, with the way guarded by the cherubim (3:24). Hebrews 11:4 indicates that Abel brought his offering by faith; and Rom. 10:17 teaches that "faith comes by hearing, (NKJV)." This means that God must have taught Adam and his family how to approach Him, and 3:21 indicates that sacrifice of blood was involved. Hebrews 9:22 states that there must be the shedding of blood before there can be the remission of sin, but Cain brought a bloodless offering from the cursed earth. His offering may have been sincere, but it was not accepted. He had no faith in God's Word or dependence on the sacrifice of a substitute. God probably "answered by fire" (Lev. 9:24) and burned up Abel's offering, but Cain's offering lay there on the altar.

Cain had a form of godliness and religion, but he denied the power (2 Tim. 3:5). First John 3:12 indicates that Cain was a child of the devil, and this means he practiced a false righteousness of the flesh, not the righteousness of God through faith. Jesus called the self-righteous Pharisees "children of the devil" and blamed their kind for the death of Abel (Luke. 11:37-51). Jude 11 talks about "the way of Cain," which is the way of religion without blood, religion based on religious good works and self-righteousness. There are only two religions in the world today: (1) that of Abel that depends on the blood of Christ and His finished work on the cross; and (2) that of Cain that depends on good works and man-pleasing religion. One leads to heaven, the other to hell!

## II. The Murderer (4:6-8)

James 1:15 warns us that sin begins in a small way, but grows and leads to death. So it was with Cain. We see disappointment, anger, jealousy, and finally murder. The hatred in his heart led to murder with his hand (Matt. 5:21-26). God saw Cain's faithless heart and fallen countenance and warned him that sin was crouching like a wild beast, waiting to destroy him. God said, "Its desire is for you, but you should rule over it." Alas, Cain fed the wild beast of temptation, then opened the door and invited him in! Cain invited his brother to talk with him, then killed him in cold blood. A child of the devil (1 John 3:12), Cain, like his father, was a liar and a murderer (John 8:44). In chapter 3, we have man sinning against God by disobeying His Word; in chapter 4, we have man sinning against man.

## III. The Wanderer (4:9-16)

"Adam, where are you?" "Where is Abel your brother?" How significant are these first two questions in the Bible! Sin always finds us out, even though we try (like Cain) to lie about our sin. Abel's blood cried out for vengeance; Christ's blood cries out peace and forgiveness (Heb. 12:24). God had cursed the serpent and the ground; now He curses Cain. "You are cursed away from the earth . . ." (v. 11) is a suggested translation. In other words, the ground would not yield increase to Cain, and he would have to wander from place to place in order to live. He would be a fugitive, a wanderer.

Cain did not repent of his sin; instead, he showed remorse and despair. Like his parents, he blamed God. "You have driven me out!" (v. 14, NKJV) He was rejected by heaven and refused by earth! He was condemned to a restlessness that could be cured only by faith.

Note also Cain's fear and hopelessness: "Anyone who finds me will kill me!" (v. 14, NKJV) In grace, God promised to protect Cain and gave him a sign (mark) to verify His promise. (It is not likely that there was a literal mark on Cain; rather, God gave a sign to Cain to assure him. What grace!) Why did God release Cain? For one thing, Cain became a "walking sermon" on the grace of God and the tragic consequences of sin. What a picture of humankind today: restless, hopeless, wandering, defeated!

Did Cain spend the rest of his life wandering? No! He settled down and built a city! We have here the origin of "civilization"—man's substitute for God's spiritual gifts.

## IV. The Builder (4:17-26)

"Nod" means "to stray, to wander", so the very land of Cain's choice speaks of his wandering away from God. He went away from the presence of God (4:16); he had no need for a religion of blood. Cain certainly married one of his sisters, for by then there were many descendants of Adam (5:3 indicates 130 years had passed). Abraham later married his half-sister; why could Cain not marry his full sister, especially in a day when sin had not yet taken its toll in the human body? His son's name "Enoch" means "initiation" and suggests a new beginning, but it was a beginning without God.

Evaluated from a human point of view, Cain's descendants are an admirable lot. Jabal ("wanderer") founded the science of agriculture (v. 20); Jubal founded "culture"—music; and Tubal-Cain founded the metal industries. In outward appearances, Cain's "city" was a great success, but God made it clear that He had rejected the whole thing. In v. 25, God gave Adam and Eve another seed—Seth—which means "the appointed, the substitute" (taking Abel's place). God did not try to reform the Cainites. He rejected them and ultimately would condemn them in the flood. As the Cainites were gradually wandering away from the true worship of God, the Sethites were returning to Him (v. 26) and establishing again their worship of the Lord.

Civilization today is Cainite in origin. It has such elements as agriculture, industry, arts, great cities, and religion without faith in the blood of Christ. Also, like Cain's civilization of old, it will be destroyed. We still have boasting murderers like Lamech, and we still have people (like Lamech) who violate the sacred vows of marriage. "As the days of Noah were, so also will the coming of the Son of man be" (Matt. 24:37, NKJV). Men still reject divine revelation and depend on their own human resources. The true Christian does not belong to this "world system" that is passing away (1 John 2:15-17), and should not get involved with it (Rom. 12:1-2; 2 Cor. 6:14-7:1).

We must take special note of "Lamech's Message" (vv. 23-24). This passage is not clear, and not all Bible students interpret it the same way. Lamech was the seventh from Adam on Cain's side and was a man who displeased God, while Enoch was the seventh from Adam on Seth's side (5:3-27) and walked with God and pleased God (Heb. 11:5). Note that the Cainite line even copied the names of the true believers in Seth's line (Enoch–Enos; Irad–Jared; Mehujael–Mahalaleel; Lamech–Lamech). Some suggest that Lamech had been wounded by a young man, so had killed his attacker in self-defense. If God had avenged Cain, who was guilty of gross murder, surely He would defend Lamech who had killed in self-defense. Another suggestion is that Tubal-Cain had devised the first weapons of brass and iron and that Lamech had proudly demonstrated them to his wives. The Hebrew verbs can be translated in the future tense: "I will slay anyone who wounds me and will not need God's protection, for with these weapons I can avenge myself seventy-seven fold!" Seen in this light, it is the first expression of arrogant defiance and warfare in the Bible.

# GENESIS 5–8

These chapters deal with the flood and the faith of Noah. Since it is impossible for us to mine all of the spiritual treasures here, we will limit ourselves to four aspects of this important event in Bible history.

## I. The Flood Considered Historically

### A. The fact of the flood.

That there actually was a flood is proved by the Genesis record, as well as by Christ (Matt. 24:37-39; Luke 17:26-27), the prophets

(Isa. 54:9), and the apostles (1 Peter 3:20; 2 Peter 2:5; 3:6). Archaeologists tell us that many ancient civilizations have a flood tradition with details paralleling the Genesis account. It is likely that these stories (involving their fanciful gods and goddesses) were corruptions of the original history of the flood that was handed down from generation to generation.

## B. The purpose of the flood.

Stated in 6:5-13, because people had become corrupt, and the earth was filled with violence, God sent the flood in order to destroy humankind. There must always be judgment and death before there can be a new beginning. We will study the details later.

## C. The schedule of the flood.

If we count the year of Adam's creation as 1, then Noah was born in the year 1056. Genesis 6:3 indicates that God gave Noah 120 years to build the ark and preach (1 Peter 3:20), which means he was 480 years old when he started (7:11). This would be the year 1536. The flood came in Noah's 600th year, which would be 1656, and in the year 1657, his 601st year, Noah and his family were back on dry ground (8:13ff). The events on the ark began on the tenth day of the second month (2/10) of 1656, when Noah and His family entered the ark (7:1-9). The floods came on 2/17 (7:10-11); the rains stopped on 3/26 (7:12); and the ark rested on Mt. Ararat on 7/17 (8:1-4). On 10/1 the family could see the tops of the mountains (8:5). On 11/11, Noah sent out the raven (8:6-9). On 11/18, he sent the dove, which brought back the olive branch (8:10-11). A week later on 8/25, Noah again sent out the dove and it did not return (8:12). On the first day of the first month of the next year (1657), Noah removed the covering of the ark and surveyed the earth (8:13). On 2/27, they all left the ark (8:14ff).

## D. The ark.

It was not a boat, but was rather a "floating box" made of cypress wood and pitched with bitumen. If we use a 24" cubit, the ark's size would be 600 feet long, 100 feet wide, and 60 feet high. With an 18" cubit the size becomes 450 x 75 x 45. In either case, the ark was large enough to hold the collection of animals, the food needed, and the members of Noah's family. We do not know how many species of animals there were in that day. Note that 6:20 indicates that God brought the animals to Noah. There were three levels to the ark, with a window either in the roof of the top level or running all around the top level (6:16); and there was one door.

## E. *The flood itself.*

The deluge was caused by rain falling and water erupting from under the earth (7:11). One can well imagine the tremendous effects this would have on the surface of the earth, as well as on the climate. Gigantic tidal waves followed these eruptions. Genesis 2:5-6 suggests that the falling of rain was something new on the earth in Noah's time, which makes the faith of Noah even more wonderful.

## II. The Flood Considered Typically

The ark is an illuminating picture of our salvation in Christ (see 1 Peter 3:18-22). The salvation and the ark were planned by God, not invented by humans. There is only one way of salvation and there was only one door in the ark. The ark was made of wood, speaking of the humanity of Christ: He had to be born as man in order to save us. The word for "pitch" in 6:14 is the same as the word "atonement" used later in the OT. God invited Noah and his family into the ark (7:1); then, once they were in, God shut them in so that they were secure (7:16). The ark saved not only humankind, but also the creatures within it, just as Christ's death will one day deliver creation from the bondage of sin (Rom. 8:18-23). The ark saved Noah and his family from judgment because they believed God's promise (Heb. 11:7); Christ saves us from the wrath to come as we believe Him. First Peter 3:18-22 connects the ark with the resurrection of Christ; the waters buried the old world but raised Noah to a new life. Noah was faithful to obey all that God commanded; Jesus said, "I do always those things that please Him" (John 8:29). Noah was brought safely through the floods; Christ went through the flood of suffering (Ps. 42:7) and came out in victory. Noah went out of the ark, the head of a new creation with his family; and Christ came out of the tomb, the Head of the new creation, and the Father of a new family.

Noah went through the judgment and was kept safe, just as the believing Jewish remnant will go through the Tribulation to establish the kingdom on the earth. Enoch was raptured before the judgment came (5:21-24; Heb. 11:5), just as the church will be raptured before the wrath of God is poured out upon the world. See 1 Thes. 1:10 and 5:9-10.

## III. The Flood Considered Prophetically

Christ teaches that the days before the rapture and the Tribulation will be like the days of Noah (Luke 17:26, Matt. 24:37-39). We are living in the "days of Noah" today. We see such parallels as the multiplication of people in the "population explosion" (6:1); moral corruption of every kind (6:5); violence (6:11, 13); the expansion of arts and industry (4:16-22); lack of conscience, even for murder (4:23-24); and true believers being in a minority (6:8-10). But keep in mind that "the days of Noah" were also days of witness. In fact, God had told Enoch that judgment was coming, and he warned the people (Jude 14-15). Methuselah, Enoch's son, was born in the year 687 and lived 969 years. He died in the year 1656 — the very year the flood came! In other words, God gave the wicked world 969 years of grace. And for the last 120 years of that period, Noah was preaching and preparing the ark (Gen. 6:3; 1 Peter 3:20). Today, God warns that judgment is coming (2 Peter 3 — fire not water), but few listen, and even fewer believe.

## IV. The Flood Considered Practically

We see in the flood account at least these six practical considerations: (1) God must punish sin. There must be death to the old before He can establish the new. (2) God gives warnings but eventually His patience ends and judgment comes. (3) God has always saved people the same way: by grace (6:8), through faith (Heb. 11:7). (4) True faith leads to obedience (6:22; 7:5). (5) True witness demands separation from sin, and Noah and his family kept themselves unspotted from the world. (6) Whether "the sons of God" in 6:1-4 were angels or the family of Seth, the same lesson is seen: God condemns compromise and rebellion, but rewards the separated saint.

# GENESIS 9–11

## I. God's Covenant with Noah (9:1-17)

The word covenant means "to cut," referring to the cutting of the sacrifices which was a definite part of making an agreement (see Gen. 15:9ff). Through Noah, God made an agreement with all mankind, and its terms still stand today. The basis of the covenant was the shed blood of the sacrifice (8:20-22), just as the basis of the New Covenant is the shed blood of Christ.

The terms of the covenant are these: (1) God will not destroy mankind with a flood of waters; (2) man may eat animal flesh, but not blood (see Lev. 17:10ff); (3) there is fear and terror between man and beast; (4) human beings are responsible for human government, seen in the principle of capital punishment (see Rom. 13:1-5). God set apart the rainbow as the token and pledge of the covenant. This does not mean that the rainbow first appeared at that time, but only that God gave it a special meaning when He made this covenant. The rainbow is a product of sunshine and storm, and its colors remind us of the "manifold (many-colored) grace of God" (1 Peter 4:10). The rainbow appears to be a bridge between heaven and earth, reminding us that in Christ, God bridged the chasm that separated man from God. We meet the rainbow again in Ezek. 1:28 and Rev. 4:3.

We must keep in mind that the covenant was with Noah's "seed" after him, and this includes us today. It is for this reason that most Christian people have supported capital punishment (9:5-6). God had promised to avenge Cain (4:15), but in this covenant with Noah God gave men the responsibility of punishing the murderer.

## II. Noah's Curse upon Canaan (9:18-29)

### A. The sin.

It was a seasoned saint, over 600 years old, and not a young prodigal, that fell into this sin and shame. The Hebrew text suggests that Noah deliberately uncovered himself in a shameful manner; intemperance and impurity often go together. Some excuse Noah by suggesting that the new atmospheric conditions of the earth since the flood would lead to the fermentation of wine, and that Noah did not fully know what he was doing. But the Bible does not excuse the sins of the saints. This is the third failure on the part of man. He had disobeyed in Eden, resulting in his expulsion; he had corrupted the earth, resulting in the flood; and now he had become a shameful drunk! To make matters worse, Ham did not respect his father; instead, he "told with delight" what Noah had done.

### B. The curse.

Noah learned what Ham had done and pronounced his famous

curse. (This is the third curse in Genesis. See 3:14-19 and 4:11.) The fact that he curses Canaan, Ham's youngest son (10:6), suggests that the boy was involved in the sin along with his father and that God would punish the sins of both the father and the son. Canaan and his descendants (nations named in 10:15-20) were to be the lowest of servants to their brethren. It is easy to see that they were ultimately made slaves by the Jews and Gentiles. Of course, the Shemites (Semites) were the Jews. Their tribes are listed in 10:21-32, and 11:10-26 traces the line to Abraham. The descendants of Japheth are the Gentiles (10:1-5). The enslavement of Canaan's descendants is mentioned in Gen. 15:13-21 with 10:15-20. We are not told how the various racial distinctions appeared, but Acts 17:26 teaches that God made all men of "one blood."

### C. The blessing

Noah blessed the Jews (Shem) and gave the Canaanites to them as their servants. He promised that the Gentiles (Japheth) would be spread abroad, but that (spiritually speaking) they would dwell in the Jewish tents. Paul explains this in Romans 9–11.

## III. Nimrod's Confederation against God (11:1-9)

### A. The dictator (10:6-14).

Nimrod was a grandson of Ham through Cush, and his name means "rebel." He was a mighty tyrant in the sight of God, the first dictator. The word "hunter" does not refer to the hunting of animals, but rather to the hunting of men. He was the founder of the Babylonian empire and the organizer of the enterprise that led to the construction of the tower of Babel. History informs us that Nimrod and his wife devised a new religion built around "the mother and child." For details, read Alexander Hislop's book *The Two Babylons* (London: S.W. Partridge, 1956). "Babylon" in the Bible symbolizes rebellion against God and confusion in religion. We see Babylon opposing the people of God throughout the Bible, culminating in the "Great Babylon" of Rev. 17–18.

### B. The rebellion.

God had commanded men to replenish the earth (9:1, 7, 9), but they decided to settle down on the plain of Shinar where Babylon was located (10:8-10). This was deliberate rebellion against God's Word. They journeyed "from the east" which suggests that they were turning their backs on the light. They decided to unite and build both a city and a tower. Their purposes were to (1) maintain unity in opposition to God, and (2) make a name for themselves. This entire operation is a foregleam of the final opposition of man (and Satan) against Christ, centered in the Babylon of Rev. 17–18. Men will unite then in a world church and world political organization; they will be led by the Antichrist, the last world dictator; and their plans will be frustrated. It is interesting to note that today the world is rapidly moving toward the "one world" concept, thanks to the United Nations and other international alliances.

## C. The judgment.

God knew the designs of the rebels and judged them. The Godhead held another conference (see 1:26 and 3:22) and decided to confound the languages of the workers, thus making it impossible for them to work together. This was really an act of mercy as well as judgment, for had they persisted in their plan, a more terrible judgment would have followed. The name "Babel" comes from a Hebrew word which means "gate of God." It sounds like the word *balal* which means "confusion." The description of God's action here explains the origin of the languages of mankind. It has often been pointed out that Pentecost was a reversal of Babel — there was true spiritual unity among God's people; they spoke with other tongues but were understood; and their work glorified God, not men.

## IV. God's Call of Abraham (11:10-32)

We had the family tree of Shem in 10:21-32, but here the writer repeats the line to show how Abraham fits into the plan. He takes the line to Terah, the father of Abraham (11:26). We see here another evidence of divine election: God chose Abraham in His grace! He bypassed Ham and Japheth and chose Shem. Of Shem's five sons (10:22), God chose Arphaxad (11:10). And of Terah's three sons (11:26), He chose Abraham. This is the beginning of the Hebrew nation.

Genesis 12:1 indicates that the Lord had said (past tense) to Abraham, "Get out." But 11:31-32 states that Abraham did not fully obey. Instead of leaving his father behind, he took him along (NKJV); and the pilgrimage was delayed at Haran, where Terah died. Often our half-way obedience becomes costly, both in time and treasure. Abraham lost the time he could have spent walking with God, and he lost his father too. Abraham took Lot with him on the next stage of the journey, but Lot also had to be taken away from Abraham (13:5-14).

Hebrews 11:8-19 is a summary of the faith of Abraham. Someone has said that Abraham believed God when he did not know where (Heb. 11:8), when he did not know how (11:11), and when he did not know why (11:17-19).

We must emphasize again that God did not call Abraham because of his own merits. He had none. He was a citizen of an idolatrous city, Ur of the Chaldees. Had not God revealed Himself to him, he would have died an unbeliever. From a human point of view, God's choice of Abraham and Sarah — who had no children — was a foolish one. But ultimately it brought great glory to God and great blessing to the world.

# GENESIS 12–13:4

This chapter begins the account of Abraham's walk of faith. (His given name, of course, was Abram, "high father," which was changed to Abraham, "father of a multitude." We will use his more familiar name for the sake of convenience.) The flood had destroyed a corrupt civilization, but another sinful society soon took its place. God called one man to begin the fulfillment of His promise in Gen. 3:15, to send a Savior to the world. This man was of the line of Shem (11:10ff) and was the father of the Jewish nation. From this one man, God was to bless the whole world!

## I. Abraham's Response of Faith (12:1-9)

### A. The covenant (vv. 1-3).

God had called Abraham in Ur of the Chaldees (Acts 7:2-4), but he had lingered at Haran until the death of his father (11:27-32). God demands total separation to Himself, even if death must accomplish it. This call was completely of grace and the blessings of the covenant wholly from the Lord's goodness. God promised to give Abraham (1) a land; (2) a great name; (3) a great nation; and (4) a blessing that would spread to the whole world. It took a good deal of faith for Abraham to respond to these promises for he had no children, and he and his wife were getting old (11:30). Note the repeated "I will" from the lips of God. God would do it all if only Abraham would believe. Certainly God has fulfilled His promises; for Israel has her land (and will get more); the Jews have blessed all nations by giving us the Bible and Christ; and Abraham's name is revered by Jews, Moslems, Christians, and even unbelievers. The men of Babel wanted to make a name for themselves and failed (11:4); but Abraham trusted God and God gave him a great name!

### B. The compromise (vv. 4-6).

"Lot went with him"—this was mistake number two. Lot's father, Haran, was dead (11:28), so Abraham took the young man under his protection, only to have him create serious problems. Later, God had to separate Lot from Abraham before He could advance His plan for the patriarch's life. Their long journey from Haran to Canaan is not recorded, but it certainly took faith and patience to complete it. It is easy to see that Abraham was a wealthy man, but that his wealth was no barrier to his walk with God. The travelers came to Shechem, "the place of the shoulder." How wonderful it is for the believer to live in "the place of the shoulder," where "underneath are the everlasting arms" (Deut. 33:27).

### C. The confession (vv. 7-9).

Obedience always leads to blessing. After Abraham arrived in Canaan, the Lord appeared to Abraham to further assure him. Abraham did not hesitate to confess his faith before the heathen in the land. Wherever he went, he pitched his tent and built his altar. (See 13:3-4, 18.) The tent speaks of the pilgrim, the person who trusts God a day at a time and is always ready to move. The altar speaks of the worshiper who brings a sacrifice and offers it to God. Interestingly at Abraham's location, Bethel ("the house of God") was on the west, Ai ("the heap of ruins") was on the east, and he was traveling toward "the house of God." In 13:11, Lot turned his back on the house of God and took his journey eastward, back into the world with disastrous results. Also, whenever Abraham stepped out of God's will, he lost the tent and the altar.

## II. Abraham's Lapse of Faith (12:10-20)

### A. The disappointment (v. 10).

A famine in the place of God's leading! What a great disappointment this must have been to the pilgrims. God was testing their faith, to see if they were trusting the land or the Lord. Instead of remaining in Canaan and trusting God, they went down to Egypt, possibly at the suggestion of Lot (see 13:10). Egypt symbolizes the world, the life of self-confidence; Canaan illustrates the life of faith and victory. Egypt was watered by the muddy Nile river; Canaan received the fresh rains from God (see Deut. 11:10-12). Abraham abandoned his tent and altar and trusted in the world! See Isa. 31:1.

## B. The deception (vv. 11-13).

One sin leads to another: first Abraham trusted Egypt; now he trusted his wife's lie to protect him. Genesis 20:13 makes it clear that Sarah was equally guilty with Abraham, and 20:12 indicates that the "lie" was really a half-truth, for she was his half-sister. It seems that Abraham was more concerned for his own safety than the safety of his wife—or the safety of the promised seed. Had Sarah been kept in that harem, God could not have fulfilled His promise! Without his tent and altar, Abraham was acting like the people of the world (Ps. 1:1-3).

## C. The discipline (vv. 14-20).

What a shame that believing Abraham should be rebuked by an unbelieving king. Until he knew the truth about Sarah, Pharaoh "bestowed favors" upon Abraham, but once God stepped in and exposed the lie, Pharaoh had to ask them to leave. What a poor testimony the Christian is when he or she mingles with the world and compromises. Someone has said, "Faith is living without scheming." Abraham and all his descendants have needed to learn that lesson! Lot lived with the world and lost his testimony (19:12-14); and Peter sat by the enemy fire and denied his Lord.

## III. Abraham's Return of Faith (13:1-4)

Christians enmeshed in the world cannot be happy with themselves. They must go back to the very place where they abandoned the Lord. This is repentance and confession, to feel sorry for sin and to make amends. Abraham could not have confessed his sin and remained in Egypt! No, he had to get back to the place of the tent and the altar, back to the place where he could call upon the Lord and receive blessing. This is a good principle for Christians to follow: go nowhere in this world where you must leave your testimony behind. Any place where we cannot build the altar and pitch the tent is out of bounds.

It seems that Abraham's restoration should have undone all his disobedience, but such is not the case. Certainly God forgave Abraham and restored him to fellowship, but God could not overrule the sad consequences of the trip to Egypt:

## A. Lost time.

The weeks that Abraham and his household were away from the Lord were lost and could not be regained. All believers must pray to avoid such losses, "Teach us to number our days that we may gain a heart of wisdom" (Ps. 90:12, NKJV).

## B. Lost testimony.

Could Abraham ever witness to Pharaoh of the true God, after deceiving him? Probably not. How sad it will be when we face God at the judgment seat of Christ and discover how many souls have gone to hell because of the poor testimony of carnal Christians!

## C. Hagar's place in the family.

Sarah's maid, Hagar, came from Egypt (16:1ff), and brought untold trouble to the family. Of course, the suggestion that she bear a child came from Sarah, but the presence of Hagar helped to bring about the carnal scheme. Whatever we bring with us from Egypt (the godless world) will ultimately cause us trouble. We must be crucified to the world and make sure that the world is crucified to us (Gal. 6:14).

## D. More wealth.

The increase in possessions helped to cause the later dispute between Abraham's herdsmen and Lot's herdsmen. Later, Abraham would refuse the world's wealth (14:17-24).

## E. Lot's enjoyment of Egypt.

This young man developed a taste for Egypt (13:10), and though Abraham took Lot out of Egypt, he could not take Egypt out of Lot! It is always tragic when a mature believer leads a younger Christian astray. In 12:8, Lot shares Abraham's tent and altar, but when Lot comes out of Egypt, he has only tents, no altar (13:5). No wonder Lot gravitated toward Sodom — and ended up a moral and spiritual wreck.

# GENESIS 13:5–14:24

We begin here the tragic account of Lot's backsliding and failure. Were it not for 2 Peter 2:7-8, we might wonder whether Lot was even saved. He is an illustration of the worldly believer who loses everything to the fire of judgment (1 Cor. 3:11-15). Saved, yet so as by fire!

## I. The Conflict (13:5-7)

Lot was walking in the flesh, and Abraham was walking in the Spirit. This always leads to conflict. The outward cause was increased wealth; the real cause was Lot's unbelief and carnality. Christ is a divider (John 7:43; 9:16; 10:19). His presence brings conflict between people of the same family (Luke 12:49-53). The conflict with Lot must have been a burden to Abraham and Sarah at the same time as a poor testimony to the heathen then living in the land.

## II. The Choice (13:8-18)

People reveal their true selves by the choices they make. Note what Lot reveals here:

### A. His pride (vv. 8-9).

The younger should submit to the elder (1 Peter 5:5), yet Lot put himself ahead of Abraham. What a gracious man Abraham was. He was anxious to make peace (Ps. 133). While Abraham was concerned about maintaining a good testimony, Lot was concerned only about himself. But "pride goes before destruction" (Prov. 16:18, NKJV), and Lot was to lose everything!

### B. His unbelief (v. 10a).

He "lifted up his eyes"—he lived by sight, not by faith. Had Lot consulted God, he would have discovered that Sodom was on the agenda to be destroyed, but instead he trusted his own sight and chose the wealthy, wicked city.

### C. His worldliness (v. 10b).

The land Lot saw was "like the land of Egypt"—that was all that mattered! Lot was walking according to the flesh, living for the things of the world. The area around Sodom looked well-watered and fruitful to Lot, but to God, it was wicked (v. 13). Unbelievers today, like Lot, anchor their hopes on this world and laugh at the idea that God will one day destroy the world with fire (2 Peter 3).

### D. His selfishness (v. 11).

Lot's success was due mainly to Abraham's kindness, yet the young man left his generous uncle and tried to take "the best" for himself. Of course, God wanted to separate Lot and Abraham (12:1), but from a human standpoint, it was a painful separation.

### E. His heedlessness (v. 12).

First, Lot looked toward Sodom. Then he moved toward Sodom. Before long (14:12 and 19:1), he was living in Sodom. Verse 11 tells us that Lot journeyed east; instead of walking with the light, he went toward the darkness (Prov. 4:18).

While Lot was getting farther from the Lord, Abraham was drawing closer! Lot was becoming a friend of the world (James 4:4); Abraham was becoming the friend of God (James 2:23). God told Abraham to lift up his eyes (see v. 14-15) and behold the entire land. The people of the world claim what their eyes can see, while the people of faith claim what God's eyes can see! Lot took a part of the land, but Abraham was given all of the land. God always gives His best to those who leave the choice with Him (Matt. 6:33). God promised to bless Abraham's seed, but Lot's family was either destroyed in Sodom or defiled in the cave (19:12-38). Verse 17 makes it clear that the believer must step out on God's promises and claim them by faith (Josh. 1:3). Lot had lost his altar and would soon lose his tent (19:30), but Abraham still had his tent and altar. It pays to walk by faith and trust the Word of God!

## III. The Captive (14:1-12)

Archaeologists have confirmed the historical accuracy of this account of the first war in the Bible. When Lot moved into Sodom (v. 12), he lost the protection of "the Judge of all the earth" (18:25) and had to suffer the consequences. Lot followed the path of friendship with the world (James 4:4), then love of the world (1 John 2:15-17), then conformity to the world (Rom. 12:2), and finally, judgment with the world (1 Cor. 11:32). Lot thought that Sodom was a place of peace and protection; however, it turned out to be a place of warfare and danger!

Saints rarely are "captured by the world" suddenly. They enter into the place of danger by degrees. With Lot, the process began when he adopted Egypt as his standard and began to walk by sight instead of by faith. He preferred the people of the world to his godly uncle, and the houses of Sodom to the tents of God. The result: he was captured!

## IV. The Conquest (14:13-24)

Godly Abraham was in the place of safety, even though he lived in a tent. Hearing of Lot's plight, Abraham did the generous thing and went to rescue him. Only the separated believer has the power to help the backslider, and it is to such a faithful saint that the backslider turns when in trouble. In this chapter, Abraham delivers Lot by his sword. By faith, he overcomes the enemy, covering 120 miles to do it. See 1 John 5:1-4. In 19:29 Abraham delivers Lot by his prayers (18:23-33). A worldly Christian is truly fortunate if he has a dedicated loved one praying for him!

Following the victory, Abraham faced a greater temptation as he met the King of Sodom. It is usually true that Satan tempts us immediately after a great spiritual victory. Satan met Christ in the wilderness after His baptism. Elijah fled in fear after his great work of faith on Mt. Carmel (1 Kings 19). The King of Sodom wanted to bargain with Abraham and get him to compromise by accepting the wealth of Sodom, but Abraham refused. The wealth of Egypt had proved a snare. The wealth of Sodom would be worse. Had Abraham not been on his guard, he would have fallen for this subtle temptation and would have taken all the glory away from God. The people would have said, "Abraham rescued Lot for what he could get out of it, not because of his faith and love. Abraham refuses to live in Sodom with Lot, but he enjoys the goods of Sodom just the same." Abraham would have lost his testimony.

Abraham ignored the king of Sodom, but he honored the king of Salem. Hebrews 5–7 makes it clear that Melchizedek ("king of righteousness") is a type of Christ, our heavenly High Priest. As King of Salem ("peace") Christ gives us peace through His own righteousness, made possible by His death on the cross. What an encouragement it is to see Melchizedek meeting Abraham just when the king of Sodom tempts him! As King and Priest, Christ is able to give us "grace to help in time of need" (Heb. 4:16). The bread and wine (v. 18) typify Christ's body and shed blood, for it is the cross that makes possible the heavenly priesthood of Christ. Melchizedek met Abraham, fed him, and blessed him. What a wonderful Savior!

Abraham honored Melchizedek by paying him tithes of all. This is the first instance of tithing in the Bible, and it occurs years before the giving of the Mosaic Law. Hebrews 7:4-10 indicates that these tithes were paid (in type) to Christ, suggesting that believers today are following Abraham's example as they bring tithes to the Lord. Abraham refused the riches of the world but shared his wealth with the Lord, and God richly blessed him.

Did this battle and night of danger bring Lot to his senses? Alas, it did not! In 19:1 we see him right back in Sodom. Lot's heart was in Sodom, so that is where his body had to go.

# GENESIS 15–17

In these chapters we have a rich mine of spiritual truth that reaches into the NT, particularly to Romans and Galatians. God had outlined His promises in 12:1-3 and expanded them in 13:14-18, but at this point, He reveals the covenant promises more fully. This covenant has to do with Abraham's son and the coming of the promised Seed, Christ. It also deals with the land of Canaan and the wonderful program God has for His people, Israel.

## I. The Terms of the Covenant (15)

### A. The setting.

Abraham had just defeated the kings (chap. 14) and overcome a great temptation from the King of Sodom. Now God stepped in to encourage him. How wonderful that Christ comes to us when we need Him! (14:18) God is our protection (shield) and provision (reward); we need never fear. Abraham did not need the protection of the King of Sodom or the treasures he offered. Abraham had all he needed in God.

### B. The supplication.

Abraham did not want a reward; he wanted an heir. He was now 85 years old, and for 10 years he had been waiting for his promised son to be born. If he had no son, all his inheritance would fall to Eliezer, his steward. Had not God promised in 12:2 (NKJV), "I will make you a great nation"? Then why was He not fulfilling His promise? God answered Abraham's supplication by lifting his eyes from himself and his steward to the heavens (v. 5). Verse 6 is a key verse in the Bible which can be translated: "And he said AMEN to the Lord, and He put it to his account for righteousness" (see Gal. 3:6; Rom. 4:3; James 2:23). How was Abraham saved? Not by keeping the Law, for the Law had not yet been given, nor by circumcision, for that was not established until he was ninety-nine years old. He was saved by faith in God's Word.

## C. The sacrifice.

Salvation is based on sacrifice, for the covenant requires the shedding of blood. It was customary in that day for the contracting parties in an agreement to walk between the pieces of the slain animals; this sealed the agreement. The sacrifices in v. 9 all speak of Christ and the cross. Abraham offered the sacrifices and labored to keep Satan (the birds in v. 11, Matt. 13:4, 19) away. But nothing really happened until Abraham went to sleep. Abraham never did walk between the pieces. It was God alone (v. 17) who went between the pieces; the covenant was all of grace and depended solely upon the Lord. Like Adam (2:21), Abraham was in a deep sleep and could do nothing to help God. When we are helpless God is able to do great things for us.

## D. The surety.

Abraham wanted to know for sure what God would do (v. 8), and God met his need. Salvation is based on the sacrifice of Christ and the grace of God; assurance comes from the Word of God. God gave Abraham a capsule forecast of events: the sojourn of Israel in Egypt, their suffering in Egypt, their deliverance in the fourth generation (see Ex. 6:16-26), and their possession of the Promised Land. Note that God says, "I have given this land" (v. 18), and not, "I will give" as in 12:7. God's promises are as good as His performances!

Note that at least seven words or phrases appear in this chapter for the first time: "The Word of the Lord" (v. 1); "Fear not" (v. 1); reward (v. 1); heir and inherit (vv. 3, 7); believe, counted, righteousness (all in v. 6). This chapter shows us that there can be no heirship without sonship (Rom. 8:16-17), no righteousness without faith (Rom. 4:3ff), no assurance without promises, and no blessing without suffering. It had to become dark before Abraham could see God's stars!

## II. The Test of the Covenant (16)

God had made the covenant, and God would fulfill it. All Abraham and Sarah had to do was wait by faith (Heb. 6:12). Alas, the spirit is willing but the flesh is weak! In the previous chapter, Abraham listened to God and exercised faith, but here he listened to his wife and revealed his unbelief. He ceased to walk in the Spirit and began to walk in the flesh. We have seen that "faith is living without scheming," but at this point both of them tried to help God accomplish His plan. This explains why God had to wait until they were old before He gave them the child. They had to be dead in themselves before He could work (Heb. 11:11-12).

In v. 2 Sarah blames God for her barren condition and hints that He is not good to them (see 3:1-6). She turns to the world for help—to Hagar, the Egyptian—but the whole scheme fails. The works of the flesh now appear (Gal. 5:16-26).

God did not recognize the marriage. He called Hagar "Sarah's maid" (v. 8). This is the first mention of the Angel of the Lord in the OT, and is none other than Christ. God cared for Hagar, instructed her to submit to Sarah, and promised that her son, Ishmael, would be a great man, but a wild man. "Ishmael" means "God will hear" (see v. 11).

When Isaac, Sarah's son, entered the family, there was no room for Ishmael and he was cast out (21:9ff). Eventually, Ishmael fathered twelve sons (25:13-15), and their descendants have been enemies of the Jews for centuries. Galatians 4:21-31 teaches that Sarah pictures the New Covenant and Hagar the Old Covenant. Hagar was a slave, and the Old Covenant enslaved people (Acts 15:10); Sarah was a free woman and Christ makes us free (Gal. 5:1ff). Ishmael was born of the flesh and could not be controlled. Likewise, the Law appeals to the flesh but cannot change it or control it. Isaac was born of the Spirit, a child of promise (Gal.4:23) who enjoyed liberty.

Do not miss the practical lessons here: whenever we run ahead of God, there is trouble. The flesh loves to help God, but true faith is shown in patience (Isa. 28:16). We cannot mix faith and flesh, law and grace, promise and self-effort.

## III. The Token of the Covenant (17)

There are thirteen years of silence between Ishmael's birth and the events of this chapter. God had to wait for Abraham and Sarah to die to self so that His resurrection power might be displayed in their lives. God revealed Himself as "God Almighty" — *El Shaddai*, "the all-sufficient One." Note the repetition of "my covenant" in this chapter. Its fulfillment rests upon God, not upon man. Note too the repeated "I will" statements.

### A. The new names.

"Abram" means "high father"; "Abraham" means "father of a multitude." "Sarai" is said to mean "contentious"; but "Sarah" means "a princess." Their new names were preparation for the new blessing about to enter their home. Only the grace of God could take two idol-worshiping heathen and make godly kings and queens out of them!

### B. The new sign.

This is the first mention of circumcision in the Bible. Nowhere does the OT teach that circumcision saves a man. It is but the outward symbol of the covenant between God and men. It was to remind them of the inward circumcision of the heart that accompanies true salvation (Deut. 10:16 and 30:6; Jer. 4:4; and see Rom. 4:11 and Gal. 5:6). The ritual was to be performed on the eighth day (v. 12), and significantly, eight is the number of resurrection. Sad to say, the Jews depended on the fleshly ritual and not the inner reality (Acts 15:5). Believers today are in the New Covenant and are the true circumcision (Phil. 3:1-3), which is experienced spiritually through the death of Christ (Col. 2:9-15). The entire body of sin (the old nature) has been put off, and we may live in the Spirit, not in the flesh.

Abraham's laughter in v. 17 was that of joyful faith; Sarah's (18:12) was that of unbelief. "Isaac" means "laughter." God rejects Ishmael and establishes His covenant with Isaac and his seed; however, in grace He does appoint special blessing for Ishmael.

# GENESIS 18–20

Three visits are recorded in these chapters, and each one carries a spiritual lesson.

## I. Christ's Visit with Abraham (18)

Verses 17-22 make it clear that the Lord Jesus Christ was one of the three heavenly visitors; note also Abraham's words in v. 3. The great theme of this chapter is the believer's fellowship with Christ, for Abraham was "the friend of God" (James 2:23). In chapter 19 we will see Lot, the friend of the world.

### A. Abraham's communion with Christ (vv. 1-8).

These verses picture the believer in loving communion with Christ. Abraham is in Mamre, which means "fatness"; he is enjoying the fullness of God's blessing. The tent speaks of his pilgrim life; "the heat of the day" indicates that he is walking in the light (1 John 1). His haste proves his loving desire to please the Lord. And he spares no pains to make Christ feel at home. Paul prays in Eph. 3:17, "That Christ may dwell in your hearts," which literally means "That Christ may settle down and feel at home in your hearts." How important it is for the Christian to make Christ feel at home. He yearns to have communion with us.

### B. Sarah's confession of unbelief (vv. 9-15).

The birth of Isaac is connected with laughter. In fact, the name "Isaac" means "laughter." Abraham had laughed in joyful faith when he heard the news that God would give him a son (17:15-18), but here Sarah seems to laugh in carnal unbelief. Why should we doubt the promises of God? "Is anything too hard for the Lord?" Note Mary's faith in Luke 1:34, when she asked, "How shall this be?" Alternatively, Sarah was saying, "How can this be?" When Isaac was born, however, Sarah did laugh in spiritual joy (21:6-7).

### C. Christ's confidence in Abraham (vv. 16-22).

The angels left and went to Sodom, but Christ stayed behind to visit with Abraham. What a scene! Christ would not hide anything from His friend. See John 15:14-15, where Christ promises to reveal His will to His friends. Read also Ps. 25:9-14, and see how Abraham meets all the conditions given there. Abraham knew more about Sodom than Lot did, and Lot was living in Sodom! The separated obedient Christian knows more about this world than the atheistic philosophers do!

### D. Abraham's concern for Lot (vv. 23-33).

Abraham had such love for Lot, in spite of the man's worldliness and unbelief. Note that Abraham was not pleading the grace of God, but the justice of God: how could God destroy the righteous with the wicked? (At Calvary, God punished the Righteous One

instead of the wicked.) Persistently and tenderly Abraham interceded on behalf of Sodom. If only ten believers could be found,
God said he would spare the whole city. Chapter 19 indicates that
Lot had at least two married daughters (v. 14) and two single
daughters (v. 30ff), so, with his wife and sons-in-law, there were
eight in the family. If Lot had won his own family, plus only two
neighbors, God would have spared a whole city! But he failed to
meet even those conditions.

## II. The Angels' Visit with Lot (19)

Christ did not accompany the angels; He would not have felt "at
home" in the house of a worldly backslider. Second Peter 2:7-8
indicates that Lot was a saved man. He had union with the Lord,
but not communion; sonship, but not fellowship. He was "saved,
yet as by fire" (1 Cor. 3:14-15). Note that Lot had lost his tent.
For at this time he lived in a house (v. 3), and there is no mention
of the altar. It was evening when the angels arrived, and most of
the chapter events take place at night. Lot was not walking in the
light. Not only had worldly Lot lost his tent and altar and his
fellowship with God, but he had also lost his spiritual standards: he
dared to suggest that his single daughters go out in the street to
satisfy the lusts of the crowd! Lot had also lost his testimony with
his own family (vv. 12-14). Where did it all start? When he "lifted
up his eyes" (13:10) and chose his land. He started walking by
sight, not by faith, living for the things of the world. He must have
married a worldly woman, for her heart was in Sodom and she could
not bear to leave the city behind.

That morning dawned bright and beautiful. People started about
their daily tasks—and then judgment came! The wicked cities
were completely destroyed. Only Lot and his two single daughters
escaped alive. Sodom's fate is a picture of the wrath to come. When
men think there is peace and safety, then destruction will fall
(1 Thes. 5). Lot's rescue, meanwhile, is an illustration of the rapture of the church prior to the pouring out of the wrath of God.
The Lord rescued Lot for Abraham's sake (19:29), and He will
deliver His church from the wrath to come for Jesus' sake (1 Thes.
1:10; 5:9).

Lot's final days were full of darkness and sin as he committed
incest in a cave. He forsook a tent for a house in the city, and
ended up in a cave, made drunk by his own daughters! The children of this horrible scene, the Moabites and Ammonites, have

been enemies of the Jews for centuries, illustrating that the flesh fights against the Spirit. We must be sure we are in the will of God when we settle down with our family. Lot chose the wrong place and ruined himself and his loved ones.

It is interesting to contrast the two visits in chapters 18 and 19. Christ Himself visited Abraham, but only the angels went to Sodom to visit Lot. Christ had a message of joy for Abraham and Sarah, but the angels gave a message of judgment to Lot. Abraham was visited in the daytime but Lot in the evening. Abraham was at a tent door; Lot at the city gate. Abraham had power with God but Lot had no influence even with his own family. Abraham saw Sodom destroyed and lost nothing, but Lot lost everything. Only his life was spared. Abraham brought the world blessing, but Lot brought trouble into the world (the Ammonites and Moabites).

### III. Abraham's Visit in Gerar (20)

Lot is forgotten, but the story of Abraham continues. "He who does the will of God abides forever" (1 John 2:17, NKJV). Unfortunately, this chapter records the repetition of an old sin—Abraham lying about his wife (see 12:10-20). Even the most dedicated saint must constantly be on his guard lest Satan trip him up.

Why was this sin repeated? Because Abraham had not judged it in his life. Certainly he had confessed it to the Lord and been forgiven, but confessing sin is not the same as judging sin. To judge our sins means to see them in their true light (as God sees them), to hate them, and to put them out of our lives. In v. 13 Abraham admitted that this sin came with him out of Ur of the Chaldees.

There is a difference between the believer and the unbeliever, even though the believer might commit sin. God plagued the heathen court but protected Abraham. God said to the ruler, "You are a dead man" (v. 3, NKJV), but He called Abraham a "prophet" (v. 7). This does not mean that believers have license to sin, but it does show that God is faithful even though we might be unfaithful (2 Tim. 2:12-13). Certainly Abraham suffered shame and reproach because of his sin, but God protects His own. Actually, had Abimelech taken Sarah, it would have altered God's plan for the birth of Isaac the very next year. Abraham's selfishness and unbelief almost wrecked his own life and the future of the Jewish nation. Sadly enough, his son Isaac would use this same scheme in later years (26:6ff), and with the same bitter results.

# GENESIS 21–22

These two chapters record three tests that came into the life of Abraham. True faith is always tested, for it is only through testing that we discover what kind of faith we have. Tests of faith are opportunities for growth and victory.

## I. A Test from the Family (21:1-21)

It is often hardest to live for Christ at home. Abraham had already been tested in his family by his father (11:27-32), by his nephew Lot (chaps. 12–13), and by his wife (chap. 16). Here we see conflict between the two sons, Ishmael (who would be in his late teens according to 16:16), and Isaac (who was weaned at about the age of 3). At first, Isaac's birth brought joy and laughter (compare 21:6 with 17:17 and 18:12) for the very name "Isaac" means "laughter." But soon there was conflict as Ishmael constantly persecuted his younger brother. There are some valuable lessons here:

### A. The flesh vs. the Spirit.

Ishmael was a child of the flesh (chap. 16), while Isaac was a child of promise, born miraculously. Isaac's presence in the home was not due to Abraham's strength (for Abraham was as good as dead, Rom. 4:19-20), but to God's promise and power. There is always conflict between the flesh and the Spirit, the old nature and the new, (Gal. 5:16-24). Salvation does not change the old nature, nor can the old nature be improved or disciplined (see Rom. 6–7). The only way to overcome the old nature is to accept God's estimate of it and obey God's Word. Abraham loved Ishmael and longed to hold to him (21:10-11, and see 17:18); but God said, "Cast him out!" Romans 6 informs us that our only victory over the flesh is crucifixion—reckoning ourselves dead. Christians who cater to the old nature (Rom. 13:14) will always have conflict and trouble.

### B. The Old Covenant vs. the New Covenant.

Galatians 4:21-31 explains that these events with Ishmael and Isaac are an allegory that symbolizes God's Old Covenant with Israel and His New Covenant with the church. We may briefly summarize the main ideas as follows: Hagar symbolizes the Old Covenant of law, identified with the earthly Jerusalem in Paul's day. Sarah symbolizes the New Covenant of grace, identified with the heavenly Jerusalem. Ishmael was born of the flesh and was the son of a slave. Isaac was "born of the Spirit" and was the son of a freewoman. The two sons, then, picture the Jews under the slavery of law and the true Christians under the liberty of grace. Paul's argument is that God commanded Abraham to cast out Hagar (the Old Covenant) because His blessing was to be upon Isaac. All of this fits into Paul's argument in Gal. 3–4 that Christians today are not under the law.

### C. Man's way vs. God's way.

The best way to solve any problem is God's way. Hagar had forgotten God's promise in 16:10; otherwise she would not have lost heart. God did sustain them and keep His Word. If we obey Him, He will always open the way and solve the problem.

## II. A Test from the Neighbors (21:22-34)

Believers must be careful in the relationship to "those who are outside" (Col. 4:5; 1 Thes. 4:12; 1 Tim. 3:7, NKJV). Abraham had a good testimony before his unsaved neighbors, and the conflict over the well could have ruined it for good. Note that Abraham agreed to settle the problem in a businesslike way—"Let all things be done decently and in order" (1 Cor. 14:40). Abraham and his neighbors exchanged the proper gifts and made the proper sacrifices for sealing a covenant. The place where the covenant was made was called Beersheba, "the well of the oath," and it became a place of prayer and communion for Abraham. It is important that tests that we face in the neighborhood or business be settled in a Christian way. See Rom. 12:18 for further clarification.

## III. The Test from the Lord (22:1-24)

Satan tempts us to bring out the worst in us, but God tests us to help bring out the best. See James 1:12-15. The most severe tests do not come from people, but from the Lord, and yet the greatest blessings always accompany them. God never tested Lot in this way. Lot lived on such a low level that Sodom and the world tested him. It is the saint that walks closest to the Lord that God tests the greatest for His glory.

### A. The typical lesson.

This event is a wonderful type of Christ, the only Son who was willing to give His life to please His Father. Both Isaac and Christ were promised sons; both were born miraculously (of course, Christ was born of the Virgin Mary and was sinless); both brought joy to the heart of the father; both were born at the set time. Both were persecuted by their brethren and both were obedient unto death. Christ was crucified between two thieves, and the two young men went with Isaac (v. 3). Isaac questioned his father, and Jesus asked, "My God, why have You forsaken Me?" (Matt. 27:46, NKJV) Of course, Christ actually died, while Isaac was spared. However, in God's sight Isaac had "died." Hebrews 11:19 says that "in a figure" (that is, symbolically) Isaac was raised from the dead. Verse 19 indicates that Abraham returned to the waiting servants, but nothing is said about Isaac. This too is a type; for the next time we see Isaac, he is receiving his bride! (24:62ff) Even so Christ gave Himself on the cross and went back to heaven, and one day will come forth to receive His Bride, the church.

### B. The practical lesson.

True faith is always tested. Of course, God did not want Isaac's life; He wanted Abraham's heart. Isaac was dear to Abraham, and God wanted to be sure that Isaac was not an idol standing between Him and Abraham. It was possible that Abraham was trusting Isaac to fulfill the promises and not trusting God. How did Abraham go through this test? For one thing, he rested on God's promises (Heb. 11:17-19). God had promised Abraham many descendants, and this promise could not be fulfilled unless Isaac lived or God raised him from the dead. Abraham knew that God would not lie, so he rested in His unchanging Word. "Never doubt in the dark what God has told you in the light." Abraham obeyed without delay. If we do the one thing God tells us to do, He will reveal the next step when the right time comes. God's answers never arrive a minute too late! God supplied a ram just when one was needed. This is why Abraham called the name of the place "Jehovah-Jireh — the Lord will see to it!"

### C. The prophetic lesson.

This event took place on Mt. Moriah (22:2), the place where the temple was eventually built (2 Chron. 3:1). Isaac had asked, "Where is the lamb?" but God had supplied a ram. The answer to his question came in the Person of Christ: "Behold! The Lamb of God!" (John 1:29) Abraham had said, "In the mount of the Lord it shall be seen" (v. 14); Christ was seen in the temple, and then slain on Mt. Calvary. See John 8:56 also.

### D. The doctrinal lesson.

James 2:14-26 discusses the relationship between faith and works, and James uses this event to illustrate his main point: true faith is always proved by obedience. Note the accurate translation of James 2:21 — "Was not Abraham our father justified by works in that he offered his son upon the altar?" Abraham was not saved when he offered Isaac, for he had been saved years before when he trusted God's promise (Gen. 15:6). James is not telling us that we are saved by works or by sacrifices, but that the proof of saving faith is an obedient life (see Rom. 4:1-5 and Gal. 3:6ff).

# GENESIS 23–24

These two chapters stand in contrast to one another, for in one we have a funeral and in the other a wedding. The land of Canaan is "a land of hills and valleys" (Deut. 11:11); the Christian life has both its sorrows and joys. Yet in both, Abraham walked by faith (Heb. 11:13-17). Chapter 23 shows Abraham as a mourner, one who sorrows yet not "as others which have no hope" (1 Thes. 4:13ff). What a testimony he was before his lost neighbors! How different Sarah's burial was from the heathen burials of that day. How strange that the first plot of ground Abraham possessed in Canaan was a tomb! Genesis 49:31-33 indicates that six people were eventually buried there. Note too how carefully Abraham handled his business matters, making sure that everything was done "decently and in order." It is shameful when believers carry out questionable business deals, especially with those who are lost.

We will concentrate on chapter 24, which is rich in spiritual lessons. We see in Abraham, his servant, and Rebekah three wonderful examples.

## I. Abraham's Example of Dedication (24:1-9)

At this point, Abraham is 140 years old (see 25:20 and 21:5). God has blessed him spiritually and materially, but he wants to be sure that the right bride is chosen for Isaac. Of course, we see here a picture of the Heavenly Father choosing a bride (the church) for

His Son (Christ). How did Abraham know that God would provide the right woman for his son? He trusted the promises of God! Isaac was God's possession. Abraham had laid him on the altar years before, and he knew that God would supply the need. Otherwise, the promised seed could never be born.

The woman must come from within the family of God; she must not be one of the heathen women. No doubt there were many beautiful and talented Canaanite women who would have gladly married Isaac and shared his wealth, but this was against God's will. In vv. 6 and 8, Abraham emphasizes this fact; and we need to emphasize it today. "Only in the Lord" is the admonition of 1 Cor. 7:39-40 (see also 2 Cor. 6:14-18). It is tragic when parents push their children to marry "into society" and out of the blessing of the Lord! Abraham would rather his son remain single than go back to Ur for a wife, or take a wife from the Canaanite nations.

## I. The Servant's Example of Devotion (24:10-49)

In a spiritual sense, the servant is a picture of the Holy Spirit whose work is to bring the lost to Christ and thus make up His bride. The servant's name is not given, for the ministry of the Spirit is to point to Christ and glorify Him. Note how often the servant mentioned his master and his master's son. He lived to please his master, for the word "master" is found twenty-two times in this chapter. The Spirit has been sent to represent Christ and do the Savior's will here on earth. The servant carried with him a portion of his master's wealth (vv. 10, 22, 30, 53), just as the Holy Spirit today "is a deposit guaranteeing our inheritance" (Eph. 1:14, NIV), sharing with us but a small portion of the great wealth we shall one day enjoy in glory.

In addition, the servant is an example for us as we seek to serve the Lord. As already mentioned, the servant thought only of his master and his master's will. In fact, he was so anxious to finish his task that he cared nothing for food (v. 33; John 4:31-34). Too often we put physical things ahead of the spiritual. The servant received his orders from his master and did not change them one bit. He believed in prayer (see Isa. 65:24) and knew how to wait on the Lord. There is no place for rash impatience in the service of Christ.

The servant knew how to trust in the leading of the Lord: "I being in the way (of willing obedience), the Lord led me" (v. 27). See the claim of John 7:17. Once he knew what God's will was, he did not delay, but hastened to perform his task (v. 17). The hospitality of the home was delightful, but he had a job to do for his master and everything else could wait. Note too that the servant reported to his master when he returned home (v. 66), just as we must give an account when we see Christ. It is interesting to conjecture if the servant taught the bride as they journeyed, and revealed the bridegroom to her. "He shall glorify Me," said Christ concerning the Holy Spirit (John 16:14).

## III. Rebekah's Example of Decision (24:50-67)

Again, we see a picture of Christ and His church. Rebekah was a pure virgin, just as the church will be when the marriage in heaven takes place (Rev. 19:7-8). Note that Rebekah identified with the flock, just as the church is both the bride of Christ and the flock (John 10:7-18).

Rebekah had to make an important decision: would she stay home with her family and continue to be a servant, or would she by faith believe the words of the servant and go to be with Isaac, a man she had never seen? Certainly there were obstacles in the way: her brother wanted her to stay awhile (v. 55); the trip would be long and difficult; Isaac was a pilgrim without a settled home; and she would have to leave her loved ones.

The world often advises the sinner to wait, just as Laban advised his sister. (Note, however, that when it came to getting material things, Laban could be in a hurry, vv. 28-31. We wonder if he invited the servant home out of courtesy or covetousness!) Sinners generally are not in a hurry about the salvation of their souls. Up to this point, Rebekah had been hastening (vv. 18-20, 28), but now they wanted her to slow down. "Seek the Lord while He may be found (Isa. 55:6, NIV).

We cannot help but admire her decision: "I will go." This act of faith ("Whom having not seen you love . . ." 1 Peter 1:8, NKJV) changed her life. She was changed from being a servant to being a bride, from the loneliness of the world to the joy of love and companionship, from her poverty into Isaac's wealth. Did she see all of Isaac's wealth? Of course not! That would be impossible! Did she know all about him? No. But what she saw and heard convinced her that she must go. Similarly, with lost sinners today, the Spirit speaks and shows them the things of Christ, sufficient for them to make a right decision.

We left Isaac (as far as the record is concerned) on Mt. Moriah, for 22:19 mentions Abraham alone. Isaac is a picture of our Lord who went to Calvary to die for us, then returned to heaven to wait for His bride. In chapter 24, the servant (the Holy Spirit) went forth to seek the bride. Then, when the bride approached, Isaac appeared to receive her. What a scene, it may take place today! Just as it was "eventide" when they met, so it will be dark in this world when Christ returns for His bride.

Rebekah's faith was rewarded. Her name was recorded in God's Word; she shared Isaac's love and wealth, and she became an important part of God's plan. Had she refused to go, she would have died an unknown woman. "He who does the will of God abides forever" (1 John 2:17, NKJV).

# GENESIS 25–27

Isaac was the son of a famous father (Abraham), and the father of a famous son (Jacob), and sometimes people "lose" him as they study Genesis. While he lived longer than any of the other patriarchs, his life was less exciting. Unfortunately, he does not seem to be as strong in faith at the end of his life as he was at the beginning.

## I. Isaac the Father (25)

### A. A distinguished home (vv. 1-11).

Abraham's marriage after the death of Sarah brought him six more sons and at least seven grandsons and three great-grandsons. However, note that these additional sons of Abraham do not have the status given to Isaac, for (like Christ) he is the heir of all things (Heb. 1:2). Abraham's death shows what faith can do for a man. He died in peace (see 15:15); he died "full" (satisfied), and he died in faith (Heb. 11:13ff). This is the heritage Abraham left his son: his godly example (18:19), the tent and altar (see 26:25), and the wonderful promises of God (26:2-5). These spiritual blessings mean far more to a son than any material wealth.

### B. A disappointed home (vv. 12-23).

The fulfillment of God's covenant promise demanded that Isaac and Rebekah have a son, yet for the first twenty years of their married life, she was barren (vv. 20, 26). What a delight it is to see how this spiritually-minded husband and wife took their burden to the Lord. Surely they reminded God of His promises, and surely He was pleased with their prayers. The struggle of the unborn children perplexed Rebekah, so she asked God for wisdom (James 1:5). God told her that two nations were to be born and that, contrary to custom, the elder would serve the younger.

This is a clear evidence of God's sovereign election (Rom. 9:10-16). His choice was not based on the deeds of the boys, for they were unborn and had done neither good nor evil. As far as character is concerned, Esau was the more acceptable of the two—yet Jacob was the one chosen by God (Eph. 2:8-10).

## C. A divided home (vv. 24-34).

The twin boys were opposite each other in appearance and temperament. The first boy was hairy and was named "Esau" (hairy); later his connection with the red pottage gave him the nickname "Edom" which means "red" (v. 30). Jacob's laying hold of Esau's heel (as though to catch him and trip him) gave him the name "Jacob"—the "heel-gripper" (supplanter, schemer, deceiver). Jacob was a quiet man who stayed at home; Esau was a man of the world, full of vigor and adventure. Alas, Esau had no spiritual appreciation. He would rather feed his body than enjoy the promises of God. Of course, Jacob's scheme to get the birthright showed that he doubted that God would fulfill His promise of 25:23. "Faith is living without scheming!" Esau despised his spiritual privileges as the firstborn (see Deut. 21:17 and 1 Chron. 5:1-2); he chose the flesh, not the Spirit. We never read of Esau having a tent or an altar, and 26:34-35 indicates that he loved worldly women. Hebrews 12:16 describes Esau as "profane" which means "of the world, common" (La., *profanus*—"outside the temple"). Like many people today, Esau was a success in the world and a failure with God.

## II. Isaac the Pilgrim (26)

### A. He faced his father's temptations (vv. 1-5).

Review 12:10ff. Isaac started toward Egypt, but God in His grace interrupted the trip and stopped him. Human nature does not improve from generation to generation. Isaac dwelt at Gerar which is on the borderline (10:19). Likewise, we have many "borderline

Christians" today. Isaac had material blessings there, but not the spiritual blessings God gave him later when he left that place.

## B. He repeated his father's sin (vv. 6-11).

See 12:10-20 and 20:1-5. This "half-lie," that they were brother and sister, was adopted by Isaac and Rebekah, with the same sad results—loss of blessing, loss of testimony, and a public rebuke by the heathen king.

## C. He dug again his father's wells (vv. 12-22).

Wells of water speak of the divine resources of God for the spiritual life (John 4:1-14). Abraham had dug these wells, but the enemy had either stolen them or stopped them up. How true this is today. The spiritual wells at which our fathers drank have been taken from us by the world. How we need to get back to the old wells (such as prayer, the Bible, the family altar, the church). Isaac not only opened them again, but he called them by the same names that Abraham had used (v. 18). Then he went on to dig some new wells to meet the needs of the day.

## D. He trusted his father's God (vv. 23-35).

As long as he was away from Canaan, Isaac would have conflict, but when he went back to Beersheba ("the well of the oath"), God met him and gave him peace with the enemy (Prov. 16:7).

## III. Isaac the Blesser (27)

Sad to say, this chapter depicts the whole family in a bad way spiritually. In 25:28 we saw the division of the home, and now we will see the sinful results of this carnal division.

## A. A declining father.

Isaac was about 137 years old at this point, yet he acted as though he would die very soon. Actually, he lived to be 180 (35:28). His impatience to give Esau the blessing suggests that he was following his own carnal plans, not God's will. Had he forgotten the Word in 25:23, or was he trying to change God's plan? Note how he depended on his senses (feeling, eating, smelling). Note also that feeding the body took priority over doing God's will. Isaac at one time laid himself on the altar and was willing to die for the Lord. What a change!

## B. A doubting mother.

Rebekah had been told by God that Jacob would receive God's blessing, yet she schemed and plotted to make sure that Esau was left out. Instead of going to God in prayer as she had years before, she depended on her own plans, a practice that would be characteristic of Jacob in later years. Rebekah paid dearly for her sin: she never saw her son again (see vv. 43-45). Esau deliberately acted to hurt her; and her bad example before Jacob cost him twenty years of trial.

## C. A deceiving son.

Certainly Jacob knew God's promise for his life, yet he listened to his mother instead of to God. How the two of them hurried to finish the plot! "Whoever believes will not act hastily" (Isa. 28:16, NKJV). Rebekah must have been a good cook to be able to make goat's meat taste like venison. Jacob is a perfect picture of the hypocrite: his voice and his hands do not agree (what he says and what he does), and he deceives others. In v. 19 alone, Jacob tells his father three lies: "I am Esau" (he was Jacob); "I have done" (his mother did it all); "eat of my venison" (it was goat's meat). And his kiss in v. 27 was equally as deceitful. Did Jacob pay for this sin? Yes, many times. Laban deceived him about his wives and repeatedly changed his wages. In addition, Jacob's own sons would one day kill a kid (37:31) and put its blood on Joseph's coat to deceive their father. "Be sure your sin will find you out" (Num. 32:23).

## D. A despairing brother.

Hebrews 12:17 indicates that Esau sought the blessing with tears, yet found no place for real repentance for his sins. Remorse, yes, but not sincere repentance. He was sorry for what he had lost, not sorry for what he had done. In v. 33, Isaac trembled when he realized that God had overruled his plans. Esau's tears could not change Isaac's mind or alter the blessing. Esau retaliated by plotting to murder his brother, and he deliberately hurt his parents by stirring up trouble with his marriage to heathen wives. The grace of God did not fail, but Esau failed the grace of God.

Sin in the home always brings heartache and misunderstanding. Had Isaac and Rebekah not "taken sides" with their two boys; had they continued to pray about matters as in their early married life; had they allowed God to have His way; then affairs would have been different. As it was, all of them suffered because of their unbelief and disobedience. We never get too old to be tempted — or to fail!

# GENESIS 28

## I. The Venture (28:1-9)

We can accurately say that the rest of Genesis presents the life of Jacob, including his trials with Laban (28-31), with Esau (32-33), and with his sons (34ff). The story of Joseph is actually a part of Jacob's history.

The real reason Rebekah engineered Jacob's departure from home was to avoid the anger of Esau (27:41-46), but her excuse was that she wanted Jacob to find a godly wife (see 24:1-9). Esau's worldly wives were causing trouble in the home, as is always the case when God's people marry outside of God's will. Rebekah actually planned to send for Jacob when the time was right (27:45), but this plan failed. Jacob never did see his mother again. Once again, "faith is living without scheming." We all need to heed the warning of James 4:13-17.

It is wonderful when a son can leave home with his father's blessing! But Jacob could not depend on his father's faith. He had to meet God and make some decisions of his own. Unfortunately, it took more than twenty years for Jacob to come to a place of real surrender, and how dearly he paid for his unbelief and rebellion! Verses 6-9 illustrate the conflict of the flesh and the Spirit: Esau (the flesh) deliberately disobeyed the Lord and brought even greater sorrow into the home. Note that Jacob was not a young man when he started out on this venture. He was at least seventy-seven years old. Genesis 47:9 states that Jacob was 130 when he went to Egypt. Joseph was seventeen when he was sold into Egypt, and was thirty when he was presented to Pharaoh (41:46). Add, then, Joseph's thirteen years as a servant to the seven years of plenty and two years of famine, and you have Joseph at about thirty-nine years of age when Jacob came to Egypt. This means Joseph was born when Jacob was ninety-one, and Gen. 30:25 indicates that when Joseph was born Jacob had already fulfilled his fourteen years of service for his wives. This indicates that Jacob was about seventy-seven years old when he began to walk "on his own."

## II. The Vision (28:10-12)

Jacob traveled about seventy miles from Beersheba to Bethel, a three-day journey. That night, he took "one of the stones" to rest against as he slept, and God gave him a vision of a ladder (or staircase, as some translate it) from heaven to earth. John 1:43-51 is the NT explanation of this verse. The ladder symbolizes Jesus Christ. Jacob is a perfect picture of the lost soul — in the darkness, fleeing for his life, away from the father's house, burdened with sin, and ignorant of the fact that God is near him and wants to save him. The ladder pictures Christ as the only way from earth to heaven. He opens heaven for us and brings heaven's blessings to our lives. And He alone can take us to heaven. Jacob thought he was in a lonely wilderness and awakened to discover he had been at the very gate of heaven! Relating this further to John 1:43-51, we note that Jacob was an Israelite who was full of guile (deceit), while v. 47 describes Nathanael as an Israelite without guile.

This is the first of at least seven recorded revelations from God to Jacob (see 31:3, 11-13; 32:1-2; 32:24-30; 35:1, 9-13; 46:1-4). The angels on the ladder were an indication of God's care. They appeared again to protect Jacob when he was about to face Esau (32:1-2).

## III. The Voice (28:13-15)

Visions apart from the Word of God can be deceiving, so God spoke to Jacob to assure him. A person is not saved by angels or visions; he is saved by faith in God's Word. Note the promises that God gave to Jacob:

### A. The land (v. 13).

This promise was first given to Abraham (13:14ff) and was reaffirmed to Isaac (26:1-5). The Holy Land belongs to the Jews, even though they do not possess all of it. One day, Israel will "possess her possessions" (Obadiah 17).

### B. The multiplied seed (v. 14).

This assured Jacob that God would give him a wife; otherwise he could not have descendants (see also 13:16 and 22:17). Today, there are Jews at every point of the compass.

### C. God's personal presence (v. 15).

This verse suggests that Jacob would wander about but God promised to be with him. Why? Because God had a plan for Jacob's life, and He would see to it that His plan was fulfilled (Phil. 1:6; Rom. 8:28-29). Though in the hard years ahead Jacob had to reap the consequences of his sins, God was still with him to protect him and bless him.

## IV. The Vow (28:16-22)

"This is the house of God!" exclaims Jacob, for the name "Bethel" means "house of God." His experience that night not only changed him, but it changed the name of the place where he slept. To commemorate the event, Jacob set up a pillar and made it into an altar, pouring out a drink offering to the Lord. Years later, when he came back to Bethel, Jacob repeated this act of consecration (35:9-15). This act of faith (even though caused by fear) was Jacob's way of dedicating himself to God. (See Phil. 2:17, where "offered" is literally "poured out.") It is a wonderful thing that by faith a believer can turn a "pillow" into a "pillar"!

There are two interpretations suggested of Jacob's vow: (1) that he is bargaining with God by saying "If . . . if . . ."; (2) that he is showing faith in God, for the Hebrew word can be translated "Since . . . since. . . ." This is actually the first vow recorded in the Bible. It is likely that both interpretations are true: Jacob believed God's Word, but there was still enough of the "old man" in him to try to bargain with God the way he bargained with Esau and Isaac. He was so accustomed to "scheming" that he tried to scheme his way into God's blessing! This was finally exposed and dealt with at Jabbok (Gen. 32). Jacob did return home in peace (Gen. 35:27-29), and he practiced tithing (v. 22). He realized that his dedication to God meant nothing unless his material goods were under His control as well. Abraham had practiced tithing (14:20), and in both cases the Law had not yet been given. Those who say that the tithe is not for this age of grace miss the fact that the early saints practiced tithing. It was their expression of faith and obedience to the Lord who guided them, guarded them, and provided for them.

Jacob did not always live up to this vow in the years that followed. He "met his match" in Laban, who was a schemer himself! For twenty years the two of them tried to outsmart each other, but, in the end, Jacob had been disciplined and God had kept his promises. It is good for us believers to have a "Bethel" in our lives, a place where we meet God in a serious way and make some definite commitments to Him. If we get away from the Lord, we can always come "back to Bethel" (Gen. 35:9-15) and renew our dedication. Jacob is an illustration of the conflict between the two natures, for he was always battling the flesh and trying to depend on his own abilities and plans. How good to know that God watches over His wayward children!

# GENESIS 29–31

From the spiritual mountaintop of Bethel (chap. 28), Jacob descended into everyday life at Haran, and here he "met his match" in scheming Laban, his uncle. Jacob spent about 20 years with Laban. During this time he reaped the sad consequences of his own sins, but, at the same time, God was disciplining him and preparing him for future service.

## I. Jacob's Service for Laban's Daughters (29:1–30:24)

### A. Decision (29:1-20).

God providentially directs Jacob to the house of Laban, but note that Jacob did not pause to pray, as did Abraham's servant when he was on his important errand (24:12). Jacob encouraged the other shepherds to go back to the pastures (v. 7) because he wanted to greet Rachel in private. He was still the schemer. Note how Rachel and Laban ran when they discovered who Jacob was (vv. 12-13). Jacob made his decision: he wanted beautiful Rachel for his wife. Rachel means "ewe," while Leah means "wild cow." Leah's eyes lacked that deep sparkle that, in Middle Eastern cultures, is a mark of beauty. Jacob agreed to serve Laban for seven years, and as always, where there is love, the time and labor passed quickly. Note that in v. 15 we have the first "installment" of Jacob's discipline: he became a servant. In 25:23, it had been promised that "the elder shall serve the younger"; but now the younger was a servant himself.

### B. Deception (29:21-30).

Here is discipline "installment" number two—the deceiver himself is deceived. Laban was not about to forfeit his elder daughter's chances for marriage, so he forced Jacob to marry her. Jacob had lied about the firstborn (27:19); now he is lied to about the firstborn (29:26). "The way of transgressors is hard" (Prov. 13:15). He fulfilled the week of marriage celebration for Leah, then married Rachel and began his second term of service for another seven years. Laban was careful that all the men of the area witnessed the marriage to Leah (v. 22). Having consummated the marriage, Jacob could not back out. No doubt he realized that God was disciplining him for his own scheming.

### C. Division (29:31–30:24).

When a marriage begins with sin, there is usually division and unhappiness in the home. At first, neither of the two wives bore children, but it was obvious that Jacob loved Rachel more and that he "slighted" (hated, v. 31) Leah. So, God honored Leah by giving her four sons: Reuben ("Look, a son!"), Simeon ("hearing"), Levi ("joined"), and Judah ("praise"). This was in answer to Leah's prayers (see 29:33 and 30:6, 17, 22). Rachel could not help but envy her sister, and her envy created anger and disagreement between her and Jacob. Instead of losing his temper, Jacob should have prayed about the problem, as his parents had done years before (25:19-23). The man-made solution was that Jacob marry Bilhah, who bore him Dan ("judgment"), and Naphtali ("wrestling"). Leah followed by giving him Zilpah, and she bore Gad ("a troop") and Asher ("good fortune"). It is obvious that Jacob did not have a spiritual home: his wives disagreed and used him as a pawn in their plans (30:14-16). Rachel even had an interest in idols (31:19). We read of no altar in his house, and the sad results are not difficult to see. Leah bore two more sons: Issachar ("reward, hire") and Zebulun ("dwelling"); and Rachel bore Jacob's beloved Joseph ("may He add"). Later she would bear Benjamin ("son of my right hand") and then die (35:16-20). Jacob also had several daughters (30:21; 37:35; 46:7, 15).

This account covers fourteen years in Jacob's life—years of toil, trial, and testing. God used Laban and the difficult circumstances of life to discipline Jacob and prepare him for the tasks that lay ahead.

### II. Jacob's Scheme for Laban's Cattle (30:25-43)

Jacob had served for fourteen years, and he realized that he must strike out on his own and provide for his large family. He asked Laban to send him away; however, the crafty Syrian was not about to lose so valuable a son-in-law. Jacob had worked fourteen years for his two wives; now he could work for the cattle he would need in order to get established on his own. Of course, Laban covered the evil motive of his plan by using the Lord's name (v. 27) and by asking Jacob to choose the terms. "Name me your wages, and I will give it." Laban asked, but Jacob refused a gift, for the last time he accepted Laban's "gift" he was deceived (29:19). Jacob offered to work as Laban's shepherd, if Laban would give him the "rejects" of the flocks and herds. Oriental sheep are white and goats brown or black. By accepting the striped, spotted, and speckled animals, Jacob was apparently giving Laban the better deal. It was certainly an act of faith on Jacob's part.

But the schemer went to work. Instead of trusting God to meet the need (see 31:9, and 28:15, 20), Jacob used his own plan. The special rods and sticks at the troughs probably did not influence the sheep; it was God who determined what kind of sheep and goats would be conceived. However, Jacob did use "selective breeding" (vv. 40-43) so that only the stronger cattle conceived. We learn from 31:7-8 that Laban changed the terms of the contract several times as he saw Jacob's flocks increasing, but God overruled Laban and made Jacob a wealthy man.

## III. Jacob's Flight from Laban's House (31)

### A. The conference (vv. 1-16).

Three factors entered into Jacob's decision to leave: the changed attitude of Laban; the need for establishing his own home; and, most of all, the direct leading of the Lord. God had reminded Jacob of his Bethel vow. The backslider now had to return and fulfill his promises to the Lord who had blessed him. Rachel and Leah agreed to go, but their decision was based on material considerations, not the will of the Lord. We wonder if the wives knew anything about Jacob's Bethel experience until now.

### B. The chase (vv. 17-35).

Instead of trusting God to protect him, Jacob steals away in haste while Laban was away shearing sheep. What a poor testimony when believers choose to act in secrecy. Laban was already three days' journey from Jacob (30:36), so he did not catch up with him for a week. God warned Laban before he even faced Jacob, so there was no reason for Jacob's fear (v. 31; see also Prov. 16:7). Laban "put on a front" and made it look as though he was offended, when he was probably glad to be rid of the man who was outsmarting him and getting richer. His real concern comes out in v. 30—someone had stolen his idols! Hidden sin led to more sin as Rachel, the thief, lied to her father and her husband, while angry Laban examined everything in the caravan.

### C. The conflict (vv. 36-42).

Twenty years' pent-up anger now revealed itself, and Jacob "laid it on the line" to his father-in-law. Laban was an idolater, and Jacob a backslider—how could there be any agreement between them? The only redeeming thing in Jacob's angry speech is that he gave God the glory for his success (v. 42).

### D. The covenant (vv. 43-55).

The so-called "Mizpah Blessing" found in many hymnals is not at all scriptural. These two men did not trust each other, so they set up a pillar to remind both of them that God was watching. Instead of witnessing to their friendship (as the "Mizpah Blessing" states), these stones witnessed to their mutual distrust of one another. Note that in v. 47, the two men did not even speak the same language! (Both names mean "heap of witness" or "heap of testimony.") It is truly sad when family members cannot trust each other. How much better it would have been had they forgiven each other and turned the whole thing over to God. Verse 52 indicates that the pillar Laban erected was also a boundary marker beyond which Jacob dare not go.

Jacob's twenty years of servitude were over, but he needed still to go back to Bethel and make things right with God.

# GENESIS 32–36

These chapters record several crucial experiences in Jacob's life as he made his way from Laban's house to Bethel. They give us three vivid pictures of this man who illustrates for us the conflict between the flesh and the Spirit, the old life and the new.

## I. Jacob the Wrestler (32)

Esau was coming and Jacob was about to meet up with his forgotten past. Would Esau forgive him or fight him? Would Jacob lose everything he had schemed to acquire? How tragic it is when the past catches up with sinners. Geography could not erase Jacob's past nor could twenty years of history change it. But before Jacob met Esau, he experienced three other meetings:

### A. He met God's angels (vv. 1-20).

He had first seen these angels at Bethel (chap. 28), and they should have been a reminder to Jacob that God was in control. He named the place "the two camps" (his own camp and the camp or army of angels), but he failed to put his faith in God who had promised years before to protect him. Believers today may claim Heb. 1:14 and Ps. 91:11-13 as they are walking in the will of God. Alas, Jacob started trusting himself and his own schemes again! He tried to appease Esau with gifts. He divided his company into two bands (v. 7) and ignored the protecting army of angels. Then, after taking these steps in carnal confidence, he asked for God's help! Had he forgotten the way God had protected him from Laban? (31:24)

### B. He met the Lord (vv. 21-26).

It is when we get alone with God that good things begin to happen. Christ came to wrestle with Jacob, and the struggle lasted all night. Keep in mind that Jacob was not wrestling to get a blessing from God; rather, he was defending himself and refusing to yield. The Lord wanted to break Jacob and bring him to the place where he would honestly say, "Not I, but Christ" (Gal. 2:20). All night long, Jacob defended himself and refused to surrender or even admit that he had sinned. Then God weakened Jacob, and the wrestler could only cling! Now instead of scheming for a blessing or bargaining for a blessing, he asked God for the blessing—and he received it.

### C. He met himself (vv. 27-32).

We don't truly see ourselves until first we see the Lord. "What is your name?" (v. 27, NKJV) was the question that forced Jacob to confess his true self—"Jacob, the schemer." Once he faced himself and confessed his sin, Jacob could be changed. God gave him a new name—"Israel, prince with God" or "a God-governed man." The way to have power with God is to be broken by God. God also gave him a new beginning and a new power as he began "walking in the Spirit" and not in the flesh. This was illustrated by a new walk, for now Jacob limped. He had been broken by God, but his limp was a mark of power and not weakness. Verse 31 indicates the dawning of a new day, as the sun rose and Jacob limped out to meet Esau — with God's help!

## II. Jacob the Backslider (33–34)

It would have been wonderful had Jacob lived up to his new name and new position with God, but he did not. The chapter begins with "Jacob" the old name, not "Israel" the new name, and we see him "lifting up his eyes" — walking by sight, not by faith. See what Jacob lost because he did not claim his spiritual privileges:

### A. His limp (33:3).

He bowed before Esau instead of walking (limping) and faced him man-to-man. It is always tragic when a "prince with God" cringes before a man of the world! Better to limp by faith than to bow in self-trust.

### B. His power (33:1-2, 8-11).

See Jacob scheming again, bargaining with the enemy. Did God not assure him of His power? Had God not promised to see him through?

### C. His testimony (33:12-17).

Jacob lied to Esau about the flocks and traveled in the opposite direction. The two never did meet until they buried their father (35:29). No doubt, at that meeting, Esau asked Jacob what had happened to him after they parted.

### D. His tent (33:17).

Jacob built a house and settled down in Succoth.

### E. His vision (33:19).

He moved again and pitched his tent toward the city of Shechem, not unlike Lot (13:12). He lost the vision of God's city (Heb. 11:13-16).

### F. His daughter (34).

Like Lot, Jacob put his family in a place of temptation, and, when his daughter investigated the city, she was violated. Sad to say, Jacob's sons were liars like their father. In fact, they used the sacred rite of circumcision to accomplish their wicked scheme. Verses 30-31 suggest that Jacob was selfishly more concerned with his own safety and welfare than he was with the sins of his family.

When did all of this begin? When Jacob failed to live up to his new standing with God. Why do NT Christians today scheme and sin and fail? Because they fail to live up to their heavenly position in Christ (Eph. 4:1ff).

### III. Jacob the Traveler (35–36)

Note how often Jacob "journeyed" in these chapters (35:5, 16, 21). God had called him to go "back to Bethel" (v. 1), back to the place of the vision and the vow. When a person is backslidden (as Jacob was), there is nothing else for him to do but go back to the place of dedication and renew his vows. Before he could take his company back to the altar, however, Jacob had to "clean house"—the strange gods and the jewelry associated with heathen worship had to be buried. The only place for sin is in the grave. In fact, there are four graves in this chapter: the grave of the idols (v. 4), Deborah's grave (v. 8), Rachel's grave (v. 19), and Isaac's grave (v. 29).

Jacob returned to Bethel and built an altar. God met him in a new way and reminded him of his new name, Israel. God reaffirmed the promises He gave to Abraham and Isaac, and Jacob responded by erecting a new pillar and anointing it as he had done years before. A backslidden believer does not need a new experience to get right with God. He needs only to reaffirm the old experience in a new way.

How strange that Rachel should die soon after Jacob is restored to fellowship with God. Great spiritual experiences are not security against the sorrows and trials of life. And certainly Jacob was better able to bear this sorrow now that he had again built his altar. Everything that Jacob had lost before had been regained because he had met God at the altar.

Not only are there sorrows in the family of the dedicated believer, but there are also sins (v. 22). Reuben was born amid great expectations (29:32), and Jacob said in later years that Reuben could have accomplished much (49:3). But Reuben was unstable; he lacked godly character (49:4); and, as a consequence, he lost the birthright that belonged to the firstborn son (1 Chron. 5:1-2) and had to give it to Judah and Joseph. Sin never brings blessing; it is always costly.

The final act on this journey was for Jacob and Esau to bury their father. Jacob had planned to see his mother again, but she died before he arrived home. Chapter 36 gives the history of Esau, for God did make him a mighty nation. Unfortunately, the Edomites were the enemies of God's people for centuries.

# GENESIS 37–40

We begin now a study of one of the most exciting biographies in the Bible, that of Joseph and his brothers. The entire story illustrates the sovereignty of God and God's providential care of His own. While Joseph had his faults, he still stands out as a spiritual giant in his own family.

## I. Joseph the Favored Son (37)

### A. Jacob's love (vv. 1-4).

Since Rachel was Jacob's favorite wife, and Joseph was her firstborn son (30:22-24), it is easy to see why Jacob favored him in his old age. This kind of partiality in a home is bound to cause trouble. Joseph at seventeen was helping with the sheep, but soon Jacob relieved him of that duty and made him an "overseer" by giving him a "tailored coat." Jacob wanted to make Joseph a ruler before he had really learned how to be a servant! The result—Joseph's brothers hated him (v. 4) and envied him (v. 11).

### B. Joseph's dreams (vv. 5-11).

That these dreams came from God, there is no question; and certainly the assurance that one day he would rule helped to keep Joseph faithful during those many years of testing in Egypt. Note that the first dream had an earthly setting, while the second dream was set in heaven. This suggests Abraham's earthly children (the Jews) and his heavenly seed (the church). Joseph's brothers did one day bow down to him! See also 42:6; 43:26; and 44:14.

### C. Judah's scheme (vv. 12-28).

We are not told which of the brothers first suggested doing away with Joseph. Possibly it was Simeon, who resented Joseph's intrusion on the rights of the firstborn (which would finally be taken away from Reuben, 49:3-4). We know from chapter 34 that Simeon was crafty and cruel, and in 42:24, Joseph was rather harsh on Simeon. At any rate, the brothers were back in the region of Shechem (where they had gotten into trouble before, chap. 34), and they plotted to slay Joseph. It is to Reuben's credit that he tried to spare Joseph's life, although he used the wrong method to accomplish a noble deed. God overruled the hatred of the men, and Joseph was sold into slavery instead of slain in cold blood.

### D. Jacob's sorrow (vv. 29-36).

Years before, Jacob had slain a kid to deceive his father (27:9ff), and now his sons deceived him the same way. We reap what we sow. Jacob spent the next twenty-two years in sorrow, thinking that Joseph was dead. He thought that everything was working against him (Gen. 42:36), when in reality everything was working for him (Rom. 8:28). God had sent Joseph ahead to prepare the way for Israel's preservation as a nation.

## II. Joseph the Faithful Steward (38–39)

Chapter 38 presents a sordid picture, showing Judah yielding to the lusts of the flesh. It is quite a contrast to Joseph's purity (39:7-13). Judah was willing to sell his brother for a slave, yet he himself was a "slave of sin" (John 8:34). Even so, "where sin abounds, grace much more abounds" (Rom. 5:20), for we see that Tamar is included in the human lineage of Christ (Matt. 1:3). Note that Judah was harder on others than on himself (v. 24). Like David, he wanted the "sinner" judged—until he discovered that he was the sinner!

Jacob had tried to shield Joseph from the responsibilities of work, but God knew that Joseph could never be a ruler until first he was a servant (Matt. 25:21). God used three disciplines in Joseph's life to prepare him to be the second ruler of Egypt:

### A. The discipline of service (39:1-6).

Joseph exchanged his "tailored coat" for a servant's garb, and God forced him to learn how to work. This way, he learned humility (1 Peter 5:5-6) and the importance of obeying orders.

Because Joseph was faithful in the small things, God promoted him to greater things. See Prov. 22:29 and 12:24.

### B. The discipline of self-control (39:7-18).

Joseph's mother was a beautiful woman, and no doubt the son inherited her features (29:17). Egyptian women were known for their unfaithfulness, but Joseph did not yield. God was testing Joseph, for if Joseph could not control himself as a servant, he could never control others as a ruler. He could have argued, "Nobody will know!" or "Everybody else is doing it!" But, instead, he lived to please God and made it a point to make no provision for the flesh (Rom. 13:14). "Flee youthful lusts!" Paul admonished (2 Tim. 2:22)—and that is just what Joseph did. As the Puritan preacher said, Joseph lost his coat, but he kept his character. Too many people have failed in this discipline, and God has had to put them on the shelf (1 Cor. 9:24-27; Prov. 16:32; 25:28).

## C. The discipline of suffering (39:19-23).

Not only was Joseph able to control his appetites, but he was also able to control his tongue; for he did not argue with the officers or expose the lie Potiphar's wife was spreading about him. Control of the tongue is a mark of spiritual maturity (James 3). It is likely that Potiphar was the captain of the guards in charge of prisoners; he may even have been the chief executioner. At any rate, he saw to it that Joseph was put in the king's prison (v. 20), and Joseph's faithfulness and devotion again brought him favor with the officers. "The Lord was with Joseph" is the key to his success (39:2, 5, 21). Joseph had to suffer as a prisoner for at least two years, and probably longer. Psalm 105:17-20 explains that this suffering put "iron" in his soul. It helped to make a man out of him. People who avoid suffering have a hard time developing character. Certainly Joseph learned patience from his suffering (James 1:1-5) as well as a deeper faith in God's Word (Heb. 6:12). This suffering was not enjoyable, but it was necessary, and one day it turned into glory.

## III. Joseph the Forgotten Servant (40)

Joseph was now a servant in the royal prison (41:12), faithfully doing his work and waiting for the day when his prophetic dreams would come true. One day two new prisoners were added—the cupbearer to Pharaoh and the chief baker. What their crimes were is not stated; it may have been some minor thing that upset Pharaoh. However, we know that God arranged their arrest for Joseph's sake. Joseph had been treated unjustly, but he knew that one day God would fulfill His Word.

Note Joseph's humility as he interpreted the two dreams (v. 8). He gave all the glory to the Lord. "Humble yourselves under the mighty hand of God, that He may exalt you in due time" (1 Peter 5:6).

The two prisoners were in bonds because of something they had done, while Joseph was innocent. His interpretation of the dreams came true: the cupbearer was restored, and the baker was hanged. Yet Joseph was left in prison! We may wonder why others experience the blessings that we so desperately need; yet God has His plan and His time.

There is a hint of discouragement and unbelief, however, in Joseph's request in v. 14. Was Joseph leaning on the arm of flesh? If so, the arm of flesh failed him, for the butler completely forgot about Joseph for the next two years. This was a good lesson to Joseph never to trust in men. God was ultimately going to use the butler's bad memory to deliver Joseph, but the right time had not yet come. The butler forgot Joseph, but God did not forget him!

Joseph was seventeen years old when he went to Egypt and thirty years old when he was delivered from the prison (41:46). This means he spent thirteen years as a servant and a prisoner, years of discipline and training, and years of preparation for his lifelong ministry as the second ruler of Egypt. God prepares us for what He is preparing for us, if we will but yield to Him.

In many ways, Joseph is a picture of our Lord Jesus Christ, even though nowhere in the NT is he specifically called a type of Christ. Joseph was a beloved son who was hated and rejected by His own brothers. They sold him for a slave and then one day met him as their king. Joseph had to suffer before he could enter into his glory. He was victorious over temptation and yet arrested and treated unjustly. Joseph was a faithful servant who ministered to others. Eventually he was exalted to the throne and was responsible for saving the nations. His brothers did not recognize him the first time, but he revealed himself to them the second time they came to Egypt. So it will be with Israel: they did not know Christ when He came the first time, but they will see Him when He comes again and will bow before Him.

# GENESIS 41–45

This section records Joseph's elevation from prisoner to second ruler of the land. He was given a new name—"the revealer of secrets" (41:45). Note the three secrets that Joseph revealed.

# I. The Secret of Pharaoh's Dreams (41)

Joseph had hoped that the butler would remember him and intercede for him (40:13-15), but the man did not remember Joseph until the day Pharaoh became disturbed because he could not find the meaning of his strange dreams. God's ways are past finding out, but God's time to act is never too early or too late. Note the humility of Joseph as he stood before the mightiest monarch on earth: "God shall give Pharaoh an answer of peace" (v. 16). He explained the dream: there would be seven years of plenty followed by seven years of famine. Then he gave wise counsel: appoint a wise man to administer the food supply. God directed Pharaoh to appoint Joseph, so now he was exalted to the throne! See also 1 Peter 5:6.

Joseph's marriage to a Gentile bride is a type of Christ's marriage to the church during this age when His brothers after the flesh have rejected Him. "Manasseh" means "to forget" and suggests that Joseph's new position in God's will had caused him to forget the trials of the past; and "Ephraim" means "doubly fruitful," suggesting that all his trials had, in the end, led to fruitfulness and blessing. Like the grain of wheat, Joseph "died" that he might not abide alone (John 12:23-26). God kept His Word to Joseph, and Joseph's predictions came true. The Word of the Lord stands when man's wisdom fails (41:8).

However, all of this was but a part of a greater plan, a plan to preserve Israel and prepare the way for the birth of Christ.

# II. The Secrets of His Brothers' Hearts (42–44)

The plan was now set in motion, for Jacob heard that there was grain in Egypt and sent his sons to secure food. Consider their two visits to Egypt.

## A. The first visit (v. 42).

Ten of the sons went down to Egypt, and Joseph recognized them even though they did not recognize him. Certainly his appearance had changed in twenty years, and his Egyptian speech and dress would lead them to believe he was a native. Note that the ten men bowed down (42:6), but that Joseph's dreams had predicted that eleven would bow (37:9-10). This explains how Joseph knew the men would return with his brother, Benjamin.

Why was Joseph so hard on his brothers? And why did he wait so long to reveal himself to them? Because he wanted to be sure they had repented of their sins. To excuse people who are not sincerely repentant is to make them a worse sinner (see Luke 17:3-4). How did Joseph deal with his brothers? He spoke roughly to them and accused them of being spies (7-14); he kept them locked up for three days (v. 17); and then he kept Simeon as hostage and bound him before their eyes (vv. 18-24). His crowning act was to give them back their money (vv. 25-28). This rough treatment had its designed result, for the men confessed, "We are guilty!" See vv. 21-23. This statement indicated to Joseph that their hearts were softening. Their report to Jacob back home and their discovery of the money in their sacks only complicated their problem. What would they do? If they stayed home, they were thieves, but if they went back to Egypt, they had to risk taking Benjamin with them. We wonder if v. 36 indicates that Jacob knew what they had done to Joseph years before.

### B. The second visit (chaps. 43–44).

God made Jacob's family hungry again, and like the prodigal son of Luke 15, these men had to go back or starve to death. We see here other indications of their change of heart: Judah's willingness to be surety, to bear the blame for young Benjamin; their willingness to return the money; and their confession of the truth to Joseph's steward (43:19-22). However, they were making some mistakes too—taking a present to Joseph and confessing their sins to the servant instead of to Joseph himself. We cannot help but see in this whole episode the way God deals with the lost sinner. God controls circumstances to bring the sinner to himself and to the end of himself. But, sad to say, too many convicted sinners try to win their salvation by offering a present, or by confessing to a human servant, or by making some great sacrifice (as Judah did when he offered his own life as surety for Benjamin). The only way Joseph could excuse their sins was by receiving their honest confession and repentance.

Joseph used two devices to bring them to the place of confession: the feast of joy (43:26-34—note that in v. 26 and v. 28 all eleven men bowed before him) and the discovery of the cup in Benjamin's sack. Again in 44:14 all eleven men fell down before Joseph in true contrition. "God has found out the iniquity of your servants!" they confess (44:16, NKJV). We cannot help but admire Judah's speech in 44:18-34, not only for its humility and confession but also for the love that it shows toward his father and his youngest brother. He was willing to be surety, to bear the blame, even though it would cost him his life.

What a beautiful spiritual lesson we have here. Judah thought that Joseph was actually dead (44:20), and therefore, that he himself was guilty of murder. What he did not realize was that Joseph was alive—and was his savior! The lost sinner stands before God's bar of judgment and confesses his guilt, thinking that his confession will mean certain wrath. But Jesus Christ is alive, and because He is alive, He is able to save to the uttermost. Christ does not expect us to be surety for our sins, or for the sins of another, for He Himself is our surety before God (Heb. 7:22). As long as Christ lives, God can never condemn us. And He will live forever!

It was not their confession of guilt, their sacrifices, or their gifts that brought salvation to the brothers. It was the gracious forgiveness of Joseph, a forgiveness purchased by his own suffering on their behalf. What a picture of Jesus Christ!

## III. The Secret of God's Purpose (45)

It was now time for Joseph to reveal himself and the purpose for which God had sent him. Acts 7:13 makes it clear that it was "the second time" that he revealed himself, just as it was the second time that Israel received Moses after rejecting his leadership forty years before (Acts 7:35). This is the theme of Stephen's speech recorded in Acts 7: the chosen people Israel have always rejected their saviors the first time and received them the second time; they will do the same with Jesus Christ.

Joseph's revelation of himself brought his brothers terror, for they fully expected him to judge them for their past sins. But he had seen their repentance; they had bowed before him; and he knew he could forgive them. He explained that five more years of famine would follow, but that he had prepared a place of refuge for them and their families there in Egypt. God had sent him before to save their lives.

Joseph promised to nourish them (v. 11) and protect them. He wept over them and kissed them, and he sent gifts to his father to assure him of the riches that lay in Egypt. "Come unto me!" was his invitation (45:18). Then, what a change took place in Jacob after he discovered that Joseph was alive—a change not too different from the change in the disciples when they discovered that Christ was alive! Before, Jacob had said, "All these things are against me (42:36), but now he could say, "All things are working together for good!"

# GENESIS 46–50

These chapters cover the last days of Jacob. We see him performing several acts for the last time. It's a sobering reminder that one day each of us will face the end.

## I. Jacob's Last Journey (46–47)

By faith, Jacob left Hebron and started for Egypt, and God honored his faith by revealing Himself again and renewing His promises (46:2-4). Jacob no doubt remembered that Abraham had sinned in going to Egypt (12:10ff), and that Isaac had been forbidden to go there (26:2), so he was reassured by God's Word. Instead of being a place of defeat, Egypt would be a place of blessing, for the nation would increase in spite of suffering. The whole family went with Jacob: the thirty-three descendants of Leah (vv. 8-15); the sixteen descendants of Zilpah (vv. 16-18); the fourteen descendants of Rachel (vv. 19-22); and the seven descendants of Bilhah (vv. 23-25). Actually sixty-six traveled with Jacob, and when we add Jacob and Joseph and his two sons (v. 27), we get a total of seventy. See Ex. 1:5. Acts 7:14 says that there were seventy-five in the family, but this may include the five children of Ephraim and Manasseh, listed in 1 Chron. 7:14ff. Note that Judah was now the trusted one, for Jacob sent him ahead as the leader. Meanwhile, Joseph was preparing the way with Pharaoh, finding them places to live and occupations to follow while in the land. Since Egypt is a picture of this present world system, it does not surprise us that shepherds were an abomination to the unsaved people. Our Lord is the Good Shepherd, and the world will have nothing to do with Him!

Jacob met Pharaoh, testified of God's goodness during his long life, and then blessed him. The only blessing this world has comes from God through God's people Israel (John 4:22).

Verses 13ff describe the way Joseph managed the affairs of Egypt giving us an illustration of dedication: the people  him their money, their lands, their possessions, and their own bodies (Rom. 12:1-2). We should give our all to Christ who has saved us and who cares for us daily.

## II. Jacob's Last Blessing (48)

Jacob spent the last 17 of his 147 years with Joseph in Egypt, so he had his favorite son the first 17 years of Joseph's life and then the last 17 years of his own life. Knowing that he was to die, the aged patriarch called Joseph to his bed (47:31) that he might bless his two sons. See Heb. 11:21. The two boys were at least in their early 20s (see 41:50 and 47:28). Jacob claimed the boys as his own, comparing them in status with his firstborn, Reuben and Simeon. (We will see in 49:5-7 that Simeon and Levi would disappear as separate tribes, so that Ephraim and Manasseh would take their places.) Knowing that Manasseh was the firstborn, Joseph put the boy at Jacob's right, with Ephraim on the left, but Jacob crossed his arms and gave the blessing of the firstborn to Ephraim. This displeased Joseph, but Jacob was guided by God, for God was going to give the greater blessing to Ephraim. This is another example of the divine principle of setting aside the first to establish the second (Heb. 10:9). We saw this before in Seth and Cain, Isaac and Ishmael, and Jacob and Esau. The fact that Jacob crossed his hands brings the cross into the picture. It is through the cross that God crucified the old nature and now sets aside the natural that He might establish the spiritual. When you are born again, God rearranges your spiritual "birth order."

Jacob also blessed Joseph in the name of the God who had "shepherded" him all his years, and he gave to Joseph a special parcel of land (v. 22, and see John 4:5). This was a token of the total inheritance they were yet to receive.

## III. Jacob's Last Message (49)

This is a difficult chapter and we cannot go into all the details. In this final message to his sons, Jacob revealed their character and predicted their history. Reuben was the firstborn and should have inherited might and glory, but because of his sin, he lost the blessings of his birth (Gen. 35:22, 1 Chron. 5:1-2). Simeon and Levi both were sons of Leah, and both were cruel and self-willed as seen in their crime of murdering the men of Shechem (Gen. 34). Simeon's descendants were later absorbed into the tribe of Judah (Josh. 19:1), and Levi became the priestly tribe (what grace!) having no inheritance of their own. Simeon's numerical decline is seen when we compare Num. 1:23 (59,300) with Num. 26:14 (22,200).

Judah is identified with the lion, the kingly beast; for out of

Judah, the lawgiver (Christ) would come, as would all the rightful kings of Israel. Jesus is the Lion of the tribe of Judah (Rev. 5:5). Verse 10 predicts that Shiloh ("The Rest-Giver" Christ) would not come until Judah had lost his rule, and certainly this was true when Jesus was born. Verses 11-12 promise great material blessings to Judah. Zebulun would stretch from the Sea of Galilee to the Mediterranean Sea, thus its connection with ships. Issachar is pictured as a humble servant to others, willing to bear their burdens that they might enjoy rest, rather than resisting and having liberty. Dan is connected with the serpent and deceit. It is no surprise that idolatry in Israel started with Dan. Gad means "a troop" (30:11) and is connected with war; Asher is connected with riches, especially the kind that would please a king. Naphtali is compared to a beautiful deer let loose, and it is promised that he will know how to use powerful language; see the victory and the song of Barak and Deborah in Jud. 4–5 (note 4:6).

The blessing on Joseph is longest. He is a fruitful bough, attacked by his brothers, but victorious in the end. Jacob gives Joseph a variety of blessings, material and spiritual, and he assures Joseph of ultimate victory through the God of Israel. Joseph is a "prince among his brethren" (end of v. 26). Benjamin is compared to a wolf catching the game he pursues and then enjoying his prey at night. King Saul came from this tribe and was a conqueror; Saul of Tarsus, who became Paul the apostle, also came from Benjamin.

It is difficult to press all the details of this amazing prophecy. History has shown that Jacob's words came true. Certainly there is a lesson here of personal responsibility, for some of the tribes lost their blessings because of the sins of their founders. Joseph suffered the most during his early life, yet he received the greatest blessings.

## IV. Jacob's Last Request (50)

In 49:29-33, the aged man had asked to be buried with his family in the cave of Machpelah. Already Abraham, Sarah, Isaac, Rebekah, and Leah were there, and Jacob's body would be the seventh. When Jacob died, his sons mourned for him and gave him an honorable burial. Apparently the entire land mourned for him for seventy days, and during forty of these days, the embalmers were preparing his body. This is the first case of an embalmed body and an elaborate funeral in the Bible. Why did Jacob (and Joseph after him,

50:24-26) want to be buried in Canaan? This was the land God had given him; he did not belong to the world (Egypt). Perhaps we have a spiritual lesson here as well: not only does the believer's spirit go to heaven when he or she dies, but the body will also be taken from this world at the resurrection.

It is unfortunate that Joseph's brothers did not believe his words when he told them years before that he had forgiven them! In fact, their unbelief and fear caused him to weep. They illustrate weak Christians today who cannot accept God's Word, and, as a consequence, live in fear and doubt. "Fear not!" is Christ's Word to us just as it was Joseph's word to his brothers. In their blindness, they wanted to work for his forgiveness ("We are your servants," v. 18, NKJV), but he gave them full pardon through grace.

Genesis begins with a garden and ends with a coffin. What a commentary on the results of sin in this world! But the Bible ends with a description of a beautiful "garden city" (Rev. 21–22), the home of all who put their trust in Jesus Christ.

# EXODUS

## A Suggested Outline of Exodus

I. Redemption—God's Power (1–17)

    A. The slavery of sin (1–4)

    B. The stubbornness of Pharaoh (5–11)

    C. The salvation of God (12–17)

        1. Passover—Christ the slain Lamb (12–13)

        2. Crossing the sea—resurrection (14–15)

        3. Manna—Christ the Bread of Life (16)

        4. Smitten rock—the Spirit—(17:1-7)

        5. Amalek—flesh vs. the Spirit—(17:8-16)

II. Righteousness—God's Holiness (18–24)

    A. The nation prepared (18–19)

    B. The law revealed (20–23)

        1. The commandments (Godward) (20)

        2. The judgments (manward) (21–23)

    C. The covenant ratified (24)

III. Restoration—God's Grace (25–40)

    A. The tabernacle described (25–31)

    B. The tabernacle needed—Israel sins (32–34)

    C. The tabernacle constructed (35–40)

# Introductory Notes to Exodus

## I. Name

In the Greek language, *exodus* means "the way out." (See Heb. 11:22, "departing.") This book describes Israel's bondage in Egypt and the wonderful deliverance (or "way out") that God gave them. One of the key words in Exodus is redemption, since "to redeem" means "to set free." The book presents many pictures of our salvation through Christ. The word *exodus* is used in two places in the NT: Luke 9:31 ("decease"), where Christ's redeeming work on the cross is the theme; and 2 Peter 1:15, where "decease" means a believer's "death." In other words, there are three exodus experiences in the Bible — Israel's deliverance from Egypt; Christ's deliverance of the sinner through the cross; and the believer's deliverance from the bondage of this world at death.

## II. Author

There is no reason to doubt that Moses wrote this book. The unity of the book (see outline) suggests that there was one author, and the eyewitness accounts indicate that the author was present at those events. Christ affirmed the Mosaic authorship of the book (John 7:19: 5:46-47).

## III. Purpose

Genesis is the book of beginnings; Exodus is the book of redemption. It records the deliverance of Israel from Egypt and presents the basic historical facts about the origins of the Hebrew nation and its religious ceremonies. These accounts are also pictures of Christ and the redemption He purchased at the cross. There are many types and symbols of Christ and the believer in Exodus, especially in the tabernacle furnishings and ceremonies. Exodus also records the giving of the Law. It would be impossible to understand much NT doctrine apart from an understanding of the events and symbols in Exodus.

## IV. Types

There are several basic types in Exodus: (1) Egypt is a type of the world system, opposing God's people and trying to keep them in bondage. (2) Pharaoh is a type of Satan, "the god of this world," who demands worship, defies God, and thinks to enslave God's people. (3) Israel is a type of the church—delivered from the bondage of the world, led on a pilgrim journey, and protected by God. (4) Moses is a type of Christ, God's Prophet. (5) The crossing of the Red Sea is a picture of the resurrection, which delivers the believer from this present evil world. (6) The manna pictures Christ the Bread of Life (John 6). (7) The smitten rock is a type of the smitten Christ, through whose death the Holy Spirit is given. (8) Amalek is a picture of the flesh, opposing the believer in the pilgrim journey. The key type in Exodus is Passover, picturing the death of Christ, the application of His blood for our safety, and the appropriation of His life (feeding on the lamb) for our daily strength.

## V. Moses and Christ

Here we could list many comparisons and one major contrast between the two, since Moses is a wonderful picture of Jesus Christ. In his offices, Moses was a prophet (Acts 3:22); a priest (Ps. 99:6, Heb. 7:24); a servant (Ps. 105:26, Matt. 12:18); a shepherd (Ex. 3:1, John 10:11-l4); a mediator (Ex. 33:8-9, 1 Tim. 2:5); and a deliverer (Acts 7:35, 1 Thes. 1:10). In his character, he was meek (Num. 12:3, Matt. 11:29), faithful (Heb. 3:12), obedient, and mighty in word and deed (Acts 7:22, Mark 6:2). In his history, Moses was a son in Egypt and was in danger of being killed (Matt. 2:14ff), but was providentially cared for by God. He chose to suffer with the Jews rather than reign in Egypt (Heb. 11:24-26, Phil. 2:1-11). Moses was rejected by his brothers the first time, but received the second time; and, while rejected, he gained a Gentile bride (picturing Christ and the church). Moses condemned Egypt, and Christ condemned the world. Moses delivered God's people through the blood, as did Christ on the cross (Luke 9:31). Moses led the people, fed the people, and carried their burdens. The contrast, of course, is that Moses did not take Israel into the Promised Land; Joshua had to do that. "The law was given by Moses, but grace and truth came by Jesus Christ (John 1:17).

# EXODUS 1–2

## I. The Persecution of God's People (1)

### A. A new generation (vv. 1-7).

The bondage of Israel in Egypt had been predicted in Gen. 15:13-16. The fourth generation would be equal to 400 years, since Abraham was 100 years old when Isaac was born. Of course, a generation would be fewer years today. God also fulfilled the promise of multiplying the people (Gen. 46:3), and Jacob's original seventy became over a million! They increased in spite of persecution and suffering. See Acts 7:15-19.

### B. A new king (vv. 8-14).

Acts 7:18 says this was "another king of a different kind" (literal Gk.). That is, the new king was from a different people. History tells us that about this time the "Hyksos" invaders took over in Egypt. They were Semites, probably from Assyria (Isa. 52:4). The new king warned his own people (not the Egyptians) that the presence of so many Jews was a threat to their own rule; so they decided to deal vigorously with the Children of Israel. Since Joseph had been the savior of Egypt, it is unlikely that an Egyptian king would not know him, but this new king was an outsider. Of course, the bondage in Egypt is but a picture of the sinner's spiritual bondage to this world. The Jews went down to Egypt and lived in the best of the land (Gen. 47:6), but this luxury later turned into trial and suffering. How like the path of the lost sinner today; sin promises pleasure and freedom, but it brings sorrow and bondage.

### C. A new strategy (vv. 15-22).

The king's plan to kill all the male babies would have met with great success except for the intervention of God. He used the midwives to confound the king, just as later He used a baby's cry to reach the heart of Pharaoh's daughter. God uses the weak things of this world to defeat the mighty. Of course, the king's strategy was born of Satan, the murderer. This was but another attempt on Satan's part to destroy the Jews and keep the Messiah from being born. Later, Satan would use King Herod to try to slay the baby Jesus. Was it right for the women to defy the orders of the king? Yes, for "we ought to obey God rather than men" (Acts 5:29). When the laws of the land are definitely contrary to the commandments of God, then the believer has the right and duty to put God first. While God did not approve of the excuses the midwives gave Pharaoh (although their words may have been true), He did bless them for their faith. Keep in mind that this same ruler who wanted to drown God's people saw his own army drowned in the Red Sea (Ex. 15:4-5). We reap what we sow, even though the harvest may be slow in coming (Ecc. 8:11).

We also see in this chapter Satan's attempt to bring the people of God into bondage. Verse 1 calls the Jews "the Children of Israel" and Israel means "a prince with God" (Gen. 32:28) — the prince of the world (Satan) defying the prince with God! But God's people are not of this world and will be delivered from Satan's bondage!

## II. The Preparation of God's Prophet (2)

It seemed as though God was doing nothing. The Jews prayed and cried out for help (2:23-25) and wondered where God's deliverance was. Had they only remembered the Word in Gen. 15, they would have known that 400 years had to elapse. During these years, God was preparing his people, but He was also waiting in mercy and giving the wicked nations of Canaan time to repent (Gen. 15:16). God is never in a hurry; He had His leader chosen for the Hebrews and was preparing him for his mighty task. Note the means God used to prepare Moses:

### A. A godly home (vv. 1-10).

Read Acts 7:20-28 and Heb. 11:23. In Ex. 6:20, we learn that the godly parents of Moses were Amram and Jochebed. That they should wed during such difficult times was an act of great faith and love, and God rewarded them for this. Since they acted by faith (Heb. 11:23), they must have had a communication from God concerning the birth of their son, Moses. He was a "goodly child" (beautiful in the sight of God), and so they gave him to God by faith. Parents never know what God sees in each child that is born, and it is important that parents raise their children in the fear of God. It took real faith to put the child in the river, the very place where the young boys were being destroyed! Note how God used a child's tears to touch the princess, and how He arranged for the child's own mother to raise him. Read Job 5:13.

### B. A special education (Acts 7:22).

Raised in the palace as the adopted son of the princess, Moses was trained in the great Egyptian schools. Even today, scholars marvel at the learning of the Egyptians, and no doubt Moses stood at the head of his class. There is nothing wrong with education. Certainly Moses made use of his training. But it was no substitute for the wisdom of God that came through suffering and trial and his personal walk with God.

### C. A great failure (vv. 11-15; Heb. 11:24-26).

Moses was forty years old when he made his great decision to leave the palace and become the deliverer of Israel. We admire him for his love for his people and for his courage, but we must confess that he ran ahead of the Lord in the way he acted. Verse 12 indicates that he was walking by sight, not by faith, for "he looked this way and that" before he killed the Egyptian who was beating a Hebrew. Like Peter in the Garden of Gethsemane, Moses depended on the sword in his hand and the energy in his arm. Later he was to exchange that sword for a rod, and the power would be from God's hand, not his own (see 6:1). He buried the body, but this was no proof that the deed went unseen. The next day he found two Jews fighting and tried to help them, only to discover that friends and enemies alike knew he had killed a man. (Note: The text in Acts 7:24 may indicate that Moses killed the man in self-defense, but even if he did, he was still a criminal in the eyes of the Egyptians.) His only recourse was to flee from the land.

While we may justly criticize Moses for his misdeeds, we must admire his courage and convictions. As Dr. Vance Havner has said (commenting on Heb. 11:24-26): "Moses saw the invisible, chose the imperishable, and did the impossible!" Faith has its refusals, and these refusals lead to rewards. Unfortunately, Moses was too hasty in his actions, and God had to set him aside for further training. The weapons of our warfare are not fleshly, but spiritual (2 Cor. 10:3-6).

### D. A long delay (vv. 16-25).

Moses' life is divided into three equal periods: forty years as a prince in Egypt; forty years as a shepherd in Midian; and forty years as leader of Israel. Beginning this second period, Moses assisted the women as they tried to water their flocks, and this kindness led to his meeting Jethro and marrying Jethro's daughter Zipporah. Note that the girls identified Moses as "an Egyptian." This suggests that he was more like the Egyptians than he was like the Jews. Moses spent forty years as a faithful servant in Midian, and here God prepared him for the difficult tasks that lay ahead. Rejected by his nation, he took a Gentile bride, and is thus a picture of Christ who is today getting a bride for Himself from the nations. "Gershom" means "a stranger" and suggests that Moses knew his real place was with the people of Israel back in Egypt.

It seemed that God was doing nothing, yet He heard the groans of His people and was waiting for the right time to act. Whenever God works, He chooses the right worker, uses the right plan, and acts at the right time. Moses was taking care of a few sheep; soon he would be shepherding a whole nation. The shepherd's crook would be exchanged for the rod of power, and he would be used of God to help create a mighty nation. Because he was faithful to do the humble job of shepherding, God used him to accomplish greater tasks as liberator, lawgiver, and leader.

# EXODUS 3–4

A new day dawned and everything had to change for Moses. When he went out with his sheep that morning, he had no idea that he would meet God. It pays to be ready, for we never know what God has planned for us.

## I. God Appears to Moses (3:1-6)

The burning bush had a threefold significance. It was a picture of God (Deut. 33:16), for it revealed His glory and power, yet it was not consumed. Moses needed to be reminded of the glory and power of God, for he was about to undertake an impossible task. Second, the bush symbolized Israel going through the fire of affliction, but not consumed. How often nations have tried to exterminate the Jews, yet have failed! Finally, the bush illustrated Moses—a humble shepherd, who with God's help would become a fire that could not be put out! Note that Moses was brought to the place where he bowed before God and adored Him in wonder, for this is the true beginning of Christian service. Servants who know how to take off their shoes in humility can be used of God to walk in power. Later we see that before God called Isaiah, He revealed His glory (Isa. 6). The memory of the burning bush must have encouraged Moses during many a trying mile in the wilderness.

## II. God Appoints Moses (3:7-10)

"I have seen . . . I have heard their cry . . . I know . . . I have come
down!" What a message of grace! Moses often had wondered about
the condition of his beloved people, and now he was shown that
God had been watching over them all the time. We might easily
apply these verses to the situation when Christ was born: it was a
time of bondage, trial, and sorrow, yet God came down in the
Person of His Son, to deliver men from sin. God had a definite
plan, to bring them out and then to bring them into the Promised
Land. What He starts, He finishes.

Moses rejoiced to hear that God was about to deliver Israel, but
then he heard the news that he was the deliverer! "I will send
you!" God uses human instruments to accomplish His work on
earth. There had been eighty years of preparation for Moses; now it
was time to act. Unfortunately, Moses did not reply, "Here am I;
send me" (Isa. 6:8).

## III. God Answers Moses (3:11–4:17)

Moses did not immediately agree with God's plan to send him. Was
he not a failure? Did he not have a family? Was he not too old?
Perhaps these and other arguments went through his mind, but he
voiced at least four objections that day as he argued with God
about God's will for his life.

### A. "Who am I?" (3:11-12)

We admire Moses for his humility, for forty years before he would
have told God who he was! He was "learned . . . and mighty in
words and in deeds" (Acts 7:22). But years of communion and
discipline in the desert had humbled Moses. A person acting in the
flesh is impulsive and sees no obstacles, but a person humbly
walking in the Spirit knows the battles that lie ahead. God's reply
was to assure him: "I will be with you!" This promise sustained
him for forty years, as it later did Joshua (Josh. 1:5). Who we are is
not important; that God is with us is important, for without Him
we can do nothing (John 15:5).

### B. "Who is sending me?" (3:13-22)

This was no evasive question, for the Jews would want assurance
that the Lord had sent Moses on his mission. God revealed His
name, *Jehovah*—"I AM WHO I AM" or "I was, I am, I always will

be!" Our Lord Jesus added to this name in the Gospel of John where we find the seven great I AM statements (6:35; 8:12; 10:9 and 11; 11:25; 14:6; and 15:1-5). If God is "I AM," then He is always the same, and His purposes will be fulfilled. God promised Moses that He would see to it that the work was done, in spite of the opposition of Pharaoh.

### C. "They will not believe me" (4:1-9).

But God had just said that they would believe him (3:18), so this statement was nothing but open unbelief. God gave Moses two miracles — the rod changed to a serpent and the hand made leprous. These would be his credentials before the people. God takes what we have in our hands and uses it, if we but trust Him. Of itself, the rod was nothing, but in God's hands it became power. Moses' own hand had killed a man, but in the second miracle God showed him that He could heal the weakness of the flesh and use Moses for His glory. His own hand was nothing, but in God's hand, it would do wonders! Then God added a third sign — turning water into blood. These signs did convince God's people (4:29-31), but they were only imitated by the godless Egyptians (7:10-25).

### D. "I am not gifted" (4:10-17).

God had said "I AM" — and all Moses could say was, "I am not!" He was looking at himself and his failures instead of to God and His power. In this case, Moses argued that he was not a gifted speaker. But the same God who made the mouth could use it. God does not need eloquence or oratory; He needs only a clean vessel that He can fill with His message. "Send anybody, but not me!" is Moses' cry in v. 13. This attitude of unbelief angered God, but He gave Aaron to Moses to be his helper. Unfortunately, more than once, Aaron turned out to be more of a hindrance than a help! He led the nation into idolatry (32:15-28) and murmured against Moses (Num. 12). How tragic that Moses was willing to trust a weak man of flesh instead of the living God of heaven. Verse 14 teaches us that God works "at both ends of the line" when He is moving His people. He brought the two brothers together to serve Him.

## IV. God Assures Moses (4:18-31)

Moses had God's Word, the miraculous signs, and the assistance of his brother Aaron; yet these verses make it clear that he still was not ready to walk by faith. He did not tell his father-in-law the truth about his trip to Egypt, for God had told him that his brothers were yet alive. We appreciate the fact that Moses took care of his earthly tasks in a faithful manner before leaving, but he was not much of a testimony to Jethro. Note the assurances God gave Moses as he started in his new life of service:

### A. His Word (vv. 19-23).

The people who wanted to slay Moses were dead, and God wanted Moses to trust Him and not be afraid. How patient God is with His own. How encouraging are His promises.

### B. His discipline (vv. 24-26).

Circumcision was an important part of the Jewish faith, yet Moses had neglected to bring his own son into the covenant (Gen. 17). God had to discipline Moses (perhaps by sickness) to remind him of his obligation. How could he lead Israel if he was failing to lead his own household in things spiritual? Moses later sent his family back to Midian (see 18:2).

### C. His leading (vv. 27-28).

God had promised that Aaron was coming (v. 14), and now He fulfilled that promise. While both Moses and Aaron had their weaknesses, and each failed God and each other more than once, it was a great help to Moses to have his brother at his side. They met in "the mount of God" where Moses had seen the burning bush (3:1).

### D. The acceptance of the people (vv. 29-31).

This too was a fulfillment of God's Word (3:18). Sad to say, these same Jews who received Moses and bowed their heads to God, later hated him and criticized him because of their increased labor (5:19-23). It is wise not to fix our hopes on the reactions of people, for people often fail to live up to their commitments.

# EXODUS 5–10

## I. The Command

Seven times in these chapters, God says to Pharaoh, "Let my people go!" (See 5:1; 7:16; 8:1, 20; 9:1, 13; 10:3.) This command reveals that Israel was in bondage, but God wanted them to be free that they might serve Him. This is the condition of every lost sinner: enslavement to the world, the flesh and the devil (Eph. 2:1-3).

"Who is the Lord, that I should obey His voice?" was Pharaoh's response to God's command (5:2). The world has no respect for God's Word; it is "vain words" to them (5:9). Moses and Aaron presented God's command to Pharaoh, and the result was more bondage for Israel! The sinner will either yield to God's Word, or resist it and become hardened (see 3:18-22 and 4:21-23). In one sense, God hardened Pharaoh's heart by presenting His claims, but Pharaoh himself hardened his own heart by resisting God's claims. The same sun that melts the ice also hardens the clay.

Unfortunately, the people of Israel looked to Pharaoh for help rather than to the Lord who had promised to deliver them (5:15-19). No wonder the Jews were unable to agree with Moses (5:20-23) and accused him instead of encouraging him. Believers who are out of fellowship with God bring grief to their leaders instead of help. Moses certainly was discouraged, but he did what is always best—he took his problem to the Lord. God encouraged Moses in chapter 6 by reminding him of His name (6:1-3), His covenant (6:4), His personal concern (6:5), and His faithful promises (6:6-8). God's "I AM" and "I WILL" are enough to overcome the enemy! God's purpose in allowing Pharaoh to oppress Israel was that His own power and glory might be known to the world (6:7; 7:5, 17; 8:10, 22; see Rom. 9:17).

The stage is set: Pharaoh refused God's command, and now God would send His judgments on Egypt. He would fulfill His promise in Gen. 12:3 to judge the nations that persecute the Jews. He would reveal His power (9:16), His wrath (Ps. 78:43-51), and His greatness, showing that the gods of Egypt were false gods, and that Jehovah alone is the true God (12:12; Num. 33:4).

## II. The Conflict

The ten plagues of Egypt accomplished several things: (1) they were signs to Israel, assuring them of God's power and care, 7:3; (2) they were plagues of judgment to Egypt, punishing the people for persecuting Israel and revealing the vanity of their gods, 9:14; and (3) they were prophecies of judgments to come, as revealed in the Book of Revelation.

Note the sequence of the plagues. They fall into three groups of three each, with the tenth plague (death of the firstborn) set off last:

1. Water to blood, 7:14-25 (warning given, 7:16)
2. Frogs, 8:1-15 (warning given, 8:1)
3. Lice, 8:16-19 (no warning, and magicians could not duplicate, 8:18-19)
4. Flies, 8:20-24 (warning given, 8:20)
5. Murrain on cattle, 9:1-7 (warning given, 9:1)
6. Boils on the people, 9:8-12 (no warning given, magicians afflicted, 9:11)
7. Hail, fire, 9:13-35 (warning given, 9:13)
8. Locusts, 10:1-20 (warning given, 10:3)
9. Thick darkness, 10:21-23 (no warning, Pharaoh refused to see Moses again, 10:27-29)
10. Death of the firstborn, 11–12 (the final judgment).

The plagues were actually a "declaration of war" against the gods of Egypt (see 12:12). The Nile River was worshiped as a god since it was their source of life (Deut. 11:10-12), and when Moses turned it into blood, God showed His power over the river. The goddess Heqt was pictured as a frog, the Egyptian symbol of resurrection. The plague of frogs certainly turned the people against Heqt! The lice and flies brought defilement to the people—a terrible blow, for Egyptians could not worship their gods unless they were spotlessly clean. The murrain attacked the cattle which were sacred to the Egyptians; Hathor was the "cow-goddess" and Apis was the sacred bull. The gods and goddesses that controlled health and safety were attacked in the plagues of boils, hail, and locusts. The plague of darkness was the most serious, since Egypt worshiped the sun god, Ra, the chief of the gods. When the sun was blotted out for three days, it meant that Jehovah had conquered Ra. The final plague (the death of the firstborn) conquered Meskhemit the goddess of birth, and Hathor, her companion, both of whom were supposed to watch over the firstborn. All of these plagues made it clear that Jehovah was the true God!

We may trace these same plagues in the Book of Revelation, when God describes His final conflict with the god of this world, Satan: water to blood (Rev. 8:8 and 16:4-6); frogs (16:13); disease and afflictions (16:2); hail and fire (8:7), locusts (9:1ff); and darkness (16:10).

The Egyptian magicians were able to imitate some of Moses' miracles—turning the rod into a serpent (7:8-13) and the water into blood (7:19-25), and bringing forth the frogs (8:5-7). But they could not turn the dust into lice (8:16-19). Second Timothy 3:8-9 warns us that in the last days false teachers will oppose God by imitating His miracles. See 2 Thes. 2:9-10. Satan is a counterfeiter who deceives the lost world by imitating what God does (2 Cor. 11:1-4, 13-15).

## III. The Compromises

Pharaoh is a type of Satan: he was the god of Egypt; he had supreme power (except where limited by God); he was a liar; he was a murderer; he kept people in bondage; he hated the Word of God and the people of God. Pharaoh did not want to release the Jews, so he offered four subtle compromises:

### A. *Worship God in the land (8:25-27).*

God demands complete separation from the world; the friendship of the world is enmity with God (James 4:4). Since the Egyptians worshiped cows, they would be offended if they saw the Jews sacrificing their cattle to Jehovah. The believer must "come out and be separate" (2 Cor. 6:17).

### B. *Do not go too far away (8:28).*

"Don't be a fanatic!" says the world. "It's fine to have religion, but don't get too serious about it." Here we have the temptation to be "borderline believers," trying to stay close to the world and close to the Lord at the same time.

### C. *Only the men should go (10:7-11).*

This meant leaving the wives and children in the world. Faith involves the whole family, not the men only. It is the privilege of the husband and father to lead the family into the blessings of the Lord.

### D. *Keep your possessions in Egypt (10:24-26).*

Satan loves to get hold of our material wealth so that we cannot use it for the Lord. All that we have belongs to Christ. And Jesus tells us, "Where your treasure is, there will your heart be also" (Matt. 6:21). What a tragedy to rob God by leaving our "flocks and herds" for Satan to use (Mal. 3:8-10).

Moses refused each of these compromises because he could not compromise with Satan and the world and still please God. We may think that we have won a victory by pacifying the world, but we are mistaken. God demands total obedience, complete separation. This was to be effected by the blood of the lamb and by the crossing of the Red Sea, pictures of Christ's death on the cross and our resurrection with Him, delivering us from "this present evil world" (Gal. 1:4).

# EXODUS 11–13

The key to this section is the lamb. The Passover marks the birth of the nation of Israel and its deliverance from bondage. This great event also pictures Christ and His work on the cross (John 1:29; 1 Cor. 5:7-8; 1 Peter 1:18-20).

## I. The Lamb Needed (11)

"One plague more!" God's patience had run out and His final judgment—death to the firstborn—was about to fall. Note that death was to come to all (11:5-6; 12:12-13), unless they were protected by the blood of the lamb. "All have sinned" (Rom. 3:23) and "the wages of sin is death" (Rom. 6:23). God specifies that the "firstborn" will die, and this speaks of God's rejection of our first birth. All people are "firstborn" who have not been "twice-born." "That which is born of the flesh is flesh . . . you must be born again" (John 3:6-7). People cannot save themselves from the penalty of death; they need Christ, the Lamb of God.

For years, the Jews had slaved for the Egyptians without pay, so now God permits them to ask for (not "borrow") their just wages. See Gen. 15:14 for God's promise, and Ex. 3:21 and 12:35ff.

From a human point of view, there was no difference between the firstborn of Egypt and the firstborn of Israel. The difference was in the application of the blood (v. 7). All are sinners, but those who have trusted Christ are "under the blood" and saved. This is the most important difference in the world!

## II. The Lamb Chosen (12:1-5)

The Jews have a religious and a civil calendar, and Passover marks the beginning of their religious year. The death of the lamb makes

96

a new beginning, just as the death of Christ makes a new beginning for the believing sinner.

## A. *Chosen before it is slain.*

Selected on the tenth day, and slain "between the evenings" of the fourteenth and fifteenth days, the lamb was set aside for death. So Christ was the Lamb foreordained before the foundation of the world (1 Peter 1:20).

## B. *Spotless.*

The lamb was to be a male without blemish, a picture of the perfect Lamb of God in whom there was no spot or stain (1 Peter 1:19).

## C. *Tested.*

From the tenth to the fourteenth days, the people watched the lambs to make sure they were satisfactory; similarly, Christ was tested and watched during His earthly ministry, especially during the last week before He was crucified. Note the progress: "a lamb" (v. 3), "the lamb" (v. 4), "your lamb" (v. 5). This parallels "a Savior" (Luke 2:11), "the Savior" (John 4:42), and "my Savior" (Luke 1:47). It is not enough to call Christ "a Savior" (one among many), or "the Savior" (for somebody else). Each of us must be able to say, "He is my Savior!"

## III. The Lamb Slain (12:6-7)

A living lamb was a lovely thing, but it could not save! We are not saved by Christ's example or His life; we are saved by His death. Read Heb. 9:22 and Lev. 17:11 to see the importance of the shed blood of Christ. Of course, killing a lamb seemed like foolishness to the wise Egyptians, but it was God's way of salvation (1 Cor. 1:18-23).

The blood of the lamb had to be applied to the door of the house (12:21-28). The word "basin" in 12:22 can mean "threshold," so that the blood of the lamb was caught in the hollow place at the threshold. The blood was then applied to the lintel over the door and the posts at the sides of the door. Anybody who went out of the house walked on the blood (see Heb. 10:29). Christ was slain on the fourteenth day of the month, just at the time when the Passover lambs were being offered. Note that God speaks of Israel killing it (the lamb), not them (lambs); for to God, there is but one Lamb—Jesus Christ. Isaac asked, "Where is the lamb?" (Gen. 22:7), and John the Baptist answered in John 1:29, "Behold, the Lamb of God!" All of heaven says, "Worthy is the Lamb!" (Rev. 5:12)

## IV. The Lamb Eaten (12:8-20, 43-51)

We often neglect this important part of the Passover, the Feast of Unleavened Bread. Leaven (yeast) in the Bible is a picture of sin: it works silently; it corrupts and puffs up; and it can only be removed with fire. The Jews had to put all leaven out of their homes at Passover season, and they were not allowed to eat leavened bread for seven days. Paul applies this to Christians in 1 Cor. 5; read the chapter carefully.

The blood of the lamb was sufficient to save from death, but the people had to feed on the lamb to get strength for their pilgrim journey. Salvation is just the beginning. We must feed on Christ if we are to have the strength to follow Him. Christians are a pilgrim people (v. 11), always ready for their Lord's orders to move on. The lamb was to be roasted with fire, which speaks of the sufferings of Christ on the cross. Nothing was to remain to be eaten later; no "leftovers" can satisfy the believer, for we need a whole Christ. We need a completed work on the cross. Furthermore, leftovers would become corrupt, and this would ruin the type; for Christ did not see corruption (Ps. 16:10). Alas, too many people receive the Lamb as their salvation from death, but they do not feed on the Lamb daily.

Verses 43-51 give further instructions concerning the feast. No stranger could participate, nor could a hired servant or one who was uncircumcised. These regulations remind us that salvation is a birth into God's family—no strangers are there. It is by grace—no one can earn it. And it is through the cross—for circumcision points to our true spiritual circumcision in Christ (Col. 2:11-12). The feast was not to be eaten outside the house (v. 46), for the feast cannot be separated from the shed blood. Modernists who want to "feed on Christ" apart from His shed blood are fooling themselves.

## V. The Lamb Trusted (12:21-42)

It took faith to be delivered that night! The Egyptians thought all these things were foolishness, but God's Word had spoken and that was enough for Moses and his people. Please keep in mind that the people were saved by the blood and assured by the Word (v. 12). No doubt many of the Jews were safe under the blood who did not "feel safe," just as we have saints today who doubt God's Word and worry about losing their salvation. God did exactly what He said He would do. And the Egyptians urged the Jews to leave the land, just as God said they would (11:1-3). God was not one day late. He kept His Word.

## VI. The Lamb Honored (13)

The lamb had died for the firstborn; now the firstborn would belong to God. The Jews were a "purchased people" just as we are God's purchased people (1 Cor. 6:18-20). The nation would forever honor the Lamb by giving their firstborn — their best — to the Lord. The hands, eyes, and mouth would be given to Him for His service (v. 9).

God led His people, not on the nearest way, but on the way that was best for them (vv. 17-18), just as He does today. The pillar was a cloud by day and a fire by night. God always makes His will clear to those who are willing to follow (John 7:17). He saves us, feeds us, guides us, and protects us — and yet we do so little for Him!

Joseph knew what he believed and where he belonged. His tomb in Egypt was a reminder to the Jews that one day God would deliver them. On Joseph's bones, see Gen. 50:24-26, Joshua 24:32, and Heb. 11:22.

# EXODUS 14–15

The Passover illustrates the Christian's salvation through the blood of the Lamb, but there is more to the Christian life than being saved from judgment. Israel's experiences in their journey from Egypt to Canaan are pictures of the battles and blessings of the Christian life. God wanted Israel in Canaan, and Canaan is a picture of the victorious Christian life — the life of claiming our inheritance in Christ (Eph. 1:3). Alas, too many Christians (like the Jews of old) are delivered from Egypt, but they get lost in the wilderness of unbelief! Yes, they are saved by the blood, but they fail to claim their rich spiritual inheritance by faith (Heb. 3–5). We see in these two chapters four different experiences of God's people on their pilgrim journey.

## I. Israel Crying Out in Fear (14:1-12)

God specifically directed Israel to their place of encampment by the Red Sea, and He told Moses that the Egyptians would pursue them. Similarly, God has explained the Christian life to us in His Word so that we know what to expect. Satan is not pleased when sinners are set free from his grasp, and he pursues the Christian to try to get him back into bondage. New Christians in particular must be warned that their adversary is coming!

Sad to say, the Jews were walking by sight, not by faith; for when they saw the Egyptian army coming, they gave up in despair and cried out in fear. Fear and faith cannot dwell in the same heart; if we trust God, we need not be afraid. As is often the case, the Children of Israel criticized their spiritual leader instead of praying and seeking to encourage one another. They were actually complaining to God, for Moses had led them to the very place God had appointed. Instead of looking up to God in faith, they looked back to Egypt and said, "We were better off in bondage to Pharaoh!" What poor memories they had! God had smitten Egypt with His judgments and delivered Israel with great power, yet they did not believe that He could see them through. Undoubtedly, the "mixed multitude" that went with them (12:38) led in this chorus of complaint, just as they were to lead in later years (Num. 11:4). The "mixed multitude" represents unconverted and worldly people among the children of God.

## II. Israel Walking in Faith (14:13-31)

Moses knew that the way of victory was through trusting the Lord (Heb. 11:29). Note his three commands: "Fear not" for God is on your side; "stand still," for you cannot win this battle in your own strength; "see the salvation of the Lord," for He will fight for you. It is important that we stand still before we "go forward" (v. 15), for unless we are standing by faith, we can never walk by faith. Moses lifted his rod, and God began to work.

God protected His people by coming between Israel and the Egyptian armies (vv. 19-20). The workings of the Lord are darkness to the world, but light to God's people. God kept the army at a distance that whole night. Then, God opened the way forward by sending a strong wind. No doubt the Jews were fearful as they heard the wind blow, but the very wind that frightened them was the means of their salvation. The entire nation walked through the

Red Sea on dry land! Yet the same sea that was salvation to Israel was condemnation to Egypt, for God used the waters to drown the Egyptians and to separate Israel from Egypt permanently. Pharaoh reaped what he had sown, for he had drowned the Jewish infant boys, and now his own army was drowned.

We must grasp the spiritual meaning of this event (1 Cor. 10:1-2). The crossing of the Red Sea is a type of the believer's union with Christ in death to the old life and resurrection to a whole new life. Israel was "baptized unto Moses" (identified with Moses) in going through the waters, and we are identified with Christ and therefore separated from the world (Egypt). The Egyptians could not pass through the sea because they had never been sheltered by the blood.

Passover illustrates Christ's death for us, while the crossing of the Red Sea pictures His resurrection. The blood has delivered us from the penalty of sin and the resurrection, from the power of sin. The first experience is substitution, for the lamb died in the place of the firstborn. This is Romans 4–5. The second experience is identification, for we are identified with Christ in His death, burial and resurrection; and this is explained in Romans 6–8. The crossing of Israel through Jordan into Canaan in Josh. 3–4 is a type of believer entering into his spiritual inheritance by faith and claiming it for his own. In each case, it is by faith that the Christian claims the victory.

## III. Israel Praising in Triumph (15:1-21)

This is the first recorded song in the Bible, significantly coming after redemption from bondage. Only the Christian has a right to sing songs of redemption (Ps. 40:1-3). Exodus began with sighing (2:23), but because of redemption, we now see the nation singing. Note that this song exalts God, for the Lord is referred to at least forty-five times in these eighteen verses. Too many songs exalt men instead of the Person and holy character of God, and His wonderful works of power.

Note the key refrain in v. 2. It is repeated in Ps. 118:14, at the time the Jews returned from captivity and rebuilt the temple under Ezra, as well as in Isa. 12:2, referring to that day in the future when God will restore the nation to their land. See Isa. 11:15-16. Israel sang this song when delivered from Egypt, led by Moses the prophet and when delivered from Babylon, led by Ezra, a priest. They will yet sing it when delivered from the Gentile nations, when they turn to Christ, their king.

We will not linger over the details of this song. Note that they praised God for His redemption (vv. 1-10), guidance (vv. 11-13), and victory (vv. 14-17). And the song ends on a note of glory, looking ahead to His eternal reign (v. 18). Miriam led the women (see 1 Cor. 14:34, 1 Tim. 2:11-12) in a separate choir, for certainly women have reason to praise the Lord for the redemption He has given them in Christ.

## IV. Israel Complaining in Unbelief (15:22-27)

It would be wonderful to linger at the seaside and praise the Lord, but the believer is a pilgrim and must follow God's leading. How strange that God should lead them to a place without water. Yet God must discipline His children so that they may discover their own hearts. When the Jews did see water, they discovered that it was bitter, and immediately they complained to Moses and to God. How wicked the human heart is! We praise God one day for His glorious salvation and then complain to Him the first time we find bitter waters. This experience taught the people of Israel some valuable lessons:

### A. About life.

Life is a combination of the bitter and the sweet, triumphs and trials. If we are following God, however, we never need fear what comes our way. And after the trial there is often a spiritual "Elim" (v. 27) where God refreshes us. We must accept the bitter waters with the sweet, knowing that God knows what is best for us.

### B. About themselves.

Life is a great laboratory, and each experience x-rays our hearts to reveal what we really are. The waters of Marah revealed that the Jews were worldly, thinking only of bodily satisfaction; they were walking by sight, expecting to be satisfied by the world; they were ungrateful, complaining to God when trials came their way.

### C. About the Lord.

God knows the need because He plans the way. He used the tree (suggesting the cross, 1 Peter 2:24) to make the bitter waters sweet. He is Jehovah-Rapha, "The Lord Who Heals."

# EXODUS 16

This chapter should be read in connection with John 6, for the manna from heaven is a type of Jesus Christ, the Bread of Life. It also illustrates the written Word of God on which God's pilgrim people feed from day to day (Matt. 4:4).

## I. The Manna Explains Who Jesus Is

The Hebrew word *manna* means "What is it?" (v. 15), the statement of the Jews when they could not explain this new food that God had sent. "Great is the mystery of godliness," writes Paul in 1 Tim. 3:16. "God was manifest in the flesh." Consider how the manna pictures Jesus Christ:

### A. His humility.

It was small (v. 14), which speaks of His humility; for He became a baby, and even a servant.

### B. His eternal nature.

It was round (v. 14), which reminds us of the circle, symbol of His eternality; for Jesus Christ is eternal God (John 8:53-59).

### C. His holiness.

It was white (v. 31), a reminder of His purity and sinlessness; He is the holy Son of God.

### D. His sweetness.

It was sweet (v. 31). "Taste and see that the Lord is good" (Ps. 34:8). Note in Num. 11:4-8 that the "mixed multitude" that went with the Jews did not appreciate the taste of the manna but asked for the "leeks, onions, and garlic" of Egypt. They were not satisfied with simple manna. They "ground it, beat it, and baked it," but then it tasted like "oil" and not like honey. There is a spiritual lesson here for us; we cannot improve upon the simple Word of God (Ps. 119:103).

### E. His nourishment of us.

It was satisfying and strengthening, for the nation lived on manna for nearly forty years. All that we need for spiritual nourishment is Jesus Christ, God's heaven-sent Bread. We are to feast on the Bread that will never leave us hungering.

## II. The Manna Illustrates How Jesus Came

### A. *It came from heaven.*

It was not imported from Egypt, or manufactured in the wilderness; it was given from heaven, the gift of God's grace. Jesus Christ came down from heaven (John 6:33) as the Father's gift to hungry sinners. To say that Christ is "just another man" is to deny the teaching of the whole Bible that He is God's Son sent from heaven.

### B. *It came at night.*

The people gathered the manna early each morning, for the manna fell at night. This suggests the darkness of sin in this world when Jesus came. It was night when Jesus was born, for He came to be the Light of the World (John 8:12). And it is still night in the hearts of all who have rejected Him (2 Cor. 4:1-4).

### C. *It came on the dew (vv. 13-14).*

The dew kept the manna from being defiled by the earth (see Num. 11:9). This is a type of the Holy Spirit for when Jesus came to earth, it was through the miracle ministry of the Spirit (Luke 1:34-35). Had Jesus not been born of the virgin, He could never be called "that Holy One."

### D. *It fell in the wilderness.*

This world is not a paradise. To the unsaved person, it is a wonderful place, but to the Christian on his pilgrimage to glory the world is but a wilderness. Yet Christ came to this world in love to give men life. What grace!

### E. *It came to a rebellious people (vv. 1-3).*

What poor memories Israel had! They had been away from the bondage of Egypt only six weeks and had already forgotten God's many mercies. They murmured against Moses and against God (see 15:22-27), and they longed for the fleshly diet of the old life; yet God in His grace and mercy supplied them with bread. Verse 4 could well have read, "I will rain fire and brimstone upon those ungrateful sinners!" But, no, God proved His love toward them by raining bread upon them. See Rom. 5:6-8. Someone has calculated that to supply six pints (an omer) of manna each for two million people daily would have required four freight trains of sixty cars each. How generous God is to us!

## F. It fell right where they were.

How easily accessible the manna was to the Jews! They did not have to climb a mountain or cross a deep river; the manna came where they were (see Rom. 10:6-8). Jesus Christ is not far away from sinners. They can come to Him at any time.

## III. The Manna Shows What We Must Do with Jesus Christ

### A. We must feel the need.

There is a spiritual hunger within that can be satisfied only by Christ (John 6:35). It was when the Prodigal Son said, "I perish with hunger" that he decided to go back to the father and seek forgiveness (Luke 15:17-18). Much of the unrest and sin in the world today is the result of unsatisfied spiritual hunger. People are living on substitutes and rejecting the nourishment that God freely provides (Isa. 55:1-3).

### B. We must stoop.

The manna did not fall on the tables or on the trees but on the ground, and the people had to stoop to pick it up. Many sinners will not humble themselves. They will not bend! They will not repent and turn to the Savior!

### C. We must take for ourselves.

The hungry Jews were not fed by looking at the manna, admiring it, or watching others eat it; they had to pick it up and eat it themselves. Christ must be received inwardly by faith if the sinner is to be saved. This is what Christ meant in John 6:51-58 by "eating His flesh and drinking His blood." John 6:63 makes it clear that Christ was not speaking about literal flesh and blood, and John 6:68 tells us that it was His Word that He was referring to. When we receive the Word inwardly, we are feeding on Christ, the Living Word.

### D. We must do it early (v. 21).

"Seek the Lord while He may be found!" is the warning of Isa. 55:6 (NKJV). The manna disappeared when the sun became hot, and this suggests that the day of judgment will arrive when it will be too late to turn to Christ (Mal. 4). It also suggests that, as believers, we must get our spiritual nourishment from the Word early in the day as we meditate on it and pray.

### E. We must continue to feed on Him.

Once we receive Christ as Savior, we are saved eternally (John 10:27-29). It is important, however, that we feed on Christ to have the strength for our pilgrim journey, just as the Jews fed on the Passover lamb (Ex. 12:11ff). How do believers feed on Christ? By reading, studying, and meditating on His Word. God invites each of us to get up early in the day and gather from the Word the precious manna to nourish our souls. We cannot hoard God's truth for another day (vv. 16-21); we must gather fresh food for each new day. Too many Christians mark their Bibles and fill their notebooks with outlines, yet never really feed on Christ.

Note that the spiritual manna (Christ) accomplishes more than did the physical manna that God sent to the Jews. The OT manna sustained physical life, but Christ gives spiritual life to all who receive Him. The OT manna was for the Jews only, but Christ offers Himself to the whole world (John 6:51). It did not cost Moses anything to secure the manna for Israel, but to make Himself available to the world, Christ had to die on the cross. How sad it is that most of the people in the world walk on Christ as if he were unused manna on the ground, rather than stooping to receive Him that they might live.

The daily gathering of the manna was God's test of Israel's obedience (v. 4), and it is still God's test for His people. Those Christians that begin their day with the Bible, gathering spiritual food, are the ones God can trust and use. Alas, many Christians still hunger for the carnal diet of the world! (v. 3) And many expect the pastor or the Sunday School teacher to gather the manna for them and "spoon-feed" them. The test of our spiritual walk is this: do I think enough of Christ and His Word to start my day gathering manna?

Joshua 5:10-12 tells us that the manna ceased when the Jews entered Canaan at Gilgal, and that they ate the "old corn of the land." The manna came down from heaven, speaking of Christ in His incarnation and crucifixion. The corn grew up out of a place of burial and death, and speaks of Christ in His resurrection and heavenly ministry. To enter Canaan means to enter into our heavenly inheritance in Christ (Eph. 1:3), and this means laying hold of the blessing we have in His resurrection, ascension, and heavenly priesthood. Too many saints "know Christ according to the flesh" (2 Cor. 5:16, NKJV) in His earthly life and ministry and have never graduated into His heavenly priestly ministry. When they do take that step, they are "eating the old corn of the land"—feeding on His resurrection power.

# EXODUS 17–18

As Israel followed the leading of the Lord, they experienced tests and trials which helped them understand themselves better and see more fully the power and grace of God. There are three such experiences in these chapters.

## I. Water from the Rock (17:1-7)

The congregation had thirsted before (15:22) and God had met their needs, but, like people today, they forgot God's mercy. After all, if they were in the place of God's leading, it was His responsibility to take care of them. The people criticized Moses and murmured against God, a sin about which we are warned in 1 Cor. 10:1-12. They were actually "tempting the Lord" by their attitude, for they were saying that God did not care and that He would not help them. They were trying His patience by their repeated complaints.

Moses illustrates what the trusting Christian does in the hour of trial: he turned to the Lord and asked for guidance (James 1:5). The Lord instructed him to take his rod and to smite the rock and water would come out. This rock is Christ (1 Cor. 10:4), and the smiting of the rock speaks of Christ's death on the cross, where He felt the rod of the curse of the law. (It was this same rod, you will recall, that turned into a serpent, Ex. 4:2-3, and that helped to bring the plagues on Egypt.) The order here is wonderful: in chap. 16 we have the manna, illustrating Christ's coming to earth; in chapter 17 we see the smiting of the rock, which pictures His death on the cross. The water is a symbol of the Holy Spirit, who was given after Christ had been glorified (John 7:37-39).

Read Num. 20:1-13 for a second experience with the rock. God commanded Moses to speak to the rock, but in his self-will, Moses smote the rock. Then, because of this sin, he was not permitted to enter Canaan. By once again striking the rock, Moses spoiled the type—Christ can die only once. See Rom. 6:9-10 and Heb. 9:26-28. The Spirit was given once, but the believer may receive added fillings by asking God.

First Corinthians 10:4 says that Israel "drank of that spiritual rock that followed them." Some have interpreted this to mean that the smitten rock traveled with the Jews through the wilderness, but this explanation is unlikely. The word "them" is not in the original Greek text; the sentence says that they drank of the water from the rock, and that this event followed the giving of the manna (cf. 1 Cor. 10:3 with Ex. 16).

## II. Warfare with the Enemy (17:8-16)

The new Christian sometimes is amazed that the Christian life is one of battles as well as blessings. Up to this point, Israel had not had to fight; the Lord had fought for them (13:17). But now, the Lord chose to fight through them to overcome the enemy. The Amalekites were descendants of Esau (Gen. 36:12, 16) and can illustrate the opposition of the flesh (Gen. 25:29-34). Israel was delivered from the world (Egypt) once and for all by crossing the Red Sea, but God's people will always battle the flesh until Christ returns.

Note that the Amalekites did not appear until after the water was given; for when the Holy Spirit comes in to dwell, then the flesh begins to oppose Him (Gal. 5:17ff). Deuteronomy 25:17-19 tells us that the Amalekites pulled a "sneak attack" and came up from the rear. As Christians we must always "watch and pray."

How did Israel overcome the enemy? They had an intercessor on the mountain and a commander in the valley! Moses' role on the mountain illustrates the intercessory work of Christ, and Joshua with his sword illustrates the Spirit of God using the Word of God against the enemy (Heb. 4:12 and Eph. 6:17-18). Of course, Moses is an imperfect picture of Christ and His intercessory work, since our Lord never wearies and needs no assistance (Heb. 4:16; 9:24). Paul says that believers can "help together by prayer" (2 Cor. 1:11), which is what Aaron and Hur did. Moses had the rod of God in his hand, which speaks of God's almighty power. Moses had defeated every enemy in Egypt, just as Christ has overcome the world in mighty victory.

It is important that God's people cooperate with God in gaining victory over the flesh. Romans 6 tells us to reckon and to yield, and by faith to put to death the deeds of the body. Moses alone on the mount could not win the battle, nor could Joshua alone on the battlefield: victory required both of them. How wonderful that we have the interceding Son of God who is for us (Rom. 8:34), and the indwelling Spirit of God who is for us (Rom. 8:26), plus the inspired Word of God in our hearts!

Note that Joshua did not completely destroy the Amalekites; he "discomfited" them (v. 13). The flesh will never be destroyed or "eradicated" in this life; Christ will give us new bodies when He returns (Phil. 3:21). In 1 Sam. 15 we will see that Saul's sin was in refusing to deal completely with the Amalekites; and 2 Sam. 1:6-10 informs us that it was one of the Amalekites Saul spared that killed him! "Make no provision for the flesh" (Rom. 13:14, NKJV).

Jehovah-Nissi means "The Lord our banner." We have our victory not through our own efforts but through Christ alone (John 16:33; 1 John 2:13-14; 5:4-5).

## III. Wisdom from the World (18)

Bible students disagree as to the interpretation of this chapter, whether Jethro's advice to Moses was of the Lord or of the flesh. Some point to Num. 11 where God took of His Spirit and distributed the power among the seventy officers, suggesting that Moses already had all the power he needed to get the job done. God had told Moses back in chapters 3–4 that He alone would supply the needed grace to do the job. In v. 11, Jethro called Jehovah "greater than all gods," but this is a far cry from a definite confession of faith in the true God. Furthermore, in v. 27, we see Jethro refusing to stay with Israel, but going back to his own people.

Certainly our God is a God of order, and there is nothing wrong with organization. In the NT the apostles added the deacons to assist them when the burdens of ministry became too great (Acts 6). God's people can learn even from outsiders (Luke 16:8), but we must test everything by the Word of God (Isa. 8:20). We wonder if this "worldly wisdom" from Jethro was pleasing to God, for Jethro himself was not sure (see v. 23). He was willing to rejoice in all that the Lord had done (vv. 9-10), but he was not willing to believe that God could help Moses with the everyday burdens of life. Moses adopted Jethro's scheme, and the people agreed to it (Deut. 1:9-18), but we have no assurance that God approved the new arrangement. In fact, God's attitude in Num. 11 suggests otherwise.

Believers face open and obvious attacks of the flesh, as with Amalek (17:8-16); but also subtle ideas of the flesh, as with Jethro. Certainly Moses could have done whatever work God called him to do, for "God's commandments are His enablements." How easy it is for us to pity ourselves, to feel that nobody else cares and that God has given us too great a burden! Read Isa. 40:31 for God's solution to this problem.

# EXODUS 19–20

## I. Introductory Notes: The Law's Importance

No topic has been more misunderstood among Christians than the Law of Moses and its application to the NT believer today. To confuse the covenants of God is to misinterpret the mind of God and miss the blessings of God, so the believer is wise to examine the Word to determine the place and purpose of the whole Mosaic system.

## II. Name

Beginning with Ex. 19 and continuing to the cross of Christ (Col. 2:14), the people were under the Mosaic system. This is called "the Law of Moses," "the Law," and sometimes "the Law of God." For the sake of convenience, we often speak of "the Moral Law" (referring to the Ten Commandments), "the Ceremonial Law" (relating to the types and symbols found in the sacrificial system), and "the Civil Law" (meaning the everyday laws that governed the lives of the people). Actually, the Bible seems to make no distinction between the "moral" and "ceremonial" laws, since the one was definitely a part of the other. For example, the fourth commandment about the Sabbath Day is found in the Moral Law yet is certainly a part of the ceremonial system of Jewish holy days as well.

## III. Purposes

To understand the Law, we must remember that God had already made an everlasting covenant with the Jews through their father Abraham (Gen. 15). He promised them His blessing and gave them the ownership of the land of Canaan. The Mosaic Law was "added" to the Abrahamic Covenant later, but it did not disannul it (Gal. 3:13-18). The law "entered in alongside" God's previous covenant (Rom. 5:20) and was but a temporary measure (Gal. 3:19) on His part. It was given only to Israel to mark them as God's chosen people and His holy nation (Ex. 19:4-6; Ps. 147:19-20). God did not give the Law to save anybody, because it is impossible to be saved by the keeping of the Law (Gal. 3:11; Rom. 3:20). He gave the Law to Israel for the following reasons:

*A. To reveal His glory and holiness (Deut. 5:22-28).*

*B. To reveal man's sinfulness (Rom. 7:7, 13; 1 Tim. 1:9ff; James 1:22-25).*

*C. To mark Israel as His chosen people, and to separate them from the other nations (Ps. 147:19-20; Eph. 2:11-17; Acts 15).*

*D. To give Israel a standard for godly living so that they might inherit the land and enjoy its blessings (Deut. 4:1ff; 5:29ff; Judges 2:19-21).*

*E. To prepare Israel for the coming of Christ (Gal. 3:24).*

The "schoolmaster" was a trained slave whose task it was to prepare the child for adult living. When the child matured and entered adulthood, he received his inheritance and no longer needed the schoolmaster. Israel was in her "spiritual childhood" under the Law, but this prepared her for the coming of Christ (Gal. 3:23–4:7).

*F. To illustrate in type and ceremony the Person and work of Christ (Heb. 8–10).*

The Law is compared to a mirror, because it reveals our sins (James 1:22-25); a yoke, because it brings bondage (Acts 15:10; Gal. 5:1; Rom. 8:3); a child-trainer, because it prepared Israel for the coming of Christ (Gal. 3:23–4:7); letters written on stones (2 Cor. 3) in contrast to the law of love written on our hearts by the Spirit; and a shadow in contrast to the reality and fulfillment we have in Christ (Heb. 10:1; Col. 2:14-17).

## IV. Weakness

It is important to note what the Law cannot do. It cannot accomplish these things: (1) make anything perfect, Heb. 7:11-19, 10:1-2; (2) justify from sin, Acts 13:38-39 and Rom. 3:20-28; (3) give righteousness, Gal. 2:21; (4) give peace to the heart, Heb. 9:9; and (5) give life, Gal. 3:21.

## V. Christ and the Law

"The Law was given by Moses, but grace and truth came by Jesus Christ" (John 1:17). There is obviously a contrast between the legalistic system of Moses for Israel and the gracious position the Christian has in the body of Christ. Christ was made under the Law (Gal. 4:4-6) and fulfilled the Law in every respect (Matt. 5:17). His Person and work are seen in the Law (Luke 24:44-47). He is the end of the Law for righteousness to the believer (Rom. 10:1-13). He paid the penalty of the Law and bore the curse of the Law on the cross (Gal. 3:10-14, Col. 2:13-14). The Law no longer separates Jew and Gentile, for in Christ we are one in the church (Eph. 2:11-14).

## VI. The Christian and the Law

The NT makes it very clear that the Christian is not under the Law (Rom. 6:14 and Gal. 5:18) but lives in the sphere of grace. In Christ, we died to the Law (Rom. 7:1-4) and have been delivered from the Law (Rom. 7:5-6). We must not become entangled again in the bondage of the Law (Gal. 5:1-4), which means falling out of the sphere of grace and living like a servant, not a son.

Does this mean that the Christian is supposed to be lawless and ignore the holy demands of God? Of course not! This is the accusation Paul's enemies threw at him because he emphasized the believer's glorious position in Christ (Rom. 6:1). Second Corinthians 3 makes it clear that the glory of the Gospel of God's grace far surpasses the temporary glory of the OT Law, and that we Christians go "from glory to glory" (3:18) as we grow in grace. Actually, the NT Christian is under a more demanding way of life than was the OT believer; for the OT Law dealt with outward acts, while the NT law of love deals with inward attitudes. Being free from the Law does not mean being free to sin—liberty is not license. We have been called to liberty, and we must use that liberty for the good of others and the glory of God (read Gal. 5:13-26). We are under the higher law of love, the law of Christ (Gal. 6:2). We do not try to obey God in the energy of the flesh because this is impossible (Rom. 7:14); the flesh is sinful and weak and cannot submit to the law. But as we reckon ourselves dead to sin (Rom. 6) and yield to the Holy Spirit (Rom. 8), the Spirit fulfills the law in us and through us (Rom. 8:1-4).

To go back to the Law is to exchange reality for shadows and liberty for bondage. It is to forfeit the high calling we have in grace. Law means that we must do something to please God; grace means that God works in us to fulfill His perfect will.

## VII. The Ten Commandments Today

All of the OT Law is but an amplification and application of the Ten Commandments. Nine of the Ten Commandments are repeated in the NT for believers today:

*A. Have no other gods before Me (Acts 14:15; John 4:21-23; 1 Tim. 2:5; James 2:19; 1 Cor. 8:6).*

*B. Make no idols or images (Acts 17:29; Rom. 1:22-23; 1 John 5:21; 1 Cor. 10:7, 14).*

*C. Do not take His name in vain (James 5:12; Matt. 5:33-37 and 6:5-9).*

*D. Remember the Sabbath Day.*

This is not repeated anywhere in the NT for the church to obey today. Keeping the Sabbath is mentioned in Matt. 12, Mark 2, Luke 6, and John 5; but these all refer to the people of Israel and not to the church. Colossians 2 and Rom. 14-15 teach that believers should not judge one another with reference to holy days or Sabbaths. To say that a person is lost or unspiritual for not keeping the Sabbath is to go beyond the bounds of Scripture.

*E. Honor father and mother (Eph. 6:1-4).*

*F. Do not murder (1 John 3:15; Matt. 5:21-22).*

*G. Do not commit adultery (Matt. 5:27-28; 1 Cor. 5:1-13, 6:9-20; Heb. 13:4).*

*H. Do not steal (Eph. 4:28; 2 Thes. 3:10-12; James 5:1-4).*

*I. Do not bear false witness (Col. 3:9; Eph. 4:25).*

*J. Do not covet (Eph. 5:3; Luke 12:15-21).*

Note these "summaries of the Law" in the NT; not one of them mentions the Sabbath: Matt. 19:16-20; Mark 10:17-20; Luke 18:18-21; Rom. 13:8-10. Of course, the "New Commandment" of love is the basic motivation for the Christian today (John 13:34-35; Rom. 13:9-10). This love is shed abroad from our hearts by the Spirit

(Rom. 5:5), so that we love God and others, and therefore should need no external law to control our lives. The old nature knows no law, and the new nature needs no law. The Sabbath was God's special day for the Jews under the Old Covenant; the Lord's Day is God's special day for the church under the New. The Sabbath symbolizes salvation by works: six days of labor, then rest; the Lord's Day symbolizes salvation by grace: first rest, and then the works follow. The Sabbath, the sacrifices, the dietary laws, the priesthood, and the tabernacle services were all done away in Christ.

# EXODUS 21–23

Having given Israel the Law of God in the Ten Commandments, Moses then explained and applied that Law to various aspects of human life. Wherever there is law, there must be interpretation and application; otherwise the law is impractical and not at all helpful. In the beginning, it was the priests who taught and applied the Law in Israel; but in later years, it was the scribes and rabbis who became the professional teachers of the Law. Unfortunately, their interpretations became as authoritative as the original Law, and it was this error that Jesus exposed through His teachings, especially the Sermon on the Mount (Matt. 5-7). See also Mark 7:1-23 for further insight.

## I. Caring for Servants (21:1-11)

The Jews were allowed to buy and sell servants, but they were forbidden to treat them as slaves. Sometimes people had to sell themselves into service because of their poverty (Lev. 25:39; Deut. 15:12), but their service was limited to only six years. Then they had to be freed. If a servant wanted to remain with the master, the servant was marked in the ear and would remain in the household for life. See Deut. 15:17, Ps. 40:6. The Law gave special protection to female servants to make sure their masters did not abuse them and deprive them of their rights.

## II. Compensating Personal Injuries (21:12-36)

These regulations were given to assure fairness in compensating people for injuries. "Eye for eye, tooth for tooth" (v. 24) is not a "law of the jungle" but an expression of fair payment for injuries received, so that the judges would not demand more or less than what was right. It is the basis for law today, although it is not always justly applied. Our Lord's words in Matt. 5:38-42 have to do with private revenge rather than public disobedience to the Law. There were several capital crimes in Israel, among them: murder (vv. 12-15), kidnapping (v. 16), cursing one's parents (v. 17), causing the death of a pregnant woman and/or her fetus (vv. 22-23), trafficking in demonism (22:18), and practicing bestiality (22:19). The basis for capital punishment is God's covenant with Noah (Gen. 9:1-6) and the fact that man is created in the image of God. It is God who gives life and only He has the right to take it away or authorize it to be taken (Rom. 13).

God makes a distinction between deliberate murder and accidental death or manslaughter (vv. 12-13). The cities of refuge were provided for the protection of the person who accidentally killed someone (Num. 35:6ff). There were no police in that day, and a slain person's family would feel obligated to avenge the death of their loved one. Therefore it was necessary to protect the innocent until the case could be investigated by the elders.

Note that God held the owner of an animal responsible for what it did to others (vv. 28-36), if that owner knew already that the animal was dangerous. The law made sure that nobody could take advantage of such situations and profit from them.

Verses 22-23 are basic to the pro-life position on abortion, for they indicate that the aborting of a fetus was equivalent to the murdering of the child. The guilty party was punished as a murderer ("life for life") if the mother or the unborn child, or both, died. See also Ps. 139:13-16.

## III. Protecting Personal Property (22:1-15)

Here Moses dealt with several kinds of thievery, and he stated once again that the thief must make compensation to those who are wronged. But note that God holds sacred even the life of a thief who is breaking into a house! If he breaks in at night and is slain, the slayer is not charged. But if his crime is in the daytime, when the owner could call for help or even recognize the intruder and accuse him later, then the slayer is guilty of homicide.

Moses also deals with property damage caused by animals who eat in a field other than their master's (v. 5) or by uncontrolled fire

(v. 6), and with loss of property entrusted to others (vv. 7-15). From these specific instances, the judges could derive principles that would help them decide cases that Moses did not explain in detail.

## IV. Respecting Humanity (22:16-31)

This series of miscellaneous laws reveals God's concern for humanity and His desire that people not be exploited. This includes virgins (vv. 16-17; see Deut. 22:23-24), foreigners in the land (v. 21), widows (vv. 22-24), and the poor (vv. 25-27). God promises to hear the cries of those who are wronged and defend the poor and oppressed.

Witches and wizards were not permitted to live because they were in league with the demonic powers that operated in the godless religions of the nations around Israel. See Lev. 19:31, 20:27 and Deut. 18:9-12. Modern occult practices are an invitation for Satan to go to work and destroy lives.

God also condemned sexual intercourse with animals (see Lev. 20:15-16; Deut. 27:21). Not only were these practices a part of the heathen worship of idols, but they debased human sexuality which is a precious gift from God.

The people were to respect their rulers and refrain from cursing them, even as they would refrain from cursing God. According to Romans 13, the powers that be are ordained of God. If we curse a leader, we are in danger of cursing the God who established the authority of human government.

Verses 29-31 get to the heart of obeying the law: put God first in your life and gladly obey what He says. This is the OT version of Matt. 6:33.

## V. Dispensing Justice (23:1-9)

The judicial system in Israel, like our system of courts today, depended on just laws, honest judges, and faithful witnesses. God's laws were just, but they could be deliberately misinterpreted by an unjust judge, or a lying witness could give false testimony. Judgment was not to be influenced by numbers (v. 2), money (vv. 3, 6, 8), personal feelings (vv. 4-5), or social status (v. 9).

When it comes to applying the law, God does not want the wicked to be justified (v. 7; 2 Chron. 6:23). But when it comes to saving lost sinners, God in His grace justifies the ungodly. (Rom.

4:5) He can do this because the penalty for our sins was borne on the cross by the Son of God.

## VI. Celebrating Holy Times (23:10-19)

The worship of God and the working of the land (which belonged to God) were bound together. Israel's religious festivals were tied to the agricultural year in a series of "sevens." See Lev. 23. The seventh day was the Sabbath and the seventh year was the Sabbatical Year. The Feast of Unleavened Bread was celebrated for seven days after Passover. The seventh month opened with the Feast of Trumpets and included the Day of Atonement and the Feast of Tabernacles (Booths).

The weekly Sabbath not only reminded the Jews that they belonged to God, but it also showed God's care for the health of man and beast and the "health" of the land. The Sabbatical Year gave even more opportunity for rest and restoration. God is concerned about the way we use the natural resources He has graciously given us. If people kept this in mind today, there would be less exploitation of both human and natural resources.

Passover speaks of the death of Jesus Christ, the Lamb of God (Ex. 12; John 1:29); the Feast of Firstfruits is a type of His resurrection (1 Cor. 15:23); and the Feast of Tabernacles reminds us of His coming again and the future kingdom of joy and fullness (Zech. 14:16-21).

The puzzling statement about the kid and its mother's milk relates to a heathen practice that was a part of an idolatrous fertility rite (see 34:26 and Deut. 14:21). Moses connected this law with the harvest festivals because that is when heathen fertility rites were practiced.

## VII. Conquering the Promised Land (23:20-33)

God promised His people victory because His angel would go before them and help them defeat their enemies, if the nation faithfully obeyed God's commandments. Their ownership of the land was purely by God's grace, but their enjoyment of the land depended on their faith and faithfulness.

Once in their land, the people were to beware not to imitate the idolatrous practices of the other nations. God promised His people health, prosperity, and safety if they obeyed Him, for these blessings were a part of His covenant. He has not guaranteed these same blessings to His new covenant people today, but He has promised to supply all our needs and enable us to live in victory over our spiritual enemies. Much of the "prosperity preaching" of our modern day is based on a misinterpretation of the Old Covenant that God made with the Jews.

Israel did conquer the Promised Land and destroy the cities and idols of the godless inhabitants. But gradually, God's people began to make peace with their neighbors and learn to worship their false gods and goddesses. This led to discipline in the land (the Book of Judges) and eventual captivity away from the land. Before we judge Israel too severely for this, however, we need to ask how much God's people today are compromising with the gods of this world, such as money, pleasure, and success.

# EXODUS 24

Moses is about to receive from God the divine pattern for the tabernacle and the priesthood. Whenever God calls us to do a work, He gives us the plans and expects us to follow His will. Ministry is not accomplished by our trying to invent ways to serve God, but by seeking His will and obeying it (Isa. 8:20).

## I. Confirming the Covenant (24:1-8)

Before Moses and the leaders of the nation could ascend the mountain to meet with God, the people had to enter into covenant relationship with God. Moses shared the Word of God with the people, and they agreed to obey it. How little they understood their own hearts! They should have said, "With the Lord's help, we will obey His Law." Within a few weeks, the nation would be worshiping an idol and violating the very Law they agreed to obey.

The covenant was confirmed with sacrifices and the sprinkling of the blood on the Book of the Law and on the people who agreed to obey it. The twelve stones of the altar represented the twelve tribes of Israel, indicating that each tribe was committed to obey the voice of God. The blood on the altar spoke of God's gracious forgiveness of sin, while the blood sprinkled on the people committed them to a life of obedience. Believers today have been sprinkled by the blood of Christ in a spiritual sense and are committed to obey His will (1 Peter 1:2).

## II. Seeing the Lord (24:9-18)

Seventy-five men went up the mountain: Moses, Joshua, Aaron and his two sons Nadab and Abihu, and seventy of the elders of the people. They beheld the glory of God on the mountain and ate and drank in His presence. You would think v. 11 would read, "They saw God and did fall on their faces in fear." But it says that they saw God and "did eat and drink." Because of the blood on the altar, they were able to have fellowship with God and with one another. We should eat and drink to the glory of God (1 Cor. 10:31) and live each day in the presence of God, even though we cannot be on the mountain.

God called Moses to go up higher so that He might give him instructions for building the tabernacle and establishing the priestly ministry. He left Aaron and Hur with the elders and took Joshua with him into the cloud of glory. First mentioned in Ex. 17:9, Joshua eventually became Moses' successor. We do not know who Hur was, but he, with Aaron, assisted Moses in praying for the success of Joshua in the battle against the Amalekites (Ex. 17:8-16). Aaron must have gone down from the mount, because we find him in chapter 32 helping the people make the golden calf. When we abandon our place of ministry, we not only sin ourselves, but we may lead others into sin. See John 21.

In OT days, God often revealed His glory in a cloud (19:9, 16). He led the nation with a pillar of cloud and fire (Ex. 13:21-22). "God is a consuming fire" (Deut. 4:24; Heb. 12:29). Moses did not dare approach God until God summoned him, but when God called, Moses obeyed.

It is possible to believe in God and be a part of His covenant and yet not be close to God. The nation was at the base of the mountain; the seventy elders with Aaron, Hur, Nadab, and Abihu were farther up the mountain; Moses went higher with his assistant Joshua; and then Moses left Joshua behind as he entered the cloud into the presence of the Lord. Under Law, God determined how near people could be to Him. But under grace, we are the ones who determine our nearness to God. God invites us to fellowship with Him. The elders worshiped God "afar off" (v. 1), but we today are invited to "draw near" (Heb. 10:22; James 4:8). What a privilege it is to fellowship with God, and what a tragedy it is that we too often fail to spend time in His presence.

Nadab and Abihu were given the gracious privilege of seeing the glory of God, and yet later they presumptuously disobeyed God and were slain (Lev. 10:1-5). It is possible to come near to God and still go away and sin. How important it is that our personal worship of the Lord result in a clean heart and a right spirit (Ps. 51:10), for great privileges bring with them even greater responsibilities.

# EXODUS 25

In the Book of Genesis, it is recorded that God walked with His people (Gen. 3:8; 5:22, 24; 6:9; 17:1). But in Exodus, God said that He wanted to dwell with His people (Ex. 25:8; 29:46). The tabernacle built by Moses is the first of several dwellings that God blessed with His glorious presence (Ex. 40:34-38). However, when Israel sinned, the glory departed (1 Sam. 4:21-22). The second dwelling place is the temple of Solomon (1 Kings 8:10-11). The prophet Ezekiel saw that glory depart (Ezek. 8:4; 9:3; 10:4, 18; 11:23). The glory of God returned to earth in the Person of His Son, Jesus Christ (John 1:14, where "dwelt" means "tabernacled"), and men nailed Him to a cross. God's people today are the temple of God, universally (Eph. 2:20-22), locally (1 Cor. 3:16), and individually (1 Cor. 6:19-20). Ezekiel 40–46 promises a kingdom temple where God's glory will dwell (Ezek. 43:1-5). We also see that the heavenly home will be a place where God's presence is eternally with His people (Rev. 21:22).

## I. Offerings for the Sanctuary (25:1-9)

God gave Moses the pattern for the tabernacle (v. 9), but He asked the people to contribute the materials needed for its construction (vv. 1-9). This was a one-time offering that had to come from willing hearts (see 35:4-29). Fourteen different kinds of material are listed here, from precious stones and gold to various colors of yarn. Paul later used the image of "gold, silver, and precious stones" when he wrote about the building of the local church (1 Cor. 3:10ff.). It is important to note that the various pieces of furniture were constructed so that they could be carried; for the tabernacle emphasizes that we are a pilgrim people. The design was changed for Solomon's temple, for the temple illustrates the people of God permanently dwelling in God's glorious kingdom. Without going into tedious detail, we will consider the various pieces of furniture of the tabernacle and the spiritual lessons that they convey.

## II. The Ark of the Covenant (25:10-22)

God began with the ark because it was the most important piece of furniture in the tent proper. It was the throne of God where His glory rested (v. 22; Pss. 80:1 and 99:1). It speaks of our Lord Jesus Christ in His humanity (wood) and deity (gold).

Within the ark were three special items: the tables of the Law (v. 16), Aaron's rod that budded (Num. 16–17), and a pot of manna (Ex. 16:32-34). It is interesting that each of these three items is connected with rebellion on the part of God's people: the tables of Law with the making of the golden calf; Aaron's rod with the rebellion led by Korah; and the manna with Israel's complaining in the wilderness.

These three items within the ark could have brought judgment to Israel were it not for the mercy seat upon the ark, the place where the blood was sprinkled each annual Day of Atonement (Lev. 16:14). The shed blood covered the sins of the people so that God saw the blood and not their rebellion. The phrase "mercy seat" also means "propitiation," and Jesus Christ is the propitiation (mercy seat) for us today (Rom. 3:25; 1 John 2:2). We come to God through Him and offer our spiritual sacrifices (1 Peter 2:5, 9).

The phrase "under His wings" sometimes refers to the wings of the cherubim rather than the wings of the mother hen. To be "under His wings" means to dwell in the holy of holies in close communion with God. See Pss. 36:7-8 and 61:4.

## III. The Table of Showbread (25:23-30)

The twelve tribes of Israel were represented in the tabernacle in three ways: by their names on the two engraved stones on the high priest's shoulders (Ex. 28:6-14); by their names on the twelve stones on the high priest's breastplate (28:15-25), and by the twelve loaves of bread on the table in the holy place. These loaves were a reminder that the tribes were constantly in the presence of God and that God saw all that they did (see Lev. 24:5-9).

The bread was a reminder too that God fed His people ("give us this day our daily bread"), that His people were to "feed on" God's truth (Matt. 4:4), and that Israel was to "feed" the Gentiles and witness to them. God called Israel to be a blessing to the

Gentiles, just as bread is food for humanity; but the people of Israel did not always fulfill their calling.

The loaves were changed each week and only the priests were allowed to eat this holy bread. See Lev. 22. David was allowed to eat the bread because he was God's anointed king, and the bread was no longer on the table. God is more concerned with meeting human needs than protecting sacred rituals (Matt. 12:3-4).

## IV. The Golden Lampstand (25:31-40)

The word "candlestick" is misleading, for this was a lampstand whose light was fed with oil (see Lev. 24:2-4; Zech. 4). Local churches are represented by individual golden lampstands (Rev. 1:12-20), giving God's light to the dark world. The lampstand in the holy place speaks of Jesus Christ, the light of the world (John 8:12). The oil for the lamps reminds us of the Holy Spirit, who has anointed us (1 John 2:20). Some students see the golden lampstand as a picture of the Word of God that gives us light as we walk in this world (Ps. 119:105). Israel was to be a light to the Gentiles (Isa. 42:6; 49:6) but failed in their mission. Today, each believer is God's light (Matt. 5:14-16), and each local church is to shine in this dark world (Phil. 2:12-16).

# EXODUS 26–27

## I. The Curtains and Coverings (26:1-14)

Within the tabernacle, seen only by the ministering priests, were colorful curtains of linen, hung upon the wooden framework. God built beauty into the walls and ceiling of the tabernacle, not only with the colors used but also with the images of the cherubim on the curtains. The commandment against making graven images did not prohibit the people from engaging in artistic work and making beautiful things, for they did not intend to worship these things they made for God's glory.

Keep in mind that the tabernacle proper was a tent located within a courtyard, with the various coverings placed over a wooden framework. There were four different coverings, the inner two of woven fabric and the outer two of animal skins. The innermost covering was of beautifully-colored linen, covered by fabric of woven goat's hair. Then came two protective coverings for the tent—

ram's hide dyed red and leather-like badger's skins. These materials were in common use among the nomadic peoples of that day.

## II. The Framework (26:15-30)

The combination of wood and its gold covering suggests the humanity and deity of our Lord Jesus Christ. There were many parts to the tabernacle, but it was considered one structure. And what set it apart as truly special was that the glory of God dwelt there.

The silver sockets were necessary to hold the structure level and secure on the desert ground. The silver for these sockets came from the "redemption price" given by each male who was twenty years old or older (Ex. 30:11-16). The tabernacle boards rested on silver sockets, and the curtains hung from silver hooks. The basis for our worship today is the redemption that we have in Christ.

## III. The Veils (26:31-37)

The inner veil hung between the holy place and the holy of holies and was passed only once a year by the high priest on the Day of Atonement (Lev. 16). Hebrews 10:19-20 teaches that this veil represents our Lord Jesus Christ's body which was given for us on the cross. When He offered up His spirit, the veil in the temple was torn from top to bottom, thus allowing anyone to come at any time into God's presence (Matt. 27:50-51).

The outer veil hung across the five pillars that formed the entrance to the tent of meeting, and it was visible to those who came to the brazen altar with their sacrifices. However, this veil prevented anyone on the outside from looking into the holy place.

## IV. The Bronze Altar (27:1-8)

There were two altars associated with the tabernacle—a bronze altar for sacrifices, and a golden altar for the burning of incense (Ex. 30:1-10). The bronze altar stood in the courtyard of the tabernacle, just inside the entrance of the court. There was one entrance and one altar, just as there is only one way of salvation for lost sinners (Acts 4:12).

God lit the fire on the altar when the tabernacle was dedicated, and it was the responsibility of the priests to keep the fire burning (Lev. 6:9-13). Pans and shovels were available for cleaning out the ashes, basins for handling the blood, and fleshhooks for taking the priests' share of the offerings. This altar speaks of the sacrificial death of our Lord on the cross. He is pictured in all the sacrifices God commanded Israel to bring (Lev. 1–5; Heb. 10:1-14). He went through the fire of judgment for us and gave Himself as the sacrifice for our sins.

## V. The Court of the Tabernacle (27:9-19)

Surrounding the tent of meeting was a linen fence with a beautiful woven "gate," opening to the place where the brazen altar stood. Looking at the total picture, we see that there were three parts to the tabernacle: the outer court that everybody could see; the holy place, containing the table, the lampstand, and the incense altar; and the holy of holies, containing the ark of the covenant.

This threefold division suggests the tripartite nature of human beings—spirit, soul, and body (1 Thes. 5:23). Just as the holy place and the holy of holies were two parts of one structure, so our soul and spirit comprise our "inner person" (2 Cor. 4:16). Moses could take down the fence of the outer court, and it would not affect the tent. So with our own death, the body may turn to dust, but the soul and spirit go to be with God and are not affected by the change (2 Cor. 5:1-8; James 2:26).

## VI. Oil for the Lampstand (27:20-21)

Zechariah 4:1-6 indicates that oil for the lampstand is a type of the Holy Spirit of God. One of the ministries of the Spirit is to glorify the Lord Jesus Christ, just as the light shone on the beautiful golden lampstand (John 16:14). As the priests ministered in the holy place, they walked in the light that God provided (1 John 1:5-10). The lamp was to "burn always" (27:20; Lev. 24:2). It would appear that only the high priest was permitted to dress the wicks and replenish the oil supply. When the high priest burned the incense each morning and evening, he also tended to the lamps (Ex. 30:7-8).

# EXODUS 28

This chapter focuses on the clothing of the priests, while chapter 29 deals primarily with the consecration of the priests. As you study these two chapters, keep in mind that all of God's people are priests (1 Peter 2:5, 9); therefore, the Aaronic priesthood can teach us much about the privileges and obligations we have as God's priests. (Our Lord's priesthood comes from the order of Melchizedek and not the order of Aaron. See Heb. 7–8.) Note that the priests ministered first of all to the Lord, even though they also ministered to the Lord's people. The priests represented the people before God and ministered at the altar, but their first obligation was to serve the Lord (vv. 1, 3, 4, 41). If we would serve the people rightly, we must serve the Lord acceptably. The innermost garment of the priests was a pair of linen breeches (v. 42), which was covered with a fine linen coat (vv. 39-41). Over these the high priest wore the blue robe of the ephod (vv. 31-35), and over that the ephod itself and the holy breastplate (vv. 6-30). The high priest also wore a linen turban (mitre) with a golden plate on it that read "holiness to the Lord" (vv. 36-38).

## I. The Ephod (28:6-14)

"Ephod" is a transliteration of the Hebrew word that describes a particular garment—a sleeveless coat made of the same material and colors as the hangings in the tabernacle. It was held together at the shoulders by special clasps, and on each clasp was an onyx stone engraved with the names of six of the tribes of Israel. The high priest carried his people on his shoulders as he served the Lord. The high priest wore a beautiful girdle around the ephod as a reminder that he was a servant.

## II. The Breastplate (28:15-30)

This was a beautiful cloth "pouch" that had twelve precious stones on the outside and the Urim and Thummim in the pocket. It hung over the high priest's heart, held by golden chains and blue lace. The high priest carried the twelve tribes not only on his shoulders, but also over his heart. Jesus Christ, our high priest in heaven, has His people on His heart and His shoulders as He intercedes for us and equips us to minister in this world.

The names of the tribes on the two shoulder stones were positioned according to their birth order (v. 10), while the order on the breastplate was according to the tribal order established by the Lord (Num. 10). God sees His people as precious jewels—each one is different, but each one is beautiful. *Urim* and *Thummim* mean "lights and perfection" in Hebrew. It is generally thought that these were stones that were used to determine God's will for His people (Num. 27:21; 1 Sam. 30:7-8). In the East, it was common to use white and black stones in making decisions. If the person drew a white stone out of the bag, it meant "Yes," while the black stone meant "No." It is unwise to be dogmatic about this interpretation because we do not have enough information to guide us. Suffice it to say that God provided His Old Covenant people with a way to determine His will, and He has given us today His Word and His Holy Spirit to direct us.

## III. The Robe of the Ephod (28:31-35)

This was a seamless blue garment with a hole for the head and golden bells and fabric pomegranates decorating the hem. The fabric pomegranates kept the bells from hitting each other. As the high priest ministered in the holy place, the bells would jingle and let the outsiders know that their holy representative was still serving them and the Lord. The bells suggest joyfulness as we serve the Lord, and the pomegranates suggest fruitfulness.

Note that the high priest laid aside these glorious robes when he ministered on the annual Day of Atonement (Lev. 16:4). On that day, he wore the simple linen garments of the priest or Levite, a picture of Christ's humiliation (Phil. 2:1-11).

## IV. The Holy Crown (28:36-39)

The turban (mitre) was a simple white linen cap, perhaps not unlike the cap worn by a modern chef, only not as high. On the turban, held by a lace of blue, was a golden plate that said "holiness to the Lord." It was called "a holy crown" (29:6; 39:30; Lev. 8:9) and emphasized the fact that God wanted His people to be holy (Lev. 11:44; 19:2; 20:7). The nation was accepted before God because of the high priest (v. 38), just as God's people are accepted in Jesus Christ (Eph. 1:6). Because of Jesus Christ, God's people today are a holy priesthood (1 Peter 2:5) and a royal priesthood (1 Peter 2:9).

## V. The Garments for the Priests (28:40-43)

Aaron's sons served as priests and had to wear the assigned garments. The fine linen of all the garments reminds us of the righteousness that ought to characterize our walk and our service. If

126

the priests did not wear the proper garments, they were in danger of death. The priests of the heathen cults sometimes conducted their rituals in a lewd manner, but the Lord's priests were to cover their nakedness and practice modesty.

# EXODUS 29

The consecration of the priests teaches us much about our own relationship to the Lord.

## I. The Ceremony (29:1-9)

Aaron and his sons did not choose the priesthood for themselves but were chosen by God. It was an act of God's grace. No stranger (outsider) was allowed to intrude into the priesthood (Num. 3:10), not even a king (2 Chron. 26:16-23).

The washing speaks of the cleansing we have through faith in Jesus Christ (1 Cor. 6:9-11; Rev. 1:5; Acts 15:9), a once-for-all washing that needed never to be repeated (John 13:1-10). It was necessary for the priests to have daily washing at the laver, which speaks of our daily cleansing as we confess our sins (1 John 1:9).

In Scripture, clothing often symbolizes character and conduct. Our righteousnesses are like filthy rags before God (Isa. 64:6), and we cannot clothe ourselves with good works as Adam and Eve tried to do (Gen. 3:7). When we trust Christ, we are clothed with His righteousness (2 Cor. 5:21; Isa. 61:10). We should put off the "graveclothes" and put on the "grace clothes" (Col. 3:1ff). The distinctive garments of the priests identified them as the holy servants of God, set apart to minister to the Lord. As we noted before, the holy anointing oil is a type of the Spirit of God who alone can empower us for service (30:22-33).

## II. The Sacrifices (29:10-37)

According to OT law, there were three agents for cleansing: water, blood, and fire. It was necessary that the priests be cleansed by the sacrificial blood (Lev. 17:11). A bullock was slain as a sin offering each day for the entire week of consecration (v. 36), and the first ram was given as a burnt offering, a picture of total dedication to God. The blood from the second ram was applied to the right ears, thumbs, and great toes of Aaron and his sons, picturing their consecration to hear God's Word, do God's work, and walk in God's way. This second ram became a wave offering and then a burnt offering.

Part of the second ram was kept back for a special meal that only the priests could eat (Lev. 7:28-38). God ordained that certain parts of some sacrifices belonged to the priests as payment for their ministry to the people.

### III. The Continual Burnt Offering (29:38-46)

Now the Lord began to describe the ministerial duties of the priests, beginning with the burnt offerings that were to be offered morning and evening each day. The first responsibility of the priests each morning was to remove the old ashes from the altar, get the fire burning, and then offer a lamb to the Lord, a symbol of total devotion to God. See Lev. 6:8-13. This is a beautiful picture of what our morning "devotional time" ought to be like. "Stir up the gift of God" (2 Tim. 1:6) literally means "fan into full flame." How easy it is for the fire to get low on the altar of our hearts (Rev. 2:4) so that we become lukewarm (Rev. 3:16) and even cold (Matt. 24:12). The tabernacle was sanctified (set apart) by God's glory (v. 43) when the glory of God moved into the holy of holies (Ex. 40:34). Israel was the only nation to have "the glory" (Rom. 9:4). God's Spirit lives within us and therefore we should be a separated people who bring glory to God (2 Cor. 6:14–7:1).

# EXODUS 30

God wanted His people to be "a kingdom of priests" (19:6). Today, all of God's people are a priesthood (1 Peter 2:5, 9; Rev. 1:6), but in OT days, the nation of Israel had a priesthood that represented them before God. What the priests were, the whole nation should have been. What kind of people make up "a kingdom of priests"?

### I. A Praying People (30:1-10, 34-38)

As we have noted, there were two altars involved in the tabernacle services—a bronze altar for the blood sacrifices and a golden altar for the incense. The gold covering the wood speaks of the deity and humanity of the Savior and reminds us that we can pray to the Father only because of the intercessory work of His Son. We bring our requests in the name of Jesus Christ (John 14:12-15).

The burning of the incense pictures the offering up of our prayers (Ps. 141:2; Luke 1:10; Rev. 5:8). The fire that consumes the incense reminds us of the Holy Spirit, for without His aid we cannot truly pray (Rom. 8:26-27; Jude 20). The golden altar stood before the veil, outside the holy of holies, but we are privileged to come boldly into God's presence and bring our requests to Him (Heb. 4:14-16; 10:19-22). The high priest burned the incense each morning and evening, a reminder that we should open and close the day with prayer and during the day "pray without ceasing" (1 Thes. 5:17). The priest carried the fragrance of the incense with him all the day.

The special composition of the incense is given in vv. 34-38, and this formula was not to be used for common purposes. Likewise, prayer is special, and God dictates what the requirements are for effective praying. "Strange incense" (v. 9) and "strange fire" (Lev. 10:1) were not to be used on God's altar. No matter how fervent a prayer might be, if it is not according to God's will, it will not be answered.

## II. A Grateful People (30:11-16)

The annual Passover celebration would remind the people that the nation had been redeemed from bondage, and this annual "census tax" would be another reminder of their redemption (see 1 Peter 1:18-19). The silver was originally used for the sockets and hooks for the tabernacle (38:25-28); in later years, it helped to pay for the upkeep of the house of God (Matt. 17:24-27). When David impetuously took a census without receiving the "redemption money," God sent a plague to the nation (1 Chron. 21:1-17). It is dangerous to use "religious statistics" for the praise of man and not for the glory of God. We should be grateful to God for the redemption we have in Christ, and we should be willing to give to Him for His glory.

## III. A Cleansed People (30:17-21)

This bronze basin stood between the bronze altar and the tent, and the water in it provided ceremonial cleansing for the hands and feet of the priests. With no floor in the tabernacle, their feet would get dirty. In addition, the handling of the sacrifices would defile their hands. It is possible to be defiled even while serving the Lord.

The laver was made out of brass mirrors (38:8). Since the mirror is a picture of the Word of God (James 1:23-25), the laver illustrates the cleansing power of God's Word (John 15:3; Eph. 5:25-27; Ps. 119:9). When we trust Jesus Christ, we are "washed all over" once and for all, but it is necessary to confess our sins and "wash our hands and feet" if we want to enjoy fellowship with the Lord (John 13:1-11; 1 John 1:9).

## IV. An Anointed People (30:22-33)

Like the incense for the golden altar, the anointing oil for the priests was to be a special commodity, not to be duplicated or desecrated by common use. It could only be poured on the priests; the common people could not use this special ointment. How wonderful that all of God's people today have been anointed by the Spirit (1 John 2:20, 27; 2 Cor. 1:21).

# EXODUS 31

## I. The Ability to Work (31:1-11)

Whenever God calls us to do a job for Him, He gives us the enablement we need and the helpers we need. This He did for Bezaleel and Aholiab. Bezaleel means "in God's protection"; his father Hur we have met before (Ex. 17:10-16; 24:14). God gave these men the ability they needed to follow the heavenly pattern and make the things necessary for the tabernacle. Their wisdom and skill came from the Lord, and they used their abilities in obedience to God's command.

Artistic skills can be dedicated to God and used for His glory. Not everybody is called to be a preacher, teacher, or missionary. There is also a need for Christian writers, artists, musicians, architects, doctors, gardeners—in fact, in every legitimate vocation we can serve the Lord (1 Cor. 10:31).

## II. The Responsibility Not to Work (31:12-18)

There is a time to labor for the Lord and a time to rest, and both are a part of His plan for His people (Mark 6:31). Bezaleel and Aholiab were constructing the holy tabernacle, but they were instructed to be careful not to violate the Sabbath. The Sabbath was not given to the Gentile nations but only to Israel as a sign of their special relationship to the Lord. As we have noted before, the Sabbath commandment is nowhere given to the church, for the church honors the first day of the week, the Lord's Day, the day of His resurrection from the dead. The Sabbath belonged to the old creation (v. 17), but the Lord's Day belongs to the new creation.

# EXODUS 32–34

While Moses was having a "mountaintop" experience with the Lord, the people were sinning in the valley below. Spiritual leadership is not all blessing; there are burdens as well.

## I. Moses the Intercessor (32:1-35)

### A. *God's people sinning (vv. 1-6).*

No matter how you look at this sin, it was a great offense against God. The Jews were God's people, chosen by His grace and redeemed from Egypt by His power. He had led them, fed them, protected them from the enemy, and made them a part of His covenant. He had given them His holy laws and the people had agreed to obey (19:8; 24:3-7). Here at Sinai, the people had seen the awesome display of God's glory and had trembled at His power. Yet, in spite of all these marvelous experiences, they impudently disobeyed the Lord and lapsed into idolatry and immorality.

Moses had agreed to God's giving him Aaron as a helper (4:10-17), but now Aaron had become a leader in helping the people sin. When did Aaron come down from the mountain? Why did he not rebuke the people and turn to God for help? To say that Aaron made the calf as a symbol of Jehovah, stooping to the weakness of the people, does not excuse him; for Aaron knew what the Lord had said about idols (20:1-6).

The basic cause of this sin was unbelief: the people became impatient while waiting for Moses, and without true faith they decided they had to have something they could see. Impatience and unbelief led to idolatry, and idolatry led to immorality (see Rom. 1:18-32).

### B. *God's servant interceding (vv. 7-14).*

Of course the Lord knew what was going on in the camp of Israel.

131

See Heb. 4:13. Note how God seemed to "blame" Moses for what had happened, but Moses was quick to remind the Lord that Israel was His people. It was Jehovah's glory that was at stake and not Moses' reputation, so Moses reminded the Lord of His promises to the patriarchs. When Scripture says that the Lord "repents," it is using human language to describe a divine response (Num. 23:19; Jer. 18:7-10; Amos 7:1-6). Twice during Moses' lifetime, God offered to destroy Israel and use Moses to found a new nation (v. 10; Num. 14:12), but he refused. The Jews never knew the price Moses paid to be their leader. How much they owed to him, and yet how little they showed their appreciation! God was even going to kill Aaron, but Moses interceded for him (Deut. 9:20).

## C. God's wrath judging (vv. 15-35).

In His grace, God forgave their sins, but in his government, He had to discipline the people. How many tears have been caused by the painful consequences of forgiven sins! Moses had a right to be angry and to humble Aaron and the people. By breaking the two tables of the Law, written by God, Moses dramatically showed the people the greatness of their sin. Instead of confessing his sins, Aaron made excuses. He blamed the people for their depravity (v. 22), Moses for his delay (v. 23), and the furnace for its delivery of a calf! After dealing with the people, Moses returned to the Lord on the mountain and offered to give up his own life that the people might be spared. See Rom. 9:3. When a person dies, his or her name is removed from the book of life (Ps. 69:28; Ezek. 13:9). The book of life (or "the living") should not be confused with the Lamb's Book of Life, which records the names of the saved (Rev. 21:27; Luke 10:20).

## II. Moses the Mediator (33:1-17)

As intercessor, Moses stood between the nation and their past sins. As mediator, he stood between the nation and their future blessings. Moses was not content just to have the nation forgiven; he wanted to be sure that God would go with them as they continued their march to the Promised Land. When the people heard that God would not go with them, they humbled themselves and mourned. It is one thing to mourn because of God's discipline of our sins and quite something else to mourn because of God's distance resulting from our pride. "An afflicted people is an object of grace," wrote C. H. Macintosh, "but a stiff-necked people must be humbled."

The tent described in vv. 7-11 is not the tabernacle, for the tabernacle had not yet been constructed. This was the tent where God met with Moses and shared His plans with him (Num. 12:6-8; Deut. 34:10). As a symbolic gesture to show Israel how wicked they had been, Moses moved the tent outside the camp. Some of the people went out to meet with God while others merely watched as Moses went out. Joshua was one who stayed with Moses and kept vigil at the tent of meeting. "Every one of us is as close to God as he has chosen to be," said J. Oswald Sanders; and this is true.

Moses asked for God's grace to bless the people and God's presence to go with the people, and the Lord granted his request. After all, it was the glorious presence of God that distinguished Israel from all the other nations. Other nations had laws, priests, and sacrifices. Only Israel had the presence of God among them.

## III. Moses the Worshiper (33:18–34:35)

### A. Seeing the glory (33:18–34:9).

Moses knew what many in the church today have forgotten — that the most important activity of God's people is the worship of God. Moses had been given a guarantee of God's presence with His people, but that was not enough; he wanted a new vision of the glory of God. God's "goodness" (33:19) means His character and attributes. The word "back" (33:23) carries the idea of "what remains," that is, the afterglow of the glory of God — what was "left over" after God passed by. Since God is spirit, He does not have a body as humans do. These are only human representations of divine truths about God.

Moses returned for another forty days with God on the mountain (34:28; Deut. 9:18, 25), and God gave him new tables of Law. The Lord's proclamation in 34:6-7 became a standard "statement of faith" for the Jews (Num. 14:18; 2 Chron. 30:9; Neh. 9:17; Jonah 4:2). The earlier declaration in Ex. 20:5 states that God sends judgment "unto the third and fourth generation of them that hate me." Children and grandchildren are not condemned for the sins of their ancestors (see Ezek. 18:1-4), but they may suffer because of those sins. Once again, Moses bowed and worshiped as he communed with the Lord.

### B. Protecting the glory (34:10-28).

God reminded Moses that the people of Israel were to be different from the people living in the land of Canaan, and He warned Moses against the sin of idolatry. What is idolatry? It is exchanging the glory of the incorruptible God for an image (Rom. 1:23) and worshiping and serving the creature instead of the Creator (Rom. 1:25). God gave Israel His Law so that they might live godly lives and manifest His glory.

### C. Reflecting the glory (34:29-35).

You will want to read 2 Cor. 3 to get the spiritual lessons for today. The glory of the OT Law was temporary and finally faded away, but the glory of new covenant grace grows brighter and brighter. Moses only reflected God's glory and had to wear a veil so the people could not see the glory disappear, but God's people today radiate God's glory from within as they see Jesus Christ in the Word (the mirror) and become more like Him (2 Cor. 3:18). Ours is to be a constant "transfiguration" experience as we walk with the Lord. ("Transformed" in Rom. 12:2, and "changed" in 2 Cor. 3:18 are both the Gk. word "transfigured" as used in Matt. 17:2.)

# EXODUS 35–40

## I. The People Bring Their Gifts (35:1-29)

Moses had already told the people that God wanted their willing gifts so that the tabernacle could be built (25:1-8). What grace that God would accept gifts from a people who had disobeyed Him and grieved His heart. These were to be willing gifts from the heart (vv. 5, 21, 26, 29), for the Lord loves a cheerful giver (2 Cor. 9:6-8). Most of this wealth probably came from the people of Egypt (12:35-36) — delayed wages for all the work the Jews had done for the Egyptians. It was "the Lord's offering" (vv. 22, 24, 29), and therefore, they wanted to give their best. In fact, they gave so generously that Moses had to stop them from bringing more (36:4-7). We wonder if that problem ever exists in the church today!

## II. The Gifted People Give Their Service (35:30–39:43)

The Holy Spirit gave Bezaleel and Aholiab the wisdom to know what to do and the ability to do it. In like manner, God has given gifts to His people today so that the church might be built up (1 Cor. 12–14; Eph. 4:1-17; Rom. 12). Bezaleel and Aholiab did not do all the work themselves but taught others who assisted them.

In the succeeding verses, Moses names the various parts of the tabernacle one by one, as well as the garments of the priests. God is concerned with every detail of our work and does not minimize any aspect of it. The smallest hook for the curtains was as important to Him as the brazen altar. If we are faithful in the small things, God can trust us with the bigger things (Luke 16:10).

Scholars have estimated that in the construction of the tabernacle, the people used nearly a ton of gold, about three and a quarter tons of silver, and two and a quarter tons of bronze. It was not an inexpensive structure!

## III. The Lord Gives His Glory (40:1-38)

Israel had arrived at Sinai three months after their exodus from Egypt (19:1), and it was now the first day of the second year of their pilgrimage (40:2); so nine months transpired from the giving of the Law to the dedicating of the finished tabernacle. Nearly three months of that time, Moses had been with God on the mountain (24:18; 34:28). We see then that the construction of the tabernacle took about six months.

As he was setting up the tabernacle this first time, Moses put up the tent, and then, working outward from the holy of holies, he put the pieces of furniture in place. When that was done, he set up the outer court. With everything in its proper place, Moses then anointed the structure and its contents (vv. 9-11) and set it apart for the Lord. His final act of dedication was the consecration of Aaron and the priests (vv. 13-16), which was followed by their presenting the sacrifices to the Lord (Lev. 8–9).

The climax of the dedication service was the revelation of the glory of God in the fire on the altar (Lev. 9:24) and the cloud in the tent (Ex. 40:34-38; see also 1 Kings 8:10). No matter how expensive the tabernacle was, without the presence of God it was just another tent. The glory not only resided in the tabernacle, but it guided the Israelites on their pilgrim journey. When we speak of the "shekinah glory of God," we are referring to God's dwelling in the tabernacle or the temple. The Hebrew word transliterated "shekinah" means "dwelling of God," from the Hebrew word *shakan* which means "to dwell" (Ex. 29:45-46).

# LEVITICUS

## *A Suggested Outline of Leviticus*

I. God's Provision for Sin (1–10)

  A. The sacrifices (1–7)

    1. Burnt offering (1; 6:8-13)

    2. Meal offering (2; 6:14-23)

    3. Peace offering (3; 7:11-34)

    4. Sin offering (4; 6:24-30)

    5. Trespass offering (5:1–6:7; 7:1-7)

  B. The priesthood (8–10)

II. God's Precepts for Separation (11–24)

  A. A holy nation (11–20)

    1. Clean and unclean—laws of purity (11–15)

    2. The Day of Atonement (16–17)

    3. Various laws of separation (18–20)

  B. A holy priesthood (21–22)

  C. Holy days—the feasts of the Lord (23–24)

III. God's Promise for Success (25–27)

  A. The Sabbath of the land (25)

  B. The importance of obedience (26)

  C. The seriousness of vows (27)

# Introductory Notes to Leviticus

## I. Name

Leviticus means "pertaining to the Levites." The Levites were the members of Aaron's family who were not ordained as priests but were responsible to help the priests in the service of the tabernacle (Num. 3:1-13). This book contains the divine instructions for the priests concerning the various sacrifices, the feasts, and the laws of separation (what was clean and what was unclean).

## II. Theme

Genesis explains man's sin and condemnation, while Exodus is the book of redemption. Leviticus deals with separation and communion. The nation was led out of Egypt and brought to Sinai in Exodus, but in Leviticus the Lord speaks from the tabernacle (Lev. 1:1) and explains how sinful man may walk in communion with God. The words "holy" or "holiness" are found more than eighty times in this book. The first section of the book deals with the sacrifices, for we cannot approach God apart from the shed blood. The word "blood" is found eighty-eight times in Leviticus. The second half of the book covers the laws of purity, explaining how the people must live separated lives to please their Lord. God had redeemed the nation from bondage; now He wanted to see that nation walk in holiness and purity for His glory. If we have been saved by the blood of the Lamb and delivered from the bondage of the world, then we too ought to walk in fellowship with our Lord (1 John 1:5-10). We need the blood of Christ, the Perfect Sacrifice, to cleanse us from sin, and we need to obey the Word and walk in purity and holiness in this present evil world. All of this is seen in type and symbol in Leviticus.

## III. Sacrifice

Leviticus is a book of sacrifice and blood, themes that are repulsive to modern minds. People today wants a "bloodless religion," salvation without sacrifice, yet this is impossible. Leviticus 16 is perhaps the key chapter of the book, and chapter 17 makes it clear that the shed blood is what takes care of the sin problem (17:11). The word "atonement" means "to cover"; it is used about forty-five times in the book. The blood of the OT sacrifices could never take away sin (Heb. 10:1-18). This was accomplished by the once-for-all sacrifice of Christ on the cross. The blood of the OT sacrifices could only cover sin and point ahead to the Savior whose death would finish the work of redemption. By itself, the bringing of sacrifices could never save the sinner. There had to be faith in God's Word, for it is faith that saves the soul. David knew that sacrifices alone could never take away his sins (Ps. 51:16-17); the prophets also made this clear (Isa. 1:11-24). However, when the sinner came with a contrite heart, putting faith in God's Word, then his sacrifice was acceptable to God (see Cain and Abel, Gen. 4:1-5).

Leviticus presents many pictures of Christ and His work of redemption on the cross. The five sacrifices illustrate various aspects of His Person and work, and the Day of Atonement beautifully pictures His death on the cross. Do not try to press every detail of each type. Some of the instructions for the sacrifices, for example, had practical purposes behind them and need not be made to carry special spiritual lessons.

## IV. Practical Lessons

We do not practice the Levitical sacrifices today, but this book still carries some weighty practical lessons that we would do well to ponder.

### A. The awfulness of sin.

There must be the shedding of blood to atone for sin. Sin is not something light and unimportant; it is hateful in the eyes of God. Sin is costly—every sacrifice was an expensive thing to the Jewish worshiper.

### B. The holiness of God.

God makes a distinction in this book between the clean and the unclean. He also warns His people, "Be holy for I am holy" (11:44).

### C. The graciousness of God.

He provides a way of forgiveness and restoration! Of course, this "Way" is Christ, "the new and living way" (Heb. 10:19ff). The OT sacrifices pointed to the coming Savior. The phrase "it shall be forgiven" is used at least ten times in Leviticus.

# LEVITICUS 1–7

Hebrews 10:1-14 makes it clear that in Christ we have the complete fulfillment of each of the OT sacrifices. These five special sacrifices illustrate to us the various aspects of the Person and work of our Savior.

## I. The Burnt Offering—Christ's Complete Dedication (1)

This sacrifice had to be a perfect male of the first year, the very best that was in the herd. The sacrifice would be brought to the door of the tabernacle, for there was but one place of sacrifice acceptable to God (see Lev. 17). The offerer would then place his hands on the head of the sacrifice, thus identifying himself with the beast, and as it were, transferring his sin and guilt to the innocent animal. The beast was killed and the priest caught the blood and sprinkled it around the brazen altar at the door of the tabernacle. The animal was then skinned (and the skin given to the priest), cut into pieces, and burned completely on the altar. "All on the altar" (v. 9) is the key phrase: the entire animal was given to God as it was burned in the fire. This is a picture of our Lord's complete dedication of Himself to God. "I have come to do Your will, O God" (Heb. 10:9). See also John 10:17 and Rom. 5:19. Leviticus 6:8-13 points out that the priest offered a burnt offering the first thing each morning, so that every other sacrifice during the day was offered on the foundation of the burnt offering. Romans 12:1-2 instructs Christians to give themselves as living sacrifices—as living burnt offerings—wholly dedicated to God. Just as the priests were to maintain a "continual burnt offering" (6:12-13), so we are to be constantly dedicated to the Lord for His glory.

## II. The Meal Offering—Christ's Perfections (2)

The word "meat" means "meal"; there is no blood involved in this offering. It could be fine flour, flour baked into cakes, or even dried ears of corn. The fine flour speaks to us of Christ's perfect character and life—there was nothing rough or uneven in Him. The oil symbolizes the Spirit of God. And note the two-fold use of the oil: (1) mingled, v. 4, which reminds us that Christ was born of the Spirit; and (2) poured, v. 6, which speaks of Christ's anointing by the Spirit for His ministry. The frankincense added a wonderful fragrance to the offering, illustrating the beauty and fragrance of

Christ's perfect life here on earth. The offering had to go through the fire, just as Christ had to endure the fire of Calvary. There must always be salt with the offering (v. 13), symbolizing purity and absence of decay, for there was no corruption of any kind in Christ. However, the offering was never to have leaven, which symbolizes sin (1 Cor. 5:6-8; Matt. 16:6; Mark 8:15), for there was no sin in Christ. Nor was the offering to have honey, which is the sweetest thing nature has to offer. There was nothing of "human, natural sweetness" in Christ; He was divine love in the flesh.

How wonderful are Christ's perfections! May the Spirit of God so work in us that we might become more like Him—balanced, even, fragrant, pure.

## III. The Peace Offering—Christ Our Peace (3)

This procedure was about the same as the procedure for the burnt offering, except that the offerer received back some of the animal and feasted upon it. The best was first given to God (vv. 3-5), but the rest was to be eaten by the offerer according to the rules laid down in 7:11-21. This was to be a joyful feast, illustrating the fact that there was peace between the offerer and the Lord, that the barrier of sin had been removed. For the NT truth, see Eph. 2:14, 17 and Col. 1:20. Note too in Lev. 7:28-34 that the priests received the breast and the shoulder as their own, reminding us that God's people must feed on Christ if they are to be strong. Leviticus 17:1-9 points out that every time an Israelite slaughtered a beast, it was to be treated like a peace offering. Would it not be wonderful if we regarded each of our meals as a peace offering to God and spent our time at the table in communion with Him and one another?

Apart from Christ, there can be no peace. It required the blood of the cross for the sin problem to be settled once and for all.

## IV. The Sin Offering—Christ Made Sin for Us (4)

There was no offering for deliberate "high-handed" sin (Num. 15:30-31), but there was provision made for sins of ignorance. Note that the blood had to be sprinkled before the veil (v. 6) and applied to the horns of the incense altar (v. 7), which shows the seriousness of sin. In vv. 3-12 we have the instructions for the sins of the priest; in vv. 13-21 we have the instructions for the sins of the whole congregation—and note that the same sacrifice was required for both! The sins of a priest (being the anointed of God) were equal to the sins of the whole nation! In vv. 22-26 we have the regulations for rulers, and in vv. 27-35, the regulations for the common people. The offering, then, depended on the status and responsibility of the person who had broken the Law of God.

Note that the sacrifice was not burned on the brazen altar; it was taken outside the camp and burned in a clean place. This reminds us of Heb. 13:11-13 and the fact that Christ was crucified "outside the camp," rejected by the nation He came to save. The NT parallel for the sin offering is 2 Cor. 5:21 where we are told that Christ was made sin for us; see also 1 Peter 2:24.

It is wonderful to see that even the poorest offender could provide a sin offering, for in 5:7 we are told that God would accept turtledoves or pigeons. It was this humble sacrifice that Mary and Joseph brought (Luke 2:24) showing the poverty of our Lord's family.

## V. The Trespass Offering—Christ Paying Sin's Debt (5:1–6:7)

The sin offering and trespass offering are closely related. In fact, they picture two aspects of the death of Christ for lost sinners. The sin offering dealt with sin as a part of human nature, the fact that all people are sinners, while the trespass offering emphasized the individual acts of sin. You will note in the trespass offering that offenders had to make restitution for what they had done (5:16; 6:4-5). This offering, then, reminds us that sin is costly, and that where there is true repentance there will be restitution and repayment. In 5:14-19 we have trespasses against God emphasized, while in 6:1-7, the emphasis is on trespasses against other people. In both cases, sin was looked upon as a debt to be paid; and, of course, that debt was fully and finally paid by Christ.

It is interesting to look at the order of these sacrifices as they are recorded in the Bible. God begins with the burnt offering, the complete consecration of His Son to the work of redemption, for this is where the plan of salvation begins in eternity past. But from man's point of view, the order is reversed. First, we see ourselves as having committed sins of various kinds, and we realize that we are in debt to God and man. This is the trespass offering. But as the work of conviction continues, we realize that we are sinners—our very nature is sinful! This is the sin offering. Then the Spirit reveals Christ to us, the One who made peace by the blood of His cross, and we discover the peace offering. As we grow in grace, we come to understand the perfections of our Lord, and that we are "accepted in the Beloved"; this is the meal offering. The result of all of this must be our complete consecration to the Lord—the burnt offering.

We do not need any sacrifices today. "For by one offering He has perfected forever those who are being sanctified" (Heb. 10:14, NKJV). Hallelujah, what a Savior!

# LEVITICUS 10

In the previous chapter, Moses and Aaron had set up the tabernacle and dedicated it to the Lord, the fire of God had fallen on the altar, and the glory of God had filled the sanctuary. It was a high and holy experience for the priests and the nation of Israel. However, two of the sons of Aaron, Nadab and Abihu (Ex. 6:23; 28:1), presumptuously sinned against God and were judged by Him. The fire of God that consumed the sacrifice on the altar (9:24) brought about their sudden death. "Our God is a consuming fire" (Heb. 12:29).

The central theme of the chapter is stated in v. 3, "I will be sanctified in them that come near me, and before all the people I will be glorified." The phrase "them that come near me" refers to the priests, who had the privilege of ministering in the tabernacle where God dwelt in the holy of holies. See Ezek. 42:13 and Ex. 19:22. Privilege always brings responsibility, but Nadab and Abihu proved themselves to be irresponsible.

It's a privilege to be a servant of the Lord. God admonished His servants to honor and glorify Him in three special areas of life.

## I. Honoring God (10)

### A. In their serving (vv. 1-5).

Nadab and Abihu had been on the holy mount with Moses and their father Aaron (Ex. 24:1-2, 10), so they were a privileged pair. They had heard the words of the Law and knew what God required of His priests, so theirs was not a sin of ignorance.

*What was their sin?* The text says they offered "strange fire" to the Lord. The word "strange" means "unauthorized by the Word of God" (see Ex. 30:9). They were enthusiastic, but what they did was not according to the Scriptures. It has been suggested that they failed to use the fire from the altar (9:24), so God couldn't accept their worship. But much more is involved than that.

Once a year, on the Day of Atonement, the high priest was privileged to enter the Holy of Holies with incense (Lev. 16:12). The rest of the year, incense was burned morning and evening on the golden altar that stood before the veil (Ex. 30:1-10, 34-38). The two sons of Aaron had devised a new ceremony for worshiping Jehovah, and He would not accept it. They were not high priests, it was not the Day of Atonement, and they did not burn the incense on the golden altar.

*Why did they sin?* Perhaps they were carried away by the enthusiasm of the hour as they saw the glory of God fill the sanctuary and the fire of God come down from heaven. What they did was an example of "will worship" (Col. 2:23) and is a warning to all who lead God's people in the service of worship. Carnal enthusiasm is no substitute for the fullness of the Spirit, and one of the fruits of the Spirit is self-control (Gal. 5:23). We must worship God "in spirit and in truth" (John 4:24). The Spirit of God will never lead believers to do anything contrary to the Word of God, no matter how "happy" or enthusiastic they may feel.

Judgment begins at the house of the Lord (1 Peter 4:17; see also Ezek. 9:6). This was the beginning of a new period in the history of Israel, and God used this judgment as a warning to His people. You will find similar judgments occurring when Israel entered the Promised Land (Josh. 7), when David sought to bring the ark to Jerusalem (2 Sam. 6), and during the first days of the church (Acts 5). Whenever sinful men and women take to themselves the glory that belongs only to God, judgment will come in one form or another. God will not give His glory to another (Isa. 42:8; 48:11; 52:11).

### B. In their mourning (vv. 6-7).

Moses warned Aaron and his two remaining sons not to mourn the death of Nadab and Abihu the way the common people would mourn (see 21:1-12 and Ezek. 24:16-17). They had to remain in the tabernacle precincts during the time of dedication (8:33). If they disobeyed, wrath would come upon all the people and not just on the priests. By staying at their posts and serving the people, they were honoring God and showing the people the importance of obeying His Word, no matter what the cost.

Of course, no such commandment applies to God's people today, who are also His priests (1 Peter 2:5, 9). We sorrow at the death of loved ones, but we must not sorrow "as those who have no hope" (1 Thes. 4:13-18). By sorrowing in a godly manner, we bear witness to the lost world that we have hope in Jesus Christ and are not in despair.

### C. In their eating and drinking (vv. 8-20).

These admonitions relate to the daily duties of the priests, but they have practical applications for believers today.

*(1) Strong drink (vv. 8-11).* This is the only place in Leviticus where God speaks directly to Aaron, so it must be an important commandment. The Jews were not forbidden to drink wine or strong drink, but they were warned against drunkenness and the sins that often accompany it (Prov. 20:1; 23:20, 29-31; Isa. 5:11; Hab. 2:15). Those who serve the Lord must be an example to others and be filled with the Spirit and not with wine (Eph. 5:18). By their teaching and example, they must "put a difference" between the holy and the unholy (see Ezek. 22:26; 42:20; 44:23; 48:14-15). The NT follows this same approach (Rom. 14:14-23).

*(2) The sacrifices (vv. 12-20).* The priests were given a certain portion of some of the sacrifices and were to eat this food at the tabernacle. It was holy and must not be treated like common food. During the dedication ceremony recorded in chapter 9, they had offered the meal offering, sin offering, burnt offering, and peace offering; and the priests were to eat their portions as a part of the service. It was another reminder to them and the people that the sacrifices were holy unto the Lord. See Lev. 6:14-30 and 7:11-38 for more detail.

There were two kinds of sin offerings, one whose blood was sprinkled in the holy place, and one whose blood was sprinkled on the altar of burnt offering. On that day, the sin offering was of the second kind (9:9; 10:18), so Aaron and the priests should have eaten it; but they didn't. It was bad enough that Nadab and Abihu did what they weren't supposed to do and brought judgment, but now the priests weren't doing what they were supposed to do and were inviting more judgment!

Moses rebuked Aaron's two sons, but Aaron spoke up in their defense. The family had not been allowed to mourn over the sudden loss of two sons, so they had fasted instead and did not eat the meat of the sin offering. Had they eaten the sacrifice, it would have been only a mechanical routine and not a holy meal; for their hearts wouldn't have been in it. Would God want that kind of service? He wants obedience, not sacrifice (1 Sam. 15:22) and hearts that are right with Him.

This chapter is a stern warning against worship and service that go beyond the boundaries set by the Word of God. It's also a warning against carnal enthusiasm that imitates the work of the Spirit. Counterfeit worship grieves the Spirit of God who wants to lead us in worship experiences that are based on Scripture and that glorify the Lord. Our worship must show forth the praises of God (1 Peter 2:9) and be acceptable to God (1 Peter 2:5). Worship that exalts men and women and fails to glorify God is not acceptable to Him.

"Therefore, whether you eat or drink, or whatever you do, do all to the glory of God" (1 Cor. 10:31, NKJV).

# LEVITICUS 11

From the emphasis on *atonement* in chapters 1–10, Moses now turns to the theme of *defilement*. In chapters 11–15 and 17–22, he teaches his people the difference between the clean and the unclean in the areas of food, birth and death, diseases and personal relationships. Chapters 21–22 instruct the priests as to their responsibility to be separated from sin and devoted to the Lord.

## I. Guidelines for God's People (11)

### A. The diet of God's people (vv. 1-23).

We don't know when God's people first received the law about clean and unclean foods, but it was known in Noah's day (Gen. 7:1-10). Perhaps this was a part of the teaching God gave Adam and Eve in the Garden of Eden. There were at least two reasons for this dietary law: (1) the health of God's people, and (2) the distinction of Israel as a separated people. In a day when there was neither refrigeration nor adequate means for cooking, many of these forbidden foods were potentially dangerous to the health of the people. See Ex. 15:26 and Deut. 7:15. However, the main reason was that the Jews might be reminded daily, at each meal, that they were a separated people who were not to live like the Gentile nations around them. See Deut. 14:1-20 for more information.

These dietary laws were given only to the Jews and were abolished with the fulfillment of the Mosaic Law in Jesus Christ (Col. 2:11-17). Jesus made it clear that these laws were temporary and did not determine the condition of the heart (Mark 7:1-23). The early church found itself divided over these laws (Rom. 14:1–15:7). Peter apparently kept a "kosher house" even after Calvary and Pentecost (Acts 10:9-16), but he soon learned that God had made some drastic changes. ("Kosher" comes from a Hebrew word meaning "right, fit." People in a kosher Jewish home ate only those foods that God said were right and fit.) In the church today, diets are not a means of salvation or holiness (Col. 2:20-23; 1 Tim. 4:1-5); and Christians must not judge one another in these matters. While some foods may not be physically good for some people, what a Christian eats or drinks must not be made a test of spirituality.

Moses first deals with *land creatures* (vv. 1-8) and states that only those animals may be eaten that have the split hoof and that chew the cud. The *water creatures* (vv. 9-12) must have both scales and fins. This would eliminate the creatures that wallow in the mud where they could pick up all sorts of parasites. The free swimming fish would be safe to eat. (Of course, this was long before the days of the pollution of the earth's water systems.) Next come the *flying creatures* (vv. 13-23), including fowl (vv. 13-19) and insects (vv. 20-23). Here the Lord names specific creatures and doesn't give any general standard to follow as He did with land and water creatures. The fourth category is *creeping things* (vv. 29-31a, 41-43). Again, specific creatures are named as being unclean to the Jews.

Some well-meaning students try to "spiritualize" these laws to find some "deeper" truth in them, but the results are contradictory and questionable. To make "chewing the cud" refer to meditating on Scripture, and "the cloven hoof" picture a separated walk in Christ, is to twist the Scriptures and rob them of their true meaning.

Christians today are free to eat what they please, but they must keep 1 Cor. 10:31 in mind.

### B. The defilement of God's people (vv. 24-40).

Not only did Moses warn the Jews to beware of what they ate, but they must also beware of what they touched; for the carcass of an animal was unclean to them. If a Jew touched a carcass, he would be unclean until evening, the beginning of the new day. He would then have to wash both his clothes and his body, and then he was permitted to enter the camp.

In vv. 24-28, the law deals with *people* being defiled by dead animals; and in vv. 31b-38, it deals with the defilement of *things*, particularly things in the home. Vessels, clothing, furniture, food, and water could all be defiled by that which was unclean. This "ritual uncleanness" had to be dealt with seriously if the people and the home were to be pleasing to the Lord. In vv. 39-40, Moses deals with defilement from the carcasses of clean animals used for food. The Jew didn't eat much meat since it was very expensive to lose an animal that was useful for breeding, wool, and milk. They were to be careful not to kill their animals carelessly, for it was against the law to eat blood (Lev. 3:17; 7:26-27; 17:14).

### C. The dedication of God's people (vv. 44-47).

Here Moses gives three motives for purity on the part of the Jewish nation. They would be tempted to follow the filthy customs of their pagan neighbors, but these truths would motivate them to obey the Lord and refrain from defilement.

*(1) God is a holy God (v. 44).* "Be holy for I am holy" is repeated in various forms nine times in the Book of Leviticus (11:44; 19:2; 20:7, 26; 21:8, 15; 22:9, 16, 32) and it is quoted in 1 Peter 1:15-16 as applying to the NT Christian today. If we are God's people, and He is a holy God, then it's logical that we live holy lives. The dietary laws reminded the Jews to be a separated people, a holy people (Ex. 19:5-8; see 1 Peter 2:9).

*(2) God redeemed us for Himself (v. 45).* The Lord often reminded the Jews that they were a redeemed people and that He had rescued them by His grace and power (19:36; 22:33, 43; 25:38, 42, 55; 26:13, 45). Had He not redeemed them, they would still be slaves in Egypt. Of course, the Exodus is a picture of the redemption we have in Jesus Christ, for He is the Passover Lamb sacrificed for us (John 1:29; 1 Cor. 5:7; 1 Peter 1:18-19). If we are a redeemed people, then we ought to live holy lives to please the God who set us free.

*(3) God wants His people to be different (vv. 46-47).* These laws taught the Jews that they were a special people to the Lord and were supposed to be different from the nations around them. See Lev. 10:10 and 20:22-26, as well as Ezek. 22:26, 42:20, 44:23, and 48:14-15. Because the people forgot their debt to the Lord, they began to mingle with the Gentile nations and learn their godless ways. They stopped making a difference between the holy and the unholy, the clean and the unclean; and this led to their chastening

and captivity. Of course, today "there is no difference" between the Jew and the Gentile, either in condemnation (Rom. 3:22-23) or salvation (Rom. 10:12-13). Believing Jews and Gentiles are "all one in Christ Jesus" (Gal. 3:26-29).

It's significant that the Lord Jesus established an ordinance for His church that involved eating and drinking (1 Cor. 11:23-34). Each time we share the bread and the cup, we do it to remember Him and what He did for us on the cross. The observing of the Lord's Supper (the Eucharist) should encourage us to be a holy people, a grateful people, and a people who are different from the people of the world.

# LEVITICUS 13–14

When He was ministering on earth, our Lord healed lepers (Matt. 10:8; 11:5; Mark 1:40-45; Luke 17:11-19). This was called cleansing, since leprosy was looked upon as defilement as well as disease. The leper was barred from normal society and was prohibited from going to the temple. These two chapters in Leviticus deal with leprosy as a picture of sin, and they illustrate what Christ has done to cleanse sinners. (Note that the Hebrew word translated "leprosy" could be applied to several different skin ailments.)

## I. The Characteristics of Sin (13)

If people thought they had leprosy, they were required to go to the priest for an examination. Note the characteristics of leprosy and how they picture sin:

### A. It is deeper than the skin (v. 3).

Leprosy was not merely a surface eruption; it was deeper than the skin. How like sin! The problem is not on the surface. Deeper than the skin, the problem lies in sinful human nature. The Bible has nothing good to say about the flesh (the old nature) because our sinful nature is the source of so many of our troubles. Sinners cannot be changed by shallow surface remedies; they need to have their hearts changed. See Jer. 17:9, Rom. 7:18, Ps. 51:5, and Job 14:4.

### B. It spreads (v. 7).

Leprosy was not an isolated sore on one part of the body; it had a way of spreading and defiling the whole body. Sin also spreads: it begins with a thought, then follows a desire, then an act, then the terrible results (James 1:13-15). Read 2 Sam. 11 and see how sin spread in David's life. David left his army when he should have been fighting; he allowed his eyes to wander to his neighbor's wife; he lusted; he committed adultery; he lied; he made Uriah, the neighbor, drunk; and finally, he murdered the man.

### C. It defiles (vv. 44-46).

This means, of course, ceremonial defilement; lepers were not allowed to participate in the religious services. They were forced to mark themselves as lepers and to cry, "Unclean! Unclean!" to warn the people around them. Anyone who touched a leper was also defiled. This is the tragedy of sin: it defiles the mind, the heart, the body, and all that it touches. One sinner can defile a whole household; think of Achan (Josh. 7). No person was ever made cleaner because of sin, for sin is the great defiler of mankind.

### D. It isolates (v. 46).

"He shall dwell alone!" What sad words. "Outside the camp" in the place of rejection was the only place for a leper. Sin always isolates people. It takes them away from family, friends, and, ultimately, from God. When Christ was made sin for us He cried, "Why have You forsaken me?" Sin separates people from God—and this is what hell is.

### E. It destines things for the fire (v. 52).

Any garment that was found defiled with leprosy was burned. There is only one place for sin, and that is in the fires of judgment. Jesus described hell as a place where the fire never burns out (Mark 9:43-48). It is sad to think of millions of "spiritual lepers" being consigned to the eternal fires of judgment because they have never trusted Christ as their Savior. How important it is that we tell the world the good news of the Gospel!

People may laugh at sin, excuse it, or try to explain it away, but to God sin is serious. Note Isa. 1:4ff for the prophet's use of leprosy as a picture of sin.

## II. The Cleansing of the Sinner (14)

This chapter explains the ritual for the ceremonial cleansing of lepers so that they might enter society again.

## A. The priest goes to the leper (v. 3).

Of course, the leper was barred from coming into the camp, so the priest had to go "outside the camp" to him. What a picture of Christ who came to us and died "outside the camp" that we might be saved (Heb. 13:10-13). We did not seek Him; He came to seek and to save the lost (Luke 19:10).

## B. The priest offers the sacrifices (vv. 4-7).

This ceremony is a beautiful picture of the work of Christ. The priest took one of the birds and placed it in an earthen vessel (clay jar), and then he killed it. Of course, the birds were not created to live in jars, but to fly in the heavens. Christ willingly left heaven and took upon Himself a body, put Himself, as it were, in an earthen vessel, that He might die for us. Note that the bird was killed over running water, a picture of the Holy Spirit. The priest then took the living bird, dipped it in the blood of the dead bird, and set it free. Here is a vivid illustration of Christ's resurrection. Christ died for our sins and was raised again, and He took the blood (spiritually speaking) back to heaven that we might be cleansed from sin. The priest finally sprinkled some of the blood on the leper, for "without shedding of blood there is no remission" (Heb. 9:22, NKJV).

## C. The leper washes and waits (vv. 8-9).

The priest had already pronounced him clean, so he was accepted as far as the Lord was concerned, but now he had to make himself ritually acceptable. This washing is a picture of the believer cleansing himself from filthiness of the flesh and spirit (2 Cor. 7:1). After we have been saved, it is our responsibility to keep our lives blameless and holy for His sake. Note that the leper's wait was until the eighth day, for eight is the number of resurrection, the new beginning.

## D. The leper offers the sacrifices (vv. 10-13).

He was now back in the camp at the door of the tabernacle. He offered a trespass offering, a sin offering, and a burnt offering. The sin offering took care of his defilement; the burnt offering represented his renewed dedication to God. Why the trespass offering? Because while he had been defiled, the man had not been able to serve God as he should, and he owed God a great debt. The trespass offering was his only way to repair the damage done by that wasted segment of his life. Every lost sinner is robbing God of the honor due His Name, and each day the debt becomes greater.

### E. The priest applies the blood and oil (vv. 14-20).

This is a touching part of the ritual. The priest took the blood and applied it to the right ear, the right thumb, and the right great toe of the man, symbolizing that his whole body had now been purchased and belonged to God. He was to listen to God's Word, work for God's glory, and walk in God's ways. Then the priest put the oil on the blood, symbolizing the power of the Spirit of God for the doing of God's will. The blood could not be put on the oil; the oil had to be put on the blood. For where the blood has been applied, the Spirit of God can work. The rest of the oil was poured on the man's head, and thus, he was anointed for his new life. If you will read Lev. 8:22-24, you will see that a similar ceremony was performed for the consecration of the priests. In other words, God treated the leper as he would a priest.

Of course, all of this is accomplished today through faith in Jesus Christ. He went "outside the camp" to find us. He died and rose again to save us. When we trust Him, He applies the blood and oil to our lives and restores us to fellowship with God. One day a leper said to Christ, "If You are willing, You can make me clean." He replied, "I am willing; be cleansed." See Mark 1:40-45. Christ is willing to save and able to save.

# LEVITICUS 16–17

The Day of Atonement was Israel's highest religious holiday, for on that day God dealt with all the sins that had not been covered during the year. Hebrews 10:1ff is the NT commentary on this chapter.

## I. The Preparation of the Priest (16:1-14)

### A. He had to be alone (vv. 1-2, 16:17).

No Levite could assist in this important ritual. The high priest had to officiate alone. So with our Lord: He alone could pay the price for sin. His nation rejected Him, His disciples forsook Him and fled, and the Father turned from Him when He died on the cross. Alone our Lord settled the sin question once and for all.

### B. He laid aside his glorious garments (v. 4).

What a picture of our Lord's coming to earth as a human being. He laid aside the garments of His glory and took upon Him the form of a servant. See also Phil. 2:1-11.

### C. He washed (v. 4).

For the priest, this meant getting rid of any ceremonial defilement. As a picture of Christ, it shows Him sanctifying Himself for our sake (John 17:19). He willingly dedicated Himself to the task of giving His life a ransom for many.

### D. He offered a sin offering (vv. 6-11).

Our Lord did not have to offer any sacrifices for Himself. Read carefully Heb. 7:23-28.

### E. He entered the holy of holies (vv. 12-13).

The high priest actually entered the holy of holies three times: first, with the incense, which pictures the glory of God; then, with the blood from the sacrifice for himself; and finally, with the blood shed for the people. The incense preceded the blood because the purpose of salvation is the glory of God (Eph. 1:6, 12, 14). Jesus died not simply to save lost sinners and give them life, but that God might be glorified (John 17:1-5).

All of this was preparation for the main task of the Day of Atonement, the giving of the sin offering for the nation.

## II. The Presentation of the Goats (16:15-34)

Note that the two goats were considered one sin offering (v. 5). They illustrate two aspects of the work of the cross. After the high priest returned from sprinkling the blood of his sin offering, he took the goat that was designated to die and killed it as a sin offering for the entire nation. He then entered the holy of holies for the third time, this time with the blood of the goat. He sprinkled the blood on the mercy seat and before it, and thus covered the sins of the nation. Note that v. 20 indicates that the blood of the sin offering "reconciled" the people and the tabernacle to God (see Heb. 9:23-24).

Having applied the blood, the high priest then took the live goat, laid his hands on its head, and confessed the sins of the people, thus symbolically transferring their guilt to the innocent animal. The word "scapegoat" comes from a Hebrew word which means "to remove." This goat was then sent away into the wilderness, never to be seen again, and this illustrated the removal of the nation's sins (Ps. 103:12). Of course, these rituals did not remove sin, since the ceremonies had to be repeated year by year. But they illustrated what Christ would do when He died once for the sins of the world. The believing Israelite was saved by his faith, just the way people have always been saved. Only after the sin offering had been completed, and the nation's iniquity carried away (symbolically), did the high priest lay aside his humble linen garments and put on his garments of glory. This is a picture of the resurrection and ascension of Christ. After He had finished His work on the cross, He went back to the Father in glory, where He is seated today. The Day of Atonement was to be a serious day for the Jews, and they were not to do any work. Salvation is not by works, it is wholly by the grace of God.

## III. The Prohibition Concerning Blood (17)

Leviticus 17:11 is a key verse of the Bible, for it states emphatically that the only way of atonement is through the blood. Long before science discovered the marvel of blood, the Bible taught that the life is in the blood. Doctors used to take out blood to try to make people well; today they give blood transfusions!

This chapter prohibited the Jew from slaughtering his animals carelessly. He was to make each animal a peace offering to the Lord by bringing it to the door of the tabernacle for the priest to offer. The danger, of course, was that they would be tempted to sacrifice to idols or demons (v. 7), a practice they had learned in Egypt; or that the blood would not be taken from the animal and thus the people would sin by eating blood. The blood was something special; it was not to be treated as common food.

Throughout this chapter the emphasis is on the one place of sacrifice. There was only one price that God would accept—the blood—and only one place where God would accept it—the door of the tabernacle. So it is today. God accepts but one price for sin—the blood of His Son. And that blood was shed at the one place God appointed—Calvary's cross. To depend on any other sacrifice at any other place is to be rejected by God.

The life is in the blood, both physically and spiritually. Our spiritual life depends on the shed blood of Christ (see 1 John 1:7; Eph. 1:7; Col. 1:14; Heb. 9:22).

We live in a day when liberal theologians reject the doctrine of the blood of Christ. They call it "slaughterhouse religion." It needs to be made clear that the Bible is a book of blood, from Genesis (where God slew animals to clothe Adam and Eve) to Revelation (where John beheld Christ "as a Lamb that was slain"). It is not Christ the Example, or Christ the Teacher who saves us; it is Christ the Lamb of God, crucified for the sins of the world.

# LEVITICUS 21–22

The priests in general, and the high priest in particular, were to maintain the highest standards of character and conduct; and they were never to offer sacrifices that were below standard. In this, they pictured our Lord Jesus Christ, the perfect High Priest and the perfect sacrifice (Heb. 7:26-28; 10:1-14). They also challenge God's people as priests (1 Peter 2:5, 9) and sacrifices (Rom. 12:1) to give their very best to God.

Note the repetition of the words defile, profane, blemish, unclean, holy, and sanctify. The theme is the holy character and conduct of God's servants as they minister to the Lord and His people. God warns that, as we serve Him, we not profane ourselves (21:5), God's name (21:6; 22:2), God's sanctuary (21:12), our children (21:15), or the holy things that we handle in ministry (22:15).

One of the tragedies throughout Israel's history was the defilement of the priesthood, which led ultimately to the defilement of the nation. If the greatest sin is the corruption of the highest good, then the Jewish priests succeeded in committing the greatest sin; for they corrupted the priesthood by their godless character, their evil conduct, and their careless ministry of the holy things of God (see Mal. 1:6–2:9). Unfortunately, the church today has made both merchandise and mockery of the ministry; and the church is desperately in need of a revival of holiness.

## I. Perfect Priests (21:1–22:16)

These laws concern the conduct of the priests with reference to mourning for the dead, marriage, and the conduct of family relationships.

### A. Conduct of the priests (21:1-9).

In the camp of Israel, a person was defiled if he or she touched a dead body or even entered a dwelling where there was a dead body (Num. 19:11-22). The ordinary priest could defile himself for close family members but not for other relatives or for friends. No Jew was to follow the mourning practices of the pagans (19:27-28; Deut. 14:1). The reason for these laws is given in vv. 6 and 8: the priests offer the sacrifices of God and have been set apart by God (see 21:15, 23; 22:9, 16, 32). No priest was to marry a harlot or a divorcée, for this might bring into the priestly clan children not begotten by a man from the tribe of Levi (see v. 15). No daughter of a priest was permitted to live, if she became involved in immorality (see 20:14 and Gen. 38:24).

### B. The conduct of the high priest (21:10-15).

Because of his position before God and anointing from God, the high priest was expected to be even more exemplary than the ordinary priests. God always expects more from leaders. He couldn't even defile himself for his father and mother, nor could he show the normal signs of mourning. Verse 11 doesn't teach that the high priest lived in the tabernacle, for Num. 3:38 tells us his tent was pitched at the east side of the tabernacle. This verse instructs the high priest always to be on duty and not to leave the tabernacle precincts even for a funeral. He had to marry a virgin to assure the nation that the next high priest was actually his son.

### C. The characteristics of the priests (21:16-24).

Both the priests at the altar and the sacrifices on the altar (22:17-25) were to be without blemish. While we're not certain what handicaps are indicated by some of these terms, it's clear that God wanted His ministers to be perfect physically. Once again, this magnifies the perfections of our High Priest, Jesus Christ. The Lord certainly doesn't include physical perfection as a requirement for ministry today (1 Tim. 3); the emphasis is on moral and spiritual maturity. Paul had a thorn in the flesh which made him even more qualified to serve!

### D. The contacts of the priests (22:1-16).

The priests must "treat with respect" (NIV) the holy things of God by keeping themselves separated from defilement. What a tragedy if the holy servant of God made everything he touched unclean because of his own defilement (see Matt. 23:25-28). Moses repeated some of the causes of defilement that had already been explained in detail in previous chapters: leprosy (chaps. 13–14), running sores (chap. 15). A priest who presumptuously ministered while unclean was in danger of death (vv. 3, 9).

Beside avoiding the unclean things, the priests had to be careful how they dispensed the holy things. Only the priests could eat portions taken from the meal offerings, the sin offerings, and the trespass offerings; but members of the priest's family could share in eating the other offerings. The person had to be an official member of the family by birth or purchase. A daughter married to a non-priest was excluded. Anybody who ate the holy food unwittingly had to pay a penalty.

## II. Perfect Sacrifices (22:17-33)

God always deserves the very best and we dare not bring Him that which is blemished (Mal. 1:6–2:9). The blood of a blemish sacrifice could never please God or atone for sin. Furthermore, these sacrifices were types of the Lord Jesus Christ, and He is the perfect sacrifice (Heb. 9:14; Eph. 5:27). To offer God blemished sacrifices was to profane His name.

The laws relating to the killing of the sacrifices shows the tenderness God has toward animals (vv. 27-28). He will not take the young from the mother too soon. God also has concern for the birds (Deut. 22:6-7) and the trees (Deut. 20:19-20).

The chapter closes with God's reminder of the reasons that ought to motivate His people as they sacrifice: He is the Lord who has set them apart as His own people, He delivered them from the bondage of Egypt, and these are His commandments.

Believers today don't bring animal sacrifices to God because that whole system was ended at the cross. But we do present to Him our bodies (Rom. 12:1-2), the people we have won to Christ (Rom. 15:16), our praise (Heb. 13:15), our good works (Heb. 13:16), a broken heart (Ps. 51:17), and our prayers (Ps. 141:2). Since nothing that we offer Him is perfect, we must offer our sacrifices through Jesus Christ so that they will be acceptable to God (1 Peter 2:5).

# LEVITICUS 23

The seven feasts of the Lord are full of rich spiritual food and bear careful study. Some of these feasts we have already studied, so we will not deal with them in detail, but others are new in our studies. It is important to note the order of these seven feasts, for they give us a "prophetic calendar" for both Israel and the church. The religious year opened with Passover, which pictures the death of Christ. On the day following the Passover Sabbath (a Sunday), the Israelites celebrated Firstfruits, picturing our Lord's resurrection from the dead. The week following Passover was devoted to the Feast of Unleavened Bread, when all the leaven was put out of the houses. This illustrates the sanctification of believers as they put sin out of their lives. All of this took place in the first month of the year. Fifty days after Firstfruits is the NT Pentecost, the coming of the Holy Spirit on the church. In the seventh month, three feasts were celebrated. The Feast of Trumpets opened the month, reminding us of the gathering of God's people when the Lord returns. On the tenth day was the Day of Atonement, illustrating the cleansing of God's people; and from the fifteenth to the twenty-first days, the Jews joyfully celebrated the Feast of Tabernacles, picturing the blessings of the future kingdom. God's people are a scattered people who must be gathered, a sinful people who must be cleansed, and a suffering people who must be given joy. The long period (about three months) between Pentecost and the Feast of Trumpets speaks of this present age of the church, when Israel is set aside because she rejected her Messiah.

## I. Passover (23:4-5)

We have already considered this feast, so refer to the notes on Ex. 11–13. Everything depends on the blood of the lamb: there could be no other feasts if there were no Passover. People today who want to do away with the blood are undermining the very foundation of God's plan of the ages!

## II. Unleavened Bread (23:6-8)

This too has already been considered. It pictures God's people putting sin out of their lives (2 Cor. 7:1) and feeding on the Lamb that they might have strength for the journey. Do not reverse these two feasts. Nobody is saved by putting away leaven (sin), and nobody will want to put away sin until first he or she has been saved by the blood! This is the difference between religious reformation and spiritual regeneration, being born again by the Spirit of God.

## III. Firstfruits (23:9-14)

This feast was reserved for the land of Canaan, when the people would have fields and harvests. It would be impossible to celebrate such a feast in the wilderness. On the day after the "Passover Sabbath" (a Sunday, the first day of the week), the priest would wave the first sheaf of grain before the altar as a token that the whole harvest belonged to the Lord. This is a picture of our Lord's resurrection, since 1 Cor. 15:20-21 definitely calls Him "the first-fruits." Worshiping on the Lord's Day is not the invention of the church, as some people teach. It was written into God's calendar centuries before! Because Christ, the Firstfruits, is alive, the entire "resurrection harvest" belongs to God. Not one person will be forgotten. The promise is certain: "Because I live, you shall live also" (John 14:19, NKJV).

## IV. Pentecost (23:15-22)

"Pentecost" means "fifty," and fifty days after Christ's resurrection, the Holy Spirit came to believers (Acts 2). For forty days, Christ had ministered to His disciples (Acts 1:3), and for another ten days they had prayed and waited for Pentecost to arrive. The "new meal offering" (v. 16) was composed of two loaves of bread, symbolizing Jews and Gentiles baptized into one body, the church, by the Holy Spirit (1 Cor. 12:13). The fact that leaven was allowed illustrates to us that there is sin in the church on earth today. Thank God the day will come when there will be no leaven among God's people! Note too that the priest presented loaves and not sheaves of grain, for now the believers have been united in Christ by the Spirit. It is after Pentecost that we have the long gap when there are no feasts. There are three feasts in the first month and three in the seventh, with Pentecost between. This long gap speaks of the present age, the age of the church. Israel has rejected her Lamb; she cannot receive the Spirit until she receives her Messiah; and she is scattered across the world. She has no temple, no priesthood, no sacrifice, and no king. What is her future? It is seen in the next three feasts.

## V. Trumpets (23:23-25)

As a nation, Israel was instructed by signals from the priests blowing trumpets (Num. 10). The Feast of Trumpets illustrates the regathering of Israel when God's trumpets shall call them from the ends of the earth. Read Isa. 27:12-13, and the words of Christ in Matt. 24:29-31.

Of course, there is an application here to the church, for we await the sound of the trumpet and the return of our Lord in the air (1 Cor. 15:52ff; 1 Thes. 4:13-18). The Jews sounded the trumpets to gather the assembly together, and this is what our Lord will do when He gathers His children. The Jews also sounded the trumpets for war, and once Christ has His children off this earth, He will declare war on the nations.

## VI. Day of Atonement (23:26-32)

This has previously been discussed in our notes on Lev. 16–17. When God has finally gathered the Jews together, He will reveal Christ to them, and "they shall look upon Him whom they have pierced." Israel's future Day of Atonement is described in Zech. 12:10–13:1. Read these verses carefully. It will be a day of mourning for sin, a day of cleansing by the blood of the Lamb. There are some who apply the Day of Atonement to the Judgment Seat of Christ, when the saints of God will give account for the deeds done in the body. Its primary application, however, is to the nation of Israel. Certainly at the Judgment Seat of Christ, the church will be cleansed of all defilement and be made beautiful for the marriage of the Lamb.

## VII. Tabernacles (23:33-44)

For seven days, the Jews were to live in booths, reminding them of God's provision and protection when they were in the wilderness. But there is also a future Feast of Tabernacles for Israel that will take place when the King has been received and the nation restored. Read Zech. 14:16-21 for more detail. Thus, this feast speaks of the future millennial kingdom that God has promised the Jews. This feast followed the harvest (v. 39), which teaches us that God will have gathered all of His harvest before Christ establishes His earthly kingdom. This was to be a feast of rejoicing, not sorrow; and certainly all heaven and earth will rejoice when Christ reigns from Jerusalem. This chapter is God's "prophetic timetable," and we know not when the trumpets will sound. How important it is for us to be ready for the sound of the trumpet and the coming of the Lord!

# LEVITICUS 25

The economic system in Israel was based on three fundamental principles: (1) God owned the land and had a right to control it, v. 23; (2) God owned the people, because He had redeemed them from Egyptian bondage, vv. 38, 42, 55; and (3) the Jews were a family ("your brother," NKJV) and should care for each other, vv. 25, 35-36, 39, 47. Joshua and the Jewish army conquered the land of Canaan, but it was God who assigned their inheritance (Joshua 13–21). The people "possessed" the land and enjoyed its products, but God owned it and determined how it would be used.

This chapter focuses on three topics relating to the economy of the nation.

## I. The Sabbatic Year (25:1-7, 18-22)

The OT Jewish calendar functioned on a series of "sevens." The seventh day of the week was the Sabbath. Seven weeks after Passover came Pentecost, and the seventh month of the year introduces the Feast of Trumpets, the Day of Atonement, and the Feast of Tabernacles. Every seventh year was a "Sabbatic Year," and after seven Sabbatic years came the Year of Jubilee.

The Sabbatic year was God's way of allowing the land to lie fallow and restore its fruitfulness. The people were not permitted to have a formal harvest that year, but anyone could eat from the produce of the fields and orchards. God promised to provide abundant crops during the sixth year, so observing the Sabbatic Year was really a test of faith for the people. It was also an expression of God's love for the poor of the land (Ex. 23:10-12). According to Deut. 15:1-11, all debts were to be remitted at the end of the seventh year. Jewish servants were supposed to serve only six years (Ex. 21:2), and the Jewish people were encouraged to be especially generous to the poor.

The Sabbatic year was a time of rest and restoration for the land, the people, and the animals who worked on the land. It was an opportunity for a new beginning for those who had experienced difficulties financially. Unfortunately, there's no evidence that the nation ever faithfully obeyed this law (2 Chron. 36:21). The prophets often condemned the Jewish leaders and wealthy people for their ruthless treatment of the poor. Had the Sabbatic year law been observed, it would have prevented the poor from losing their

161

lands and the rich from amassing huge estates. The economy wouldn't have been perfect, but it would have been balanced much better.

During the Feast of Tabernacles in each Sabbatic year, the priests were to read and explain the Book of Deuteronomy to the people (Deut. 31:9-13). It was something like a week-long Bible conference during which the people were reminded of what God had done for them and what He expected them to do in return. God's people need to be taught His Word, for each new generation has not learned it; and the older generations need to be reminded of it.

## II. The Year of Jubilee (25:8-17, 23-24)

The word "jubilee" comes from the Hebrew word *yobel* which means "ram's horn." This special year was announced by the blowing of trumpets on the Day of Atonement. Thus, the year began with fasting and repentance as the nation confessed its sins to the Lord (Lev. 16).

During that year, the people reclaimed the land that had been sold so that it would not go out of the control of the family or clan. Any Jew purchasing property would calculate the price until the next Year of Jubilee when the land would revert back to the original owner. How much food it could produce in that time was a major consideration. As in the Sabbatic year, the land was to lie fallow during the Year of Jubilee. The people would have to trust God to provide what they needed for the Sabbatic year (the forty-ninth), the Year of Jubilee (the fiftieth), and the fifty-first year when they would again plant seed. There would not be a new harvest until the next year.

The people did not own the land, therefore they couldn't sell it permanently. God gave them the land (Gen. 12:1-3; 15:7; 17:8; Deut. 5:16) and permitted them to use it, and He would always control it. The people were to walk in the fear of the Lord and not use their wealth to oppress one another.

The slaves were released during this special year, so that families would be reunited. The statement "Proclaim liberty throughout all the land" (v. 10) is engraved on the Liberty Bell in Philadelphia.

The Year of Jubilee looks forward to the kingdom age when Jesus Christ will reign in glory and fulfill the promises made to the Jewish people. Read Isa. 61 and see what God has planned for the nation of Israel. In a spiritual sense, the Year of Jubilee also pictures our Christian life (Luke 4:16-21, which is quoted from Isa. 61:1-2). In His reading of the OT in the synagogue that Sabbath in Nazareth, Jesus stopped with "the acceptable year of the Lord" (Luke 4:19), which refers to the Year of Jubilee. He did not read "the day of vengeance of our God" (Isa. 61:2), for that day of judgment will not come until after God has finished His present program of "calling out a people for His name" (Acts 15:14).

## III. The care of the poor (25:25-55)

These laws applied regardless of whether it was a Sabbatic year or a Year of Jubilee. The general principle is laid down in vv. 25-28 and then is applied to specific situations. A person who had to sell property because of a financial need could redeem it at any time, or a brother could redeem it for him. But the price would be determined by the number of years remaining until the Year of Jubilee.

### A. A house in a city (vv. 29-34).

This would be very valuable property because of the security afforded in a walled city. For this reason, the seller had only one year's time in which to buy it back. After that, the owner held the property as long as he pleased; and it would not revert to the original owner during the Year of Jubilee. However, this rule didn't apply to houses owned by the Levites. For a Levite who gave his property to the Lord, see Acts 4:34-37.

### B. A poor brother (vv. 35-46).

The Jews were not to oppress one another or take advantage of each other in financial matters. If they loaned money, they were not to take interest; if they sold food, they were not to make an exorbitant profit. See Neh. 5. If a Jew had a fellow Jew as a servant, working off a debt, he was not to treat him like a slave; and the servant was to go free at the Year of Jubilee.

### C. The Kinsman-Redeemer (vv. 47-55).

The best illustration of this law is in the book of Ruth where Boaz redeemed Ruth and Naomi and their property. A kinsman could rescue his relative by paying his debts and recovering his land. The "redeemer" had to be a near kinsman who was able and willing to redeem. The poor relative would be set free from both bondage and debt. The kinsman-redeemer is a picture of our Lord Jesus Christ who became our "close relative" by becoming a man (Phil. 2:1-11; Heb. 2:9-18) and paying the price for our redemption by dying on the cross. He was both able to save and willing to save.

It must be noted that the economic system in Israel was not a form of communism. People possessed private property which could be bought and sold, but God owned the land and would not permit it to be sold permanently. The Sabbatic year and the Year of Jubilee, if obeyed, would have prevented the rich from getting richer and thus making the poor poorer. But the Jews didn't obey these laws and the results were tragic. They also enacted laws that favored the rich and crushed the poor, and God judged them for it. See Isa. 3:12-15 and 10:1-3; Amos 2:6-7 and 5:11.

Finally, these special laws also show God's concern for the land. By allowing the land to lie fallow every seventh year, and then two years in a row at the Jubilee, they were restoring its productivity and increasing its value. Of course it took faith to do this, but God promised to meet their needs. After all, the food we eat comes from the hand of God, not from the supermarket; and we all need to pray, "Give us this day our daily bread" (Matt. 6:11).

# NUMBERS

## *A Suggested Outline of Numbers*

I. The Old Generation Set Aside (1–20)
- A. Counted (1–4)
- B. Counseled (5–10)
- C. Chastised (11–12)
- D. Condemned (13–20)

II. The New Generation Set Apart (21–36)
- A. Their journeying (21–25, 33)
- B. Their numbering (26–27)
- C. Their offerings (28–30)
- D. Their dividing of the inheritance (31–36)

# *Introductory Notes to Numbers*

## I. Name

The book takes its name from the two numberings of the men of war in chapters 1–4 and 26–27. The first census was made the second year after the nation had left Egypt, and the second was made thirty-eight years later when the new generation was about to enter Canaan. These numberings were not of the entire nation, but only of the men able to fight. The first census revealed that there were 603,550 available men; the second, that there were 601,730.

## II. Theme

Numbers is the wilderness book of the OT. It describes the failure of the nation at Kadesh-Barnea and their wanderings in the wilderness until the unbelieving older generation died. Someone has described Israel's wilderness wanderings as "the longest funeral march in history." Only Caleb and Joshua of the older generation were permitted to enter Canaan, because they had trusted God and opposed the decision of the nation to turn back at Kadesh-Barnea. Even Moses was forbidden to go into the Promised Land because of his sin when he smote the rock instead of speaking to it.

## III. Spiritual Lesson

Numbers has an important spiritual lesson for Christians today, as explained in Hebrews 3–4 and 1 Cor. 10:1-15. God honors faith and punishes unbelief. At the root of all of Israel's sins in the wilderness was unbelief: they did not trust God's Word. At Kadesh-Barnea they doubted God's Word and failed to enter into their inheritance. Instead of claiming Canaan by faith, they wandered in the wilderness in unbelief. Many Christians today are "in between" in their spiritual lives. They have been delivered from Egypt by the blood of the Lamb, but they have not yet entered into their inheritance in Christ. Canaan is not a picture of heaven. Rather, it is an illustration of our spiritual inheritance in Christ (Eph. 1:3), an inheritance that must be claimed by faith. Canaan was a land of battles and blessings, as is the Christian life today. Alas, too many Christians come to the place of decision (their own Kadesh-Barnea), and they fail to enter into their inheritance by faith! Instead of being conquerors (as described in Joshua), they become wanderers, as described in Numbers. Yes, they are saved, but they fail to fulfill God's purpose for their lives. They will not trust God to overcome the giants, knock down the walls, and give them the inheritance that He has promised. They will not cross Jordan (which illustrates death to self) and step out by faith to claim what Christ has promised them.

It is interesting to note that the nation did not grow during their wilderness wanderings. In fact, the second census showed 1,820 fewer men of war. The nation wasted thirty-eight years, endured unnecessary afflictions, failed to grow, and failed to honor God all the while they were on their "death march." This is what unbelief does to Christians. It wastes time, effort, and manpower and brings no real blessing. How sad it is when churches fail to step out by faith and, as a result, start to degenerate spiritually, numerically, and materially. May God help us to trust His Word!

# NUMBERS 9–12

These chapters describe some of the wilderness experiences of the nation of Israel, and in them we see the experiences of Christians today.

## I. God Leading His People (9–10)

### A. He gives wisdom in problems (9:1-14).

It was now the second year after Israel's wonderful deliverance from Egypt, and the nation was to observe the Passover. This feast was the constant reminder that their redemption depended on the blood of the lamb and the power of God. Every blessing they experienced came through the blood, even as with the church today (Eph. 1:3ff). However, certain men had been ceremonially defiled by a dead body, and they needed to know the mind of God about whether they could participate in the feast. Moses graciously admitted that he did not know the answer, but that he would ask the Lord. See James 1:5. The Lord permitted these men to observe the feast later, in the second month, which shows that even under the rigid Law of Moses there was freedom when circumstances demanded it (see 2 Chron. 30:13-15). Interestingly, when Nicodemus and Joseph took the body of Jesus down from the cross on Passover, they defiled themselves and could not participate in the feast (John 19:38-42). However, they had found salvation in Christ, the true Lamb of God.

### B. He gives direction in our daily walk (9:15-23).

We have seen the guiding cloud before in Ex. 13:21-22. It is encouraging to know that the same God who saves and keeps us also guides us in our journey. Of course, God wanted to guide the nation into the place of His blessing, but their unbelief hindered Him. It is likely that the pillar of cloud and fire is a picture of the Word of God that is our counselor and guide in this present life. Using the Word, the Spirit leads us "always . . . by day and . . . by night" (v. 16). It would have been foolish, in fact, dangerous, for the camp or any part of it to move without direction from God. The Jews were a pilgrim people, living in tents, and they had to be ready to move at a moment's notice. Verse 22 makes it clear that God's leading is beyond human calculation: sometimes the cloud would tarry a few days, sometimes a month, and sometimes as long as a year. At times God would lead them in the daytime, and at other times in the darkness (v. 21). But it made no difference so long as God was the one leading.

### C. He gives warning when we need it (10:1-10).

These two trumpets were made of silver (a metal that speaks of redemption) and were used to call the assemblies for the journeying of the camp. The priests and Levites lived right next to the tabernacle, and they would be the first ones to see the cloud moving. It would be their responsibility to warn the camp. As we read these verses, we see that the trumpets were used for several other purposes: to assemble the camp at the door of the tabernacle (vv. 3, 7); to call the heads of the tribes together (v. 4); to sound an alarm, either for war or for the journeying of the camp (vv. 6, 9); and to announce the special days, the new moons, etc., (v. 10). It is interesting that trumpets are associated with both Israel and the church. The rapture of the church, when God calls His heavenly people together, will be with the sound of the trumpet (1 Cor. 15:51-53; 1 Thes. 4:16-17; see also Rev. 4:1). He will also use the trumpet to gather scattered Israel (Matt. 24:31, and see the Feast of Trumpets in Lev. 23:23-25).

### D. He leads His people in an orderly way (10:11-28).

Each tribe was camped at a specific place around the tabernacle, and each section moved as the trumpets commanded.

### E. He does not need the world's wisdom (10:29-36).

Hobab was Moses' brother-in-law; Raguel (or Reuel) was Moses' father-in-law, also named Jethro (see Ex. 2:18-21 and 3:1). God had promised to guide His people, yet Moses wanted to lean on the arm of flesh.

## II. God Chastening His People (11–12)

After the remarkable evidences of God's love in chapters 9–10, it is amazing that we read of the people complaining. Yet such is human nature—we fail to appreciate what God has done for us.

### A. The people complained and God sent fire to chasten them (11:1-3).

The same people who complained, begged Moses for help, and he

169

was gracious enough to pray for them. Taberah means "burning." It is a serious thing to complain against God.

### B. The people lusted and God provided flesh for them (11:4-35).

The "mixed multitude" were traveling with Israel, but, like worldly church members today, their hearts were still in Egypt. Instead of remembering God's goodness, they remembered the carnal things of Egypt! And they complained about the heavenly manna that God gave them daily. Verse 8 indicates that the people did their best to improve on the manna, for they ground it, beat it, and baked it. They would do anything to make God's bread taste like the food of Egypt, but the problem was their appetite and not God's bread. Exodus 16:31 says that the manna tasted like honey, but v. 8 states that when the Jews tried to "improve" upon the manna, they made it taste like oil!

One of the sad results of carnality among God's people is discouragement on the part of the leaders (v. 10ff). Now Moses himself complained to God! Notice how often he said "I" and "my" and "me" in his prayer, for his concern was himself and not God's glory. Moses should have known that the same God who delivered them, led them, and provided for them, would give them flesh in the wilderness; but, as often happens, self-centered praying killed his faith. Finally, Moses was about to give up: "I am not able!" (v. 14). See what his father-in-law said back in Ex. 18:18. Of course, in himself, Moses was not able to lead Israel, but with God leading him, he could do the impossible. Yet Moses was so discouraged that he even asked to be killed!

God met both needs: He gave Moses seventy elders to assist him in his work, and He gave the lusting Jews the meat that they craved. Note, however, that in both cases, the answers God gave were costly. God took of the same Spirit that empowered Moses and gave Him to the seventy elders to assist him, but could not the Spirit have given Moses all the power he needed for his work? And the people who ate the flesh died of a great plague even as they ate (Ps. 78:25-32; 106:13-15). God sometimes answers our prayers, and we find that the answer is not a blessing at all! Note in vv. 26-30 that Moses manifested no envy toward the two men empowered by the Spirit to prophesy. This is the sign of a great man. Moses certainly had his days of discouragement, as we all do, but he was a man of God in spite of his failings.

In v. 31 we see that the quails were blown in from the sea and flew about two cubits over the face of the earth, near enough for the Jews to catch them. The people spent two days and one night gathering their meat, yet how many of them were faithful to gather the heavenly manna? The name "Kibroth-hattaavah" means "graves of lust." "To be carnally minded is death" (Rom. 8:6).

### C. The leaders criticized and God chastened them (chap. 12).

Aaron, the high priest, and Miriam, a prophetess (Ex. 15:20-21), both were leaders in Israel with their brother Moses. The apparent cause of their argument was Moses' wife, who was a Cushite (Ethiopian, and therefore a Gentile). But the real cause was their jealousy over Moses' leadership (v. 2). Moses proved his meekness (humility) by refusing to fight them; he left his cause in the hands of God. God has promised to defend His servants (Isa. 54:17). Apparently Miriam was the ringleader, for she was made leprous, and her sin held up the march of the camp for seven days. Aaron confessed his guilt, and Moses prayed for his sister Miriam, an evidence of true love and humility. It is a serious thing when spiritual leaders become envious of one another, because their sin affects the whole congregation.

Whether this was a new wife, or Zipporah, Moses' wife of years before, we do not know. It could have been a second marriage for Moses, but there is no hint anywhere that Zipporah had died. Note that the word "apparently" in v. 8 means "plainly"; God spoke to Moses face to face.

# NUMBERS 13–14

Hebrews 3–4 is the NT commentary on these chapters. The key thought is that unbelief robs us of blessing. Notice the evidences of unbelief in the nation and its leaders.

### I. Sending in the Spies (13:1-27)

Here read Deut. 1:20-23, where Moses makes it clear that the sending of the spies was the desire of the people, not the commandment of the Lord. He permitted this plan to be used so that He might reveal to the people what their hearts were really like. God had already told them many times what Canaan was like, what nations were there, and how He would defeat their enemies and give them their promised inheritance; so what need was there for men to go in and spy out the land? Sad to say, human nature prefers to walk by sight, not by faith.

The spies searched the land and even brought back some of the wonderful fruit, but they also brought back an evil report and discouraged the hearts of the people. Except for Moses, Caleb, and Joshua, nobody in the nation believed that God would keep His promises! The ten unbelieving spies illustrate many Christians today: they have "spied out" their inheritance in Christ and have even tasted some of the fruits of His blessing; but their unbelief keeps them from entering in by faith.

It is interesting to note the "promotion" of Joshua. In Num. 11:28 he is called "Moses' servant"; ultimately, he becomes Moses' successor (Josh. 1). We see him as a soldier in Ex. 17:8-16; Ex. 24:13 shows him with Moses on Sinai; Ex. 33:11 has him in charge of the tent of meeting; and Num. 13 shows him as one of the spies. Because he was faithful in whatever task God gave him, Joshua was advanced from one responsibility to another.

## II. Refusing to Go into the Land (13:28-33)

The ten spies described the glories of the land, and then added, "Nevertheless . . ." This word is usually a sign of unbelief. The people were strong; the cities were walled up; and giants were in the land. They saw the giants and saw themselves as grasshoppers—but they did not see God. Their eyes were on the obstacles, not on the God who had led them there. Caleb showed true faith when he said, "We are well able!" The people showed unbelief when they said, "We are not able!" Instead of reporting the blessings of the land, the ten spies emphasized the difficulties, giving an "evil report" of God's holy land. Unbelief always sees the obstacles; faith always sees the opportunities.

This refusal to enter the land is a type of the believer's refusal to claim his or her inheritance in Christ (Heb. 3–4). Instead of entering into full rest in Christ, and trusting Him for every need, doubting Christians see the problems and obstacles, and wander around restlessly, blind to their blessings.

## III. Rebelling against Their Leaders (14:1-39)

In Ex. 15, we see Israel singing in great victory, but here they are weeping in defeat! Had they forgotten their song? See Ex. 15:14-18.

Had they forgotten all that God had done for them in the past two years? They had seen His power and glory, yet now were tempting Him by their attitude of rebellion and unbelief (vv. 22-23).

God waited until the people expressed a desire to replace Moses and return to Egypt; then He began to act. Caleb and Joshua realized that the nation's response was nothing but rebellion (v. 9). God's glory suddenly appeared, and God spoke to Moses.

## A. God's offer (vv. 11-12).

God was willing to destroy the entire nation and make a new nation through Moses' family, but Moses rejected this offer. What humility and love! You can be sure Moses realized that his descendants would not be any different from the nation he was now leading, for "all flesh is as grass." See Ex. 32:10 for a similar offer from God.

## B. Moses' intercession (vv. 13-19).

A short time before, Moses was complaining because the people were such a burden, and now he was pleading on their behalf. He had the heart of a true shepherd—he loved his people and prayed for them. Note that Moses reminded God of His promises and performances: it was the glory of God that was at stake! Moses also reminded the Lord of His mercy and forgiveness (see Ex. 33:18-23 and 34:5-9). In this scene, Moses is a picture of Christ who was willing to give up His own life that He might save us.

## C. God's judgment (vv. 20-39).

In His grace, God pardoned their sin; but in His government, He had to allow that sin to produce its bitter fruit (see 2 Sam. 12:13-15). First, God gave the people their request, announcing that they would die in the wilderness (vv. 2, 28-30). Only Caleb and Joshua were excluded from this judgment because of their faith and faithfulness. The people had fretted about their little ones, yet the children would be the very ones to live and enter into the land. Since the men had spied out the land forty days, God gave the Jews forty years to wander in the wilderness while they died one by one. What a contrast to the church today: when the last unbelieving Jew died, the nation could enter Canaan; but when the last unbelieving sinner enters the body of Christ, the church will leave this world and enter her inheritance! Finally, the ten spies who brought the evil report were killed immediately by a plague (v. 37).

It cannot be emphasized too much that God honors faith and

judges unbelief. Faith leads to obedience and glorifies God; unbelief leads to rebellion and death. We have the Word of God filled with His promises and assurances. There is no reason why any of us should wander in unbelief when we can be walking in victory and enjoying the spiritual riches we have in Christ.

## IV. Attempting to Battle without God (14:40-45)

How fickle is human nature! One day the nation was mourning because of their plight, and the next day they were recklessly trying to accomplish God's work apart from God's will and God's blessing. They thought that because they had confessed their sin, God would change His mind and give them victory. Moses warned them, but they ignored his warning, proving that they were not walking by faith in the power of the Spirit. The flesh is always self-confident and self-sufficient, as illustrated by Peter (Luke 22:31-54).

The men advanced to the top of the hill, and the enemy defeated them. The whole venture was "presumption" on their part; they were living by chance, not by faith. The Lord was not with them in spite of their seeming repentance and their zeal. We can never do anything by faith that contradicts the Word of God. How many Christians today realize their failings and then try to make up for them in fleshly activities that only lead to discouragement and defeat. All the Israelites could do was to accept God's judgment and surrender to His will. Far better to wander in the wilderness in the will of God than to fight a losing battle out of the will of God.

These two chapters emphasize again the importance of faith. Faith is not blind; it has all of the promises and assurances of God's Word for its foundation. "Today, if you will hear His voice, harden not your hearts" (see Heb. 3:7-8).

# NUMBERS 16–17

The "gainsaying (saying against) of Korah" is mentioned in Jude 11 as one of the marks of false teachers in the last days; and certainly today we see a united rebellion against the authority of Moses and the priesthood of Aaron (God's way of salvation by blood). Korah was evidently a cousin of Moses (Ex. 6:21), which makes the rebellion even more serious.

## I. Korah Defies Moses and Aaron (16:1-18)

Korah was a Levite who was not content to assist in the tabernacle; he wanted to serve as a priest as well (v. 10). Of course, this attitude was a direct rebellion against the Word of God as given by Moses, since it was God who made the tabernacle appointments. Not content to rebel alone, Korah gathered 250 princes of Israel, well-known men (most of them probably Levites), as well as three men from the tribe of Reuben, Jacob's firstborn son. In name, number, unity, and attitude, those rebels seemed to have a strong case against Aaron and Moses. It appears that Korah and his followers defied Aaron, while Dathan, Abiram, and On (being descendants of Reuben, the firstborn) questioned the authority of Moses. However, they were united in their plot.

Rebels rarely give the real reason for their attacks; in v. 3 the men argued that all of the nation was "a kingdom of priests" (Ex. 19:6), and therefore Moses and Aaron had no right to take the places of leadership. Of course, this rebellion was based on self-seeking and envy. These men wanted to "lift themselves up" before the congregation. Certainly the whole nation was holy to God, but He had placed some people in positions of leadership as He willed. The same is true of the church today: all saints are beloved of God, but some have been given spiritual gifts and spiritual offices for the work of the ministry (Eph. 4:15-16; 1 Cor. 12:14-18). We are encouraged to "desire spiritual gifts" (1 Cor. 14:1) but not to covet another person's spiritual office. If a believer wants a place of spiritual leadership, let him prove himself worthy of it by his character and conduct (1 Tim. 3:1ff). The church must heed Paul's warning in Acts 20:28-31.

Moses and Aaron did not defend themselves; they let God do the defending. Moses instructed Korah and his followers to bring censers (pots for burning incense) to the tabernacle where God would demonstrate who was right in the dispute. He called for Dathan and Abiram to come, but they defied Moses' authority and refused to obey. In v. 25, Moses went to them, but his visit meant condemnation, not blessing. Note how the men blamed Moses for their failure to enter the Promised Land (vv. 13-14), when it was their own unbelief that brought this defeat. To rebel against Moses meant rejecting the Word of God, for he was God's prophet; and to rebel against Aaron meant rejecting the work of God on the altar, salvation by the blood.

## II. God Defends Moses' Authority (16:19-35)

The next day God stepped in and judged the rebels. Fire from the Lord killed the followers (v. 35), and the earth opened up and swallowed the leaders, Korah, Dathan, Abiram, and their possessions. In 26:11 we learn that Korah's family was not destroyed. This explains why we have psalms titled "For the sons of Korah" in our Bible (Pss. 84, 85, 87, 88). Apparently Korah's descendants were content to be humble ministers and not priests, for they wrote in Ps. 84:10 (NKJV), "I would rather be a doorkeeper in the house of my God than dwell in the tents of wickedness." For "tents of wickedness" see Num. 16:26. It is tragic when a few people sin and cause the deaths of many others. Before this rebellion was over, nearly 15,000 people had died (see v. 49). Read 2 Peter 2:10-22 for God's estimate of those who "despise authority" and rebel against God's truth.

## III. God Defends Aaron's Authority (16:36–17:13)

### A. By giving Aaron the censers of the rebels (16:36-40).

Moses told Aaron's son, Eleazar, to gather the censers and have them made into brass plates for a covering for the brazen altar. When worshipers came to the altar, they would see these plates and be reminded that the sin of rebellion is severely judged by God. Why were these censers "hallowed" (sanctified)? Because God had used them in a special way to teach Israel a lesson. To allow the censers to be treated as "junk" or as ordinary implements would have lessened the impact of the judgment.

### B. By having Aaron intercede (16:41-50).

You would think that the deaths of all these people would strike terror and awe into the hearts of the nation, but it did not. The very next day the entire congregation rebelled again! Only the grace of God can change the human heart; no amount of law or judgment will ever make the heart new. The congregation gathered against Moses and Aaron and accused them of being murderers, but God stepped in and defended his servants. Had Moses been of a bitter spirit, he would have allowed the plague to destroy the people. Instead, he commanded his brother Aaron to go into the midst of the plague with his censer to stop the judgment. How little the people realized Moses' love and sacrifice for them. Aaron literally became their savior—he stood between the living and the dead and stayed the plague. His one censer accomplished more than the 250 censers of the rebels! In a sense, Aaron illustrates the work of our Savior, for Christ left the place of safety to stand between the living and the dead and rescue sinners from death.

### C. By causing Aaron's rod to bud (17:1-13).

God was now going to declare once and for all the authority of the Aaronic priesthood. The people had not learned their lesson, so Moses instructed each tribe to bring a rod—a dead stick—to be placed before the ark in the tabernacle. God announced that the rod that blossomed would indicate the one He had chosen for the priesthood. Verse 8 tells us that Aaron's rod not only budded, but it blossomed and bore fruit! The other rods were still dead, and each of the princes took back his dead rod, leaving Aaron's rod to be placed in the tabernacle as a testimony to the nation's rebellion and God's appointment of Aaron as the high priest.

The budding of the rod is a beautiful picture of the Resurrection of Christ. By means of the Resurrection, God has declared that Christ is His Son and the only Priest that God accepts. All other priesthoods are rejected by God. It matters not how many people are involved, how great their names, or how sincere their work—all other priesthoods are rejected. There is One High Priest, one sacrifice, and only one open way to heaven; read Hebrews 10. We have many today like Korah who presume to take over the priesthood, but they have no heavenly authority.

Note in vv. 12-13 that the people were fearful after they had seen this demonstration of God's power. What the death of nearly 15,000 people could not do, the silent blossoming of a dead stick did accomplish! "Not by might, nor by power, but by My Spirit . . ." (Zech. 4:6).

# NUMBERS 20–21

In these two chapters, we have two wonderful types of Christ.

## I. Christ the Smitten Rock (20:1-13)

We have already been introduced to this type in Ex. 17:1-7. In many places in Scripture, God is pictured as a Rock; and 1 Cor. 10:4 makes it clear that the Rock in Exodus and Numbers is a picture of Christ. The people could not live without water, nor can we live today without the water of life (John 4:13-14; 7:37-39). In the Bible, water for drinking is a type of the Holy Spirit, who comes within and satisfies our spiritual thirst. Water for washing is a type of the Word of God, which has cleansing power (John 15:3; Eph. 5:26).

The events here contrast with those in Ex. 17. In the Exodus passage, God told Moses to smite the rock, picturing our Lord's death on the cross. But here He told him to speak to the rock, for Jesus Christ died but once. All we need do now is ask, and He will give of His Holy Spirit (John 7:37-39). When Moses smote the rock, he used Aaron's rod, not his own. This is the priestly rod of life (Ex. 17:1ff). Here is the explanation of why Moses was to speak to the rock and not smite it: Christ our rock has risen from the dead; He is our living High Priest; and He gives us the spiritual blessings we need as we ask for them. A person does not have to be saved over and over again, nor does the gift of the Holy Spirit have to be repeated. We receive the Spirit once when we trust Christ; we receive fillings of the Spirit many times as we come to Christ and ask.

The main reason, though, that God judged Moses and kept him out of the Promised Land was this: he exalted himself and failed to glorify God. In calling the people "rebels" and in saying, "Must we [Aaron and I] fetch you water out of this rock?" (v. 10) Moses was not giving God the glory due His Name. It was an evidence of pride and unbelief (v. 12). Moses' strongest point was his meekness (12:3), yet this was where he failed. No doubt Peter was a brave man, yet he failed in that very thing when he denied the Lord. Unless we glorify God in all that we do, God will deal with us and we will miss the blessing He has planned for us.

## II. Christ the Uplifted Brazen Serpent (21:1-9)

John 3:14 is our authority for making this a type of Christ. Note how it pictures for us the salvation we have in Christ.

### A. The need.

The people had sinned in two ways: they had spoken against God, and they had spoken against Moses. Because of this, they were dying. "The wages of sin is death" (Rom. 6:23). Here we have the two aspects of the Law of God: behavior toward God and behavior toward one another. Because of sin, death is in the world and all are condemned (John 3:16-18). Every person born into this world has been bitten by the fiery serpent of sin and is destined to die.

## B. God's grace.

God could have ignored his people's plight, for they deserved to die, but in His love and grace He provided a remedy. The intercession of Moses in v. 7 reminds us of the prayer of Christ, "Father, forgive them; for they know not what they do" (Luke 23:34).

## C. Another serpent.

How strange that Moses should make another serpent when it was serpents that caused all the trouble to begin with! Were there not enough of them in the camp already? But the serpent of brass pictures Christ, who became sin for us (2 Cor. 5:21). Brass is the metal that speaks of judgment, and on the cross, Christ bore our judgment for us. Note that the serpent was not effective in Moses' hand, or on a shelf. It had to be "lifted up"—Christ had to be crucified. See John 3:14, 8:28, and 12:30-33.

## D. By faith.

The people had prayed, "Take away the serpents!" But God's method was to overcome the sting of death by faith. "Look and live!" was the answer. It was not by ignoring the bites, beating the serpents, applying medicine, or trying to flee that the afflicted people were saved. Salvation came through looking by faith to the uplifted serpent in the center of the camp (cf. Isa. 45:22). Note that the serpent was not connected with the tabernacle in any way. No amount of sacrifices could have saved the people from death.

## E. Available.

The serpent was not lifted up in some hidden corner. It was lifted up in the center of the camp where all could see it and live. Christ is available today; He is not far away. See Rom. 10:6-13 for fuller application. The remedy was available to all; "whosoever will, let him take" (Rev. 22:17).

## F. Free.

It cost dying sinners with Moses nothing to look and live. They may not have understood the how and why of it all (and who does understand salvation?) but they could believe and live!

## G. Sufficient.

The one uplifted serpent sufficed for the whole camp. Christ alone is sufficient for our salvation; we need nothing more. The dying were not saved by looking at the serpent and then keeping the law, or looking and bringing a sacrifice, or looking and making promises to do better. They were saved by faith alone. Christ is sufficient to take care of all our needs for time and eternity.

## H. Immediate healing.

Salvation is not a process; it is an immediate miracle that takes place when the sinner looks to Christ by faith. Christ in His death and resurrection does not save us "a little bit at a time." He saves instantly, immediately, and completely.

## I. One remedy for all.

Thoughtless people say, "As there are many roads leading to Rome, so there are many roads to heaven, many ways to be saved!" There was only one way to be saved in the camp of Israel, and there is only one way today. Read John 14:6 and Acts 4:12. Unless a sinner looks to Christ by faith, he or she is lost forever.

## J. Double assurance.

How did the dying people know the remedy would work? First, they had the assurance of the Word of God. God had promised that if anyone would look, he or she would live. Second, they could see what had happened in the lives of others. God would give no special revelation, no special feeling; sinners had to depend on what God had promised.

All of this seems so foolish to the people of the world (1 Cor. 1:18-31). Imagine, looking at an uplifted serpent to be saved from death! People today scoff at the cross, while they try to kill the snakes and manufacture new anti-snake remedies. Yet every remedy man has manufactured has failed! Reformation, education, better laws, religion—all have had their day. And still people are dying in sin. The only answer is the cross of Jesus Christ, the uplifted Savior.

Read 2 Kings 18:4 and you will discover that the Jews had preserved this brazen serpent and made an idol out of it. This is human nature, to look at the material thing and ignore the God who deserves our trust. It was not the serpent that healed the people; it was the God who commanded the serpent to be made.

This is idolatry, to "worship and serve the creature rather than the Creator" (Rom. 1:25). Hezekiah broke the serpent idol in pieces and named it, "Nehushtan" — "a piece of brass." We wonder what God thinks of the millions of idols scattered across this world, pieces of wood or metal that are robbing God of the trust and glory that He deserves.

# NUMBERS 22–25

Few men in the Bible raise as many problems as Balaam. He was apparently of a heathen nation, yet he knew the true God. He was a soothsayer, yet was able to predict the future of Israel. He listened to God's Word and faithfully proclaimed it, yet turned right around and led Israel into sin and judgment. What an enigma he is!

## I. Balaam's Visits from Balak (22)

### A. The first visit (vv. 1-14).

Balak was the king of Moab and apparently was allied with the Midianites in some way. He had seen the conquests of Israel (Num. 20–21) and was afraid his people would be overcome too. He realized that physical force would never defeat the Jews, so he resorted to spiritual deception by hiring Balaam to curse Israel. He offered Balaam a good price for doing the job, but the prophet (having consulted the Lord) refused to agree. Balak's messengers went home and reported failure.

### B. The second visit (vv. 15-41).

Balak was not one to give up easily; he sent princes more noble than the first, promised Balaam greater wealth and honor, and suggested that the prophet reconsider the matter. This is what Satan often does once we have made a definite decision to obey God's Word. Deep in his heart, Balaam wanted to go with the messengers because he was greedy of gain. This is "the way of Balaam" (2 Peter 2:15-16), using religion as a means of getting wealth. God permitted Balaam to go with the princes, but He did so only to test him (vv. 20-22). It is here that the well-known episode with the angel and the ass takes place. The angel stood in Balaam's way, but the prophet did not see him! The ass did see, and acted so strangely that Balaam struck her. This should have been a warning to

Balaam, but he was intent on his selfish mission and was not sensitive to God's will. When his eyes were opened, Balaam saw the angel and realized his mistakes. God said plainly, "Your way is perverse" (v. 32, NKJV), so there was no reason for Balaam to say, "If it displeases You, I will turn back" (v. 34). Balaam was playing with God's will, seeing how far he could go. God permitted Balaam to meet Balak, who gave him a great feast ("offered" in v. 40 means "slew, as for a feast") and took him out to view Israel.

The main lesson here is to find the will of God and obey it, regardless of personal desires or subsequent circumstances.

## II. Balaam's Visions of Israel (23–24)

Balak wanted Balaam to curse Israel and in this way protect Midian and Moab, but every time Balaam opened his mouth, he blessed Israel instead!

### A. *First vision — Israel's calling (23:1-12).*

Balaam makes it clear that he cannot curse Israel because God has blessed Israel. He sees the nation as a special people, called by God and separate from the other nations (Deut. 26:18-19; 32:8-9; Lev. 20:26). He sees the increase of Israel (as the dust) and expresses his desire to die as a righteous Jew would die, in the blessing and favor of God. This vision, of course, displeased Balak, who took Balaam to "another place" for a "different viewpoint."

### B. *Second vision — Israel's acceptance (23:13-30)*

This time Balaam makes it clear that God speaks and keeps His Word. He is not like men who change their minds or who fail to keep their promises. He announces the amazing fact that God sees no iniquity in Israel. Certainly the Jews had sinned often, but as far as their standing before God was concerned, they were accepted. They had been delivered from Egypt by the blood of the Lamb, and they were God's own purchased possession (Ex. 19:1-6). Humanly speaking, they were failures, but from the divine viewpoint, they were the people of God forever. By now, of course, Balak was furious, but he took Balaam for another look at Israel from a new place.

### C. *Third vision — Israel and Canaan (24:1-9).*

This time Balaam did not use any of his enchantments; instead, the Spirit of God came upon him and opened his eyes. This vision describes Israel enjoying her blessings in the Promised Land, with the other nations defeated. Note the emphasis on water in this vision, a precious item in the wilderness. This vision was more than Balak could bear. He threatened Balaam, hinting that "the Lord" had kept him from receiving wealth and honor (vv. 10-11). Then the prophet had a fourth vision.

### D. *Fourth vision—Israel's future glory (24:10-25).*

There are probably two ways to look at this symbolic message. Certainly King David fits the description, since he did defeat the Moabites, Edomites, and other peoples (see 2 Sam. 8:2, 14). But the greater fulfillment is in Christ, the Messiah, the "Star of Jacob and Scepter of Israel." Israel will have complete dominion when Christ returns and establishes the millennial kingdom. Israel's many enemies will be defeated. See Luke 1:68-79.

Balaam gives a wonderful history of Israel in these four visions, all the way from their election as a nation to their exaltation in the kingdom. We may apply these truths, of course, to the NT believer, who has been chosen of God, justified (so that we are accepted in the beloved), given a rich inheritance in Christ, and promised future glory.

## III. Balaam's Victory over Israel (25)

Had Balaam stopped with his visions from God, he would have been safe, but he wanted the money and the honor that Balak promised. So he told the king how to defeat Israel. His plan was simple: invite the Jews to share in the heathen sacrificial feasts and corrupt them with idolatry and lust. The ceremonies involved in Baal worship were very wicked, and Balaam knew that the Jewish men would be tempted to join with the Moabite women. This is exactly what happened. In fact, one Israelite was bold enough to bring a heathen woman home right in the sight of Moses (v. 6). What the armies of the other nations could not do, the women of Moab and Midian were doing. If Satan cannot overcome God's people as a lion (1 Peter 5:8), then he comes as a serpent. Beware of the friendliness of God's enemies! Their smiles are snares.

Aaron's grandson Phinehas took a definite stand for the Lord and opposed this compromise of God's people with the heathen (2 Cor. 6:14-18). A plague from the Lord had already begun. When

Phinehas slew the guilty man and woman, the plague stopped, but not before 24,000 people had died. See Num. 31:16. In this age when people are telling Christians to become friendly with their spiritual enemies, we need more courageous men like Phinehas who will take a stand for separation and holiness.

Of course, Balaam thought that Israel's sins would destroy the nation. This is "the error of Balaam" mentioned in Jude 11. People look at the church today and condemn her for her "spots and wrinkles and blemishes," but God sees His church from a different viewpoint. True, He punishes our sins and chastens us when we disobey, but He will never leave us or forsake us. It is this blessed fact of grace that Balaam did not understand. Revelation 2:14 mentions the doctrine of Balaam. This was his counsel to Balak that he invite the Jews to mix with the Gentiles, marry Moabite women, and share in their evil feasts. Such a "doctrine" is nothing but compromise. It is interesting that the NT warning comes in the letter to the church at Pergamos, because "Pergamos" means "married." This is the great danger today: Christians individually and churches (and denominations) collectively are forgetting their calling to be separate and are joining themselves to the world. This can only mean judgment.

For other references to Balaam, see Deut. 23:4-5, Josh. 24:9-10, Neh. 13:2, Micah 6:5, 2 Peter 2:15-16, Jude 11, and Rev. 2:14.

# NUMBERS 33–36

These chapters deal with the assigning of the tribes' inheritance, looking ahead to the time when the nation would possess Canaan. The tribes are assigned their portions, the Levites their special cities, and, most important of all, the cities of refuge are defined. We will consider these six cities from three viewpoints. (Read Deut. 19 and Josh. 20 for additional facts.)

## I. The Practical Meaning

The nation had no police force, and the elders in each city constituted a "court" to consider capital crimes. If a person accidentally killed another person, he or she needed some kind of protection; for it was legal for a member of the slain person's family to try to avenge the blood of the slain relative. Genesis 9:6 established the principle of capital punishment, which was affirmed by Moses in Ex. 21:12-14. (Note in v. 13 the suggestion of the cities of refuge, however.) In other words, the person who killed another was in danger of his own life, because the "avenger of blood" (the kinsman) could kill him before the slayer had a chance to prove himself innocent.

Numbers 35:16-23 makes it clear that God considers murder (by deliberate intent) and manslaughter (by accident) two different things. We follow this distinction in modern law. The murderer has deliberate intent to kill; he has a history of hating the victim. But the person who slays another by accident has no murderous intent. He deserves the right to state his case and save his life. This was the purpose of the cities of refuge. The slayer had to flee to the nearest such city, where the elders would meet him, hear his case, and hold a trial. If they decided he was guilty of murder, he would be turned over to the proper authorities and then slain (Deut. 19:11-13). If it was clear that the slaying was accidental, then the person would be allowed to live in the city under their protection, and the avenger of blood could not touch him. If, however, the person left the city, he could be slain. When the high priest died, the person would be free to return to his own city safely.

Note that the aim of this law was to keep the land from being polluted (Num. 35:29-34). Murder would defile the land, and uncondemned murders would lead the land into greater sin. This law provided for the protection of the innocent and the condemnation of the guilty. It was a just law. It is unfortunate that our laws today often are misapplied so that it is easy for the guilty to go free. No wonder our nation is defiled with blood and there is little respect for law and order.

## II. The Typical Meaning

These six cities of refuge are beautiful types of Christ, to whom we "have fled for refuge to lay hold upon the hope set before us" (Heb. 6:18).

### A. They were appointed by God.

This was an act of grace, for all men are sinners and deserve to die. Moses did not choose the cities, for the Law cannot save anyone. Though these were priestly cities, it was not an earthly priest who appointed them. Their appointment and the sending of the Messiah both came from the loving heart of God. "God so loved the world that He gave His only begotten Son" (John 3:16).

## B. They were announced in the Word.

The six cities are named in Joshua 20:7-8, and they could never be changed. On the authority of the Word of God, a slayer could enter a city and no one could forbid him! So with our salvation: it is promised to us in the Word, and this can never change. There were cities in Israel that were larger and more prominent, but none of them could shelter the sinner. There are many "religions" today, but there is only one way of salvation as announced in God's Word—faith in Jesus Christ (Acts 4:12).

## C. They were accessible to all.

If you will consult a map of the Holy Land, you will find that the six cities were arranged so that no tribe was too far from the place of safety. On the west side of Jordan were Kedesh in the north, Shechem in the central area, and Hebron in the south. Right across the river on the east side (where Reuben, Gad, and Manasseh chose to settle) were Golan in the north, Ramoth in the central section, and Bezer in the south. These cities were accessible. Some of them were located on mounts so as to be even more prominent. Tradition tells us that the priests made sure the roads were in good repair leading to these six cities, and that regular landmarks were put up to guide the fleeing person. We are also told by the rabbis that the gates of these cities were never shut. What a picture of Christ! Certainly the "way to the city" is clear! No one need ever wonder who the Savior is or how to come to Him, for we come to Him by faith. He will never turn any sinner away (John 6:37). There is one point of contrast between the cities and Christ: when the slayer came to the city, he was admitted but he was also tried. With us, there is no trial, for we are already condemned! See also John 3:18. The elders of the city admitted someone who was innocent of murder, but Christ receives guilty sinners. What grace!

## D. They were adequate to meet the need.

So long as the slayer remained in the city, he was safe, and he would be freed when the high priest died. This does not suggest that we may "leave Christ" and lose our salvation, for we do not build doctrines on types; rather we interpret types on the basis of doctrines. The true Christian can never perish, but by failing to "abide in Christ" he or she opens the door to spiritual and physical dangers. Our High Priest will never die, and because He lives, we live also.

To see the adequacy of Jesus Christ to meet our every need, consider the names of the cities. Kedesh means "righteousness," and this is our first need. When we come to Christ, He gives us His righteousness and forgives all our sins (2 Cor 5:21, Col. 2:13). Shechem means "shoulder," and suggests that we find in Christ a resting place, a friend on whom we can lay our burdens. "Can I hold out?" is always the question a new believer asks. The answer is, "He will hold you!" Hebron means "fellowship," suggesting our fellowship with God in Christ, and also our fellowship with other believers. Bezer means "fortress," suggesting the protection and victory we have in Christ. The safest place in the world is in the will of God. Ramoth means "heights" and reminds us that believers are seated "together in heavenly places in Christ" (Eph. 2:4-10). Sin always leads a person down, but Christ lifts us up; and one day we shall be caught up together in the clouds to meet the Lord in the air! Finally, Golan means "circle" or "complete" and suggests that in Christ we are complete (Col. 2:9-10). Some say it means "happiness," and certainly the Christian is a happy person, in spite of the trials and problems of life.

Note that the slayer is told to flee to the city. Such a person could not afford to delay! Nor can lost sinners today afford to delay in fleeing to the only refuge, Jesus Christ.

### III. The Dispensational Meaning

There are some students who see in these cities a picture of Israel and her rejection of Christ. Israel killed Jesus Christ in ignorance and blindness (Acts 3:14-17; 1 Cor. 2:8). Jesus prayed, "Father, forgive them; for they know not what they do" (Luke 23:34). This means Israel is treated like a manslayer and not a murderer, and that there is forgiveness and safety for Israel. However, Israel is now "in exile" as was the manslayer in the city of refuge. In other words, God is protecting Israel and one day will bring her forth in forgiveness and blessing, when she sees her Messiah (Zech. 12:10–13:1).

These same ideas would apply to Paul, who was guilty of slaying others (see 1 Tim. 1:12-16). He is a "pattern" for Jews who will be saved in the future, for they will see Christ in glory just as Paul did (Acts 9).

# DEUTERONOMY

## *A Suggested Outline of Deuteronomy*

## *Introductory Notes to Deuteronomy*

## I. Name

"Deuteronomy" in Greek means "second law." It comes from Deut. 17:18, and also from the fact that in this book Moses was restating the Law to the new generation. This book does not contain a new Law, it is a second stating of the original Law.

## II. Purpose

There are several reasons why Moses restated the Law on the border of Canaan.

### A. A new generation.

The old generation (except for Caleb and Joshua) had perished in the wilderness, and the new generation needed to hear the Law again. We all have short memories, and these people were twenty years of age and under when the nation failed decades before at Kadesh-Barnea.

It was important that they know God's Word afresh and realize how important it is to obey God.

### B. A new challenge.

Up to now, the nation's life had been unsettled; they had been pilgrims. But now they were to enter their Promised Land and become a settled nation. There would be battles to fight, and they needed to be prepared. The best way to prepare for the future is to understand the past. "Those who cannot remember the past are condemned to repeat it," a famous philosopher has said. Moses wanted the nation to remember what God had done.

### C. A new leader.

Moses was about to die, and Joshua would take over the leadership of the nation. Moses knew that the success of the nation depended on the people obeying God, no matter who their human leader might be. If they were grounded in the Word and loved the Lord, they would follow Joshua and win the victory.

### D. New temptations.

A settled people in the land would face different problems than a pilgrim people in the wilderness. Moses wanted them not only to possess the land, but also to maintain that possession, so he warned them of the dangers and gave them the way of success.

In a spiritual sense, too many Christians stand with Israel in Deut. 1:1-3. They are redeemed from Egypt, but they have not yet entered into their spiritual inheritance. They stand "on this side of Jordan" instead of in the Promised Land of blessing. They need to hear God's Word again and step out by faith to claim their inheritance in Christ.

### E. A deeper message.

As we read Deuteronomy, we cannot help but be impressed with the deeper message Moses gives concerning the spiritual life of his people. We find the word "love" repeated at least twenty times in the book, an emphasis not found in Genesis through Numbers. "Love for God and God's love for the people" is a new theme in Deuteronomy (4:37; 6:4-6; 7:6-13; 10:12; 11:1; 30:6, 16, 20). While the previous books certainly speak of love and prove God's love for Israel, Deuteronomy emphasizes this theme as never before. The word "heart" is also important: the Word must be in their hearts (5:29; 6:6); sin begins in the heart (7:17ff and 8:11-20); and they must love God from the heart (10:12). In other words, Moses makes it clear that blessings come when the heart is right. In order for the people to possess and enjoy the land, their hearts had to be filled with love for God and His Word.

### F. A book for everyone.

Exodus, Leviticus, and Numbers were "technical books" belonging in a special way to the priests and Levites, but Deuteronomy was written for everyone. While it repeats many of the laws found in previous books, it gives a new and deeper meaning to these laws and shows what they meant in the everyday lives of the people. All of us today can learn much from Deuteronomy about loving God and obeying His will.

We list here several of the key words of this book and the number of times they are found in the King James Version: land (153); inherit (36); possess (65); hear (44); hearken (27); heart (46); love (20). Putting these repeated words together, we can quickly see the emphasis of the book: you will go in and possess the land if you hear God's Word, love Him, and hearken (obey). If we love God, we will obey Him; and if we obey, He will bless.

# DEUTERONOMY 1–6

As Moses begins this series of addresses to the new generation in Israel, he reviews the past history of the nation. It is a sin to live in the past, but we can never understand the present or prepare for the future if we are ignorant of the past.

## I. He Reminds Them of God's Guidance (1–3)

The nation was gathered on the Plains of Moab "on this side of Jordan." It had taken them forty years to get there, yet v. 2 states that the journey should have taken eleven days! This is the tragedy of unbelief: it wastes time, energy, and manpower; and it robs God of the glory due His Name. Moses began to "declare" God's Law, and this word "declare" literally means "to engrave." He wanted to make it clear, to write it on their hearts.

### A. From Sinai to Kadesh-Barnea (1:1-46).

The nation had camped at Horeb from the third month of the first year (Ex. 19:1) until the second month of the second year after their exodus from Egypt (Num. 10:11). During this time, Moses had received the Law and the tabernacle had been constructed and erected. It is interesting that Moses reviews his own failure (vv. 9-18) as well as the failure of the nation (vv. 19-46). The new generation certainly should know why the nation was organized as it was, and why the nation had not entered its inheritance sooner. Moses makes it clear that their sin at Kadesh-Barnea was rebellion (v. 26) based on unbelief. For a review of these events, see your notes on Numbers 9–14.

### B. The nations they avoided (2:1-23).

Moses passes over the years of "wandering" with one sentence (1:46), and now takes up their journey to the borders of Canaan. Three nations were avoided: Edom (the descendants of Esau, Jacob's brother); and Moab and Ammon (the descendants of Lot, Abraham's nephew). Since these nations had blood relation to Israel, God did not permit the Jews to fight them. And God protected Israel as they passed through the borders of these great nations.

### C. The nations they defeated (2:24-3:29).

There were two reasons why God allowed Israel to fight and conquer these nations: (1) as a warning to the nations in Canaan, v. 25; and (2) to make the land available for the two and a half tribes that would settle east of Jordan (3:12-17). The Jews were kind to these nations when they arrived, offering to pass through peacefully. When the nations attacked them though, God conquered them. The great walled cities like those that had frightened the older generation were captured by the new generation (3:5). Certainly this would be an encouragement to them as they prepared to enter Canaan. Note that Joshua received a special commission at this time. Moses prayed to be allowed to enter the land, but God would not permit it.

God had guided and protected Israel in the past, and certainly He would be with them in the future.

## II. He Reminds Them of God's Glory and Greatness (4–5)

In this section, Moses takes the nation back to Sinai where God's glory and greatness were revealed, and where the nation trembled at God's Law. The people were in danger of forgetting the glory and greatness of God (see 4:9, 23, 31). Moses points out three dangers:

### A. Forgetting the Word (4:1-13).

What other nation had been blessed with God's Word? God's Word was Israel's wisdom and their power. If they obeyed His Word, He would bless them and they would possess the land. If they changed His Word (v. 2) or disobeyed it, He would chasten them and they would lose the enjoyment of their land. When God's Word becomes commonplace to the children of God in any time, and they no longer respect it, then they are heading for serious trouble.

### B. Turning to idols (4:14-49).

"Take heed!" is Moses' warning, repeated in 4:9, 15, and 23. He reminds the people that they saw no image of God at Sinai, and he warns them that they must not make any images (vv. 15-19; see Rom. 1:21-23). God proved Himself greater than all the gods of Egypt, so why worship them? In love, God had called the nation to Himself. If they turned to idols, it would be spiritual adultery. In vv. 25-31, Moses summarizes the future of Israel: they would turn to idols, be cast out of the land and scattered, and serve other gods in captivity. It was in captivity that Israel would learn her lesson and abandon false gods once and for all.

## C. Neglecting His Law (5:1-33).

Here Moses repeats the Ten Commandments, the basis for God's Moral Law. In fact, the rest of Deuteronomy is actually an amplification and application of these commandments. Israel was to hear, learn, keep, and do these laws (v. 1), for in obeying the Law they would be honoring God and opening the way for victory and blessing. "Hear, O Israel!" is an important phrase in this book (see 5:1; 6:3-4; 9:1; 20:3). God gave this Law to reveal sin (Rom. 3:20); to prepare the nation for the coming of Christ (Gal. 3:19-24); and to make them a separated nation on the earth (Deut. 4:5-8). Note that Moses reminds them that their responsibility is based on God's redemption, for He had delivered them from Egypt (vv. 6 and 15; cf. 6:12; 8:14; 13:5, 10). "You are not your own; you were bought at a price; therefore . . ." (1 Cor. 6:19-20, NKJV). Note that v. 10 introduces the fact of God's love; compare 4:37. Verse 29 makes it clear that the Law must be in the heart, or there can be no true obedience. See also Heb. 8:8-12; Jer. 32:39-40 and 31:31-34. Second Corinthians 3 teaches that the NT believer has the Law written in his heart by the Spirit of God; and Rom. 8:1-4 explains that we obey the Law by the power of the Spirit.

## III. He Reminds Them of God's Goodness (6)

Verses 10-12 illustrate a basic weakness of human nature: we take God's blessings for granted. "Beware lest you forget the Lord!" How prone we are to think that our wisdom and our strength have gotten us all that we have. See 8:17-18. God chose Israel in His love; He endured their sins in His grace; He guided them and protected them; and then He gave them a wonderful land. What ingratitude it would show if Israel deliberately (or carelessly) ignored God and failed to obey Him. Too often we want to enjoy the blessings, but we do not want to obey the One who gives us the blessings!

"God . . . is a jealous God" (v. 15). This takes us back to Sinai (Ex. 20:5) where God entered into covenant relationship with Israel. Just as a husband has the right to be jealous over his wife, so God has the right to be jealous over His people. See Josh. 24:19 and James 4:5. Idolatry is spiritual adultery, and Israel was often guilty of this sin.

The parents were to remind their children of what God had done for the nation, just as Moses was that day reminding Israel of God's care (vv. 20-25). Verses 6-9 make it clear that the Word was to be made a part of the home, the center of conversation, and the means of instructing the children to love the Lord and obey Him. Unfortunately, the Jews took the letter of this law and not the spirit, and ended up making phylacteries (Matt. 23:5), little boxes containing passages from the Law. They wore these boxes on their arms and heads, but this did not mean they had the Word in their hearts.

New Testament Christians need all these warnings too. How prone we are to forget God's guidance and complain when circumstances get uncomfortable. He has helped us in the days gone by; He will not forsake us now. We need to remember God's glory and greatness, for it is easy for idols to creep into our lives. And we need to remind ourselves of His goodness. How wonderfully He has cared for us. If we love Him and His Word with all our hearts, then He will bless us and we will be a blessing to others.

# DEUTERONOMY 7–11

Having reminded the people of the events of the past (chaps. 1–6), Moses now warns them of the perils of the future. For centuries Israel was a slave nation and for forty years it had been a pilgrim people. Now the people were to settle down in their own land, so they needed to beware of the dangers that would come with this new environment. Notice at least five dangers the people had to recognize and avoid.

## I. Compromise with the Enemy (7:1-16)

It was God's purpose to drive out the heathen nations and establish Israel in Canaan. But He had to warn Israel to utterly destroy these nations and in no way compromise with them. There was a two-fold reason for this complete destruction: (1) the nations were wicked and ripe for judgment (Gen. 15:16; cf. Deut. 9:4-5); and (2) if left in the land, the nations would lead Israel into sin. People who do not understand the judgment of God or the awfulness of sin argue that God was "wicked" to destroy these nations. If they understood the sinfulness of these pagan religions and the way these nations had resisted God, such critics would instead be grateful that Israel wiped them out. A defiled Israel could never give the world God's Word and God's Son.

195

Moses' argument in this passage is simple: Israel is God's special nation, a chosen people, separate from all other nations. God chose them because He loved them, and He proved His love by bringing them out of Egypt and faithfully caring for them in the wilderness. This principle of separation runs throughout the Bible; God separated light from darkness (Gen. 1:4) and the waters under the firmament from those above (Gen. 1:7). He commanded Israel to be separate from the other nations (Ex. 23:20-23; 34:11-16). He commanded the church to be separate from the world (2 Cor. 6:14–7:1; see Rev. 18:4). When God called Abraham to found the Jewish nation, He separated him from the heathen around him. God promises to bless when His people are separated from sin (Deut. 7:12-16).

We live in a day when the church and the world are so mingled that it is difficult to tell who really belongs to Christ. We have been called out of the world that we might be a testimony to the world (John 15:16-27). Worldly Christians hinder the work of God.

## II. Fear of the Enemy (7:17-26)

Fear usually leads to compromise; we "give in" that we might protect ourselves. Moses warns the people not to be afraid of the enemy because God will be with Israel to give them the victory. Did He not deliver them from Egypt, and from the kings in the wilderness? Then He would give them victory in Canaan! The victory would be in stages (v. 23, Judges 2:20-23, NIV), so that they might be able to possess the land safely. God would do the delivering, but they had to do the destroying (vv. 23-26) — eliminating the heathen kings, idols, and altars. Anything that remained would be a snare to them and lead them into sin. Read 2 Cor. 7:1 and Rom. 13:14.

## III. Prosperity and Self-satisfaction (8)

The "wiles" of the devil are more dangerous than his armies! In this section Moses warns his people about the perils of prosperity. They would forget the forty years of God's care, when He alone provided food to eat and plentiful clothing. They would even forget God's chastening hand when they had sinned. And this forgetting would lead them into sin: in their prosperity and blessing in the "land of milk and honey," they would become self-satisfied and think their own strength had accomplished all these things.

Is this sin not with us today? Often when times are hard and we have to depend on God for our daily needs, we remember Him and obey Him. But when "things are going well" and we have more than we need, we become self-sufficient and forget God. "It is He who gives you power to get wealth" (v. 18, NKJV) is a statement we all need to remember. Sometimes God has to chasten us to remind us who is in control of the wealth of this world.

## IV. Pride (9:1–10:11)

After they had conquered the heathen nations in Canaan, Israel would be tempted to be proud, thinking it was because of their own righteousness that God had given the victory. Moses reminds them that their victories will all be by the grace of God. To begin with, God would give them the land to fulfill His promises to their fathers (Gen. 15), promises that He had made because of His grace. The Jews did not deserve the land. It was given to them because God loved them. Furthermore, He would drive out the heathen nations because of those nations' sins, not because of Israel's goodness. Moses reminds the Jews that their whole history has been one of rebellion, not righteousness! They provoked God in the wilderness; they made an idol at Mt. Sinai; they rebelled in unbelief at Kadesh-Barnea. Had it not been for the intercession of Moses, the whole nation would have been destroyed.

The application is true for Christians today. We dare not forget the grace of God! We are saved by grace (Eph. 2:8-10), and any work we do for Him is by grace (1 Cor. 15:10; Rom. 12:6). If we have material and spiritual blessings, it is because of His grace and not our goodness. Such blessings ought to humble us, not make us proud, and we should want to use what we have for His glory in the winning of souls. Just as Moses interceded for the nation and saved them, so Christ died for us and ever lives to make intercession for us. It is all because of Him that we have such great blessings today.

Perhaps the worst kind of pride is "spiritual pride," such as we see in the Pharisees. If people are spiritual, they cannot be proud. To boast of spiritual gifts or graces is to invite the chastening hand of God.

## V. Deliberate Disobedience (10:12–11:32)

This section is Moses' closing appeal before he starts to review and apply the various laws that will govern their lives in the Promised

Land (12:1ff). "I will be giving many laws," Moses is saying, "but the Lord actually requires only this: fear Him, love Him, serve Him, and He will bless you" (v. 12). Circumcision was the sign of the covenant (Gen. 17), but this rite had been ignored during Israel's wanderings (Josh. 5). However, the important thing was not physical circumcision; it was spiritual circumcision — the yielding of their hearts to God (v. 16).

Moses makes it clear in chapter 11 that the real issue is the heart: if they truly loved God, they would obey His Word (John 14:21). Yes, they should fear God, having seen his miracles and judgments; but this fear should be a loving reverence for the God who chose them above all other nations. God could not bless them if they refused to obey His Word.

Some of the Jews might have been saying, "Once we get into the land, we can live as we please and still enjoy its wealth." Not so, for the Promised Land was not like Egypt (vv. 10-17). In Egypt, the people depended on the dirty Nile River to irrigate their crops, but in Canaan, the rains would come from heaven twice a year to give the people their needed harvests. The fruitfulness of the Promised Land depended on the rain from heaven, just as we today depend on the "showers of blessing" if our lives are to be fruitful for God. If Israel disobeyed, God would not send the rain, an event repeated several times in the nation's history.

The time of decision had come (vv. 26-32). They had to choose between a blessing and a curse. This basic principle has never changed: if we obey God's Word from the heart, He will bless us and our labors; but if we disobey Him, He will send a curse and chasten us. Obedience is the key to happiness.

# DEUTERONOMY 27–30

This section is prophetic and gives us four pictures of Israel in relationship to the land.

## I. Israel Entering the Land (27)

We find the fulfillment of this prophecy in Josh. 8:30-35. Deuteronomy 27:3 teaches that the nation's conquest of the land depended on their obeying this set of instructions. The valley between Mt. Ebal and Mt. Gerizim is a beautiful place, with the city of

Shechem in it. The entire area forms a natural amphitheater about two miles wide, and it would not be difficult for the people to hear the Law read.

The elders of the tribes were to set up the "great stones" on Mt. Ebal and write on them the Ten Commandments. At the foot of the mount they were to erect an altar, where burnt offerings and peace offerings would be sacrificed. The Law brings condemnation (2 Cor. 3:7-9), but the altar met the need of the condemned sinner. The burnt offerings speak of Christ's complete sacrifice on our behalf, and the peace offerings remind us that, in spite of a broken law, He has brought us peace with God (Rom. 5:1). Six tribes were to stand on Mt. Gerizim, the mount of blessing; and note that all of them were from Leah and Rachel. Reuben and Zebulun were sons of Leah, but they were to stand with those on the mount of cursing (v. 13). Reuben lost his rights as firstborn when he sinned against his father (Gen. 49:4). The Levites, with the ark, were to stand in the valley between the two mounts and call out the Law. Note that none of the blessings were to be recited, for the Law brings a curse, not a blessing (Gal. 3:10).

This entire ceremony would be a striking reminder to Israel that they were a covenant nation (v. 9), obligated to obey God's Law. Read 2 Cor. 3 to see the contrasts between the ministry of law and the glorious ministry of grace.

## II. Israel Possessing and Enjoying the Land (28:1-14)

"Obedience brings blessing" (vv. 1-2); this is the theme of the Word of God. See Eph. 1:3, where the NT believer already has "all spiritual blessings" in Christ, and he enjoys them as he trusts God and obeys Him. Of course, this principle of obedience is found in every period of salvation history, for God cannot bless those who rebel against Him.

Note that God promised Israel material blessings in all areas — city, farm, fruit, cattle, coming in, going out. He promised to defeat their enemies and to establish them in the land as a holy people. Verse 10 indicates that the nation was to be a worldwide witness of God's grace. Alas, they have become a worldwide witness of God's chastening (vv. 45-46). God promised them the rain in its season. He stated that He would make Israel the leading nation (v. 13), His instrument of blessing in the world.

Keep in mind that Israel owned the land because of God's covenant with Abraham, but the people possessed and enjoyed the land only if they obeyed God's covenant as a holy nation. We today have all the blessings we need in Christ because of His grace, but we enjoy these blessings only as we trust Him and obey His voice.

## III. Israel Being Plucked off the Land (28:15–29:29)

Here is the prophecy of Israel's chastening, captivity, and scattering, as well as her future return in blessing. To "spiritualize" these blessings and curses, and apply them to the church is to twist the Scriptures and to fail to "rightly divide the Word of truth." These are literal curses, and they later fell upon Israel because she broke her covenant with God by worshiping idols and disobeying His Law.

The curses in 28:15-19 parallel the blessings in 28:3-6. God warned them that the very diseases and pestilences they had seen among their enemies would visit them, including the plagues God sent to Egypt (28:27). One evidence of His wrath would be the withholding of the former and latter rains (28:23-24; see 11:10-17; 2 Chron. 7:13-14; 1 Kings 17:1ff; Jer. 14:1ff). Their enemies would defeat them; they would be scattered like blind slaves across the face of the earth. In 28:36 we have a hint that Israel would ask for a king (see 1 Sam. 8). Their rich land, flowing with milk and honey, would turn into a wilderness. And instead of being the first nation of the earth, Israel would be "the tail" (28:44).

The word "destroyed" in v. 45 does not mean annihilated; for God could not violate His covenant and completely destroy the nation of Israel. It means "crushed," referring to the terrible trials and disciplines that would fall on Israel because of disobedience. The nation would be "a sign and a wonder" to the world, even as it still is today.

In 28:48-68 we have the prediction of the captivities of Israel and the nation's removal from the Promised Land. Verse 49 refers to Babylon immediately, but remotely to Rome (note the eagle as well as the yoke of iron; see Jer. 5:15ff). The terrible sieges of Jerusalem are pictured here (see Lam. 2:20-22, 4:10; Matt. 24:19). Verses 63-65 make it clear that continued disobedience would result in Israel being plucked off the land and scattered among the nations where there would be "no ease," a perfect picture of the Jews of the world today. What other nation has suffered more than Israel? Verse 68 predicts that some of the Jews would be taken to

Egypt, and this took place after Titus conquered Israel in A.D. 70, and transported a number of Jews to Egypt.

Chapter 29 summarizes the basic facts of the covenant: God had redeemed them and they were responsible to obey Him; if they obeyed, He would bless; if they disobeyed, He would judge. Moses warned that even one person could defile the whole nation (29:18-19). Finally, there are some secrets God has not revealed, but what He has revealed, we are obligated to obey (29:29).

### IV. Israel Being Restored to the Land (30)

Israel enjoyed the blessings for less than 1,000 years. They entered Canaan about 1400 B.C., and Babylon conquered Israel about 587 B.C. In addition, many times during this period Israel disobeyed God and was chastened.

This chapter promises that God will "turn the captivity" of Israel and restore the nation to the land, if they will but return to the Lord and obey His voice. Of course, a remnant returned to the land in 536 B.C., but this was not a great national return. Moses is here predicting the *final* return of the Jews to their land (see Isa. 11:10–12:6). Of course, they return to the land in unbelief, even though they have turned again to the Law of God. Even today we see Jews going back to Palestine and returning to the "old ways" of their fathers. God is starting to bless the land once again with the former and latter rains, and the desert is starting to blossom like the rose. When the nation sees their pierced Messiah, they will repent and be cleansed of all sin (Zech. 12:9–13:1).

Paul quotes 30:11-14 in Rom. 10:6-8 and applies it to Christ. Christ is not far away from His people, even though they have turned away from Him. If they will call, He will save!

The grand conclusion of Moses' address is in 30:15-20. The nation had to choose between life and death, blessing and cursing. As always, such a choice is a matter of the heart (v. 17). Mere outward obedience will not do; it must come from within.

# DEUTERONOMY 31–34

The old generation had died off, except for Caleb, Joshua, and Moses; and now Moses was to move off the scene. These are "transition chapters" as Moses gives his final words to the people he has loved and led for forty years. It is amazing that Moses remained so loyal to his people, for they were guilty of criticizing him, rebelling against him, and lying about him. Moses knew that he himself would not enter Canaan, yet he did everything possible to enable Israel to enter! Of course, Moses was faithful to the Lord (Heb. 3:1-6), and this is why he was so faithful to Israel.

## I. The New Leader (31)

First, Moses announced the new leader for the people (vv. 1-6), explaining that he would not be able to lead them any longer because of God's judgment. Moses gave the people that wonderful promise of God's victorious presence in v. 6. This was repeated to Joshua in v. 8 and (by God Himself) in Josh. 1:9. It is also given to us today (Heb. 13:5).

Then Moses called Joshua and commissioned him (vv. 7-13), laying his hands on him and thereby granting the spiritual power he would need for his great task (34:9). "God changes His workers but continues His work." Moses put a copy of Deuteronomy in the hands of the priests to place in the ark, and to read at the Feast of Tabernacles. He knew that only God's Word could make the people the kind of nation God wanted them to be.

Finally, God summoned both Moses and Joshua to the tabernacle (vv. 14-30) where He told them that the nation would rebel and turn away from the Law. He commissioned both of them to write a "song" (see 32:44) to be taught to the people. The song would be a witness against them (v. 19), as would be the Law in the ark (v. 26). Once again, Joshua was encouraged (v. 23), and then Moses gathered the elders together to teach them the song, which is recorded in chap. 32.

Moses was not permitted to lead Israel into Canaan for two reasons: (1) he had sinned against God at Meribah (Num. 20:7-13; Deut. 3:23-29); and (2) Canaan is a type of the "rest" we have in Christ, and Moses the lawgiver could never bring rest. Only Joshua, the type of Christ the conqueror, could do that (Heb. 4; and note that Heb. 4:8 calls Joshua "Jesus," which is the Gk. spelling).

## II. The New Song (32)

Israel had sung the "Song of Moses" at the Red Sea (Ex. 15), celebrating their victory and God's power; but this new song laments Israel's apostasy and God's chastening of His own people. In

31:19-30, God made it clear that the song was to be a witness to remind them of their sins. The key name of God in this song is "the Rock" (vv. 4, 15, 18, 30-31). Moses thus reminded them of the water from the rock (Ex. 17; Num. 20) and the goodness of God to the nation. In v. 6, God is pictured as a Father, as a Redeemer who has purchased the people. Yet in vv. 5-6, the nation is described as corrupt, perverse, and crooked.

In vv. 7-14, Moses reminded the people of God's blessings: He found them in the desert; He loved them and sheltered them; He lifted them up to "high places" of victory; He gave them the richest blessings of the land. But what does Israel do? The nation rebells. In vv. 15-18 we have a description of Israel's apostasy and idolatry, their forsaking their Rock and forgetting His love. How does God respond to their sins? In vv. 19-25 we have God's judgments: hiding His face; provoking Israel by turning to the Gentiles (v. 21, see Rom. 10:19); and heaping His wrath upon them as He scatters them across the world. God would blot out Israel but for her enemies (v. 27) who would take advantage of the judgment of God and pour out their hatred upon the Jews. In past ages, God has used Gentile nations to chasten Israel, but when those nations have gone beyond God's commands and poured out their own wrath upon Israel, God has stepped in and judged those nations (vv. 35-43). The day will come when He will avenge Israel and restore Israel to the place where the nations will rejoice with her (v. 43).

Unfortunately, Israel was not mindful of her Rock, nor did she remember this song and take warning. One day though, these words will speak to Israel, and she will turn to her Rock and discover that He is Jesus Christ whom she crucified!

## III. The New Blessing (33)

We cannot study these verses in detail, except to note that Moses does not name any sin in the tribes as Jacob had done in his blessing (Gen. 49). Moses' heart was filled with love for his people, and in this chapter he gives his parting benediction as he asks God's blessing on the various tribes. Note that he begins with the sons of Leah, but leaves out Simeon. This tribe was eventually absorbed into Judah, so Judah's blessing was shared with Simeon.

Reuben had shared in the rebellion of Num. 16, but Moses prays that the tribe might live and increase. Judah was the kingly tribe. When Moses asks God to "bring him unto his people" (v. 7), he is probably referring to Messiah, the Lawgiver promised in Gen. 49:10. Levi was Moses' own tribe, and he prays that God will bless their spiritual ministry to the nation. Note the special blessing for Joseph (vv. 13-17), fulfilled in the wealth of Ephraim and Manasseh.

It is interesting to note the spiritual position of God's people as described in this chapter: in God's hand and at His feet (v. 3); between His shoulders (v. 12); and upheld by His everlasting arms (v. 27). "As your days, so shall your strength be" is a good promise for us today (v. 25, NKJV). "Who is like you, a people saved by the Lord!" (v. 29, NKJV) What a privilege it is to be a child of God!

## IV. The New Home (34)

Moses had prayed that God would repent and allow him to enter the Promised Land, but God had refused (Deut. 3:23-29). God knew that Joshua ("Jehovah is salvation") would lead the people into their earthly rest, just as the heavenly Joshua, Jesus Christ, would lead His people into spiritual rest. This the Law (Moses) could never do. However, Moses did visit the Promised Land on the Mount of Transfiguration, with Elijah; and he discussed with Christ the "exodus" (decease) He would accomplish at Jerusalem (Luke 9:27-31).

God permitted Moses to view the land, which is all the Law can do when it comes to holy living. The Law sets forth a divine standard, but it cannot help us to attain it. Apart from the death of Christ and the gift of the Spirit (Rom. 8:1-4), we cannot have the righteousness of the Law fulfilled in our lives. We can view the land but never enter it. Those who follow Moses (legalism) will never enter the land of blessing.

God alone was present when Moses died, and God buried him. If people knew the location of his grave, they would undoubtedly make it an idolatrous shrine. Jude 9 suggests that Satan wanted the body of Moses, perhaps arguing that Moses was a murderer (Ex. 2:11-12) and had sinned at Meribah when he smote the rock.

The people wept for Moses for thirty days. Often a leader is more appreciated after death than during his or her life. The book closes by reminding us of the unique character of Moses' minis-try—he was a man to whom God talked face to face.

The people were now ready to enter and claim the land, and this will be our study in Joshua.

# JOSHUA

## *A Suggested Outline of Joshua*

I. Crossing the River (1–5)

   A. The commission to Joshua (1)
   B. The covenant with Rahab (2)
   C. The crossing of Jordan (3–4)
   D. The circumcision at Gilgal (5)

II. Conquering the Enemy (6–12)

   A. The central campaign: Jericho; Ai; Gibeon (6–9)
   B. The southern campaign (10)
   C. The northern campaign (11)
   D. The defeated kings (12)

III. Claiming the Inheritance (13–24)

   A. The tribal territory assigned (13–19)
     1. Eastern Canaan (13–14)
     2. Western Canaan (15–19)
   B. The special cities appointed (20–21)
     1. The cities of refuge (20)
     2. The priestly cities (21)
   C. The border tribes allotted (22)
   D. The entire nation admonished (23–24)

# Introductory Notes to Joshua

## I. Theme

It has been pointed out before that Canaan is a type of the Christian's inheritance in Christ. Canaan is not a picture of heaven, because the believer does not have to battle to gain his heavenly home. Canaan represents God's inheritance, given to the believer and claimed by faith. The victorious Christian life is a life of battles and blessings, but it is also a life of rest. In Heb. 4–5 we see that the entering of the nation into Canaan is a picture of the believer entering into a life of rest and victory through faith in Christ. Too many Christians are "in between" in their spiritual lives — between Egypt and Canaan. They have been delivered from the bondage of sin, but they have not by faith entered into the inheritance of rest and victory. How to enter and claim this inheritance is the theme of Joshua.

## II. Joshua the Man

Joshua was born in Egyptian slavery. His father was Nun, of the tribe of Ephraim (1 Chron. 7:20-27); we know nothing about his mother. Originally his name was Oshea or Hoshea, which means "salvation," but Moses changed it to Jehoshua (or Joshua), which means "Jehovah is salvation" (Num. 13:16). He was a slave in Egypt and served as Moses' minister during the journeys of the nation (Ex. 24:13). He also led the army in the battle against Amalek (Ex. 17), and was one of the two spies who had the faith to enter Canaan when the nation rebelled in unbelief (Num. 14:6ff). As a result of his faith, he (with Caleb) was permitted to enter the Promised Land. Jewish tradition says that Joshua was eighty-five years old when he took Moses' place at the head of the nation. Joshua 1–12 (the conquest of the land) covers roughly the next seven years; he spent the remainder of his life dividing up the inheritance and ruling the nation. He died at 110 (Josh. 24:29). The NT makes it clear that Joshua is a type of Christ (Heb. 4:8, where "Jesus" (KJV) should be translated "Joshua"). The name "Jesus" in Greek is equivalent to "Joshua"; both mean "God's salvation" or "Jehovah is the Savior." Just as Joshua conquered earthly foes, so Christ has defeated every enemy through His death and resurrection. It was Joshua, not Moses (representing Law), who brought Israel into Canaan, and it is Jesus who leads us into spiritual rest and victory. As Joshua assigned the tribes their inheritance so Christ has given us our inheritance (Eph. 1:3ff).

## III. The Defeated Nations

Those who oppose the inspiration of the Bible enjoy attacking the passages in Joshua that tell about war and slaughter (6:21, for example). "How can a God of love command such bloodshed?" they ask. Keep in mind that God had given these nations hundreds of years to repent (Gen. 15:16-21), yet they refused to turn from their filthy ways. If you wish to know what "the doings of Canaan" were, read Lev. 18, and keep in mind that these immoral practices were a part of heathen religious worship! Any sinner in the nation (such as Rahab, Josh. 2 and 6:22-27) could be saved by faith; and there was adequate warning sent ahead (read Josh. 2:8-13). God sometimes uses war to chasten and even to destroy nations that forget Him. God had these wicked nations destroyed to punish them for their sins and, something like a doctor who disinfects his instruments to kill the germs, to protect His people from their evil ways.

# JOSHUA 1–2

"God buries His workmen, but His work goes on." Israel has finished mourning for Moses, and now God speaks to Joshua concerning his responsibilities as the new leader of the nation.

## I. The Commission to Joshua (1)

### A. God speaks to Joshua (vv. 1-9).

God had chosen Joshua to be Moses' successor as far back as the battle with Amalek (Ex. 17:8-16; note v. 14). Moses was told to remind Joshua, and write it in his book, that Amalek would be exterminated. In Num. 27:15ff God instructed Moses to "ordain" Joshua; and in Deut. 31:7ff, Moses gave a final word of blessing and encouragement to his successor. It must have fortified Joshua greatly to know that he was called of God, for he had a tremendous task ahead of him.

Notice that God gives every encouragement to Joshua: (1) the promise of the land, vv. 2-4; (2) the promise of His presence, v. 5; and (3) the assurance that God would keep His word, vv. 6-9. It is interesting to study the verbs God uses: "the land which I do give . . ." (v. 2); ". . . that have I given" (v. 3); ". . . to this people you shall divide . . ." (NKJV, v. 6). He had already given them the land; all they had to do was step out by faith and claim it! God has already given us "every blessing of the Spirit" in Christ (Eph. 1:3). All we need do is step out by faith and possess our possessions.

As God was with Moses, so He would be with Joshua: "I will not leave you nor forsake you" (v. 5). This promise was repeated to Solomon (1 Chron. 28:20), and is given to us in Heb. 13:5-6. Leaders change, and times change, but God changes not. Notice that courage is demanded in the Christian life (vv. 6-7, 9), but this courage is supplied by the Word of God (v. 8). Moses had been writing "the Book of the Law" (Ex. 17:14; 24:4-7; Num. 33:2; Deut. 31:9-13), and this Book was now given to Joshua. He was to read the Book, meditate upon it night and day, and obey its commands. See Pss. 1:1-3 and 119:15. If Joshua was able to conquer Canaan having only the first five books of the Bible, how much more ought we to overcome now that we have a complete Bible!

### B. Joshua speaks to the people (vv. 10-15).

We have here a "spiritual chain of command." God commanded

Joshua (v. 9); Joshua commanded the leaders (v. 10); the leaders were to command the people (v. 11). This is spiritual leadership under the command of God, and this same pattern ought to prevail in the NT church. Joshua told the leaders what God had told him, and they quickly passed the message along to their people. Three days later, they would cross the Jordan and enter the Promised Land, and they had to prepare for the event. "Three days" suggests resurrection—the nation was about to have a new beginning in a new land. The three tribes that were singled out had chosen to live on the other side of Jordan (see Num. 32:16-24), but they had promised to help conquer the land before claiming their own inheritance. Joshua reminded them of their obligation.

## C. The people speak to Joshua (vv. 16-18).

How wonderful it is when God's people honor God by respecting and following their spiritual leaders. See Deut. 34:9. Unlike the carnal Christians at Corinth (1 Cor. 1:11-17), they did not divide up into groups, with the followers of dead Moses opposing the followers of Joshua. They all followed the Lord! Note their prayer for Joshua in v. 17 and their encouragement in v. 18. Joshua had seen their division and heard their murmuring years before. How grateful he must have been for this spirit of harmony!

## II. The Covenant with Rahab (2)

Archaeologists have done a great deal of research at Jericho. They tell us the city covered about eight acres, with inner and outer walls surrounding the city. The inner wall was twelve feet thick, the outer wall six feet thick, and there were houses upon the walls (v. 15). The walls stood about thirty feet high, and excavations show that these walls were "violently destroyed." Of the many people who lived in Jericho, we know the name of only one— Rahab, the harlot (see Heb. 11:31; James 2:25). She pictures to us the spiritual history of the believer in Jesus Christ:

## A. She was a sinner.

The sin in this case was moral impurity, but "all have sinned and come short of the glory of God" (Rom. 3:23). It was not uncommon in that day for harlots to manage inns.

## B. She was under condemnation.

Rahab's city had already been declared condemned by God; it was

just a matter of time before the sentence of death would be executed. Everything and everyone in the city would be destroyed
(6:21), whether the people "felt" condemned or not! Jericho is a
picture of the condemned world today. The people could not feel
confident and peaceful, for death was coming.

### C. She was given a period of grace.

The city had been set aside for judgment for many years (Deut.
7:1-5, 23-24; 12:2-3). Genesis 15:13-16 reminds us that God waited
400 years before He permitted judgment to come to the land!
Rahab and all the other residents of Jericho had heard about the
Exodus from Egypt (Josh. 2:10), which had taken place forty years
before. Joshua 4:19 and 5:10 add other days of waiting, leading up
to the additional week that Israel marched around the city (6:14).
How patient God is!

### D. She heard the Word of God.

It was a message of judgment that Rahab heard, but it introduced
her to the true God. Note how she calls God "the LORD" in her
conversation.

### E. She believed the Word.

"Faith comes by hearing, and hearing by the Word of God" (Rom.
10:17, NKJV). It is faith that saves the sinner, even the most ungodly (Rom. 4:5). We are told in Heb. 11:31 that Rahab was saved by
faith. Note that her assurance came from the Word: "I know that
the Lord has given you the land" (v. 9, NKJV).

### F. She proved her faith by works.

The fact that she risked her life to receive, hide, and protect the
spies is proof that Rahab trusted God. She identified herself with
God's people, not with the heathen around her. See James 2:25.

### G. She sought to win others.

Think of the risk Rahab was taking in sharing the Word with her
family! When people trust Christ, their first desire will be to share
it with others, especially their own family (John 1:35-42; Mark
5:18-20).

### H. She was delivered from judgment.

There was a two-fold judgment on the city: first, the shaking that destroyed the city; then, the fire that destroyed all its contents. Rahab's house was on the wall (2:15), but apparently that section of the wall did not fall! After Rahab and her loved ones were taken from her house, Joshua commanded the rest of the city to be destroyed with fire. Rahab and her family may have been troubled when things began to shake, but they were perfectly safe in the hands of God (6:22-25). Christians today see the world shaking all about them, but they can be sure God will rescue them before He sends His fiery judgment on the world (1 Thes. 1:10; 5:9).

## I. *She went to a wedding.*

In Matt. 1:5, we find Rahab included by marriage in the Jewish nation and named as an ancestress of the Messiah! While the people of Jericho suffered death, Rahab and her family were to enjoy a marriage feast! See Rev. 19:7-9 and 17-19. Rahab was saved by faith, not by character or by religious works. This is the only way God saves people (Eph. 2:8-9). Have you trusted Jesus as Rahab trusted Joshua?

# JOSHUA 3–5

## I. The Miracle of the Crossing (3)

### A. *The people sanctified (vv. 1-5).*

Like our NT Joshua (Mark 1:35), Joshua arose early in the morning to meditate on the Word (1:8; 3:1) and to prepare himself for the day's duties. It was not left for Joshua to invent a method of crossing the flooded Jordan, for God gave him all the instructions necessary. The key word in this chapter is *ark*, used ten times. Of course, the ark symbolized the presence of God. The ark went before the people to lead them, and it was kept in the midst of the river until all the nation had passed over. Christ always goes before His people and opens the way, but the people must sanctify themselves (see 2 Cor. 7:1) and be ready for God's leading. God was going to lead the Jews in a new way (v. 4), and they had to be ready.

### B. *Joshua magnified (vv. 6-8).*

Of course, to God all the glory is due, but God sees fit to magnify His servants that their people might honor them (1 Chron. 29:25;

2 Chron. 1:1; see Josh 4:14). It was Joshua who commanded the priests and gave directions to the leaders for the people. God's people ought to magnify Christ (Phil. 1:20-21), but God also delights in magnifying His people when they obey Him (Acts 5:12-13).

### C. The Lord glorified (vv. 9-13).

At the Exodus, God had proved Himself LORD and the true God beside whom the gods of Egypt were but harmless idols. Now God would prove Himself the "Lord of all the earth" (vv. 11, 13; see Ps. 97:5; Micah 4:13). All the gods of the heathen nations would fall before Him! God would prove His power by holding back the waters of the flooded Jordan and permitting His people to cross over on dry land.

### D. The Word verified (vv. 14-17).

It happened just as God said it would! The priests went before, bearing the ark, and when they dipped their feet into the water, God opened the river before them! (Sometimes God's people have to "get their feet wet" by faith before God goes to work! See Josh. 1:2-3.) The priests then walked to the midst of the river and stood there while all Israel passed over to the other side. Then they followed to the opposite side themselves. What a perfect picture of Christ! He goes before us to open the way; He stands with us until we cross over; and He follows behind to protect us! God kept His Word as His people trusted Him and obeyed Him.

It is instructive to contrast the crossing of the Red Sea (Ex. 14–15) and the crossing of the Jordan. The first crossing illustrates separation from the past (Egypt, the world), while the second crossing pictures entrance by faith into our spiritual inheritance in Christ. The enemy was defeated once and for all when the Egyptian army was drowned in the Red Sea, but the Jews had to win one victory after another when they crossed Jordan and entered Canaan. On the cross, Jesus defeated our enemies, but we have to walk and war by faith if we are to have daily victory. We "cross the Jordan" when we enter by faith into the victory experience of Rom. 6–8.

## II. The Memorials of the Crossing (4)

There were two piles of stones built: one by the twelve chosen men on the bank of the river (3:12; 4:1-8), and one by Joshua in the midst of the river (4:9-10). They were to be memorials of the crossing, and to us they convey wonderful spiritual truths.

The twelve stones on the bank of the Jordan came out of the midst of the river (v. 8) as evidence that God did part the waters and take His people safely across. The twelve stones hidden in the midst of the river could be seen only by God, but they too spoke of Israel's marvelous crossing. These two piles of stones picture Christ's death and burial (the hidden stones), and resurrection (the stones on the bank). At the same time, they illustrate the believer's spiritual union with Christ: when He died, we died with Him; we were buried with Him; we arose with Him in victory! See Eph. 2:1-10; Gal. 2:20; Col. 2:13; Rom. 6:4-5. Today the church has two memorials of this great truth: (1) baptism reminds us that the Spirit of God has baptized us into Christ, 1 Cor. 12:13; (2) the Lord's Supper points back to His death and ahead to His coming again.

The Jews could not get victory in Canaan and overcome the enemy without first going through Jordan. Nor can Christians today overcome their spiritual foes unless they die to self, reckon themselves crucified with Christ, and allow the Spirit to give them resurrection power. Review *Wiersbe's Expository Outlines on the New Testament* on Romans 5–8 for the NT explanation of this truth.

## III. The Mark of the Covenant (5)

The Jews were no sooner safe on the other side than God commanded them to receive the mark of the covenant, circumcision (Gen. 17). Collectively as a nation they had gone through the experience of "death" in crossing the river. Now they were to apply that "death to self" individually.

Throughout the Bible, physical circumcision is always a picture of a spiritual truth. Unfortunately, the Jews made the physical rite more important than the spiritual truth it taught (see Rom. 2:25-29). Circumcision pictures putting off that which is sinful, and in the NT it illustrates putting off the "old man" of the flesh (Col. 3:1ff; Rom. 8:13). It is not enough for me to say, "I died with Christ"; I must make this truth practical in my daily life by "putting to death" the deeds of the flesh. The OT Jew put off but a small portion of his flesh. Through Christ, however, the NT Christian has put off "the body of the sins of the flesh" (Col. 2:9-13). This operation at Gilgal, then, is an illustration of the truth that each believer must live "crucified with Christ" (Gal. 2:20).

The Jewish males had not received this mark of the covenant during their years of wandering in the wilderness, and for a very good reason: their unbelief had temporarily suspended their covenant relationship with God (Num. 14:32-34). When they refused to enter Canaan because of their unbelief, God "gave them up" to years of wandering until the old generation died. Now the new generation was to receive the mark of the covenant. "The reproach of Egypt" probably means the reproach the Egyptians (and other nations) heaped upon the Jews while they wandered in the wilderness (see Ex. 32:12ff; Deut. 9:24-29). Their unbelief did not glorify God, and the heathen nations said, "Your God is not strong enough to take you into Canaan!" Now God had taken them into the Promised Land, and the reproach was gone.

The new generation crossed Jordan, but they did not immediately attack Jericho. Many of today's Christians would have rushed right into battle! But God knew that His people needed to be prepared spiritually for the battle that lay ahead, so He caused them to wait and to rest. While waiting, they commemorated the Passover. It had been forty years before when the nation was delivered from Egypt on that first Passover night.

God gave them new food—the "produce" (old corn) of the land. The manna was food for the nation when they were pilgrims, but now they would be settling down in the land. See Deut. 6:10-11 and 8:3. The corn speaks of Christ in resurrection blessing, for the seed must be buried before there can be fruit (John 12:24). The order of events reminds us again of His death, burial, and resurrection—they kept the Passover (His death), and they ate the fruit of the land (resurrection).

The main lesson of these chapters is clear: there can be no conquest without death to self (crossing the Jordan) and identification with Christ's resurrection (the two memorials of stone). Before the Jews could get victory over the enemy, they had to experience victory over sin and self.

# JOSHUA 6

Israel's conquest of this mighty city is an illustration of several practical spiritual truths: (1) It is faith that overcomes obstacles, Heb. 11:30 and 1 John 5:4; (2) The weapons we use are spiritual, 2 Cor. 10:4; (3) Christ is the victor and we can trust Him fully,

John 16:33. Christians face many "Jerichos" in daily life, and often they are tempted to give up, as the spies did at Kadesh (Num. 13:28ff). But no wall is too high or too strong for the Lord. By faith we win the victory and claim the inheritance!

## I. The Captain of the Host (5:13–6:5)

Jericho was a closed city. Joshua stood by the city and saw a man there with a drawn sword. Fearlessly, Joshua asked the man to declare himself, and he discovered that the Man was the Lord of Hosts! This is the "battle" title of the Lord; it speaks of His supreme command of the hosts (armies) of Israel and of heaven. See Pss. 24:10 and 46:7, 11; 1 Kings 18:15; Isa. 8:11-14; Hag. 2:4; James 5:4. Jesus Christ had come down to direct the battle, and Joshua was quick to acknowledge His leadership. The first step toward victory is to confess that you are second in command.

There can be no victory for the Lord in public unless we experience worship of the Lord in private. Joshua fell on his face in worship; he took off his shoes in humility; and he turned all his plans over to his Commander when he said, "What does my Lord say to His servant?" As Christian soldiers (2 Tim. 2:3; Eph. 6:10ff), we must submit to Christ and listen to His orders in the Word. Christ gave to Joshua the exact orders for overcoming the city (6:2-5), and all he had to do was obey by faith. "I have given Jericho to you!" Christ promised. But the people had to step out by faith and claim the victory.

The armed men were to lead the procession (vv. 3, 7), with seven priests following with trumpets (v. 4). The ark was to follow (vv. 4, 7), and then the rest of the people ("the rereward") finished the procession (v. 9). The procession was to march around Jericho once a day for six days in absolute silence except for the trumpets blowing (v. 10). On the seventh day, they were to march around seven times (making a total of thirteen marches), and on the seventh march they were to blow the trumpets and shout. What a strange plan for fighting a war! But God's ways are not our ways, and He uses what the world calls "foolish" to confound the mighty (1 Cor. 1:26-31).

God has outlined for us in His Word all we need to know about spreading the Gospel and conquering the enemy. Sad to say, too many Christians (and churches) invent their own plans, borrowing man-made schemes from the world, and their efforts ultimately fail.

If we will listen to our Captain's orders and obey them, He will give the victory.

## II. The Capture of the City (6:6-25)

It is easy to see why Israel was victorious over the enemy:

### A. They obeyed their leaders (vv. 6-9).

We noted God's "spiritual chain of command" in Josh. 1, and here we see it in operation. The people respectfully listened to God's Word from their leaders and obeyed what God commanded. They manifested unity, cooperation, and singleness of mind in the ranks; and God gave them the victory.

### B. They had patience and faith (vv. 10-14).

Could God have delivered the city to Joshua on the first day? Certainly! But the requirement of six days of marching (during which the people were not allowed to talk) was a great means of discipline for the nation. Faith and patience go together (Heb. 6:11-15). Maintaining silence and waiting for God's appointed time also required discipline. James 3:1-2 teaches us that people who can control their speech are mature in the faith; also see Prov. 16:32.

### C. They trusted God for the impossible (vv. 15-16).

Who ever heard of taking a city using weapons like shouts and trumpets? But the ark (representing Christ's presence) was with them, and this meant that God would do the work. With God, all things are possible. See Jer. 33:3.

### D. They obeyed Him in every detail (vv. 17-25).

The loot of the city was to be "devoted to God" (accursed, consecrated); the animals and citizens were to be slain; Rahab and her family were to be saved alive. Sometimes we obey God before the battle, but (like Achan, chap. 7) disobey Him after the victory. God gave the Jews a total victory over Jericho because they trusted His Word. Note that Rahab and her family were taken out of the city before the fire was lit. See 1 Thes. 1:10; 5:9.

As you read the Book of Acts, you see how God's "spiritual army" conquered one city after another by faith. Even the mighty city of Rome fell before the power of the Gospel! Today, God's people again need to learn how to capture cities, and this chapter tells us how.

## III. The Curse of the Lord (6:26-27)

The "them" in v. 26 probably means the people who were saved alive, for they might be tempted to rebuild their city. Just as some of the Jews wanted to go back to Egypt, so some of Rahab's family might want to go back to Jericho. For this reason, God put a special curse on the city and on any man who would rebuild it. See Deut. 13:15-18.

This curse was fulfilled in 1 Kings 16:34. During the reign of wicked King Ahab, a man named Hiel of Bethel rebuilt Jericho. When he laid the foundation, he lost his firstborn son; and when he set up the gates, he lost his youngest son. What a sacrifice to make for a city! How foolish people are to defy God's Word and rebel against His will!

Jericho figures in the NT in several places. The man in the Parable of the Good Samaritan was going from Jerusalem to Jericho (Luke 10). Zacchaeus was of Jericho (Luke 19:1-10); and in that city, Christ healed blind Bartimaeus (Mark 10:46-52). The NT Jericho was not on the site of the OT city, but was a completely new city known for its beauty.

Some practical points to consider as we face our own "Jerichos":

### A. The soldier who wants to fight the best must bow the lowest before the battle (5:13-15).

We win our battles on our knees and on our faces before the Lord.

### B. No one can take a city alone.

Joshua had the loyal cooperation of the priests and people, and together they overcame the enemy.

### C. When we follow God's methods, He wins the battle and He gets the glory.

This is why He uses such "foolish methods." When we use our own schemes and systems, we might get the glory but the victory never lasts.

### D. Unbelief looks at the walls and giants (Num. 13:28ff), but faith looks to the Lord.

"Obstacles are those nasty little things we see when we take our eyes off the goal." And, we might add, when we take our eyes off the Lord. God's commandments are God's enablements.

*E. We see the grace of God at work even in judgment, for Rahab and her family were saved by faith.*

Is there a suggestion here that "few will be saved" when God's judgment finally does fall on this world?

# JOSHUA 7–9

Joshua's military strategy was to cut across Canaan and divide the land, beginning at Jericho and continuing with Ai, Bethel, and Gibeon. He then would conquer the southern cities and complete his conquest by defeating the northern cities. However, he experienced a setback at Ai and was deceived by the leaders of Gibeon.

## I. The Disobedience of Achan (7)

### A. Defeat (vv. 1-5).

God had made it clear that the spoils of Jericho were to be "devoted" or dedicated to Him and placed in His treasury (6:18-19), but Achan had disobeyed this law. It is possible that Joshua was too hasty in his attack on Ai, that he did not wait for the Lord's direction. Furthermore, he acted upon the suggestions of the spies rather than on God's Word. Later, God rejected the plan given by the spies (compare 7:3 with 8:1). There is a hint of overconfidence in these verses: Jericho had fallen to Israel, and they were confident that the smaller city of Ai would be a "pushover." Self-confidence, dependence on human wisdom, impatience, lack of prayer, and a secret sin were behind Israel's defeat at Ai.

### B. Discouragement (vv. 6-9).

The hearts of the Jews melted (v. 5) instead of the hearts of the enemy melting (Josh. 2:11). Joshua and his leaders spent the whole day in prayer before the ark, and even Joshua wanted to "back up" and settle for an inheritance on the other side of Jordan! Note, however, that Joshua was more concerned about the glory of the Lord and the testimony of Israel before the heathen nations, than he was about the discouragement of the defeat. It is a mark of true spirituality when God's glory is what motivates a servant's life.

## C. Discovery (vv. 10-18).

God spoke sternly to His servant: "Get up! Israel has sinned!" Of course, only one man had sinned, but this involved the entire nation (v. 1; 1 Cor. 12:12ff). It is a solemn truth that one person's disobedience can cause the sorrow and failure of a whole nation, family, or church. Achan thought he could hide his sin, but God saw what he did. And because an "accursed thing" was in the camp, God could not dwell with His people. This caused their defeat at Ai. Joshua and the high priest perhaps used the Urim and Thummim to determine the culprit (Ex. 28:30), or they may have cast lots. "Be sure your sin will find you out!" Achan was discovered and his sin exposed.

## D. Destruction (vv. 19-26).

"I have sinned!" confessed Achan, explaining how he "saw . . . coveted . . . and took" the spoils from Jericho (see Gen. 3:6). Undoubtedly the members of his household knew about the loot and were sharing in his sin. All of them had to be judged for their disobedience, so the people took them to the valley and stoned them. That place was called the "Valley of Achor" (trouble) in memory of the trouble Achan had brought to the people. Hosea 2:15 promises that God will make the Valley of Achor "a door of hope" for the Jews. Certainly Israel has been in the "valley of trouble" because of her rejection of Christ, but one day the nation will turn to Him and find hope.

## II. The Destruction of Ai (8:1-29)

Now that the nation had been sanctified (7:13) and their sin judged, God could again lead His people to victory. Note how the Lord used the defeat to good advantage, for the people of Ai were confident that they could overcome Israel again. Note too that God allowed the people to take the loot from Ai. Had Achan waited but a few days, he would have had all the wealth he could have carried! Read Matt. 6:33.

The plan was a simple one. Joshua sent 30,000 men to Bethel at night (v. 3), and placed another five thousand between Bethel and Ai (v. 12). Some of the soldiers attacked Ai and drew the men out of the city. At that point Joshua signaled the ambush, and his men entered the city and captured it. It was a complete victory! Joshua holding up his spear in v. 26 reminds us of Moses holding up his hands when Joshua fought Amalek (Ex. 17:8ff). Ai was made such a desolation that archaeologists cannot be certain of its location even today.

## III. The Declaration of the Law (8:30-35)

Joshua interrupted his military campaign to take the nation thirty miles to Shechem where he obeyed the commandments of Deut. 27:4-6. We are told that this valley is a natural amphitheater with wonderful acoustics. Joshua put the tribes of Reuben, Gad, Asher, Zebulun, Dan, and Naphtali on Mt. Ebal (the mount of the curses); and he put Simeon, Levi, Judah, Issachar, Ephraim, Manasseh, and Benjamin on Mt. Gerizim (the mount of blessing). Joshua well knew that Israel's victory and possession of the land depended on their obedience to the Word of God. It was more important for the nation to hear the Word than to fight any more battles. Note that he also built an altar (vv. 30-31), for apart from the blood of Christ, we have no righteousness before God. The Law would have condemned and slain them had they neglected the sacrifices. We must admire and imitate Joshua's respect for the Word of God (see 1:8; 24:26-27; also 23:14).

## IV. The Deception of the Gibeonites (9)

The heathen tribes of Canaan were divided into many little "nations" (city-states) with key cities as their centers. They usually fought each other, but when God's people arrived, these petty kings united to oppose Israel. It is amazing how enemies unite against God! However, the people at Gibeon, the next city to be taken, decided to use deceit instead of force. (Satan is both a lion and a serpent.) They dressed themselves to appear like men who had been on a long journey, with old sacks, patched (clouted) shoes, and moldy food, and their plan worked. God had commanded Israel to make no covenant with the nations in Canaan (Deut. 7), but the Gibeonites knew that if they did get a covenant, Israel would keep it. They lied when they said they came from a far country. Note also that they said nothing about Israel's victories at Jericho and Ai.

Joshua and his leaders failed to seek God's mind in the matter; instead, they judged by appearances. The Gibeonites' story sounded reasonable; the food and clothing certainly seemed to be old and worn out; and everything appeared to be in order. Consequently,

Joshua made a pact with the men and then discovered that they were from Gibeon! Three days later, Israel came to Gibeon and its allied cities (v. 17), but they could not attack them because of their promise. This caused murmuring among the people, who probably wanted more spoils. But God's people could not go back on their word. All Israel could do was make slaves out of the Gibeonites—they put them to work cutting wood and drawing water for the tabernacle service. At least they made their mistakes work for them!

What Jericho could not do with walls, or Ai with weapons, the Gibeonites accomplished with deceit. Satan tries one device after another to defeat God's people, and we must constantly be on guard. Note that it is usually after a great victory that Satan begins his subtle attacks. It was after the victory at Jericho that Israel was defeated by Ai, and it was after Israel's defeat of Ai that Joshua was deceived by Gibeon. We must beware of "judging after the flesh" (John 8:15) and depending on our own wisdom (Prov. 3:5-6). James 1:5 promises that God will give us wisdom if we ask for it. Christians must beware of worldly alliances (2 Cor. 6:14-18). We shall see in chapter 10 that Joshua was forced to defend his enemies because of his hasty covenant. Moses warned Israel in Deut. 7 that friendship with these heathen nations would only lead Israel into sin, and that is what happened.

# JOSHUA 14–15

Caleb stands out in the Bible as a great hero of faith. Six times we are told that he "wholly followed the Lord" (Num. 14:24; 32:12; Deut. 1:36; Joshua 14:8-9, 14). Caleb was "an overcomer" (1 John 2:13-14 and 5:4), a man who surrendered wholly to the Lord and fully obeyed His Word. We may trace his spiritual history in four stages.

## I. Caleb the Sufferer

Since Caleb was forty years old at Kadesh-barnea (Josh. 14:7), he had to have been born in Egypt while the Jews were enduring great suffering (Ex. 1–2). He was born a slave, yet he died a hero! His parentage is given in Josh. 14:13-14. Some think that Caleb (whose name means "dog") was of mixed parentage, his father being a

Kenezite and his mother from the tribe of Judah (Josh. 15:13). If so, this makes his faith an even greater wonder! However, 1 Chron. 2:18 makes Caleb the son of Hezron, a descendant of Pharez (1 Chron. 2:5); and this would put him in the ancestry of Christ (Matt. 1:3). In either case, Caleb was redeemed by the blood of the Passover lamb, delivered from Egypt, and given the prospects of a great inheritance in Canaan. He would have had no inheritance under Joshua had he not first experienced redemption under Moses.

## II. Caleb the Defender (Num. 13–14)

The rebellion of Israel at Kadesh-barnea has already been discussed in previous studies. The nation had been out of Egypt about two years when they arrived at the entrance to Canaan. Instead of believing God's Word and immediately claiming their inheritance, they asked for a report from twelve spies (Deut. 1:21ff). Caleb and Joshua were among those spies, which shows the position of confidence they held in the nation. When the report was given, only Caleb and Joshua defended Moses and encouraged the nation to enter Canaan. The ten spies despised the land (14:36), while Caleb and Joshua delighted in the land. The nation wanted to go back; the two men of faith wanted to go ahead. The majority was walking by sight; the minority was walking by faith. The rebellious nation saw only the obstacles, the problems; the believing leaders saw the opportunities, the prospects. What was the result? The ten spies and the unbelieving generation died in the wilderness! But Caleb and Joshua lived to enter and enjoy the Promised Land. "To be carnally minded is death" (Rom. 8:6). It took courage for Caleb to stand against the whole nation, but God honored him for it.

## III. Caleb the Wanderer

Caleb did not die in the wilderness, but he still had to suffer with the unbelieving nation during their nearly forty years of wandering. Think of what this godly, believing man had to endure! Every single day he saw people die and miss out on their inheritance. He had to listen to the murmuring and complaining. This man of faith had to put up with the unbelief of his fellow Israelites. He loved Moses, yet he had to listen to the Jews as they criticized their leader and opposed him.

How was Caleb able to maintain his spiritual life when surrounded by so much carnality and unbelief? His heart was in Canaan! God had given him a wonderful inheritance (read Josh. 14:9-12), and though his body was in the wilderness, his heart and mind were in Canaan! He is a perfect illustration of Col. 3:1-4. He possessed what Rom. 8:6 refers to as "the spiritual mind." Caleb was able to endure the trials of the wilderness because he knew that he did not have to fear death, that he had an inheritance, and that God would not fail him. How much more we have in Christ! Yet we give up so easily and fail in our pilgrim journey.

## IV. Caleb the Conqueror

This brings us to our study of Joshua 14–15. Joshua is giving each tribe its special inheritance, and Caleb comes to claim his share. He reminds Joshua of God's promise (14:6-9), for it is only on the basis of God's Word that we can claim our blessings. Note the glorious testimony of strength Caleb gives (14:10-11). The person of faith is the person with strength. Forty-five years after the nation's failure at Kadesh-barnea, Caleb is eighty-five years old, yet he is anxious to claim his inheritance to the glory of God. It is sad when believers allow "old age" to make complainers out of them when they ought (like Caleb) to be conquerors.

"Give me this mountain!" (14:12) Caleb was a man of spiritual vision as well as spiritual vitality, and these two qualities led to spiritual victory. God had promised him the inheritance, and Caleb had faith that what God promised He was able to perform (see Rom. 4:20-21). Caleb was able to drive out the inhabitants of his inheritance (Josh. 15:13-14), the very "giants" that the ten unbelieving spies had feared (Num. 13:28, 33). Unbelief looks at the giants; faith looks to God. Unbelief depends on man's "common sense"; faith rests wholly on the Word of God.

Caleb's nephew Othniel helped him in one of his conquests (Josh. 15:15-17) and gained Caleb's daughter for a wife. This man later became the first judge of Israel (Jud. 3:9ff), and thus carried on the family leadership. Caleb's daughter illustrates a wonderful spiritual truth. After her marriage to Othniel, she returned to her father to ask for a further blessing (15:18-19). Caleb had given her a field, but she also wanted the springs of water to nourish the field. The Christian should joyfully continue to ask the Father for greater blessings, especially for the "spiritual springs" that water the fruitful life. The field that God gives us will never produce fruit apart from the springs of water (John 7:37-39).

What a difference it makes when believers "wholly follow the Lord" and exercise faith in the Word. Caleb's dedication and faith saved his life, gained him an inheritance, overcame the enemy, and enabled him to enrich his own family for years to come. The Lord certainly expects Christians today to be conquerors; in fact, Paul claims that we are "more than conquerors!" (Rom. 8:37) Joshua and Caleb conquered with physical weapons and claimed a material inheritance, but we conquer with spiritual weapons (2 Cor. 10:3-5) to claim our spiritual inheritance in Christ (Eph. 1:3). Christians are supposed to be overcomers through faith in Christ (1 John 5:4). We are to overcome the world (1 John 5:5), false doctrine (1 John 4:1-4), and the wicked one (1 John 2:13-14). Christ has already overcome Satan (Luke 11:21-22) and the world (John 16:33), so that we need only to claim His victory by faith. Note in the letters to the seven churches (Rev. 2–3) the many promises to those who overcome. "He who overcomes shall inherit all things!" promises Rev. 21:7 (NKJV).

We overcome the enemy and claim the inheritance the same way as Caleb: (1) we must be wholly yielded to the Lord; (2) we must know His promises and believe them; (3) we must keep heart and mind fixed on the inheritance; (4) we must depend on God to give the victory. "Thanks be to God who gives us the victory through our Lord Jesus Christ!" (1 Cor. 15:57, NKJV)

# JOSHUA 23–24

We commonly think of Joshua as a great soldier, and he was; but here we see him as a great shepherd with a loving concern for his people. He had served the Lord and the nation faithfully; now he was concerned lest the people depart from the Lord and lose their inheritance. This was the same concern Peter had before he died (2 Peter 1:12-15) and also the Apostle Paul (Acts 20:13ff). How tragic it is when one generation sacrifices to obtain God's blessing and a new generation comes along and loses everything.

## I. Joshua's Address to the Leaders (23)

Joshua called the leaders of the tribes together, probably at Shiloh (18:1). He wanted to instill in his leaders a sincere devotion to the

Lord. He would die, but they would be left to carry on the work. Joshua wants them to be faithful to their God.

## A. A review of the past (vv. 3-4).

These men had seen the wonders of the Lord, from the crossing of Jordan to that present day. Note how Joshua gives God all the glory for what had been achieved: The Lord fought the battles; all Joshua did was divide the land! It is good for us to remember what God has done for us.

## B. A promise for the future (v. 5).

God's workers change, but His Word remains the same. Joshua assures them that God will continue to fight for them and give them victory over their enemies.

## C. A responsibility for the present (vv. 6-16).

What God does for His people depends often on what the people do for God. Joshua reminds them of their responsibilities as the people of God, and his words take us back to Moses' warnings in Deut. 7–11. The key word here is *nations,* used seven times in vv. 3-13. Israel must beware of the heathen nations in the land. The only way Israel could ever hope to gain the land and claim their inheritance was by obeying the Law of God (see Josh. 1:7-8). It would take courage to trust the Word and oppose the enemy, but God would enable them.

Joshua's main concern was that Israel be a separated people and not mingle with the heathen nations. Verse 7 (NKJV) presents the negative ("Lest you go among these nations") and v. 8 the positive ("But you shall hold fast to the Lord"). How foolish it would be to worship the gods of a defeated enemy! If Israel would be separated unto the Lord, God would enable one man to do the work of a thousand! (v. 10) They had to cleave either to the Lord or to the heathen nations (v. 11-12); but if they mingled with the heathen, God would remove His blessings from them. The principle here in verse 13 applies to all believers: any sins we allow to remain in our lives become traps and thorns to us.

We cannot help but notice Joshua's emphasis on the Word of God (vv. 6, 14). "There has not failed one word of all His good promise!" (See 1 Kings 8:56, NKJV.) To obey His Word means victory and blessing; to disobey it means defeat and trial. See Josh. 1:8.

## II. Joshua's Appeal to the People (24:1-28)

After exhorting the leaders, Joshua calls all the people together at Shechem, a place dear to the heart of Israel since it was at Shechem that God first promised the land to Abraham (Gen. 12:6-7). Here also, Jacob built an altar (Gen. 33:20), and he exhorted his family to put away their idols (Gen. 35:1-4). While there are no "holy places" on earth, there are places that arouse sacred memories to the believer.

Joshua was concerned lest the people lapse into idolatry because of the influence of the heathen nations around them. Israel was prone to worship idols, and Joshua knew that idolatry would cause them to forfeit their inheritance. So, he uses several arguments to encourage them to devote themselves wholly to the Lord.

### A. God's goodness in the past (vv. 2-13).

Joshua goes all the way back to the birth of the nation in the call of Abraham. Abraham and his father were idolaters until God called them in His grace. ("On the other side of the flood" means "over the Euphrates River." See also vv. 14-15.) God called Abraham, not because of his goodness, for he was a heathen man, but because of God's grace and love. God gave the land to Abraham, Isaac, and Jacob. God protected the Jews in Egypt and then delivered them by His mighty hand. He led them and provided for them in the wilderness. He defeated nations for their sake. He brought them over the Jordan River into the Promised Land and drove out the enemies before them. What more could God have done for His people! Now they had claimed their inheritances and were enjoying the blessings of the land. How they ought to love and serve the Lord!

### B. Joshua's own example (vv. 14-15).

Israel had to serve some god — either the gods of the heathen or the true God, Jehovah. "As for me and my house," said Joshua, "we will serve the Lord!" It is not only encouraging but also essential that godly leaders set a good example in their own homes.

### C. The danger of discipline (vv. 16-21).

The people assure Joshua three times that they will serve the Lord (vv. 16, 21, 24). He knows that what is said by the lips is not always true in the heart. "If you continue with your idols," he warns, "then you cannot serve the Lord! He is a jealous God, a God who will not share His people with any other god." He warns them that idolatry will lead to chastening and discipline, and the loss of their land.

### D. The covenant with God (vv. 22-28).

God had made a covenant with Israel at Sinai (see Ex. 20), and this covenant had been renewed by the new generation under Moses in Deuteronomy. But each generation needs to reaffirm its faithfulness to God, so Joshua renews the covenant with the people. He writes the words in the Book of the Law, and then sets up a stone to remind the people of their vows. This recalls to mind the stones set up when Israel crossed Jordan (chap. 4). We are so prone to forget that God has to use reminders (such as the Lord's Supper) to keep His people in the path of obedience. Even with the reminders, in the years that followed, the Jews failed to keep their covenant with God. Read Jud. 21:25 for the sad report.

## III. Joshua's Achievement for the Lord (24:29-33)

Verse 31 is a great testimonial for this man of God—because of his leadership, the nation served the Lord and continued to serve Him even after he was dead. Joshua had been used of God to achieve many things for Israel. He had led them across Jordan; he had led them from victory to victory in the land; he had given them their inheritance. Certainly the tomb of Joshua was another reminder to Israel of the power and mercy of the Lord. It is right for God's people to remember godly leaders and to imitate their faith (Heb. 13:7-8).

Three burials are recorded in these verses: Joshua's, Joseph's, and Eleazar's. Joseph's brothers had promised to bury his remains in Canaan (Gen. 50:25), so the Jews had carried his coffin out of Egypt (Ex. 13:19). This is a picture of our future resurrection, for just as Joseph's body was redeemed from Egypt, so our bodies will be one day not only at rest in their rightful home, but also transformed to be like the body of Jesus Christ (Phil. 3:20-21). It is easy to believe that Joseph's grave would also be a reminder to the people of the faithfulness of God. Joseph had been used to keep the nation alive in famine, and he had been faithful to the Lord even in the heathen land of Egypt.

As we close this book, let us remember that Christ is our Joshua (Savior), and that He fights our battles for us and helps us claim the inheritance.

# JUDGES

## *A Suggested Outline of Judges*

I. Apathy (1–2)
   A. Early victories (1:1-26)
   B. Repeated defeats (1:27-36)
   C. Divine rebuke (2:1-5)
   D. Serving other gods (2:6-23)
      (summary of the entire book)

II. Apostasy (3–16)
   A. Othniel (3:1-11)
      (Mesopotamia)
   B. Ehud and Shamgar (3:12-31)
      (Moab)
   C. Deborah and Barak (4–5)
      (The Canaanites)
   D. Gideon (6–8)
      (Midian)
   E. Abimelech, Tola, and Jair (9:1–10:5)
      (Men of Shechem)
   F. Jephthah (10:6–12:15)
      (Ammon)
   G. Samson (13–16)
      (The Philistines)

III. Anarchy (17–21)
   A. Idolatry (17–18)
   B. Immorality (19)
   C. Civil war (20–21)

# Introductory Notes to Judges

## I. Theme

Just as Joshua continues the history of Israel after the death of Moses (Josh. 1:1), the Book of Judges picks up the story of Israel after the death of Joshua (Jud. 1:1). This is a book of defeat and disgrace, as we see in the key verse (17:6): "Every man did that which was right in his own eyes." The Lord was no longer "King in Israel"—the tribes were divided; the people were mixing with the heathen nations; and it was necessary for God to chasten His people. We have a summary of the entire book in 2:10-19—blessing, disobedience, chastening, repentance, deliverance. Judges is the book of incomplete victory; it is a book of failure on the part of God's people to trust His Word and claim His power.

## II. Spiritual Lesson

You will recall the three divisions of Joshua: crossing the river, conquering the enemy, and claiming the inheritance. Joshua records how Israel crossed the river and began to conquer the enemy, but the book ends with "much land yet to be possessed" (Josh. 13:1 and 23:1-11). "Crossing the river" signifies death to self and separation from sin; it means entering into our spiritual inheritance by faith (Eph. 1:3). But after we have taken this step of faith, it is easy to faint, or to compromise with the enemy. Israel entered into her land, but she failed to possess the total inheritance. She first tolerated the enemy, then took tribute (taxes) from the enemy, then mixed with the enemy, and finally surrendered to the enemy. It was only through God's deliverers (the judges) that the Israelites found victory. How easy it is for Christians to "settle down with sin" and miss the blessings of complete dedication and complete victory.

## III. The Land

The Promised Land was filled with many nations and many "petty kings" who ruled over smaller territories. Joshua had led the nation collectively in great victories over the major enemies; the way had now been paved for each tribe to go in by faith and claim the allotted inheritance. Whereas the Book of Joshua is a record of united efforts, Judges records a divided nation no longer devoted to the Lord, forgetful of the covenant that they made at Sinai.

## IV. The Judges

Named in this book are twelve different judges raised up by God to defeat a particular enemy in a particular territory and give the people rest. These judges were not national leaders; rather, they were local leaders who delivered the people from various oppressors. It is possible that some of the periods of oppression and rest overlap. Not all of the tribes participated in each battle, and often there was tribal rivalry. That God could call these "ordinary people" as judges and use them so mightily is another evidence of His grace and power (1 Cor. 1:26-31). The Spirit of God came upon these leaders for a particular work (6:34; 11:29; 13:25), though often their personal lives were not exemplary in every detail. The several hundred years of rule under the judges prepared Israel for their request for a king (1 Sam. 8).

## V. The Nations That Remained

God permitted the heathen nations to be left in the land for several reasons: (1) to punish Israel, 2:3, 20-21; (2) to prove Israel, 2:22 and 3:4; (3) to provide Israel with experience in warfare, 3:2; and (4) to prevent the land from becoming a wilderness, Deut. 7:20-24. If Israel wanted to live with this "second-class" situation, God would give them their desire. He then used these nations for His own purposes. The Jews could have enjoyed total victory; instead, they settled for a compromise. Chapters 3–16 picture the "up-and-down" experiences of some of God's people. Alas, the nation did not yield to God and obey Him; they looked instead to the human helpers He sent them. Too many Christians have their "ups and downs" and run to the pastor or another friend for help instead of first getting alone with God to permit Him to examine their hearts and give them the help they need.

# JUDGES 1–5

## I. The Failures of the Nation (1–2)

### A. They failed to conquer the land (1:1-36).

Verses 1-18 record the early victories of Judah and Simeon, while the rest of the chapter is a record of repeated defeats. These two tribes were able to take Bezek (v. 4), Jerusalem (v. 8), Hebron (v. 10), Debir (v. 11), Zephath (v. 17), Gaza, Askelon, and Ekron (v. 18). The people of Joseph took Bethel (v. 22), but the rest of the tribes were unable to drive out the enemy. What began as a series of victories, led by the Lord, ended as a series of compromises. Judah could not drive out the inhabitants of the valley (v. 19, and see 4:13ff); Benjamin could not overcome the Jebusites (v. 21); and the other tribes likewise "settled down" with the heathen nations (vv. 27-36). Of course, they were able to rationalize their failures by making slaves out of the heathen peoples; but this only led to further trouble. In Joshua 23–24, Joshua had warned them against compromising with the enemy, but now they were falling into that very trap.

### B. They failed to consider the Law (2:1-10).

This, of course, was the reason for their repeated failures and defeats. God had promised Joshua constant victory if the nation honored and obeyed the Word (Josh. 1:7-8), and Joshua had repeated this promise to the leaders (Josh. 23:5-11). Gilgal had been the scene of great victory for Israel, but now the Lord moved from Gilgal to Bochim, "the place of weeping," emphasizing Israel's tragic decline from winning to weeping! (For the importance of Gilgal, see Josh. 5:1-9; 9:6; 10:6. Gilgal was the center of Israel's military operations, the camp of Joshua. Now it had been forsaken.)

God reminded the people that they had disobeyed the Law by making covenants with the heathen nations and joining themselves to their gods. Read Deut. 7 carefully for God's instructions on this matter of separation. The nation had followed the Law during the years of Joshua and the leaders that followed him, but after they died, the nation backslid. "There arose another generation . . . which knew not the Lord." (See v. 10). They had not even brought their own children to the Lord! They had failed to teach them the Law, as God had instructed them to do in Deut. 6:1-15. How often this happens in nations, churches, and families. How easy it is for the "younger generation" to fall away from the Lord if the "older generation" is not faithful to teach them and set the best example of obedience before them.

### C. They failed to cleave to the Lord (2:11-23).

They forsook the Lord and they followed other gods. The religion of the Canaanites was horribly wicked, with practices too obscene to discuss. Worship of Baal and Ashtaroth (male and female deities, v. 13) plagued Israel throughout their history. Once it got into their lives, it was difficult to exterminate. When the people forsook the Lord, He forsook them. Time after time he "sold them" into the hands of their enemies. Instead of enjoying the "rest" God had promised, the nation was in and out of slavery for hundreds of years, with only occasional periods of "rest" from the Lord. Each time the judgment became so severe that the nation finally cried out to God. He would send a deliverer, but note that God was with the judge personally, not with the nation collectively. Sadly enough, the people turned to the Lord only when in trouble; once the judge was gone, the nation fell back into sin again.

These failures are seen in professing Christians today. At times, instead of overcoming the enemy, we compromise and let the enemy drag us down. We often deliberately disobey the Word of God, and many times we fail to love the Lord and cleave to Him by faith. When this happens, God must chasten us, and the only remedy is for us to repent and return.

## II. The Victories of the Judges (3–5)

In the Book of Joshua, there was one leader and God was with the whole nation; but in Judges, there are many leaders, and God is with these leaders only, not with the entire nation (2:18). Several minor judges are listed here whose ministries we can only study briefly.

### A. Othniel (3:1-11).

The people of Mesopotamia enslaved Israel for eight years; then God raised up Caleb's son-in-law Othniel to deliver the nation. His name means "God is might," and he lived up to his name. See Jud. 1:9-15 and Josh. 15:16-19. It must have pleased the family of Caleb to have such a courageous man in their ranks. He delivered the nation and they had rest for forty years.

## B. Ehud (3:12-30).

This time the Lord used Moab to chasten Israel, along with Ammon and Amalek, the old enemies of the Jews! The Israelites served as slaves for eighteen years until Ehud delivered them and gave them rest for eighty years. God used the fact that he was left-handed to deceive the enemy, for the king would not have known what Ehud would be drawing out from his garments on the right side (3:21). The Benjamites seemed to be gifted with left-handed men (Jud. 20:16; 1 Chron. 12:2). Once the enemy king was slain, Ehud was able to muster his army and drive out the invaders.

## C. Shamgar (3:31).

It is probable that Shamgar led in a local victory against the Philistines. He is not called a judge, although he is listed with them. God is able to use the most foolish weapons, even an ox goad.

## D. Deborah and Barak (chaps. 4–5).

The nation had fallen so low that it was now judged by a woman, which would humiliate the men in this male-dominant society (see Isa. 3:12). For twenty years the Canaanites had oppressed Israel, so God raised up this prophetess to lead the way to victory. First she called Barak to deliver the nation (4:1-7), and she even gave him the battle plan from the Lord. Usually the Kishon River was dry, but God was going to send a great storm that would flood the river-bed and trap the chariots of iron (see 4:3 and 5:20-22). Though Barak is listed as a man of faith in Heb. 11:32, we see him here as a man who had to depend upon Deborah for victory. In fact, God used two women to deliver the Jews—Deborah the prophetess and Jael (vv. 18-24). It is interesting to contrast Barak and Samson. Both were associated with women, but in one case this led to victory, while in the other it led to defeat. Barak led 10,000 men from Mt. Tabor, trusting the promise of God given by His servant, Deborah. Whatever may have been Barak's weaknesses, God still honored him for his faith. In her song of victory (chap. 5), Deborah praises the Lord for the willingness of the people to fight in the battle (vv. 2, 9). However, she also names some of the tribes that were too cowardly to fight (5:16-17). The battle was held "by the waters of Megiddo" where the Kishon River flowed down from Mt. Tabor. Sisera and his army thought their chariots of iron would give them victory, but it was the chariots that led to their defeat! God sent a great storm (5:4-5 and 20-22) that turned the plain into a swamp, and the enemy could not attack. Israel won a great victory that day, led by Barak, planned by Deborah.

But it was not given to Barak to slay General Sisera; this was left to another woman, Jael. The Kenites were a people friendly to Israel (Jud. 1:16) because of their connection with Moses' family (Jud. 4:11), but they were also friendly to Jabin, the Canaanite king. Usually a man in the cultures of the East will not enter a woman's tent, but Jael persuaded Jabin, made him comfortable, and then killed him. The "nail" was likely a wooden tent peg. Her deed is praised in Deborah's song (5:24-27), although some people find it difficult to understand this deed. Certainly Sisera would have been slain when Barak's troops caught up with him, and he was the enemy of the Lord (5:31), not of Jael personally. She was helping Israel fight the battles of the Lord. Two women rejoiced in victory (Deborah and Jael), but one woman (the mother of Sisera) wept in sorrow (5:28-30).

Note in 5:6-8 a description of the terrible state of society in Israel at that time. The people were so fearful they moved from the villages into the walled cities, and it was not safe for people to travel on the highways. A decline in the social and moral life of the nation was the inevitable consequence of the nation's spiritual decline.

# JUDGES 6–8

Hebrews 11:32 puts Gideon at the head of the list of judges. Though he sometimes wavered in his faith, he was still a "man of faith" who dared to trust the Word of God. When we realize that he was a farmer, not a trained warrior, we see how wonderful his faith was! We will trace Gideon's career in this passage.

## I. Gideon the Coward (6:1-24)

Seven years of bondage under the Midianites had brought Israel to its lowest level. Instead of "riding on the high places" (Deut. 32:13), they were hiding in the dens! The Israelites were not even allowed to harvest their grain, which explains why we find Gideon hiding in the winepress. God's prophet (vv. 7-10) reminded the people of their unbelief and sin; then God's Angel—Christ Himself—visited Gideon to prepare him for his victory. Remember that

God had forsaken His people temporarily; He was now working through chosen individuals (2:18).

When the Angel called Gideon a "mighty man of valor" (v. 12), it seemed a mockery, yet God was only anticipating what Gideon would become by faith. It reminds us of Christ's words to Peter: "You are . . . You shall be" (John 1:42, NKJV). But see Gideon's unbelief, which was the cause of his cowardice, as he questions God: "If . . . why . . . where . . . how . . . if . . . ?" Then he asks God to show him a sign! This is certainly not the language of faith. Gideon confessed that God had chastened His people justly (v. 13), but he could not understand how the Lord would use a poor farmer like himself to deliver the nation. God met his unbelief with a series of promises: "The Lord is with you"; "you shall save Israel . . . have I not sent you?" "surely I will be with you" (vv. 12, 14, NKJV). Faith comes by hearing God's Word (Rom. 10:17). Gideon required a sign, and God graciously granted it to him (vv. 19-24). However, this is not a good example for us to follow. "Jehovah-shalom" means "The Lord is our peace" (vv. 23-24).

## II. Gideon the Challenger (6:25-32)

It is one thing to meet God in the secrecy of a winepress, but quite another thing to stand up for the Lord in public. That very night God tested Gideon's dedication by asking him to tear down his father's idolatrous altar to Baal, and to build an altar to Jehovah. More than this, he was to sacrifice his father's special bullock (probably reserved for Baal) on the new altar. Christian testimony has to begin at home. Gideon obeyed the Lord, but he showed unbelief by doing the deed by night (v. 27) and by asking ten other men to help him. We can imagine the furor in the neighborhood when the people discovered the destroyed altar the next morning! Did they kill Gideon? No! Rather, Gideon became a leader, able to summon the army together to prepare to fight. God will never use a "secret saint" to win great battles. We must come out in the open and take our stand, regardless of the cost.

## III. Gideon the Conqueror (6:33–8:3)

### A. He conquered his fears (6:33–7:14).

An army of thirty-two thousand men rallied to his side, but he was still doubtful of victory. How gracious God is to minister to His feeble saints! Gideon "put out the fleece" twice, and both times God answered. It is too bad, though, when God's people trust circumstances to lead them instead of relying on God's clear Word. Gideon was not the only one afraid; 22,000 soldiers were also fearful and went home (7:1-3, and see Deut. 20:8). However, God did not need all of the remaining 10,000 men, so He tested them and sent most of them home. The 300 who drank from the hand (v. 6) would have been in better position to face and fight the enemy in a surprise attack.

On the night of the battle, God saw that there was still fear in Gideon's heart (vv. 9-14), so He graciously gave him a special sign assuring him that he would win the battle. The barley cake represented Gideon, for barley was the poorest kind of food. But God was going to use this ordinary farmer to win a great victory!

### B. He conquered his foes (7:15-25).

Note how Gideon quotes God's promise of victory to the people (v. 15, note v. 9). He was relying wholly on the Word of God. This victory was won by the power of God, for their weapons were useless in the battle. The Spirit of God was now using Gideon (6:34); see Zech. 4:6 and 1 Cor. 1:26-31. The pitchers would hide the light of the torches and would also make a great deal of noise when broken; and these effects, added to the shouting and the blowing of the trumpets, would certainly rout the enemy. The vessel, torch, and trumpet also have spiritual significance. We must be clean, yielded vessels for God to use (2 Tim. 2:21); we must let our lights shine (Matt. 5:16); and we must "trumpet out" a clear witness for Christ (1 Thes. 1:8).

The steps in Gideon's victory are easy to trace: he has a promise to believe (6:12, 14, 16; 7:7-9), an altar to build (6:25-26), a vessel to break, a lamp to burn, and a trumpet to blow. And God gave the victory!

### C. He conquered his feelings (8:1-3).

Ephraim had not been included in the original army (6:35), but Manasseh, the sister tribe, had shared in the battle. Later, Gideon called Ephraim to capture the two famous princes, which they did. But they were provoked! How easy it is for the flesh to act even when God has given a great victory. Gideon could have "told them off" but instead he practiced Prov. 15:1: "A soft answer turns away wrath" (NKJV). It is better to control our feelings than to conquer a city (Prov. 16:32); and if Gideon had offended his brethren, he might never win them back (Prov. 18:19). Godly leaders must know how to control their own feelings.

## IV. Gideon the Compromiser (8:4-35)

Gideon and his 300 men pursued the two kings of Midian, but the men of Succoth and Penuel would not assist him. Their attitude provoked Gideon and he promised to avenge himself. This seems to have been the beginning of his backsliding, for God certainly would have dealt with these rebellious men in His own way (Rom. 12:19). The army took the host of Midian by surprise when the kings were feeling confident (8:11), and on his return march, Gideon punished the men of Succoth and Penuel with thorns and briers (8:16-17). He then slew the two kings who had themselves slain Gideon's brethren.

After winning a great victory, we must always beware of the temptation to sin, for Satan attacks us subtly when we least expect it. The nation asked Gideon to become their king and to establish a dynasty; but this he refused. "The Lord shall rule over you!" However, Gideon used this opportunity to ask for "a lesser thing"—all their earrings and ornaments. This seemed like a fitting gift for a great deliverer, but keep in mind that these golden trinkets were associated with idol worship. Ornaments in v. 21 is actually "crescents"; these items were connected with moon-worship. Read Gen. 35:1-4 for the association between earrings and idolatry.

Gideon made an idolatrous "ephod" (or image) with the seventy pounds of gold he collected. What the Midianites could not do by means of swords, Satan accomplished with earrings. It is sad to see the man who overthrew Baal's altar now setting up an idol of his own. Unfortunately, the whole nation forsook God and worshiped the new god (v. 27). When Gideon died, the nation went right back to Baal worship (v. 33).

The subsequent history of Gideon's family is not encouraging. He had many sons and daughters by his "many wives" (v. 30), but these were all slain (with the exception of Jotham) by the son of Gideon's concubine, a man named Abimelech (v. 31; Jud. 9:1-6). Furthermore, before Gideon's family was slain, they were not treated kindly by the nation (v. 35). How soon the sinful hearts of humans forget both the Lord (v. 34) and the people who have served them faithfully.

# JUDGES 13–16

Few accounts in the Bible are as tragic as this one. Here is a man to whom God gave twenty years' time to begin to overcome the enemy, yet in the end, he himself was overcome by the enemy. Samson's history is an illustration of Paul's warning in 1 Cor. 9:27, for Samson was a castaway. Hebrews 11:32 cites him for his faith in God's Word, but apart from this, very little can be said on his behalf. "Let him who thinks he stands take heed lest he fall" (1 Cor. 10:12, NKJV). Note the steps that led to Samson's sin and tragic end.

## I. He Despised His Heritage (13)

Samson was born into a godly home, to parents who believed in prayer. He was God's special gift to them and to the nation. He had a father who prayed, "Teach us what we shall do unto the child" (v. 8; and see v. 12). His parents had a fear of God and tried to instill this same fear in their son. They brought offerings to God and dared to believe His wonderful promises.

God gave to Samson a special enduement of the Holy Spirit that made him a conqueror. God called Samson to be a Nazarite ("separated one"), wholly surrendered to the Lord. According to Num. 6, a Nazarite was never to drink strong drink or touch a dead body; and the mark of his dedication would be his uncut hair.

All of this wonderful heritage the grown Samson despised! Instead of putting himself in God's hands to accomplish his God-given task, he chose to live to please himself. How tragic it is when God gives a young person a wonderful heritage and a great opportunity, and he or she treats it lightly.

## II. He Defied His Parents (14:1-4)

One evidence of spiritual decline can be the way we get along with our loved ones. "Samson went down . . . " (14:1) is true both spiritually and geographically. Instead of staying in the borders of Israel, he went into enemy territory and fell in love with a heathen woman. He knew the laws of separation God had given to the Jews, but he chose to ignore them (see Ex. 34:16; Deut. 7:3; and 2 Cor. 6:14-18; also Gen. 24:1-4). Note that he *told* his parents; he did not *ask* them. And when they reminded him of God's law, he defied them. "Get her for me," he insisted, "for she pleases me well!" It did not

239

bother Samson that his desires displeased his parents. Note that in this instance God mercifully was going to overrule his sin and use it to weaken the Philistines (v. 4). Christian young people need to stop and consider carefully when they find themselves defying godly parents who know God's Word.

## III. He Defiled His Body (14:5-20)

In those days, the parents arranged for a marriage, and there was several months time between the engagement and the wedding. When Samson met the lion, God gave him the power to overcome it even though Samson was not walking completely in God's will. When he came back months later to complete the marriage, he found honey in the carcass of the lion. Numbers 6:6-9 tells us that a Nazarite was never to touch a dead body, but Samson deliberately defiled himself for the sake of the honey! How many Christians today defile themselves just to enjoy a little honey in the carcass of a lion—perhaps a popular book, a movie, or a questionable friendship. Sad to say, Samson passed the sin along to his parents, and then he made a joke about it to entertain his friends! As a Nazarite and a Jew, he had no right to be sharing in a worldly Philistine wedding. The marriage was never completed, but the seeds of sin had already been planted in his heart.

## IV. He Disregarded God's Warning (15)

This is a chapter of seeming victories, yet it ends with the "strong man" utterly exhausted for lack of water. He burned the fields of the Philistines, but they turned around and burned the house of the woman he had loved (15:6 with 14:15). Samson avenged their death, but then his own people turned against him and delivered him to the enemy (vv. 11-13). God delivered him, but then God warned him by showing him how weak he was. We find only two prayers of Samson: here, for water (vv. 18-20), and in 16:28, for strength to destroy the Philistines. His parents had been prayerful people, but Samson had not followed their example. God warned him here, but he would not heed the warning.

## V. He Deliberately Played with Sin (16)

Samson had already gotten into trouble with one woman, but now he tried again, this time going deep into enemy territory to Gaza.

Again, God warned him by allowing the enemy to almost catch him, but Samson still refused to repent. It was then that Delilah came into his life and led him to his doom. The Valley of Sorek was near his home, but Samson's heart was already far from God.

It shocks us to see this Nazarite sleeping on the lap of a wicked woman, but this is what happens when people choose to go their own way and reject the counsel of loved ones and the Lord. Three times Delilah enticed Samson, and three times he lied to her. Each time, the enemy attacked him, so he should have realized he was in danger. But read Prov. 7:21-27 to see why Samson yielded. He was asleep when he should have been awake! Remember the warning Christ gave to Peter in Matt. 26:40-41. Note that each lie Samson told actually took him closer to the truth. How dangerous it is to play with sin.

The rest of the story shows the tragic end of the believer who will not let God have his way with his life. From v. 20 on, Samson does nothing but lose. He loses his hair, the symbol of his Nazarite dedication; for that dedication had long since been abandoned. Then he loses his strength, but he is ignorant of it until he is overpowered. How futile it is for the servant of God to try to serve the Lord when out of His will. Next Samson loses the light, for the Philistines put out his eyes. He loses his liberty, for they bind him with fetters of brass. He loses his usefulness to the Lord, for he ends up grinding corn instead of fighting God's battles. Someone has said that v. 21 pictures the blinding, binding, and grinding results of sin. And all of this began when Samson despised his blessings and defied his parents!

Samson also lost his testimony, for he was the laughingstock of the Philistines. Their fish-god Dagon, not the God of Israel, was given all the glory. Apparently Samson repented of his sin, for God gave him one more chance to act by faith. His hair had begun to grow and Samson asked God for strength to win one more victory over the enemy. God answered his prayer, but in defeating others, Samson took his own life. Like Saul, Samson was a castaway; he had committed sin unto death, and God had to take him off the scene (see 1 Cor. 11:30-31; 1 John 5:16-17). His loved ones claimed his body and buried him "between Zorah and Eshtaol" — the very place where he had started his ministry (13:25).

Samson illustrates people who have power to conquer others, but who cannot conquer themselves. He set the Philistine fields on fire, but could not control the fires of his own lust. He killed a lion, but would not put to death the passions of the flesh. He could easily break the bonds that men put on him, but the shackles of sin gradually grew stronger on his soul. Instead of leading the nation, he preferred to work independently, and as a result, left no permanent victory behind. He was remembered for what he destroyed, not for what he built up. He lacked discipline and direction; without these, his strength could accomplish little. He failed to check the impulses that began early in his career, and twenty years later, they killed him.

It remained for Samuel and David in later years to finally defeat the Philistines. Samuel by one prayer accomplished more than Samson did in twenty years of fighting (see 1 Sam. 7:9-14).

# RUTH

## A Suggested Outline of Ruth

I. Ruth's Sorrow (1)

    A. Naomi's wrong decision (1:1-5)

    B. Naomi's wrong counsel (1:6-18)

    C. Naomi's wrong attitude (1:19-22)

II. Ruth's Service (2)

    A. God guides Ruth (2:1-3)

    B. Boaz shows kindness to Ruth (2:4-16)

    C. Naomi encourages Ruth (2:17-23)

III. Ruth's Surrender (3)

    A. She obeys Naomi's counsel (3:1-5)

    B. She submits to Boaz (3:6-13)

    C. She waits for Boaz to work (3:14-18)

IV. Ruth's Satisfaction (4)

    A. Boaz redeems Ruth (4:1-12)

    B. Boaz marries Ruth (4:13)

    C. Boaz and Ruth have a son (4:14-21)

# Introductory Notes to Ruth

## I. Background

It is difficult to believe that the events in this book took place during the time of the Judges, a time when Israel was a divided and defeated nation. But during the worst of times, God reveals His love and still works on behalf of those who fear and trust Him. We live today at a time when there is "no king in Israel" (Jud. 17:6; 18:1; 19:1; 21:25), for the Jews rejected their King; but during this time, a beautiful love story is taking place in this world: God is getting a Bride for His Son. The Book of Ruth is a harvest story, as the "Lord of the harvest" gathers His sheaves (John 4:31-38).

We aren't certain just where the story of Ruth fits into the history recorded in the Book of Judges. It's possible that the famine was caused by the ravages of one of the invading armies that God used to discipline His people. There must have been peace between Judah and Moab or Elimelech and his family would not have been able to move there. During the period of the Judges, peace was possible in one part of the land while there was trouble in another part.

## II. Theology

While the immediate purpose of this little book is to trace the ancestry of David the King, there is much spiritual truth found in this story. Ruth was from Moab, and the Moabites were excluded from the nation of Israel (Deut. 23:3). But because she put faith in the God of Israel, she was accepted, an illustration of God's grace to the Gentiles (Eph. 2:11-22). Boaz, the kinsman-redeemer, is a picture of our Lord Jesus Christ who paid the price to redeem us and make us His bride. The unknown kinsman was unwilling to jeopardize his inheritance for the sake of Ruth, but Boaz so loved Ruth that he made her a part of his inheritance! The grace of God and the providential leading of God are major themes of this story.

Ruth became an ancestress of the Messiah (Matt. 1:5) and of David, through whose line the Messiah was promised (2 Sam. 7). Like Rahab (Josh. 2; 6; Heb. 11:31), Ruth was a Gentile who married a Jew and became a part of "salvation history" (Matt. 1:5). This book may be a small one, but the story it tells is a part of the greatest story ever told.

## III. Practical Lessons

There are many lessons we can learn from this wonderful book:

(1) No matter how difficult the situation may be, if we surrender to the Lord and obey Him, He will see us through.

(2) No person is so far outside the reach of God's grace that he or she cannot be saved. Ruth had everything against her, but the Lord saved her!

(3) God providentially guides those who want to obey Him and serve others. Because Ruth was concerned for Naomi, God led her and brought her into a life of happiness.

(4) It does no good to get angry at God and blame Him for our mistakes. God used Ruth to lead Naomi out of despair and into His blessing.

(5) There are no "small decisions" with God. Ruth's decision to glean in the fields led to her becoming an ancestress of King David and of the Messiah. Read Ps. 37:3-7 and see how it is fulfilled in Ruth's experience.

(6) It is wise to wait on the Lord and let Him work out His loving purposes. "The one who trusts will never be dismayed" (Isa. 28:16, NIV). After we have done all that we can do, we must trust the Lord to do the rest; and He will never fail us.

# RUTH 1–4

This is the eighth book in the OT, and eight is the number of new beginning. The events in Ruth take place during the days of the Judges, but what a difference between these two books! Instead of violence and lawlessness, we see tenderness, love, and sacrifice. It is good to know that there are still good people in bad days, and that God is at work in the "corners of the land" though violence may fill the news. Ruth and Esther are the only OT books named after women. Ruth was a Gentile who married a Jew; Esther was a Jew who married a Gentile; but God used both of them to save the nation. Ruth is placed between Judges and Samuel for a definite reason. Judges shows the decline of the Jewish nation; Samuel shows the setting up of the Jewish kingdom; and Ruth pictures Christ and His bride. During this present age, when Israel is set aside, Christ is calling out His bride from among the Gentiles and the Jews. As we shall see, this brief book has a wonderful typical meaning. It is a love story and a harvest story, and that is what God is doing in our world today.

## I. Ruth's Sorrow (1)

### A. A wrong decision (vv. 1-5).

Why a famine should come to Bethlehem ("house of bread"), we do not know; possibly because of the sins of the people. Instead of trusting God in the land, Elimelech ("God is my king") and Naomi ("pleasantness") take their two sons to the land of Moab. Abraham made a similar mistake when he went to Egypt (Gen. 12:10ff). Better to starve in the will of God than to eat the enemy's bread! They plan to "sojourn" briefly, but instead they "continue" until the father and the two sons die. The names of the two sons may reflect the sorrow of their sojourn: Mahlon means "sickly" and Chilion means "pining." "To be carnally minded is death" (Rom. 8:6). Jews were not to mix with the Moabites (Deut. 23:3), so their wrong decision brought them the discipline of God.

### B. A wrong direction (vv. 6-18).

Backslidden Naomi desires to return home, but she is not wise enough to invite her daughters-in-law to accompany her! Beware of the advice of a carnal Christian. Imagine Naomi sending these women back to their heathen idols! She thought that (like her) their only interests were fleshly, but Ruth had higher desires than bread and marriage. Orpah returned to the old life, but Ruth "clung to her." She desired to follow the true God, Jehovah, and to abandon the old heathen life. "I will go!" was her steadfast decision, in spite of Naomi's unspiritual direction.

## C. A wrong disposition (vv. 19-22).

Their return home moved the city, for great changes had taken place in Naomi. Do we detect here a bitter spirit against the Lord? Is she blaming God for her sorrows? These verses certainly ought to warn the backslider of the great cost of getting out of the will of God. "Call me Mara—bitterness!" We shall see that God uses Ruth to change her mother-in-law's attitudes toward life and toward God.

## II. Ruth's Service (2)

Barley harvest was in April, and Ruth enters into the harvest as a poor gleaner; see Deut. 24:19-22 and Lev. 19:9ff. Note her dedication and determination: "Let me now go to the field" (v. 2); "Let me glean and gather" (v. 7); "Let me find favor" (v. 13). God leads in her choice of fields so that she comes face-to-face with the one man God had chosen to redeem her and marry her! "I being in the way, the Lord led me" (Gen. 24:27). God does not bless and guide lazy people; those who do the task at hand will find His direction. Boaz protects Ruth and provides for her long before he marries her, a perfect picture of our Lord. All of this comes from God's grace (v. 2), favor (v. 13), and kindness (v. 20). How good it is to see Naomi losing her bitterness. God was going to use the Gentile Ruth to restore Naomi's blessing again, just as God is saving Gentiles today and will one day restore Israel to her place of blessing.

## III. Ruth's Surrender (3)

Back in Moab, Naomi had told Ruth she would find rest among her own people (1:9), but now she realizes that there is rest only with the people of God and in the will of God. The time has come for Ruth to present her claims to Boaz and give him opportunity to be her kinsman-redeemer. The OT law provided that a kinsman could buy back an estate which had been lost through poverty (Lev. 25:23-55). This kept the land in the possession of the proper people. The kinsman, of course, had to be willing and able to redeem. Ruth followed the custom of the day and presented her case to Boaz: if he was to redeem her deceased husband's estate, he must also marry Ruth, the widow. Men often slept at the threshing floor to protect the grain. "Spread your skirt over your handmaid" (v. 9) was Ruth's legal claim to Boaz, asking him to be the kinsman-redeemer and claim her as his wife. Certainly it took faith and courage for her to take this step. Boaz rejoiced that this younger woman did not reject him because of his age, and he promised to fulfill the duty of a kinsman the next day. Note that he did not send her away empty-handed!

We can see in Ruth's actions a beautiful illustration of the believer's relationship to Christ. Certainly if we want fellowship with Him, we must be washed, anointed (the Holy Spirit), and clothed (v. 3). Our proper place is at His feet. It is "night" now, but we fellowship with Him until the morning comes (v. 13) and He claims His bride for Himself! As the result of our fellowship, we ought to have food to share with others (vv. 15-17).

## IV. Ruth's Satisfaction (4)

Another man in Bethlehem had prior claim on the estate, so Boaz approached him the next day. The man was anxious to claim the land, but he did not want Ruth! "I cannot marry her lest I mar my own inheritance!" How wonderful that Christ was willing to make us part of His inheritance and claim us as His bride! How unselfish was His love for us! The unnamed kinsman knew that any sons Ruth bore him would carry, not his name, but the name of her first husband (v. 5); and thus he would lose the estate the son would inherit. It was "a bad business deal" from his point of view; certainly he had no love for Ruth. Boaz was willing to pay any price to redeem the woman and her estate simply because he loved her. What a wonderful picture of Christ and His love for the church!

We now discover the significance of this book: Ruth becomes an ancestress of David. Deuteronomy 23:3 excludes a Moabite from the congregation of Israel "even to the tenth generation"; but the grace of God makes Ruth the Moabitess a member of the earthly family that gave Christ to the world (Matt. 1:3-6, and note the mention of Tamar and Bathsheba, further proof of the grace of God).

This book begins with a funeral and ends with a wedding! It opens with famine and closes with fullness! Ruth's love for her mother-in-law and her willingness to obey the Word brought her into joy and blessing. The decision she made in chapter 1 determined her future. Had she gone back to her heathen way of life, she would have been heard of no more. Note, in closing, some special lessons:

## A. Prophetical.

Chapter 1 shows Israel out of the will of God and suffering His chastening. But then God begins to deal with a Gentile (Ruth), just as today He is calling out from the Gentiles a people for His name (Acts 15:14). Naomi's blessing came after Ruth's wedding, just as Israel will be restored and blessed after Christ and His church are united.

## B. Typical.

Certainly Boaz is a picture of Christ, our Kinsman-Redeemer. Christ took upon Him our flesh (without sin, of course) that He might redeem us. He paid the price, and He did it because He loved us. Like Boaz, He is the Lord of the harvest; He supplies our needs; He redeems the inheritance for us; He gives rest.

## C. Practical.

Backsliding is a serious matter; it cost Naomi her husband and her sons. No matter how difficult the circumstances may be, the only place for God's people is in the will of God. When we seek satisfaction from the world, we pay a high price. However, God is willing to forgive backsliders and restore them to favor. Naomi could never regain the lost time out of God's will, but she did regain her joy and testimony.

# Introductory Notes to the Historical Books

## I. Theme

Samuel, Kings, and Chronicles are books of history that record the establishment of the kingdom, its years of victory and defeat, and the end of a divided kingdom. One lesson is obvious as you read these books: "Righteousness exalts a nation, but sin is a reproach to any people" (Prov. 14:34). Whenever the nation exalted God, God exalted the nation; but when the rulers, prophets, and people turned from the Law, God removed His blessing.

This truth is seen not only in the history of the nation collectively, but also in the lives of the leaders personally. Both David and Solomon disobeyed God and paid dearly in their own homes and personal lives.

## II. The Prophets

In a period of spiritual decline, God sent His prophets to awaken the people. There are several "unnamed prophets" in these books, as well as famous servants of God such as Elijah and Elisha, Isaiah, Joel, Amos, Jonah, and Micah. Be sure to check your Bible dictionary or Bible handbook for the parallels between the lives of the prophets and the history of the nation.

## III. The Books of Samuel

These books record the transition from the period of judges to the time when the kingdom was established. Samuel was the last of the judges and the first of the national prophets. It was he who anointed Saul the first king, and then David his successor. You may outline the books together as follows:

A. Samuel (1 Sam. 1–7)
1. Birth and childhood (1–3)
2. Early ministry (4–7)
B. Saul (1 Sam. 8–15)
1. Made king (8–10)
2. Early victories (11–12)
3. Sins and rejection (13–15)

C. David (1 Sam. 16–2 Sam. 24)
1. The shepherd (1 Sam. 16–17)
2. The servant (1 Sam. 18–19)
3. The exile (1 Sam. 20–31)
4. The King (2 Sam. 1–24)
   a. His triumphs (2 Sam. 1–12)
   b. His trials (2 Sam. 13–24)
      i. Personal sin (11–12)
      ii. Amnon's sin (13)
      iii. Absalom's sin (14–18)
      iv. National unrest (19–24)

## IV. The Books of Kings

These books, as the title indicates, deal with the kings of the nation, beginning with the glorious reign of Solomon and ending with the tragic captivity of Judah by Babylon. We may outline the books as follows:

A. The Kingdom United (1 Kings 1–11)
1. Solomon's wealth and wisdom (1–4)
2. Solomon's temple (5–9)
3. Solomon's sins (10–11)

B. The Kingdom Divided (1 Kings 12–22)
1. Rehoboam and Jeroboam (12–14)
2. A series of good and bad kings (15–16)
3. Elijah and King Ahab (17–22)

C. The Kingdom Taken Captive (2 Kings 1–25)
1. Israel's captivity (1–17)
2. Judah's captivity (18–25)

## V. The Books of Chronicles

First and Second Kings were written before the captivity of Judah and seem to emphasize a prophet's point of view, while 1 and 2 Chronicles were written after the captivity (1 Chron. 6:15) and seem to have a priest's point of view. These books remind us that "righteousness exalts a nation, but sin is a reproach to any people"

(Prov. 14:34, NKJV). Sin was a special reproach to the Jews because they were God's people and were graciously called by God to a life of holiness (Ex. 19–20). God would have destroyed the nation much sooner except for His covenant with David and His promise to keep a descendant of David on the throne in Jerusalem. The ultimate fulfillment of that promise is in Jesus Christ, the "Son of David" (Matt. 1:1), who will one day establish the throne of David (Luke 1:26-33) and rule from Jerusalem.

We have covered much of the history of Saul, David, Solomon, and the important kings in our outlines on 1 and 2 Samuel and 1 and 2 Kings. Here, we will focus on the material that is found exclusively in 1 and 2 Chronicles. The new events in these two books parallel and supplement what is given in Samuel and Kings. For this reason we will focus on material found exclusively in 1 and 2 Chronicles.

I. Genealogies from Adam to King Saul (1 Chron. 1–9)

II. The reign of King David (1 Chron. 10–29)

    A. The death of King Saul (10)

    B. David solidifies his kingdom (11–16)

    C. God's covenant with David (17)

    D. David expands the kingdom (18–20)

    E. David numbers the people (21)

    F. David prepares for the building of the temple (22–29) (The death of David)

III. The reign of King Solomon (2 Chron. 1–9)

    A. Solomon receives God's blessing (1)

    B. Solomon builds and dedicates the temple (2–7)

    C. Solomon's fame and splendor (8–9)

IV. The divided kingdom (The kings of Judah) (10-36)

    A. The reign of Rehoboam (10–12)

    B. From Abijah to Asa (13–16)

    C. The reign of Jehoshaphat (17–20)

D. From Jehoram to Amaziah (21–25)
E. The reign of Uzziah (26)
F. The reigns of Jotham and Ahaz (27–28)
G. The reign of Hezekiah (29–32)
H. The reigns of Manasseh and Amon (33)
I. The reign of Josiah (34–35)
J. The last kings and the downfall of Judah (36)

# 1 SAMUEL 1–3

The events in these opening chapters of the book center around three persons.

## I. Hannah—A Godly Mother (1:1–2:11)

### A. Her sorrow (1:1-10).

While God's perfect pattern for the family from the very beginning had been one husband and one wife, "because of the hardness of men's hearts" (Matt. 19:8), God permitted polygamy. See Deut. 21:15-17. Elkanah was a godly man but he had a divided home, and his favorite wife, Hannah ("grace"), carried a constant burden of sorrow because of her barrenness and because of the persecution of the other wife.

### B. Her supplication (1:11-19).

Hannah was a woman of prayer, so it is no surprise to find her son Samuel a great man of prayer. So burdened was her heart that Hannah left the feast without eating and went to the tabernacle to pray. (The world "temple" in 1:9 simply means "a large public building" and does not refer to Solomon's temple which had not yet been built.) Hannah did not "bargain" with the Lord; rather, she proved her spirituality by willingly offering God her best—her firstborn son. Verse 21 suggests that her husband agreed with the vow; see also Num. 30:6-16. The Nazarite regulations are found in Num. 6. Eli, the High Priest, certainly judged Hannah severely (Matt. 7:1-5), especially considering that his own sons were "sons of Belial [Satan]" (see 2:12).

### C. Her surrender (1:20-28).

God answered Hannah's prayers and sent a son, so she named him Samuel, "asked of the Lord." Jewish women weaned their children at about the age of three; at that time Hannah took Samuel to Eli and fulfilled her vow to the Lord. The three bullocks were probably for the sin offering, burnt offering, and special offering for the Nazarite vow; see Num. 15:8. "For this child I prayed." What a testimony from a godly mother! See 2 Tim. 1:5. If we had more parents like Elkanah and Hannah, we would have more godly people like Samuel. "Lent" means "given"; Samuel belonged to the Lord for the rest of his life.

## D. Her son (2:1-11).

While Elkanah was worshiping (1:28), his wife was praying and praising God. Compare this passage with Mary's song in Luke 1:46-55. In both cases, the women praise God for His victory and for honoring the prayers of the humble. Note the two names of Christ in 2:10—"His King" and "His Anointed" (Messiah, Christ)—for Hannah's burden was for the glory of the Lord among His people. Hannah certainly exemplifies a godly mother, for she put God first, she believed in prayer, she kept her vows, and she gave God all the glory.

## II. Eli—A Careless Father (2:12-36)

### A. His sinful sons (vv. 12-21).

How tragic when a servant of the Lord (and a high priest at that) fails to win his own sons to the Lord! These sons of Eli were selfish, for they put their own desires ahead of the Word of God and the needs of the people; they were overbearing; and they were lustful (2:22). Philippians 3:17-19 is a perfect description of these ungodly priests. Note the repetition of the word *flesh*. Note too the contrast between Eli's sons and young Samuel in v. 18: "But Samuel. . . ." No doubt Eli's sons laughed at young Samuel and ridiculed him for his faithful ministry; but God was going to step in and settle accounts before long.

### B. His selfish disobedience (vv. 22-26).

Eli refused to face facts honestly and obey the Word of God; see Deut. 21:18-21 and 17:12. In 3:13 God states clearly that Eli refused to restrain his sons; instead, he pampered them. His weak warning in 2:23-25 was certainly no substitute for definite discipline. Compare 2:26 with Luke 2:52.

### C. His severe judgment (vv. 27-36).

God in His grace sent a severe message to Eli by the mouth of an unknown man of God, warning him that his family would suffer because of the sins of his sons and because of his own carelessness. He honored his sons above the Lord (v. 29); this was idolatry. Eli had not been jealous for the glory of the Lord, so God had to remove him. In later years, Saul killed many of Eli's descendants (1 Sam. 22:17-20); and later Solomon replaced Eli's family with the family of Zadok (1 Kings 2:26-27, 35). Of course, the "faithful priest" of v. 35 refers immediately to Samuel, but ultimately to Christ. Verse 34 predicts the death of Eli's two sons; see 4:17-18 for the fulfillment.

## III. Samuel—A Devoted Son (3)

### A. His call from the Lord (vv. 1-10).

Tradition states that Samuel was about twelve years old at this time. He had grown up in the presence of the Lord and learned to serve in His tabernacle, yet he did not have a personal experience with the Lord (v. 7). How important it is for those who are raised in Christian homes to make their own personal decisions for Christ. Samuel had filled the lampstand with oil; it was close to daybreak and the lamp was about to go out. Samuel was sleeping and the Lord called him. He first thought was that blind Eli needed his help, so he ran to him. (See how quick this boy was to obey when called.) Verse 10 (NKJV) records Samuel's conversation: "Speak, Lord, for your servant hears." Later on, God would say to Samuel, "Speak servant, for your Lord hears!" For Samuel became a great man of prayer.

### B. His message from the Lord (vv. 11-14).

The person who surrenders to the Lord and is willing to listen will always learn God's will. Eli had disobeyed the Lord and put his family first, so God could not speak directly to him. It was a message of judgment on Eli's house, and it must have weighed heavily upon Samuel's heart. Samuel loved Eli and had learned much from him, but Samuel knew he must be true to the Lord in spite of his personal desires.

### C. His message to Eli (vv. 15-21).

This tremendous spiritual experience did not keep Samuel from doing his daily tasks the next morning. He did not "parade" himself before the people; no, he walked in great humility, carrying within his heart the burden of the Lord. Just as he had said "Here am I" to the Lord, so he replied "Here am I" when Eli called him. Those who honor the Lord will also honor their elders. Samuel would rather keep the sad message in his own heart, but Eli asked him to tell him all; so he did. While we do not admire Eli's failure with his own family, we do admire his resignation to God's will even though it meant death to him and his sons.

This event was a turning point in history. Up to now, God had not spoken to the people in frequent or wide-spread ("open") visions (v. 1); but now everyone knew that Samuel was God's prophet and that the Lord was with him. The Lord was now able to appear once again because there was a servant whom He could trust. Certainly God would do more for His people even today if He could find devoted believers willing to be His servants.

Several practical lessons are found in these chapters:

1. Never underestimate the power of sin in a family. Eli's sons needed discipline, but he pampered them instead. This cost him his life, and eventually cost the family the priesthood.

2. Never underestimate the power of prayer in a home. Hannah and Elkanah were people of prayer, and God answered their prayers. We are blessed today because of the dedication of Hannah, for through her, God gave the world Samuel, the last of the judges and the first of the national prophets.

3. God speaks to children and young people, and adults should make it easy for them to hear God's voice and respond in faith. How wise Eli was to know that God was calling young Samuel. The training of children in spiritual things is a great responsibility that we must not neglect.

# 1 SAMUEL 4–7

These chapters relate three great events in the history of Israel.

## I. God's Glory Is Departed (4)

### A. A great sin (vv. 1-5).

Israel lost 4,000 men in the first battle, and this should have been evidence to them that God was displeased. Did they repent and turn to God in prayer and confession? No! Instead they resorted to superstition and took the ark of the covenant to the battlefield. They could not take the ark out in faith because God had not commanded them by His Word. They were acting by chance and not by faith. Because the ark had gone before the nation in the wilderness and had marched in victory around Jericho, they thought its presence would assure them victory over the Philistines. Instead of revering the ark as the symbol of God's presence, they turned it into a religious relic! See Num. 10:35ff.

## B. A great slaughter (vv. 6-10).

The Philistines were first afraid, then determined; even if the God of Israel were in the camp, they were going to behave like brave soldiers! Since God had forsaken His people, the Philistines had an easy victory. Psalm 78:56ff is a vivid description of this tragedy. Israel should have known that God's presence with them depended upon their obedience to His Word. Hophni and Phinehas were ungodly priests; their presence brought judgment, not blessing.

## C. A great sorrow (vv. 11-22).

Eli, the ninety-eight-year-old blind priest, was sitting by the wayside when the messenger arrived at Shiloh with the sad news; but the messenger ran right past him and announced his message to the city. The uproar in the city aroused Eli's curiosity, for no doubt he was expecting the fulfillment of Samuel's prophecy (3:11-14; 2:34-35). Note how the messenger gives the four pieces of bad news in order of their importance: Israel is fled; many have been slaughtered; Eli's two sons are dead; and the ark has been captured by the enemy. Verse 13 tells us that the safety of the ark had been Eli's greatest concern. Now we see sorrow upon sorrow: Eli falls down in a state of shock, breaks his neck, and dies; and his daughter-in-law likewise loses her life as she delivers a son. The name "Ichabod" means "no glory" or "Where is the glory?" See Ex. 40:34ff. The word "departed" may be translated "gone into exile." Israel's history is a story of receiving and then losing the glory of God.

## II. God's Name Is Defended (5–6)

### A. Before the heathen (chap. 5).

God will not reveal His power on behalf of His sinning people, but He will not allow His glory to be mocked or His Name to be defiled by a smirking enemy. The lords of the Philistines added the ark to their other religious relics in their heathen temple and put Jehovah on the same level as their fish-god Dagon. Of course, God stands high above all other gods! No wonder the heathen idol fell on its face before the ark! See Isa. 19:1. The men put Dagon back on his feet because he was powerless to help himself; but the next day they found their beloved idol without hands and head! Jehovah had proved Dagon to be a false god; He had vindicated His Name. Dagon lost his hands, but the hand of the Lord was heavy in judgment upon Ashdod (v. 6); God sent boils ("emerods," swellings) and mice (6:4) to plague the people. The mice ruined the crops and carried disease germs to the people. The ark was then moved from Ashdod to Ekron, but the citizens there begged to have it removed! Once again, God defended His name.

### B. Before the Israelites (chap. 6).

The Philistines decided to return the ark to Israel, but nobody had the courage to undertake the task. They finally decided to put the ark on a new cart and allow the cows to walk down the road unassisted. It would be natural for the cows to seek out their calves (v. 10); but if they headed instead for Bethshemesh, it would be evidence that God was directing them and therefore that He had sent the plagues. The Philistines added a trespass offering too: five images of the boils, and five images of the mice. God directed the cows and they brought the cart to the field of Joshua, an inhabitant of Bethshemesh. The Israelites in the harvest field rejoiced to see the ark returned. However, they became curious and looked into the ark (vv. 19-20), and God had to judge them. The numbers in v. 19 have created a problem, for there were not 50,000 people in that little village. In Hebrew, letters are used for numbers, and it is easy for a scribe to miscopy or misread a letter. It is likely that seventy men were judged instantly, certainly a "great slaughter" for such a small village. The problem does not affect anything crucial. It is important that we know God did judge their sin. How many were slain is not a vital matter.

Hophni and Phinehas thought they could win victories by trusting the ark when their lives were wicked, and God killed them. Eli died because he had not disciplined his own sons who were dishonoring the Lord. The Philistines died because they treated Jehovah like one of their own gods. The men of Bethshemesh died because they presumptuously looked into the ark. It does not pay to trifle with God.

### III. God's People Are Delivered (7)

The ark was not returned to Shiloh; it remained at the house of Abinadab for twenty years. What was God doing during this time? He was preparing His servant Samuel to defeat the enemy and establish the kingdom. No doubt Samuel was ministering to the people from place to place, giving them the Word of God. Verse 3 indicates that Samuel called the people to repent and return to the Lord. This meant putting away the gods of the heathen, and then preparing their hearts to serve the Lord. How tragic that the great nation of Israel had fallen into defeat and disrepute because of their sins! Had Eli been a faithful father and his sons faithful priests, this defeat would never have occurred. Baalim and Ashtaroth represented male and female deities. Their worship was celebrated with ceremonies of abominable filth.

Samuel summoned the nation to Mizpeh for a prayer meeting! Samuel must always be associated with prayer; see 12:23. He was born in answer to his mother's prayers (chap. 1); he prayed for his nation and defeated the enemy (7:13); he prayed when Israel defied the Lord and asked for a king (8:6); and he prayed for King Saul (15:11) even after God had rejected him. Someone has called Samuel "God's Emergency Man," and the name surely fits. Samuel stepped on the scene when the priesthood was decayed, when the nation was defeated, and when God's glory had departed. Certainly Hannah must have realized how wonderfully God would use her son; see her song (and prediction) in 2:9-10.

The events at Mizpeh were these: (1) Samuel poured out water before the Lord as a symbol of the nation's repentance, their hearts poured out in sorrow for their sins; (2) He offered a burnt offering to indicate Israel's complete dedication to God; (3) He prayed for the nation while they were fearing the arrival of the Philistines; God gave the army of Israel a great victory. What a day that was! Samuel accomplished with one prayer a victory that Samson could not win during the entire twenty years of his leadership! From that day on (until David's great victory over the Philistines), the enemy kept their distance. Such is the power of a dedicated life, the power of prayer (James 5:16).

Samuel had a ministry as prophet and judge, traveling from city to city to minister to the people and settle their disputes. He was the last of the judges and the first of the national prophets. (Moses' prophetic office was of a different nature.) It is sad to see that Samuel's sons did not follow in their father's godly walk (8:5). Perhaps he was too busy with the affairs of the nation to train them. Eli had made a similar mistake.

These events show us the importance of a godly home. The nation fell into sin and defeat because Eli had neglected his home; but God saved the nation because of the prayers of a godly mother (Hannah) and her God-given son. As go the homes, so goes the nation.

# 1 SAMUEL 8–15

These chapters cover the early life of Saul and record the sins that led up to his rejection by the Lord.

## I. The Request for a King (8–10)

Jehovah God had been King of Israel and had cared for the nation since its beginning; but now the elders of the nation wanted a king to lead them. Their request was motivated by several factors: (1) Samuel's sons were not godly and the elders feared that they would lead the nation astray when Samuel died; (2) the nation had been through a series of temporary leaders during the period of the Judges, and the elders wanted a more permanent ruler; and (3) Israel wanted to be like the other nations and have a king to honor. The powerful nations around Israel were a constant threat, and the elders felt that a king would give greater security. Samuel's reaction to their request shows that he fully understood their unbelief and rebellion: they were rejecting Jehovah. In choosing Saul, the nation rejected the Father; much later in choosing Barabbas, they rejected the Son; and when they chose their own leaders instead of the witness of the Apostles, they rejected the Holy Spirit (Acts 7:51).

Here is an illustration of God's permissive will: He granted them their request, but He warned them of the cost. See Deut. 17:14-20 for Moses' prophecy of this event. The nation listened to Samuel and then asked for a king just the same! They wanted to be like the other nations, even though God had called them to be separate from the nations. Chapter 9 explains how Saul was brought to Samuel and privately anointed for the kingship. Note his humility in 9:21, and also in 10:22 when he hesitated to stand before the people. God gave Saul three special signs to assure him (10:1-7). Samuel also instructed Saul to tarry at Gilgal and wait for him to come (10:8). Verse 8 should be translated, "When you go before me to Gilgal"—that is, at some future date when King Saul would have the army ready for battle. This event took place some years later; see chap. 13.

Saul had everything in his favor: (1) a strong body, 10:23; (2) a humble mind, 9:21; (3) a new heart, 10:9; (4) spiritual power, 10:10; (5) loyal friends, 10:26; and most of all, (6) the guidance and prayers of Samuel. Yet in spite of these advantages, he failed miserably. Why? Because he would not allow God to be the Lord of his life.

## II. The Renewal of the Kingdom (11–12)

Saul returned home and was actually hesitant to talk about his great experience. Keep in mind that this was at the beginning of the kingdom when everything was new. Samuel was still the spiritual ruler of the land, and he and Saul were waiting for God's leading concerning the future of the nation. Without modern means of transportation or communication, it would take months for Saul and Samuel to rally the people. Saul's first opportunity came when Nahash threatened the nation. Certainly this national victory put Saul before the people and established his authority. Some of his associates wanted Saul to kill those Israelites who had opposed his reign (10:27), but Saul showed humility and restraint by giving the glory to the Lord and refusing to take vengeance on others.

This victory was the occasion for a renewal of the kingdom and a rededication of the nation. Samuel reviewed his own ministry and reminded the people that he had been faithful to them and to the Lord. He then reviewed the history of the nation and led the people to see that they had greatly sinned against the Lord by asking for a king. He called for rain to show the people his own faith and the power of God, and the sudden storm in harvest (an unusual event at that time of the year) brought fear to the people. They admitted their sin and Samuel reassured them of God's grace. They needed to know that their king was not going to save them; it would be their own faithfulness and obedience to the Lord that would assure them of God's blessings. They had made a mistake, but God would overrule if they would obey.

## III. The Rejection of the King (13–15)

These three chapters record three sins of King Saul, sins that ultimately cost him the kingdom.

### A. Impatience (chap. 13).

The time had now come for Israel to gather at Gilgal as Samuel and Saul had agreed months before (10:8). Note how Saul took the credit for his son's victory at Gibeah in order to impress the people and get them to follow him. The vast host of the Philistines began to assemble, and the longer Saul waited, the more dangerous his position became. If he were to strike immediately, he could defeat the enemy, but his delay only gave them opportunity to become stronger. Saul's impatience (and unbelief) led him to go ahead without Samuel, and while Saul was completing the offering, the prophet appeared. Verses 11-12 record Saul's excuses as he tried to put the blame on Samuel and the people. "I forced myself!" he told Samuel, but the prophet knew the truth. This was the beginning of the end: if God could not trust him in this little matter, how could He trust him with the kingdom? Saul's impatience cost him the kingdom.

## B. Pride (chap. 14).

Jonathan, Saul's son, was evidently a godly man; for the Lord gave him and his armorbearer a victory over the Philistines. Saul was only a spectator (vv. 16-18), but he then mustered his troops and shared in the victory. Unfortunately, however, Saul had uttered a foolish vow that day forbidding his soldiers to eat any food. How foolish to think that a sacrificial vow would give him victory when his heart was not right with God! He was later to learn, "To obey is better than to sacrifice." Jonathan knew nothing about this curse, so he went ahead and ate some honey and was strengthened (v. 27), and his example of practical wisdom encouraged the army to go ahead and eat after their victory (vv. 31-32). Alas, the Jews were so hungry they ate the meat with the blood (Lev. 17:10-14), which was far worse than breaking the vow. Saul tried to amend this by offering the spoils as a sacrifice to God. When the army went to their next engagement, they sought the guidance of God but failed to get an answer. This led to Saul's discovery of Jonathan's disobedience, and the foolish king was going to kill his own son! How easy it is to be convicted about somebody else's sins! The people rescued Jonathan, but Saul's actions revealed the darkness of his heart. Trouble was soon to come. His pride would bring him low.

## C. Disobedience (chap. 15).

God would give Saul one more chance to prove himself, this time by utterly destroying Israel's old enemies, the Amalekites (Deut. 25:17-19; Ex. 17:16). But Saul did not obey the Lord: he kept the best of the spoils for himself and failed to kill Agag, the king. God told Samuel what Saul had done, and the burdened prophet prayed all night. When Samuel approached Saul, the king lied to him and told him he had obeyed God's Word. Just about that time Saul's sins found him out, for the animals began to make noise. Once more, Saul resorted to excuses: "They" (the people) saved the animals, but "we" (himself and the leaders) have utterly destroyed the rest. Then Samuel delivered God's message to the rejected king: Saul had lost his early humility (9:21) and became proud and disobedient; he had rebelled against the Word of the Lord and had tried to make up for his disobedience by sacrifices (vv. 21-23). Saul had substituted saying for doing (15:13); excuses for confessions (15:15 and 21); and sacrifice for obedience (v. 22). He was too quick to criticize and blame others; he was unwilling to face and judge his own sins.

When Samuel was about to leave Saul, the king confessed his sins, but his confession did not impress the prophet (vv. 24-27). True confession involves more than saying "I have sinned"; it means repentance and true sorrow for sin. As Samuel turned away, Saul held to his robe and ripped it, and Samuel took this as a prophecy that the kingdom would be torn from Saul and given to another (David). Verse 30 reveals that Saul was more concerned about what the people thought than what God thought; he wanted a good reputation, but he did not want true character. Samuel worshiped with Saul, and then killed Agag as the Lord had commanded, but this was the last time Samuel walked with Saul. Saul had lost his best friend; he had lost the Lord's blessing; he had lost the kingdom. From now on, he would be on a dark, winding road that would end with him becoming a castaway and being slain by one of the very Amalekites he had refused to destroy (2 Sam. 1:13).

# 1 SAMUEL 16–17

We enter now into a study of the life of David, "the man after God's own heart." As Saul is a picture of the carnal life, so David is a picture of the spiritual life of the believer who walks by faith in the Lord. It is true that David sinned. Unlike Saul, however, David confessed his sins and sought to restore his fellowship with God. We see in these chapters three scenes in David's early life.

### I. The Obedient Son (16:1-13)

What a solemn statement: "I have rejected Saul!" This rejection was not yet known to the people, and Saul was still "putting on a front" as the king of the land. A person may be rejected by God and still be accepted by men, but ultimately God's judgment will fall. So dangerous was Saul that Samuel had to devise a plan to escape his wrath when visiting Bethlehem. See 22:17-19 for a sample of Saul's jealous rage.

When, at God's direction, Samuel arrived at the house of Jesse to invite them to the feast, David was not even there! He was in the fields caring for the sheep. We cannot help but be impressed with David's obedience and humility. As the "baby of the family" he had very little status, but he was faithful to his father and to the Lord. David's life illustrates Matt. 25:21 — he began as a servant and became a ruler; he was faithful with a few sheep and then inherited the whole nation; he knew how to work, so God gave him joy. Compare this to the Prodigal Son in Luke 15, who began as a leader and ended as a servant; began owning many things and ended up poor; and started with pleasure but finished in slavery. Matthew 25:21 outlines God's method of success, and we see it proved in the life of David.

Samuel was about to make the mistake of evaluating the men by their physical gifts (see 10:24) when God reminded him that the heart was the important thing. Read Prov. 4:23. When David appeared, summoned from the field, God told Samuel, "This is he!" David was fair of skin, and he had red hair. His handsome appearance and his surrendered heart were a wonderful combination. He was the eighth son, and eight is the number of new beginning. His anointing with oil brought him a special unction from the Spirit of God, and from that hour he was God's man. It is not likely that David or his family understood the significance of the anointing that day. Samuel would certainly explain it to David at an opportune time.

## II. The Humble Servant (16:14-23)

What a tragic contrast: the Spirit came upon David, but departed from Saul! An evil spirit was permitted by God to afflict Saul and he became, at times, like a madman. See 18:10 and 19:9. His strange behavior prompted his servants to suggest that he call a skilled musician to soothe him. How sad that Saul's servants dealt with the symptoms and not with the causes, for music could never change Saul's sinful heart. True, the king might "feel better" afterward, but it would be a false peace. The servants should have prayed for Saul to get right with God!

David was just the man Saul needed, and one of the servants suggested him. Already we can see David's abilities being recognized, yet David was not promoting himself: God was doing it. Read carefully Prov. 22:29; also 1 Peter 5:6. Too many young people today try to push themselves into prominent places without first proving themselves at home in the small matters. David came to court and immediately became a favorite. Of course, had Saul known that God had chosen David to be king, he would have immediately tried to kill the lad. When he did discover this, Saul began to persecute David and hunt him in the wilds of Israel.

David did not remain permanently at court; 17:15 should read, "But David went back and forth from Saul to feed his father's sheep." He would visit the court when needed, but he did not neglect his responsibilities at home. What humility! Here is a gifted lad, chosen to be king, anointed of God, yet he still cares for the sheep and works as a servant! No wonder God was able to use David.

## III. The Victorious Soldier (17)

The story of David and Goliath is familiar and carries with it many practical lessons for the Christian life. All of us face giants of one kind or another, but we may overcome them through the power of God. Goliath was probably ten feet tall, with armor weighing over 150 pounds. He was "the Philistine" (17:8), their great champion, and so terrifying was he that he threw the Jewish army into panic (v. 11). Had Saul been a godly leader, he would have claimed Deut. 20 and led his army to victory; but when people are out of fellowship with God, they can only lead others into defeat.

David arrived with provisions for his brothers, and immediately he was interested in the challenge of the giant. Note that his own brethren accused him and tried to discourage him; Satan always has somebody to tell us "it can't be done." Even Saul tried to dissuade him: "You are not able" (v. 33, NKJV). Well, in himself, David was not able, but in the power of the Lord he could overcome any enemy. (See Phil. 4:13; Eph. 3:20-21.) Saul tried to give David some armor, but since he had not proved it, David refused the armor. Imagine Saul telling somebody else how to have victory! David had proved the power of God privately in the fields caring for his sheep; now he would demonstrate this power publicly to the glory of God. Note how throughout this entire episode, David gives glory to the Lord.

The practical lesson here is that God gives victory in response to our faith. God had tested David privately with a lion and a bear; now he was to test him openly with a giant. If we are faithful in the private battles, God will see us through the public testings. Too often God's people faint at the smallest test that comes their way, little realizing that the "little tests" are but preparation for the bigger battles that are sure to come (Jer. 12:5). David used simple, humble weapons: a sling and five stones (see 1 Cor. 1:27-28 and 2 Cor. 10:3-5). David knew how Gideon was given victory with weak weapons, and he knew that Gideon's God was not dead. Neither his brothers' criticism nor Saul's unbelief kept David from trusting God for victory. The stone hit its mark; the giant fell down, and David used the giant's own sword to cut off his head! This one victory opened the way for Israel to attack the Philistines and spoil their camp. "And this is the victory that has overcome the world—our faith" (1 John 5:4, NKJV). We are "more than conquerors"!

There is also a typical lesson here, for David is a picture of Jesus Christ. David's name means "beloved," and Christ is God's beloved Son. Both were born in Bethlehem. Both were rejected by their brethren. (Of course, when David became king, his brethren received him, just as the Jews will receive Christ when He returns to reign.) David was anointed king years before he was permitted to reign, just as Christ is King now but will not reign on earth until Satan is banished. King Saul typifies Satan in this present age; for Saul was rejected and defeated, yet permitted to reign until David came to the throne. Satan is permitted to persecute God's people, yet one day he will be defeated.

Just as David was sent by his father to the battlefield, so Christ was sent by the Father to this world. Goliath illustrates Satan in his pride and power. Read carefully Luke 11:14-23. Satan is the strong man guarding his goods (people under his control), and Christ is the Stronger Man who overcomes him. Christ invaded Satan's kingdom, overcame his power, took his armor, and now is dividing his spoils by saving lost souls and making them children of God. This is what David did that day: he overcame the strong man and allowed Israel to divide the spoils (vv. 52-54). We Christians do not simply fight *for* victory, we fight *from* victory, the victory won at the cross (Col. 2:15). "Be of good cheer," said Jesus, "I have overcome (John 16:33)."

Why Saul did not recognize David, his own armorbearer, is not made clear. It is likely that he saw David when under the influence of the evil spirit. Another factor is that David would be but one of several servants at the court, and it would not be unusual for Saul to confuse them. Since Saul had promised his daughter to the victor, he would certainly ask about the boy's family.

# 1 SAMUEL 18–21

These chapters form the transition between David's service in Saul's court and his exile as a fugitive. They explain how David was moved from being Saul's favorite to being Saul's foe. The main issue is David's faith, and we can see in these chapters how this man of God all but lost his confidence in God because of the trials that came to his life.

## I. David Trusts the Lord (18)
David's greatest test of faith was not when he faced Goliath; it was when he had to serve daily in Saul's court. Note the different ways his faith was tested:

### A. By popularity (vv. 18:1-11).

David was beloved by Jonathan, Saul's son, and this in itself was an opportunity for testing. David would be the next king, but, by rights, Jonathan should inherit the crown. The friendship between these two men of God is a great example for us. Certainly there was no jealousy on Jonathan's part because of the honor bestowed upon David. However, with Saul it was another matter, for David was popular with the people. The fact that the women praised David and not David's God is significant. David was wise enough not to put too much stock in their words. But Saul's heart filled with envy when he heard that David had more praise than he did. "As the fining pot for silver, and the furnace for gold; so is a man to his praise" (Prov. 27:21). Praise is like a hot furnace: it reveals what a person is really made of. The praise that made David humble only brought the dross to the top in Saul's heart and revealed his pride and desire for glory.

### B. By demotion (vv. 18:12-16).

Verse 5 suggests that David was the head of Saul's personal body-guard, but now he is demoted to being merely the captain over one thousand men. Did this change David? No! His faith was in the Lord, and he continued to serve and honor his king. This made Saul all the more afraid! The king knew that God had departed from him and had given blessings to David. It takes real faith to experience a demotion before the eyes of the people and still maintain your humility and service.

### C. By disappointment (vv. 17-30).

Saul had promised one of his daughters to the man who defeated Goliath (17:25), and now he was going to fulfill his promise. Note David's humility before the king in v. 18. But, did Saul keep his word? No! The woman was given to another man. Then Saul tried to use his daughter Michal as a tool to slay David; for the king demanded an impossible dowry, hoping that David would be killed in trying to obtain it. But the Lord was with David, and he completed the mission successfully. It is unfortunate that he did marry Michal, for the union was never a happy one. While in exile, David lost Michal to another man (25:44), but he gained her back when he started to reign at Hebron (2 Sam. 3:13-16). Her attitude toward David led to a complete separation later (2 Sam. 6:20-23).

## II. David Trusts Men (19)

Saul's plan to murder David was no longer a secret, for now the king's servants were commanded to slay him. But Saul had been unable to kill David in previous attempts (18:11, 25), and now it appeared that his anger was spent and David could return to the court. Here we see David's faith wavering, for instead of trusting God and seeking His will, he trusts in human beings.

### A. He trusts Jonathan (vv. 1-10).

Certainly the king's son could intercede for David. Saul even swore that he would protect David, but these promises were never fulfilled. No sooner did David win a great victory on the battlefield than Saul's old envy returned, and he threw the spear again. David made a mistake trusting Jonathan to "patch things up" for him. Saul's heart needed to be changed before his words would be trustworthy.

### B. He trusts Michal (vv. 11-17).

Though his wife loved David, there was never a strong spiritual tie between the two, as her later actions proved. She warned David that Saul was watching him, so together they concocted a lie. This was the beginning of serious trouble for David, for it is never right to do evil that good may come of it (Rom. 3:8). Note that Michal used an idol to give the impression that David was sick in bed! She was now deceiving her own father and only making matters worse. Read Ps. 59 for additional insight into this situation.

## C. He trusts Samuel (vv. 18-24).

This perhaps was the wisest move David made, for this man of God would be able to pray for him and counsel him. Note that Samuel defeated Saul, not with lies or weapons, but with the Spirit of God. By using spiritual weapons, Samuel delayed Saul and gave David opportunity to get away.

## III. David Trusts Himself (20–21)

These chapters do not record a very beautiful picture, for in them we see the man of faith faltering and failing in his faith. Instead of waiting to seek the Lord's will, David flees in fear and tries to "scheme" his way out of his problems. Note the lies he tells.

## A. He lied to Saul (chap. 20).

David's speech to Jonathan in 20:1 suggests self-centeredness and impatience. How much better it would have been had these two friends prayed together instead of hatching their scheme. Jonathan lied to his father about David's whereabouts (vv. 6, 28), but he had to wait a few days to see how the matter would end. Meanwhile, he and David made a covenant together that David would protect Jonathan's family when he became king, a promise that David fulfilled (2 Sam. 9). Saul did not believe Jonathan's story (vv. 24-33), and his reaction almost cost Jonathan his life! When God abandons a person and the devil takes over, there is no end to the wickedness that results. Jonathan left the table and met David the next morning; they wept together and said farewell.

## B. He lied to Ahimelech (21:1-9).

David fled again, this time to Nob, where the tabernacle was established. David always had a great love for the house of God, so perhaps he wanted to visit the tabernacle again before going into hiding. But he lied to the priest by claiming to be on business for Saul (v. 2). The priest gave David and his men the holy bread to eat and also the sword of Goliath for David's protection. The whole plan seemed to be successful, except that one of Saul's spies, Doeg, was there to witness the events; and this ultimately led to treachery and bloodshed (22:9ff; see Ps. 52 and note the title).

### C. He lied to Achish (21:10-15).

Matters were going from bad to worse, just as they always do when we trust ourselves instead of the wisdom of God. David now fled into the hands of the enemy! "The fear of man brings a snare," and David almost snared himself right in enemy territory! Certainly the king would not tolerate a Jewish hero in his land, and David had to pretend to be out of his mind before he could escape. "O what a tangled web we weave, when first we practice to deceive." This might have been the end of David's life, but the Lord intervened and turned the heart of the king toward getting rid of David. He then fled to the cave of Adullam and organized his "outlaw band." See Ps. 34 and Ps. 56.

It is amazing how men and women of faith can gradually become men and women of fear and unbelief. If we get in a hurry, trust people, and trust our own plans, before long everything falls to pieces and we find ourselves out of the place of God's blessing and protection. We shall see in later chapters that David learned to wait on the Lord and seek His will.

The friendship between David and Jonathan was something rare, for actually neither of them had anything to gain. Jonathan had lost the crown, and David could lose his life. Their unselfishness and constancy in spite of trials is a beautiful example of Christian love.

# 1 SAMUEL 22–24

David is now completely separated from Saul's court and is considered an outlaw and a rebel. Psalm 34 grew out of his narrow escape from Achish (1 Sam. 21:10-15) and perhaps best expresses David's trials and triumphs during his exile period. "Many are the afflictions of the righteous, but the Lord delivers him out of them all" (Ps. 34:19, NKJV). God was with David and helped him.

## I. God Guided David's Steps (22)

David assembled a loyal band of followers at the cave of Adullam, a crowd of 400 men that eventually grew to 600 (23:13). His experiences in the cave are found in Pss. 54 and 142. David would want to protect his brethren since Saul might want to slay them as well as David. Certainly this "motley crew" illustrates the kind of people who flee to Christ for refuge: people in distress or in debt (because of our sins); people discontented with life. David's band was small and despised, *but to them belonged the kingdom!* David was able to get protection for his parents at Moab since his family (through Ruth) came from there. How thoughtful of David to care for his loved ones; see John 19:26-27.

This period of persecution in David's life was a part of the preparation for the throne. He was already a great soldier; now he needed to suffer in the wilderness to learn *not* to trust men but to trust the Lord. All of us need "wilderness testings" to bring us closer to the Lord and to make us better equipped to serve Him. Saul's persecution of David is an illustration of the conflict between the flesh and the Spirit. It also pictures Satan's persecution of the church today: Saul was not the king, yet he was reigning; David was the king, but he was not yet on the throne. Satan seems to be "reigning" today, but Christ is King and one day He will take His rightful throne.

Saul's murder of the innocent priests at Nob shows to what extent people will go once they have rejected the Lord. Saul was a liar and a murderer, just like Satan (John 8:44). Doeg was an Edomite, a descendant of Esau (Gen. 25:30), so his hatred for David and the priests is but another stage in the battle between Esau and Jacob. David's presence at Nob brought death to these people, so his deception only resulted in tragedy. Saul was unwilling to slay the Amalekites (chap. 15), yet he had no problem slaying innocent priests. This slaughter was a fulfillment of God's prophecy to Eli that his house would be judged; see 2:30-36. Saul was able to slay the priests, but he was not able to prevent Abiathar from fleeing to David with the ephod, the instrument for determining the will of God. What use had Saul for the ephod? He was determined to do his own will! Abiathar later became a help to David; see 23:9; 30:7.

## II. God Guarded David's Life (23)

It was important that David live, for it was he who would deliver Israel, establish the kingdom in glory, and become the father of Christ in the flesh (Rom. 1:3). Satan used Saul to seek to kill

David, but God was too strong for the enemy. As long as David sought the mind of the Lord, God gave him protection and victory.

### A. Victory at Keilah (vv. 1-13).

The Philistines were David's enemy and the enemy of Israel, so it was right for him to fight them. When the child of God is in the will of God, he may expect the help of God. So intense was Saul's hatred that he did not thank God for David's victory, but instead came to fight the victor himself. And the men of Keilah did not protect their deliverer; rather, they tried to turn him over to Saul! How wicked is the human heart untouched by the grace of God!

### B. Victory in the wilderness (vv. 14-18).

What patience David had, to be able to endure daily danger and persecution! He was a master strategist and could have tricked Saul into defeat, but he preferred to wait for God to give the victory. How moving it was when Jonathan met him in the wilderness (at the risk of his own life) to reassure him and encourage him. Sad to say, Jonathan was never allowed to reign with David, for he was slain in battle with his father. The righteous often suffer because of the sins of others.

### C. Victory over the Ziphites (vv. 19-29).

Ziph was in Judah and its inhabitants should have been loyal to David; but instead they betrayed their rightful king to Saul. Read Ps. 54 for David's prayer to God for deliverance. The rock stood between David and Saul (23:26), just as the cloud stood between Israel and the Egyptians. It seemed that Saul would finally capture his man, but an invasion from the Philistines forced Saul to return home. Certainly God is in control of circumstances and delivers His own at the right time.

## III. God Gave David Grace (24)

"He who is slow to anger is better than the mighty, and he who rules his spirit than he who takes a city" (Prov. 16:32). God gave David the grace needed to show kindness to his enemy, and this is even greater than defeating the giant Goliath. Saul's men had been lying about David and telling Saul that David was trying to slay him (24:9). If Psalm 7 fits into this event, as many students believe, then Cush the Benjamite was chief of the liars. This experience gave David opportunity to prove to Saul and the leaders that he was not trying to slay Saul, but that he honored the king even though the king was out of the will of God.

### A. The temptation (vv. 1-7).

Saul came into the cave to rest and relieve himself, probably laying his outer garment down as he entered. The cave was large and very dark, so he did not see David and his men hiding in the rocks. David was able to cut Saul's garment and not be detected. Certainly this would have been the time to kill his enemy! In fact, some of David's men insisted that God had arranged the circumstances so that David might so act (v. 4). It is important that we always test circumstances by the Word of God. So tender was David's heart that he repented openly of his rash deed of cutting Saul's robe; for he had not shown proper respect for the Lord's anointed. David, "a man after God's own heart," was willing for God to take care of Saul (Rom. 12:19-21).

### B. The explanation (vv. 8-15).

David and his men were safe in the cave, and Saul's men would not dare to attack them; so David boldly stepped out to speak to Saul once the king had gone some distance away. How shocked Saul must have been to hear the voice of his son-in-law! David explained that Saul was listening to lies (v. 9) and that he could have lost his life in the cave but for David's kindness (vv. 10-11). The piece of the robe was evidence enough that David was telling the truth. "I am but a flea, a dead dog!" said David. "To what advantage is it for you to chase me? But I am not going to kill you or trick you, for the Lord will fight my battles and plead my cause." What a gracious spirit God gave to David. Oh, that we might have this same attitude toward our enemies today.

### C. The supplication (vv. 16-22).

Picture the pitiful Saul as he stands before one who is his better. Saul's weeping and his admission of guilt were but shallow, passing emotions; they did not really come from his heart. He was only too glad to acknowledge David's kindness. After all, David had spared his life! And Saul was concerned primarily for his own family, that, when David did become king, he would not slay them. Verse 20 indicates the perversity of Saul's heart: he admitted that David was the rightful king, yet he persisted in opposing him!

David kept his promises to Saul and even vindicated Saul's honor after Saul's death. This beautifully illustrates Christ's words in Matt. 5:10-12. For David to show kindness to Saul, and to pray for him, was a greater victory than to overcome the Philistines. We can be sure, if we obey the Lord, that He will take care of our enemies for us in His good time.

# 1 SAMUEL 26–31

We come now to the tragic end of Saul's life. The man who "stood higher than any of the people" (10:23) now falls to the earth in a witch's house (28:20) and then falls dead on the battlefield (see 2 Sam. 1:19). Perhaps the best way to study these sad events is to notice the obvious contrasts between David and Saul.

## I. Love and Hatred (26)

Why David returned to the wilderness of Ziph when he had experienced trouble there before, is difficult to understand (23:19ff). Perhaps it's just an illustration that he, like all men of clay, made mistakes. It has been suggested that David's polygamous marriage (25:42-44) hindered his close fellowship with the Lord, since such a marriage was not in God's will. Of course, Saul pursued David! Saul's tearful confession in 24:17-21 did not last, for it was not from his heart.

Abishai was David's nephew (1 Chron. 2:15-16) and was a courageous warrior (2 Sam. 10:10). Later, Abishai was to save David's life from the giant (2 Sam. 21:17). However, Abishai was involved in the murder of Abner (2 Sam. 3:30), a crime that grieved David. God put a deep sleep upon the camp (v. 12) so David and his nephew were not in danger. The word "trench" in v. 7 indicates a barricade of baggage and wagons. Once again, Satan used others to tempt David to slay Saul (v. 8, and see 24:4), but David resisted the temptation. Vengeance was in the hands of the Lord.

David's message to Saul was actually a plea for him to return to the Lord. "If God has led you to pursue me because of some sin in my life, then I will offer a sacrifice with you and get the matter settled," he said. "But if men are cursing me, then you can be sure God will settle the matter for me." Listen to Saul's empty confession in v. 21: "I have sinned! I have played the fool!" Yes, he had—

but he still did not repent! We play the fool when we run ahead of the Lord (13:8ff); when we fail to obey completely (chap. 15); when we turn our back on our godly friends (David and Samuel); when we seek guidance from the devil (chap. 28); and when we refuse to repent even when we know we are wrong. "Be sure your sins will find you out!"

## II. Light and Darkness (27–30)

Chapters 27 and 29–30 deal with David's victories as he sought the mind of the Lord, while chapter 28 pictures Saul's terrible defeat as he sought aid in a witch's house. Of course, David was not always walking in the will of the Lord, for it seems that his faith failed him when he went back to Gath to live under the protection of the enemy (chap. 27). He had gotten into trouble there before (21:10-15), but now he was the leader of a strong band of 600 men and his reception was much better. Still, David's sojourn in enemy territory forced him to lie to the king (27:10-12), and when the Philistines did gather (29:1), David was almost forced to fight against his own people! When we lean on the wisdom of the flesh, we always end up in trouble. It was only the grace of God that kept David from having to slay his own people.

The contrast between chapters 28 and 30 is striking: Saul had departed from the Lord and therefore had no divine guidance (28:6), while David looked to the Lord for courage and direction (30:6-9). "Seek the Lord while He may be found" (Isa. 55:6, NIV) was a warning Saul did not heed. God enabled David not only to recover all his possessions and people, but also to gather the loot collected by the enemy. We appreciate his gracious spirit in sharing the spoils with those who tarried by the supplies, and also his kindness in sending gifts to the elders of Judah. The latter action probably had some political meaning as well.

It is quite another picture when we look at Saul's midnight visit to the witch's house (chap. 28). Samuel was dead, but even when he was alive, his ministry was not really appreciated by Saul. How sad when people discover their real friends too late. Saul's only recourse was to visit a witch, and this was prohibited by the Law (Lev. 20:6). It is alarming to what ends people will go when they have turned their back on the Lord. There have been endless debates over the matter of Samuel's appearance at the call of the witch. It seems likely that: (1) Samuel's coming was of the Lord and not because of the witch's art; (2) the witch was surprised when Samuel appeared; and (3) Samuel came because he had a special message for the king from the Lord. The witch could not have impersonated Samuel (in league with someone else) since she did not know Saul was coming. Nor is it possible that Satan could have accomplished this feat, since God would not allow Satan to deliver such a weighty message, nor would the Lord put His approval on a practice His Word condemned. The witch becomes a mere spectator once Samuel is on the scene. It is likely that Saul heard Samuel's words (v. 20) but did not see Samuel's form (vv. 12-14). Back in 15:35 and 16:1, Samuel's separation from Saul had been accomplished and the king would see him no more.

It is unbelievable that King Saul, a man chosen by God, could ever participate in so wicked a deed; yet the record is there—"let him who thinks he stands take heed, lest he fall" (1 Cor. 10:12). Saul walked in darkness, not in light; he disguised himself (yet was actually revealing his true character); he allowed a woman to break the law; he brought shame and defeat upon his nation, his army, his family, and himself.

## III. Life and Death (31)

While David was sending gifts to his friends, Saul and his family were being stripped on the battlefield! "To be carnally minded is death" (Rom. 8:6). Gilboa had been the scene of some great victories in the days of Deborah (Jud. 4-5) and Gideon (Jud. 7); but this day it would be the scene of a tragic defeat. God had abandoned Saul, and the only thing left for the rebellious king was death. How sad that his innocent son, Jonathan, had to suffer because of the father's sins.

Read 2 Sam. 1:1-10 for another account of the death of Saul. It is not difficult to harmonize the two accounts. Saul saw that he was defeated; he did not want to fall into the hands of the enemy alive, because they would only humiliate him. Therefore, he tried to take his own life by falling on his sword. This, however, did not kill him; and he was yet alive, leaning upon his spear (2 Sam. 1:6), when the Amalekite came along and finished the work. (However, it must be noted that there are those who believe the Amalekite in 2 Sam. 1 was not telling the truth, but only giving this story to David to explain why he possessed Saul's royal crown and bracelet. Perhaps he thought that David would reward him because he "did Saul a favor" by killing him.) There is an important lesson in Saul's death: because Saul refused to slay all of the Amalekites (15), one of them ended up killing him. The sin that we fail to deal with, eventually causes our downfall. Saul lost his crown: "Behold, I come quickly! Hold fast what you have that no one take your crown" (Rev. 3:11).

How the enemy rejoiced at the death of Saul. What triumph it brought to the temples of their false gods. Saul did not glorify his God either in life or death (Phil. 1:20-21). It was commendable that the heroic men of Jabesh-gilead rescued the desecrated bodies of the royal family and gave them decent burial. They burned them, probably to prevent any future insults. Saul had once rescued these people (chap. 11), and this was one way they could repay him. David later put the bones in a tomb (2 Sam. 21:12-14). When he became king at Hebron, David showed his appreciation to these brave men for honoring their late king (2 Sam. 2:5-7).

Saul's tragic life and death can teach us many practical lessons: (1) great sins often begin as "little matters"—impatience, incomplete obedience, excuse-making; (2) once sin gets hold of people, they go from bad to worse; (3) if we are not right with God, we will not get along with God's people; (4) excuses are no substitute for confessions; (5) natural gifts and abilities mean nothing without the power of God; and (6) there is no substitute for obedience.

# 2 SAMUEL 1–5

These chapters describe the events leading up to David's corona-
tion as king of Israel. You will want to read 1 Chron. 10:1-14, 11:1-
19, and 14:1-8 for parallel accounts.

## I. David Sorrows over Saul's Death (1)

A lesser saint would have rejoiced that his enemy was slain, but
David was a man after God's own heart and felt keenly the tragedy
of Saul's sin. Of course, David's dear friend Jonathan was also dead;
the sin of a disobedient father had brought judgment upon innocent people. We have already noted the lessons of Saul's death in
our study of 1 Samuel, but it would be profitable to consider some
of the other details.

Note that an Amalekite brought the news and claimed to be the
one who finally took Saul's life. Had Saul obeyed the Lord in
1 Sam. 15 and slain *all* of the Amalekites, this would not have
happened. The sin we fail to slay is the one that slays us. See
Deut. 25:17-19.

David's lamentation is touching; see Prov. 24:17. This "Song of
the Bow" connects with Jonathan's use of the bow (1 Sam.
20:20ff). There are no unkind words about Saul in this song. David's chief concern is that the Lord's anointed has been slain and
the Lord's glory has been dimmed. He is anxious that the unsaved
enemy not rejoice over this victory. "How are the mighty fallen!" is
his theme (vv. 19, 25, 27). In 1 Sam. 10:23, Saul "stood higher"
than any other man, but now he had fallen lower than the enemy!

## II. David Struggles against Saul's Family (2–4)

We now begin those "political intrigues" that plagued David
throughout all his life. Even though David sought the mind of God,
he could not escape the plots and plans of others; and because he
was indebted to these men, it was difficult for him to oppose them.
David's march to the throne was a difficult one.

### A. The murder of Asahel (chap. 2).

Joab, Abishai, and Asahel were all sons of David's half-sister Zeruiah (1 Chron. 2:16 and 2 Sam. 17:25). Thus, they were David's
nephews as well as valued men in his army. David first reigned over
Judah, his own tribe, with his headquarters at Hebron. However,

Abner, the commander of Saul's army, had made Saul's son Ishbosheth the king over the other tribes. He relocated the capital over the Jordan River in Mahanaim to protect himself and the new king from David's men. Of course, Abner had personal interest in the household of Saul since he was Saul's cousin (1 Sam. 14:50). It was to his advantage to see Ishbosheth reign, but he was deliberately rebelling against God's Word when he crowned him. God had made it very clear that David alone was to rule Israel. Perhaps Christians today are like the Jews of that day: we permit our King to reign over only a part of our lives, and the result is conflict and sorrow. Abner's murder of Asahel was the prelude to the "long war" between the two kings (3:1). As we shall see, the two remaining brothers avenged this death, much to David's grief.

### B. The murder of Abner (chap. 3).

David's many wives were chosen in direct violation of Deut. 17:15-17. Some students believe that this expression of David's lust eventually led to the many family problems that plagued his later days. Amnon violated his half-sister Tamar (chap. 13); Absalom rebelled against David and tried to capture the crown (chaps. 13-18); and Adonijah tried to wrest the kingdom from Solomon (1 Kings 1:5ff). Abner had problems with lust too; for he took one of Saul's concubines and incurred the displeasure of the pretended king. This led to a disruption between Abner and Ishbosheth. Abner tried to make a peaceful agreement with David, but the "sons of Zeruiah" plotted against him and killed him (vv. 26-30). While Joab did the actual killing, it is likely that his brother was in on the plans. Joab's hands were stained with blood before his own death came; for he not only killed Abner, but also Absalom (2 Sam. 18:14) and Amasa (2 Sam. 20:10). David asked his son Solomon to deal with Joab, and he did (1 Kings 2:5-6, 28-34). How different history would have been had Abner lived, it is difficult to tell. Certainly Joab held unusual power over David, particularly after he assisted the king in his murderous plot against innocent Uriah (11:14ff). Note, however, David's godly conduct in the matter of Abner's death.

### C. The murder of Ishbosheth (chap. 4).

This was the turning point: when Ishbosheth died, the way was wide open for David to rule over the entire nation. However, it must be noted that David did not approve of the method the sons of Rimmon used, and he had the murderers slain because of their crime. David knew that God was able to elevate him to the throne; he would not do evil that good might come from it (Rom. 3:8). These three murders are evidence that David's road to the throne was a bloody one. What a contrast to our Savior who shed His own blood, and not the blood of others, to gain His throne! See 1 Chron. 22:8 for God's evaluation of David's career.

### III. David Succeeds to Saul's Throne (5)

David had reigned seven years in Hebron over the tribe of Judah; now he was to reign over the entire nation for thirty-three years, making a total of forty years. This was David's third anointing—Samuel had anointed him at home in Bethlehem, and the men of Judah had anointed him at Hebron (2:4). See Ps. 18 for David's song of victory after God had defeated all his foes and given him peace. This is a good Psalm to read when you are in trouble, for it shows how the Lord brings us out and leads us into a place of greater blessing. Certainly David did not enjoy his many trials, but he could look back and thank God for them.

The king now needed a capital city, and he chose Jerusalem. This stronghold had not been captured previously (Josh. 15:63; Jud. 1:21) and the Jebusites were arrogant and defied David to attack. "The lame and the blind could defeat you!" they taunted, but David and his men turned their taunts into cries of defeat. First Chron. 11:5-8 tells us that Joab was the man God used to open the city. There are students who feel that David's men crept into the city unawares through the water system, but some archaeologists maintain that the *water system was not located at that point*. It seems clear from the text that David did use the water tunnel as his means of entry and that Joab carried out the king's master plan.

No sooner was David established in his own city than the old enemy, the Philistines, returned. How true this is in our personal lives: Satan waits for the "peace after the storm" to attack us again. David knew that the Lord's will was the only way to victory, so he immediately consulted Him. Note that the second attack (vv. 22-25) was different from the first, and that David was wise enough to seek God's guidance again. God led him in a new way. We must take care not to keep "carbon copies" of the Lord's will, but to seek Him anew for each new decision.

Certainly it was God's will that David reign over the entire nation, just as it is His will that Christ be Lord over all of our lives. Any part that is left outside His will is going to rebel and cause trouble. We are "bone of His bone, and flesh of His flesh" (5:1; Eph. 5:30), and we ought to invite Him to reign over us. Only then will we have complete peace and victory.

David's road to the throne covered many years and many trials, but throughout that journey he put God first and never sought vengeance or retaliation against Saul. God saw to it that David was protected and promoted according to His time and plan. He will do the same for us if we will but trust Him.

# 2 SAMUEL 6

You will want to read 1 Chron. 13, 15, and 16 as you study this chapter, since they give additional information about this important event in the life of David. Psalm 132:1-6 tells of David's intense desire to honor the Lord by returning the ark of the covenant to its proper place. For nearly twenty years, the ark had been in Kirjath-jearim (Baale of Judah, see 1 Sam. 6:21–7:2); so David prepared a special tent for it in Jerusalem (1 Chron. 15:1) and prepared to return the sacred ark to its home. It took more than three months for him to finish the task (6:11).

## I. David Displeases the Lord (6:1-11)

Certainly it was a noble desire on David's part to bring the ark to Jerusalem, but it is possible to have "zeal without knowledge" and do a good work in a wrong way. To begin with, David did not consult the Lord; he consulted his political leaders (1 Chron. 13:1-4; note 2 Sam. 5:19 and 23). It appears that his main motive was to unify the nation under his rule rather than to glorify the Lord. Note in 1 Chron. 13:3 that David criticizes Saul for neglecting the ark. Perhaps this statement had something to do with the behavior of Saul's daughter, Michal, as recorded in 6:20ff. All the leaders and all the congregation agreed to David's plan, but this did not make the subsequent actions right.

David's next mistake was to ignore God's Word. Instead of asking the Levites to bear the ark on their shoulders (Num. 3:27-31; 4:15; 7:9; 10:21), he followed the worldly example of the Philistines and put the ark on a new cart (1 Sam. 6). God would permit the Philistines to use this method, since they were not His covenant people, instructed in the Word. But for the Jews to ignore the divine commands and imitate the heathen nations, was to invite disaster. How many Christians and local churches today "conform to the world" (Rom. 12:2) instead of "following the pattern" given by God from heaven? (Ex. 25:40) All of the people were enthusiastic and joyful, but this did not make their method right in the eyes of God. Israel wanted to be "like the other nations" (1 Sam. 8:5), and it led to tragedy.

Naturally, the human method of doing God's work eventually fails: the oxen stumbled and the ark was in danger of falling! This led to the third mistake: a man who was not a Levite touched the ark (see Num. 4:15). God had to judge him immediately or else sacrifice His glory and permit His Word to be violated. David's reaction to this sudden judgment reveals that his heart was not completely right with God in the matter; for, first he was angry, then he was fearful. Instead of pausing and seeking God's will to discover the reason for the judgment, David stopped the procession and quickly disposed of the ark. First Chronicles 26:1-4 indicates that the family of Obed-edom belonged to the Levitical family and could safely care for the ark.

One mistake led to another! How important it is to determine God's will and then follow God's way in accomplishing that will.

## II. David Displays His Zeal (6:11-19)

During the three months' interim, David undoubtedly searched his heart and confessed his sins. He certainly turned to the Law to discover God's instructions for carrying the ark (1 Chron. 15:1-2, 12-13). God was blessing the household of Obed-edom, and David wanted that blessing for the whole nation. This time he prepared the tent and also saw to it that the Levites were properly prepared for their task.

It is thought that Ps. 24 may have been composed to celebrate this event. From 1 Chron. 16:7ff we discover that Ps. 105 also grew out of this happy event. David was used of God to give expression to the joy of his heart, and his song glorified the Lord. The king laid aside his royal robes and led the procession in the humble garments of a Levite. The Levites took six paces and then paused, waiting to see if God would accept them; when no judgment came, they offered sacrifices and then proceeded the rest of the way to Jerusalem.

It is obvious that David's "dancing" before the Lord was a spontaneous expression of his joy that the ark of God was restored to the people. Was it undignified for David to act in this way? Certainly not! While his actions are not given as examples for us to follow, we dare not go to the other extreme and rule out all outward expressions of joy and praise in our worship of God! While some believers may carry such activities to extremes, others may be guilty of grieving the Spirit by a false sobriety. Finally, David's "dancing" is in no way an excuse for modern "dancing"; for his actions were done before the Lord to glorify Him.

David blessed the people and gave them gifts to celebrate the return of the ark. Years before "the glory had departed"; now the Lord of Hosts (God of armies) was back in the midst of His people again. No wonder David rejoiced!

## III. David Disciplines His Wife (6:20-23)

We have noted before that Michal, Saul's daughter, was never a suitable wife for David. She belonged to Saul's family and never really exhibited any faith in the God of Israel. First Samuel 19:13 indicates that she worshiped idols. David did not take her as his wife because of the leading of the Lord; he "won her" by slaying Goliath (1 Sam. 17:25) and by fulfilling Saul's murderous requirements (1 Sam. 18:17-27). This life-time alliance with the family of Saul meant trouble from the very beginning, as all ungodly alliances do (2 Cor. 6:14-18). The conflict between David and Saul is an illustration of the battle between the flesh and the Spirit, and for David to be united to Michal meant yielding to the flesh.

It takes little imagination to see why Michal despised her husband. Certainly her sinful attitude had been growing within for years. She resented being married to her father's armorbearer as the "prize" for victory. She resented the fact that David had other wives (see 3:2-5; 5:13-16), all of whom were chosen after her marriage to David. Her father had died shamefully, and his enemy now reigned victoriously over all Israel. Of course, beneath all these reasons lay the basic reason: she was an unbeliever who did not understand or appreciate the things of the Lord (1 Cor. 2:14-16). She wanted David to display his royal power in great pomp and ceremony; he preferred to take his place with the common people and glorify the Lord.

Her harsh words to David after a great time of praise must have cut him deeply. It is usually true that Satan has a "Michal" to meet us whenever we have been rejoicing in the Lord and seeking to glorify Him. Her wicked words revealed a wicked heart, and David knew that she must be dealt with. "If your hand offends you, cut it off!" He realized that Michal would never help him in the work of the Lord; therefore, he put her away and refused to give her the privileges of marriage. For a Jewish woman to die without children was, of course, a great shame to her. David answered this fool according to her folly (Prov. 26:5).

When others criticize us, and we know our hearts and motives are right, we should not get discouraged. Had David been like some saints, he would have said, "All right, I just won't serve the Lord anymore! Even my wife doesn't appreciate it!" No, instead, we find in the next chapter that David planned to do even more and build a temple for the Lord. This is the proper spirit for the Christian, to honor the Lord regardless of what obstacles Satan may put in the way.

# 2 SAMUEL 7

Two phrases in this chapter summarize the main lesson: "your seed" (v. 12) and "your throne" (v. 16). This Davidic covenant (also given in 1 Chron. 17) is important to the program of God, because in it God promises certain special blessings to the Jewish nation through David. In His covenant with Abraham (Gen. 15), God had promised a seed, a land, and a blessing to all nations through Israel. In this covenant, God reveals that the promised Messiah would come through David's line (Rom. 1:3) and would rule from David's throne over the promised messianic kingdom.

## I. A Noble Purpose (7:1-3)

The days of exile and danger are over, and David is enjoying rest and blessing in his own house. The king is fellowshipping with the prophet Nathan, and they are discussing the things of the Lord.

David always had a love for the house of God (Ps. 132), and his desire was to build a beautiful house for the Lord. God would not permit this (1 Chron. 22:8), but He would acknowledge David's love, inasmuch as this desire was in his heart (1 Kings 8:18). Nathan did not know God's express will in the matter, so he merely commended David and encouraged him to do what was in his heart. Both David and Nathan kept their hearts open for God's leading; and, when the Lord spoke, they listened and obeyed. We ought always to encourage one another in spiritual matters and provoke one another to good works (Heb. 10:24-25).

David truly was "a man after God's own heart," for he had the Word of God and the house of God uppermost in his heart. Would that more of God's people were like him!

## II. A Wonderful Promise (7:4-17)

Nathan must have been meditating on the Word "in the night" (Ps. 119:55) when God spoke to him. How often God speaks to us when it is dark! See Gen. 15. "You have visited me in the night" (Ps. 17:3). God gave Nathan a message for the king, and this message involved several important factors.

### A. God's grace (vv. 5-10).

How gracious God was to "dwell in a tent" during the years since the nation had come out of Egypt! He had not asked for an elaborate temple, as housed the gods of Egypt. No, He had "humbled Himself" and dwelt in the tabernacle, journeying with His people and going before them to open the way. John 1:14 says, "And the Word (Christ) became flesh and *tabernacled* among us." Another evidence of God's grace was His treatment of David. God had called him from the pastures and put him on the throne. God had given him victory over all his enemies. God had brought Israel into a place of blessing and they would not be moved again (v. 10, where the verbs ought to be past tense, "I *have* appointed a place").

### B. God's purpose (vv. 11-16).

Please note that the word "house" has a double meaning in this passage: (1) a material house, the temple, v. 13; and (2) a human house, David's family, vv. 11, 16, 19, 25, 27, 29. It is customary to speak of a royal family as a "house," such as the "House of Windsor" in Great Britain. David wanted to build God a house of stone, but God was going to build David a royal house, a family that would reign on his throne.

The terms of this covenant are important because they involve the purposes of God in sending Jesus Christ to the world. We must note, first, that some of this covenant was fulfilled in Solomon, David's successor on the throne; see 1 Chron. 22:6-16. God did put Solomon on the throne, in spite of the wicked plots of others in the family, and God did enable Solomon to build the beautiful temple. When Solomon and his descendants sinned, God kept His promise (v. 14) and chastened them; see Ps. 89:20-37. It must be noted as well that there are some matters in this covenant that can apply only to Jesus Christ. God states that the throne would be forever (v. 13) and that David's house and kingdom would be forever (v. 16). But David does not have a descendant upon his throne today. In fact, there is no throne in Jerusalem. Did God not fulfill His promises? God states in Ps. 89:33-37 that He would never break His covenant with David, even though He might have to chasten David's children.

The ultimate fulfillment of these promises is in Jesus Christ. Read carefully the message of the angel to Mary in Luke 1:28-33, and note that God promises Christ the throne and the kingdom of David. Some "spiritualize" these verses and apply them to the church today; but if the rest of the angel's message is to be taken literally, what right do we have to spiritualize the throne and the kingdom? Led by the Spirit, Zacharias states clearly that Christ would fulfill the covenants made to the fathers (Luke 1:68-75). It is our conviction that Christ will fulfill this Davidic covenant when He sits on David's throne and rules during the millennial kingdom (Rev. 20:1-6). It is then that all the great kingdom promises in the OT Prophets will be fulfilled. The apostles in Acts 15:13-18 understood that God would build David's house (tabernacle) again *after* God was finished visiting the Gentiles and calling out a people for His name (the church).

## III. A Humble Prayer (7:18-29)

David received the message from Nathan, then went in to pray, asking God to fulfill His Word (vv. 28-29). How much more we would receive from lessons and sermons if only we spent time with God afterward and "prayed the message in."

God enjoys giving His children "exceeding abundantly above all that we ask or think." David had asked permission to build an earthly temple; God responded by promising him an eternal kingdom! This tremendous act of grace left David humbled before the Lord, and in his prayer, the king praises the greatness of the Lord.

He realized the privileged position of Israel (vv. 22-24). Oh, that God's people today would understand how great God is and what great things He has done for His own! Yet David's concern was not that his name be praised, but that the name of the Lord be magnified (v. 26; see Phil. 1:20-21). "You have spoken; now perform the promises!" prayed David. Like Abraham, David was "fully persuaded that what He had promised, He was able also to perform" (Rom. 4:21).

Was David disappointed because God would not permit him to build the house? Perhaps, however, it was not important to him who built it but that God's will be done and God's name be glorified.

# 2 SAMUEL 9

This chapter presents a moving illustration of the salvation we have in Christ. David's treatment of Mephibosheth is certainly that of a "man after God's own heart."

## I. Mephibosheth—The Lost Sinner

### A. He was born in a rejected family.

As the son of Jonathan, Mephibosheth was a member of a rejected family. He was a son of a prince, yet was living in dependence on others away from the city of Jerusalem. Every lost sinner today is born in sin, born into Adam's family, and is thus under condemnation (Rom. 5:12ff; Eph. 2:1-3).

### B. He experienced a fall and could not walk.

Mephibosheth was lame in both his feet (vv. 3, 13) and thus could not walk. All people today are sinners because of the fall of Adam (Rom. 5:12), and they cannot walk so as to please God. Instead of walking in obedience, sinners walk "according to the course of this world" (Eph. 2:2). They may try to walk to please God, but no amount of self-effort or good works will save them.

### C. He was missing the best.

Mephibosheth lived at Lo-debar which means "no pasture." That is a fitting description of this present world—no pasture, no place for the souls to be satisfied. Sinners are hungry and thirsty, but this world and its pleasures cannot satisfy.

## D. *He would have perished without David's help.*

We would never have heard of Mephibosheth were it not for the gracious steps David took to save him. His name was written down in God's Word because David reached him and helped him.

The lost sinner is in a tragic situation. He has fallen; he cannot walk to please God; he is separated from home; he is under condemnation; he cannot help himself.

## II. David—The Gracious Savior

### A. *David made the first move.*

Salvation is of the Lord! He must take the first steps, because the lost sinner will not by nature seek God (Rom. 3:10-12). David sent for poor Mephibosheth, just as God sent Christ to this earth to "seek and to save that which was lost" (Luke 19:10).

### B. *David acted for Jonathan's sake.*

This grew out of the loving covenant that David had made with Jonathan years before (1 Sam. 20:11-23). David had never seen Mephibosheth, yet he loved him for Jonathan's sake. We are not saved because of our own merit; we are saved for the sake of Christ. We are forgiven for His sake (Eph. 4:32). We are accepted "in the beloved" (Eph. 1:6). It was part of that "everlasting covenant" (Heb. 13:20-21) that the Father should save for Jesus' sake all that trust the Savior.

### C. *It was an act of kindness.*

In v. 3, David calls it "the kindness of God." Christ shows His kindness to us in saving us (Eph. 2:7; Titus 3:4-7). David's throne was a throne of grace, not a throne of justice. Mephibosheth had no claim upon David; he had absolutely no case to present. Had he appeared before that throne asking for justice, he would have received condemnation.

### D. *David called him personally and he came.*

David sent a servant to bring him (v. 5), but the servant then stepped out of the way to make room for the king. Nobody is saved by a preacher or evangelist; all the servant can do is usher the sinner into the presence of Christ. Note how Mephibosheth fell humbly before David, for he knew his place as a condemned man. How tenderly David said, "Mephibosheth."

## E. David took him into his own family.

Like many sinners today, Mephibosheth wanted to work his way into forgiveness (vv. 6, 8), but David made him a son (v. 11). The Prodigal Son wanted to be a servant too, but no one can earn salvation (Luke 15:18-19). "Beloved, now are we the sons of God!" See 1 John 3:1-2 and John 1:11-13.

## F. David spoke peace to him.

"Fear not!" were David's words of grace to the trembling crippled man; and "Fear not!" is what Christ says to every believing sinner. "There is therefore now no condemnation..." (Rom. 8:1). Through the Word of God before us and the Spirit of God within us, we experience peace.

## G. David provided for his every need.

Mephibosheth would no longer live at "no pasture"; for now he would eat daily at the king's table. Furthermore, the servant Ziba and his sons became servants to Mephibosheth. And David gave to Mephibosheth all of the inheritance that belonged to him. So Christ satisfies the spiritual and material needs of His family. He has given us an eternal inheritance (Eph. 1:11, 18; 1 Peter 1:4ff; Col. 1:12). If he gave us our rightful inheritance, we would go to hell! But in His grace He has chosen us to share His inheritance with Him, for we are "joint-heirs with Christ" (Rom. 8:17).

## H. David protected him from judgment.

In 2 Sam. 21:1-11, we see that God sent a famine to the land to chastise His people. When David sought God's will, it became evident that the famine came because of the wicked way Saul treated the Gibeonites. There is no record of Saul's exact treatment of them in the Bible, but since Israel had made a treaty with these people (Josh. 9), Saul's actions were a direct violation of the truth and were a sin against God. God had waited many years to reveal this sin and send this judgment; "Be sure your sins will find you out." See Ex. 21:23-25. It is not for us in this age of grace to judge these people for asking for the sacrifice of seven of Saul's descendants; it is sufficient that God permitted this to happen. Note that David deliberately spared Mephibosheth (v. 7). There was another Mephibosheth among Saul's descendants (v. 8), but David knew the difference! There are many today who profess to be God's children, and perhaps we cannot always tell the difference; but when the Day of Judgment comes, God will reveal those who are truly His.

Of course, as we study this illustration, we must keep in mind that the salvation we have in Christ supplies "much more." David rescued Mephibosheth from physical danger and supplied his physical needs, but Christ has saved us from eternal hell and daily meets our physical and spiritual needs. We are not sons of some earthly king; we are the very children of God.

Second Samuel 16:1-4 illustrates this difference. When David fled from Jerusalem during the rebellion of his son Absalom, Ziba the servant met him and made an accusation against Mephibosheth. David believed the accusation and rashly gave all of Mephibosheth's land to the servant. However, when David returned to Jerusalem later, he met Mephibosheth and learned the truth (2 Sam. 19:24-30). Ziba had lied. He had promised to supply an animal for Mephibosheth to use to escape with David, but had not kept his promise. Ziba had slandered an innocent man, and David had believed the slander. Of course, this could never happen between a believer and Jesus Christ. "Who shall bring a charge against God's elect? . . . Who is he who condemns?" (Rom. 8:33-39, NKJV) Satan may accuse us and slander us, but Christ will never change in His love for us or His promises to us.

We can see in Mephibosheth the attitude the believer ought to have concerning the "return of the King." This exiled lame man lived for the day his king would return! He had no thought for his own comfort; rather, he waited and prayed for the return of the one who had loved him and rescued him from death. So overjoyed was Mephibosheth at the return of David that he even forfeited his land.

# 2 SAMUEL 11–12

The Bible honestly records the sins of God's people, but never in such a way that sin is made acceptable. Unlike many so-called "true-to-life" books today, the Bible states the facts and draws out the lessons, but allows nothing for the imagination to dwell on. There are some things "it is a shame to speak of" (Eph. 5:12), and the events in this chapter must be studied with a Spirit-directed mind and heart, "considering ourselves, lest we also be tempted" (Gal. 6:1).

## I. David and Bathsheba (11:1-4)

It was not a passionate youth who deliberately walked into this sin, but a man of God who had now reached middle age. It is easy to see how David got into this sin: (1) he was self-confident, after enjoying victories and prosperity; (2) he was disobedient, staying home when he should have been on the battlefield; (3) he was idle, lying in bed in the evening; (4) he was self-indulgent, giving freedom to his desires when he should have been disciplining himself; and (5) he was careless, allowing his eyes to wander and yielding to the "lust of the flesh and the lust of the eyes" (1 John 2:16). The Christian soldier must never lay aside the armor (Eph. 6:10ff).

James 1:13-15 perfectly describes David's case: (1) his desires were activated by the sight, and he failed to curb them; (2) desire conceived the sin in his imagination; (3) his will surrendered and this led to sin; (4) his actions led to death. He did not "watch and pray" as Matt. 26:41 commands; nor did he deal decisively with his "wandering eye" (Matt. 5:29 and 18:9).

David could have defeated this temptation (for it is not a sin to be tempted) by recalling God's Word (Ex. 20:14), or by considering that Bathsheba was a man's daughter and a man's wife (v. 3). In fact, she was married to one of the bravest soldiers in David's army (23:39), and she was also the granddaughter of Ahithophel, who later rebelled against David and sided with Absalom (23:34 and chaps. 16–17). David had many wives already, and God would have given him more (12:8). It is too bad that the record of this godly man was marred forever by "the matter of Uriah the Hittite" (1 Kings 15:5). Of course, we must admit that the woman shared in the guilt, but David, being the king, surely is more to blame.

## II. David and Uriah (11:5-27)

"When desire has conceived, it gives birth to sin!" warns James 1:15 (NKJV). How true these words are in David's experience. Instead of calling on the Lord and confessing his sin, the king sent for the husband and tried to trick him into going home. This, of course, might have covered the sin. But Uriah was a better man than his king, and he refused to go home! Compare David's self-indulgence in vv. 1-2 with Uriah's discipline in v. 11. Then, his first plan having failed, David tried a new scheme and made the man drunk. But even under the influence of wine, Uriah was a more disciplined man than sober David!

Sin was still growing: David decided to have the man murdered and then to take his wife. Joab was more than willing to cooperate, since this would give him opportunity later to take advantage of the king. Uriah carried his own death warrant to the battlefield that day. The plan worked and the brave soldier was killed in battle. David "put on a front" and waited until the week of mourning was over; then he married the widow. Some in the court may have thought highly of David for comforting Bathsheba in this way, but the Lord thought otherwise.

## III. David and the Lord (12)

### A. David's confession (vv. 1-14).

At least a year passed, during which time David covered his sins. Read Ps. 32 and 51 for descriptions of David's feelings during that difficult period. He became weak and sick physically; he lost his joy; he lost his witness; he lost his power. God gave David plenty of time to make things right, but he persisted in hiding his sins. Had he come to the Lord on his own, in sincere repentance, things might have been different later on. Finally, God sent Nathan, not with a message of blessing as in chapter 7, but with a message of conviction. How easy it is to be convicted about other people's sins! But Nathan fearlessly told David, "You are the man!"

We must commend David for bowing to the authority of the Word of God and confessing his sin. He could have slain Nathan. (Note that David even named a son after Nathan, 1 Chron. 3:5; Luke 3:31). God was ready to forgive David's sins, but He could not prevent those sins from "bringing forth death" (James 1:15). God's grace forgives, but God's government must allow sinners to reap what they sow. See Ps. 99:8. "He shall restore fourfold!" David had declared punishment concerning the man in Nathan's story, so God accepted his sentence. The sword never did depart from David's household: the baby died; Absalom killed Amnon, who had ruined Tamar (chap. 13); then Joab killed Absalom (18:9-17); and Adonijah was slain by Benaiah (1 Kings 2:24-25). Fourfold! Add to these trials the awful ruin of Tamar, the shameful treatment of David's wives by Absalom (12:11; 16:20-23), plus the rebellion of Absalom, and you can see that David paid dearly for a few moments of lustful pleasure. He sowed lust and reaped the same; he sowed murder and reaped murders, for "whatever a man sows, that he will also reap" (Gal. 6:7).

## B. David's contrition (vv. 15-25).

Immediately the chastening hand of God moved, and the baby became ill. Nathan had said it would die (v. 14), but David still fasted and prayed for the life of the child. He would not even listen to his servants, but at the end of a week, the child died. David's fasting and prayers could not alter the counsel of God. He had committed a sin unto death, and it was wrong to pray about it (1 John 5:14-16). However, we appreciate David's concern for the child and mother, and his faith in the goodness of God. We appreciate too his confidence in God's Word, for he knew the child had gone to heaven (v. 23). While we abhor David's sin and all the trouble it brought, we thank God for this wonderful verse of assurance to sorrowing parents who have lost children in death. (As Vance Havner said, "When you know where something is, you haven't lost it.") "Where sin abounds, grace much more abounds!" Note too that it is wrong to pray for the dead. David stopped praying for the child.

## C. David's conquests (vv. 26-31).

This tragic episode began with David pampering himself at home, but it ends with him taking his rightful place on the battlefield and leading the nation to an important victory. It is encouraging to see that God was willing to use David again in spite of his sins. He had confessed his sins; God had forgiven him; now he could fight for the Lord again. It is bad for believers to sin; it is also bad for them to live in the past and think themselves useless even after they have confessed their sins. Satan loves to shackle God's people with memories of sins that God has already forgiven and forgotten. Satan is the accuser (Rev. 12:10; Zech. 3), but Jesus is the Advocate (1 John 2:1-2).

How the grace of God shines in vv. 24-25, for God chose Bathsheba to be the mother of the next king! "Solomon" means "Peaceable"; "Jedidiah" means "beloved of the Lord." God turned the curse into a blessing, for Solomon was the fulfillment of the promise given to David in 1 Chron. 22:9.

This event in David's life ought to be a warning to all Christians to "take heed lest we fall" (1 Cor. 10:12). First Corinthians 10:13 promises a way of escape when we face temptation. However, as in David's case, we cannot overcome temptation if we allow our desires to take over. We need to beware of the beginnings of sin and take care to keep our imaginations clean. The Apostle Paul com-

mands us to "put to death" (mortify) the members of the body
that can lead us into sin (Col. 3; Rom. 6). It is necessary for all
believers to watch and pray and not make provision for the flesh
(Rom. 13:14).

# 2 SAMUEL 15–19

David continues to reap the sad harvest of his sins; see 2 Sam.
12:10-12. While our God is gracious to forgive when we confess our
sins, He will not violate His own holiness by interfering with the
tragic results of our sins.

## I. The Rebellion of the Prince (15:1-12)

Read chapters 13 and 14 to get the complete story. Absalom's
beautiful sister Tamar was ruined by his half-brother Amnon, who
was David's oldest son (3:2). David had committed adultery with
Bathsheba; now rape invaded his own household! Absalom had a
dual purpose in mind when he found out what Amnon had done: he
wanted to revenge Tamar by killing Amnon, but at the same time
he would be removing the obvious heir to the throne. It seems that
David had no disciplinary influence over his own family. In 13:21
we read of David's anger, but we read nothing of his actions to
correct matters. Perhaps the memory of his own sins checked him.
Absalom took matters into his own hands and killed Amnon; then
he fled to Gentile territory to hide away with the relatives of his
mother (13:37 and see 3:3). In chapter 14, Joab interceded for
Absalom and tricked David into bringing his wayward son back
home.

Absalom wasted little time in building a loyal group of followers.
He openly criticized his father's administration and secretly stole
the hearts of the people. (Note that the "forty years" of 15:7 is
translated "four years" in other versions. If the number forty is the
correct number, then we do not know from which event in the past
the writer is dating.) After a time, Absalom found his movement
strong enough to risk open revolt. It is not surprising that Ahithophel, David's counselor, sided with the rebels, for it was his granddaughter Bathsheba that David had taken (11:3 with 23:34). It
looked as though Absalom would be successful and steal the crown
from his father.

## II. The Reactions of the People (15:13–16:23)

While David was reigning in power, his real enemies would not dare to oppose him, but Absalom's revolt gave them what appeared to be a wonderful opportunity to resist the king and get away with it. It was a time of sifting the true from the false.

### A. David's friends (15:13-37).

Leaving Jerusalem was a wise move for David, for it would not have taken much force to make him a prisoner in his own palace. Note that the Gentiles in his army, led by Ittai the Gittite, were loyal to their king. Undoubtedly these men had stood with David during his trying years of exile. The two priests, Zadok and Abiathar, also started to follow their king, but David sent them back to the city. This in itself was a step of faith, for David was trusting God to give him victory and return him to his throne. David did not make the mistake Eli's sons made when they rashly took the ark into battle (1 Sam. 4–5); he sent the priests and the ark back to Jerusalem. Of course, the priests could spy for him and send their sons with information. Hushai was also sent back to the city to pose as an ally of Absalom; his counsel could change that of Ahithophel. It is a sad picture as David and his small army flee the city and cross the Kidron River. It reminds us of our Lord Jesus as He was rejected in Jerusalem, left the city, and crossed the Kidron to pray in the garden (John 18:1). The "Judas" in David's situation was his former friend Ahithophel; perhaps Ps. 55:12-15 was written at this time. Psalms 3 and 4 were composed during this rebellion, and in them we see where David was putting his faith.

### B. David's enemies (chap. 16).

Times of rebellion are times of revelation; you see what people really believe and where they stand. Ziba lied to David about Mephibosheth (see 19:24-30) and David was too quick to pass judgment. Shimei was related to Saul's family and openly showed his hatred for David. David's patience under this trial was wonderful; he knew the Lord would avenge him at the right time. Abishai wanted to cut off the man's head (see Luke 9:54 and 1 Peter 2:23), but David stopped him. David was being disgraced not only in the wilderness, but also back in his own palace. For Ahithophel had counseled Absalom to take David's concubines for himself and thus openly break with his father. This was a fulfillment of the prophecy in 12:11-12.

Today, our Lord Jesus is despised and rejected of men, just as was David during the rebellion. It takes courage for men and women today to remain loyal to the King, but we can be sure that God will reward such loyalty when Jesus returns.

### III. The Reckoning of the Lord (17–19)

God permitted this rebellion as a part of the price David was to pay for the sins he committed in connection with Uriah and Bathsheba. God also overruled the events so as to purge David's kingdom and separate the loyal from the disloyal. A day of reckoning finally arrived. Sometimes God's judgments fall swiftly, while at other times He waits and acts slowly.

#### A. Ahithophel dies (chap. 17).

There is no question that Ahithophel's plan was the better of the two, but God saw to it that Absalom rejected it. Note Hushai's psychological approach to suggesting that Absalom himself lead the army in battle. This appealed to the man's vanity, but, alas, that vanity only led ultimately to his death. When Ahithophel saw that his counsel was rejected, he took his own life. This is another parallel with Christ's experience in the NT, for Judas went out and hanged himself.

#### B. Absalom dies (18:1–19:15).

The vain prince followed Hushai's advice and led his army into the wood of Ephraim. Certainly he was unprepared to wage war, but "Pride goes before destruction, and a haughty spirit before a fall" (Prov. 16:18, NKJV). Absalom caught his head and long hair (14:25-26) in a branch and could not get down. (See Job 20:1-7.) Joab disobeyed David's command (18:5) and killed the rebel; then he sent the news to the king who, when he heard it, wept bitterly. David was a man "after God's own heart" and found "no pleasure in the death of the wicked" (Ezek. 33:11). David's abnormal grief, however, almost cost him the kingdom.

#### C. Shimei is pardoned (19:16-23).

Many a rebel will try to "change his tune" when the King comes back! David was trying to gather together the fragments of his kingdom, so he could not afford to alienate any of the tribes, but later on, Solomon gave Shimei what he deserved (1 Kings 2:36-46).

## D. *Ziba and Mephibosheth are reconciled (19:24-30).*

It does not speak well of Ziba that he arrived in the company of Shimei (vv. 16-17). Certainly Ziba had lied about his master, and David sought to give a fair judgment. Sad to say, his rash decision before made it difficult to settle matters completely; but we do appreciate David's attitude. We see in Mephibosheth a good example of concern for his absent king.

## E. *Barzillai is rewarded (19:31-43).*

He had met David's company with help in their hour of need (17:27-29); and no doubt this act of kindness had cost him friends, but he was wonderfully rewarded when the king came back! Barzillai did not want to leave his home and die away from his loved ones, so he suggested that Chimham (perhaps a son or grandson) be given the blessing. Jeremiah 41:17 informs us that David gave Chimham land near Bethlehem and that his family lived there for many years.

This entire episode of David's rejection and return certainly illustrates the attitudes people today have toward Christ. There are the loyal few who stand by their absent King, and there are the selfish majority who prefer to rebel. But what will happen when the King comes back? And what are we, His followers, doing to hasten His return? (2 Peter 3:12)

# 2 SAMUEL 24

You will want to read 1 Chronicles 21, the parallel account of this great sin in David's life. Here is another example of God permitting Satan to work so that the purposes of the Lord might be fulfilled. See Luke 22:31-34.

## I. Sin (24:1-9)

What lay behind David's desire for a national census? Probably it was pride: he had won a number of great victories (1 Chron. 18–20) and perhaps wanted to bask in the glory of success. There was certainly nothing wrong with a census, since the people had often been numbered during their national history; but we must keep in mind that a census that praised men would never glorify God.

Another factor to consider is Ex. 30:11-16. In connection with a census was the matter of the "redemption money" that each one was to give, for this money was a reminder that the people were the Lord's purchased possession. Exodus 30:12 warns that God would plague the nation if the people ignored giving the redemption money, and this is just what happened.

God gave David nearly ten months to change his mind and avoid discipline (v. 8). God even used the wise counsel of Joab to discourage him, but David would not listen. It is too bad that God's children sometimes become stubborn in heart and insist on their own way.

David's sin was not a hasty thing; he carried it out with cool, calculated precision. He was rebelling against God! There is an interesting series of contrasts between this sin and his sin with Bathsheba: (1) this was a sin of the spirit (pride) while the other was a sin of the flesh; (2) here he acted with deliberate persistence, while his sin with Bathsheba came as the result of the sudden overwhelming desires of the flesh; (3) this sin involved the nation, and 70,000 people died; his other sin was a family matter, with 4 people dying. (4) Yet in both sins, God gave David time to repent, but he waited too long.

We may not think that pride and rebellion against God's Word are serious sins, but in David's life they produced greater sorrow and tragedy than did his adultery. We must beware of sins "of the flesh and of the spirit" (2 Cor. 7:1).

## II. Suffering (24:10-17)

"The wages of sin is death." Note that David was convicted in his heart before the judgment fell. He was certainly honest with himself and with the Lord, but his conviction and repentance came too late. In 12:13, David said, "I have sinned," but here he says, "I have sinned *greatly.*" From a human point of view, numbering the people does not seem a greater sin than adultery and murder; yet from God's point of view, taking the census was a sin greater in its disobedience and consequence. Jesus, when on earth, was forgiving toward the publicans and sinners but severe with the proud and rebellious. Certainly sins both of the flesh and of the spirit are evil, and a person should not be involved in either one, but we dare not underestimate the awful results of pride and stubborn disobedience.

God permitted David to choose his own discipline, and his

choice showed the compassion of his heart. ("Seven years of famine" in v. 13 should be "three years" to parallel the three months and three days of the other two punishments.) David chose to fall into the hands of his merciful Lord rather than into the hands of men. At 6:00 A.M. God's angel came and began to plague the people. By the time of the evening sacrifice (3:00 P.M.) the angel had slain 70,000 people with a plague. David and his elders saw the judging angel, and David immediately interceded for the people. "These sheep, what have they done? Let Your hand be against me!" However, we must remember that God had a definite cause against the entire nation (24:1) and was using David's sin as the opportunity to judge the people. Perhaps God was punishing the nation for its rebellion against David when many of them followed Absalom.

There is a practical warning here for those in places of authority: the higher the office, the greater the influence for good or for evil. In Lev. 4 we see that, if the high priest sinned, he was to bring a bullock for an offering (v. 3), the same sacrifice that God required if the whole congregation sinned (vv. 13-14)! David's sin involved the whole nation this time, just as his "family sin" had involved his entire household.

## III. Sacrifice (24:18-25)

Two factors were involved in the halting of the judgment: the mercy of the Lord (v. 16) and the confession and sacrifice of the sinner (vv. 17ff). God sent His servant a message to build an altar at the place where he had seen the angel, the threshing floor of Araunah (or Ornan). David and his elders went immediately to the site and settled the purchase: he paid 600 shekels of gold for "the place" (the entire area, 1 Chron. 21:25) and 50 shekels of silver for the oxen and the threshing floor (2 Sam. 24:24). Ornan would have freely given the whole thing to his king, but David would not accept it. He would not give the Lord another man's sacrifice! A cheap sacrifice is worse than no sacrifice at all. This is a good principle for us to follow in our own Christian walk.

David immediately offered the oxen as burnt offerings of dedication to the Lord, and the shedding of the blood took care of the sins. Second Chronicles 3:1 informs us that this very same area became the site for Solomon's temple. God was able to turn the curse into a blessing! It is interesting to note that Solomon was born to Bathsheba, who had been involved in David's adultery; and yet Solomon became the next king and actually built the temple on the piece of ground associated with David's greater sin of numbering the people. Such is the amazing working of the grace of God! Certainly we ought not to "do evil that good may come from it" (Rom. 3:8), but we can rest in the confidence that "all things work together for good to them that love God" (Rom. 8:28).

Let us note some practical lessons from this chapter:

### A. We never outgrow temptation.

David was not an inexperienced youth when he committed this sin! Had he been "watching and praying" he would not have entered into temptation and sin so easily.

### B. God graciously gives time to repent.

He gave David more than nine months to deal with his sins and make matters right. "Seek the Lord while He may be found."

### C. Sins of the spirit do great damage.

All sin is wicked and should be avoided, to be sure, but we must realize that the Bible repeatedly condemns stubborn pride. Once David got on his evil course, he was too proud to turn around. His predecessor, King Saul, made the same mistake. We may not be guilty of adultery and murder, but a hard heart and a proud look will lead to perhaps greater evils.

### D. Our sins involve others.

Seventy thousand people died because David disobeyed the Lord.

### E. True confession is a costly thing.

Do we realize the high cost of sinning? A true confession is more than a quick prayer and a quoting of 1 John 1:9! True confession involves facing sin honestly and obeying God's Word regardless of the price we must pay.

### F. God will forgive and bring blessing.

Let us put ourselves into the hands of the Lord, for great are His mercies toward us!

# 1 KINGS 1-4

We now begin the study of the life and reign of Solomon, David's son and successor to the throne of Israel. In David we have a type of Christ in His humiliation, exile, and rejection; but in Solomon we see the "Prince of Peace" (the name Solomon means "peaceable") reigning in glory and splendor over His people. David made the conquests that enabled Solomon to live and reign in peace and magnificent prosperity.

## I. Solomon Fulfills God's Word (1)

David was now unable to carry on his royal duties, so his son Adonijah took advantage of the situation and proclaimed himself king of Israel. "I will be king!" he announced, all the while realizing that God had appointed Solomon to succeed David (1:17; and see 2:13-15). Adonijah was deliberately rebelling against the will of God. Sad to say, some of David's confidential advisors fell in with the wicked plot, including Joab (whom David once tried to replace; see 2 Sam. 19:11-15 and 20:4-13) and Abiathar the priest. The treacherous prince followed the example of Absalom by preparing chariots and seeking to impress the people (see 2 Sam. 15:1ff).

However, three loyal servants took matters in their own hands and informed Bathsheba. She, in turn, took the message to King David, knowing that he would not break his oath that Solomon, her son, be crowned the next king. The entire plan worked smoothly, and David made it very clear that he wanted Solomon to take the throne immediately. Zadok, Nathan, and Bathsheba lost no time in putting Solomon on the royal mule and proclaiming him the new king of Israel. Verse 40 suggests that the news was received with great joy by the people of the land. However, when Adonijah and his unsuspecting crowd of admirers heard the news, it threw them into panic, for now their treachery was known. The rebellious prince ran to God's altar for protection and Solomon promised not to kill him. Too often wicked people flee to God for help without really repenting in their hearts.

## II. Solomon Executes God's Wrath (2)

### A. David's last counsels (vv. 1-11).

See also 1 Chron. 22-29. David emphasized the spiritual before the

303

political, for he wanted his son to walk in the ways of the Lord. He admonished him to study and obey the Law (see Deut. 17:14-20 and Josh. 1:8). God had made wonderful promises concerning Solomon (2 Sam. 7:8-17), but He could not fulfill them apart from Solomon's faith and obedience. David also reminded Solomon of the enemies that would oppose him and the friends that would assist him.

### B. Judgment on Adonijah (vv. 12-25).

Had Adonijah remained in his proper place, he would have lived, but he stubbornly refused to yield. In asking for the hand of Abishag, the last of David's wives (1:1-4), Adonijah was making a rash claim; for everything of David's had been turned over to Solomon. Bathsheba seems to have been an innocent go-between in this entire episode. Solomon realized the treacherous implications of his brother's request and made it clear that he knew also the treachery of Abiathar and Joab (v. 22). Adonijah had gone too far; now he had to die.

### C. Judgment on Abiathar and Joab (vv. 26-35).

Solomon honored the priest's office by not slaying him, but he banished him from service. This fulfilled 1 Sam. 2:30-36. When Joab heard of his friend's exile, he knew that judgment would soon come to him; so he, like Adonijah, fled to the altar for protection. Joab was guilty of murdering several men and he had to pay for his sins. Benaiah became the new general of the army, and Zadok was made the high priest. It's interesting to note that Benaiah was a priest (1 Chron. 27:5) who turned general.

### D. Judgment on Shimei (vv. 36-46).

This was the man who so cruelly cursed David when he was fleeing from Absalom (2 Sam. 16:5ff). Solomon ordered him to remain in Jerusalem where he could be watched, a sentence far more merciful than he deserved. However, Shimei tried to "call his bluff" by disobeying the king's order, and it cost him his life. If these many judgments of Solomon seem cruel, keep in mind that these were enemies of the king and therefore enemies of the Lord.

## III. Solomon Receives God's Wisdom (3)

Solomon's marriage to an Egyptian princess was purely a political move; later he was to wed other heathen women (11:1ff) and be turned away from the true worship of Jehovah. But at the beginning of his career, he had a sincere love for the Lord and wanted to put Him first in his life. When God gave Solomon the privilege of asking for anything he wanted, he asked for wisdom and an understanding heart; and God answered his prayer. Furthermore, God gave him all the other blessings too (Matt. 6:33). Of course, if Solomon wanted to enjoy these blessings, he would have to walk in obedience to the Word (vv. 13-14).

The account of the two mothers is but one of many illustrations of the wisdom of Solomon. The fact that these two women had access to the king's throne shows how much young Solomon loved his people and wanted to serve them. How wonderful it is that every Christian has access to the throne of one who is "greater than Solomon" (Matt. 12:42), and who promises to give wisdom and to meet every need. Certainly all of us need to depend on the wisdom of God, not the wisdom of this world (1 Cor. 1:18-31; James 3:13-18).

It is a precious truth to the Christian that God equips us for our calling. God made Solomon king, and God supplied all that he needed to serve acceptably. "Ask and it shall be given you."

## IV. Solomon Enjoys God's Wealth (4)

In vv. 1-6 we have the names of the men in Solomon's "cabinet," and in vv. 7-19 the names of those who were overseers of the divisions of Israel. Samuel's warning about the king certainly came true: read 1 Sam. 8:10-18 as well as Deut. 17:14-20. It appears that the material prosperity of the nation was not matched by a spiritual prosperity, for in a few years the kingdom would be divided and Solomon's splendor would fade away. The people were "eating, drinking, and making merry" (4:20), but we do not read of their interest in the Law of the Lord. It is possible for a person to enjoy material prosperity and still be spiritual, as in the case of Abraham, but most people cannot handle much wealth.

Solomon's kingdom was the largest in Israel's history (v. 21, and see Gen. 15:18). Those were days of peace and prosperity (v. 25). However, the seeds of sin and apostasy were being sown. Solomon brought horses from Egypt (10:26-29) in direct disobedience to the Law (Deut. 17:16). He also multiplied wives (11:1 with Deut. 17:17). These sins eventually brought ruin to the kingdom. Solomon was a great student of nature, as you cannot help but notice when you read the Books of Proverbs, Ecclesiastes, and the Song of Solomon. We do not have all of his 3,000 proverbs, and the only "songs" we have are in the Song of Solomon. Certainly we may learn much of the ways of God watching nature; Jesus pointed to the lilies, seeds, sparrows, and other forms in nature to teach us about God.

Yet Jesus Christ is "greater than Solomon." Certainly He is greater in His person, being the very Son of God; and He is greater in His wisdom (Col. 2:3) and in His wealth (see Col. 1:19 and 2:9). Solomon took foreign wives, yet Jesus Christ will one day be married to His bride, the church, made up of blood-bought sinners from every tribe and nation. Christ is greater in His power and glory, and one day He shall reign over a greater kingdom forever and forever.

# 1 KINGS 5–8

These chapters record the fulfillment of God's promise that Solomon would build a temple to the glory of God (2 Sam. 7:12-16; and see 1 Kings 8:15-21). That this was a gigantic undertaking for so young a king, it is not difficult to imagine; but the Lord had given him assurance, and Solomon trusted the Lord (see 6:11-14). The parallel passages are found in 1 Chron. 22–2 Chron. 7.

## I. Preparation (5)

David was the man who started the entire project. God approved the project but made it clear that Solomon would do the actual work. David had ready the plans (1 Chron. 28:11-21) and the costly materials (1 Chron. 22:5, 14-16). He encouraged his son in the work and assured him that God would faithfully assist him (1 Chron. 28:1-21).

Hiram, the Gentile king of Tyre, agreed to supply the wood and the skillful men to do the work. Solomon in turn paid him 130,000 bushels of wheat and 120 gallons of pure olive oil each year. See also 1 Kings 9:10-14.

Israel provided the manpower through a part-time enlistment or "draft." The heavy "slave work" was done by the Canaanites, 150,000 of them (5:15; 9:20-22), while 30,000 Jews did the other work "in courses." There would be 10,000 a month on the job, and

then they would return home for two months. This levy represented about 1/40th of the available men in the land, so it was not
oppressive, and the service was temporary.

The building of the temple represented the cooperative efforts
of many people, both Jews and Gentiles. The materials secured
were the very finest: great and costly stones that would endure, and
precious metals that would give glory to the house. It reminds us of
Paul's admonition concerning the local church that we build with
"gold, silver, precious stones" and not "wood, hay, stubble" (1 Cor.
3:9-23). While God does not dwell in material temples today (Acts
17:24), this is no reason why the work we do for Him should be
cheap or shoddy.

## II. Construction (6–7)

Please check your Bible dictionary for the floor plan of the temple.
You will note that the "temple area" included buildings in addition
to the temple proper (7:1-12). Solomon built the temple first; this
required seven years (6:38). Then he built the king's house and the
other structures and courts that made up the temple area (9:10).
The entire project took twenty years.

It is not necessary to go into all the details of the construction of
the temple. You will note that the dimensions of the temple proper
were double that of the tabernacle, so the temple itself was not a
huge structure. The temple was made of cut stone, overlayed with
wood, overlayed with gold, and embellished with precious stones.
In 6:7 we note that the building stones were precut at the quarry
and silently fitted into place. The stone cutters were following
God's plans, so everything fit together. This is a good example for
Christian workers to follow today as we assist in the building of His
temple, the church (Eph. 2:19-22, and see 1 Peter 2:5-8).

The temple was larger and more elaborate than the tabernacle. It
was not a temporary tent with skins for a covering; rather, it was a
magnificent stone building that could not be moved. There were
windows and a floor in the temple (6:4 and 6:15), both of which
were lacking in the tabernacle. Solomon added two cherubim to the
holy of holies (6:23-30) and placed the ark under them. Instead of a
dusty outer court, the temple had a beautiful porch (7:1-12) with
two pillars (13-22) called "Jachin" ("He will establish") and
"Boaz" ("in Him is strength"). Strength and stability belonged to
the Lord and now would belong to His people as they settled in

their land. Instead of the small laver, they made a large "molten sea" (7:23-26) which stood upon twelve oxen. They also made ten portable brass lavers (7:27-39) to use throughout the temple area. We are told in 2 Chron. 4:1 that the altar of brass was equal in size to the holy of holies. There were ten candlesticks instead of one (2 Chron. 4:7-8), as well as ten tables for the bread.

The NT does not give us as much instruction as to the meaning of the temple as it gives concerning the tabernacle. Some see the tabernacle as a picture of Christ in His humility on the earth, and the temple as a type of His present ministry in glory, building that "holy temple" of living stones. Or, the tabernacle typifies our pilgrim life today, while the temple (a permanent building) typifies our glorious reign with Christ when He returns. How tragic that the Jews trusted the presence of their temple instead of the promises of the Lord; for in less than 500 years, this temple was destroyed as the Jews went into captivity for their sins. In 6:11-13, God reminded Solomon that the important thing was obeying His Word, not building a great temple.

## III. Dedication (8)

God filled the temple with His glory when the ark was brought in (vv. 1-11). In later years, Ezekiel would see that glory depart (Ezek. 8–11). Solomon addressed the people (vv. 12-21) and re-minded them of God's faithfulness to keep His promises. Then he prayed to the Lord on behalf of his family (vv. 22-30), citizens who sinned (vv. 31-40), Gentile strangers (vv. 41-43), and the nation in future exile (vv. 44-53). The key thought of his prayer is that God would hear their cries and be merciful to them in spite of their sins. Solomon makes it clear in his prayer that the condition of Israel's heart was more important than the presence of the temple. He knew that sin would bring chastening, but that repentance would bring forgiveness and blessing. It was more important to dedicate the people than the building.

Verses 44-53 certainly did come true, for Israel was taken captive because of their sins, and God brought them back to their land to rebuild their temple and serve Him again. This prayer and promise will also be fulfilled in these latter days when Israel goes back to her land in unbelief.

After the prayer, Solomon blessed the people (vv. 54-61) and exhorted them to have their hearts right with God. Note that the king is concerned that other nations know the truth of the Lord (v. 60, and see vv. 41-43). It is too bad that Israel did not fulfill her mission to take the truth to the Gentiles. The celebration lasted fourteen days (v. 65), with the first week taken up with sacrifices, feasts, and the official dedication ceremonies. In the second week, the people went back to their tents to rejoice in the Lord. In 9:1-9, God appeared to Solomon to remind him that with his privileges came great responsibilities; that He would establish his throne forever if the people followed the Lord in obedience; but that He would cut off the nation if they sinned. Unfortunately, the nation lapsed into sin and unbelief, and the prophecy of 9:6-9 came true. The beautiful and costly temple was plundered and destroyed in 586 B.C. when the Babylonians took the people captive.

God originally dwelt in the tabernacle (Ex. 40:34), then in Solomon's temple. The glory of God then came to earth in the Person of Christ (John 1:12-14). Today, every true Christian is the temple of God (1 Cor. 6:19-20), as is the church collectively (Eph. 2:21) and locally (1 Cor. 3:16). There will be a future Jewish temple during the tribulation period (2 Thes. 2:1-12) in which the Antichrist will be worshiped by an unbelieving world. There will also be a glorious temple during the 1,000 year reign of Christ (Ezek. 40–48).

# 1 KINGS 9-11

See 2 Chron. 7–9 for the parallel passages. These chapters cover Solomon's life after the great building programs had been completed. They show how this wise and godly king gradually declined spiritually and brought about the division of the kingdom.

## I. Divine Admonition (9:1-9)

God had appeared to Solomon just shortly after he ascended the throne (3:5-15), at which time the young king had asked for divine wisdom to carry on his duties. God had also sent a message of encouragement to the king during the difficult years of building the temple (6:11-13). Now that his great projects were completed, Solomon received another message from the Lord, this time to admonish him to obey God's Word. We often face our greatest temptations after a period of successful ministry.

God reaffirmed his covenant with David and reminded Solomon of his responsibility to "keep his heart with all diligence" (Prov. 4:23) and walk in obedience to the Word. If Solomon obeyed God's Word, his throne would be established and God would be able to bless Israel. But if Solomon disobeyed, and his children after him disobeyed, God would have to withdraw His blessings and take the people off their good land. Then the great houses he had built would be ruined and left behind as monuments of Israel's unbelief. No matter where you turn in the Bible, the same principle holds true: obedience leads to blessing, disobedience leads to chastening. Alas, we shall see in this study that King Solomon did not heed the warning, but instead gradually drifted away from the Lord until (near the end of his life) he tried to kill an innocent man (11:40).

## II. Dangerous Alliances (9:10–10:13)

### A. With Hiram (9:10-14).

We have already seen that Solomon depended on Hiram for the wood and skilled workmen for building the temple (5:1-12). Apparently in later years, Solomon needed more money, so he "borrowed it" from Hiram, giving the twenty cities of Galilee as security. This is the "Galilee of the Gentiles" of Matt. 4:15. When Hiram saw the cities, he considered them "worthless" (which is what "Cabul" means). Second Chronicles 8:1-2 informs us that Hiram had also given some cities to Solomon as part of the transaction. In any event, such alliances with the heathen nations were prohibited by the Law, and they only led Solomon deeper into trouble. See 2 Cor. 6:14–7:1.

### B. With Egypt (9:15-24).

Solomon's marriage to an Egyptian princess was strictly a political move, for he was importing horses and other luxuries from Egypt (10:28-29). To "go back to Egypt" was contrary to God's will for the Jews. "Woe to them that go down to Egypt for help!" cried Isaiah (31:1). By marrying a heathen woman, Solomon was setting a bad example for his nation and unnecessarily involving the people in the affairs of the heathen.

### C. With other nations (9:25–10:13).

Solomon's navy must have sailed as far away as India to secure the luxuries his kingdom demanded. The visit of the Queen of Sheba too was more than a personal visit; it involved setting up trade agreements and other alliances with her country. Solomon and the Queen exchanged expensive gifts, and she went home completely overwhelmed with his wisdom and wealth. Jesus mentions her in Matt. 12:42, using her visit to warn the Jews of His day. If the Queen of Sheba expended all that effort to go hear the wisdom of Solomon, how much greater judgment will fall on the Jews who had a "greater than Solomon" in their very midst, yet rejected Him!

These accounts show the peril of fame and fortune. Note that in 10:7 we have "wisdom and prosperity," but in 10:23 it is "riches and wisdom" — riches come first. No doubt Solomon gradually declined in spiritual things as the material became more important.

## III. Destructive Ambitions (10:12-49)

"Those who desire to be rich fall into temptation and a snare," warns 1 Tim. 6:9 (NKJV); and this came true in Solomon's life. He was not content with the abundance of blessings God had given him; he had to send away for even greater luxuries to satisfy his heart. No doubt the latter years of Solomon's life are revealed in Ecclesiastes, a book that reveals the emptiness of living for material pleasures. Perhaps it is not without significance that Solomon received 666 talents of gold a year (see Rev. 13:18). He would use only vessels of gold (v. 21), unlike our Lord who will use *any* vessel that is sanctified (2 Tim. 2:20-21). Yes, Solomon lived in glory and luxury, but Jesus said that even Solomon in all his glory was not as beautiful as one of God's simple lilies (Matt. 6:28-29).

Read Deut. 17:16-20 for God's instructions to the king, and note how Solomon disobeyed these instructions. He multiplied horses and chariots, he multiplied money, and he multiplied wives. Perhaps Solomon thought that his building of the temple was sufficient for his spiritual life; now he could afford to "coast" on past blessings. Read Ecc. 2 to see Solomon's interest in material gain.

## IV. Deliberate Apostasy (11)

It is unbelievable that the man who wrote Prov. 5:20-23 and 6:20-24 would multiply wives and concubines from heathen nations. Polygamy itself was bad enough (it had caused his father David no end of trouble), but to take wives from heathen lands was deliberate apostasy. See Deut. 7:1-14. What was the cause of this repeated sin? Solomon's heart was not right with God (11:4). God wanted "integrity of heart" (9:4), which means a united heart single to the glory of God. But Solomon had a divided heart—he loved the world as he tried to serve God. What a tragedy that the man who built the temple to the one true God should begin to worship at heathen altars. God was angry at this, so He sent several disciplines to bring the erring king back to the faith.

## A. A warning message (vv. 1-13).

God threatened to take the kingdom away from Solomon and give it to another. You would think that this warning would shock Solomon back to his senses, but apparently it did not. If a person will not listen to the Word, then the Lord has to take even more drastic measures.

## B. An invasion by Edom (vv. 14-22).

Solomon's "kingdom of rest" is now upset by war. Read James 4 for the spiritual explanation of this. Apparently Solomon's alliances with Pharaoh were not accomplishing much, because Egypt turned out to be an ally with the Edomites.

## C. Trouble from Rezon (vv. 23-25).

This band of warriors harassed Solomon's borders for many years. The apostate king was losing ground rapidly.

## D. Competition from Jeroboam (vv. 26-43).

Solomon himself had promoted Jeroboam into a good position because of his bravery and industry. But God chose this obscure young man to be the king over ten tribes. The one tribe remaining would be Judah, but this southern kingdom would include "little Benjamin" (12:21). When Solomon heard that he had a rival, he tried to kill him. The king must have known that the people were groaning under the heavy taxes and forced labor programs (see 12:6-11). In fact, Adoram, who was in charge of the "public works" was stoned by the people (12:18).

Solomon's death left his son Rehoboam to reign in his place. Had Solomon remained true to the Lord, his later years would have been filled with blessing and victory instead of chastening and defeat. He left to his son the problem of winning back the love of the people and lifting the heavy tax burdens that helped to make Solomon so wealthy. Yes, Israel seemed to be basking in great glory and splendor, but all was not well. It was a hollow glory that could not last. The description in Rev. 3:17-18 fits the situation well.

# 1 KINGS 12–16

These chapters record "the beginning of the end." With the death of Solomon, the nation's glory begins to fade. First Kings covers about 125 years of history, 40 years of Solomon's reign, and about 85 years for the divided kingdom of Israel and Judah. Only five kings reigned in Judah during that period, while eight kings reigned in Israel, and all of them were wicked. Second Kings then takes up the account of the Assyrian captivity of Israel (the northern tribes) and the Babylonian captivity of Judah (the southern tribes).

## I. The Division of the Kingdom (12:1–14:20)

### A. Rehoboam's folly (12:1-15).

Solomon's vast program of building and expansion had brought fame and glory to the nation, but the taxes were heavy upon the people and they were hoping for some relief from the burden. In his later years, Solomon's values had changed and he was more interested in material wealth than spiritual blessing (see Ecclesiastes 1:12–2:26). Had his son Rehoboam listened to the wisdom of the older leaders, he would have won the hearts of the people; but he was unwilling to be a servant to the people. He listened to the younger men, who lacked experience and, as a consequence, made a foolish decision. The way to be a ruler is to be a servant (Mark 10:42-45).

### B. Jeroboam's rebellion (12:16–13:34).

God had already chosen Jeroboam to be the king of the ten tribes (11:26-40) because of Solomon's sins (11:9-13). Sin is a great divider and destroyer. Only Judah and Benjamin were left to Rehoboam, and God did this for David's sake. Alas, Jeroboam failed to live up to his opportunities, for he led the ten tribes into idolatry. He was afraid that the people of his kingdom would go up to Jerusalem for the annual feasts, and there revolt against him, so he made it "convenient" for them to worship in their own territory. He repeated Aaron's sin (Ex. 32:1-6) and made calves of gold, putting one in Dan and the other in Bethel. He also consecrated places of worship and organized his own priesthood. It was a man-made religion, designed for the convenience of the people; therefore, it had nothing of the power of God or the blessing of God. Of course, God could not permit such apostasy to continue, so He sent a message of warning and judgment to the king (chap. 13). Note that the king was burning incense at the altar, acting like a priest. The mysterious man of God announced the birth of the future king Josiah (13:2, see 2 Kings 23:15-18), and also warned that the king's man-made religion would be judged and destroyed. When Jeroboam tried to arrest the prophet, the king's extended hand was dried up and the altar broke open, just as the prophet had predicted. The king begged to be healed, and the man prayed for him. The king then tried to trap the prophet by inviting him to the palace, but the man of God refused to fall for the trick. It is unfortunate that the man of God listened to the lies of a fellow prophet and lost his life. If there is one lesson to be learned from 13:11-34, it is this: don't let other people determine the will of God for your life. Obey what God's Word says to you, regardless of the cost.

### C. God's judgment (14:1-20).

Abijah was a young man when he became fatally ill (his father reigned for twenty-two years), and, of course, the king was concerned lest there be no son to succeed him on the throne. Jeroboam could not turn to his false gods for help; he had to turn to the prophet Ahijah for guidance. This was the prophet who first told Jeroboam that he would be the new king. The king dared not go himself; he sent his wife in a disguise. But the blind prophet could see more with his spiritual eyes than Jeroboam could see with his physical eyes. Ahijah exposed the disguise and sent the wicked king a message of judgment. The message came true: the queen returned home, and, when she entered the house, her son died. It is tragic that Jeroboam turned away from the Lord, for he could have led the ten tribes into wonderful blessing and victory. Instead, he set a terrible example for other kings to follow.

## II. The Decline of Judah (14:21–15:24)

### A. Rehoboam (14:21-31).

For seventeen years, this evil son of Solomon led the people into terrible sins. Instead of walking in the laws of the Lord, he patterned himself after the wicked nations Israel had defeated. God punished him by bringing Egypt up to defeat the nation. The people had lost their spiritual values: the expensive gold shields were now replaced with cheaper bronze shields. Things "looked the same," but God knew they were not the same.

## B. Abijam (15:1-8).

"Like father, like son." God allowed him to reign only three short years. Note that his mother was related to Absalom ("Abishalom" in v. 2). He declared war on Jeroboam (read 2 Chron. 13), and God gave him victory *for David's sake.* The victory was purely military; there was no spiritual revival in the nation.

## C. Asa (15:9-24).

Read 2 Chron. 14–16. Asa was a *good* king, a welcome change after years of evil rulers. He tried to take away the sins established by Rehoboam (14:24). There was a brief period of rest and revival under his leadership. He even deposed his own mother because she was an idol worshiper (2 Chron. 15:16). Sad to say, his reign did not end as well as it began, for he trusted in men for protection and failed to trust in the Lord. He used the temple wealth to hire Syria to fight for him; and this ungodly alliance cost him much personally.

## D. Jehoshaphat (15:24).

See also 22:41-50 and 2 Chron. 17:1–21:3. The writer here does not give the history of this good king who purged out the idolatry and who sought to teach the people the Word of God. God gave him many victories, because he "sought the Lord with all his heart" (2 Chron. 22:9).

## III. The Decay of Israel (15:25–16:34)

Six kings are listed here, starting with Nadab and ending with Ahab, and all of them were evil. Nadab maintained his father's wicked idolatry; he was slain by Baasha during one of the battles with the Philistines. Baasha reigned for twenty-four years and fulfilled the prophecy of 14:14-15 that all of Jeroboam's seed would be destroyed. Jehu the prophet then came with a message for Baasha, however, predicting the destruction of Baasha's household. His son, Elah, reigned for less than two years and was killed by Zimri, one of his captains, while the king was drunk. Zimri led the nation for only one week (16:15), but during that time he wiped out the family of Baasha and fulfilled the prophecy of Jehu (16:1-4). The army revolted and appointed Omri the new king. He in turn marched against Zimri, who set fire to the palace and committed suicide by perishing in the blaze. Omri ruled for twelve years (after putting down a brief revolt of the people) and led the people into further sin. His son Ahab was married to Jezebel, and this brought Baal worship officially into the kingdom. His only claim to fame was the establishing of Samaria as the capital of the northern kingdom. Upon his death, his son Ahab came to the throne, and under his leadership the tribes declined further into idolatry and sin.

You will note that it was when the nation was moving into idolatry that God called His prophets forth to preach to the people. We have met an anonymous prophet in chapter 13, and we will yet meet Elijah and Elisha. Of course, Jehu and Ahijah should also be mentioned. When God's people sin, it is only the Word of God proclaimed by the servants of God that can call them back and save them.

"Righteousness exalts a nation, but sin is a reproach to any people" (Prov. 14:34, NKJV). When godly kings were ruling, God blessed His people; when ungodly men reigned, God sent judgment and defeat. How tragic it is to see this great nation, called by the Lord, now declining in spiritual things and turning away from the truth. Yes, they often had material prosperity, but this was no sign that God was pleased with their deeds. In fact, the lust for material things often led the people farther from God. The best way to build a godly nation is to have godly citizens in godly churches (1 Tim. 2:1-6).

# 1 KINGS 17–18

Whenever the nation fell into sin and idolatry, God sent prophets to call it back to the true faith. The prophet was not simply a "foreteller"; he was also a "forth-teller" who announced God's judgment and exposed the sins of the people. Such a prophet was Elijah the Tishbite (native of the town Tishbeh), a "man subject to like passions as we are" (James 5:17), yet a man with great courage and faith. In these two chapters we see Elijah obeying two commandments from the Lord: "Go hide yourself," and "Go show yourself."

## I. His Private Ministry: "Go Hide Yourself" (17)

Luke 4:25 tells us that the drought lasted for three years, but in 1 Kings 18:1 we find the contest on Mt. Carmel taking place "in

316

the third year." Apparently the drought had begun six months before Elijah suddenly appeared in Ahab's court to proclaim that the drought would last another three years. Lack of rain was often a punishment for the sins of the people (Deut. 11:13-17; see 2 Chron. 7:12-15). Ahab and his wicked heathen wife Jezebel had led the people into Baal worship, a religion so vile we dare not describe it. The extra three years of drought was an answer to Elijah's prayer (James 5:17). Having delivered his message, the prophet retired from public ministry for three years, and during this time, the Lord graciously cared for him. The obedient servant can always depend on his master's faithful care. Note the three disciplines Elijah experienced:

### A. The dry brook (vv. 2-7).

God told Elijah exactly where to go and what to do. See Prov. 3:5-6 and Ps. 37:3-6. God withdrew Elijah's ministry from Israel as another punishment for their sins (Ps. 74:7-9). The Lord permitted Elijah to drink of the brook, and He provided bread and meat daily, delivered to the prophet by ravens. The raven is the first bird named in the Bible (Gen. 8:7); it was an unclean bird, yet God used it to help His servant. Note that while Elijah was enjoying bread, water, and meat in the place of God's appointment, the 100 prophets hiding in the cave (18:4) had to settle for only bread and water. But there came a day when the brook dried up. Did this mean Elijah had sinned, or that he was out of God's will? No! It simply meant that God had another place for him, and it was a reminder for Elijah to trust the Lord and not the brook.

### B. The depleted barrel (vv. 8-16).

God's Word always leads God's servant in the time of testing. But what strange commandments: "Go to Gentile territory where a widow will feed you." See Luke 4:22-26. "Zarephath" means "refining"; and God was certainly putting his servant through the furnace. Imagine Elijah's feelings when he discovered how poor the widow was, and that she was about to prepare her last meal. But God's commands are never wrong; for when the widow put God first (by obeying Elijah's commands), God provided for her, her son, and her guest. Note in v. 14 that Elijah honored the Lord God of Israel before this Gentile woman. All God asks is that we give Him what we have, and He will take care of the rest. He can feed thousands with only a few loaves and fishes.

## C. The dead boy (vv. 17-24).

The dry brook was Elijah's test; the dead boy was the widow's test. Great blessings are usually followed by great testings. It is unfortunate that the widow's faith should fail as indicated in v. 18; see Ps. 119:75 and 1 Sam. 3:18 for the right way to react to disappointments and trials. "Give me the boy" is Elijah's answer, for he knew God could raise the dead boy to life again. This is the first recorded instance of resurrection in the Bible. The prophet took the corpse up to his private guestroom (an upper chamber on the roof) and there prayed to God for the boy's life. Notice that he agonized for the boy and even stretched his own body upon the dead body of the lad. What an example for us today who would seek to "raise the dead" spiritually. The miracle brought forth a testimony of faith from the woman.

## II. His Public Ministry: "Go Show Yourself" (18)

Having been trained and tested in private, the prophet is now ready for his public ministry, so God commands him to face wicked King Ahab (see 16:33). We must admire Elijah's patience as he waited three years to preach one sermon.

## A. Elijah and Obadiah (vv. 1-16).

Obadiah is a picture of the compromising believer, and his life is in direct contrast to that of Elijah. Elijah was serving the Lord publicly and without fear; Obadiah was serving Ahab (vv. 7-8) and trying to serve Jehovah secretly (vv. 3-4). Elijah was "outside the camp" (Heb. 13:13); Obadiah was inside the court. Elijah knew the will of God; Obadiah did not know what was going on. While Elijah was laboring to save the nation, Obadiah was out looking for grass to save the horses and mules. When Elijah confronted Obadiah, the frightened servant did not trust the prophet. And note that Obadiah had to "brag" about his secret service to impress Elijah with his devotion (v. 13). Alas, we have too many Obadiahs these days and not enough Elijahs!

## B. Elijah and Baal (vv. 17-29).

The prophet was not afraid to meet King Ahab; nor was he afraid to tell the king the truth. The wicked always blame the believers for the trouble in the world; they never think to blame their own sins. The contest was not between Elijah and Ahab. It was between God and Baal. The nation was "limping and tottering between two ways," and it was time to make a decision (see Ex. 32:26; Josh. 24:15; Matt. 12:30). Confronted with their sins, the people answered nothing (v. 21). Elijah asked for an impossible situation: the true God would answer with fire. Of course, he knew that God had often "answered with fire" in years past (Lev. 9:24; 1 Chron. 21:26). When the servant of God obeys and trusts the Word of God, he need not fear failure. Of course, Baal could not answer because Baal does not exist. Satan could have sent fire to deceive the people (Job 1:16; Rev. 13:13), but God would not permit this. Elijah mocked the prophets of Baal; "He who sits in the heavens shall laugh" (Ps. 2:4, NKJV). It is amazing to what wicked extremes the heathen will go trying to get their false gods to answer prayer. Look at Ps. 115. By the time of the evening sacrifice (three o'clock in the afternoon), it was obvious to all that Baal was a false god and could not answer.

### C. Elijah and Israel (vv. 30-46).

Exposing the folly and sin of Baal worship was but half of Elijah's task for the day. More important was bringing the nation back to the true worship of Jehovah. Elijah was not out only to reform the people; he wanted to revive them too. First, he repaired the altar which the people had permitted to fall down. This is the first step toward blessing—repairing the personal altar of devotion, the family altar, the altar of sacrifice, and communion with God. By using twelve stones, Elijah reminded the people of their unity, because for many years the nation had been divided. To make it impossible for anyone to ignite the fire, Elijah had four barrels of water emptied on the wood and sacrifice three times, which would mean twelve barrels of water. The prophet prayed a simple prayer of faith, and the fire of God consumed the wood, the sacrifice, the water, and the altar.

But Elijah still had work to do. To begin with, the false prophets (850 of them, v. 19) had to be slain; see Deut. 13:1-5. It is not enough for us to acknowledge that "the Lord, He is God" (v. 39); we must also hate that which is evil and remove it from our lives. Judgment always prepares the way for blessing.

Then the prophet told the king to get back home, for rain was on the way. Baal was the "rain god," but he could neither send fire nor bring rain! As the king started on his way, Elijah began to pray for rain, just as three and a half years before he had prayed for drought

(James 5:17). He knew how to watch and pray (Col. 4:2), and he knew how to persist in prayer until God sent the answer. God does not send the showers of blessing until sin has been judged. Before long, the sky was black with clouds, the wind began to blow, and the rains came. God gave Elijah superhuman strength to run ahead of the king as his chariot raced toward Jezreel.

What we do with God in private is far more important than what we do for God in public. Our hidden life prepares us for our public life. Unless we are willing to go through such disciplines as the dry brook, the depleted barrel, and the dead boy, we will never have the victories of Mt. Carmel. "They that wait upon the Lord shall renew their strength" (Isa. 40:31).

# 1 KINGS 19

What a contrast we have here to the scene of victory in chapter 18! How often our greatest trials follow our greatest blessings. Here the man of faith gets his eyes off the Lord and becomes a man of fear; yet, in spite of Elijah's failures, God tenderly deals with His servant.

## I. God Refreshes Elijah (19:1-8)

James 5:17 reminds us that Elijah was "a man of like passions," a man of clay subject to the same trials and failures as any believer. How strange that Elijah should face 850 angry prophets and not be afraid, and then run away from the threats of one woman! Certainly there was a physical cause to his failure: the great contest on Mt. Carmel had undoubtedly wearied Elijah and drained him emotionally. Christians would do well to take better care of their bodies, especially after times of intense ministry and sacrifice (cf. Mark 6:31). But the main cause for Elijah's failure was spiritual: he saw Jezebel and failed to see the Lord; he listened to Jezebel's threats and forgot to wait for God's promises. In every step he had taken, Elijah had waited for God's command (17:2, 8; 18:1, 36), but now his fear led to impatience, and impatience led to disobedience (Isa. 28:16). He was no longer risking his life for God's glory; rather, he was trying to save his life for his own sake.

The steps of a good man are ordered by the Lord (Ps. 37:23), but the steps of an unbelieving and disobedient prophet only led him into worse trouble. Elijah fled to Judah, forgetting that Ahab's daughter was reigning there with Jehoram (2 Kings 8:16-18). He traveled more than eighty miles into greater danger. Wanting to be alone with his dejection, Elijah left his servant there and traveled into the wastelands. It is better for a man to walk with another, for "it is not good for a man to be alone." Loneliness and despondency usually go together. Physically and emotionally exhausted, Elijah lay down to sleep, and his "bedtime prayer" was, "Take away my life!" Moses had prayed this prayer at a time of great discouragement (Num. 11:15), and so had Jonah (Jonah 4:3). Elijah had his eyes on himself and what he had done (and not done), instead of looking to the Lord.

How graciously God refreshed His servant. The Lord knew that Elijah needed food and rest, as well as spiritual quickening. Elijah ate the meal and then went back to sleep. We see no evidence of repentance or confession of sin; it seems as though he had given up. So, God fed him the second time, and this time Elijah got up and started his journey again. The hand of the Lord guided him to Mt. Horeb, where Moses had received his call from God (Ex. 3) and where the Law had been given. It is encouraging to know that even when the child of God is backslidden and discouraged, God cares for him in grace.

## II. God Rebukes Elijah (19:9-18)

The word of God came to him in the cave (v. 9). "What are you doing here?" is a good question to ask ourselves at any time. Elijah's answer again revealed the discouragement of his heart; he felt as though he were the only one in Israel still faithful to the Lord. Instead of confessing his pride and desire for self-vindication, Elijah continued to argue his case with the Lord, so the Lord had to use other means to teach him and to bring him to the place of surrender.

Why did the Lord bring the wind, earthquake, and fire? For one thing, He was teaching his distraught prophet that He has many tools available to do His bidding. God does not lack for obedient servants in all nature (Ps. 148:1-10); yet men, made in the image of God, will not obey Him. What a rebuke this must have been to the backslidden prophet. Furthermore when the "still small voice" came after the storm, God was showing Elijah that His work is not always done in a big, noisy way. The miracles on Mt. Carmel were wonderful, but the lasting spiritual work in the nation must be accomplished by the Word of God quietly working in the hearts of the people. Elijah wanted something accomplished that was loud and big, but sometimes God prefers that which is still and small. It is not for us to dictate to God what methods He should use. It is our duty only to trust and obey.

"Go, return!" was God's word to the prophet after he tried to defend himself the second time (vv. 14-15). God would give him another chance to serve by anointing Hazael as the new king of Syria, Jehu as the new king of Israel, and Elisha as the new prophet. God was saying to Elijah: "Stop complaining and grieving over your seeming failures. Get back to work." This is certainly good counsel.

## III. God Replaces Elijah (19:19-21)

It is wonderful the way God encouraged Elijah by assuring him that there were 7,000 faithful believers yet in the land. We wonder where these believers were when Elijah stood alone on Mt. Carmel. We never know how much good our work has done, but God knows, and that is all that matters. Elijah's ministry was drawing to a close; he was to select his successor and prepare him for the continued work of proclaiming the Word of God. This too was an encouragement to Elijah, for now he knew that his work would continue even after his departure. There is a practical lesson for us here: if we will but wait for the Lord's message from His Word, and will not run away, He will give us the encouragement we need.

Elijah's first step was to appoint Elisha as his successor. This he did by casting his mantle (or cloak) about Elisha as Elisha was plowing in the fields. This act symbolized the fact that Elisha would now be a prophet with the same power and authority of Elijah. Elisha desired to bid farewell to his loved ones, and this was permitted, although in most homes such farewells would have taken several days to complete. See Luke 9:61-62. When God has called us, it is important that we follow immediately and not put others ahead of him.

The fact that Elisha slew the oxen and used the tools for his firewood indicates how definitely he was breaking with the past. He was "burning his bridges behind him" so to speak. The feast involved the friends of the neighborhood as well as Elisha's family; they all came to wish him well in his new calling. But once the feast was over, Elisha arose and followed his master and ministered to him.

Elijah did not anoint Hazael; Elisha did this later on (2 Kings 8:8-15). It was also Elisha who anointed Jehu (2 Kings 9:1-10). However, inasmuch as Elijah anointed Elisha, he indirectly anointed the others.

The fact that Elisha was assisted in the plowing by eleven other men (probably his father's servants, v. 19) suggests that Elisha came from a wealthy family. Have you noticed in the Bible that God usually calls people who are busy? Moses was caring for the sheep; Gideon was threshing wheat; Peter, James, and John were busy in their fishing business; Nehemiah was cupbearer to the king. God has no place for lazy people. For Elisha to give up his family and home, and the wealth he would have inherited, was certainly an act of faith and surrender. Elisha stayed in the background until Elijah's ascension (2 Kings 2), at which time he took up the ministry. Elijah's ministry had been that of "the earthquake, the fire, and the wind"; but Elisha would minister as "the still small voice." Of course, there would be judgments in his ministry as well, since sin must always be judged.

This experience in the life of Elijah is a good warning against despondency and discouragement. Just about the time we feel we have accomplished nothing, God reveals that He has used us more than we realized. It is a dangerous thing to think we are the only ones holding to the truth. Of course, it would have been better had the 7,000 "hidden ones" taken their stand with the prophet. It is likely that Elijah's bitter attitude shortened his ministry. The best solution for discouragement is Isa. 40:31—waiting upon the Lord.

# 1 KINGS 20–22

Ahab has gone down in history as the wickedest king Israel ever had (see 1 Kings 16:29-33 and 21:25-26). His heathen wife, Jezebel, ruled him from behind the scenes and saw to it that Baal worship was made the official religion of the land. Ahab had "sold himself to work evil" (21:20, 25). In these chapters we see his sins and his final judgment from God.

## I. Ahab's Defense (20)

### A. The challenge (vv. 1-12).

The king of Syria brought his vast army, assisted by thirty-two other kings, and threatened Samaria. His messengers asked for the king's wealth and family, and Ahab agreed to obey. But when they asked for the privilege of looting his palace, Ahab refused. Ahab tried to put up a brave front, but he knew the end was near. Had he been walking with the Lord, he could have turned his problem over to Him, but Baal was unable to deliver the king.

## B. The conquest (vv. 13-30).

The Lord stepped in to save the king and his people, not because Ahab deserved it (for he surely did not), but because God had a cause against Syria and the time of her judgment had arrived. The anonymous prophet gave the frightened king the message (v. 13), and Ahab's immediate answer in v. 14 indicates that he believed the message. Ahab was not a man of faith but was clutching to the last hope offered him. He immediately obeyed the Word of the Lord and sent his small army out to face the vast armies of the Syrians. God gave the Israelites a great victory; then the king himself went out to take charge of the battle and finish it in great glory. The Syrians concluded that Israel's God could win victories in the hills but not in the plains and valleys, so they planned another invasion for the following year. Once again, God in His mercy sent a message of hope to the evil king, and the Lord gave Israel another tremendous victory.

## C. The compromise (vv. 31-43).

What Satan could not accomplish with force, he accomplished with guile; for he led Ahab into a wicked compromise with the enemy. The enemy king and his servants pretended to repent and to humble themselves before proud Ahab, and the vain king fell for the trick. "He is my brother!" he said of Ben-hadad, his enemy. The two kings made a covenant of peace, and Ahab sent Ben-hadad away alive, in direct disobedience to the Word of God. The anonymous prophet, his face bruised by his friend, waited to see the king and to announce God's verdict of judgment. By telling the story of the escaped prisoner, the prophet was able to get King Ahab to confess his own guilt and pass his own sentence. (Nathan used this same approach with David, 2 Sam. 12). Ahab himself would die along with many of his people because he refused to follow God's directions.

Please keep in mind that God delivered Israel from her enemies wholly because of His grace; the king did not deserve it, neither did the people. God had already decreed that Ahab would be slain, not by Ben-hadad, but by Hazael (19:15-17), so the time was not right. God will perform His Word, and He is not in a great hurry to accomplish His will, for in mercy He gives men time to repent.

## II. Ahab's Deception (21)

### A. The sin (vv. 1-16).

The heart of the wicked is constantly lusting after things, and even the king is not satisfied in his empty idolatry. Now he covets his neighbor's vineyard and "pouts" because his neighbor will not disobey the Word of God and give it to him (see Lev. 25:23 and Num. 36:7). Queen Jezebel solves the problem by bringing false witness against Naboth, forging letters in her husband's name, and hiding the entire undertaking under the disguise of a religious fast. Naboth, an innocent man, was stoned to death just to satisfy the lust of King Ahab and his Baal-worshiping wife. "The heart is deceitful above all things, and desperately wicked; who can know it?" (Jer. 17:9)

### B. The judgment (vv. 17-29).

God knew all that had happened, and He sent Elijah to settle matters with the wicked king. "Have you found me?" asked Ahab, reminding us of Num. 32:23 — "Be sure your sins will find you out." Elijah announced doom to the household of Ahab, and in a short time his prophecies came true (2 Kings 9-10). Ahab had "sold himself to do wickedness" and therefore he had to accept the wages he had earned. The king humbled himself before the Lord (whether sincerely or hypocritically, we do not know), so the Lord postponed the punishment.

## III. Ahab's Defeat and Death (22)

Ahab did not defeat Syria when he had the opportunity, so the enemy came back to attack him and finally kill him. Similarly, King Saul had failed to destroy the Amalekites, and one of their young men killed him. Since Ahab's daughter was married to King Jehoshaphat's son (2 Chron. 21:1-7), his alliance with Ahab for this battle was not surprising. Note that King Jehoshaphat wanted to know God's will about the battle, so they inquired of the prophets that ministered to Ahab.

Of course, the heathen prophets in their blindness catered to the desires of the two kings and promised victory. But their promises sounded hollow; Jehoshaphat wanted to hear from a prophet of the Lord. Micaiah was the only one available (and he was a prisoner), so they sent for him and asked for his message. In holy sarcasm, Micaiah echoed the promises of the heathen prophets, but the king knew he was pretending. Is it not strange the way the lost want to hear from the Lord, but yet they do not want to hear the truth and obey it? Micaiah told the truth: the heathen prophets were being used to tell lies, for King Ahab would die in the battle and Israel would be scattered. What did the faithful prophet receive for his ministry? Bread and water in the prison. But he had been faithful to the Lord, and that is all that counted.

Ahab thought to avoid death by disguising himself, for the soldiers would seek to kill the king first. (Paul follows this idea in Eph. 6 when he cautions us not to fight against flesh and blood, but to battle against Satan through prayer and the Word. Once you have defeated the king, the rest is easy.) Jehoshaphat went into battle in his royal robes, and the Lord protected him, but Ahab in his disguise was slain. Verse 34 indicates that the soldier shot the arrow without even aiming, yet the Lord directed it to its proper target. When the judgment of the Lord comes, no devices or disguises will protect the sinner. Israel lost the battle and also lost her king.

The king was buried at Samaria; the bloody chariot was washed at the pool; and the dogs licked the blood, as God had promised (20:42 and 21:19). Ahab's wicked son Ahaziah reigned in his place, and the nation continued in its sinful course.

King Ahab was a great soldier who could have led Israel to victory and peace had he followed the Lord in truth, but his alliance with Baal worship, and the evil influence of his godless wife, brought him defeat. Ahab experienced the goodness of God in the military victories, yet refused to submit himself to the Law. He humbled himself outwardly when judgment was announced, and even then received a "stay of execution," but his shallow repentance did not last. The three and a half years of drought and the great demonstration of God's glory on Mt. Carmel did not soften his hard heart. He had "sold himself to do evil," and he would not repent. He heard one of the greatest prophets of OT history, Elijah, and yet did not repent. His twenty-two years of reign only led the nation farther away from God.

# 2 KINGS 1–4

The ministries of Elijah and Elisha have often been contrasted. Elijah was a fiery prophet who suddenly appeared in a dramatic fashion, while Elisha was a pastor-prophet who ministered in a personal way to the people. Elijah belonged to the rugged hills, Elisha to the peaceful valleys. Elijah was a solitary servant, while Elisha enjoyed fellowship with the people. Broadly speaking, Elijah was a prophet of judgment who sought to turn the nation back to God, while Elisha was a minister of grace who called out "a remnant" before the nation was destroyed.

## I. Elisha Succeeds Elijah (1–2)

### A. The judgment of fire (chap. 1).

The last three verses in 1 Kings 22 inform us that King Ahaziah was a wicked man whose heart had been unmoved by the recent judgments of God. We see now that neither the rebellion of Moab nor the injuries from his fall brought Ahaziah to repentance. In fact, he even sent to the heathen gods to find out whether or not he would survive. The Lord instructed Elijah to send the messengers back with a true message from the Lord: the king would die. Then Elijah departed; see John 12:35-36 for a NT parallel. Rather than submit to Elijah's God, the king sought to slay the prophet, but fire from heaven destroyed his men. This judgment was from the Lord. It was not Elijah's doing. The prophet's motive was to glorify the Lord; see Luke 9:51-56 for the disciples' misuse of this event. The third company of soldiers humbled themselves (through fear, not faith), and God accepted them. Fearlessly, Elijah gave the king his message of doom—and the king died.

### B. The chariot of fire (chap. 2).

In 1 Kings 19:20, Elisha had promised to follow Elijah faithfully; and this he did in spite of opportunities to depart. He had served his master about ten years when he was told that Elijah was going to leave him. Had Elisha taken the easy route and stayed behind, he would have missed all the blessing of vv. 9-15. It pays to be faithful to your calling. For the "double portion" of v. 9 see Deut. 21:17. Years before, Elijah had wanted to die in the wilderness. How wonderful that God did not honor that request. Instead, the prophet was carried to heaven in a whirlwind. God always gives

His best to those who leave the choice with Him. Because Elisha saw his risen, glorified master, he received the double portion of the Spirit. In v. 12, Elisha compares Elijah to the armies of Israel: he was more important to the nation's safety than the horses and chariots. See also 13:14.

Elisha took Elijah's mantle (see 1 Kings 19:19) and dared to trust God for the power to do the impossible. It was one thing to cross Jordan with Elijah, but quite another to step out by faith by himself. But when you trust "the Lord God of Elijah," you do not need Elijah too. This first miracle proved to the young men in the school of the prophets that Elisha was truly God's prophet, and they honored him. However, they were not so sure that Elijah was really gone. In vv. 16-18 we have their unbelief and folly recorded. It is an illustration of people today who doubt the resurrection and bodily ascension of Christ, and who question the future rapture of the saints. The healing of the waters by the salt is quite a contrast to Elijah's miracle of stopping the rain for three and a half years.

Verses 23-25 have puzzled some people. Keep in mind that these were young men, not children, and therefore responsible for their deeds. Bethel was a headquarters for idolatry (1 Kings 12:28-33); this sacred place had been desecrated and the young men were actually ridiculing God's Word and God's servants. The fact that forty-two of them met together suggests an organized plan. Calling the prophet "baldhead" was one of the lowest forms of insults, and the words "go up" point to their ridicule of Elijah's rapture to heaven. The bears mauled them, but we do not know if any of the young men were killed. It was a divine rebuke to the flippant attitude of wicked men who should have known better.

## II. Elisha Saves the Nation (3)

It was a sin for Jehoshaphat of Judah to ally himself with Ahab's wicked son, but he did it. The two of them lined up with Edom (another enemy) to fight the Moabites. Jehoram of Israel had to unite with Judah and Edom because his armies had to cross their lands to attack Moab. Alas, their journey was a failure and they ran out of water. Jehoshaphat turned to Elisha and the Lord, and the prophet recognized David's descendant, but refused to recognize Ahab's godless heir (vv. 13-14). God miraculously provided the water in the ditches they dug, and also routed the enemy before them. The account ends on a strange note; the helpless king of

Moab offered his own son as a burnt offering, and Judah and Edom became so indignant against Israel (Jehoram) that they withdrew from the battle and went home. They should not have allied with Jehoram to begin with. It was the faithful prophet of God, not the wicked king, who saved the nation.

## III. Elisha Serves the People (4)

During his "hidden years," Elijah had helped the people, but this was not his main ministry. Elijah was primarily a prophet of fire; Elisha was a "pastor" and a minister to the people. We see several miracles performed to assist the needy people.

### A. The prophet's widow (vv. 1-7).

See Lev. 25:39-46. The Jews were not showing mercy to one another or obeying the OT laws concerning debt. God takes what we have and uses it to meet the need, if we trust him (Ex. 4:2). "Shut the door" reminds us of Matt. 6:6; note that Elisha often "shut the door" when asking for God's help (vv. 21 and 33). God filled as many vessels as the widow had faith to bring, and those who loaned her the vessels must have benefited too. "My God shall supply all your need. . . ." (Phil. 4:19)

### B. The Shunammite woman (vv. 8-37).

Two miracles are recorded here: God gave the woman a son when her husband was old, and God raised the boy back to life when he was stricken. Shunem was about seven miles from Carmel. Elisha passed by the house often; he was finally invited in to break bread with the husband and wife. We see here that the prophet (unlike Elijah) was socially inclined. We may have here a parallel with John the Baptist and Christ: John was like Elijah, living alone; but Christ was like Elisha, visiting homes and enjoying meals with the people. The woman had true spiritual values, for she made a special room on the roof for the visiting prophet—a "prophet's chamber." To reward her, God gave her a son. But the son was stricken in the field (sunstroke?) and taken home dead. However, the mother did not despair; she immediately set out for Carmel to find the prophet. She would not deal with the prophet's servant Gehazi, and when the servant tried to raise the boy, he failed. This may be because of the covetousness that was already in his heart and that showed itself later (5:20ff). Note that Gehazi even tried to get rid of her (v. 27; see Matt. 14:15 and 15:23). Elisha himself had to make the journey to raise the boy. Verse 34 is a beautiful illustration of the effort and love it takes to win a soul, for Elisha "died" with the boy as he prayed for him. See 1 Kings 17:21ff.

### C. The school of the prophets (vv. 38-44).

This may have been started by Samuel (1 Sam. 10:10) and continued by Elijah (1 Kings 20:35). Not all of the young men were men of faith, and it is possible that there were rival "apostate schools" in the land; see 2:23-25. The dearth in the land meant a lack of food, so the young preachers were making some stew. One of the students was dissatisfied with the menu, so he went to find some vegetables to improve it. None of the others knew enough about food to reject the poisonous gourds he brought. The taste warned them of the danger, and their prayer brought action from Elijah: he added the meal and healed the pottage. Sad to say, in many colleges, "schools of the prophets," and even some churches, there is "death in the pot." The only thing that will cure the poisonous diet is the pure meal of the Word of God. In vv. 42-44, we find another problem: there was good food on hand, but not enough to go around. Elisha multiplied the food to meet the needs of all the men. See John 6.

Elisha the prophet was certainly a man of miracles. No matter what the need, God was able to work through him and meet it. He is the same "yesterday, today, and forever" (Heb. 13:8). Let's trust Him!

# 2 KINGS 5

## I. Naaman's Cure (5:1-19)

We have in this miracle a beautiful picture of salvation through faith in God's Word. Every lost sinner can see himself in Naaman; he can also see the power of saving faith.

### A. He was condemned.

He was a leper. His beautiful uniform and his mighty victories could not disguise the fact that Naaman was a dead man, for he had a disease that man could not cure. Read the notes on Lev. 13 and see how leprosy is an illustration of sin.

### B. He was an enemy.

He had a Jewish maid serving in his home, a girl kidnapped during a raid. As a Gentile, Naaman was outside the blessings of Israel; see Eph. 2:11-22. God gave His Son for us while we were enemies (Rom. 5:6-10).

### C. He heard a witness.

The little Jewish maid loved her master. Even though she was far from home, she did not forget her God and she was quick to witness of His great power. Had she not been a faithful worker in the house, she would not have been an effective witness, but because of her faithfulness, her witness was rewarded. How Christ needs witnesses today!

### D. He tried to save himself.

Naaman made every mistake possible in seeking to get a cure for his leprosy. First, he went to the king of Syria, who, of course, could do nothing. Then he went to the king of Israel, who was also unable to do anything. How many lost sinners run from one person to another, seeking salvation, and all the while Christ is waiting to meet their need. Note that Naaman was also ignorant of grace, for he brought with him a great deal of wealth (v. 5). The lost sinner tries to purchase salvation or earn it, but this is impossible.

### E. He was called by God.

Elisha heard about Naaman's plight and sent for him. No sinner deserves to be saved; it is only through the gracious calling of the Spirit that anyone comes to Christ; see John 6:37. In Luke 4:27, Jesus tells us that Naaman was one of many lepers, but the Lord chose him and healed him. This is grace.

### F. He resisted God's simple way of salvation.

Elisha did not come out to see Naaman; the general was a leper and would have defiled the prophet. Elisha wanted Naaman to know he was a rejected, condemned man. He treated the proud general like a sinner, and Naaman was angry at such treatment. "Doesn't he know who I am?" he asked. Like sinners today, Naaman thought the prophet would put him through some ritual (v. 11) to make him well. He would not humble himself to go into the Jordan, the river of death. He thought that his lovely rivers closer to home were far superior.

## G. He was cured by his obedient faith.

The humble servant in v. 13 had more sense than the great general. How unreasonable it is to resist God's simple way of salvation. When Naaman obeyed in faith, he was "born again" and came out of the waters with flesh as clean as that of a little child. The seven dips in the Jordan are not a picture of baptism, for nobody was ever saved by being baptized even once, let alone seven times. Naaman's faith was proved by his works; he trusted the Word and acted upon it.

## H. He had assurance.

He had said, "Behold, I thought" (v. 11); but now he said, "Behold, now I know" (v. 15). He gave public testimony to the reality of God's power and the fact that Jehovah alone was the true God. So grateful was he that he offered wealth to Elisha, who, of course, refused to accept the gift. Had he accepted the gift, it would have ruined the lesson of salvation by grace and would have robbed God of all the glory.

## I. He went home in peace (v. 19).

Naaman knew he would face problems back in Syria, since his king was an idol worshiper, but Naaman sought to obey the Lord and honor Him fully. Every true believer has "peace with God" (Rom. 5:1).

## II. Gehazi's Covetousness (5:20-27)

Gehazi disagreed with God's Word; this was the beginning of his troubles and sins. Had he submitted to God's Word and judged the covetousness in his heart, he would never have become a leper. It is important that God's people honestly judge their own sins in their hearts. "I will" was the attitude Gehazi had, not "Your will."

Note how quick and efficient people can be when they are disobeying God's Word. Gehazi did not run in 4:29-31 to raise the dead boy, but here he runs to Naaman to get material wealth. If only Christians would be as concerned about spiritual things as material. We now have two lies:

## A. He lied to Naaman (vv. 21-23).

"My master has sent me," he told the general. "Elisha needs the money, not for himself, but for one of the students at the school."

Like Judas, Gehazi seemed concerned for the poor, when all the while he was interested only in himself (John 12:1-7). Of course, by taking the money, Gehazi robbed God of His glory, contradicted the word of the prophet, and gave the impression that salvation involved money and good works. His one selfish deed ruined the whole picture. Gehazi received so much wealth that two of Naaman's servants had to carry it back for him.

### B. *He lied to Elisha (vv. 25-27).*

He went in and acted as though nothing had happened. But the prophet knew the truth and asked him where he had been. "Your servant did not go anywhere." Another lie. Verse 26 suggests that Gehazi had planned to use the money to set himself up in a little homestead of his own. It is likely that Gehazi's covetousness was in his heart long before this event for in chapter 4 we saw how powerless the servant was to raise the dead boy. God judged Gehazi because he would not judge himself, and Naaman's leprosy clung to Gehazi and to his descendants. We find Gehazi again in 8:1-6, this time in the presence of the king. Some have suggested that he repented and was healed, but this has no support from the Scripture. Furthermore, the disease was to pass on to his children too. The answer is simple: the events recorded in *2 Kings* are not necessarily given in their actual chronological order. This conversation between Gehazi and the king probably took place in the city gate as the king was hearing the complaints of the people.

How sad it is to see a devoted servant of the Lord brought into shame and rejection because of covetousness. It was not blasphemy (as with Peter), or even adultery (as with David), but the hidden sin of covetousness. Of course, covetousness can be the cause of all kinds of sins. If people covet something (or someone), there is no sin they will not commit to get what they want. Elisha, the servant of the Lord, did not live for material gain; he lived wholly for the glory of God. Gehazi could not serve two masters—money and Jehovah. Colossians 3:5 equates covetousness with idolatry. Jesus associates covetousness with the awful sins of the flesh (Mark 7:22), and Paul lists covetousness in his catalog of Gentile sins in Rom. 1:29. In Luke 12:13ff, the Lord clearly warns of the dangers of covetousness; and in Luke 16:13ff, He shows that this sin will take people to hell. See also Eph. 5:3.

It is interesting to contrast the servant girl of vv. 2-3 with Gehazi. She was a slave, yet joyfully witnessed for the Lord; he was a free man in his own land, yet was interested only in himself. She brought Naaman to the place of salvation; he ruined the message of grace by his sin. She had no material gain, but she did have the Lord's blessing; he went home with wealth, yet he lost everything.

# 2 KINGS 6–8

In these chapters we have several miracles and ministries of Elisha, some done privately for God's people, some done publicly for the nation. In each case we see clearly that the man of God is never at a loss to know God's will or exercise God's power.

## I. Elisha Restores the Axe Head (6:1-7)

It rejoices us to see that one of the schools of the prophets was growing and needed more space. These men were in a sense "home missionaries" being trained by Elisha to take the Word to the people. Evangelical schools that train our future workers are important and merit the support of God's people. Note that Elisha was not too busy or too proud to share in the building activities. Certainly his presence encouraged the young men. The students were poor, and at least one of them had to borrow tools. When the axe head flew off into the water, the student was terrified; but Elisha restored it to him. It is no sin to borrow, provided what is borrowed is cared for and returned. God is certainly interested in the personal needs of his people, even those "little matters" that often burden our hearts.

## II. Elisha Captures the Syrian Invaders (6:8-23)

The Syrian king was sending in bands of soldiers to raid Israel (see 5:2), but God kept revealing to Elisha every movement the enemy made. "The secret of the Lord is with them that fear Him," says Ps. 25:14. Though Elisha did not honor wicked King Jehoram (3:13-14), the prophet did have a heart for the people of Israel and wanted to protect them. The king was wise enough to listen to the man of God, and God protected Israel. When the king of Syria was told that Elisha was the "hidden spy," he sent a band of soldiers to capture the prophet. Elisha's servant (who apparently had replaced Gehazi) saw the army about their city and thought the end had come, but God opened the servant's eyes to see the hosts of angels ready to deliver Elisha. Verse 16 is as true for the Christian today as it was for the Jews in that day. "If God be for us, who can be against us?"

Elisha performed a dual miracle; he opened the eyes of his servant, but he blinded the eyes of the invaders. It was thus very easy to take the band to Samaria. Imagine the surprise of the Syrians when their eyes were opened to behold the enemy city. Elisha prohibited the King of Israel from slaying the soldiers: God had captured them and God alone was to get the glory. Elisha defeated them with kindness. See Rom. 12:20-21, Prov. 25:21-22, and Matt. 5:43-45. From that time on, Syria sent no more secret "commando" bands to raid the villages of Israel. God's people, if obeying His Word, never need fear the enemy; see Ps. 46.

## III. Elisha Delivers the City (6:24–7:20)

We do not know how many years passed between verse 23 and verse 24. When Ben-hadad did decide to fight Israel, it was with a complete army and not with small bands of invaders. The capital city was besieged until there was very little food: the very worst food was selling for exorbitant prices. ("Dove's dung" in v. 25 probably means a very cheap kind of grain. However, it would not be unlikely that starving people would eat even animal refuse). Furthermore, some of the people were resorting to cannibalism. Wicked King Jehoram echoed his father Ahab's words when he blamed the famine on Elisha (6:31 and 1 Kings 18:17). The king sent a messenger (whom Elisha knew was coming) to receive a strange prediction from the man of God: by the next day, Samaria would be delivered, and there would be plenty to eat. In 7:1, Elisha predicted that they would be able to buy six times as much food for one-fifth the cost. One of the king's lords revealed his unbelief, and Elisha promised him judgment. See 7:17-20.

What weapons did God use to defeat the entrenched Syrian army? A noise and four lepers! Thinking that a hired army was coming upon them, the Syrians fled, leaving wealth and food in the camp. With good reasoning, the four lepers decided it was better to eat as prisoners (or die quickly) than to starve in freedom. Verse 9 is certainly a Gospel text and a great missionary text. How Christians need to heed it today! When the imprisoned citizens of Samaria heard the good news, they rushed out—and trampled the unbelieving lord underfoot! He heard the good news, he saw the proof of the message, but he died before he could enjoy it. What a warning to the sinner who delays receiving Christ!

## IV. Elisha Protects the Shunammite Woman (8:1-6)

Verse 1 should read, "Now Elijah had said . . ."; that is, seven years before, the man of God had warned her about approaching famine over the whole land; see 4:38. This is not the local famine in the city of Samaria described in chapter 6. The fact that Gehazi is talking to the king indicates that this event occurred before the healing of Naaman (chap. 5). The woman had obeyed Elisha and forsaken her property, finding temporary help in the land of the Philistines. But when she returned to Israel, someone had confiscated her property. Imagine her surprise to discover Gehazi talking to the king at the very moment she came to press her case. God had ordained years before that her son should die and be raised (4:18-37) and that this miracle would make it possible for her to regain her lost land. We may never understand the reasons for our trials now, but certainly they are working together for our good (Rom. 8:28). How wonderful that believers have an inheritance that cannot be taken away (1 Peter 1:4; Eph. 1:11, 14).

## V. Elisha Judges the King (8:7-29)

Back in the days of Elijah, God had told that prophet to anoint Hazael king of Syria (1 Kings 19:15). Elijah did anoint Elisha to be his successor as prophet, but it remained for Elisha to see Hazael established on the throne. God's Word is going to be fulfilled in spite of the failure of believers or the plans of unbelievers.

Ben-hadad had been an enemy of Israel, yet when a crisis came, he turned to the man of God for help. How like the people of the world today! He sent an elaborate and expensive gift to Elisha; we have no record that he accepted it. If he did, certainly he used it for the schools of the prophets. Note the cryptic reply Elisha gave to Hazael: (1) *Say to him*, "You shall certainly recover"; (2) However, the Lord has shown *me* (Elisha) that he will really die. The first statement Hazael quoted to his king in v. 14, elaborating it somewhat to make his recovery seem certain. The second statement Hazael fulfilled by murdering the king (v. 15).

Verses 11-13 must be studied carefully. After Elisha gave his strange answer to Hazael, the man of God stared at his visitor for a long time. Actually, Elisha was reading the thoughts of Hazael's wicked heart; he saw that his visitor was planning to murder the king. Hazael was so embarrassed by this peculiar behavior that he became ashamed; in return, Elisha wept. The wicked visitor tried to cover up the sins of his heart, but Elisha knew too much. "I know the evil you will do in Israel," said Elisha as he wept, and he described his terrible crimes. Hazael was shocked at this announcement; yet, no one should be shocked at the wickedness of his own heart, for the heart is "desperately wicked." Elisha's parting words were, "You will become king over Syria." Instead of allowing the Lord to accomplish the task, Hazael engineered matters himself by smothering the ailing king in his own bed. Later history reveals that Elisha's words were true, for Hazael was guilty of awful deeds during his reign; see 10:32-33, 13:3-7, 13:22.

The remaining verses of this chapter bring us up to date on Israel and Judah. It is likely that Joram and Jehoshaphat were co-regents during the last part of Jehoshaphat's reign. How sad to see the kings of these nations following the bad examples of Jeroboam and Ahab.

During those days of political decay and national sin, God was using Elisha to call out a believing remnant of people to obey God. The whole nation was not going to be saved, even as the whole world today is not going to be saved. God is calling out a people for His name. Our responsibility as believers is to be true to the Word of God and to seek to win others to Christ.

# 2 KINGS 9–10

These two chapters are filled with violence, for in them we see the Lord executing His wrath on those who had long despised Him and disobeyed His Word. King Jehu was an instrument of vengeance in the hands of the Lord (9:7), although we must confess that his zeal for the Lord (10:16) perhaps was too fanatical. In Hosea 1:4 God announced that He would judge the house of Jehu because of his deeds of ruthless murder. Jehu called his activities "zeal for the Lord," but we can see in his slaughters a carnal and sinful motive that did not honor the Lord.

## I. The Anointing (9:1-13)

Ahab's son Joram (or Jehoram) was reigning over Israel, and Ahaziah was reigning over Judah. Both kings were allied to fight against Hazael, king of Syria (2 Kings 8:25-29). Joram had been wounded in battle and was recuperating in Jezreel, and Ahaziah went to visit him. Jehu was a respected captain in the army of Israel, probably one of the key leaders in the war. He had been one of Ahab's bodyguards years before when that evil king had taken possession of Naboth's vineyard (9:25-26).

Elisha did not go to anoint Jehu; he would be recognized and perhaps assaulted. Instead, he chose one of the sons of the prophets to run to Ramoth-gilead and anoint Jehu as king of Israel. This had been commanded by the Lord years before (1 Kings 19:15-17). The young prophet obeyed quickly; he suddenly appeared in the war council, asked Jehu to step into a private room where he anointed him and gave him God's message, and then left as quickly as he arrived. Jehu knew his commission: wipe out the family of Ahab and avenge the innocent blood shed by Ahab and Jezebel and their descendants. Compare v. 9 with 1 Kings 15:29 and 16:3-11.

The soldiers thought the prophet was a madman; Jehu thought the soldiers had arranged the whole affair. "You know the man and his commission," Jehu said, thinking they had secretly set up an army rebellion against the king. But the officers admitted they knew nothing, so Jehu told them what the Lord's messenger had said. Their immediate response was to submit to him and proclaim him king. In v. 15 the new king carefully arranged to keep his anointing a secret until he could accomplish his important task. Had the word been carried to the two kings in Jezreel, Jehu's sudden attack would have been thwarted.

## II. The Avenging (9:14–10:28)

### A. The slaying of King Joram (9:14-26).

The ailing king was at Jezreel, and Ahaziah was visiting him. God arranged for both kings to be together when the hour of judgment arrived. The king sent messengers to intercept Jehu, but he refused to stop for them or give them any information. This popular soldier was known for the "furious driving" of his chariot, and the watchman recognized him from a distance. Instead of waiting in the city where they would have had some protection, the two kings went out to meet Jehu, probably because they thought their great captain had good news from the battlefield. Jehu concentrated on Joram first, but his announcement only made the evil monarch turn to flee. Jehu killed him easily with an arrow in the back. The Word of God was fulfilled, for he died in that portion of ground Ahab had stolen from Naboth some twenty years before (1 Kings 21:17-24).

## B. The slaying of King Ahaziah (9:27-29).

He too tried to run away, but Jehu's men followed him to the kingdom of Samaria (not the city) where he was slain in Megiddo (see 2 Chron. 22:9). His servants were permitted to bring him to Jerusalem for decent burial. Ahaziah was Joram's brother-in-law (8:18) and was thus included in the judgment against Ahab's house.

## C. The slaying of Jezebel (9:30-37).

The Queen Mother still exercised a great deal of power in Israel, but her hour of judgment had arrived and nothing could protect her. She heard that Jehu was coming and boldly beautified herself to meet the new king. She "put her eyes in painting" and put a crown on her head. She was going to die like a queen. Her statement in v. 31 takes us back to 1 Kings 16:9-20, where Zimri killed the king and ruled only seven days. Was wicked Jezebel trying to bribe Jehu into sparing her and thus making his throne more secure? Several servants in the palace assisted Jehu by throwing the queen down from the upper window, and Jehu finished the job by riding over her body with his chariot. He then took over the palace and enjoyed a hearty meal. He instructed the men to bury the dead queen, but the dogs had already gone to work and eaten her body. See 1 Kings 21:23.

## D. The slaying of Ahab's descendants (10:1-17).

Ahab had seventy descendants (e.g., sons, grandsons) living in Samaria, and Jehu turned his attention toward them. He wrote official letters to the elders (as Jezebel had done, 1 Kings 21:8-14) asking them to select champions from the family to fight Jehu and his men. The elders feared to fight and immediately sued for peace. Jehu's second letter suggested that they bring *only the heads* of the seventy sons. That evening the men arrived with the heads, and the next morning Jehu went to the city gate to see the horrible sight. In v. 9 he pretended to be innocent of their death, and in v. 10 he affirmed that the murders only fulfilled the Word of the Lord. Of course, in one sense Jehu was telling the truth, but we cannot help but think that he was more anxious to murder Ahab's family than to glorify the Lord. In vv. 12-14 he even killed forty-two cousins of Ahaziah. And in v. 17 we are told that Jehu destroyed the rest of Ahab's family in Samaria, the capital city. Indeed, he had a "zeal for the Lord."

## E. The slaying of the Baal worshipers (10:18-28).

The end justified the means in Jehu's mind, so he felt no qualms of conscience when he deliberately lied to the people and claimed to be more ardent in his worship of Baal than was Ahab. He was joined in this plot by Jehonadab, a dedicated Jew who was anxious to rid the land of idolatry. See Jer. 35 for more about the family of Rechab. Having arrived in Samaria, Jehu announced his intention of establishing Baal worship, and the people believed him. Once he had the faithful followers of Baal gathered in the house of Baal, he set his soldiers outside and carefully examined the crowd to be sure no faithful follower of the Lord had mistakenly entered the heathen temple. Jehu himself did not participate in the worship. Once the service was ended, the guards killed the followers of Baal and destroyed the images and the temple. It was turned into a "dunghill" and therefore defiled permanently.

We may cringe at reading of these events, but we must remember that God had given the house of Ahab many opportunities to repent and escape judgment. While Jehu's zeal may have gotten out of control, and while his motives may not have been always spiritual, we must recognize the fact that he was God's instrument of wrath against a wicked family. God waited many years and His judgment "slumbered" while His mercy was extended to an undeserving nation. Let the sinner take heed lest he try the patience of God and sin away the day of grace.

## III. The Abandoning (10:29-36)

God commended Jehu for his obedience and promised him a secure throne for four generations (see 15:1-12). However, Jehu took no heed to obey the Word of the Lord, but went back into idolatry, worshiping the golden calves. How prone we are to judge sins in the lives of other people while failing to see these same sins in our own lives; see Matt. 7:1-5. God had to chasten Jehu by allowing Hazael of Syria to capture territory from Israel. Jehu reigned twenty-eight years. The prophet Hosea (1:4) announced that God would avenge the blood of Jezreel upon Jehu's house, and this He did. Jehu had abandoned the Lord, and now the Lord would have to abandon him and his seed after only four generations.

We can discover some basic lessons in this account. (1) God fulfills His work of judgment though His mercy may tarry long. The sinner often sinks into a false peace because the sword of judgment fails to come, but we can be sure of this: it will come. (2) Godless fathers often lead their children into sin and condemnation. Ahab's marriage to a heathen woman and his following of her worship of Baal led the family and the nation into darkness and doom. How many people died because one man led them into sin! (3) A servant may fulfill God's Word and then fail to obey completely himself. Had Jehu continued zealous for the Lord, his reign would have been especially blessed. His own idolatry condemned him and his family.

# 2 KINGS 11–16

Thirteen different kings are mentioned in these chapters, five from Judah and eight from Israel. It is not necessary to examine the life of each king separately, so we will focus our attention on five kings in particular and seek to learn lessons from their lives.

## I. Joash, the Boy King (11–12) (2 Chron. 22–24)

### A. Protected (11:1-3).

When the Queen Mother Athaliah saw that her son Ahaziah was dead, she determined to wipe out the entire royal family lest any rival steal the throne from her. In the providence of God, one little boy was rescued and protected for seven years, and thus God fulfilled His promise to keep David's seed on the throne of Judah. Second Chronicles 22:11 tells us that the godly woman who saved Joash's life was actually his aunt, a half-sister to Azariah and wife to the godly high priest, Jehoiada. Satan's seed tried to exterminate God's seed (Gen. 3:15), but God won the battle.

### B. Proclaimed king (11:4-21).

Jehoiada had the entire program arranged without the Queen Mother's knowledge of the plot. He had the Levites and the guards in their places before evil Athaliah could act, and when she did appear, it meant her death. Note that the guards used weapons from the temple that had been captured years before by David

(v. 10). But it was more than a change in government; it was also a religious revival. Youthful Joash was given the Law (v. 12, and see Deut. 17:18), and the king vowed to serve the Lord and the people. Once his throne was secured, the king permitted Jehoiada to "clean house" and remove the Baal worshipers and their idols. Revival has its negative aspects of judgment as well as its positive steps of dedication.

### C. Blessed by God (12:1-16).

The high priest Jehoiada was the young king's spiritual guide, and at the beginning of his reign, Joash was willing to follow. Baal-worshiping Athaliah had allowed the house of the Lord to fall into disrepair, so Jehoiada and the king went to work to repair it and restore its use. Their first plan for financing the program was to have the priests ask for contributions from the people who came to pay their vows and to bring sacrifices (vv. 4-5). But after a long time, this policy was abandoned. Since the priests had to live by the sacrifices and money paid for vows, it was difficult to ask for even more money on a freewill basis. The high priest put an offering box right by the brazen altar by the gate of the house of the Lord. The people responded generously so that soon there was enough money to complete the work. So honest and faithful were the workers that no special accounting was even made as the funds were spent.

### D. Ruined by sin (12:17-21).

Second Chronicles 24:15-27 informs us that when godly Jehoiada died (at the age of 130), the king began to backslide and actually went into idolatry. Unfortunately, this leader's faith was tied to another leader and not to the Lord directly. God sent prophets to warn the king, but he would not listen. One of these prophets was Zechariah, the son of the high priest Jehoiada and Joash's cousin (2 Chron. 22:11); instead of listening to him, Joash commanded him to be stoned in the temple court. Jesus referred to this murder in Matt. 23:34-35. Being spiritually backslidden, Joash was unable to cope with the Syrian invasion, so he tried to bribe Hazael by giving him the wealth of God's house. How often God's people rob the Lord in trying to solve their problems, instead of turning to the Lord in confession. Alas, Joash himself was murdered by some of his own servants as they sought to avenge the deaths of Jehoiada's innocent sons.

## II. Jehoash—Lost Opportunity (13)

In the first nine verses, we read of Jehoahaz, Jehoash's father. Do not confuse this Jehoash (or Joash) with the young king of Judah in chapters 11–12. This Jehoash was king of Israel and did what was evil in God's sight. We will see in 14:8-14 that this king defeated the king of Judah, Amaziah. During his reign, Jehoash came into contact with the prophet Elisha just before the man of God died. Elisha gave him a golden opportunity to defeat Syria once and for all, but he failed to use his opportunity. Verse 25 tells us that he won only three times. How tragic it is when we fail to take advantage of the great opportunities the Lord gives us. Wrong decisions today often mean defeat tomorrow. The unusual miracle of vv. 20-21 suggests the powerful influence a godly man can have even after his death.

## III. Amaziah—Defeat by Pride (14) (2 Chron. 25)

This king got off to a good start by obeying the Lord and avenging the murder of his father Joash (v. 5, and see 12:20). Note his strict obedience to Deut. 24:16 in v. 6. God gave him great victories in Edom, but 2 Chron. 25:14-16 tells us that he brought back with him the heathen gods of Edom and worshiped these gods of the defeated enemy. This combination of idolatry and pride led him to "meddle" with Jehoash, the king of Israel (see 13:10-13), and challenge him to a war (v. 8). The king of Israel was too wise to fear the threat. As his clever parable in vv. 9-10 indicates, Amaziah was but a little thistle. The result? "Pride goes before destruction and a haughty spirit before a fall" (Prov. 16:18). Judah was soundly defeated by Israel; Jerusalem was partly destroyed, and the Lord's treasury emptied. Had Amaziah remained in his own land and given God the glory for his victories, he would not have become captive to Israel. We are told that he was slain in a conspiracy (2 Chron. 25:25-28).

## IV. Uzziah—Judah's Great King (15) (2 Chron. 26)

Uzziah means "strength of the Lord"; his other name, Azariah, means "helped of Jehovah." He was elevated to the throne at the age of sixteen, and under his sound leadership the nation took on new life and prosperity. His spiritual guide was Zechariah (2 Chron. 26:5); this is not the prophet who ministered to Joash

(2 Chron. 24:17-22). God gave Uzziah great victories over the Philistines and the Arabian nations. He led the nation in great building programs, particularly in the area of the water supply. His military establishment was remarkable; he used the latest machinery for waging war. The prophet Isaiah received his call to service in the year that King Uzziah died; Isa. 6.

Pride brought about his ruin (2 Chron. 26:16): he went into the temple to burn incense, and the Lord smote him with leprosy. His son Jotham reigned with him for several years until Uzziah died. His death brought great mourning to Judah. He had ruled for fifty-two years and the nation enjoyed its greatest safety and prosperity since Solomon.

In 15:8-31 we have a brief record of five kings of Israel: Zachariah ruled only six months and was assassinated by Shallum. Shallum reigned one month and was killed by Menahem. Menahem reigned for ten years, doing wicked deeds even surpassing the heathen, and he was succeeded by Pekahiah who ruled for two years, up to the time of King Ahaz. Those were difficult days in Israel, for the nation had turned away from the Lord.

### V. Ahaz—The Cost of Compromise (16) (2 Chron. 28)

So evil was this king of Judah that he even sacrificed his son to the god Moloch. He reigned for only sixteen years. One of his achievements was dedicating the Valley of the Son of Hinnom to Baal. Later, King Josiah desecrated that valley and made it a garbage dump, and the term "Ge-Hinnom" ("valley of Hinnom") became "Gehenna" in the Greek, a name for hell. God punished Ahaz by bringing the Syrians against him, and, like some of his predecessors, Ahaz robbed the Lord's house to bribe the Assyrians to fight for him.

His friendship with the Assyrian king led to more trouble. Ahaz saw a heathen altar at Damascus and tried to duplicate it in Jerusalem. In fact, his new altar replaced the God-ordained altar in the temple. How easy it is to imitate the world. Second Chronicles 28:20-27 tells us that this friendship with Assyria led Ahaz into idolatry, and that the king of Assyria took the money but in the end failed to help Judah at all. In vv. 17-18 we are told that Ahaz hid the extra gold decorations from the king of Assyria to keep him from taking those also. At his death, his son Hezekiah took the throne, a godly man who sought the blessing of the Lord. Ahaz had tried to compromise and to "buy his way" to victory, but it only led to shame and defeat.

# 2 Kings 17

This long chapter is the record of Israel's last king and how he led the Northern Kingdom into captivity. Assyria captured Samaria (capital of the Northern Kingdom) in 722 B.C., after subduing the nation. What could have been a great victory to the glory of God turned out to be a defeat that brought the worship of the true God to a new low.

## I. The Capture of Samaria (17:1-6)

Hoshea became king of Israel through the cooperation of Assyria, for he had promised to pay the king of Assyria tribute. See 2 Kings 15:27-31 for the story of Hoshea's conspiracy. We are told that Hoshea was an evil king (one of twenty evil kings in Israel's history) but that his sins were not as bad as those of his predecessors. Verse 2 suggests that Hoshea would have liked to lead the nation into a better way; 2 Chron. 30:6-11 indicates that he permitted his citizens to share in the "great Passover" called by godly King Hezekiah. But the king had sold himself to Assyria, and it was too late to change. Sad to say, he even revolted against Assyria by refusing to pay his annual tribute and by making a secret treaty with Egypt. How prone Israel was to "go down to Egypt" for help, just as now God's people look to "the world" for support. See Jer. 17:5-7 and Hosea 7:11-13 for the prophets' attitude toward Egyptian alliances.

Assyria did not take Hoshea's rebellion lightly. Their armies overran the Northern Kingdom and finally converged on the capital city of Samaria. It was a strongly fortified city; thus it took Assyria three years to capture it. But the case was hopeless: the nation had forsaken the Lord and He had decreed their captivity. It was the Assyrian policy to take the best citizens to their own land, and then to colonize the captive land with foreigners from other captivities. So it was, that after 250 years of constant sin and rebellion, the nation of Israel (the Northern Kingdom) was taken captive by the enemy and left a barren wilderness of shame and defeat. Had Israel's first king, Jeroboam, walked in the ways of the Lord and led his nation to obey the Law, the history of Israel would have been

different. Instead, we find Jeroboam disobeying the Lord and leading the nation away from God, and his successors walking in the
sins of Jeroboam who made Israel to sin" (see e.g., 1 Kings 16:19,
26; 2 Kings 3:3). Jeroboam's golden calves at Dan and Bethel led
Israel astray (1 Kings 12:25-33).

## II. The Causes of the Captivity (17:7-23)

History is never merely a series of accidental events, for behind
every nation is the plan and purpose of God. In these verses, the
Holy Spirit explains to us why Samaria fell. We today had better
take heed, for God is no respecter of nations; and if He so severely
chastised His own people Israel, what must He do to nations today
that rebel against Him? "History is His story."

### A. The nation forgot God (v. 7).

God had redeemed them from Egyptian slavery and had purchased
them to be His own people. The annual Passover feast was a
reminder to them of God's grace. Yet they forgot all that God had
done for them. Many times in Deuteronomy, Moses urged the
people to remember the Lord and not to forget His mercies. See
Deut. 6:10ff and 8:1ff.

### B. The nation secretly disobeyed (vv. 8-9).

God had warned them not to mingle with the heathen nations in
Canaan (Deut. 7), yet Israel secretly disobeyed. They lusted in
their hearts and gradually yielded to the heathen worship around
them.

### C. The nation openly rebelled (vv. 10-12).

What begins as secret sin ultimately becomes open sin, and the
nation deliberately provoked God. See Ex. 20:4 and Deut. 4:16 and
5:8.

### D. The nation resisted God's call (vv. 13-15).

The Lord sent godly prophets to warn them and plead with them,
but the people only stiffened their necks in stubborn rebellion (see
Ex. 32:9 and 33:3; also Acts 7:51). They rejected the Law, which
was written by the Lord and given to them for their blessing. Verse
15 is terrifying: "They followed vanity (empty idols), and became
vain." We become like that which we worship; see Ps. 115:1-8.

346

*E. The nation sold itself to do evil (vv. 16-23).*

They became slaves of sin. Jeroboam established the golden calves, but even this was not enough for Israel's lustful heart. Not only did they worship the gods of the Canaanites, but they imported gods from the other nations. God divided the kingdom (v. 18), leaving David's family to rule Judah, but then even Judah went into sin. God turned the nation over to "spoilers" (v. 20), both from within their own land and from outside the land. Their kings robbed them and their enemies attacked them. God warned them through the prophets that judgment would come, but the people blindly went on from sin to sin.

The OT lists twenty kings for the nation of Israel, all of them wicked. It took about 250 years for the kingdom of Israel to fall into ruin. They heard preachers like Elijah, Elisha, Amos, Hosea, and Isaiah, yet refused to bow the knee to the Lord. There is no cure for apostasy. All God can do is judge, and then take a "believing remnant" and start over again.

## III. The Colonization of Samaria (17:24-41)

After deporting the best of the people, the king of Assyria imported citizens from other nations under his rule, thereby preventing Israel from organizing and rebelling. These verses describe the origin of "the Samaritans," that mixed people we read about in John 4 and Acts 8. Later on a "remnant" of believing Jews did return to Samaria, but orthodox Jews would have no dealings with this "half-breed" nation. Jesus told a Samaritan woman plainly that the Samaritans did not know what they were worshiping (John 4:22) and that salvation would come from the Jews.

At first, there was no religious faith in Samaria, so God had to send lions to bring fear into the hearts of the people (see v. 25). However, the leaders solved the problem in a most peculiar way: they imported a Jewish priest, learned the way of the Lord, and then had the people worship *both* Jehovah and their own national gods. "Every nation made gods of their own," says v. 29. This was an OT ecumenical movement. Note the repetition of the phrase "they feared the Lord" (vv. 25, 28, 32-34, 41). They feared the Lord (as the "god of the land," v. 27), but they worshiped and served their own gods (v. 33). Their worship of Jehovah was an empty formality, a mere outward show of allegiance; their true worship was of their own heathen gods. Jehovah was but another "god" in their collection of deities.

In other words, even after seeing the heavy hand of judgment on their land, the people that remained still persisted in disobeying the Lord. Ultimately this cancer of idolatry spread to Judah, and in 586 B.C. the Babylonians captured and destroyed Jerusalem. A remnant returned under Ezra and Nehemiah, and the nation began to blossom again. But when God sent His Son to His people, they rejected Him, and once again divine judgment had to fall. In A.D. 70 Jerusalem was destroyed, and the nation scattered across the world.

"Blessed is that nation whose God is the Lord." These tragic events in the history of Israel ought to cause Christian citizens to fear for their country and pray for their leaders. Godless leaders produce godless generations of citizens (v. 41). Compromising priests lead worshipers farther away from the Lord. When the Word of the Lord is rejected (vv. 34-38), there is no hope for a nation's future. There may be an extension of mercy (God bore with Israel for 250 years), but ultimately judgment must fall.

There is no cure for apostasy. Once God's people have finally turned away from the Lord, God must judge. He will save for Himself a "remnant" of faithful believers and start His witness again, but He will not bless that part that has rejected His Word and refused His calls.

# 2 KINGS 18–20

(Read also Isa. 36–39 and 2 Chron. 29–32.) We enter now into the study of one of the most exciting periods in Judah's history, the reign of godly King Hezekiah. Samaria (Israel) had fallen to Assyria, and now the enemy was attacking Judah. Ahaz had made a covenant with Assyria years before (16:7-9), but Hezekiah rebelled against it (18:7; 13-16); and this invited an invasion from the enemy. Actually, the events in these chapters are not recorded in their exact order, for Hezekiah's sickness occurred during the siege (see 20:6), and the visit from the Babylonian leaders followed his recovery. He reigned twenty-nine years (18:2). Since fifteen years were given him after his recovery, and the invasion took place in the fourteenth year of his reign (18:13), then his sickness and the invasion occurred at the same period in his life. We will note three enemies that Hezekiah had to face and how he dealt with them.

## I. The Assyrian Invaders (18–19)

### A. *Hezekiah's reformation (18:1-8; 2 Chron. 29–32).*

This godly king immediately set out to rid the land of idolatry and sin. He reopened and repaired the temple, cleaned out the rubbish that had gathered there, and *reestablished* the services. He was especially interested in the singers and the sacrifices. He also called the whole nation (Israel included) to a great Passover feast. It was a time of revival, but, unfortunately, it did not get into the hearts of the people. The changes were only on the surface. However, Hezekiah proved that he did love the Lord, and God blessed him for his service.

### B. *Rebellion (18:9-37).*

For years, the nation had been under tribute to Assyria, but Hezekiah rebelled and refused to pay tribute. This brought the Assyrian army to Jerusalem, but instead of turning to God, Hezekiah feared the enemy and gave in (vv. 13-16), even to the point of robbing the temple to pay Assyria. There were actually three "parties" in Judah at this time: one wanted to capitulate to Assyria; another wanted to go to Egypt for help; and a third group (led by Isaiah) called the nation to trust in the Lord for deliverance. The king of Assyria took the money and then turned around and invaded Judah anyway. Isaiah called this move "treachery" (Isa. 33:1-8), for Assyria did not keep her promise. Three of the Assyrian officers taunted the Jews (v. 17—these are titles of offices, not personal names) and tried to undermine Hezekiah's faith and leadership. Verses 31-32 illustrate the deceitfulness of sin; he promised them peace and plenty until they were taken away into captivity. There is always an "until" to disobedience.

### C. *Request (19:1-19).*

Unable to save himself, the king went to the temple to pray. Verse 2 is the first mention of the Prophet Isaiah in the Bible. The prophet sent the king an answer of peace: God would deliver Judah and defeat Assyria. Difficulties with other nations forced Assyria to pull back their forces, but Rabshakeh sent an arrogant letter to Hezekiah to frighten him into surrendering. The king took the letter to the temple and "spread it before the Lord." Note that v. 19 emphasizes the glory of God, which is the real basis for prayer.

### D. *Reward (19:20-37).*

What a wonderful combination—the Word of God and prayer. Hezekiah prayed and God sent the answer through Isaiah—He would judge Assyria and treat them as they had treated the nations. God gave Hezekiah the promise that after two years Judah would have harvests again (v. 29). (The Assyrians had devastated the land.) Note that God answered prayer for David's sake and not because Judah or the king deserved such mercy (v. 34). God killed 185,000 soldiers in one night, and later Sennacherib's own sons assassinated him. God was able to defeat the enemy without the help of Egypt. See Isa. 30–31.

## II. Death (20:1-11)

Death is called "the last enemy" (1 Cor. 15:26). It must have been trying to the king to be very ill while Assyria was threatening to invade. Troubles many times come in pairs, but God is sufficient to meet them. We are not sure why God sent this sickness. It may have been because of Hezekiah's unbelief and willingness to pay the tribute (18:13-16). Or perhaps there was secret sin (see Isa. 38:17). Certainly the king's psalm of praise in Isa. 38:9-20 indicates that he was fearful of death and wanted to stay alive to finish his work of reformation. At any rate, he prayed to be spared, and God answered his prayer. Note that God uses means to heal His own (in this case a poultice), so it is not an evidence of unbelief to go to a doctor for help. God gave the king fifteen additional years. He strengthened the king's faith even more by causing the shadow to go back on the sundial ten degrees. (This sundial was perhaps a stone stairway with steps to mark out the hours. The king could see it from his palace window.)

Bible students have debated for years whether Hezekiah should have prayed for healing and whether his recovery was God's *perfect* will or His *permissive* will. Sometimes God does answer prayer when the answer is not the best thing for us (see Ps. 106:15). Those who feel Hezekiah was wrong, point out that the king's final fifteen years involved his sinful alliance with the Babylonians (20:12-21) and also the birth of Manasseh, who turned out to be Judah's most wicked king (chap. 21). Had Hezekiah died, Judah would have been spared the Babylonian compromise and the evil reign of Manasseh. However, Manasseh did repent and serve the Lord (2 Chron. 33:11-19).

On the other hand, others point out that Hezekiah had no heir to the throne when Isaiah gave the message of doom, so that his prayer was not for himself alone but for the nation. "Set your house in order" in 20:1 (NKJV) literally means, "Pick out a man to succeed you to the throne." God had promised that Judah would always have a descendant of David on the throne, and Hezekiah was holding God to His promise. All of his sons were born in the closing fifteen years; see 20:18. It is true that Manasseh was a godless king (which is not to Hezekiah's honor as a father), but then we must admit that Josiah was a great man of God. Had Hezekiah died, there would have been no Josiah. Furthermore, we have indications in the Bible that during Hezekiah's last fifteen years of rule, he was busy with the "men of Hezekiah" (a group of scribes, Prov. 25:1) copying out the OT Scriptures and putting them in order. Many fine scholars believe that the "Songs of Degrees" (Pss. 120–134) were especially put together to commemorate Hezekiah's sickness and recovery. Also, you find the Hebrew letters "H Z K" at the end of many OT books in the Hebrew manuscripts. It would seem that, in gratitude to God for what He did, Hezekiah devoted the last fifteen years of his life to putting the OT Scriptures in order for the people. As for Manasseh, to say that a man should die rather than beget a wicked son is to claim too much. David's sons were wicked, including Solomon; why did God allow David to live? Does God slay a man because of the future sins of a child not yet conceived? Furthermore, the healing of the king and the deliverance of Jerusalem occurred at the same time (20:5-6). Would it have been to the glory of God to rescue the city and then slay their king?

## III. The Babylonian Visitors (20:12-21)

What Assyria could not accomplish by force, Babylon accomplished by guile. Satan is either a lion or a serpent. Hezekiah's pride after the healing and the deliverance of Jerusalem got him into a wicked alliance with Babylon. Read 2 Chron. 32:25-26, 31 and see that it was his pride that brought the chastening upon him after he was healed. For the king to let the enemy see his wealth and his weapons was certainly a foolish move, and the nation ultimately suffered for it. Note the king's pride in v. 15: "my house . . . my treasures." The same prophet who brought him the joyful message of healing now had to convey a sad message of judgment: the treasures would go to Babylon, and so would his sons. In these experiences, God was testing Hezekiah's heart (2 Chron. 32:31) to see if the king would glorify Him and trust Him, not his treasures or his own strength. Manasseh was taken to Babylon and imprisoned, but he humbled himself and God delivered him (2 Chron. 33:11-19). It is sad to see Hezekiah more concerned about his own day than the future of his nation. To rest on temporary peace when ultimate defeat is around the corner, is most unwise. But in spite of his mistakes and sins, Hezekiah has gone down in Jewish history as a great king. He fortified the city, improved its water system, cleansed the land of idols, and sought to lead the people back to the Lord. He was a man of prayer who knew how to "spread it out before the Lord."

# 2 KINGS 21–23

Five kings are mentioned in these chapters, but we will concern ourselves primarily with two: Manasseh and Josiah. King Amon reigned but two years (21:19-26); and Jehoahaz only three months (23:31-33). We will meet Jehoiakim in our next study. The interesting thing about Josiah and Manasseh is that their spiritual lives were exactly opposite each other. Manasseh began his reign in sin but ended it in humble repentance, while Josiah sought the Lord early in his life but ended his reign (and his life) in disobedience.

## I. Manasseh's Reign (21)

### A. *His rebellion (21:1-9).*

Historians have calculated that Manasseh ruled jointly with godly Hezekiah for at least ten years. Manasseh was a wicked man, worse than any before him or after him. How strange that godly Hezekiah should reign but twenty-nine years while ungodly Manasseh reigned fifty-five years. But God was giving to the people just what they wanted and just what they deserved. No sooner was Hezekiah off the scene than Manasseh's true character was revealed. He built up what Hezekiah had torn down, and tore down what Hezekiah had built up. Contrast this with Isaac in Gen. 26:18. Instead of imitating godly Hezekiah, Manasseh followed the ways of King Ahab. Tradition tells us that Isaiah was sawn in two by Manasseh; Heb. 11:37. Manasseh even carried his idolatry right into the courts of the temple. He rebelled against his godly father's example and against the Law of the Lord.

## B. His removal (21:10-15).

Here we must read 2 Chron. 33:11-20 for the full story. God sent his prophets to warn the king, but the king would not listen. God announced to the nation that judgment and captivity were coming. Judah had witnessed God's judgment on Samaria, but that had not brought the people to repentance. God promised to treat the house of David the way he treated the house of Ahab (v. 13). The Assyrian captains took Manasseh to Babylon where he was put into prison.

## C. His repentance (2 Chron. 33:12).

How typical this is of many people: "When he was in affliction he besought the Lord." God in His grace forgave the evil king and permitted him to return to his throne. God works on behalf of those who sincerely humble themselves and pray.

## D. His reformation (2 Chron. 33:13-20; 2 Kings 21:17-26).

Manasseh's repentance was not a shallow "fox-hole" conversion, for once back on the throne, he immediately began to repair the damage he had done. He fortified Jerusalem against the enemy; he removed the idols and the strange altars; and he sought to lead the nation back to the Lord. Of course, it was impossible to undo all the damage he had done, but we must commend him for what he did accomplish before his death. Sad to say, God gave Manasseh the longest reign of any Hebrew king, yet he accomplished almost nothing. In fact, even his repentance did not stay God's hand of judgment; it was Manasseh's sins that moved God to send the nation into captivity (23:26-27).

King Manasseh had every opportunity to live a godly life and serve the Lord and his people with faithfulness. His father was perhaps Judah's greatest king (except for David); the prophet Isaiah was ministering in his day; yet Manasseh failed to find the Lord until the close of his life. We admire what he did after his conversion, but we cannot help but feel he did more damage in his earlier years than he ever repaired in his later years. Note that he was not buried with the kings, but rather in his private garden.

His son Amon was not affected by his father's late conversion; he imitated his father's sins, not his righteous acts. He lasted but two years, then was slain in a conspiracy and buried near his father.

## II. Josiah's Reign (22–23)

The assassination of Amon brought Josiah to the throne at the young age of eight years. Four key events summarize this godly king's brief life and reign:

### A. Salvation (22:1-2; 2 Chron. 34:3).

In the eighth year of his reign, when he was sixteen, Josiah began to seek the Lord. No doubt Hilkiah the high priest taught the lad the Word of God. It is interesting that his mother's name (Jedidah) is the same "pet name" that God gave to Solomon (2 Sam. 12:25). It means "beloved of the Lord" and may indicate that Josiah's mother was also a godly influence in his life. Jeremiah and Zephaniah were also ministering then.

### B. Reformation (2 Chron. 34:3-7).

The king was now twenty years old and mature enough to start purifying the city and the land of the idolatry of Manasseh and Amon. Josiah's ultimate goal was to restore the temple and bring the nation back to the worship of the Lord, but he knew that he would have to destroy the old sins before he could establish new obedience. Unfortunately, "Josiah's revival" was a surface thing; it never did get to the hearts of the people. While Jeremiah the prophet wept much at Josiah's death (2 Chron. 35:25; Jer. 22:10-12), we do not find him commending the youthful king for his so-called "revival." Certainly the king and his council were sincere in their attempts at reform, but the people did not follow; they remained idolaters at heart.

### C. Restoration (22:3–23:28).

Having purged away the idols, Josiah could now concentrate on re-establishing the true worship of Jehovah. It is not enough to tear down; we must also build up. He commanded the priests to gather money and repair the temple. See 2 Chron. 34:8–35:19. While repairing the temple, the high priest discovered a copy of the Law of Moses, long since discarded by an idolatrous nation. When he heard the Law read, Josiah immediately knew that Judah was in great danger, and he sent to inquire of the Lord what to do. Huldah the prophetess, who lived in the "second quarter" of the city ("college" in 22:14), gave the anxious king God's message: (1) Judah and Jerusalem would be judged for their sins, but (2) King Josiah would not see these judgments because he had humbled himself before the Lord. Josiah immediately shared the Word of God with all the elders of the land, and he led the way in a great service of dedication, reaffirming the Covenant of God. He continued further purges of the land, including the defiling of "Topheth"—the valley of the son of Hinnom where the people burned their children as sacrifices to Molech. As we noted earlier, the king made this valley a garbage dump and Ge-hinnom became, in the NT, "Gehenna"— a vivid illustration of hell. The Mount of Olives had been a "mount of corruption" (23:13), but Josiah restored it. During his purge, Josiah uncovered the altar of wicked King Jeroboam as well as the tomb of the prophet who had warned him; and thus Josiah fulfilled the prophecy of 1 Kings 13:1-5. God's Word never returns void. The king not only restored the temple and the Law, but he also restored the Passover feast that had long been neglected by the nation. He wanted to remind his people that they had been "bought with a price."

What did Josiah's reformations and restorations accomplish? During Josiah's day, there was peace and blessing; but God did not withdraw His original promise of judgment because of the sins of Manasseh (23:26-27). Josiah's godly life and ministry had stayed the hand of judgment a few more years, but captivity was coming and nothing could prevent it.

### D. Assassination (23:29-37; 2 Chron. 35:20-27).

The Egyptian army probably came by sea and landed on the coast of Palestine. Pharaoh made it clear that he was not against Judah, but only moving on his way to attack Assyria. Josiah did not seek the mind of the Lord; in fact, it appears that he deliberately disobeyed God's will; see 2 Chron. 35:22. Even his disguise could not protect him once he was out of the Lord's will, and he was slain in battle. See Zech. 12:11 for an allusion to the great mourning at Megiddo for Josiah. The king should have heeded the wisdom of Prov. 20:3 and 26:17. Perhaps Judah was an ally of Assyria at this time and the king was obligated to act, but it is clear that Pharaoh would have preferred not to battle King Josiah. Josiah's son Jehoahaz reigned only three months before Pharaoh deposed him and put him in bonds. Pharaoh chose another of Josiah's sons, Eliakim, and made him king, giving him the new name of "Jehoiakim"— "whom Jehovah will raise up." We will consider his life and reign in our next study.

# 2 KINGS 24–25

The hour of judgment finally arrives, and God keeps His Word by bringing terrible wrath upon His people in the kingdom of Judah. God had given them a throne, a temple, a city, and a land, and upon each of these He poured out His anger. Read Jer. 25–34 if you wish sidelights on these chapters; also read 2 Chron. 36. Notice the judgments that fell on Judah.

## I. The King Was Dethroned (24:1-12, 17-20)

After the reign of godly Josiah, the throne of David was occupied by a series of men who defied God by their persistent sins. Jehoahaz reigned three months, as did Jehoiachin (also called Coniah or Jeconiah, Jer. 22:24). Jehoiakim ruled for eleven years and in the third year of his reign rebelled against Babylon. (Babylon had defeated Egypt and was now the greatest nation among Judah's enemies.) Jehoiakim became subject to Babylon in 604 B.C., and in 601 he rebelled. It was this vile king who cut Jeremiah's prophecies to pieces and burned them in the fire (Jer. 36). In 597, Jehoiakim died, leaving the throne to his son Jehoiachin, who ruled for three months.

It was in 597 that the Babylonian army began its siege of Jerusalem. Of course, weak and faithless Jehoiachin immediately surrendered with his family and they were taken to Babylon. The king's uncle, Mattaniah, was made the next king and was given the new name of Zedekiah. See Jer. 52. He reigned eleven years, from 597 to 585. In the ninth year of his reign (588 B.C.), he made a secret alliance with Egypt and thus incurred the wrath of the Babylonians. It was this foolish move (which, by the way, was opposed by Jeremiah) that brought the Babylonian armies to Jerusalem for a final siege. In 25:27-30 we are told that banished King Jehoiachin was liberated from jail in Babylon halfway through the captivity.

The throne of David was now virtually empty. Zedekiah was the last king of Judah. Had Zedekiah listened to the Word of Jeremiah, the final days of Jerusalem would have been different.

## II. The People Were Deported (24:13-16)

There were actually three deportations: in 605 (when Daniel was included); in 597 (described in this passage); and in 587 (after the awful eighteen-month siege of the city). Ezekiel was taken to Babylon in the second deportation. It was Babylon's policy to take the best of the people out of the land—the princes, nobles, soldiers, craftsmen, and royal family—and to leave the poorest of the people behind to manage things under the direction of their own governors. This way a captive nation would not be able to organize any resistance. Of course, this deportation was predicted by Jeremiah (chap. 25) as well as by Moses in the Law (Lev. 26; Deut. 28). The people had defiled their God-given land with blood and with idols; they were no longer fit to live upon it. God had to "sweep them away" that He might be able to purify the land once again.

### III. The City Was Destroyed (25:1-12)

Read the Book of Lamentations for Jeremiah's graphic description of the destruction of Jerusalem. The city was besieged for eighteen months, beginning January 15, 588. On July 19, 586, a breach was made in the walls and the citizens knew that the end was at hand. Zedekiah and his men tried to flee (vv. 4-6), but they were intercepted by the Babylonian army. Jeremiah 32:4-5 and 34:1-7, as well as Ezek. 12:13, predicted that Zedekiah would not escape. He would see the king of Babylon, but he would not see Babylon itself. He did see Nebuchadnezzar; then his eyes were put out and he was taken to Babylon a blind man. A month later, the Babylonians burned Jerusalem, broke down the walls, and destroyed the temple.

### IV. The Temple Was Disgraced (25:13-17)

The Babylonian soldiers stripped the temple of all its wealth. The objects that were too large to carry whole, they broke into pieces. The brass, gold, and silver instruments were carried to a heathen land. In 24:13, we are told that Solomon's gold and the treasures in the palace were included in the spoils. In Jer. 7 we note that the Jews thought God would protect them from invasion because of the presence of the temple. The false prophets and worldly priests had the people believing lies, just as people today believe their church or their religious rituals will save them from judgment. Instead of the vessels of the house of the Lord being used for God's glory, they were carried to Babylon to embellish the temples of the idols (2 Chron. 36:7).

The presence of the temple could not save the nation; there had to be sincere confession and repentance from the heart. But it was too late. The nation had "mocked the messengers of God . . . till there was no remedy."

## V. The Land Was Left Desolate (25:18-30)

One of the Babylonian officers gathered together the nobles that were left and had them slain (vv. 18-21). All that remained on the land were the poorest people. Nebuchadnezzar set up a system of governors over the land, making Gedaliah the first governor. His father had helped Jeremiah (Jer. 26:24; 39:14), and his family was devoted to the prophet (see Jer. 39–40). Gedaliah did establish a reasonable amount of safety, peace, and security for those left behind, but the jealousy of Ishmael (probably a distant relative of the king) led to a plot and the murder of the governor (Jer. 40–41). When the plot was revealed, many of the Jews fled to Egypt for safety.

Second Chronicles 36:20-21 informs us that the seventy years of captivity (Jer. 29:10) were calculated from the "sabbatical years" of Lev. 25. Every seventh year, the Jews were supposed to let the land rest, but they had not obeyed this law for centuries. See Jer. 38:8-22. Note also that God promised to punish them for their sins "seven times over" (Lev. 26:18, 21, 28), so the number seven plays an important role in the captivity. The twenty kings of Judah (during the divided kingdom) reigned altogether approximately 390 years; and the total years of David, Solomon, and Saul is 120, making a grand total of 510 years for the monarchy. However, in some instances a father and son reigned together so that years overlapped. This means that we have less than 500 years for the kingdom of Judah from Saul to Zedekiah, and 500 divided by seven (for the sabbatical years) gives us approximately 70 years. Just as Israel chose 40 years of wandering in the wilderness by spying out the land forty days, so her neglect of the sabbatical years for nearly five centuries brought her 70 years of captivity.

Everything that God had given the Jews was taken from them. They had no king on David's throne, nor do they have one today. They had no temple, for it had been burned and its sacred vessels confiscated. Today they have no temple. Their holy city was destroyed, and ever since that time has been the focal point for war and unrest in the Mideast. Their land was taken from them, and they were scattered among the nations. Of course, this awful siege was but a forerunner of the terrible destruction of Jerusalem in A.D. 70. "Be sure your sins will find you out."

# 1 & 2 CHRONICLES

## *A Suggested Outline of 1 and 2 Chronicles*

I. Genealogies from Adam to King Saul (1 Chron. 1–9)

II. The reign of King David (1 Chron. 10–29)
   - A. The death of King Saul (10)
   - B. David solidifies his kingdom (11–16)
   - C. God's covenant with David (17)
   - D. David expands the kingdom (18–20)
   - E. David numbers the people (21)
   - F. David prepares for the building of the temple (22–29) (The death of David)

III. The reign of King Solomon (2 Chron. 1–9)
   - A. Solomon receives God's blessing (1)
   - B. Solomon builds and dedicates the temple (2–7)
   - C. Solomon's fame and splendor (8–9)

IV. The divided kingdom (The kings of Judah) (10–36)
   - A. The reign of Rehoboam (10–12)
   - B. From Abijah to Asa (13–16)
   - C. The reign of Jehoshaphat (17–20)
   - D. From Jehoram to Amaziah (21–25)
   - E. The reign of Uzziah (26)
   - F. The reigns of Jotham and Ahaz (27–28)
   - G. The reign of Hezekiah (29–32)
   - H. The reigns of Manasseh and Amon (33)
   - I. The reign of Josiah (34–35)
   - J. The last kings and the downfall of Judah (36)

# Introductory Notes to 1 and 2 Chronicles

The books of Samuel, Kings, and Chronicles record the history of the Jews from the last judge (Samuel) and the establishment of the first king (Saul), to the exile of the nation to Babylon. The books of 1 and 2 Kings were written from the viewpoint of the prophets, while 1 and 2 Chronicles present the priestly viewpoint of Jewish history. There is an emphasis in Chronicles on the Levites, the building of the temple, God's covenant as recorded in Deuteronomy, and the holy city of Jerusalem. You might say that 1 and 2 Kings give us the political record and 1 and 2 Chronicles the religious record. Second Chronicles records at least five "revivals" in the history of Judah (chaps. 15, 20, 23–24, 25, and 29–31).

The chronologies in 1 Chron. 1–9 belong before 1 Sam. 1 and are the "living links" with the past. It was important to the Jews that they know their family history and be able to claim their place in the nation. This was especially true of the priests and Levites who served in the tabernacle and then the temple.

The writer of 1 Chronicles picks up the royal record at the death of Saul (1 Chron. 10). It is interesting to note what he omits from the record: David's long conflict with Saul; the rivalry with Ishbosheth (2 Sam. 2–4); David's sin with Bathsheba; David's family problems with Amnon and Absalom; Adonijah's attempt to get the throne from Solomon; the sins of Solomon; and much of the history of the kings of Israel (the Northern Kingdom). The record focuses on the kings of Judah and emphasizes God's choice of David and his descendants to reign from Jerusalem. If you studied only the record in 1 and 2 Chronicles, you would never know that David and Solomon had ever sinned! According to the writer of 2 Chronicles, it was not Solomon's sin that caused the division of the kingdom, but Jeroboam's political scheming. Both are true, but it is interesting to see the priestly viewpoint that almost idealized both David and Solomon. After all, David provided the wealth for the building of the temple, as well as the songs, musical instruments, and organization for the Levites; and Solomon built the temple.

The book shows that God blesses His people when they obey His will and disciplines them when they disobey. God is true to His covenant even if His people prove false to Him. When God's longsuffering ended, He turned the people of Judah over to the Babylonians and permitted the enemy to destroy the temple and the city of Jerusalem. Second Chronicles ends with a copy of the decree of Cyrus allowing the Jews to return to their land, and thus parallels the beginning of Ezra. The writer sees continuity in the history of the people, because God is guiding them and accomplishing His purposes through them, in spite of their sins.

A helpful volume to use in studying 1 and 2 Chronicles is *A Harmony of Samuel, Kings and Chronicles* by William D. Crockett (Baker Book House).

# 1 CHRONICLES 1–9

Genealogies make boring reading for most people today, but they were essential to the Jews who had to keep accurate records of their family ties for many reasons. You had to know your tribe, clan, and family relationships because property ownership was supposed to stay within the tribe. In situations where a kinsman redeemer would rescue a poor person, he had to prove that he was indeed a near relative. (See the Book of Ruth.) The firstborn son received twice as much inheritance as did the other sons. Of course, the priests and Levites had to prove that they were from the tribe of Levi or they were not permitted to serve.

These hundreds of names, some of them difficult to pronounce, represent people whom God used to maintain the "living link" with the promises and covenants of the past. The Jews were chosen by God and given promises that would ultimately affect all the world. Had there been a break in this chain of "living links," the Savior could not have been born into this world.

Most of these people are unknown while a few of them are very famous, but God used all of them to accomplish His purposes. When you read your Bible, you remember people like Abraham, Isaac, Jacob, Moses, Joshua, Samuel, and David, but were it not for a great many lesser-known people, these men would not have been on the scene. Let's thank God for the "forgotten people" who helped the "famous people" get there!

Scattered throughout these genealogies are the names of people who are given special identification, and reflecting on them can teach us some important spiritual lessons.

## I. Nimrod, the Mighty Hunter (1:10)

The reference is to Gen. 10:8-10. The word "hunter" carries the connotation of hunting people, not hunting animals. He was a rebel who defied God and set up the infamous kingdom of Babylon. After the sons of Noah began to replenish the earth, it didn't take long for their descendants to turn against the Lord. The lesson of the flood didn't penetrate very deep.

## II. Er, the Wicked Son (2:3)

See Genesis 38. We don't know the nature of Er's sin, but it was something serious enough for God to slay him. His brother Onan refused to marry the widow and carry on the brother's name and family, so he was also killed. See Deut. 25:5-10. It was important to God that the Jewish people continue to multiply, for He had some special tasks for them to fulfill. It's unfortunate that Onan's name has gotten into the English dictionary ("onanism") as a synonym for masturbation, for that was not his offense. The whole story about Judah and Tamar seems repulsive to us, yet Tamar is listed in the genealogy of Jesus Christ (Matt. 1:3).

### III. Achan, the Troubler of Israel (2:7)

Read Joshua 6–7. His sin was in violating a ban that Joshua had put on all the spoil of Jericho because it was dedicated to the Lord. Achan thought he had gotten away with stealing the loot, but the defeat of Israel's army at Ai led to his discovery and execution. Had Achan waited a few days, he could have had all the loot he wanted at Ai! One sinner can bring trouble to a whole nation.

### IV. Amnon, the Unclean (3:1)

He violated his half-sister Tamar and was eventually slain by Absalom (2 Sam. 13–14). Some of the firstborn sons listed in these chapters are not models of virtue. Er was killed by the Lord (2:3); Amnon was killed by his brother (3:1); and Reuben lost the birthright because he violated his father's concubine (5:1-2). In Israel, the firstborn had special privileges, but these three men threw away their privileges for the "pleasures of sin for a season."

### V. Jabez, the Undaunted (4:9-10)

In Hebrew, the name "Jabez" means "to grieve." It certainly wasn't the fault of Jabez that his mother had such a difficult delivery, but she gave him a name that would remind him and others of her pain. See Gen. 35:18-19. It would seem from the text that his brethren rejected him and were not "noble" men of character. Jabez overcame his name and his family problems by turning to God in prayer and asking for His blessing.

### VI. Reuben, the Uncontrollable (5:1-2)

How strange that a man's sins should get into an official genealogy! The deed is recorded in Gen. 35:22; and in Gen. 49:3-4, Jacob brought it up publicly at his deathbed and judged him for his lack of self-control. Reuben lost the birthright, which was given to Ephraim and Manasseh (Gen. 48:15-22). One act of sin can be costly for the sinner and for his or her family!

## VII. Beriah the Unfortunate (7:20-23)

When Ephraim's two sons, Ezer and Elead, tried to seize some cattle, they were killed, and their father was plunged into grief. He found solace in loving his wife, and she gave birth to a son whom Ephraim named Beriah, which means "misfortune." He and Jabez and Benjamin (Benoni) could have formed a fellowship of men with miserable names.

# 1 CHRONICLES 22–29

Since the record in Chronicles was written from the priestly viewpoint, we would expect the strong emphasis here on the building of the temple. It's remarkable that the temple was built on the property David purchased from Ornan, a reminder of David's great sin in numbering the people (1 Chron. 21). The temple was built by Solomon, a son of Bathsheba, the woman with whom David had committed adultery. Only God can take a man's two greatest sins and build a temple out of them. "But where sin abounded, grace did much more abound" (Rom. 5:20).

## I. The Builder of the Temple (22:1-19)

David's heart had always been set on building a temple for the Lord (see 2 Sam. 7), but since he had been fully occupied fighting wars, he was not able to do the work. The fact that he was a warrior and had shed blood was another reason. Throughout his life, David had gathered treasures to be used for the temple, and these he now turned over to his son Solomon. God gave David the plans for the temple (1 Chron. 28:11-12, 19) just as He had given Moses the plans for the tabernacle (Ex. 25:40). When you are going to do something for the Lord on earth, be sure you get the plans from heaven. And if the Lord won't let you do something that is really on your heart, try to help the other person do it.

Solomon was anointed king privately, in the presence of the leaders, so that the throne would be secure (vv. 17-19); and then the new king was publicly presented to the people (chap. 28). Our Lord Jesus has been anointed King, but His public presentation has yet to be made. Meanwhile, we who trust Him should assist Him in the building of His temple, the church (Matt. 16:18; Eph. 2:19-22). David drafted the "aliens and strangers" in the land (non-Israelites) and forced them to work on the temple (v. 2). But the Lord has taken sinners who were "outsiders" and made them fellow citizens and living stones in His temple (Eph. 2:19-22; 1 Peter 2:5). What a grace!

David admonished Solomon to trust the Lord and obey Him; otherwise, he could never build the temple to the glory of God. God gave Solomon and the nation rest from war (the name Solomon is related to the Hebrew word "shalom" which means "peace"), and He would give him wisdom in doing the work. We can't begin to calculate the purchasing power of the wealth that David gathered (v. 14).

So, David gave Solomon the wealth to build the temple, the plans, the workers, and the cooperation of the princes of the land (vv. 17-19). But the "heart" of the matter was the heart of Solomon (v. 19). If Solomon's heart was right with God, then God would bless his endeavors. There is nothing "automatic" about the service of the Lord. If we are right with Him, He will prosper our efforts (Josh. 1:8; Matt. 6:33).

## II. The Ministers in the Temple (23:1–26:32)

Second Chronicles 29:25 informs us that David's plan for organizing the priests and Levites was given to him by the Lord through his two prophets, Gad and Nathan. Not only the plan for the temple itself, but also what went on in the temple and how it was organized, were commanded by the Lord. The local church today needs to heed the directions given in the NT for its organization and ministry. Too often, we import the ideas of the world and reject the ideals of the Word.

There were 38,000 Levites available and David divided them into four units: 24,000 to supervise the work in the temple; 4,000 as musicians; 4,000 as doorkeepers, which involved the temple treasuries and storerooms; and 6,000 to be scattered throughout the nation to minister as judges and teachers of the law. It is not enough for the people to come to God's house; the servants of God must also go to the people. Note that David provided the instruments for the musicians to use (23:5), and he wrote many of the songs that they used to worship the Lord.

During the years of Israel's wandering, the descendants of Levi were assigned to take down the tabernacle and carry its various parts, reassembling the tabernacle at the place God told the people to camp (see Num. 3–4). Now that they would be serving in a permanent sanctuary, the three clans of the sons of Levi were assigned to other duties.

The priests were divided into twenty-four courses (chap. 24; see Luke 1:5), which means they served in "shifts," possibly two weeks each month. David did things "decently and in order" (1 Cor. 14:40). The specific assignments were given by lot (Luke 1:8-9).

The gatekeepers (chap. 26) guarded the temple and the storerooms in it. You will recall that Obed-edom (26:4) was the man who guarded the ark of the covenant before it was finally placed in the tent (1 Chron. 13:13-14). The gatekeepers cast lots to see where they would be assigned (26:13). Keep in mind that the Jewish people brought tithes and offerings to the temple as a part of their worship, and all these commodities had to be stored, inventoried, and protected. Most of all, the temple treasury contained valuables dedicated to the Lord, as well as material needed for the service of the Lord (see 1 Chron. 9:27-34). It was important that the spices, flour, and other items be kept from contamination. How unfortunate it is when that which defiles gets into the house of the Lord.

As we review these chapters and their many names, we are struck with the fact that God uses people to accomplish His work, people with different talents and different ministries. Some of the temple servants led in singing praises to God; others played the instruments; some guarded the treasures; some kept the inventory of the gifts brought to the temple. The priests offered the sacrifices to the Lord and cared for the daily service of worship. Everything was organized for efficiency, and the total temple ministry brought glory to the Lord. Even those who had to work "the night shift" praised the Lord for the privilege of worshiping and serving Him. (Ps. 134)

## III. The Protectors of the Temple and the Land (27:1-34)

### A. The army (vv. 1-15).

We move now from the temple organization to the civil government, for in the nation of Israel, both were ordered by God and governed by His divine law. There were twelve army units and each one served for one month of the year. Of course, when needed, the units could be called together quickly.

If you compare 1 Chron. 11:10ff with the list of leaders in vv. 2-15, you will see that David's "mighty men" were in charge of the army. He had proved these men in many places of testing, and he knew he could trust them.

### B. The civil servants (vv. 16-24).

Not only were there capable soldiers to lead each of the twelve units of the army, but there were capable officers assigned to the tribes of Israel (vv. 16-22). David had a "chain of command" in the nation so that each tribe had a representative before the king. We have no record of David's brother Elihu anywhere else in Scripture (v. 18). It's possible that this is a variation of the name "Eliab" (1 Chron. 2:13). The Hebrew word "brother" was often applied to any relative, but it would seem that an official listing such as this would aim for accuracy.

How interesting that a son of Abner was one of David's trusted officers (v. 21). Abner had tried to maintain Saul's dynasty after Saul was slain and had created problems for David (2 Sam. 1–4). David obeyed Deut. 24:16.

### C. David's overseers (vv. 25-34).

In modern society, government leaders must divest themselves of anything that would lead to conflict of interest, but not so in ancient monarchies. The king was a very wealthy man, thanks to the spoils of war, the tribute brought by conquered rulers, and the profit made from his lands. In fairness to David, we should recognize that, since there were no taxes on the citizens, he had to use much of this income for the administration of his own government. All of these holdings had to be supervised, the laborers paid, and the profits guarded.

## IV. The Encouragement to Build the Temple (28:1–29:30)

The writer is giving us "the last words of David" (1 Chron. 23:27) as well as the last works of David as he prepared Solomon and the people for the building of the temple. What a wonderful thing that David sought to build a temple to the glory of God and not a monument to his own glory. He could die knowing that future generations would have a beautiful house of prayer and praise where they could honor the Lord. David not only "served his own generation" (Acts 13:36), which every child of God should do, but he also served generations to come. He provided the materials to build the temple; he organized the temple ministry; he wrote songs for the temple singers; and he even designed musical instruments for the Levites to play.

David gathered all the leaders of Israel and exhorted and encouraged them to support Solomon in his administration, especially in the building of the temple.

### A. God's choices (28:1-7).

David emphasized the fact that it was God who chose the tribe of Judah to be the royal tribe (v. 4; Gen. 49:8-10); and from Judah, God chose David's family to be the royal family (1 Sam. 16:6-13; 2 Sam. 7). Then God chose Solomon to be David's successor and the one to build the temple. It was a solemn obligation on Solomon's part, for these were God's chosen people; and the temple was for the God of Abraham, Isaac, and Jacob.

### B. David's charges (28:8-10, 20-21).

First, David charged all the officers and people to obey all of God's commands (v. 8). What good was a beautiful temple if the people were disobedient to their God? They owed it to the Lord and to one another, as fellow citizens in God's assembly, to live according to the Law that God had graciously given to them. The Jews owned the land by virtue of God's covenant with Abraham (Gen. 12:1-3; 13:14-18), but they possessed and enjoyed the land only so long as they obeyed God's Word. See Deut. 27–30. If they wanted to maintain possession of the land and leave it to the next generation, then they had to be an obedient people. It's a solemn thought that we are stewards of all that God gives us, and, if we aren't faithful to the Lord, there will be nothing to leave our children and grandchildren.

Then David charged Solomon (28:9-10, 20-21) to be faithful to discharge his responsibility as king and builder of the temple. "Be strong and of good courage" (vv. 10, 20) reminds us of God's admonitions to Joshua (Josh. 1:6-7, 9, 18). The tragedy is that Solomon did not maintain a perfect heart before the Lord, but loved foreign women and worshiped their false gods (1 Kings 11). A perfect heart is not a sinless heart, for nobody can live without sinning in some way. It means a heart totally devoted to the Lord, a sincere heart. When Solomon began to worship other gods along with Jehovah, he had a divided heart and was not true to the Lord. It was when Solomon forsook the Word of God that he began to worship idols (see Deut. 17:14-20; Josh. 1:8).

## C. David's contributions (28:11-19).

Everything Solomon needed for the great building project was provided by the Lord through David: the plans for the building, the organization of the priests and Levites, the material wealth, and the people to do the job. Since we don't know the buying power of gold and silver in that day, we can't accurately calculate the worth of all this material; but certainly it was in the tens of millions of dollars.

## D. David's challenge (29:1-9).

David knew that his people must have a share in the cost of the temple, so he asked the leaders of the nation to contribute, and they did so willingly. David had first set the example in giving, and he reminded the people that they were giving to the Lord (29:1). Their giving was an act of worship (29:5b), and they gave generously. The mentioning of "gold, silver, and precious stones" reminds us of 1 Cor. 3:10-23 and the language used to describe the building of the local church.

## E. David's consecration (29:10-19).

David prayed and dedicated the offering, the new king, and the people to the Lord. He blessed the Lord and extolled Him for His wonderful attributes. He expressed his humility before God (29:14) and acknowledged that even the wealth that he and his people had brought originally came from the Lord! "Everything comes from you, and we have given you only what comes from your hand" (NIV). The fact that we are "strangers and sojourners" in this world (v. 15) ought to encourage us to give generously to the Lord, for only what we give to Him will last (Matt. 6:19-21). Life is brief and we can't keep anything for ourselves or take it with us when we go (1 Tim. 6:7; see Ps. 90:1-11).

Read chapter 29 carefully and note how the people gave and why they gave; then read 2 Cor. 8–9 and note how Paul taught many of these same truths about giving.

### F. Solomon's coronation (29:20-30).

In a great worship service where the Lord was glorified, David passed the scepter to his son Solomon, and the people rejoiced at God's goodness. God was able to magnify Solomon because Solomon magnified the Lord (see Phil. 1:20; Josh. 3:7). David died but the throne of Israel continued. God buries His workmen but continues His work.

# 2 CHRONICLES

## I. The Kingdom Declines (1–9)

Most of the information in these chapters is also found in 1 Kings 1–11. Solomon began his reign in fellowship with the Lord, but gradually his heart turned away, and he began to worship the gods of his many foreign wives. Deuteronomy 17:14-20 warned the Hebrew kings not to multiply horses and chariots, wives, or gold, but Solomon did all three (1 Kings 10:14, 26, 28; 11:1-8).

While the years of Solomon's reign were undoubtedly Israel's greatest in terms of wealth, fame, and political power, they were also the worst in terms of spiritual devotion to the Lord. Yes, Solomon began his reign at the altar, sacrificing to the Lord and asking Him for wisdom, but that didn't continue. Furthermore, the king lived in luxury because he collected food and taxes from the people. Solomon reorganized the twelve tribes into twelve tax districts, with each district responsible to provide his food one month (1 Kings 4:7-19). When you read the menu for each day, you can well understand why the people felt burdened by his yoke (1 Kings 4:22-25; 12:1-5). Yes, the kingdom was indeed glorious, but it was declining in every way.

## II. The Kingdom Divides (10–12)

Solomon's son Rehoboam inherited the throne and was given a golden opportunity to bring the nation back to the Lord. Had he listened to the older advisors, he would have saved the nation from division. Instead, he heeded the unwise counsel of the young men who knew little about life or service. This doesn't mean that the aged are always wise or that the young are always foolish, for such is not the case. Like his father Solomon, Rehoboam had been reared in luxury and was out of touch with the burdens of the common people. He lacked the perception to recognize good counsel when it was given to him.

When Rehoboam tried to go to war with Jeroboam and unite the tribes, God stopped the endeavor because the division was from Him. But both Rehoboam and Jeroboam sinned against the Lord. Rehoboam "forsook the law of the Lord" (12:1) because "he prepared not his heart to seek the Lord" (12:14). When God sent the Egyptian army to chasten the nation, it is to Rehoboam's credit that he repented and sought the Lord's help. But he didn't lead the people back to the Lord.

Jeroboam, king of Israel (the Northern Kingdom), was afraid that the people would go back to Jerusalem to worship God, so he set up his own system of worship which was idolatrous. Israel never did come back to the Lord, and the kingdom was eventually swallowed up by Assyria.

The only reason God preserved the Southern Kingdom of Judah as long as He did was for the sake of His beloved David (1 Kings 11:34-39; 15:4). How much the people owed to David and to the longsuffering of the Lord!

From this point on (about 930 B.C.), the kingdom is divided: Judah and Benjamin form the Southern Kingdom of Judah, and the other ten tribes form the Northern Kingdom of Israel or Samaria. The record in Kings goes back and forth from Israel to Judah, but the record in 2 Chronicles focuses primarily on the kings of Judah.

## III. The Kingdom Decays (13–36)

While the kings of Israel were for the most part apostates, several kings in Judah were men of God who sought to bring the people back to the Lord. However, the infection of sin had already gotten into both kingdoms and it was only a matter of time before they would collapse.

### A. Asa (chaps. 14–16).

Asa led the nation in two reforms as he removed the altars to the foreign gods and commanded the people to return to the Lord. God honored his efforts by giving the nation ten years of peace, during which the king fortified the cities. His victory over the Ethiopians and the message from the prophet Azariah motivated the king to gather all the people together to reaffirm their covenant with Him

(15:12). Asa even deposed the Queen Mother and destroyed her idols! How sad it is that in his latter years, Asa stopped trusting the Lord and robbed God's temple to buy protection from a heathen king. When rebuked by the prophet Hanani, the king didn't repent; then, when afflicted with an illness, he didn't turn to the Lord. Good beginnings are no guarantee of good endings.

### B. Jehoshaphat (chaps. 17–20).

In spite of the fact that he made some unwise decisions, he was one of Judah's greatest kings. He not only sought God himself, but he sent the priests among the people to teach them the way of the Lord. His first mistake was to marry into the godless family of Israel's King Ahab, a worshiper of Baal and the husband of wicked Queen Jezebel. It was a marriage of political convenience so that Ahab would be allied with Jehoshaphat. Solomon used this approach to secure treaty rights with other nations (1 Kings 3:1). By making peace with the king of Israel, Jehoshaphat compromised his position politically and religiously.

Jehoshaphat's second mistake was to unite with Ahab in fighting Israel's enemies. Ahab talked Jehoshaphat into wearing royal robes into battle, which made him a ready target, but God protected Jehoshaphat and saw to it that Ahab was slain. This event ought not to encourage us to sin, because God isn't obligated to protect us when we are out of His will (Ps. 91:9-16).

His third mistake was to ally himself with wicked King Ahaziah in an attempt to gain wealth (20:35-37). God wrecked the ships and put the whole enterprise to an end. It's unfortunate when godly people sometimes lack discernment and get themselves involved in alliances that can only help the enemy and bring disgrace to the name of the Lord.

When faced by a combined army of the Moabites and the Ammonites, two ancient enemies of Israel (Gen. 19:30-38; Deut. 23:3; Neh. 13:1ff), Jehoshaphat put his faith in the Lord, and God gave him a great victory. The combination of prayer (20:3-13), prophecy (20:14-17), and praise (20:18-22) brought him the victory. (We wonder how the choir of Levites felt about going out before the army. But worship is a great weapon against the enemy.)

### C. Joash (chaps. 23–24).

Joash was a miracle boy because his evil grandmother Athaliah had killed all of his siblings, and he alone had survived. The future of

David's line and the messianic promise rested on that little boy! How often in Jewish history Satan tried to kill those who were a part of God's plan (Gen. 3:15). The godly high priest, Jehoiada, protected Joash and then installed him as king. At the same time, Jehoiada saw to it that Athaliah and her followers were put out of the way. Through the continued spiritual influence of Jehoiada, the king brought about many reforms, especially the restoring of the temple. When the high priest died, however, the king made the same mistake that Rehoboam made in listening to worldly counsel. Joash ended up killing Zechariah, son of Jehoiada, instead of heeding his message from the Lord, and repenting.

Joash is a warning to all who profess to do God's will but really don't have the love of God in their hearts. If your faith is "propped up" by someone else, what will you do when the "prop" is gone?

### D. Uzziah (chap. 26).

He is also called Azariah. After a long and prosperous reign, he ended up trying to become a priest, and God struck him with leprosy. "God helped him" (v. 7) and he went from victory to victory. "He was marvelously helped, till he was strong" (v. 15). Overcome by pride, he intruded into the ministry of the priests in the temple, something forbidden by God. Jesus Christ is the only King-Priest that God will accept. Uzziah is a warning to all of us not to become proud and seek to get involved in things that are outside the will of God.

### E. Hezekiah (chaps. 29–32).

He was one of Judah's greatest kings and most devoted spiritual leaders. He repaired the temple and restored the true worship of Jehovah on a scale not seen before. He called the whole nation—Israel and Judah—to observe the Passover together, and he cleansed the land of idols. You would think that such devotion to the Lord would have kept him from problems, but not so. Second Chronicles 32:1 reads, "After all that Hezekiah had so faithfully done, Sennacherib king of Assyria came and invaded Judah" (NIV). Obedience sometimes leads to greater testing, for our good and the glory of God. See the notes on 2 Kings 18–20, and read Isa. 37–39.

### F. Josiah (chaps. 34–35).

Manasseh followed the great King Hezekiah and led the nation into abominable sin. He rebuilt everything evil that his father had destroyed, and destroyed the good things his father had restored. However, in his latter years, Manasseh did repent, and God forgave him. He was followed by Amon, who reigned only two years. Then Josiah came to the throne. If Hezekiah is faulted for his son Manasseh, he certainly must be praised for his grandson Josiah. At the age of sixteen (34:3), Josiah sought the Lord and began to reform the nation and wipe out idolatry. He repaired the temple and restored the Book of the Law. He too celebrated a great Passover and sought to lead the people back to the Lord their God. Unfortunately, King Josiah meddled with a war that was not his concern, and he was wounded in battle and went home to Jerusalem to die. His pride got the best of him, and he thought he could defeat the king of Egypt.

After Josiah's death, the kings of Judah were weaklings, mere puppets in the hands of the politicians in Jerusalem or the nations around Judah. The last king was Zedekiah, and then the nation fell to Babylon in 586 B.C.

Why did Judah decay? Because the people turned from the Lord and worshiped false gods. At first, their godless worship was in secret: they worshiped the Lord in the temple, but also worshiped Baal and other gods in secret. Then they openly turned from the Lord to worship the gods of their enemies. When the Lord sent chastening to them, they repented for a time, but soon they went back to their evil ways. Whenever the Lord would raise up a godly king, his influence didn't last, because the people "reformed" but didn't repent and turn to God with all their hearts. Whatever the king did was the popular thing to do, so they did it.

The church today must beware of the same kind of spiritual decay. Are we worshiping the gods of the enemy? Are we proud of our buildings and budgets and statistics? Is there evidence of true holiness and a fear of God in our worship? Are we dependent on the spiritual leaders God gives us? Are we experiencing success because the Lord is with us or because we cooperate with the world? Do we think that because we have the Bible and church buildings and "successful ministries" that God will overlook our sins and stay His hand of discipline? "For the time has come for judgment to begin at the house of God" (1 Peter 4:17).

At any time during those centuries of spiritual decay, the people of Judah could have met the conditions of 2 Chron. 7:14, and God would have healed their land. But they would not turn back to God, so God had to turn against them.

What a lesson for God's people today!

# EZRA

## A Suggested Outline of Ezra

I. National Restoration under Zerubbabel (1–6)

  A. Returning to the land (1–2)
    1. Proclamation of Cyrus (1)
    2. Registration of the people (2)
  B. Rebuilding the temple (3)
    1. Establishing the altar (3:1-6)
    2. Laying again the foundation (3:7-13)
  C. Resisting the enemy (4–6)
    1. The building ceases (4)
    (Note: 4:6-23 is a parenthesis describing opposition at a later date)
    2. The prophets begin their ministry (5)
    3. The building is completed (6)

II. Spiritual Reformation under Ezra (7–10)

  A. Ezra comes to Jerusalem (7–8)
  B. Ezra confesses the sins of the people (9)
  C. Ezra cleanses the nation (10)

# Introductory Notes to Ezra and Nehemiah

## I. Background

Ezra and Nehemiah form one book in the Hebrew Bible because they tell one story—the return of the remnant to Jerusalem and the rebuilding of the city and the temple. The Babylonian Captivity began in 606 B.C.; Jerusalem fell to the enemy in 587 B.C. The Babylonians deported many of the people between 606 and 586, including Daniel and Ezekiel. Jeremiah had predicted a seventy-year period of captivity (Jer. 25:12-14; 29:10-14). It would extend from the beginning of the invasion in 606 to the return of the remnant in 536, at which time the altar was set up and the animal sacrifices instituted again. So, Ezra and Nehemiah tell the story of the return to the land and the city, the rebuilding of the temple, and the rebuilding of the walls. The Book of Esther also fits into this period, as do the books of the prophets Haggai and Zechariah (see Ezra 5:1ff).

## II. Chronology

A brief chronology of the period would look like this:

| | |
|---|---|
| 606–605 | Babylon begins invading and deporting people |
| 587 | Jerusalem falls to the enemy |
| 539 | Babylon falls to Cyrus and the Media-Persian empire begins |
| 538 | Cyrus permits the Jews to return; about 50,000 return |
| 535 | The Jews begin to rebuild the temple, but the work stops |
| 520 | After fifteen years, the work begins again |
| 515 | The temple is completed and dedicated |
| 476 | Esther becomes Queen of Persia |
| 458 | Ezra travels to Jerusalem (see Ezra 7–10) |

## III. The Leaders

Ezra is presented to us as a godly and patriotic Jew who was a priest and a scribe (Ezra 7:1-6). He was a devoted student of the Scriptures and helped to restore the Law to the nation. He was also a man of prayer (8:21-23) and a man who was greatly burdened for the spiritual welfare of his people (9:3-4). His name means "help." Ezra's faith in the Lord is seen by his willingness to undertake the dangerous journey from Babylon to Jerusalem without the aid of a military escort. Please note that Ezra did not lead the first group of Jews back to Jerusalem; this was done by Zerubbabel and Joshua. Ezra does not come on the scene until chapter 7 of his book, when he led a second company (and a smaller one) to the Holy Land. Ezra remained there to labor, and finally joined hands with Nehemiah (Neh. 8:9; 12:26). Nehemiah was an officer in the king's court when God called him to return to the city of Jerusalem to rebuild the walls. He was what we would call a "layman" today, since he had no prophetic call or priestly lineage. He was promoted from cupbearer to governor. Zerubbabel was one of the leaders under Ezra (2:2; 3:8); he was also called Sheshbazzar (1:8, 11; 5:16). His official title was "tirshatha" (2:63), which means "governor." First Chronicles 3:17-19 indicates that Zerubbabel was in the royal line of David. He served as the political leader of the restored nation. Joshua was the high priest at this time (Ezra 3:2; Hag. 1:1, 12, 14; see Zech. 3:1-10). As we mentioned before, the two prophets were Haggai and Zechariah.

## IV. The Lessons

God had promised captivity to the sinning nation, and He fulfilled His promise. He also promised that a remnant would return. (See Jer. 25:12-14 and 29:10-14). It was Jeremiah's prophecy that Daniel read in Babylon that encouraged him to pray for the return of the people (Dan. 9:1ff). God kept a "lamp lit" at Jerusalem in order that His Son might be born through the Hebrew nation and come to save the world. The captivity cured the Jews of idolatry and gave them a desire to know and obey the Word. Alas, they forgot their lessons quickly!

# EZRA 1–5

These chapters describe four key events in the history of the remnant of Israel that had returned to their land.

## I. Returning to the Land (1–2)

### A. The proclamation (1:1-4).

These verses are almost identical with 2 Chron. 36:22-23. Isaiah 44:28–45:3 contains an amazing prophecy of Cyrus before the great Persian ruler was born. In 539 B.C. Cyrus conquered Babylon and established the Persian empire. His policy with prisoners of war was opposite that of Babylon, for he encouraged the Jews to return to their land, rebuild their temple, and pray for his welfare. No doubt Cyrus extended this same privilege to other displaced nations and their gods. His decree was in 538 B.C. Do not confuse this decree with the one in Dan. 9:25, which refers to the rebuilding of the city and is dated 445 B.C. Cyrus's decree had to do with the people returning to the land and rebuilding the temple. This decree was a marvelous fulfillment of Scripture.

### B. The precious things (1:5-11).

The Spirit of God worked in the hearts of the people and of their captors. The temple treasures were restored to the Jews, and the Gentiles also gave them freewill contributions for their temple. See 2 Chron. 36:7; Dan. 1:2. "Sheshbazzar" in vv. 8 and 11 is Zerubbabel, the appointed governor. The Jews could not restore the temple worship without the appointed furnishings. How unlike our NT worship (John 4:19-24).

### C. The people (chap. 2).

About fifty thousand Jews were concerned enough to leave the safety and luxury of Babylon and return to their own land. This same list is cited in Neh. 7:6-73. Note that this register is in special groups: the leaders (vv. 1-2); certain families (vv. 3-19); certain towns (vv. 20-35); the priests (vv. 36-39); the Levites (vv. 40-42); the Nethinim, or temple helpers (vv. 43-54); Solomon's servants (vv. 55-58); and those with no genealogy (vv. 59-63). The word "tirshatha" in v. 63 refers to Zerubbabel. In vv. 64-70 we have the totals of the men and beasts: there were 49,897 people registered, along with a multitude of animals. Much has been said about the so-called "lost tribes of Israel," but the NT makes it clear that *all twelve tribes* were represented in this remnant (see Acts 26:7 and James 1:1). Ezra 2:70 says "all Israel." In Ezra 6:17 we see the priests offering twelve male goats for the twelve tribes; see also 8:35. Jesus will one day judge twelve tribes (Luke 22:30). Most of the Jews had settled down in Babylon and had no desire to return to their Promised Land. Content with security and material gain, they abandoned the land of their fathers and stayed with the captives in Babylon.

## II. Rebuilding the Temple (3)

### A. *Establishing the altar (vv. 1-6).*

The altar was the center of the Jewish worship for without their sacrifices they could not approach God or expect His blessing. The exiles feared their powerful neighbors, but they knew God would protect them if they obeyed Him. You will recall that Elijah had to set up the altar again (1 Kings 18:30ff). Joshua and Zerubbabel led the people to establish the sacrifices and also to keep the feasts. It was the seventh month (our Sept.–Oct.), the month of the Feast of Trumpets and the Feast of Tabernacles (Num. 29:1-6; Lev. 23:23-25).

### B. *Laying the foundation (vv. 7-13).*

The people apparently gave offerings, adding these to the gifts from the king (1:5-11) who also provided materials to rebuild the temple. In the year 535 they started the work, in the second month (our April-May). The Levites led the way in doing the work, assisting the other workers on the job. So grateful were the people that they sang and shouted when the foundation was laid. God was doing the impossible in this situation (Jer. 33:1-11). Of course, there were older people there who remembered the former temple in its glory, and they could only weep as they saw the plainness of this second temple (see Hag. 2:3). However, it is not good to live in the past.

## III. Resisting the Enemy (4)

Our enemy, Satan, never wants the Lord's work to prosper. Christ is the Builder; Satan is the destroyer. We now see the hand of the enemy as he seeks to oppose and hinder the work.

### A. Compromise (vv. 1-3).

The people of the land offered to assist the Jews in their work, but Zerubbabel and Joshua refused their aid. These people were the Samaritans, a half-breed nation of mixed Jews and Gentiles. Read 2 Kings 17 for a description of the Samaritans and their false religion. (In John 4:20-24, Jesus clearly rejected Samaritan religion.) The Samaritans finally built their own temple on Mt. Gerazim and remained separated from the Jews.

### B. Interference (vv. 4-5).

The people of the land hired men at court to resist the Jews, and this device succeeded in stopping the work; see 4:24. For nearly fifteen years (534–520) the work ceased on the temple.

Verses 6-23 have posed a problem to the Bible student because they seem to be out of place chronologically. The kings mentioned in vv. 6-7 ruled later than the time covered in Ezra 4. There are two possible explanations. It may be that the kings had more than one name, so that the Ahasuerus and Artaxerxes of vv. 6-7 are really the names of the kings that ruled during this era. Merrill Unger believes that "Ahasuerus" was an official title (like Pharaoh), and that Artaxerxes was another name for Cambyses. These verses, then, would contain the official records filed by the enemy to stop the work of the Jews. A second possibility is that these verses may have been included as examples of opposition from a later time, to show that the Jews had constant trouble with their enemies. In either case, the lesson is clear: worldly people use every means they can to hinder the work of the Lord. The king listened to the accusations and the work ceased.

## IV. Resuming the Work (5)

Fifteen years go by between chapters 4 and 5. It is not until the Word of God is proclaimed by the two prophets Haggai and Zechariah that the work of the temple begins again. The Word of God had begun the work (Ezra 1:1), and now the Word of God would encourage the workers and ultimately finish the work (6:14). From 520–515 the people labored and finished the temple. The preaching of God's Word by His servants is the secret of victory in any work of God. God's Word encouraged Joshua and Zerubbabel, and God's eye was upon them (Ezra 5:5).

You will note in Haggai four different messages: (1) Rebuke of the people for building their own houses and neglecting God's house, 1:1-15; (2) Encouragement of Zerubbabel that God is with him, 2:1-9; (3) Conviction to the priests for refusing to cleanse themselves of defilement, 2:10-19; and (4) Promise to Zerubbabel that the Messiah would one day rule in glory, 2:20-23. Haggai even dated each of these messages.

The Book of Zechariah is more complicated, but it too deals with the same period of time. In Zech. 1:1-6, the prophet called the nation to repent; this was in November. Later, in February, he gave several visions of encouragement to the people (1:7–6:15). In the last half of his book (chaps. 9–14), Zechariah pictured Christ in His rejection, second coming in glory, and future kingdom. All of these messages, of course, were meant to encourage the people to get to work and finish the temple.

Tatnai the governor was within his rights asking about the building program, since the materials were being supplied partly by the royal treasury. We have his letter to the new ruler, Darius, and in chapter 6, the reply of the king. Verse 8 indicates that the ministry of the two prophets had stirred up the people, for the work was progressing rapidly. "Sheshbazzar" in v. 16 is Zerubbabel. The Jews knew that they were in the right and suggested that the governor investigate the records to find the decree of the king. It is not wrong for God's people to claim their rights as citizens; see Acts 16:35-40 and Acts 22:25.

# EZRA 6–10

## I. The Completion of the Temple (6)

Darius became ruler in 522 B.C.; it was he who established the great empire of the Persians by defeating Babylon. (This was *not* Darius the Mede mentioned in Daniel 5, 6, and 9.) He had a friendly attitude toward his subjects and was kindly disposed toward the Jews. We have in 6:3-5 a detailed record of the original decree of Cyrus, mentioned in Ezra. 1:1. To this original decree, Darius added his own decree (6:8-12): the governor must assist the Jews in their work and see that there is no opposition, and the supplies are to be provided out of the king's treasury. Of course, Darius had a strong motive for his kindness: he wanted the Jews to pray to Jehovah for the king's health and for the welfare of his family.

The governor hastened to obey the decree. Haggai and Zechariah provided the spiritual encouragement; the governor supplied the material needs; and thus the work was completed. The Jews joyfully dedicated the house of the Lord, even though the building was not as grand and glorious as Solomon's temple had been. They kept the Passover and the Feast of Unleavened Bread. God had answered prayer and turned the king's heart (see Prov. 21:1); the nation had its temple again. Between chapters 6 and 7 is a period of fifty-eight years. The Book of Esther fits in here.

## II. The Coming of Ezra to Jerusalem (7–8)

The Artaxerxes of 7:1 is "Artaxerxes Longimanus," who ruled Persia from 465 to 425. In his seventh year, he permitted Ezra the priest-scribe to return to Jerusalem to assist the people in their spiritual needs. In vv. 1-5 we have Ezra's genealogy, the proof that he was a priest from the family of Aaron. He was also a ready student of the Law, a scribe; see Jer. 8:8. Apparently Ezra had requested permission from the king, realizing that the remnant in the restored nation desperately needed spiritual guidance. It took Ezra four months to make the journey of nearly a thousand miles from Babylon to Jerusalem. The good hand of God was upon him and he prospered; see Neh. 1:10; 2:8; 18.

The king decreed that any Jew could go up with Ezra and return to the land. These Jews would take with them a large freewill offering from Babylon to assist in the work of the Lord. Darius also gave Ezra an "expense account" (vv. 20-22) up to about $100,000, to be taken from the king's treasury. Ezra's task was to establish order and religious worship in the land (vv. 25-26). Ezra's doxology in 7:27-28 shows how grateful he was to the Lord for answering prayer.

Chapter 8 lists the names of the families and the men who accompanied Ezra on his hazardous trip to Jerusalem. It was important that the Levites go along because it was their duty to study the Word and teach it to the people. Unfortunately, Ezra had to "draft" some of the Levites, because they did not volunteer to go (vv. 15-20). Ezra proclaimed a fast, because he knew that God alone could prosper their journey. The very testimony of the nation was at stake—for Ezra had told the king that they would not require a military escort, for the Lord would take care of them. Their fasting and prayer and the Lord's response should encourage similar behavior in us today (vv. 21-23). Ezra chose twenty-two godly men to carry the treasures (vv. 24-30), and he warned them that God would require an accounting when they reached Jerusalem. What a beautiful picture of Christian stewardship today. God has entrusted us with spiritual treasures, and at the Judgment Seat of Christ we will give an account of our stewardship. The group departed in April 458 and arrived at Jerusalem in July, traveling at an average of seven miles a day. The people deposited their treasures, and it was found that each man had been faithful. They had heeded Ezra's warning, "Watch and keep!" (8:29)

## III. The Confession of Sin (9)

No sooner had a teacher of the Word arrived than the Word began to reveal sin (Heb. 4:12). Ezra discovered that the Jews had mingled with their heathen neighbors and married heathen wives. See Deut. 7; Ex. 19:5-6; and Ps. 106:35. Ezra was so burdened at hearing this report that he publicly tore his garment in sorrow and repentance and sat like a dumb man until the hour for the evening sacrifice. The people who knew God's Word began to tremble (v. 4; see Isa. 66:1-2), fearing what the Lord might do to the feeble nation.

Ezra's prayer of confession should be compared with Daniel's prayer (Dan. 9) and the prayer of Nehemiah (Neh. 9). "I am ashamed and blush to lift up my face!" Ezra prayed. He looked back to Israel's past sins (v. 7) and admitted that the nation deserved captivity. But now the Lord had sent deliverance; they had been restored by His grace; and yet the nation was sinning again. The future of the kingdom was hanging, as it were, like garments on a tent nail, so feeble was the restored remnant of Israel. God had given them a wall of protection (v. 9) and graciously answered their prayers. What more could Ezra say? "We have not learned our lessons," he says, "for God has punished us for our sins, yet we go on sinning still!"

It is interesting to note that Daniel, Ezra, and Nehemiah all had to confess national sin and plead for forgiveness. Second Chronicles 7:14 applies here. However, it was not enough for the religious leader to pray. The entire nation had to face its sins and make matters right with the Lord.

## IV. The Cleansing of the Nation (10)

Read Neh. 8–13 for parallel accounts of the religious revival in Jerusalem. God answered Ezra's prayer by touching and convicting the hearts of the people. Some of the men came to him openly and confessed that they had married heathen wives and disobeyed the Law of the Lord. They offered to make a covenant with God and to put away their unclean wives. What a great revival would come to our churches today if all God's people would humble themselves before God, confess their sins, and obey the Word of God!

The result was a proclamation throughout the land, calling the people to gather in Jerusalem to settle this important matter. Whoever was guilty and did not come would forfeit his place in the land. It was on December 20, 457, when the great multitude assembled in spite of the terrible rain that usually fell at that season. But the people trembled not only for the rain, but also because of their fear of the Lord. Ezra presented the ultimatum to the people: confess your sins and put away your wives. This is repentance and restitution, and both must go together. The people agreed to obey, but they admitted the problem was too widespread and complicated to be settled in a day. The people suggested that the rulers straighten out their houses first (v. 14), and then, having made matters right, assist Ezra in the work of purging the nation of sin. Verse 15 tells us that only four men "stood up against" this suggestion ("were employed"); the rest of the leaders approved it. We cannot always expect 100 percent cooperation, especially in matters of discipline.

It took from December to April to straighten out this problem. Verses 18-44 indicate that seventeen priests, ten Levites, and eighty-seven other men were found guilty of marrying heathen wives. It is frightening to find priests deliberately disobeying God, for when the spiritual leaders are backslidden, what can we expect of the rest of the people? So thorough was the investigation that even the heathen children were exposed and expelled. Of course, we realize that the Jewish husbands and fathers made provision for the welfare of these expelled people, but they were to live with them as husband and father no more. How long did this reformation last? About twenty-five years later, Nehemiah faced the same problem (Neh. 13:23ff). It was a repeated sin and required repeated discipline. God's servants must "watch and pray" if the work of God is to prosper.

To rebuild the temple without reforming the people would have been folly. It was easier for Ezra to rebuild the temple than it was to bring the sinful nation back to God.

# NEHEMIAH

## A Suggested Outline of Nehemiah

# NEHEMIAH 1–3

Whenever God wants to get a work done, He lays hold of willing people. The walls of Jerusalem had been ruined; a small remnant had returned; and there was much work that needed to be done. In 536, Zerubbabel and Joshua had taken about 50,000 Jews back and had (by 516) rebuilt the temple. In 457 there had been a small revival under Ezra, but now it was 445, and God was looking for someone to go to the ruined city and restore safety and order. Nehemiah was to be that person. Notice Nehemiah's activities in these three chapters.

## I. Nehemiah Prays for the Work (1)

### A. The report (vv. 1-3).

As cupbearer to the king, Nehemiah (a Jew) held a high position in the court. He was close to the king and could share his confidence. But Nehemiah was not forgetful of his own people, for he eagerly asked his brother for news about Jerusalem. Read Pss. 122 and 137:5-6. Oh, that saints today had as much interest in their heavenly Jerusalem! The news was distressing: the remnant was suffering shame, the walls were broken down, and the gates were burned. See Ps. 79:1-4. Instead of being a city of praise and glory, it was a city of shame and reproach.

### B. The response (v. 4).

Nehemiah was immediately burdened for his city. The fact that he was more than 700 miles away made no difference; nor did it matter that he was enjoying luxury and prestige in the palace of the king. He did not say, "The city's plight is not my fault!" Immediately his heart was touched and he wanted to do something to save his city. For four months (from Dec. to April; see 1:1 and 2:1) he wept and prayed. See Dan. 9 and Ezra 9.

### C. The request (vv. 5-11).

This book shows Nehemiah to be a man of prayer (1:4-11; 2:4; 4:4; 4:9; 5:19; 6:9, 14; 13:14, 22, 29, 31). The book starts and ends with prayer! Verse 6 tells us he prayed day and night, so burdened was he for the city. Note that Nehemiah confesses his sins and the sins of his people. He also reminds the Lord of His gracious promises (vv. 8-9) and then offers himself to be God's servant to do something about Jerusalem's plight. "Here am I, Lord, send me!" In v. 11 we see that he has faith to ask God for servants, other Jews who would help him in the task.

## II. Nehemiah Prepares for the Work (2)

Four months passed during which Nehemiah waited for God's time to approach the king. "Whoever believes will not act hastily," says Isa. 28:16 (NKJV). Indeed, faith and patience go together (Heb. 6:12). But Nehemiah had a plan in his mind, given to him by the Lord, and he knew just what to do when the right hour arrived. How like the Lord Jesus Christ (John 6:5-6).

### A. Nehemiah and the king (vv. 1-8).

No one was to appear before the king with sadness or bad news (Esther 4:1-2), but the burden on Nehemiah's heart revealed itself on his face. He was a man of sorrows, and the king noticed it. Were it not for the providence of God, this sadness might have caused Nehemiah's death. Before taking his burden to Artaxerxes, Nehemiah quickly went to the throne of grace in prayer; then he told the king all his heart. He knew God would open the way (Prov. 21:1). So thoroughly had Nehemiah worked out his plan that he was able to give the king a time schedule (v. 6) and a list of the materials he would need to do the task (vv. 7-8). God's strong hand (1:10) and good hand (2:8) did the impossible!

### B. Nehemiah and the ruins (vv. 9-16).

It took three months for Nehemiah to arrive at the city, and he arrived as a governor, not a servant. A man of patience, Nehemiah waited three days before taking any steps. The enemies were watching and Nehemiah had to be wise and cautious. Later he would discover that some of the nobles of Judah were allied with Tobiah, the enemy of the Jews (6:17-19). By night he investigated the situation, keeping his counsel to himself. He was awake when others were sleeping and concerned while others were at ease. He saw more of the situation at night than others could see in the light.

### C. Nehemiah and the Jews (vv. 17-20).

Nehemiah did not believe in a one-man ministry; he challenged the leaders of the remnant to work with him (not *for* him) in repairing the walls. The motive? "That we may no longer be a reproach." He was concerned with the glory of God as well as the good of the nation. Nehemiah showed them the need, outlined the task, and assured them of God's blessing. Immediately the opposition was aroused (as it always is), but Nehemiah knew that God's hand was upon him and his work.

## III. Nehemiah Prospers in the Work (3)

### A. The pattern.

The work was organized and directed, with the spiritual leaders taking the lead (v. 1) and the people cooperating. God noted each worker and put their names in the book. Each one had a specified area of responsibility. No one can do everything, but every person can do something. Of course, you will never have 100 percent cooperation; in v. 5 we find some of the nobles refusing to get involved. There were forty-two groups of workers.

### B. The people.

What a variety of workers—priests (v. 1), rulers (vv. 12-19), women (v. 12), craftsmen (vv. 8, 32), and even Jews from other cities (vv. 2, 5, 7). Note that some were willing to do extra work (vv. 11, 19, 21, 24, 27, 30). Some did their work at home (vv. 10, 23, 28-30), and this is where Christian service ought to begin. Some workers were the only ones from their families (v. 30), and some workers were more zealous than others (v. 20). Compare v. 11 with Ezra 10:31 and you will see that even some former backsliders joined in the work.

### C. The places.

There is a definite spiritual lesson in each of these gates. *The sheep gate* (v. 1) reminds us of the sacrifice of Christ on the cross (John 10). This was the first gate repaired, for without the sacrifice, there is no salvation. Note that the sheep gate had no locks or bars, for the door of salvation is ever open to the sinner. This is the only gate that was sanctified, setting it apart as a special gate. *The fish gate* (v. 3) reminds us of soul-winning, being "fishers of men" (Mark 1:17). *The old gate* (v. 6) speaks of the old paths and the old truths of the Word of God (Jer. 6:16 and 18:15). The people of the world are forever looking for "some new thing" (Acts 17:21), and they refuse to go back to the basic truths that really work. *The valley gate* (v. 13) reminds us of humility before the Lord. In Phil. 2 we see Christ descending from the glories of heaven into the valley of human limitation and even death. We do not enjoy the valley, but often God must take us there to bring a blessing to our lives.

Verse 14 introduces *the dung gate.* Apparently this is the gate through which the waste and refuse of the city were taken. Imagine how difficult it would be to repair a gate in such a place! Certainly this speaks to us of the cleansing of our lives (2 Cor. 7:1; Isa. 1:16-17). Later some of the Jews were to complain about the rubbish; see 4:10. *The gate of the fountain* (v. 15) illustrates the ministry of the Holy Spirit; see John 7:37-39. It is interesting to note the order of these gates: first, there is humility (the valley gate), then cleansing (the dung gate), and then the filling of the Spirit (the fountain gate). *The water gate* (v. 26) speaks of the Word of God, which cleanses the believer (Eph. 5:26; Ps. 119:9). Note that this is the seventh gate mentioned, and seven is the Bible number for perfection — the perfect Word of God. Note too that this gate needed no repairs! "Forever, O Lord, Your Word is settled in heaven" (Ps. 119:89, NKJV).

*The horse gate* (v. 28) introduces the idea of warfare. Certainly there are battles in the Christian life, and we must be ready to fight. See 2 Tim. 2:1-4. *The east gate* (v. 29) makes us think of the second coming of Jesus Christ (Matt. 24:27). In Ezek. 10:16-22, the prophet saw God's glory depart from the temple by the east gate; see also 11:22-25. But later (43:1-5) he saw God's glory return "from the way of the east."

*The gate Miphkad* (v. 31) speaks of God's judgment. The Hebrew word *miphkad* means "appointment, account, census, mustering." It carries the idea of troops showing up for review. Certainly God is going to call all souls up for judgment one day.

As you review these gates and their order, you can see the suggestion of the full picture of the Christian life, from the sheep gate (salvation) to the final judgment. Praise God the Christian shall never face judgment because of his sins! See John 5:24, Rom. 8:1-2.

# NEHEMIAH 4–7

Whenever the people of God start doing the work of God, there will be opposition. A worker of weak faith and purpose will quit, but a person of resolution and confidence will overcome the opposition and finish the task. Nehemiah was such a person. Notice in these chapters the opposition that he faced (from both within and without the city) and the victories that he won.

## I. Ridicule (4:1-6)

God's people always have enemies. In this case, they were Sanballat, a government official in Samaria; Tobiah, the Ammonite; and Geshem, an Arabian, who is also called Gashmu (6:1, 6). These three wicked men were outside the nation of Israel; in fact, the Ammonites were definite enemies of the Jews (Deut. 23:3-4). Their first weapon was ridicule; they mocked the "feeble Jews" openly before the leaders of Samaria. Satan is a mocker (Luke 22:63; 23:35-37). Ridicule is a device used by ignorant people who are filled with jealousy. They mocked the people ("feeble Jews"), the plan ("will they finish in a day?"), and the materials ("stones and rubbish"). How did Nehemiah answer them? He prayed to his God! His concern was only for the glory of God and the testimony of the nation, so do not read personal revenge into his prayer (see Ps. 139:19-24). Note that the people still worked as they prayed, for prayer is no substitute for work. Satan would have loved to see Nehemiah leave the wall and get involved in a dispute with Sanballat, but Nehemiah did not fall into Satan's trap. Never allow ridicule to stop your ministry; "take it to the Lord in prayer" and keep on working.

## II. Force (4:7-9)

What Satan cannot accomplish by deceit he attempts to do by force. What a confederation of people we have in v. 7! And all of them conspired against the Jews. It is amazing how the devil seems to have no manpower shortage. We have two enemies in 2:10, three in 2:19, and a whole multitude in 4:7. But "if God be for us, who can be against us?" How did Nehemiah face this new attack? He prayed and set a watch. "Watch and pray!" is a repeated admonition in the NT; see Mark 13:33 (the world), Mark 14:38 (the flesh), and Eph. 6:18 (the devil). Note that Nehemiah did not depend on prayer alone; he also set a watch.

## III. Discouragement (4:10)

The battle moves now from outside the city to inside. Satan followed this same tactic in Acts 5–6 when he used Ananias and

Sapphira and the complaining widows inside the fellowship of the church. He also used Judas inside the ranks of the apostles. How discouraged the workers were, with all that rubbish on the inside of the city and the danger lurking on the outside. Why did the tribe of Judah complain? Perhaps it was because they were secretly in league with Sanballat (6:17). Note in 13:15 Judah's disobedience to the Law of God. When they said, "We are not able!" (v. 10), they were actually agreeing with the enemy (4:2). Discouragement and complaining spread rapidly and hinder God's work. We do not read that Nehemiah paid much attention to their complaint; he kept on building, watching, and praying.

## IV. Fear (4:11-23)

Fear and faith can never abide in the same heart. In v. 11, we have a rumor the enemy started that their armies would suddenly invade Jerusalem. The Jews living outside the city heard this report and carried it to Nehemiah ten times. How persistent Satan's workers can be. Finally, Nehemiah set the guard on the walls and encouraged the people not to fear. Note that the work stopped from v. 13 to v. 15 — exactly what the enemy wanted. Nehemiah saw the folly of this plan, so he put the workers back on the job, a weapon in one hand and a tool in the other. He also set a special watch with trumpets (vv. 19-20), but he did not allow the work to stop. These Jews are wonderful examples of what a Christian worker ought to be: they had a mind to work (4:6), a heart to pray (4:9), an eye to watch (4:9), and an ear to hear (4:20).

## V. Selfishness (5)

This is a sad chapter, for in it we see the Jews selfishly preying upon one another. No building is recorded in this chapter. There were great economic burdens upon the Jews, not only because of the famine (Hag. 1:7-11), but also because of the taxes and tributes. The Jews were being robbed by their own people through mortgages and servitude. How did Nehemiah act in this crisis? First, he was angry (v. 6) because his people were so spiritually backslidden as to rob one another. He saw it not as an economic problem, but as a spiritual problem. He consulted with his own heart (v. 7) and certainly prayed to God for wisdom. Then he rebuked the people (vv. 7-11), reminding them of God's goodness to their nation. "We have been set free by the Lord," he argued;

"will you now put one another in bondage again?" He appealed to the OT Law as he commanded them to restore their ill-gotten profits (Ex. 22:25). How the enemy enjoyed seeing the Jews rob one another (v. 9)! Note that Nehemiah also appealed to his own good example as a leader (v. 10). The people vowed to obey the Word — and they did!

## VI. Guile (6:1-4)

The people went back to work, and so did the enemy. This time Sanballat and his men aimed their attacks on Nehemiah the leader. Many of God's people will never realize here on earth the special temptations and testings God's servants face day after day. Spiritual leadership is a costly thing. Sanballat invited Nehemiah to a friendly meeting on the Plain of Ono, and Nehemiah refused. God's separated servants dare not walk "in the counsel of the ungodly" (Ps. 1:1). Beware of the smiles of the enemy, for Satan is more dangerous when he appears to be your friend than at any other time. Four invitations came (v. 4) and Nehemiah refused them all. "I am doing a great work and cannot come down!" Stay on the job when Satan invites you to quit, and God will bless you.

## VII. Slander (6:5-9)

The fifth time the messenger came, he brought an "open letter" filled with slanderous accusations against Nehemiah and his people. "It is reported" is one of the devil's chief weapons. "They say" or "I have heard" are phrases that usually introduce gossip and lies. Who are "they"? Nehemiah detected the scheme and immediately exposed the lies in the so-called "open letter." His life and character refuted every lie in the letter. In vv. 1-4, the enemy offered to work with the Jews; here in vv. 5-9, the enemy wanted to defame Nehemiah's name. Note how Nehemiah again prayed for God to overrule (v. 9). Servants of God cannot help what people say about them, but they can help what kind of character and testimony they have. If Nehemiah had stopped the work to defend his reputation, the walls would never have been built.

## VIII. Threats (6:10-14)

Shemaiah had shut himself up in his house, apparently afraid of the enemy, but in reality he was working with the enemy. Why was he not helping the Jews build the wall? It pays to be cautious around so-called Christians who always have advice but never seem to get any work done for Christ themselves. Paul warned about false brethren (2 Cor. 11:26). Shemaiah lied to Nehemiah and tried to frighten him into going out to the enemy for safety. But Nehemiah saw through the scheme and openly refuted Shemaiah's lies. Again, he prayed for God's help and then went right back to work.

The walls were completed in fifty-two days. And the people worked during the hottest part of the year. God was glorified, the enemy was embarrassed (v. 16), but the compromising Jews were still at work trying to get Nehemiah to accept Tobiah. What a burden these nobles of Judah must have been to godly, courageous Nehemiah. The work had been completed. To God be the glory!

# NEHEMIAH 8–13

The walls were completed on the twenty-fifth day of the sixth month (6:15). This second half of the book begins on the first day of the seventh month (8:2), and the emphasis is on the people of the city and their dedication to God. The material building was now over. It was time to begin to build the people spiritually.

## I. Proclamation of the Word (8–10)

Ezra returned to Jerusalem to assist Nehemiah in the dedication of the walls and the sanctifying of the people. Do not confuse this scene with that in Ezra 3. It is significant that they gathered at the water gate, since this gate symbolizes the Word of God (3:26). The people had an appetite for the Word, for they asked Ezra to bring the Book and preach it. The first day of the seventh month marked the Feast of Trumpets; the tenth day would be the Day of Atonement; and the fifteenth to twenty-second days, the Feast of Tabernacles (see Lev. 23:23-44). Ezra read the Word and explained it for many hours, assisted by the Levites. Verse 8 describes a perfect church gathering: the people all assembled to listen; the Word was exalted; the preacher read and explained the Word so that people could understand it. The people wept at hearing the Word, overcome, no doubt, with grief for their sins. But this was to be a day of rejoicing. They would weep on the Day of Atonement! Ezra commanded them to feast and rejoice; see Ecc. 3:4.

The next day, the leaders met with Ezra and discovered the law concerning the Feast of Tabernacles. They proclaimed this law throughout the land, and as the people obeyed, there was "very great gladness" (v. 17). There is joy in hearing the Word, but greater joy at obeying it. The result of this "Bible conference" (which was held daily for a week, v. 18) was a great convocation of convicted people on the twenty-fourth day of the month. Ezra and the Levites taught the Word for three hours, then led the people in confession and prayer for three hours, and so on throughout the day. The prayer in chapter 9 is a spiritual summary of the OT history of the Jews: the Creation (v. 6); the call of Abraham (vv. 7-8); the Exodus (vv. 9-14); the nation's wilderness experiences (vv. 15-23); the conquering of the land (vv. 24-25); the period of Judges (vv. 26-29); the period of prophets up to the captivity (vv. 30-31). "Now therefore . . ." (v. 32) brings us up to Ezra's day and the need of the nation to repent and confess sin. Note in v. 36 that the Jews admit that the "deliverance prophecies" in Isaiah and Jeremiah did not apply to their return from captivity. They will apply at a future date when God gathers Israel again to Palestine. To say that these OT promises were fulfilled when Israel returned from exile, and are now being fulfilled "in the church," is to twist Scripture.

Chapter 10 gives the names of the brave and godly people who entered into the covenant with God that day. Little did they realize that their names would be recorded eternally in the Word! In vv. 28-39, we see the people applying the Word to their everyday lives. It is one thing to pray and sign a covenant; it is another thing to separate from evil, straighten out our homes (vv. 28-30), honor the commandments (v. 31), contribute to the house of God (vv. 32-33), and serve God with tithes and offerings (vv. 34-39). Too many "Bible conferences" end with the people stirred and blessed, but not obeying what they have heard.

## II. Dedication of the Walls (11–12)

Nehemiah returns now to the story of the walls, which he had interrupted to tell about the spiritual work under Ezra. Everything from 7:5 to 10:39 has been parenthetical. The events in Nehemiah are not given in their exact order. It was necessary to get the Jews to live in the city, for both the good of the city and the glory of God. This, of course, demanded faith. The leaders were dwelling in the city, but now they wanted the citizens to join them, so they cast lots and moved one out of ten into the city. Verse 2 indicates that there were also some volunteers. The numbers in vv. 3-19 total 3,044. If this represented 10 percent of the male population, we can see how small the remnant was in the land. Note the mention of singers (vv. 22-23). The Jews had no song during their years of exile (Ps. 137), but now they had the joy of the Lord as their strength.

The actual dedication of the walls is described in 12:27-47. Ezra and Nehemiah divided the people into two great companies, with Ezra leading one and Nehemiah following the other (see vv. 31, 36, 38). They started probably at the valley gate. Ezra led his company along the east side of the city, then north to the temple area. Nehemiah and his company went straight north and then east, meeting the other company at the temple area. It was a reminder, perhaps, of when Israel marched around Jericho and won a great victory. It was also an opportunity to publicly thank the Lord as they witnessed the work accomplished. Verse 43 indicates that the joy of the city was heard miles away. What a day of dedication that was! When dedicated people unite joyfully to dedicate God's work, they will always experience God's blessing.

## III. Condemnation of the Wicked (13)

From 13:6 and 7:2 we learn that Nehemiah returned to Babylon for a time, leaving the governing of the city in the hands of his brother. When he returned, he discovered that the people had fallen back into their old ways. Verses 1-3 speak of a cleansing that took place the very day of the dedication, when they separated the heathen wives in the families; see Deut. 23:1-5. Years before, Ezra had faced this problem (Ezra 10). Sin has a way of repeating itself. When Nehemiah returned to Jerusalem, he found that the Jewish men had repeated this sin (vv. 23-31). In fact, even the priests had sinned in this way. It was necessary for this courageous leader to face sin honestly and judge it.

He started at the house of God, where he discovered (v. 4) that the high priest was allied with the Jews' enemy, Tobiah. ("Allied" perhaps means "related to"; see 6:18 and 13:28.) It is a sad thing when the servants of God compromise with the enemies of God. The priest even gave Tobiah a chamber in the temple and provisions from the temple store, provisions that really belonged to the priests and Levites. Nehemiah lost no time in throwing out Tobiah and his goods, and having the temple chamber sanctified for its proper use.

Another sin was the failure of the people to support their spiritual servants, the priests and Levites. Malachi had something to say about this; read Mal. 3. Nehemiah reproached the people and set up a dependable system for the priests to follow. Note how he asks for God's help in all his ministry (v. 14).

Sabbath disobedience was another problem. The workers were employed on the Sabbath (v. 15), and the merchants were selling on the Sabbath (v. 16). While we do not believe that the Lord's Day today is the same as the Jewish Sabbath, we do feel that God's people ought to set apart the Lord's Day and use it to glorify Him. Our economic system requires that some people must work on Sunday, but it is far better for workers and the nation if they are allowed to honor the Lord's Day. Certainly no Christian should use Sunday as a day for shopping or for doing work that can wait. Nehemiah reproved the Jews for dishonoring the Sabbath, and he closed the gates of the city against the Sabbath salesmen. See Jer. 17:21-27 with reference to v. 18.

But note that even the Levites were guilty of desecrating the Sabbath (v. 22). Read Mal. 1–2 and you will see that the priesthood had fallen into shameful sins. Unless the leaders of God's people set the example, the people will not easily obey God. Of course, it may be that the failure of the people to support the temple (vv. 10-13) forced the Levites into working on the Sabbath to keep themselves alive.

The book closes with three prayers (vv. 22, 29, 31). Nehemiah has done his work, but only God can bless it and keep it going. Nehemiah would one day die, and the people would forget him. But God would never forget him!

# ESTHER

## *A Suggested Outline of Esther*

I. The Selection of Esther (1–2)

    A. The king loses Vashti (1)

    B. The king chooses Esther (2)

II. The Detection of Haman (3–7)

    A. Haman's evil plot (3)

    B. Mordecai's great concern (4)

    C. Esther's courageous intercession (5–7)

III. The Protection of Israel (8–10)

    A. The king's new decree (8)

    B. The Jews' new victory (9)

    C. Mordecai's new honor (10)

# Introductory Notes to Esther

## I. The Book

The events recorded in Esther take place between Ezra 6 and 7. The "third year of Ahasuerus" (1:3) would be 483 B.C. "Ahasuerus" is the title of the Persian ruler, just as Pharaoh was the title of the Egyptian ruler. The book nowhere mentions the name of God, while the name of the king is mentioned at least twenty-eight times! The Jewish rabbis have found the name "Jehovah" hidden in five different verses in the original Hebrew (1:20; 5:4, 13; 7:5, 7). Though Jehovah's name is not mentioned, His overruling providence is seen in every chapter of the book. "Esther" means "star"; "Hadassah," her Jewish name, means "myrtle" (2:7).

## II. The Theme

Esther tells how the Jewish nation was rescued from extinction. It explains the origin of one of the Jews' most festive holidays, the Feast of Purim. The word "Purim" means "lots," and refers to the casting of lots by Haman to determine the day of the slaughter of the Jews (9:26-31; 3:7). Purim is held the fourteenth and fifteenth days of the last month of the Jewish calendar (our Feb.–March). It is usually preceded by a fast on the thirteenth day in memory of Esther's fast (4:16). That evening the Book of Esther is read publicly in the synagogue. Each time the name of Haman is read, the Jews stamp on the floor, hiss, and cry, "Let his name be blotted out!" The next day, they again meet at the synagogue for prayers and the reading of the Law. The rest of the day and the next day are given over to great rejoicing, feasting, and giving gifts. There is no OT authorization from God for this feast, but the Jews have been observing it faithfully for centuries.

## III. A Spiritual Lesson

In Esther, we see once again Satan's hatred for the Jews. Had Haman succeeded in his plot, the Jewish nation would have been exterminated! Think of what this would have meant to God's gracious covenant with Abraham. Any man or nation that has tried to wipe out the Jews has failed, as did Haman. See Gen. 12:1-3. Since God declared war on Satan (Gen. 3:15), Satan and his seed have been fighting against Christ and His seed: Cain killed Abel; Pharaoh sought to drown the Jews; Haman plotted to destroy Israel; Herod tried to slay Christ. We have here also an illustration of the warfare between the flesh and the Spirit (Gal. 5:16-23). Haman was a descendant of the Amalekites, the archenemies of the Jews (compare Es. 3:1 with Deut. 25:17-19; Ex. 17:8-16; and 1 Sam. 15). Amalek symbolized the flesh, and Haman, being in that family, pictures to us the hostility of the flesh against the Spirit, as well as the children of Satan vs. the children of God.

## IV. God's Providence

God's name is nowhere seen in this book, but God's hand is nowhere missing! He is "standing somewhere in the shadows" ruling and overruling. As you study the book, note the following evidences of God's providential workings: (1) Esther being chosen queen over all the other candidates, 2:15-18; (2) Mordecai discovering the plot to kill the king, 2:21-23; (3) the casting of lots for the day to destroy the Jews resulting in a date late in the year, giving time for Mordecai and Esther to act, 3:7-15; (4) the king's welcome to Esther after ignoring her for a month, 5:2; (5) the king's patience with Esther in permitting her to hold another banquet, 5:8; (6) the king's insomnia that brought to light Mordecai's deed of kindness, 6:1ff; (7) the king's apparent lapse of memory in 6:10-14, that led him to honor one of the Jews he had agreed to slay; (8) the king's deep concern for Esther's welfare, when he had a harem to choose from, 7:5ff.

## V. The Dates

The king in the Book of Esther is Xerxes, the son of Darius I, Darius the Great. He ruled the Persian empire from 486 to 465 B.C. Vashti was dethroned in the third year of his reign (1:3), which would be 483. History tells us that Xerxes held a great feast for his princes in that year in preparation for his invasion of Greece. The campaign lasted until 479 and was a disaster. It was probably his shame and defeat that led Xerxes to wish he had not deposed Vashti. Esther was made queen in the seventh year of his reign (2:16), the year 479. It was in the twelfth year of his reign that the plot of Haman was hatched (3:7), the year 474; so Esther had been queen about five years when Haman went to work. Xerxes was assassinated in 465.

## VI. Esther and Proverbs

There is an interesting parallel between some verses in Proverbs and the events in Esther. Look up these references: Prov. 16:33 with Es. 3:7; Prov. 16:18 with Es. 5:9-14; Prov. 11:8 with Es. 7:10; Prov. 21:2 with Es. 5:1-4.

## VII. Haman and the Antichrist

Many Bible students see in wicked Haman a picture of the future Antichrist who will persecute the Jews and seek to destroy them. The phrase "this wicked Haman" in 7:6 adds up to 666 in the original Hebrew, and this is the number of the Beast (Rev. 13:18). Haman plotted his murders secretly while appearing to be friendly to the Jews openly; Antichrist will make a covenant with Israel for seven years, but break it after half that time. Haman possessed tremendous power, given to him by the king; the Beast will possess great power, given to him by Satan. Haman's pride was obvious, for he wanted all men to bow down to him; the Beast will cause all men to worship him and his image. Haman hated the Jews, and Antichrist will hate the Jews. But Haman was doomed, even though for a time he seemed to have power. Satan's masterpiece, the Beast, will appear to be indestructible, but Christ will destroy him and his followers when He returns.

## VIII. The Courage of Esther

Some have criticized Esther for her seeming lack of concern over the plight of the Jews. It is true that when Mordecai first began to fast and mourn, Esther sought to change his mind (4:1-4). But we must keep in mind that Esther was rather isolated from the actual affairs of court and had not been in the king's presence for a month. Once she did get the news of the danger at hand, she was willing to cooperate with Mordecai. Certainly she was taking her life in her hands, for Xerxes was a creature of his moods, and he could kill Esther just as easily as he deposed Vashti! While at the beginning Esther did not display the same faith in God's covenant that Mordecai did, as the events continued, she turned out to be a courageous woman with strong faith in God. It is interesting to note that as long as Esther was out of contact with Mordecai, everything went badly for the Jews, but when she started obeying Mordecai's word, everything turned out well for the Jews.

# ESTHER 1–4

These first four chapters of the book introduce us to the four main characters in the drama.

## I. Ahasuerus the King (1)

As mentioned before, "Ahasuerus" was the title of the Persian ruler; his given name was Xerxes, and he ruled from 486 to 465 B.C. History tells us that he was an impulsive ruler, and we can see this displayed in the Book of Esther. Note how quickly the king gave great authority to Haman and then forgot what his decree involved! Note too how impulsively he put away his lovely wife, and then later regretted it.

### A. The banquet (vv. 1-12).

This royal affair was for the purpose of conferring with his chiefs and leaders in preparation for his war against Greece. Xerxes had put down a rebellion in Egypt and felt confident he could conquer the Greeks. The gathering lasted for 180 days; the huge banquet was at the end of that period. This was in Xerxes' third year, or 483 B.C. The Medes and Persians were in power as Daniel had prophesied (Dan. 2:36ff). The feast lasted for seven days (v. 5) in the king's beautiful garden. Of course, there was drinking, and each guest was permitted as much as he wanted. The women, following a Persian practice, had a separate banquet. Anxious to please his guests, Xerxes asked the queen to come to the men's banquet, but Vashti refused. (The name "Vashti" means "beautiful woman.") Vashti knew the king and his guests were under the influence of wine and that the banquet hall was no place for a woman, especially a queen.

### B. The banishment (vv. 13-22).

The king was stunned by Vashti's public refusal to cater to his whims. He turned to his wise men for counsel. (You will note in this book that Xerxes listened to the advice of many people. History tells us he was a "puppet" with several of his chiefs pulling the strings.) The men advised him to depose Vashti and make her a public example to the entire nation. The Persian "postal system" was perhaps the finest in the ancient world. It operated somewhat like the old pony express, with fresh horses and riders waiting at various points along the route. The king hoped that his decree would strengthen the homes of the land. Whether it did or not, nobody knows. We do know that he later regretted his decision.

## II. Esther the Queen (2)

Between chapters 1 and 2, at least four years pass, during which Xerxes went on his disastrous Greek campaign (481–479). He came home a bitter man, and it was only natural that he should seek some kind of comfort in his own home. But then he remembered that Vashti had been dethroned and he was without a queen. Of course, he had many women available in his harem, but he missed his beautiful queen. The counselors advised him to seek another queen. (If Vashti had gotten back on the throne, she might have punished her husband's counselors.) Thus began the great search for the ideal queen, and this is where Esther comes in.

Esther and Mordecai were cousins; Mordecai had raised her like his own daughter. Mordecai was known at the palace and probably held some minor office, for we find him seated at the gate. He advised Esther to "enter the contest" but not to make known the fact that she was a Jewess. This meant that Esther probably had to eat unclean foods and break some of the OT laws; otherwise she could not have held her own among her Gentile competitors. (However, see Daniel's experience in Dan. 1.) Does this mean that "the end justifies the means"? Of course, these laws were temporary rules and not basic, eternal laws involving salvation, but they were still the Word of God. However, we are not to judge, for Esther did prove herself a courageous woman. After a year of special preparation (v. 12), Esther was presented to the king—and chosen! Verse 15 says that "she required nothing"; that is, she did not decorate herself with gaudy jewels as did the other women. She depended on her beauty and her character; see 1 Peter 3:3-4. She was made queen in the year 479 and a great feast was held in her honor. In vv. 21-23 we have what appears to be a minor incident, but later it becomes an important matter. Perhaps these men tried to slay the king because they disapproved of his treatment of Vashti.

## III. Haman the Enemy (3)

Five years pass (v. 7) and Satan begins to work. Haman's promotion went to his head and turned him into a murderer. Being a faithful

Jew, Mordecai would not bow down to Haman, and this made the proud ruler excessively angry. The palace knew Mordecai was a Jew (v. 6) but they did not know that Esther was one also. Haman decided to destroy *all* the Jews just because of his malice toward Mordecai. Satan is the destroyer Apollyon (Rev. 9:11). Haman and his fortune-tellers cast lots ("pur" in Hebrew) to find what day should be set aside for the execution, and it fell nearly a year later! Haman then offered to get for the king over $25,000,000 in silver if the king would authorize the slaying of the Jews. Haman lied about the Jews, of course, for Satan is both a liar and a murderer. Foolishly, Xerxes gave Haman his ring and the authority to act, not realizing that he was risking the life of his own queen. Haman wasted no time, for that very month he had the decrees written and sent out (vv. 7, 12), ordering the Persians to destroy, kill, and plunder all the Jews in the vast reaches of the kingdom. It is difficult to see how the king could make a law to wipe out millions of people one minute, then sit down to eat and drink the next minute (v. 15). But dictators in our modern history have done the same thing. (For additional material about Haman, consult the Introductory Notes.)

## IV. Mordecai the Protector (4)

The Jew that sat at the king's gate now comes to the fore; he is God's prepared vessel to save the nation. Immediately, Mordecai went into mourning publicly, even at the king's gate! He was not ashamed of his people or his God, although he had counseled Esther to hide her nationality. No doubt he became quite a "pest" as he sat at the gate and "cried with a loud and bitter cry." Esther sent him some new clothes and suggested that he stop, but he sent her the explanation for his actions. Esther in the palace was not likely to know all the policies and politics going on, and she had not seen the king for a month (v. 11). Mordecai sent her a copy of the decree that she might realize how desperate the situation really was. We see here two kinds of saints: those who are in joy because they are ignorant of what is going on, and those who are in sorrow because they know the signs of the times.

Is Esther making excuses in v. 11 or merely explaining the situation? Certainly she must have realized that she was the only one who could save the Jews. Keep in mind that Esther probably knew nothing about Haman's true character. Haman was a favorite of the king, and Esther would have no reason to doubt his sincerity. Mordecai reminded her that she would not escape death even in the palace. He added, "If you hold your peace, God will send deliverance some other way!" Mordecai knew God's covenant with Abraham, that He would never allow the nation to perish.

We must admire Esther's sensible, spiritual reaction: she asked for prayer! She realized that entering into the king's presence could mean death, but she presented herself as a "living sacrifice" to do God's will. "If I perish, I perish!" was not the desperate cry of a martyr; it was the testimony of a believer willing to give all for her God. See Dan. 3:13-18. Esther was now forced to reveal her people. You cannot hide the light under the bushel very long! Esther in the OT and Joseph of Arimathaea in the NT (John 19:38-42) were both "hidden believers" whom God had placed in special circumstances to perform a special ministry. (The word "secretly" in John 19:38 is literally "secreted." God had hidden him for the special purpose of burying the body of Jesus.)

We cannot help but see a modern spiritual application of these chapters. Satan is the destroyer, and millions of people are going to go to hell unless somebody rescues them. Some Christians are like the king—eating and drinking and enjoying life, unconcerned about the danger. Others, like Mordecai, are deeply concerned to save the condemned people. And there are the Esthers too who sacrifice themselves to intercede on behalf of the lost. Which are you?

# ESTHER 5–10

The events in these chapters center around three feasts.

## I. A Feast of Rejoicing (5–6)

The Jews have fasted and prayed with Esther for three days; it is now time to step out by faith and intercede before the king's throne. Keep in mind that Oriental rulers were almost like gods to their people, and their commands, right or wrong, were obeyed. Esther was taking her life in her hands, but she had already put her life into God's hands. No sooner did she appear at the entrance to the throne room than the king lifted his golden scepter and called her in! "The king's heart is in the hand of the Lord!" (Prov. 21:1) Acting very wisely, Esther did not immediately tell Xerxes her true request. Instead, she invited him and Haman to a banquet that very day. She knew the king's weakness for food and drink and, with womanly intuition, she prepared him for the important request. Furthermore, she gave Haman a false feeling of security by including him. After several full courses of food, the time would come for the wine course, a time when the king would be exceptionally happy. He knew that Esther had a matter on her heart, so he asked about it. But the wise queen delayed another day, and the king yielded to her wishes. Haman went home elated, puffed up with pride that he should enjoy such an exclusive banquet with royalty. But his peace and security were not to last long; like the lost sinner today, Haman was already under condemnation.

Only one thing ruined the day for Haman: he had to see the Jew Mordecai at the gate, and Mordecai refused to bow down to him. In his proud wrath, Haman decided to trump up some charge against Mordecai and have him executed. Like Adam, Haman listened to his wife and followed her advice. He had a 75-foot gallows erected, intending to have Mordecai hanged from it. The height of the gallows enabled the whole city to see the victim; in fact, in 7:9-10 the servants of the king seem to indicate the gallows could even be seen from the palace. Haman's fleshly rejoicing was not to last long, for in chapter 6 we find Mordecai finally rewarded for saving the king's life. Perhaps Mordecai had been meditating on Ps. 37:1-15; he knew that God would one day honor him for his good deed. But think of how humiliated Haman must have been! This event should have humbled him and forced him to change his wicked plans. In fact, his wife even warned him that now he could not overcome the Jews. While Haman and his wife were discussing the matter, the servant came to take Haman to the second banquet.

## II. A Feast of Reckoning (7)

The conflict between Haman and Mordecai, and the fact of Haman's eventual downfall, are perfect illustrations of Ps. 37. Read this psalm carefully and see how it fits. Read also Ps. 73. Haman came to the feast, with no doubt some fear and trembling in his heart. It was too late, however; his sin was going to find him out. See Prov. 16:18 and 18:12. The king asked Esther for her request, and this time she opened her heart to plead for the salvation of her people. Note that she uses the very words of the king's decree in v. 4; see 3:13. Undoubtedly, she had often read the decree and "spread it before the Lord." The king was not amazed at discovering she was a Jewess. What did amaze him was that such a wicked man should be in his employ! And the king was even more shocked to discover who the enemy was—Haman! How blind this monarch was to the true character of the people around him. He kept godly and wise Mordecai outside the gate, but he allowed Haman the run of the palace. No wonder the king was assassinated later on.

"The wrath of a king is as messengers of death" (Prov. 16:14). So disturbed was the king that he left the banquet hall and went to the garden. This gave evil Haman opportunity to humble himself before the queen, begging her for mercy. So zealous was Haman in his begging that he fell on the queen's couch, and this was too much for the king. He commanded the man to be executed, and this was done—on the very tree Haman had prepared for Mordecai! "The righteous is delivered from trouble, and it comes to the wicked stead" (Prov. 11:8). The servants were only too glad to obey, for Haman had made many enemies during his selfish, proud administration.

### III. A Feast of Remembering (8–10)

Once Haman was out of the way, peace reigned in the palace. Mordecai was given the authority once held by Haman, and by now everyone knew that Esther was a Jewess. One problem remained, however: the king could not cancel his decree and the Jews would be robbed and slain in nine months (compare 8:8 with 3:13). We can certainly see the providence of God in the casting of the lots (3:7), for it left time for the king to get the word of the new decree throughout the empire. Esther once again begged the king to act for the salvation of her people. The king turned to Mordecai and gave him authority to act for him. The new decree permitted the Jews to protect themselves and to destroy anyone in the kingdom who was an enemy of the Jews. The king did not cancel the old law; he merely gave a new law that superseded it. This is true in the Christian life; the law of sin and death has been overcome by the law of the Spirit of life in Christ (Rom. 8:1-12).

Verses 10-14 are a beautiful illustration of spreading the Gospel. This message was a matter of life and death! The scribes hurried and wrote the messages, and the official ambassadors hastened to get the message to every corner of the kingdom. If Christians today would be half as eager to get out the message of the Gospel, more souls would be rescued from eternal death. See Prov. 24:11-12.

Note that many different people were employed in spreading the good news, just as God uses many workers today. Of course, when the Jews heard and believed the message, it brought them joy and deliverance. They knew that the Persians would not dare to fight them and incur the wrath of the king. In fact, many of the Persians "called themselves Jews" to escape punishment!

When the twelfth month arrived (chap. 9), the Jews were ready for victory; they had the edict of the king on their side. Hundreds of the Jews' enemies were slain, including the ten sons of Haman (9:6-10). In the Hebrew Bible, the names of these ten sons are listed in a long column that looks like a gallows! Note that the Jews did not take any spoil (v. 10), although the decree in 8:11 permitted this. Certainly their enemies would have taken the Jews' wealth as the king commanded (3:13), but God's people have to prove themselves better than their enemies. Verse 16 states that 75,000 of their enemies were slain. On the fourteenth day of the month, the Jews rested and rejoiced at God's deliverance. Mordecai felt led to make the fourteenth and fifteenth days of the twelfth month holidays for the Jews to commemorate the great deliverance; and to this day the Jews celebrate the Feast of Purim. Verse 26 explains the meaning of "Purim." It is the plural of *pur*, which is Hebrew for "lot" (see 3:7). While we have no divine authorization in the OT for this feast, it has been celebrated for centuries and is a testimony to the power of God and the grace of God toward His people.

The book closes reporting the promotion and prosperity of Mordecai, the man of faith who believed God's promises and dared to act. Of course, we dare not forget Esther who gave her all that her people might be saved. The entire Book of Esther is a marvelous testimony of the overruling power and providence of God. Romans 8:28 is illustrated by this book.

# JOB

## *A Suggested Outline of Job*

I. Job's Distress (1–3)

   A. His prosperity (1:1-5)

   B. His adversity (1:6–2:13)

   C. His perplexity (3)

II. Job's Defense (4–37)

   A. The first round (4–14)

      1. Eliphaz (4–5) – Job's reply (6–7)

      2. Bildad (8) – Job's reply (9–10)

      3. Zophar (11) – Job's reply (12–14)

   B. The second round (15–21)

      1. Eliphaz (15) – Job's reply (16–17)

      2. Bildad (18) – Job's reply (19)

      3. Zophar (20) – Job's reply (21)

   C. The third round (22–37)

      1. Eliphaz (22) – Job's reply (23–24)

      2. Bildad (25) – Job's reply (26–31)

      3. Elihu (32–37)

III. Job's Deliverance (38–42)

   A. God humbles Job (38:1–42:6)
     (see 40:3-5 and 42:1-6)

   B. God honors Job – 42:7-17

      1. God rebukes his critics (42:7-10)

      2. God restores his wealth (42:11-17)

# *Introductory Notes to Job*

Too many Bible readers avoid studying the Book of Job, with the exception perhaps of the first two and last chapters, which are quite dramatic. The rest of the book appears at first to be a collection of long poetic speeches, and the conversation never seems to make much progress. A careful reading of the Book of Job, however, will reveal to you that its very modern message deals with a problem believers face repeatedly.

## I. The Book

As you study the Book of Job, keep these facts in mind: (1) This is an Oriental book, filled with the thoughts and expressions of Eastern peoples. (2) This is a poetical book (except for chaps. 1–2 and 42:7-17), and Hebrew poetry is very unlike Western poetry. (3) This book wrestles with a difficult problem, the presence of suffering in a world where God rules. These three characteristics alone make the Book of Job difficult to read and interpret, but we must not ignore it.

## II. The Man

Job was not a fictional character invented for this dramatic poem; he was a real man in history. Ezekiel names him (14:14-20) and so does James (5:11). Job was a godly man, a wealthy man, and a man with sincere concern for the needs of others. However, he was also a perplexed man, for he could not explain why God should permit him to experience so much trial.

## III. The Theme

Most people say that the theme of Job is the age-old question, "Why does a loving and righteous God permit the godly to suffer?" But if that is the theme of the book, the question is never answered! The theme is better stated, "*How* do the righteous suffer?" In just a few days, Job lost his business, his wealth, his family (except for his wife), and his health. Why should this happen? His three friends had it figured out that Job was really a hypocrite, that there was hidden sin in his life and the Lord was chastening him. Job insisted that he knew of no hidden sin, so they kept arguing with him. Please note in 2:3 that God states clearly that He had no cause against Job. And in 42:7 God rebukes the three friends for not speaking the truth about Him. Job was not a hypocrite, although (like any of us) he certainly had room for improvement in his life; and this he admitted in the end (42:1-6).

It is true that God sends chastening when His children persist in sin (Heb. 12:1-13), and that this chastening is evidence of His love. It is also true that the wicked have their enjoyment today but will soon be cut down (Pss. 37; 73). But neither of these facts met the need in Job's life. Nevertheless, God had divine purposes in mind in permitting Job to suffer. For one thing, He revealed through Job to Satan and the angels the testimony of a man of faith. (Only in eternity will we discover how much the angels have learned from the lives of the saints; see Eph. 3:9-10 and 1 Peter 1:12.) The main lesson in Job is this: God is completely sovereign in His dealings with His people and will never permit anything to come to the life of an obedient Christian that is not for his good and God's glory. God does not have to explain His ways to us. It is enough for us to know that He cares and that He never makes a mistake. We do not live by explanations; we live by promises. The Book of Job shows us how the righteous should suffer. "You have heard of the perseverance of Job" (James 5:11, NKJV).

## IV. Job's Friends

Four other men are involved in this drama, all of them friends of Job. Keep in mind that the events in this book cover several months (7:3) and that friends and neighbors discussed Job's case (6:15; 12:4; 16:10; 17:1-9). *Eliphaz* from Teman was the first speaker, and he based all his ideas on a "spiritual experience" he had one night (4:12-16). *Bildad* was a "traditionalist" who knew some "wise sayings" and tried to build a case on them. Like Eliphaz, he was certain Job was a hypocrite. *Zophar* was very dogmatic and certain that he knew more about God than anyone else. Each of these men argued with Job, and he argued back. At the end (chaps. 32–37), a new voice appeared, that of the younger man *Elihu*, who waited until his elders had spoken before advancing his ideas. While the three older men insisted that God always blessed the righteous and judged the wicked, Elihu said that God sometimes chastened (not punished) the righteous in His own will. He asked Job to submit to God and trust Him, but his attitude was still that of a judge and a critic. When God did appear, He made no reference to Elihu's great speeches at all!

## V. The Blessing of Endurance

The Book of Job does not give a "pat answer" to the problem of why the righteous suffer. Certainly Job was a better man after the trials were over, for suffering can have a purifying effect if we will surrender to the Lord. James 5:11 commends Job for his endurance, which literally means "faithfulness under trial." (The word "patience" here can be misleading, for Job certainly did get impatient with his friends and with his circumstances!) Job maintained his faith in God and believed that, in the end, God would vindicate him. And He did. Perhaps this is the greatest lesson of the book: that God is completely sovereign in our lives and does not have to explain His ways to us. God works out His purposes (Rom. 8:28), and this is all that matters. When trials come, we should not ask, "How can I get out of this?" but "Lord, what can I get out of this?"

# JOB 1–3

The land of Uz was probably in what we would know as northern Arabia. The greatest man in all the east lived there; his name was Job. See how great he was.

## I. Job's Prosperity (1:1-5)

In every way, Job was a rich man. He was rich in character, for he was "perfect and upright." He was not sinless, but he was sincere and obedient before the Lord. He feared God, not with a terror but with a humble trust, and he separated himself from evil. He was also rich in his family, having seven sons and three daughters. Large families (especially many sons) were greatly desired in the East. Note in v. 5 that Job had a spiritual concern for his sons and daughters and prayed for them at the altar. How fortunate these children were to have a godly father. As for Job's wife, she did not seem to have the faith and wisdom that Job possessed (see 2:9-10), although we can understand that she would rather see her husband dead than having to endure such pain. In the end, however, God proved that she was wrong. See also 19:17.

Job was rich in possessions, "a very great household." His livestock numbered in the thousands. Certainly God had blessed Job, and Job was not hesitant to praise God for all He had done. Paul wrote, "I know both how to be abased, and I know how to abound . . ." (Phil. 4:12). Most of us have no problem turning to God when we are "abased" and things are going wrong, but how difficult it is to serve God and remember Him when things are prosperous. Job did not permit his money and possessions to take the place of God.

## II. Job's Adversity (1:6–2:13)

### A. Satan's first accusation and attack (1:6-22).

Satan has access to heaven and must "report" to God. See Rev. 12:7-12. In heaven, Satan accuses the saints before God; see Zech. 3. Thank God for our Advocate in heaven, Jesus Christ the Savior (1 John 2:1-2)! Unknown to Job, God and Satan discussed his case. Had Job known about this conversation, he would have had no room for doubt or concern. He would have known that God was using him as a weapon to refute Satan's lies. But he did not know

413

what was happening in the councils of heaven; therefore, he had to take his trials by faith. Satan admitted that he had been going up and down the earth (see 1 Peter 5:8-9), and God pointed to Job as "Exhibit A" of what a godly man ought to be. But immediately Satan, who will *never* agree to God's Word, accused Job of being a hypocrite. "The only reason Job is obedient is because he is so rich. Take away his wealth and he will curse you to your face!" Note that the believers are "hedged about" by the Lord and that Satan cannot touch them without God's express permission. See Luke 22:31-34. Satan is not equal to God either in wisdom or in power. Satan is not all-powerful, for he is but a created being limited in power. Satan is not everywhere-present; he is limited to one place at one time. And Satan is not all-knowing; for had he known how this contest would turn out, he would never have entered it. Satan holds this world in his lap (1 John 5:19), but "greater is He that is in you, than he that is in the world (1 John 4:4). The moment he had the divine permission, Satan left to attack Job's personal possessions, and in a brief time, Job was left a pauper. Note that Satan used common things to attack Job—enemy armies, fire, and a strong wind. Job's friends thought these destructive forces came from God when they really came from Satan. In fact, one man called the fire (possibly lightning) "the fire of God" (1:16). How did Job respond? He mourned for the dead and worshiped God. "The Lord gave" (this is easy to say) "and the Lord has taken away" (this is harder to say). "Blessed be the name of the Lord" (it takes real faith to say that).

### B. Satan's second accusation and attack (2:1-13).

Think of how the angels in heaven praised God as they saw Job remain faithful. What a rebuke to Satan! "Still he holds fast to his integrity," God reminded Satan (2:3). But Satan had another lie on his tongue: "Let me touch his *body* and give him pain, and you will see how faithful he is." God permitted this, but limited Satan again, for Satan (who has the power of death when God permits) cannot go beyond God's will. What Job's "sore boils" were, we do not know; possibly he had a form of leprosy or elephantiasis. At any rate, he was filled with pain, his appearance was horrible (19:13-20), and there seemed to be no hope. His wife could not bear to see him suffer, and in a moment of unbelief, she suggested he curse God and let God kill him (vv. 9-10). The word "evil" in 2:10 does not mean "sin," for God is not the author of sin. It means "calamity, affliction." God does permit calamities in our lives.

Then Job's three friends made an appointment to come to comfort him, and they sat in sympathetic silence for a week after weeping with him and joining in his acts of humiliation. It is possible that Satan had his hand even in the words and deeds of Job's wife and his three "friends." Satan used Judas, Peter, and Ananias and Sapphira. Certainly he could use even Job's well-meaning friends.

## III. Job's Perplexity (3)

Do not misunderstand this chapter; Job did not curse God as Satan predicted he would do (1:11; 2:5) or as his wife suggested he do (2:9). It is good to know that Satan cannot predict the future. What Job did curse was his birthday; he wished he had never been born. He felt he would have been better off to have died at birth than to live and endure such grief. Job's description of the grave in vv. 13-19 must be supplemented with the revelation we have in the NT. Certainly Job is not suggesting that all men, sinners and saints alike, go to one place of rest and blessing; for we know that the lost die and go to a place of punishment, while believers go immediately to the presence of God. "Surely I was born for something better than this!" Job is saying. He was perplexed; he did not know the purpose of God in this suffering.

In vv. 20-24, Job asks, "Why should miserable people such as I have to live at all? Is our misery accomplishing anything? I long to die, but death will not come." Does suffering accomplish anything? When we yield to God, yes, it does. Suffering works for us, not against us (read 2 Cor. 3:7–5:9). Job could not see the "end [purpose] of the Lord" (James 5:11); we can see it because we have had a glimpse into the court of heaven.

Verses 25-26 indicate that Job had often thought about trials and feared he might have to face them. He was a prosperous man, and he wondered what he would do if he lost his wealth and health. He was not living in carnal security or false peace, for his faith was in the Lord and not in his possessions. "Yet trouble came!" Until we have "sat where he sat," let us not be too hard on Job. In the midst of prosperity, it is easy to trust God, but when we lose everything and our pain is so intense we want to die, exercising faith is another matter. Please remember that Job did not curse God; nowhere in the book does Job deny the Lord or question His holiness or His power. In fact, God's justice was Job's real problem: how could such a holy God permit such awful calamity?

For a godly man to wish he were dead should not be a surprise to us. Moses asked God to take his life (Num. 11:10-15) because of the persistent rebellion of the nation, and Elijah prayed to die after his escape from Jezebel (1 Kings 19). Jonah also wanted to die (Jonah 4:3). Please note in chapter 3 that Job asks "Why?" five times (vv. 11-12, 23). Job could have endured the pain and grief had he only understood why God was permitting it. "Why?" is an easy question to ask, but it is not always a question that God immediately answers. Job should have realized that God was in control, that these events were part of a loving plan, and that one day God would make His purposes known.

When you become perplexed over the trials of life, remember that God is still on the throne. See Job 23:10 for an expression of Job's faith: "But he knows the way that I take; when He has tested me, I shall come forth as gold" (NKJV). Job was going through the furnace. But when one of God's children is in the furnace, God is there with him (Isa. 43:1-2 and Dan. 3:25).

# JOB 4–37

We cannot examine each chapter in detail, for the chapters are too long and involved. If you read these chapters in a modern translation along with your King James Version, you may be able to follow the arguments of the men better.

## I. Job's Accusers

Job's three friends came to comfort him, but they ended up criticizing him! Each of them used the same argument in one way or another: (1) God blesses the righteous and afflicts the wicked; (2) God has afflicted Job; (3) therefore, Job must be wicked. Of course, their thinking seemed logical, but it was not spiritual. Mortal human beings are far too ignorant to understand fully the ways of God. For us to fit God into our own little "theological boxes" is to limit Him and make Him less than God. We must keep in mind that these friends did not have the full revelation that we have in the NT, showing more fully that suffering is not always caused by sin, and that, through our faith in Christ, we can turn suffering into glory. It is a dangerous thing for believers to "explain the ways of God" to other believers if they do not understand God's Word and God's ways.

In his first speech, Eliphaz argues that Job is a sinner (4:7-11). He bases his thinking on a special vision he once experienced (4:12-21), so we might say that Eliphaz argues from personal experience—the hard "facts of life." Bildad picks up the argument in 8:1-7 and very bluntly states that God does not do things unjustly. In 8:8-10, Bildad argues from tradition, and then quotes a series of "old sayings" to support his argument. *Zophar* rebukes Job in chapter 11 and tells him he needs to repent and get right with God! All three "friends" make the same mistakes: (1) they fail to enter into Job's sorrows and sympathize with him; (2) they have a rigid concept of God and His works, one that is not fully true; and (3) they are too dogmatic and proud to listen to Job and honestly examine their own beliefs.

The problem of human suffering is too deep and complex for the simple answers the three friends gave. Jesus never sinned, yet He suffered more than any person! Neither Job nor his friends knew about the conference in heaven, that God was using Job as "Exhibit A" before Satan and the angels to prove that people will trust God even when they do not understand what God is doing. The friends called Job a "hypocrite" (8:13; 15:34; 20:5; 34:30); God called him "a perfect and an upright man" (1:8; 2:3). Job would not bargain with God just to regain his material prosperity, for his greatest asset was his personal integrity.

In 2:3 God makes it clear that He had no cause for afflicting Job, that Job was not a hypocrite or a sinner. This is why God rejected the speech of Elihu (38:1-2) and the speeches of the three men (42:7).

While the three friends argued that Job's suffering was a punishment for sin, Elihu had a different idea (chaps. 32–37): God sends suffering to chasten us and teach us (33:9-20; 35:10-16). Elihu shows a higher view of God, and in his speeches he beautifully points out the power and wisdom of God; read chapter 37 especially. But he fails to help Job, and God Himself rebukes Elihu for his "dark counsel" (38:1-2).

## II. Job's Arguments

After each man spoke, Job replied, except in the case of Elihu, where God Himself stepped in to answer. Job's argument went something like this: (1) I believe God is just and powerful as you do; (2) But I am not a hypocrite—I know of no sin between me and God; (3) I would argue my case with God but I cannot find Him; (4) Nevertheless, I will trust Him, for He will vindicate me either in this life or in the life to come. It took a great deal of faith for Job to argue this way in the light of his circumstances. No wonder James 5:11 points to the endurance of Job.

The three friends argued that God always afflicts the wicked, but Job pointed out to them that the wicked seem to be prospering! In chapter 18 Bildad pictures the awful doom of the wicked like a light going out (vv. 5-6), a bird being trapped (vv. 7-10), a criminal being chased (vv. 11-13), a tent torn down (vv. 14-15), and a tree dried up (vv. 16-17). Then in chapter 20, Zophar argues that the seeming prosperity of the wicked is only brief. Job rejects their arguments in chapter 21 and points out the obvious health and wealth of the wicked. In chapter 24 Job asks, "Why doesn't God intervene and do something about sin?" He lists the sins of the wicked, and in chapter 31, he recounts his own godly life. The three friends are silenced because they know Job's arguments are right. Elihu's wordy speech adds little to the solution of the problem.

## III. Job's Appeals

The most important verses in this section are those that state Job's heart appeals to God and to his friends.

### A. *He appeals for sympathy.*

His friends did not show love and understanding; to them Job was a theological problem, not a suffering saint (see John 9:1-3). In chapter 6 Job states he has lost his taste for life (vv. 6-7) and wants to die (vv. 8-13). He compares his friends to a brook that dries up just when thirsty travelers need water (vv. 14-20). Chapter 7 gives us several pictures of life with its trials and its brevity: a warfare (v. 1, where "appointed time" means "warfare"); a slavery (vv. 1-5); a swift weaver's shuttle (v. 6); the wind (vv. 7-8); a cloud (vv. 9-10; and see James 4:13-17). In 9:25 he compares life to a swift messenger ("post," see Es. 8:9-14), and in 9:26 to a swift ship.

### B. *He appeals for a chance to confront God.*

In chapter 9 Job complains that he has no way to present his case before God, because he cannot find Him. Note in v. 33 his appeal for a "daysman" or umpire to stand between him and God. "How should a man be just with God?" (9:2) means, "How can a man ever plead his case with God?" Thank God for the Mediator, Jesus Christ, who represents us before God! See 1 Tim. 2:5; 1 John 2:1-2; and Zech. 3. See Job 16:19-22; 23:3.

## C. He appeals to his basic integrity.

In each of his speeches, Job denies that he is secretly a sinner. He knows his own heart and he confesses that his friends have cruelly misjudged him. At the end of the book, when God reveals Himself to Job, the man does bow in dust and ashes and confess his worthlessness (40:3-5; 42:1-6); but this was not a confession of sins. Rather, it was a humbling of himself before God as he realized his own ignorance and worthlessness in the presence of the Almighty. God never does accuse Job of sin. He accuses him of not realizing the greatness of God and of trying to fit God into the confines of a little argument, but He does not judge him for the sins that his friends accused him of committing. See chapter 31 for Job's defense of his godly life.

## D. He appeals to his faith in God.

This is what created the problem: Job trusted God, yet God seemed to have abandoned Job. Had Job once denied God or cursed God, the problem would have been solved, for the friends would have known that God was punishing Job for his unbelief. But Job had faith. "Though He slay me, yet will I trust Him!" (13:15) "I know that I shall be justified [vindicated, proved true]" (13:18). So great was Job's faith that he states that God will vindicate him in the resurrection in the next life, if not in this life (19:25-29; 14:1-14). Job knew that God would work out some purpose, but he thought God should tell him what He was doing (see chap. 23). Of course, if Job had known about the conference in heaven between God and Satan, there would have been no need for faith.

## E. He appeals to die.

From his first complaint in chapter 3 to the end of the argument, Job asks to die. Read 6:8-12 and 7:15-21. Do not be too critical of Job for wishing to die. He was suffering great physical affliction; friends and neighbors were abusing him (chap. 30); and it seemed that God had abandoned him. Moses, Elijah, and Jonah fell into the same error.

The ways of God are above and beyond the mind of mortal men and women. Even Bildad admitted, "Lo, these are parts of His way," literally, "these are but the outskirts of His ways, the hem of His garment." God is greater than man's theology. When we cannot understand, we can worship and trust Him.

# JOB 38–42

We now reach the climax of the book and God Himself steps on the scene! In 9:35, 13:22, and 31:35-37, Job had challenged God to appear and talk with him face to face, and now God does just that. The first thing God does is to sweep aside the vain ideas of Elihu, who had darkened God's purposes and brought no light into the situation at all. Now God proceeds to deal with his servant Job in a personal way.

## I. God Humbles Job (38:1–42:6)

God asks Job a series of simple questions about the universe and its operation. "Since you seem to know so much about God, let me ask you whether or not you could run the universe I have made!" This seems to be the main thrust of these chapters. "You challenged me; now I am going to challenge you!"

God begins with Creation (38:4-11). Of course, there are no "foundations" to the globe; God is using figurative language, not scientific terms. In fact, Job 26:7 clearly states that the world hangs on nothing, and this was written in a day when learned men taught that the world was held up by huge turtles or other creatures! And 26:10 teaches the sphericity of the earth: "He draws a circle over the deep, a boundary between light and darkness" (MLB). This verse also teaches that one part of the globe is light while the other part is in darkness. Job 38:7 refers to the rejoicing of the angels when God created the universe. In 38:12-15, God asks Job about the dawn of the sun and the spread of the light; in 38:16-21, He inquires about the measurements of the earth and the sea. How foolish to think that a mere human being could measure God's Creation!

Then God turns to inanimate nature — the snow and hail, the rain and ice (38:22-30). The phrase in verse 22 could be translated "the treasuries of the snow," that is, the hidden treasuries where

God stores the snow and hail. However, there is a real sense in which snow does contain treasures, for snow helps to capture nitrates from the air and deposit them into the ground. What man would want the responsibility of deciding where it should rain and snow! Only God can govern this universe and make everything work harmoniously. In 38:31-38, God asks about the stars and constellations, as well as the clouds and rains.

He next asks about animal life (38:39–39:30). Does a man hunt for prey to feed a lion? Do the ravens depend on man for food? Jesus answers this in Luke 12:24. The wild goats on the mountain, the wild asses in the plains, and the wild oxen ("unicorn" in 39:9-10) all look to God to protect them and provide for them. Even the stupid ostrich, which often forgets where its nest is, enjoys the care of the Almighty (39:13-18). Verse 18 is a reminder of the great speed of the ostrich. In 39:19-25, the horse is pictured as he faces the enemy in war; and in 39:26-30, the hawk and the eagle are mentioned. Wherever Job looks at animate creation, he sees the hand of God at work.

"Now," says God, "you have reproved me and argued with me. Give me your answer!" There is only one answer Job can give (40:3-5): "I am vile; I have talked too much about things I do not understand. I will say nothing more." This is one step closer to blessing, but Job has not yet repented of the way he talked about God. So, God takes up the questioning again, and this time focuses attention on two great beasts—the hippopotamus ("behemoth," 40:15-24) and the crocodile ("leviathan," chap. 41). Both of these beasts were greatly admired and feared in Job's day, although neither one was native to Palestine. The Hebrew word for "behemoth" simply means "large beast," but most students take it to refer to the hippopotamus. Certainly Job could not face such a beast, let alone create it! Likewise the crocodile; Job could not dare to fish for it, harness it, or make it a pet (41:1-8). "Who then is able to stand before me?" asks Jehovah, "for the Creator is surely greater than the creature!" "Neesings" in v. 18 is a word for "sneezings" and refers to the snorting of the crocodile. Some students suggest the spout of the whale from vv. 18-21. At any rate, the entire chapter serves to reveal the greatness of God's creatures and, therefore, the greatness of God.

The result? Job humbles himself and repents (42:1-6). God does not charge Job with the sins that his friends accused him of committing, but God does charge him with not seeing himself in the light of the greatness and majesty of God. Job's religious experience is no longer second-hand; he has met God personally, and this makes all his sufferings worthwhile.

## II. God Honors Job (42:7-14)

Now that Job has humbled himself, God can exalt him (1 Peter 5:6; James 4:10). The first thing God does is rebuke the friends. He speaks to Eliphaz because he was apparently the eldest of the friends and therefore the most accountable. God makes it clear that their many arguments were in error; they did not understand either God or Job. He commands the friends to offer burnt offerings, and He instructs Job to pray for them. It must have taken grace for Job to pray for men who had treated him so severely, but he was a man of God and he obeyed the Lord. God "turned Job's captivity" when he prayed not for himself, but for his friends. God healed his body.

After rebuking Job's friends, God then restored Job's fortunes. God knew He could trust Job with wealth and prestige because Job was a humble servant. Note that four times in vv. 7-8 God calls him "my servant Job." God gave Job twice what he had before. Compare 1:3 and 42:12. God did not give Job another fourteen sons and six daughters (double what he had before, 1:2), because the ten children who had died were still alive in heaven. Job had not lost them. So, God gave Job seven sons and three daughters, and the grand total was twice the number of children he had before.

Once his fortunes were restored, Job's friends and acquaintances returned to him to comfort him and encourage him. Some of these same people had undoubtedly criticized him and judged him in the past, but now that was all over. They brought gifts to Job, perhaps as evidence of their sincere sorrow for the mistakes of the past. It was customary in Oriental countries for people to give gifts at happy occasions.

The names of Job's daughters are interesting. "Jemima" means "dove"; "Kezia" means "cinnamon"; and "Keren-happuch" means "box of eye-paint" or "cosmetic box." Each of these names indicates that the girls were attractive and honorable. Job even gave them an inheritance with their seven brothers.

Job lived for another 140 years, which suggests (from the doubling of everything) that he may have been seventy when these events took place.

Of course, not every saint who suffers in the will of God (1 Peter

3:17) is going to be so honored in this life. The main lesson in the Book of Job is not that you will be rich and powerful when suffering is over, but rather that Almighty God has a purpose in suffering and nothing can thwart that purpose. Even Satan must bow to God's control, for God always writes the last chapter. Job was not suffering for sins, but his suffering still made him a better man. God gave him great honor after he suffered as a testimony in an age when there was no written Bible to teach people divine truth. Christians who suffer during this present age may not be rewarded here, but they will be rewarded hereafter. See Rom. 8:18-39; 2 Cor. 4–5; and 1 Peter 4:12-19. The secret of Job's life was endurance (James 5:11); he trusted God in spite of Satan, circumstances, friends, or loved ones. His faith at times wavered, and sometimes he accused God, but he still endured "as seeing Him who is invisible."

# Introductory Notes to Psalms

## I. Name

The word *psalm* comes from a Greek word that means "a poem sung to musical accompaniment." The Hebrew name is *tehillim*, which means "praises." Not all of the psalms are hymns of praise, but many of them are. The Book of Psalms is the hymnal of the Jewish nation, and some of the psalms have found their way into the Christian hymnal. Psalm 46 is the basis for Luther's "A Mighty Fortress Is Our God," and Isaac Watts used Ps. 90 to write "O God, Our Help in Ages Past." The familiar Doxology (or "Old Hundredth") is based on Ps. 100.

## II. Purpose

The Book of Psalms is a collection of very personal songs and poems. As the book grew over the centuries, its contents were adapted by the Jews for their corporate worship as well as for their personal devotions. In this collection you find prayers from sufferers, hymns of praise, confessions of sin, confessions of faith, nature hymns, and songs that teach Jewish history, and in each one the focal point for faith is the Lord. Whether the writer is looking back at history, looking up into the heavens, or looking around at his problems, he first of all looks by faith to the Lord. The psalms teach us to have a personal relationship with God as we tell Him our hurts and our needs and as we meditate on His greatness and glory.

## III. Hebrew Poetry

Western poetry is often based on rhyme, but not so Eastern poetry. It is based primarily on what we call "parallelism"; that is, the relationship of the lines to each other. In *synonymous* parallelism, the second line restates the first, as in Ps. 15:1 (NKJV) — "Lord, who may abide in Your tabernacle? Who may dwell in Your holy hill?" *Antithetic* parallelism is just the opposite: the lines are in contrast to each other. One example is Ps. 37:9 (NKJV) — "For evildoers shall be cut off; but those who wait on the Lord, they shall inherit the earth." Psalm 19:8-9 (NKJV) is an example of *synthetic* parallelism as each successive line expands the meaning: "The statutes of the Lord are right, rejoicing the heart; the commandment of the Lord is pure, enlightening the eyes. The fear of the Lord is clean, enduring forever; the judgments of the Lord are true and righteous altogether."

## IV. Christ in the Psalms

Jesus said that the psalms spoke about Him (Luke 24:44), and we can see that they do. He is the crucified Savior in Ps. 22; the shepherd in Ps. 23 (see John 10); the sacrifice in Ps. 40:6-8 (see Heb. 10:1-10); the high priest in Ps. 110 (see Heb. 7:17-21); the stone in Ps. 118:22-23 (see Matt. 21:42); and the coming King in Ps. 2 (see Acts 4:25-26 and 13:33).

## V. Special Psalms

Seven of the psalms are called "penitential psalms" because they are confessions of sin (6, 32, 38, 51, 102, 130, and 143). Psalms 120–134 are called the "Songs of Degrees" and are thought to be a collection of the songs that the Jewish pilgrims sang as they made their way to the annual festivals in Jerusalem. There are several "imprecatory psalms" in which the writers call down God's wrath upon their enemies (35, 37, 69, 79, 109, 139, 143). These are not so much personal expressions of vengeance as national petitions for the justice of God to be manifested for His chosen people. Psalm 119 extols the virtues of the Word of God (see also Ps. 19), and Pss. 113–118 are used by the Jews when they celebrate Passover.

## VI. Authors

Though we usually associate David with the Book of Psalms (his name is on seventy-three of them), some of the psalms are anonymous and some list other authors: Asaph (50, 73–83), Solomon (72, 127), the sons of Korah (42–49, 84–85, 87–88), Ethan (89), and Moses (90). Some of David's psalms reflect the experiences he was going through, such as the rebellion of his son Absalom (3), his victory over Saul (18), his sin with Bathsheba (32, 51), his strange behavior in Gath (34, 56), and his years of exile in the wilderness (57, 63, 142).

## VII. Outline

Since each of the psalms is a separate unit, there is no need for an analysis of the structure of the book. There are five divisions, each ending with a benediction: 1–41, 42–72, 73–89, 90–106, 107–150.

# PSALM 1

The theme of this psalm is the happiness of the godly and the judgment of the ungodly. Verse 1 can be translated, "O the happinesses of the man." No matter where we turn in the Bible, we find that God gives joy to the obedient (even in the midst of trial) and ultimately sorrow to the disobedient. God sees but two persons in this world: the godly, who are "in Christ," and the ungodly, who are "in Adam." See 1 Cor. 15:22, 49. Let us look at these two persons.

## I. The Person God Blesses (1:1-3)

From the beginning of creation, God blessed mankind (Gen. 1:28); it was only after sin had entered the world through Adam's disobedience that we find the word "curse" (Gen. 3:14-19). It has always been God's desire that mankind should enjoy His blessings. Ephesians 1:3 tells us that the believer in Christ has been "blessed with all spiritual blessings." How rich we are in Him! Sad to say, many Christians do not "possess their possessions" (Obad. 17) and enjoy their blessings in Christ. In these verses we have a description of the kind of Christian God is able to bless.

### A. A person who is separated from the world (v. 1).

The Christian life is compared to a walk (see Eph. 4:1, 17; 5:2, 8, 15). It begins with a step of faith in trusting Christ and it grows as we take further steps of faith in obedience to His Word. Walking involves progress, and Christians are to make progress in applying Bible truths to daily life. But it is possible for the believer to walk "in the darkness," outside the will of God (1 John 1:5-7). The people God blesses are careful in their walk: though they are in the world, they are not of the world. By contrast, it takes little imagination to see the person walking near sin, then standing to consider it, and finally sitting down to enjoy "the pleasures of sin for a season" (Heb. 11:25). We see this sad development in Peter's disobedience. Jesus said he should go away (John 18:8), but instead, Peter walked after Jesus (18:15). Next we see him standing with the wrong crowd (18:18), and before long he is sitting by the fire (Luke 22:55). You know what happened: he walked right into temptation and three times denied his Lord. If Christians start listening to the counsel (advice, plans) of the ungodly, they will soon be standing in their way of life, and finally will sit right down and agree with them.

### B. A person who is saturated with the Word (v. 2).

Those whom God blesses are not delighted with what pertains to sin and the world; they delight in the Word of God. It is love for and obedience to the Bible that brings blessing on our lives. See Josh. 1:8. The people God blesses not only read the Word daily, but they study it, memorize it, and meditate on it during the day and night. Their mind is controlled by the Word of God. Because of this, they are led by the Spirit and walk in the Spirit. Meditation is to the soul what "digestion" is to the body. It means understanding the Word, "chewing on it," and applying it to our lives, making it a part of the inner person. See Jer. 15:16, Ezek. 3:3, and Rev. 10:9.

### C. A person who is situated by the waters (v. 3).

Water for drinking is a picture of the Holy Spirit of God (John 7:37-39). The Christian is here compared to a tree that gets its water from the deep hidden springs under the dry sands. This world is a desert that can never satisfy the dedicated believer. We must send our "spiritual roots" down deep into the things of Christ and draw upon the spiritual water of life. See Jer. 17:7-8, Ps. 92:12-14. There can be no fruit without roots. Too many Christians are more concerned about the leaves and the fruit than they are the roots, but the roots are the most important part. Unless Christians spend time daily in prayer and the Word, and allow the Spirit to feed them, they will wither and die. The believer who draws upon the spiritual life in Christ will be fruitful and successful in the life of faith. When Christians cease to bear fruit, it is because something has happened to the roots (Mark 11:12-13, 20; and see Luke 13:6-9). What kind of fruit are we to bear? See Rom. 1:13 and 6:22, Gal. 5:22-23, Heb. 13:15, and Col. 1:10.

Of course, the perfect example of this godly person in vv. 1-3 is Jesus Christ. He is the Way (v. 1), the Truth (v. 2), and the Life (v. 3); see John 14:6.

## II. The Person God Judges (1:4-6)

"Not so!" This means that all that the godly person enjoys and experiences is not true in the life of the ungodly. The godly are compared to a tree—strong, permanent, beautiful, useful, fruitful. The ungodly are compared to chaff—they have no roots; they are blown with the wind; they are useless to the plans of God; they are neither beautiful nor fruitful. John the Baptist used a similar picture in Matt. 3:10-12 when he described God as a harvester, visiting the threshing floor and separating the grain from the chaff. "He will burn up the chaff!" See also Ps. 35:5 and Job 21:18. What a tragedy for people to spend their whole life on earth as chaff and, as far as eternal things are concerned, amount to nothing.

Is there a future judgment? Verse 5 informs us that there is. Of course, in the OT we do not find the full explanation of the future judgments as we do in the NT. For the believer in Christ, there is no judgment of sin (John 5:24; Rom. 8:1), but for the unbeliever, there is "a fearful looking for of judgment" (Heb. 10:27). This judgment of the lost is described in Rev. 20:11-15. There will be no Christians at that scene, only unsaved people. The true character of the wicked will be revealed at that judgment; they will be seen as chaff, worthless lost souls. When v. 5 says the wicked "shall not stand" in the judgment, it does not mean they will be absent; rather, it means they will not be able to endure the judgment. When the books are opened, these individuals will be flung to their knees in confession of sin and of the truth of God's Word and God's Son (Phil. 2:9-11). These ungodly people will never be allowed to enter the heavenly congregation of the righteous, even though on earth they might have been members of religious groups. See Matt. 7:21-23.

The word "know" in the Bible means much more than the mental understanding indicated when we say, "I know the names of the twelve Apostles." In addition, it carries the idea of choosing and caring. "The Lord knows those who are His" (2 Tim. 2:19, NKJV). "I know my sheep. . . . As the Father knows me, even so I know the Father (John 10:14-15, NKJV). Christ's statement to the lost is, "I never knew you" (Matt. 7:23). The Lord knows the way of the righteous: He has planned it and marked it out (Eph. 2:10), and He keeps His eyes upon the righteous as they walk this way. The life of the godly person is an eternal plan of God! What he says, where he goes, what he does—all of these have eternal consequences. But the ungodly have "turned every one to his own way" (Isa. 53:6). The path of the righteous leads to glory (Prov. 4:18), but the way of the ungodly shall perish.

Verse 6 sets before us the familiar teaching of the "two ways."

Jesus concluded His Sermon on the Mount with this picture (Matt. 7:13ff), and we see it mentioned throughout the Book of Proverbs (Prov. 2:20; 4:14; 4:24-27; etc.). Why are the ungodly lost? Because they will not submit to Christ and His Word. They prefer the counsel of the ungodly to the "whole counsel of God" in the Word (Acts 20:27). They prefer the friendship of godless people to the congregation of the righteous. They spend their days thinking about sin, not about the Word of God (Gen. 6:5). They think they are secure in the earth—but they are only chaff!

How can the believer practice Ps. 1:1-3? It begins with surrender to the Lord, a daily surrender of all that we are and all that we have (Rom. 12:1-2). It involves spending time with God's Word, reading it and meditating upon it. It means living a life separated from the world (not isolated, of course, but separated from its defilement). It demands a life with roots that draw upon the hidden resources of God. What a blessed life, one that gives satisfaction here and hereafter.

# PSALM 2

There is an interesting contrast between the first two psalms. Psalm 1 is personal and focuses on the Law, while Ps. 2 is national and focuses on prophecy. In Ps. 1, we see Christ the Perfect Man; in Ps. 2, He is the King of kings. Psalm 1 deals with the blessing of the Jew (although it certainly applies to the Christian today), while Ps. 2 presents the judgment of the Gentile nations. Both psalms use the word *perish* (1:6 applies it to the individual sinner; 2:12 to the rebellious nations), and both psalms use the word *meditate* (translated "imagine" in 2:1). We have the right kind of meditation in 1:2 and the wrong kind in 2:1. The twelve verses of Ps. 2 may be divided into four sections of three verses each, and in each section we can hear a different voice.

## I. The Voice of the Nations (2:1-3)

This is a voice of rebellion—the word "rage" means "to assemble tumultuously." It is the Gentiles that are in view ("heathen" and "people" in v. 1), and they are rebelling against God and His rule. The nations are led in rebellion by their kings, and all are resisting God and Christ. Of course, this voice has been heard down through the centuries, but it is being heard in a greater way in these last days. As never before, there is a united voice of rebellion against the rule of God and Christ. What do the nations want? Freedom from God's rule! "Let us break their bands asunder!" According to Gen. 10:5, God divided the Gentile peoples into their lands and nations; see also Acts 17:26 and Deut. 32:8. History shows that the Gentile nations have rejected God's people (Israel), God's Word, and God's Christ. The nations do not want to submit to God's rule. Like proud Nebuchadnezzar, they want their own way, and they refuse to admit that God rules in the affairs of men. See Dan. 4:28-37. This Gentile rebellion grew more fierce with the establishing of the church (Acts 4:23-30). But in the last days, it will have its complete fulfillment as the "kings of the earth" unite to fight against God (see Rev. 1:5; 6:15; 16:12-16; 17:2, 18; 19:11-21).

## II. The Voice of the Father (2:4-6)

How does God respond to the threats of men? He laughs! It is the holy voice of derision, for God is greater than man and need not fear the proud attacks of puny kings. God does not speak today in judgment; He speaks in grace from the cross. But the day is coming when God will have "the last laugh" (Ps. 37:1-15; 59:1-8). Remember how proud Sennacherib defied God and the Jews and then was suddenly wiped out? (2 Kings 19) This will happen again when God decides to deal in judgment with the nations of the world.

There is also the voice of displeasure (v. 5). We can say it again: today God is not speaking in wrath; He is speaking through His Son in grace (Heb. 1:1-2); one day, however, He will send His wrath upon the nations of the world. The word "displeasure" here means "fiery anger." This is the tribulation, described in detail in Rev. 6–19. It will be a time of awful judgment upon the land and sea, the heavens, the world of nature, and people and nations. Millions of people will die in plagues and heaven-sent disasters. During the tribulation period, the nation of Israel will be "purged" to prepare a believing remnant for the return of Christ to establish His kingdom from Jerusalem. Multitudes will be saved during this time, but many of them will seal their decision with their own lives.

Finally, God's voice is a voice of declaration (v. 6); God has set ("anointed") His King upon His holy hill. This is Christ (Isa. 9:6-

7; Dan. 7:13-14). Though He is not yet seated on His own throne of glory, or upon the throne of David, He is seated at the Father's right hand; and His throne is as certain as the Father's word! Today, Christ is a priest-king like Melchizedek (Heb. 6:20–7:17). He intercedes for His own. One day He will return in glory and sit upon the throne to judge and rule the nations (Matt. 25:31-46).

## III. The Voice of the Son (2:7-9)

Christ speaks in these verses and tells us what the Father said to Him in His eternal decree. How good to know that God has decreed the fulfillment of His plan, and that man will not hinder God's working. "You are My Son, today I have begotten You." When did the Father say this to the Son? Not when He was born into the world, but when He came out of the tomb. Read Acts 13:28-33 carefully. Christ was "begotten" from the virgin tomb into a glorious life of resurrection power. (This verse is quoted again in Heb. 1:5 and 5:5.)

Because of His victory over sin and death, Christ is given an inheritance; see Heb. 1:4-5. You will recall the Father saying to the Son at His baptism, "This is my Beloved Son" (Matt. 3:17, NKJV). He repeated this at the Transfiguration where Jesus faced His death on the cross (Matt. 17:5). Jesus has all the nations as His inheritance because of His faithful work on the cross. However, Satan offered Him these same kingdoms apart from the cross; see Matt. 4:8-10. Jesus could have received the nations without suffering had He yielded to the devil, but then He would have stepped outside the Father's will. (Of course, it was impossible for Christ to sin, but the temptation was still just as real.) Satan will offer these kingdoms to Antichrist, and he will rule the nations for a brief season. See Rev. 13:1-10.

When will Christ receive "the uttermost parts of the earth" for His possession? When He returns to the earth in power and glory; see Rev. 19:11-21. Psalm 2:9 is referred to in Rev. 12:5 and 19:15; and in Rev. 2:26-29, we are told that Christians will reign with Him. See also Dan. 2:42-44.

## IV. The Voice of the Spirit (2:10-12)

The closing three verses are an appeal from the Spirit to the sons of men to submit themselves now to Jesus Christ. The Spirit appeals to every area of the personality:

432

## A. The mind (v. 10).

"Be wise . . . be instructed!" The "counsel of the ungodly" (Ps. 1:1) has led the ungodly astray. The wisdom of the world is foolishness with God (1 Cor. 1:18-31). Our world boasts of its knowledge, and it seems that there is more knowledge than ever before, but there also seems to be less wisdom. God's wisdom is found in God's Word, yet the kings and rulers do not want the Word of God.

## B. The heart (v. 11).

"Serve Him!" Instead of rebelling and resisting, people should bow down to Christ and serve Him. A reverential joy is what will result from yielding to Christ.

## C. The will (v. 12).

"Kiss the Son" implies paying homage to Him, showing loving surrender to Him. A kiss speaks of love and reconciliation. God has been reconciled to the world by the Cross of Christ (2 Cor. 5:14-21); righteousness and peace kissed each other on the cross (Ps. 85:10). Now God is able to save lost sinners and still uphold His holy law. It is tragic that most of the people of the world are saying, "We will not have this Man to reign over us!" When Jesus returns, they will be forced to bow before Him (Phil. 2:10-11), but then it will be too late. All God has to do is kindle His wrath "but a little"—and sinners perish! What will it be like when His wrath burns on this earth in great judgment?

Psalm 1 opens with a beatitude; Ps. 2 closes with one: "Blessed are all they that put their trust in Him." "Whosoever shall call on the name of the Lord shall be saved" (Acts 2:21).

# PSALM 8

Hidden in this beautiful psalm's poetic description of man's place in creation lies much teaching for practical people today. With the aid of the NT references to Ps. 8, we will be able to discover some of the lessons found here.

## I. The Setting Historically

You have noted that there are two types of inscriptions in the psalms: historical and musical. For example, at the beginning of Ps.

8 we read, "To the chief Musician upon Gittith, a psalm of David." *Gittith* means "winepress" and probably referred to the use of the psalm in the harvest season. However, some Bible students have concluded that the musical directions belong at the end of the preceding psalm, as seen in Hab. 3. This means that *Muth-labben* at the beginning of Ps. 9 really belongs at the end of Ps. 8.

The term *Muth-labben* means "death of the son" or "death of the champion," and could refer to David's slaying of Goliath (1 Sam. 17). It is easy to see young David alone with God that evening after he had killed the giant, looking up to heaven and marveling at God's concern for His own. David was but a "babe and suckling" compared to the giant, yet God used the babe to silence the enemy. Note that in 1 Sam. 17:4 Goliath is called "a champion" and that he proudly challenged the fearful Jews for forty days (17:16). When David offered to silence the enemy, Saul said, "You are but a youth" (17:33, NKJV)—a babe, a suckling. Note another parallel between 1 Sam. 17 and Ps. 8 in "the fowl of the air" and "the beasts of the field" (1 Sam. 17:44 and Ps. 8:7-8). Also, Ps. 8 glorifies the "name of the Lord" (8:1, 9), and David defeated Goliath in the "name of the Lord" (17:45).

Here we have youthful David praising the Lord for the great victory that He gave. "What is man that You are mindful of him?" Why would God pay any attention to a shepherd boy? What a wonderful type of Jesus Christ we see in David: (1) both were born at Bethlehem; (2) both were shepherds; (3) both were rejected temporarily by their brethren; (4) both faced an enemy in the wilderness and won; (5) both were exiles before being made kings; (6) both took a bride while in exile; and (7) both were beloved—for the name David means "beloved."

## II. The Meaning Doctrinally

Any time a psalm is quoted in the NT and applied to Christ, this makes it a messianic psalm. Psalm 8 is applied to Christ in several places in the NT: Matt. 21:16; Heb. 2:6-8; 1 Cor. 15:27; and Eph. 1:22. Read these references carefully, especially Heb. 2.

The main teaching from Ps. 8 in Heb. 2 and 1 Cor. 15 is this: Christ has regained all that Adam lost because of sin. Christ has been exalted above the heavens and thus has glorified God's name (Eph. 1:19-23; Heb. 1:1-3). God's glory is no longer in a tent or a temple; it is "above the heavens" in Christ and in the hearts of ordinary believers. When Christ was ministering on earth, He was not praised by the priests or kings; it was the little children who praised Him in the temple.

Read Gen. 1:26-28 carefully, and note that God gave the first man dominion (rule) over the fish, the fowl, and the cattle. Actually, man was made "a little lower than God" and was appointed God's deputy to rule over the earth. But when Adam sinned, he lost that dominion. Romans 5 points out that there was a change of "kings": death reigned (5:14, 17), and sin reigned (5:21), but Adam no longer reigned. Instead of a king, Adam had become a slave!

When Christ came to earth, He exercised the dominion that Adam lost. Christ ruled over the fish (Luke 5:1-6; Matt. 17:24-27; John 21:1-6), over the fowl (Luke 22:34), and over the beasts (Mark 1:13; 11:1-7). No one on earth today could control nature the way He did. When Jesus came to earth, it was God "visiting" men (Ps. 8:4 with Luke 1:68, 78). Note that David is picturing a night scene (v. 3) because it certainly was night spiritually when Jesus came to earth. But by humbling Himself and becoming a servant and dying on the cross, Jesus glorified God and purchased the salvation of a lost people and a lost world. Hebrews 2:8 points out that we do not yet see all of nature put in subjection to man. There are still floods and earthquakes and plagues. Yes, but we see Jesus! (v. 9) And the fact that He died for us is all the assurance we need that one day, when He returns, His people will reign over a renewed earth.

One final thought: Christ's work on the cross did not merely undo Adam's sin and put us back where Adam was. Rather, it gave us much more: it made us like Christ. Note the repetition of "much more" in Rom. 5:9-21.

## III. The Living Practically

### A. Praise.

If David had reason to praise God for his position and his victory, how much more should we praise Him. Who are we that God should visit us? Who are we that Christ should die for us and lift us with Him above the heavens?

### B. Position.

This psalm exalts the dignity of man. Verse 5 should read, "You have made him a little lower than God." Man is certainly the greatest of God's creations, for man is made "in the image of God." Because modern teaching has lowered man to an animal and rejected the image of God, the world is in chaos. James 3:9 reminds us that we will treat people better if we remember they are made in God's image. No wonder we have so much civil unrest, so much brutality. We have dethroned God and debased humanity. Let us never forget our obligation as creatures made in God's image, and our greater obligation as saints being renewed in this image through Christ (Col. 3:9-10; Rom. 8:29).

### C. Power.

Christ has given us dominion; this means that we reign as kings. We can reign in life through Christ (Rom. 5:17), getting victory over sin and temptation. We reign in death (1 Cor. 15:54-57), for death no more has dominion over us. We shall reign in His kingdom here on earth, our place of service to be determined according to our life and faithfulness here today (Matt. 25:14-30; Luke 19:12-27). Finally, we shall reign with Him forever and ever.

### D. Promise.

This psalm makes it clear that God is concerned with creation, and the interpretation in Heb. 2:6-9 indicates that Christ will one day deliver creation from the bondage of sin. See Rom. 8:18-24. This will include the "redemption of our body" (Rom. 8:23) when we shall see Christ and become like Him (1 John 3:1-3; Phil. 3:20-21). The fact that Jesus Christ is today on the throne is proof that one day all creation will be redeemed. What a glorious promise!

Of course, Ps. 8 applies only to believers in Jesus Christ. The unbeliever may admire God's creation, the work of His fingers (v. 3), but those who are saved have experienced the power of His arm. "Who has believed our report? And to whom has the arm of the Lord been revealed?" (Isa. 53:1) How wonderful that God should visit this earth for salvation, but one day He will visit it in judgment. Have you trusted Christ as your Savior? Are you permitting Him to rule and reign in your life?

# PSALM 19

God's revelation to man is the theme of this psalm. It is amazing that God speaks to us at all. Men and women are sinners and have no desire to listen to God, yet He graciously continues to speak. God speaks to us in three ways:

## I. He Speaks in the Skies (19:1-6)

God's wisdom, power, and glory are seen in His creation. Modern science would have us study "natural laws" and leave God out, but the psalmist looked at the marvels of heaven and earth and saw God. See also Pss. 8 and 29, as well as Isa. 40:12-31. Jesus saw His Father's handiwork in the lilies and the birds (Matt. 6:24-34). Both by day and by night, God's creation is speaking (v. 2), but this speech is not heard with the human ear. Verse 3 should read, "There is no speech or language where their voice is not heard" (NIV). We hear the voice of God in creation by seeing His wisdom and power. Certainly so complex an entity as our universe (and the universes beyond our own universe) demands a Creator and Sustainer. To believe that the universe evolved out of nothing and arranged itself in this orderly manner is folly.

Creation speaks a universal language to all nations (vv. 3-4). It is this fact that Paul used in Rom. 1:18-32 to prove that all people everywhere are under the wrath of God. "Are the heathen lost?" is an oft-repeated question, and the answer is "Yes." On what basis are they lost if they have never heard the Gospel? On the basis of God's revelation in creation. The heathen see God's power and wisdom, His "eternal Godhead," in creation and know that they have a responsibility to Him. Paul uses Ps. 19:4 again in Rom. 10:18.

Nature preaches a thousand sermons a day to the human heart. Each day begins with light and moves to darkness, from waking to sleeping, a picture of life without God. Each year moves from spring to winter, from life to death. We see the grass mowed down (Isa. 40:6-8), the tree cut down (Luke 13:6-9; Matt. 3:10), the fire destroying the waste (Matt. 13:40-42). The activities of nature, under the hand of God, are vivid object lessons to the hearts of sinners but, alas, many do not want to see or hear. The lost sinner, wherever he or she may be on this globe, stands condemned before the throne of God.

## II. He Speaks in the Scriptures (19:7-11)

The heavens declare God's glory, and the Scriptures declare His grace. See Heb. 1:1-3. This law, testimony, commandment, word, of course, is a personal revelation from God, for the name used is not "God" but "LORD," meaning "Jehovah." This is the personal, covenant name for God.

## A. *What the Bible is.*

(1) The perfect law—There is no error in the Bible, either in historical fact or in spiritual truth. Of course, the Bible records the lies of men and of Satan, but the total message of the Bible is that of truth. See Ps. 119:128 and 160.

(2) The sure testimony—The Word does not change; it is sure and steadfast, Ps. 119:89. It is God's testimony to man, His witness of what is true and right. See Matt. 5:18.

(3) The right statutes—"Statutes" means "precepts, rules for daily living." Some rules are wrong rules; God's Word is right. Obeying the Word brings blessing to daily life.

(4) The pure commandment—See Pss. 12:6; 119:140; Prov. 30:5. The "sacred books" of some world religions are anything but pure, but God's Word is pure, even when dealing with sin. Nothing in the Bible, rightly understood, could lead a person into sin.

(5) The clean fear of the Lord—The phrase "fear of the Lord" (v. 9) is another reference to "the Law," since the Word of God produces a reverence for God. See Deut. 4:10; Ps. 111:10. To fear God makes a person clean; to worship heathen idols makes a person filthy.

(6) True, righteous judgments—God's evaluations of men and things are true; He knows all things completely. It pays for the Christian to believe what God says and not to depend on his own evaluation. Lot made this mistake and lost everything.

(7) Better than gold—What a treasure is the Bible (Ps. 119:72; Prov. 8:10; 16:16).

(8) Sweeter than honey (Ps. 119:103)—The spiritual Christian does not need the artificial things of this world for satisfaction; the Word satisfies the spiritual appetite.

## B. *What the Bible does.*

(1) Converts—This is the same as "restores" in Ps. 23:3. The Word converts the sinner from his ways and restores the saint when he wanders. It refreshes and heals.

(2) Makes wise—Read Ps. 119:97-104; Isa. 8:20; Jer. 8:9; Col. 1:9; James 1:5.

(3) Rejoices—The spiritual believer finds joy in the Word (Jer. 15:16).

438

(4) Enlightens—"The entrance (opening) of Your words gives light" (Ps. 119:130, NKJV).

(5) Endures—Other books fade and are forgotten, but God's Word remains. Many a hammer has been worn out on the anvil of God's Word!

(6) Enriches—It is better than gold or silver (Prov. 3:13-15).

(7) Satisfies—The honey satisfies the body; the Word satisfies the soul.

(8) Warns—It is better to prevent sin and avoid trouble than to confess sin and try to remedy mistakes. Knowing the Word and obeying it guides the believer on the safe path. See Prov. 2.

(9) Rewards—Money cannot buy the rewards of a godly life: a clean conscience, a pure heart, joy, peace, and answered prayer. Note that v. 11 says there is a reward *in* keeping the Word, not *for* keeping it. The reward comes in the doing: "This man shall be blessed in *his doing*" (James 1:25).

## III. He Speaks in the Soul (19:12-14)

No person can understand his or her own heart (Jer. 17:9). We need the mirror of the Word to reveal our sins to us (James 1:22-25). The psalmist closes by asking God to reveal his secret sins to him; see Ps. 139:23-24. The OT law provided for sins of ignorance (Lev. 4–5; Num. 15:22ff). But for sins of open defiance and rebellion, there was no sacrifice; see Num. 15:30-31. David asks not only to be cleansed of secret faults, but to be restrained from running head-long into open sin. "Watch and pray, that you enter not into temptation." This kind of wicked abandonment to sin leads to slavery, and sin becomes the master of the life. Romans 6 tells us that sin should not have dominion over us. Of course, it is by allowing the Word of God to control our lives that we get victory over sin. By "great transgression" in v. 13, the psalmist seems to mean a "sin unto death" or a repeated rebellion against God that brings forth His wrath. It is by an accumulation of the little secret sins of v. 12 that the person gradually walks into the great sin. It is important that Christians confess their sins immediately and allow the Word and the blood to cleanse the heart.

The prayer of v. 14 ought to be on our lips and in our hearts all day long. The meditation of the heart controls the words of the mouth (Mark 7:14-23). The word "meditation" here has the image of a musician plucking the strings of a harp. Who controls the music of your heart, God or Satan? Meditation is to the heart what digestion is to the body; it is the taking in of the Word of God and making it a part of the inner being. As the heart and mind think on the Word all day long, the Spirit guides the life. This is what it means to walk in the Spirit (Gal. 5:16) and to have the spiritual mind (Rom. 8:1-8).

Is your Bible all to you that God wants it to be? Read this psalm again and ask God to enable you to love the Word, live in it, and obey it—and He will bless you.

# PSALMS 22, 23, 24

These three familiar and beloved psalms present Christ as the Shepherd, each one emphasizing a different aspect of His Person and His work. Psalm 22 pictures the Good Shepherd dying for the sheep (John 10:11); Ps. 23 the Great Shepherd caring for the sheep (Heb. 13:20-21); and Ps. 24 the Chief Shepherd coming for the sheep (1 Peter 5:4). In other words, Christ died for us (past), Christ lives for us (present), and Christ will come for us (future).

### I. The Good Shepherd (22)

This psalm presents the crucifixion of Christ in vv. 1-21 and His resurrection in vv. 22-31. Since the Jews did not know of crucifixion back in David's time, this vivid description of Christ's death on the cross could only have been penned by inspiration of the Spirit. It is interesting to contrast the two sections of this psalm. In vv. 1-21 we see Christ's suffering and crucifixion, while in vv. 22-31 we see His glory and resurrection. The first passage depicts pain and prayer; the second passage depicts praise and promise. And the first shows Christ in the midst of His enemies; the second, Christ in the midst of the church.

It is not difficult to see the fulfillment of this chapter in the NT story of the cross:
- v. 1—Matt. 27:46; Mark 15:34—Christ spoke these words
- v. 2—Alternate light and darkness; Matt. 27:45
- vv. 6-8—The reproach of the people; Matt. 27:39-44
- vv. 11-12—No help was offered Him; Matt. 26:56
- v. 16—His hands and feet pierced; Matt. 27:35
- v. 17—People staring at Him; Luke 23:35

● v. 18—Gambling for His garments; John 19:23-24

At v. 22, the scene changes, and we move into resurrection. See Heb. 2:11-12 for the NT explanation of this. Christ is no longer on the cross; He is in the midst of His brethren (the church) declaring the glory of God. Verse 24 must be read in connection with Heb. 5:7. This final section is filled with praise: in the church (v. 22), in Israel (vv. 23-26), and among the Gentiles (vv. 27-31). Verse 31 (NKJV) ends, "He has done this," paralleling Jesus' words, "It is finished." Because of Christ's work on the cross, salvation has been accomplished and all who come to Him by faith will be saved.

## II. The Great Shepherd (23)

Hebrews 13:20-21 informs us that today Jesus is the Great Shepherd who cares for the sheep. We are His sheep, and as we follow Him He ministers to us. Christ did not simply die for us; He rose again and lives for us. He is the Great Shepherd, the Great High Priest. "I shall not want" is the theme of Ps. 23. "I shall not want" for: rest and refreshment (v. 2), restoration and righteousness (v. 3), protection in trouble (v. 4), provision in the wilderness (v. 5), and a home to go to at the end of the day (v. 6).

Of course, the picture here is that of the Oriental shepherd and his flock. Such a shepherd knows each sheep by name. The shepherd goes before the sheep and makes sure they are not walking into danger (John 10:27-28). The sheep never need worry when they follow the shepherd, for he will protect them and provide for them. Even when they go through a dangerous valley (v. 4), the shepherd is beside them, and beyond the valley is the house of rest. At the end of the day, the shepherd leads the flock back to the fold and stands by the open door to examine each one as it enters. If he sees one that is bruised or weary, he puts the refreshing oil upon it to soothe and heal it, and gives it a drink of cool water. How gracious our Shepherd is to care for us!

Each of the OT names for God is seen in this psalm: *Jehovah-Jireh,* "The Lord will provide" (Gen. 22:13-14); *Jehovah-Rapha,* "The Lord will heal or restore" (Ex. 15:26); *Jehovah-Shalom,* "The Lord our peace" (Jud. 6:24); *Jehovah-Tsidkenu,* "The Lord our righteousness," (Jer. 23:6); *Jehovah-Shammah,* "The Lord is there," (Ezek. 48:35); *Jehovah-Nissi,* "The Lord our banner" (Ex. 17:8-15); and *Jehovah-Raah,* "The Lord my shepherd" (Ps. 23:1). In other words, Jesus Christ is to His sheep all that they ever need. As the little child said when misquoting this psalm, "The Lord is my shepherd—what more shall I want?"

## III. The Chief Shepherd (24)

Jewish tradition says that this psalm was written to commemorate David's returning the ark to Jerusalem (1 Chron. 13–15). It was probably sung by different choirs and soloists, each answering the other. The choir would sing vv. 1-2, a voice would respond with v. 3, and then another voice would answer with v. 4. Then the chorus would sing vv. 5-6. As the people entered the gates of the city, the chorus would sing out vv. 8-9, and the voice would ask again, "Who is this king of glory?" Then the entire group would shout, "The Lord of hosts! He is the king of glory!" What a wonderful spectacle it must have been!

But an even greater wonder awaits Jerusalem when the Chief Shepherd, Jesus Christ, appears to claim David's throne. This psalm describes the return of the King to Zion; see Rev. 19:11-16. This present earth is under the sway of sin and Satan. Though it is the Lord's by creation and redemption, it has not yet been delivered from bondage. But thank God, one day Jesus will return to the earth to claim His inheritance. Then the earth will be filled with the glory of the Lord.

The question in v. 3 is important: who is worthy to rule over the earth from Mt. Zion? It reminds us of Rev. 5 when the question is asked, "Who is worthy to open the book and break the seals?" There can be only one answer: Jesus Christ the Son of God. Psalm 24:4 describes Him as the Perfect Man, the Perfect King. David did not have clean hands, for he murdered a man; nor did he have a pure heart, for he lusted and committed adultery. He lifted up his soul to vanity and pride when he numbered the people. Solomon could not qualify, for he was an idolater. Even great King Hezekiah fell because of pride. No, the only king who can qualify is Jesus Christ.

When Jesus Christ claims Jerusalem, He will come as one fresh from the battle (v. 8), for He will have defeated the nations of the world at Armageddon (Rev. 19:19-21). Before Jesus was born, it was promised that He would sit on David's throne (Luke 1:30-33). Today He is seated on His Father's throne (Rev. 3:21), but when He returns to this earth in judgment and glory, He will claim David's throne and reign over the house of Jacob. Of course, He will first return in the air to take the church to heaven (1 Thes. 4:13-18). Then will follow seven years of awful tribulation on the earth, "the time of Jacob's trouble." When Satan and his evil associates have done their worst, Jesus Christ will return to judge and to deliver the world from evil. Then there will be a renewed earth, a restored Israel, and a righteous kingdom for a thousand years (Rev. 20:1-5).

If Christ is your *Good* Shepherd because you have received Him as Savior, then let Him be your *Great* Shepherd to guide and bless your life. Then when He returns as the *Chief* Shepherd, you will be ready to meet Him.

# PSALMS 32 and 51

The background for these two psalms is 2 Sam. 11–12. David lusted after his neighbor's wife, committed adultery, made the husband drunk, had him killed, and then covered the whole affair for at least a year. He was not a youth when he fell into these sins; he was a mature man, ruling over a great kingdom. "Let him who thinks he stands take heed lest he fall" (1 Cor. 10:12, NKJV). Psalm 51 was David's prayer of confession, and Ps. 32 his song of forgiveness. Read 1 John 1:5–2:2 for God's provision for cleansing.

## I. David's Prayer of Confession (51)

This is a very personal prayer; note how often David uses "me" and "my sin." His eyes are not on someone else; his eyes are on himself and on his Lord.

### A. The cost of committing sin.

Falling into lust and adultery seemed momentary acts, but what a tremendous price David paid. (It is possible, though, that David had "planned to sin" when he came home from the battle.) As we shall see in Ps. 32:3-4, David paid for his sins physically and became ill. But the spiritual cost was also great. He lost the purity of his heart (vv. 1-2) and therefore needed to be washed and cleansed (v. 7). Note the words used for sin here: transgressions means acts of rebellion, defying God by crossing over the line God has drawn; iniquity means inward crookedness, perversity; sin means missing the mark, failing to meet God's standard. Verse 17 suggests that

David's heart not only became defiled, but it also became hard. When we harbor sin, it hardens the heart. David's eyes were also affected; all he could see were his sins (v. 3). People with a dirty conscience are usually on the defensive, wondering what other people may know. Sin also affected his ears, for he lost the sound of joy and gladness (v. 8). Nothing sounds good to a person out of fellowship with God. Even David's lips were affected, for he could no longer testify or witness, or even sing God's praises (vv. 13-15). Nothing shuts a Christian's mouth like unconfessed sin. His mind was affected, for he begged for wisdom (v. 6). The inner person (heart and spirit, v. 10) was out of fellowship with God (v. 11), and there was no joy. God does not take away the Holy Spirit when we sin (John 14:16), but we do grieve the Spirit and thereby lose His fellowship and help (Eph. 4:30-32). May we never forget the high cost of committing sin!

## B. The cost of confessing sin.

True confession of sin involves repentance, a sincere change of mind. During that year when David covered his sins, he thought he would "get away" with something. But when Nathan confronted him with his sins, David's heart smote him and he repented. There is a difference between admitting sins and confessing sins. Confession (1 John 1:9) literally means "to say the same thing." If we say the same thing about our sins that God says about them, and we truly mean it, then we are confessing sin. David even went so far as to admit his sinful nature, born in sin (v. 5). Beware of "cheap confession." Merely praying with the lips, "Lord, I have sinned, please forgive me!" is not confession. True confession costs something—a broken spirit and a contrite heart (v. 17). This does not mean that we do penance and earn forgiveness, but it does mean that we are so broken by our sins that we hide nothing from God.

## C. The cost of cleansing sin.

Good works cannot cleanse sin, not even religious works and sacrifices (vv. 16-17). Only the blood of Jesus Christ can wash away sins (Heb. 10:1-18; 1 John 1:7–2:2). Forgiveness is not a cheap thing; it cost Jesus Christ His life. We receive forgiveness because of what He has done, not because of our prayers or tears. God is willing to blot out sins (vv. 1, 9; see Isa. 43:25) and purge us completely. The high cost of cleansing alone ought to make us hate sin and want to turn from it.

## II. David's Praise for God's Cleansing (32)

The first two verses are quoted by Paul in Rom. 4:7-8, so be sure to read that passage. Literally, David sang: "Oh, the happiness of the man whose rebellion has been forgiven, whose failure to hit the mark has been covered. How happy is the man on whose account the Lord does not put his crookedness, and in whose spirit there is no deceit." David had been guilty of all of this: he had rebelled against the Law and failed to meet God's righteous standard; he had allowed his crooked nature to control him; and he had deceitfully covered the whole matter up for a year. See Prov. 28:13 and apply it to David's case.

### A. The silence of conviction (vv. 3-4).

What happened to David when he refused to confess his sins? He suffered. He suffered spiritually (as we saw in Ps. 51), but he also suffered physically. He became like an old man. God's hand of conviction was heavy upon him day and night. He "dried up" like a brook in a drought. Some people who go to the doctor to take care of their symptoms ought to go to the Lord to take care of their sins. This does not mean that all sickness is caused by sin, but it does mean that unconfessed sin can cause physical affliction. See 1 Cor. 11:29-32.

### B. The sob of confession (v. 5).

Literally, "I began to make known to You my sin." David immediately confessed that he had sinned when Nathan spoke to him (2 Sam. 12:13), but then, privately, he allowed the Spirit of God to uncover his sins one by one. David's prayer was no "general confession"; he named his sins specifically. Because he confessed, God forgave. One writer has said, "The less you spare yourself, the more God will spare you." Paul said, "For if we would judge ourselves, we should not be judged" (1 Cor. 11:31). God does not forgive us because we feel sorry, or because we pray; He forgives us when we confess our sins because He is "faithful and just" — faithful to His promise, and just with reference to the Cross. God will not make us pay for sins that Christ has already paid for. Read Rom. 8:31-39.

### C. The song of cleansing (vv. 6-7).

David's sighing has been replaced by singing. He is surrounded by "songs of deliverance"; and wherever he turns, he discovers something to sing about. It used to be that wherever he turned, he saw his sins (51:3). He warns us that we should pray to God for forgiveness "in a time of finding." This may have two meanings: in a time when we find out our sins, and in a time when God may be found (Isa. 55:6-7). If a believer allows sins to accumulate, God will have to step in and chasten (Heb. 12). David is no longer afraid, for God is his hiding place. Let troubles come; he is not afraid.

### D. The shout of confidence (vv. 8-11).

God is now speaking to David and assuring him that He will direct his steps. "He restores my soul; He leads me in the paths of righteousness for His name's sake" (Ps. 23:3, NKJV). God wants to guide us, not with a heavy rod, but with His eye. An obedient child watches his parents' eyes, to see what their will is. The Christian must constantly stay under the Father's eye and live to please Him. In v. 9 David talks about two extremes: the horse that rushes ahead impulsively, and the mule that lags behind stubbornly. Christians should avoid both of these patterns of behavior. We should walk with the Lord a step at a time in loving obedience. Horses and mules must be controlled by bits and bridles "else they will not come near you." Alas, some Christians must have "bits and bridles" before God can control them. But the normal way is for God to guide us with His eye upon us. Dumb animals have no understanding, but God's people can understand what the will of the Lord is (Eph. 5:15-17).

After we as Christians have sinned and been restored, Satan tries to undermine our peace and confidence. We begin to worry about the past and the consequences of our foolishness. Yes, there are bitter fruits from disobedience (and how David found that out!), but vv. 10-11 assure us that God protects and upholds those who belong to Him. The wicked have many sorrows, and sorrows come to the lives of disobedient saints, but the cleansed Christian experiences the loving-kindness and mercy of the Lord. No wonder David ends by shouting. The past is forgiven—the present is joyful—and the future is secure in the hands of God.

# PSALM 40

This psalm may be called "The Christmas Psalm" because it looks forward to the birth of Christ. Verses 6-8 are quoted in Heb. 10:5-

10 and applied to Jesus Christ. Historically, the psalm grew out of a crisis in the life of David. He was in "a horrible pit" and cried out to God, and God delivered him. In the first half (vv. 1-10), David testifies of God's mercy and shows his gratitude by yielding himself anew to the Lord. In the closing verses (vv. 11-17) David calls to God for further help as new enemies approach him. What a strength there is in v. 17, NKJV—"The Lord thinks upon me." Since this is a messianic psalm (a psalm that speaks of Jesus Christ), we want to study that aspect of it especially.

## I. The Birth of Christ (40:6-7)

You will want to read Heb. 10:1-18 carefully. The chapter begins by saying that God has set aside all the Hebrew sacrifices which could never take away sins. In vv. 5-9, the writer argues that Jesus Christ came to do what those sacrifices could never do. But in order for Jesus to die, He had to come to earth as a man in a body of flesh (without sin, of course). As He came into the world, the Son said to the Father, "Lo, I come—in the volume of the book (the OT prophecies) it is written of Me."

Hebrews 10:5, NKJV, quotes Ps. 40:6, NKJV, as "a body You have prepared for Me" instead of "my ears You have opened." Of course, the same Holy Spirit who wrote the Word can quote it and expand or explain it as He wills. Jesus Christ came in a prepared body; He was born of the Virgin Mary, conceived by the Holy Spirit (Luke 1:26-38). God has four ways to make a body: (1) out of clay, as with Adam; (2) out of man, as with Eve, Gen. 2:21-25; (3) out of woman married to man, as in every normal human birth; and (4) out of woman without man, as with the birth of Christ. Jesus Christ came in a prepared body, a body that was not tainted by sin. Though He felt all the *sinless* infirmities of flesh (hunger, pain, weariness, death), He never shared in the *sinful* weaknesses of flesh. If Jesus Christ did not have a sinless nature, then He could not be the Savior of the world.

For the phrase "my ears you have opened," see Ex. 21:1-6 and Isa. 50:5. The OT Jew would pierce the ear of the servant who wanted to remain with him forever. It is a beautiful picture of dedication. Note too that the birth of Christ was "written in the book." The first promise is in Gen. 3:15, where God announced that the "seed of the woman" (not the man, therefore a virgin birth) would defeat the seed of Satan. Later, God announced to

Abraham that the Savior would come through the Jews, and then He revealed that He would come through the tribe of Judah. Isaiah 7:14 announced the virgin birth, and Micah 5:2 informed the people that He would come to Bethlehem.

## II. The Life of Christ (40:8-10)

These verses beautifully summarize what Jesus did: He loved the Word, He lived the Word, and He preached the Word to the people. Nobody could ever accuse Jesus of sin; see John 8:46. The Jews had to hire liars to bring false testimony against Him at His trial. Even Judas (who would have had good excuse to accuse Christ) admitted that He was innocent (Matt. 27:1-5). Jesus delighted in the Word and will of God. "I do always those things that please Him," He said in John 8:29. His life and His lips magnified the righteousness and the loving-kindness of the Lord.

## III. The Death of Christ (40:6)

He came in that perfect body to be the perfect sacrifice for sins. Read 1 Sam. 15:22, Ps. 51:16-17, Hosea 6:6, and Micah 6:6-7 to see that nowhere in the OT are we taught that the blood of animals could wash away sins. Many Jews trusted the sacrifice instead of looking by faith to the Lord. How like many church members today who are trusting baptism or membership for salvation. Verse 6 mentions four kinds of offerings: (1) *sacrifice*, any kind of bloody offering; (2) *offering*, the non-bloody offerings, such as the meal offerings; (3) *burnt offering*, offering picturing total dedication to God; and (4) *sin offering*, offering dealing with the sin of the person.

All of these OT offerings (outlined in Lev. 1–5) are pictures of the atoning work of Jesus Christ. The burnt offering pictures His total surrender to God; "I delight to do Your will." The meal offering (Lev. 2) illustrates His perfect nature and reminds us that we feed on Him to satisfy the soul. The peace offering (Lev. 3) pictures peace with God, a peace between the sinner and the Savior that Jesus made at the cross (Col. 1:20; 2 Cor. 5:18). The sin offering (Lev. 4) deals with sin in our nature, while the trespass offering (Lev. 5) deals with acts of disobedience. Christ died for our sins, but He also condemned our old nature on the cross and thereby is able to give us victory over sin (Rom. 6–8).

The important thing is this: all of these offerings are fulfilled in Jesus Christ. By one offering He settled the sin question completely and eternally. What millions of lambs and goats could never do, Jesus Christ did in His hours of agony on the cross. Hallelujah, what a Savior!

### IV. The Resurrection of Christ (40:1-3)

These verses describe David's deliverance from some trouble, but they also illustrate Christ's resurrection. Jesus had gone down into the pit of sin for us; He was made sin for us (1 Peter 2:24; 2 Cor. 5:21). Certainly it was a "horrible pit" when you consider that Jesus bore on His sinless body all the sins of all mankind for all time. But He did not stay in the pit; God raised Him from the dead. Hebrews 5:7 suggests some of the horror of that Gethsemane and Calvary experience, and informs us that Jesus prayed to be "delivered *out of* death" (not *from* death, for He came to die). The Father answered that prayer and raised Him from the dead.

Christ today is raised to die no more. His work is finished; His feet are on the rock. The new song is a song of victory and praise to God; see Ps. 22:22-25, and compare these verses with Ps. 40:9-10. He has put all enemies under His feet.

# PSALM 90

Since Moses was the author of this psalm, it makes it the oldest of all the psalms. It was probably written in connection with Israel's failure at Kadesh-barnea (Num. 13–14). The people (except for Joshua and Caleb) refused to follow Moses and to trust God. Instead of entering the land by faith, they turned back in unbelief, and God judged them. He made the nation wander for forty years in the wilderness until all the people who had been over twenty years of age at Kadesh-barnea died. Keep this in mind as you read Ps. 90 (especially vv. 7-11), and it will take on new meaning. This psalm is Moses' personal reaction to the crisis; he turned to God in prayer and sought an eternal abiding place in the Lord. Years later he would say to Israel, "The eternal God is your refuge, and underneath are the everlasting arms" (Deut. 33:27). It was this kind of faith that sustained Moses during those trying years in the wilderness. Isaac Watts used Ps. 90 as the basis for his majestic hymn, "O God, Our Help in Ages Past." Read through the hymn with this psalm in mind.

## I. God's Eternality and Man's Frailty (90:1-6)

What a contrast we see here. The eternal God exists far above history. Generations come and go, but God is still the same. "For I am the Lord, I change not" (Mal. 3:6). "Jesus Christ the same yesterday, and today, and forever" (Heb. 13:8). There is a difference between being immortal and being eternal. Man is immortal—that is, his soul will never die; but God is eternal—He has neither beginning nor ending. God existed before the mountains (the most durable thing known in Moses' day); in fact, He gave birth to the mountains. Through faith in Jesus Christ, we become a part of eternity and possess eternal life.

The illustrations of the frailty of man are these: dust (v. 3); a watch in the night, about three hours long (v. 4); a brief flood after a shower that soon dries up (v. 5); a sleep that seems but a few minutes long (v. 5); the grass that suddenly shoots up, but before evening has been cut down (vv. 5-6). For other pictures of the brevity of life, see Job 7–9. Verse 3 takes us back to Gen. 3:19; see also Ecc. 12:7. It has well been said that humans are part dust and part divinity. We are made in the image of God, yet we are made of dust. Were it not for sin, there would be no death or decay in our world.

These verses explain why human beings need an eternal refuge. We are frail, we are dust, we are creatures of time; unless we are rightly related to the eternal God, we are nothing. Only through faith in Christ can we know God and share His eternal life.

## II. God's Holiness and Man's Sins (90:7-12)

Israel's rebellion at Kadesh-barnea brought forth the wrath of God. See Num. 14:11-25. God offered to strike the nation with disease and disinherit them, but Moses pled with Him on the basis of His own promises and covenants. Moses asked God to pardon their sins, but the Lord still judged Israel by causing the older generation to die in the wilderness during the next forty years. It was the world's longest funeral march. "The wages of sin is death."

Sinful humans live under the wrath of God. "He who does not believe is condemned already," announces John 3:18, NKJV. God sees the secret sins (v. 8; Heb. 4:13) as well as the open ones. Human days "decline like a sunset" (v. 9), from light to darkness. Our days are "as a sigh" (not a "tale"), they are so brief and empty and pass by so quickly. How long do humans live? Well, that generation in Moses' day (from twenty years up, Num. 14:29) would live but forty more years. Add twenty to forty and you get sixty years. Moses speaks of seventy years as the limit, unless God grants an extra ten years. The older people in Israel at that time would not live to reach their eightieth birthday because of their sins. Note that believing Caleb was forty years old at Kadesh-barnea and was allowed to enter Canaan at the age of eighty-five (Josh. 14:6-15).

Verses 11-12 draw a practical conclusion: number your days and make your life count. Who really understands the power of God's anger? If we did understand it, we would not waste our lives as we do in useless endeavors. We must fear the Lord and honor Him, and use our brief lives for His glory. The fear of the Lord is the beginning of wisdom. Since we are frail, and we are sinners, we need a Savior; and the only Savior is Jesus Christ.

## III. God's Blessing and Man's Yearnings (90:13-17)

This final section contains a series of prayers that God will bless His people and crown their lives with glory. Man is not just an animal that lives and dies. He is made in the image of God, and he yearns to have his life accomplish something and mean something. Multitudes of people today are caught in a meaningless existence without purpose or challenge. How they need to yield to Jesus Christ and say with Paul, "For to me to live is Christ, and to die is gain" (Phil. 1:21).

Moses prays for God's favor (v. 13). Of course, God does not "repent" as man does, for God never sins. When God repents, He changes His dealings with His people. See Ex. 32:12 and Deut. 32:36. God had just judged Israel; now Moses prays that He will forgive Israel and restore them to the place of favor and blessing.

He prays for joy (vv. 14-15). Imagine facing forty years of constant wandering and death. Imagine having to bury hundreds of people day after day. How could there be any joy or gladness in such a situation? Only through the Lord. Verse 14 can carry the meaning, "Satisfy us in the morning with Your mercy." What were the Jews to do every morning? Go out early and gather the heavenly manna. See Ex. 16. Moses is saying, "Meet us each morning, Lord, as we awaken to the new day. Feed us on Your Word. Give us joy in Your presence." It is just as important for the NT Christian today to start the day with the Lord, reading the Word and praying. In v. 15 Moses asks for gladness in proportion to the sorrows they have tasted. As Christians, we have an even greater promise in 2 Cor. 4:16-18. "For our light affliction, which is but for a moment, is working for us a far more exceeding and eternal weight of glory" (v. 17, NKJV). See also Paul's statement in Rom. 8:18.

Moses prays for God's work to be done (v. 16). He longs to see God's power work on behalf of the people. Historically, of course, this referred to Israel's possession of the land of promise; see Moses' argument with God in Num. 14:13-19. It was certainly no glory to God while Israel wandered in the wilderness; however, it was to His glory when Israel crossed the Jordan and claimed her inheritance in power. Note that Moses in v. 16 is more concerned with God's glory than his own enjoyment.

He prays for God's blessing on man's work (v. 17). There is a wonderful connection between vv. 16 and 17: "Your work — the work of our hands"; "Your glory — the beauty of the Lord our God upon us." The word "beauty" means "God's grace and kindness." In Ps. 27:4, we behold the beauty of the Lord, but here we share the beauty of the Lord. "We shall be like Him, for we shall see Him as He is" (1 John 3:1-2). What does Moses mean when he prays about the work of our hands? Simply this: that our lives might not be wasted, but that God would guide us and bless us so that what we do will last for eternity. "He who does the will of God abides forever" (1 John 2:17). As Moses watches the Jews wander in the wilderness, their lives seem so wasted and useless. Being a man of God, he does not want his life to be wasted; he wants it to count for God's glory. Therefore, he prays that God would establish his works in and through His people. Jesus had the same idea in mind in the Parable of the Two Builders (Matt. 7:21-29).

Apart from Jesus Christ, life would be unbearable. Why endure the trials of life if there is no God and no glory? Then we would be like the sinners who say, "Let us eat and drink, for tomorrow we die" (1 Cor. 15:32). But life is not a burden, a sigh, a sleep in the night. With Jesus Christ in control, life is an adventure, a challenge, an investment for eternity. "Teach us to number our days, Lord, and help us to live every day for Jesus Christ with Your wisdom!"

# PSALM 119

This psalm is special in several ways. It is the longest psalm (176 verses), and it is an acrostic psalm, following the letters of the

Hebrew alphabet. In most editions of the Bible, the twenty-two sections of this psalm are headed by the successive letters of the Hebrew alphabet (Aleph, Beth, Gimel, etc.). In the Hebrew Bible, each verse in a section begins with that Hebrew letter. For example, all the verses in the "aleph" section (vv. 1-8) begin with the Hebrew letter "aleph." Look at the "teth" section (vv. 65-72) and start v. 67 with "Til" and v. 71 with "Tis," and you will have each line starting with the English letter "T" (which is the same as the Hebrew "teth"). The Jews wrote in this fashion to help them memorize the Scriptures so they could meditate on God's Word.

We do not know who wrote this psalm, although the writer refers to himself many times. He was suffering for his love for God's Law (vv. 22, 50-53, 95, 98, 115), yet he had determined to obey the Word regardless of the cost. All but five verses mention the Word of God in one way or another. The exceptions are vv. 84, 90, 121, 122, and 132. God is referred to in every verse. The number eight is stamped all over this psalm. Each section has eight verses; there are eight special names for God's Word listed; there are eight symbols of the Word given; the believer has eight responsibilities to the Word. The word "eight" in Hebrew literally means "abundance, more than enough"; it is the number of new beginnings. It is as though the writer is saying, "God's Word is enough. If you have the Scriptures, that is all you need for life and godliness." Indeed the Bible points us to Christ: He is the Living Word about whom the written Word speaks. In one sense, Ps. 119 is an expansion of Ps. 19:7-11. Note the eight basic titles of the Bible in the first nine verses of the psalm: law of the Lord, testimonies, ways, precepts, statutes, commandments, judgments, and word. These are repeated many times throughout the psalm.

## I. What the Bible Is

### A. Water for cleansing (v. 9).

This whole section (vv. 9-16) deals with victory over sin. Young people in particular need to learn to *heed* and *hide* the Word that they might overcome temptation. As you read the Word and meditate on it, it cleanses your inner being, just as water cleanses the body. See John 15:3 and Eph. 5:25-27.

### B. Wealth and treasure (vv. 14, 72, 127, 162).

Many people do not know the difference between prices and values. Your Bible may cost but a few dollars, but what a treasure it is. How would you feel if you lost God's Word and could not replace it?

### C. A companion and friend (v. 24).

The writer was a stranger (v. 19), rejected by the proud (v. 21) and by princes (v. 23), but he always had the Word to be his counselor. Read Prov. 6:20-22.

### D. A song to sing (v. 54).

Imagine making a song out of statutes—laws! Life is a pilgrimage; we are "tourists" and not residents. The songs of the world mean nothing to us, but God's Word is a song to our hearts.

### E. Honey (v. 103).

The sweetness of the Word is like honey to the taste. It is sad when the Christian must have the "honey" of this world to be satisfied. See Ps. 34:8 and Job 23:12.

### F. A lamp (vv. 105, 130).

This is a dark world and the only dependable light is the Word of God (2 Peter 1:19-21). It leads us a step at a time, as we walk in obedience. First John 1:5-10 tells us we walk in the light as we obey His Word.

### G. Great spoil (v. 162).

Poor soldiers were made rich from the spoil left by the defeated enemy. The riches of the Word do not come easy; there must first be that spiritual battle against Satan and the flesh. But it is worth it. Read Luke 11:14-23.

### H. A heritage (v. 111).

What a precious inheritance is the Bible! And think of those who had to suffer and die that we might have this inheritance.

## II. What the Bible Does

### A. It blesses (vv. 1-2).

It is the book with a blessing (Ps. 1:1-3). We are blessed in reading the Word, understanding the Word, and obeying the Word. We are also blessed when we share the Word with others.

454

## B. It gives life (vv. 25, 37, 40, 50, 88, 93).

"Quicken" means "to give life." The Word gives us eternal life when we believe (1 Peter 1:23). It is the living Word (Heb. 4:12). But the Word also quickens us when we are weak, discouraged, and defeated. Revival comes when we yield to God's Word.

## C. It gives strength (v. 28).

Trusting the Word encourages us (Matt. 4:4). God's Word has power (Heb. 4:12) and can empower us when we believe and obey.

## D. It gives liberty (v. 45).

A law that gives liberty—what a paradox! Sin would have dominion over us (v. 133), but the Word sets us free (John 8:32). True liberty comes in obeying God's will. His Word is "the perfect law of liberty" (James 1:25).

## E. It imparts wisdom (vv. 66, 97-104).

We may get knowledge and facts in other books, but true spiritual wisdom is found in the Bible. Note in vv. 97-104 that there are various ways to discover truth—from your enemies, from your teachers, from your older friends—and all of these are good. But above them all is a knowledge of the Bible. Teachers may know from books, and elders may know from experience (both deserving respect), but these without the Bible are not sufficient.

## F. It creates friends (v. 63).

Knowing and obeying the Bible will bring into your life the very finest friends. Those who love God's Word are friends indeed. There are false friends who may dazzle you with their worldly wisdom and wealth, but their friendship will lead you astray. Stick with those who "stick" with the Bible (v. 31).

## G. It gives comfort (vv. 50, 76, 82, 92).

More than sixty verses in this psalm mention trial and persecution (vv. 22, 50-53, 95, 98, 115, etc.). The believer who obeys the Word will have trials in this world, but the Bible gives him lasting comfort. The Comforter, the Spirit of God, takes the Word of God and applies it to our hearts to comfort us.

## H. It gives direction (v. 133).

The Christian life is a "walk," a day at a time and a step at a time

(vv. 1, 3, 45). The Word directs our steps, both for walking and for running (v. 32). Note the prayers in vv. 35 and 116-117. As we pray for guidance, the Lord answers through His Word.

## III. What We Must Do with the Bible

### A. *Love it (vv. 97, 159).*

The way you treat your Bible is the way you treat Christ. To love Him is to love His Word. The Word is a delight (vv. 16, 24, 16, 35, 47, 70) and not a disappointment; we rejoice to read it (vv. 14, 162).

### B. *Prize it (vv. 72, 128).*

To hold the Bible in high esteem is the mark of a true saint. It should be more precious to us than any earthly treasure.

### C. *Study it (vv. 7, 12, 18, 26-27).*

At least twelve times the psalmist prays, "Teach me." The Christian who *daily* studies his Bible will be blessed of God. Bible study is not always easy, for it takes the "whole heart" (vv. 2, 10, 34, 69, 145).

### D. *Memorize it (v. 11).*

"The best Book, in the best place, for the best purpose!" is the way Campbell Morgan explained this verse. All ages need to memorize the Word, not children and young people alone. Joshua was not a youth when God commanded him to memorize the Law (Josh. 1:8). Jesus was able to quote Scripture when He faced Satan in the wilderness (Matt. 4:1-11).

### E. *Meditate on it (vv. 15, 23, 48, 78, 97, 99, 148).*

Meditation is to the soul what digestion is to the body. To meditate means to "turn over" God's Word in the mind and heart, to examine it, to compare Scripture with Scripture, to "feed on" its wonderful truths. In this day of noise and confusion, such meditation is rare but so needful. Meditation is impossible without memorization.

### F. *Trust it (v. 42).*

We trust the Bible about everything, because it is right about everything (v. 128). It is true and can be trusted wholly. To argue with the Bible is to argue with God. We test every other book by what God says in His Word.

### G. Obey it (vv. 1-8).

To keep the Word is to obey it, to walk in its commandments. Satan knows the Word, but he cannot obey it. If we know God's truth and fail to obey it, we are only fooling ourselves.

### H. Declare it (vv. 13, 26).

As we obey, we should also witness to others about the Word and tell them what the Lord has done for us.

# PROVERBS

## *A Suggested Outline of Proverbs*

Introduction (1:1-19)

I. Wisdom's Calls and Folly's Calls (1:20–9:18)

    A. Wisdom's first call—to salvation (1:20-33)

    B. Wisdom's Path—righteousness and safety (2–4)

    C. Folly's first call—condemnation (5)

    D. Folly's second call—poverty (6)

    E. Folly's third call—death (7)

    F. Wisdom's second call—to wealth (8)

    G. Wisdom's third call—to life (9)

II. Wisdom's Contrasts (10–15)

    A series of proverbs contrasting wisdom and folly

III. Wisdom's Counsels (16–31)

    A series of proverbs on practical matters

# Introductory Notes to Proverbs

## I. Title

Our English word "proverb" is made up of two Latin words: *pro* (instead of) and *verba* (words). So, a proverb is a sentence that is given "instead of many words"; it is a short statement that summarizes a wise principle. The Hebrew word translated "proverb" means "a comparison." As we shall see, many of the proverbs of Solomon are comparisons and contrasts. Like most Oriental peoples, the Jews did much teaching through proverbs. These short, "catchy" sentences were easy to remember, and they condensed much wisdom in a small space.

## II. Author

In Prov. 1:1, 10:1, and 25:1, we are told that Solomon wrote most of the proverbs in this book. First Kings 4:32 informs us that Solomon spoke 3,000 proverbs, and these were undoubtedly recorded in the official records. The men of Hezekiah (a group of writers in King Hezekiah's employ who assisted in copying out the Scriptures) copied out the material in Prov. 25–29 (see 25:1), while King Solomon himself wrote or dictated Prov. 1–24. In Prov. 30–31 we have material from other writers, although many believe that "King Lemuel" in 31:1 was really Solomon. Solomon was certainly known for his wisdom, even though later in his life he turned to idolatry and folly.

## III. Theme

The key word is wisdom. We commonly think of wisdom as the ability to use knowledge in the right way, and this is a practical definition. But, in the Bible, wisdom means so much more. True wisdom is a matter of the heart and not the mind alone. It is a spiritual matter. There is a "wisdom of this world" (1 Cor. 2:1-8; James 3:13-18), and there is a divine wisdom from above. In Proverbs, wisdom is actually pictured as a lovely woman who calls people to follow her into a life of blessing and success. Folly is pictured as a wicked woman who tempts the foolish and leads them to hell. Of course, Jesus Christ is the Wisdom of God to the believer (1 Cor. 1:24, 30; Col. 2:3). When you read Solomon's description of wisdom in Prov. 8:22-31, you cannot help but see Jesus Christ. Wisdom is described as eternal (vv. 22-26), the creator of all things (vv. 27-29), and the beloved of God (vv. 30-31). Immediately you think of John 1:1-2 and Col. 1:15-19. To yield your life to Christ and obey Him is true wisdom.

## IV. The Fool

Proverbs often mentions three classes of people who desperately need wisdom: the fool, the simple, and the scorner (see 1:22). The fool is the person who is dense, sluggish, careless, and self-satisfied. Nabal in 1 Sam. 25 is a good example; the name "Nabal" means "fool." The fool hates instruction (1:7, 22) and is self-confident (12:15). He talks without thinking (29:11) and mocks at sin (14:9). The simple are those who believe everything and everybody (14:15) and lack discernment. They are easily led astray by others because they lack understanding (7:7). They cannot see ahead (22:3) and, as a result, repeatedly walk into trouble. Scorners mock at God's wisdom because it is too high for them (14:6), but they will not admit it because they know everything (21:24). The Hebrew word for "scorner" literally means "to make a mouth"; and we can easily picture them sneering and curling up their lips in scorn. They never profit from rebuke (9:7-8; 13:1) and, as a result, they will one day be judged (19:29).

## V. The Wise

Proverbs outlines for us the character of the wise: they listen to instruction (1:5); obey what they hear (10:8); store up what they learn (10:14); win others to the Lord (11:30); flee from sin (14:16); watch their tongue (16:23); and are diligent in their daily work (10:5).

## VI. Value

Proverbs is valuable to us as a guidebook for practical wisdom in everyday life. It teaches us about such things as the tongue, money matters, friendship, the home, and business contracts. It would be well for believers (especially young people) to read one chapter of Proverbs a day, and thus read the entire book through each month. The NT quotes Proverbs in: Rom. 3:15 (Prov. 1:16); Heb. 12:5-6 and Rev. 3:19 (Prov. 3:11-12); James 4:6 and 1 Peter 5:5 (Prov. 3:34); Rom. 12:20 (Prov. 25:21-22); and 2 Peter 2:22 (Prov. 26:11).

## VII. Interpretation

Proverbs are generalizations about life and not promises for us to claim, although there are some great promises found in the Book of Proverbs. The basic requirement for understanding and applying these proverbs is the fear of the Lord (1:7) and a willingness to obey (3:5-6; see John 7:17). The aim of the book is to give the godly person skill in human relationships and endeavors. This begins with submission to the Lord. It is dangerous to lay hold of one or two statements in Proverbs but ignore the total message of the book. Also, though we can find examples of exceptions to some of the proverbs, this does not minimize the lesson they contain. Not all godly people live long lives (3:1-2) or become wealthy (3:10). In some parts of the world, believers are dying from famine and poverty. But generally speaking, those who obey God do not ruin their bodies or waste their substance. The Book of Proverbs summons us to understand and apply all of God's revealed wisdom for all of life.

# PROVERBS 1–9

In this lesson we want to consider Wisdom and Folly, the two "women" who are out to woo and win the hearts of people. You will note in the suggested outline of Proverbs that there are three calls from Wisdom and three from Folly. Wisdom calls us to God and life; Folly calls us to sin and judgment. We want to study these six important invitations and contrast them.

## I. Wisdom's First Call—Salvation (1:20-33)

This is an open call out in the streets where people can see and hear. God's call to hearts is not a secret matter; His Spirit invites people openly to come to Christ. Note that Wisdom invites all three classes: the simple, the scorner, and the fool (1:22). Wisdom can see judgment coming and she wants sinners to escape it. What a wonderful offer she makes to those who will hear: the gift of the Spirit of God and the Word of God (v. 23).

How do sinners respond to this call? It seems that they totally reject it. Verses 24-25 indicate their responses: they refused to heed; they did not regard God's outstretched hand; they even made light of it. What will the result be? Destruction. And God will laugh at them just as they laughed at Wisdom. "Then shall they call upon me, but I will not answer" (v. 28). They will reap just what they have sown (v. 31). Why did they refuse God's gracious offer? Verse 32 indicates that the "ease" (turning away) of the simple and the prosperity of the fools gave them a false assurance; they thought they would never see judgment.

Following Wisdom's first call we have three chapters that present the path of wisdom. The words "path" and "way" are each used thirteen times in these chapters. The message of chapter 2 is that Wisdom *protects* our paths (2:8), of chapter 3 that Wisdom *directs* our paths (3:5-6), and of chapter 4 that Wisdom *perfects* our paths (4:18).

Wisdom offers people salvation, but in chapter 5 we see Folly offering them condemnation. Wherever God gives His gracious invitation, Satan is there with an alluring offer of his own. Read this description of the wicked woman and see how Satan tries to make sin appear attractive. But note 5:5—"Her feet go down to death; her steps take hold on hell." God warns us not even to come near her door (5:7-8). Sin is always a costly thing: you can lose your reputation (5:9), your possessions (5:10), your health (5:11), and your very life (5:22-23). The "cords of sins" bind slowly, but they bind surely, until one day the sinner discovers escape is impossible.

## II. Wisdom's Second Call—Wealth (8)

Wisdom is back in the streets again, calling sinners to follow God's path. In v. 5 she calls the simple and the fools, but not the scorner. He was the one who laughed and mocked (1:25-26), so God now passes him by. How solemn to think that hearts can be so hard that they no longer hear the voice of God.

The invitation is to true wealth, the wisdom that is far above silver, gold, and precious jewels (vv. 10-11). See Prov. 4:1-10 for a similar exhortation. In fact, to know God's wisdom is to reign like a king (vv. 15-16). Verses 18-19 affirm again that wisdom and godly living are greater in value than all worldly wealth. After all, to know the Lord and obey Him is to have all the wealth of heaven and earth at your disposal. In vv. 22-31, Solomon introduces an OT picture of Jesus Christ, the Wisdom of God (1 Cor. 1:24, 30). As you read this description, you see Christ, the beloved Son of God, the Creator of the universe. To know Him is to have true wisdom. (Of course, Christ was not "brought forth" [vv. 24-25] in the sense of being created by the Father, since the Son existed from all eternity. This is symbolic language.)

Wisdom invites us to wealth, but in chapter 6, Folly invites us to poverty (6:20-35). Here is the "strange woman" again, all painted up, flattering the young man, tempting him to sin. In 6:26, we see that sin leads to poverty; see also 6:31. True, many ungodly people today seem prosperous, but their wealth will not last.

## III. Wisdom's Third Call—Life (9)

Wisdom's first invitation was to the fool, the scorner, and the simple; her second invitation was only to the fool and the simple (8:5); but her third invitation is only to the simple (9:4). The fool decided to follow Folly, and in 8:36 he experienced death (see 1:22). Alas, the simple too will reject Wisdom's gracious call and end up in the depths of hell (9:1-18). Here are the results of these invitations:

(1) The scorner rejected Wisdom and met destruction (1:24-27); he listened to Folly and received destruction (6:32)

(2) The fool rejected Wisdom and was led to death (8:36); he

listened to Folly and received death (5:22-23)

(3) The simple rejected Wisdom and went to hell (9:18); he listened to Folly and ended up in hell (7:27)

The lesson is obvious: to reject Wisdom is to accept Folly. There is no middle ground. "He that is not with Me is against Me," said Jesus. "No man can serve two masters," and nobody can live without having some master. We either follow Wisdom or Folly, Christ or sin.

Verses 1-6 picture Wisdom preparing a wonderful banquet. This reminds us of the several "banquet" parables of Christ, especially Luke 14:15-24. Salvation is not a funeral; it is a feast. "Forsake the foolish, *and live*," Wisdom calls, for receiving Christ is the only way to receive life (1 John 5:11-13). "By me your days will be multiplied," Wisdom promises in v. 11 (NKJV).

But Folly is busy inviting people to her banquet (chap. 7). It takes little imagination to see the foolish young man as he toys with temptation and finally listens to Folly and goes to her feast. But he goes like an ox to the slaughter (7:22). When you yield to this particular temptation, you become like a dumb animal. Wisdom is offering life, but Folly offers death (7:26-27). Temptation looks fascinating and enjoyable, and there are pleasures in sin "for a season" (Heb. 11:25), but in the end, sin leads to death and hell. See James 1:13-15.

These, then, are the invitations we face in this life. We can listen to Wisdom and enjoy salvation, true wealth, and life; or we can listen to Folly (temptation and sin) and experience condemnation, poverty, and death. There are several practical lessons that we ought to note before closing this study.

### A. We cannot avoid decisions.

"Decision determines destiny." We choose either the path of Wisdom or the path of Folly; we cannot postpone this decision or avoid it. To choose one is to reject the other; to reject one is to choose the other. What decision have *you* made?

### B. Sin is always alluring.

Folly does everything she can to make sin attractive. She never reveals her true nature; she never tells people that her house is the way to hell. The only way to detect Folly is to walk with Wisdom; read Prov. 2:10-22 carefully. Those who walk with Wisdom, obeying the Word of God, will not easily be tricked by Folly.

## C. It takes time for judgment to fall.

The simple, the fool, and the scorner all thought they "had it made" when they rejected Wisdom, because nothing disastrous immediately happened. But judgment eventually caught up with them. "Whatever a man sows, that he will also reap" (Gal. 6:7, NKJV).

## D. Satan appeals to the flesh.

It is clear in these chapters that the "wicked woman" (or "strange woman") is appealing to the young man's appetites. She tells him he can use his body as he pleases and not suffer for it. But Prov. 5:1-14 makes it clear that sexual sin leads to tragic results, both in body and soul. In these days of flagrant immorality (in movies, TV, music, advertising, etc.), it is important that young and old people keep their hearts and minds pure.

## E. God continues to call.

So long as people will hear, God's Spirit continues to call. But when sinners refuse to obey, their ears become deaf to the Word of God. Beware! "Today, if you will hear His voice, do not harden your hearts" (Heb. 3:7ff, NKJV).

# PROVERBS 2–4

When you know Jesus Christ, you know true wisdom (1 Cor. 1:24, 30), and through His Word, you receive wisdom for daily living. In these three chapters, Solomon is urging the young man ("My son" is repeated five times) to lay hold of divine wisdom because of the blessings it will bring to his life. Of course, these instructions apply to anyone who will hear and obey.

## I. Wisdom Protects Our Paths (2)

The key idea here is that of God's protection over His own (vv. 7-8, 11-12, 16). The path of life is not an easy one, and the older we get, the more dangers we face. The world, the flesh, and the Devil are out to defeat us, and we need the wisdom of God to keep us out of their power. Sinners are out to entice the young (Prov. 1:10-19), and too often their temptations are so alluring they are difficult to resist. But the Christian who knows the Bible and seeks to obey it will be kept safe from their power.

### A. God's commands to His own (vv. 1-9).

Note what we are to do with God's Word: receive it, hide it in the heart, incline the heart toward it, apply it to our lives, cry out to God for wisdom, and search the Word to find God's will. Solomon is not talking about simply "reading a chapter a day" and letting it go at that. He insists that we live in the Word of God and allow the Word to live in us. Verse 4 compares Bible study to the mining of precious metal. The truths of the Word must be "dug out" and put through the furnace of personal experience. They must be "minted" into spiritual coins that we can keep in our treasury for future use (Matt. 13:52). Furthermore, this wisdom will become a shield to our lives (v. 7) so that God can protect our paths. When Christians deliberately turn from the wisdom of God found in the Bible, they are putting themselves (and others) in danger.

### B. God's care for His own (vv. 10-22).

Solomon sees two great dangers in the world: the evil man (vv. 10-15) and the strange woman (vv. 16-22). The evil man is known for his "big talk" (v. 12). He always has some scheme for the young man to consider. But he is walking in the paths of darkness and being controlled by the Prince of Darkness, Satan. Instead of walking on a straight path, the evil man walks on a crooked path; you simply cannot trace him. The evil man wants you to believe that there are "shortcuts" to wealth and success, and that you can profit by disobeying the Lord.

The "strange woman" uses flattery and appeals to the appetites of the flesh. She has forsaken her own husband and broken her marriage vows (v. 17). She leads the foolish young man to death and hell. How believers today (especially young men and women) need the wisdom of God from the Word to protect their paths!

## II. Wisdom Directs Our Paths (3)

Proverbs 3:5-6 are precious promises to Christians who want to know and do God's will in every area of life. God wants us to know and do His will; He is eager to reveal His will to us (Eph. 5:8-10; John 7:17). There are certain conditions that we must meet before God can direct our paths.

### A. Listen to the Word (vv. 1-4).

God's will is found in God's Word (Col. 1:9-10). It is not only the mind, but also the heart that should remember and consider the Word. We must ask the Spirit to write the Bible on our hearts (2 Cor. 3:1-3). We must receive the Word every opportunity we have—in class, in church services, through reading. The better you know your Bible, the better you will know God's will for your life.

### B. Obey the Word (vv. 5-10).

If we really trust God, we will obey Him. We may think that our own wisdom is sufficient, but it is not; we need the wisdom of God. Verse 5 does not teach that Christians should fail to think and consider facts when making decisions, because God expects us to use our brains. Rather, it means that we should not *trust* our own ideas or wisdom; we must ask God to direct us (James 1:5). A willingness to obey is the first step toward knowing God's will (John 7:17). Note that faithful giving is a part of obeying.

### C. Submit to the Word (vv. 11-12).

Sometimes God has to chasten us to bring us into His perfect will; see Heb. 12:5-11. If we submit, God will turn it into blessing.

### D. Treasure the Word (vv. 13-26).

Matthew 6:33 summarizes this perfectly. Put Christ first. Solomon lists in vv. 21-26 the blessings that come to believers who let the Word direct their paths. Note how every part of the body should be controlled by the Word (Rom. 12:1-2).

## III. Wisdom Perfects Our Paths (4)

In vv. 14-19, there is a contrast between the path of the wicked and the path of the righteous. The path of the wicked is darkness, and it keeps getting darker; but the path of the just is light, and it keeps getting brighter. Salvation begins with the "dawning" in our hearts ("Dayspring" in Luke 1:77-79). As we walk with the Lord, the light gets brighter, until one day we shall step into God's eternal light, in a land where there is no night.

God wants to perfect the path of the believer. He has a plan for each life, and He wants to bring that plan to completion (Eph. 2:10; Phil. 2:12-13; 1:6). Solomon gives us several instructions to follow if God is to perfect our paths:

### A. Seek after wisdom (vv. 1-13).

Solomon seems to be saying, "I recall when I was a young man and

468

my father tried to teach me the right way. Now that I'm older and a father myself, I know that he was right." It is not enough merely to *get* wisdom; we must also *keep* it and not allow it to slip away. "Take fast hold of instruction." Get your hands on it. Verse 12 promises that the path of the wise person will not be "straitened" ("hindered"). The believer who obeys the Bible will avoid the pitfalls and obstacles that others encounter on their detours away from the will of God.

### B. Avoid temptation and sin (vv. 14-19).

Here Solomon is teaching separation from sin and evil. We as Christians cannot be isolated from the world, because we must live with people and seek to win them to Christ, but we must not be infected by their sins or led into their ways. The old illustration is still good: it is fine for the boat to be in the water, but not for the water to be in the boat. The Christian must be in the world, but the world must not get into the heart of the Christian. There are wicked people in this world just waiting to take advantage of foolish young people who ignore the warnings of the Bible.

### C. Guard your life (vv. 20-27).

Verse 23 reads, "Guard your heart above anything else you have, because it determines the kind of life you will live." The heart is the "master-control" of the life; a wrong heart always produces a wrong life. To allow sin into the heart is to pollute the entire life. Solomon also warns us to *guard our lips* (v. 24) because they can get us into sin. The heart controls the tongue (Luke 6:45), so a guarded heart should result in guarded lips. A "froward" mouth is a proud mouth, a mouth that speaks scornfully and arrogantly. A Christian's words must always be spoken in love (Eph. 4:15, 31), seasoned with salt (Col. 4:6). We must *guard our eyes* (v. 25) to be sure that we are keeping them on Jesus Christ and the goal He has for us (Heb. 12:1-2; Phil. 3:12-16). Eve permitted her eyes to wander and it led to sin (Gen. 3:6), and John warns about the "lust of the eyes" (1 John 2:15-17). Samson did not "look straight before" himself, but looked at the polluted honey in the carcass of the lion, and this led him into defilement and disobedience (Jud. 14:8ff). Finally, Solomon urges us to *ponder our path* (v. 26), to examine our lives, to see where we are going. "The unexamined life is not worth living," said Socrates. The Lord is pondering (examining) our lives (5:21), and we must examine them too.

Live in God's Word and He will protect your path, direct your path, and perfect your path, for the glory of Jesus Christ.

# PROVERBS 12, 18

There are many references to *the tongue* in Proverbs. We have suggested reading chapters 12 and 18 because they mention the tongue frequently, but you will want to follow the cross references and examine other verses as well. We so often take the wonderful gift of speech for granted and abuse an ability that ought to be guarded and used to the glory of God.

Before we consider some of the sins of the tongue, we ought to note the blessings of a godly tongue. (This demands a godly heart, because the tongue only speaks what the heart treasures.) When used for good, the tongue is like valuable silver (10:20); a beautiful and fruitful tree of life (15:4; see 12:14 and 18:20); a refreshing well of water (18:4; 10:11); and a healthy dose of medicine (12:18). See also James 3.

The tongue should be used for right purposes: bringing peace (15:1, 26); giving wise reproof to the erring (25:12; 28:23); delivering lost souls from death (11:9; 14:3-5, 25; 12:6); teaching people the things of the Lord (15:7; 16:21, 23; 20:15); and carrying the good news of the Gospel (25:25).

But Satan and the flesh want to control the tongue, and the results are sad. Perhaps more damage is done to lives, homes, and churches by the tongue than by any other means. It is sobering to realize that the tongue can be used to damage reputations and cause trouble, when it ought to be used to praise God, pray, and witness to others about Christ. The tongue is a "little member" of the body (James 3:5), but it is one member that must be yielded to God as a tool of righteousness (Rom. 6:12-13). Perhaps if we consider some of the sins of the tongue, it might encourage us to use our gift of speech more carefully.

## I. Lying (12:17-22)

God hates a lying tongue (6:16-17). Sometimes a lying tongue is only covering up sin in the heart (10:18), such as we see in Ananias and Sapphira (Acts 5) and Judas (John 12:1-8). In 12:18, Solomon suggests that lies are like cutting swords, but the truth is like a healing medicine. The truth is eternal, but lies will one day be revealed and the liars judged (v. 19). See Ps. 52:4-5. Verse 20 explains that it is deceit in the heart that makes a statement a lie. After all, the lips can utter true words, but if the intent of the heart is evil, the statement is false. Likewise, if we ignorantly speak an untrue statement, the statement may be a lie, but the speaker cannot be condemned as a liar. The Bible tests and reveals the intents of the heart (Heb. 4:12), so the best way to be sure of telling the truth is to allow the Word and the Spirit to control the tongue. The truth will deliver souls (14:25), but lies only lead to bondage and shame. Proverbs 17:4 indicates that liars enjoy listening to liars. People who enjoy listening to gossip will turn around and gossip themselves. The heart controls the ear as well as the lips. But all liars will be punished (19:5, 9); and when they "eat their own words," it will be like gravel (20:17). Hell is waiting for the one who "loves and practices a lie" (Rev. 22:15, NKJV).

## II. Talebearing (18:8)

Moses warned about this sin in Lev. 19:16. A "talebearer" is one who runs from person to person telling matters that ought to be concealed, whether they are true or false. See 11:13. "Love covers all sins," says 10:12. See also 17:9, 1 Peter 4:8, and James 5:20. When we love others, we seek to help them privately, and we try to win them back to the right way (Matt. 18:15-18). Think how many people have been wounded by the talebearer. Words can be as deadly as weapons; in 25:18 Solomon compares deceitful words to three different weapons: a maul (battle-ax) that crushes at close range; a sword that cuts; and an arrow that pierces and can be shot from a distance. Stay away from the talebearer (20:19). He or she is a kindler of fires (26:20) and a destroyer of friendships (17:9).

## III. Talking Too Much (12:13; 18:6-7)

The idea behind these verses is that the fool talks too much and talks his way right into trouble. His mouth becomes a trap, and he himself is snared by it. Read 6:1-5 to see how this sin gets people into trouble. "In the multitude of words sin is not lacking," warns 10:19 (NKJV). A controlled tongue means a safe life (13:3); a loose tongue means poverty (14:23 — many people would rather talk than work) and foolishness (15:2). The person of few words is a person of knowledge (17:27-28). Unfortunately, there is sometimes a "multitude of words" even in God's house, and Ecc. 5:1-7 has some good counsel about this.

## IV. Talking Too Soon (18:13, 17)

"Let every man be swift to hear, slow to speak," commands James 1:19. Too often we are slow to hear—we never really listen to the whole matter patiently—and swift to speak; and this gets us into trouble. It is wise to "restrain the lips" until you really have something to say (10:19). A godly person will study to answer, but a fool will open his mouth and pour out foolishness (15:28). Potiphar did not listen to Joseph's side of the story and committed a great crime because of it. Jesus and the Apostles were not permitted to tell their whole story; the verdicts were passed by their enemies before the cases were honestly tried. God wants us to search out each matter carefully (25:2) and then give fair judgment. Proverbs 18:17 warns us not to agree with the "first cause" that we hear but to seek to understand both sides of a matter. Even where dedicated Christians are involved, there are two sides to a story. This is not because people necessarily lie, but simply because no two people see and hear the same matter in the same way. David jumped to conclusions about innocent Mephibosheth because he failed to get the other side of the matter (2 Sam. 16:1-4; 19:24-30). All of us need to pray, "Set a watch, O Lord, before my mouth; keep the door of my lips" (Ps. 141:3). See Ps. 39:1.

## V. Flattering (26:28)

Flattery, of course, is a form of lying, but it is so dangerous that it deserves separate attention. "A flattering mouth works ruin," warns 26:28 (NKJV); and 29:5 compares flattery to a dangerous net spread before an innocent man's feet. For an X ray of the flatterer's mouth read Ps. 5:9. Flattery is insincere praise given by one who has selfish motives. "Flatter" and "flutter" belong to the same family of words, and you can just see the flatterer as he "flutters" around his victim, trying to impress him. Satan used a form of flattery to tempt Eve: "You will be like God." The evil woman uses flattery to tempt the young man (5:3; 7:5, 21). "The rich has many friends" mainly because they want to flatter him and get something out of him (14:20; 19:4-6). We are warned not to meddle with people given to flattery (20:19). Sad to say, sometimes the righteous will flatter the wicked in order to get advantages (25:26); and this will pollute a home, a church, or a nation like a poisoned spring. Honest rebuke is better than flattery (28:23). "Faithful are the wounds of a friend," says 27:6, "but the kisses of an enemy (like Judas) are deceitful."

Of course, there is a place for honest praise in the Christian life; see 1 Thes. 5:12-13. Honest praise is like a furnace (Prov. 27:21); it brings to the top either the pure gold or the dross. Some Christians are so carnal they cannot take praise; it goes to their heads. Worse still, they cannot stand to see another person praised. When the Jews praised David for his victories, this praise made David humble, but it revealed the envy and pride in Saul's heart (1 Sam. 18).

## VI. Quarreling (12:16, 18)

There is a righteous anger (Eph. 4:26), but too often it becomes unrighteous anger and leads to arguing and displays of temper. See 29:22. An angry person keeps adding fuel to the fire only to make the matter worse (26:21), and angry words are the fuel. The best way to stop an argument is with soft words (15:1-2); this is the best way to "break the bones" (25:15). Being able to control one's temper is the same as ruling an army or an empire (16:32). See also 14:17, 29, and 17:14.

# PROVERBS 23

Our emphasis will be on vv. 15-35 in which the godly father warns his son against the sin of drunkenness. We will also study other Scripture passages to show that the Bible magnifies total abstinence. There are millions of alcoholics in the United States and millions more "problem drinkers." At least 70 percent of the problem drinkers started when they were in their teens. No wonder brewers and distillers focus a large part of their annual advertising budget on winning the young people.

## I. The Bible Warns against Strong Drink

The concerned father tells his son what evil results will take place in his life if he takes to drink:

### A. Poverty (vv. 20-21; 21:17).

The liquor ads often show a "man of distinction" and give the impression that drinking goes along with success and fortune. Yet drinking and poverty have always gone together. Americans spend billions of dollars a year on alcohol, much of it money that ought to purchase clothing, food, and education for the drinkers' families. Alcoholics lose many days from work every year, costing industry millions of dollars in man hours, all of which help to raise prices for the consumer, drinker or nondrinker.

### B. Misery (vv. 29-32).

Alcohol is a great deceiver (see 20:1); it promises joy, but brings sorrow; it pretends to bring life, but really produces death. It has never made a home happier or a person healthier. Look at the results: woe, sorrow, contentions (this means "arguments, brawls"), babbling, wounds, redness of the eyes. Over 55 percent of fatal auto accidents involve drinking drivers. Anyone who thinks that drinking makes a person successful ought to visit a city rescue mission or listen to the testimonies at a local Alcoholics Anonymous meeting. Alcoholism is the #3 health problem in the United States, after heart disease and cancer.

### C. Immorality (vv. 26-28, 33).

Many a woman has lost her virtue and character because of drink; and many a man has done likewise. Drinking and disobeying the seventh commandment often go together. Alcohol is *not* a stimulant; it is a narcotic that affects the brain and makes a person lose control. Alcohol is *not* a food; it is a poison. When young people lose control of themselves, there are many temptations that prove alluring and lead to sin.

### D. Instability (vv. 34-35).

What a vivid picture of a staggering drunk! (And there is nothing comical about a drunk, no matter what the entertainers may do on TV.) Drink robs a person of stability; he or she can't walk straight or think straight. This is why the king is warned not to drink (Prov. 31:4-5).

### E. Eternity in hell (1 Cor. 6:9-10).

Drunkards go to hell. Of course, drunkards can be saved; see v. 11. But once alcohol gets ahold of a person, conversion to Christ can become very difficult. The drunkard may intend to trust Christ someday, but his or her life may be taken before that day comes.

## II. The Bible Magnifies Total Abstinence

Keep in mind that the word "wine" in your Bible can refer to many different drinks, including simple grape juice. "New wine" was grape juice that had not yet fermented; see Matt. 9:14-17. The Jews sometimes mixed their wine with spices or other fruit beverages (Isa. 5:22; 24:9). Wine and strong drink are often mentioned separately (Deut. 14:26; Prov. 20:1). Note how the Bible magnifies total abstinence by giving many examples:

(1) Israel in the wilderness did not drink wine (Deut. 29:6). Wine was not used in the Passover (Ex. 12:8-10), for fermented wine contained leaven, and leaven was prohibited. Wine was added to the ceremony later; it was not commanded by God.

(2) The priests had to abstain when serving in the temple (Lev. 10:8-10). As NT priests (1 Peter 2:5, 9), should today's Christians have a lower standard as we serve the Lord daily?

(3) Nazarites were forbidden to drink wine (Num. 6:1-3). John the Baptist was such a person (Luke 1:15), and Jesus called him the greatest preacher born of woman.

(4) Daniel refused to "follow the crowd" (Dan. 1:5, 8, 16, and 10:3), and God honored and promoted him. Contrast this with drunken Belshazzar in Dan. 5, and Herod in Mark 6:21ff.

(5) Paul warned Christians to do nothing that would cause their brother to stumble (Rom. 14:19-21). See 1 Cor. 8:13 also. The "social drinkers" who belong to our churches are supporting a wicked industry just as much as the skid-row drunks, because they are influencing others to drink. In fact, a "moral church-going drinker" is a better advertisement than is the drunk in the gutter. Paul contrasts being filled with the Spirit to being drunk (Eph. 5:18), and in Gal. 5:21 he lists drunkenness as one of the sinful works of the flesh. First Timothy 5:23 refers to a medicinal use for grape juice in a day when doctors did not have modern medicines. To say that we have the right to use alcohol because it is used in some medicines is as reasonable as saying we can use morphine or some other narcotic because the dentist or the surgeon uses it on his patients.

(6) Peter warns Christians to "abstain from fleshly lusts which war against the soul" (1 Peter 2:11); and since drunkenness is such

a fleshly lust (Gal. 5:21), total abstinence is the best way to obey this admonition. How does one begin a drunkard's life? By taking the first drink.

(7) The OT prophets thundered out against strong drink. Habakkuk 2:15 pronounces a curse on those who give a drink to their neighbor; see Isa. 5:11-22. Amos condemned the idle Jews who had to drink their wine out of bowls because their cups were too small (6:3-6).

(8) Jesus Christ is our greatest example. "But didn't Jesus turn water into wine?" Yes, He did; any person who can do the same thing today ought to be allowed to drink the wine. At the end of His ministry, Jesus said, "I will not drink henceforth of this fruit of the vine" (Matt. 26:29). Today, Jesus is a total abstainer! He refused the cup at the cross (Mark 15:23). Those who want to make Christ their "example" in drinking usually point to verses such as Matt. 11:18-19 and forget Matt. 26:29. What about the Lord's Supper? Nowhere in the Bible is the word "wine" associated with the Lord's Supper; it is either "the cup" or "the fruit of the vine" (Matt. 26:27-29).

The Japanese have a proverb: "First the man takes a drink; then the drink takes a drink; then the drink takes the man." What is the right course to take? Refuse the first drink and keep refusing it for the rest of your life.

# PROVERBS 25

We must notice from the start that there is a righteous anger against sin that itself is not sinful. Verse 23 teaches that an angry look will silence a gossip. Jesus "looked round about on them with anger" (Mark 3:5), and Paul advises us to "be angry, and do not sin" (Eph. 4:26). Of course, we should be angry at *sin* and not at people. Proverbs 27:4 warns us that anger is cruel and outrageous; it can lead to physical hurt and even murder (Matt. 5:22). Angry parents can permanently wound the body and emotions of a child. Sinful anger is of the flesh (Gal. 5:19-21) and does not accomplish God's will (James 1:19-20). Satan can work through our angry words and attitudes (Eph. 4:26-27), so God warns us to "put off anger" (Eph. 4:31; Col. 3:8). An angry person is a dangerous friend (Prov. 22:24; 29:22), and an angry woman makes a poor wife (Prov. 21:9, 19; 25:24).

In this chapter we are given the instructions for dealing with anger in our lives and in the lives of others.

## I. Patience (25:8)

The minute we hear something that disturbs us, how easy it is to become angry and to rush into the matter without thinking or praying. The wise thing to do is to think the matter through and wait upon God. This does not mean we look for an excuse to pass over some sin, even though love does cover a multitude of sins (Prov. 10:12; 12:16). Rather, it means we act prudently, knowing first what is involved. It is a wonderful gift of God to be "slow to anger" (Prov. 15:18); the person who is quick to get angry will deal foolishly (Prov. 14:17). "Cease from anger, and forsake wrath; do not fret—it only causes harm," counsels Ps. 37:8 (NKJV). So, before rushing into a matter, stop to pray and to think. Take time to read God's Word and to allow the Spirit of God to give you inward peace.

## II. Privacy (25:9-10)

Our first desire is to "tell the whole world" and get everybody on our side. But the Bible counsels just the opposite: talk to the person alone and do not allow others to interfere. This is what Jesus commanded in Matt. 18:15-17, and if this policy were followed in families and churches, there would be fewer fights and splits. It is sad when professing Christians tell everybody but the one involved. Certainly, it takes courage and Christian love to talk over a difference with a brother or sister, but this is the way to grow spiritually and to glorify Christ. Perhaps the matter cannot be settled by you two; then ask two or three spiritual people to assist you. If this fails, then the church must step in, and if the party refuses to hear the church, he or she must be disciplined. "As much as depends on you, live peaceably with all men," says Rom. 12:18 (NKJV). Unfortunately, there may be some people we cannot live with peaceably because they will not obey God's Word.

## III. Wisdom (25:11-14)

Words are not just sounds that we hear; they are living, powerful realities that can either help or harm. In Prov. 25:18 Solomon compares lies to three weapons—a battle-ax, a sword, and an arrow.

But in vv. 11-14, he states that words can also be lovely fruit ("apples of gold" are citrons or oranges), beautiful ornaments, and refreshing cold water from the mountain snows. In dealing with a matter, we must use the right words and present them in the right way. Our words must be "fitly spoken," arranged like lovely fruit in a silver basket. See Job 6:25. Proverbs 19:11 states that discretion (prudence) will cause people to hold their anger. Only a fool utters all his mind (Prov. 29:11); wise people ponder what they will say, how they will say it, and when they will say it; see Prov. 15:23. Of course, this spiritual wisdom must come from God (James 1:5).

## IV. Gentleness (25:15)

What a contradiction: "a gentle tongue breaks a bone." This parallels Prov. 15:1 (NKJV), "A soft answer turns away wrath, but a harsh word stirs up anger." Our first reaction to someone's meanness is to be mean in return, but this only adds fuel to the fire (see 26:20-21). See also James 3:5. We are commanded not to return evil for evil (Rom. 12:21), and not to revile others who revile us (1 Peter 2:20-23). If we are seeking to restore a sinning believer, we need a spirit of meekness (Gal. 6:1) and not an attitude of anger. This is the way Paul ministered to his converts (1 Thes. 2:7), and this is what he commands believers to do (2 Tim. 2:24). Elijah had to learn that God sometimes uses the "still small voice" and not the tornado (read 1 Kings 19:11-13). Many have the idea that gentleness is weakness, but it is not: it is power under control. It is the gentleness of the surgeon that makes him great, and only the Holy Spirit can give us this precious grace (Gal. 5:22-23).

## V. Kindness (25:21-22)

Gentleness ought to lead to kindness; see Rom. 12:19-21, where these same verses are quoted by Paul and applied to NT Christians. Instead of adding coals to the fire of anger (Prov. 26:20-21), we help to put out the fire by showing love and kindness. Read Christ's commandment in Matt. 5:9-12. If the person needs to be chastened, God will take care of the matter: "Vengeance is mine, I will repay." We must be careful, however, to perform these kind deeds with the right motive. If we try to obligate people to us, or if we try to "buy them off," God will not bless. But if we sincerely love them and want to help them, God will honor and reward us. Of course, these good deeds must not be done to impress people;

Prov. 21:14 says they ought to be secret. Solomon is not suggesting a bribe here; rather, he is saying that kindness will be like oil that will heal the troubled waters.

## VI. Self-control (25:28)

This lies at the very heart of the matter: the Christian who practices self-control will not be destroyed by anger, nor will he or she destroy others. This verse ought to be compared with 16:32, "He who is slow to anger is better than the mighty, and he who rules his spirit than he who takes a city." For people to rule their own spirit, the "inner kingdom," is better than to rule the world. Alexander the Great was able to conquer the known world, yet he could not conquer himself. Of course, the only way for us to have this self-control is through the kingship of the Lord Jesus Christ in our lives. We "reign in life" through Christ (Rom. 5:17). Self-control (temperance) is one of the fruit of the Spirit (Gal. 5:22-23); the flesh cannot produce self-control, for the flesh is at war with God.

It is self-control that gives us the patience we need, as outlined at the beginning of this study. If we exercise self-control at the very start of a problem, it will save us all kinds of trouble later on. Proverbs 17:14 compares the beginning of strife to a small leak from a dam; if you are not careful, the break will enlarge and you will have a flood on your hands. It is easier to stop the small leak at the start than to try to control a raging flood. Proverbs 30:33 presents a different picture: the churning of butter and the wringing of the nose. The lesson is clear: to force wrath and encourage trouble only produces more trouble. Self-control, produced by the Spirit, will enable a believer to handle these matters patiently and wisely.

The ability to be angry about the right matters in the right way helps to build character. Certainly we ought to be aroused about injustice and sin. But when anger flares up in temper, it becomes destructive. Godly anger is like the steam power in the boiler: if it is directed to the right matters it accomplishes much good. Unrighteous anger—losing one's temper—is more like a forest fire that gets out of control and destroys much good. Psalm 19:14 (NKJV) is a good prayer for us to use: "Let the words of my mouth and the meditation of my heart be acceptable in Your sight, O Lord, my strength and my redeemer."

# PROVERBS 31

Only in eternity will we fully see the blessing that godly women have brought to this world. Proverbs has much to say about wicked women in chapters 1–9, and about nagging wives (21:9 and 25:24); the book closes, however, with a glorious tribute to the godly, dedicated woman who brings honor to God and joy to her family. Many servants of God thank God for godly mothers and godly wives. Next to making a decision for Christ, the most important decision a Christian will make is the choice of a life's mate. "A virtuous woman is a crown to her husband" (Prov. 12:4). "He who finds a wife finds a good thing, and obtains favor from the Lord" (Prov. 18:22, NKJV). "A prudent wife is from the Lord" (Prov. 19:14). Christians must not be unequally yoked together with unsaved mates (2 Cor. 6:14-18). They are to marry "in the Lord" (1 Cor. 7:39). A Christian woman who marries an unsaved man may be endangering her life in childbirth; see 1 Tim. 2:12-15. This chapter of Proverbs describes the "virtuous woman" and lists her fine qualities.

## I. Her Spirituality (31:1-9)

The king's mother is teaching her son to obey the Word of God. Some students think that "King Lemuel" is actually King Solomon, but we have no proof of this. The most important ministry mothers and fathers have is the spiritual training of their children. See 2 Tim. 1:5 and 3:15. The mother boldly warns Lemuel of some of the dangers he will face in life: sinful companions, strong drink, and a temptation to disobey the Word of God. Happy is that person who had a God-fearing mother who warned about sin, and happier is the person who heeded her warnings.

## II. Her Loyalty (31:10-12)

The two key words here are heart and trust—love and faith. Marriage is a matter of the heart; there must be true love between husband and wife. What kind of love should a man show to his wife? The same kind of love that Christ shows to the church (Eph. 5:18ff): sacrificial, patient, suffering, tender, constant. A wife has no problem submitting herself in obedience to a husband who loves her *and shows it*. Husbands need to take care that their jobs and household chores do not take them away from their wives and children. A happy home does not "just happen"; it is the result of hard work, prayer, and real love. When husbands and wives trust the Lord and each other, there will be happiness and blessing. The marriage vows are promises that must be taken seriously. To break these vows is to sin against God and each other.

## III. Her Industry (31:13-22)

This priceless woman is a worker. Whether it be sewing or cooking, taking care of the children or assisting her husband in family business, she is faithfully doing her share. Note that she works willingly (v. 13); it is not a matter of compulsion but compassion. She loves her husband and therefore seeks to please him. (See 1 Cor. 7:32-34 for a wonderful principle of marriage—live to please the other person.) This ideal woman does not spend the morning in bed; she is up early to do her tasks (v. 15) and, if necessary, she stays up late at night (v. 18). Note Paul's instructions to young women in 1 Tim. 5:14. While there are sometimes emergencies and situations that require women to work outside the home, it must be remembered that even there her first responsibility is to her family.

Proverbs has nothing good to say about laziness, whether it involves a man or a woman. See 6:6-11; 10:4, 26; 13:4; 15:19; 18:9; 19:15, 24; 20:4, 13; 21:25; 22:13; 24:30-34; 26:13-16. In these days of "labor-saving devices," there is still no substitute for hard work and diligence.

## IV. Her Modesty (31:23-26)

Her husband is known in the gates; she is known for her faithfulness at home. Man and woman both have a place in the economy of God, and when either one steps out of place, there is confusion and trouble. Of course, the headship of the man does not mean dictatorship; rather it means example and leadership in love. Verse 25 suggests that the godly woman does not depend on fancy clothing to be successful; she wears "strength and honor" on the inner person. Peter writes about the outward adorning of extravagance and the inward adorning of a "meek and quiet spirit" (1 Peter 3:3-4). Paul commands women to wear "modest apparel" (1 Tim. 2:9) and to depend on spiritual beauty, not the artificial beauty of the world. Verse 26 tells us that the godly woman is careful in her speech as well as in her dress. How wonderful it is when the "law of kindness" rules the tongue.

## V. Her Piety (31:27-31)

"A woman who fears the Lord, she shall be praised." This is the secret of her life: she fears God and seeks to obey His Word. No doubt she would arise early in the morning to meditate on the Word and to pray. All day long she would pray for her husband and her family. Her true beauty is within; though the years might change her body, her beauty in the Lord only grows greater. Her praise comes from God. "I do always those things that please Him."

How does God praise this woman? By blessing her labors and her life. The fruit of her life will praise her. She will certainly reap "life everlasting" because she has sown to the Spirit, not to the flesh (Gal. 6:7-8).

Her husband and children also rise up and praise her. What a need there is today for husbands and children to show constantly their appreciation for what the wife and mother does in the home. One of the greatest weaknesses in many homes today is that family members take each other for granted. Husbands need to set the right example before their children by openly praising the Lord and the wife for the blessings of the home. How often a dedicated wife sacrifices for the happiness of the home and never receives so much as a simple "thanks." What a sin lack of appreciation is in our homes. This kind of appreciation must not be reserved for Mother's Day or Christmas; rather, it must be shown sincerely all year long. Gratitude is a wonderful Christian virtue. It needs to be cultivated in every home.

Of course, these same qualities ought to be seen in the man of the house as well. How often we see a godly woman patiently suffering with a carnal, worldly husband. The Bible knows nothing of a "double standard" for husbands and wives. It is important that the husband be spiritual, loyal, industrious, etc. In God's gracious plan, He has ordered that *both* husband and wife are needed in the home and that each one must fulfill certain ministries. One cannot replace the other, although in some emergencies (such as death of one mate) God has given grace for a person to be both "father and mother" in the home.

Husbands and wives must constantly be on guard lest Satan move in and break up the home. They have spiritual, material, and physical responsibilities to each other, and if these are not met, Satan goes to work (1 Cor. 7:1-6; 1 Tim. 5:8; Eph. 5:21-33; 1 Peter

3:7). It is especially important to be on guard after the children have grown up and left home, for then the true strength of the home is tested. A man and woman can no longer say, "We will stay together for the children's sake." May God help us all to choose the right mates in His will, and to build the kind of homes that glorify His Name.

# ECCLESIASTES

## A Suggested Outline of Ecclesiastes

Introduction (1:1-3)

I. His Initial Reasons (1:4–2:26)

    A. Man is just a "cog in the wheel" (1:4-11)

    B. Man's wisdom cannot understand life (1:12-18)

    C. Wealth and pleasure do not satisfy (2:1-11)

    D. Death comes and ends it all (2:12-23)

    E. Conclusion — enjoy God's blessings (2:24-26)

II. His Deeper Observations (3–10)

    A. God has a purpose in this "weary cycle of life" (3)

    B. Wealth and pleasure can glorify God (4–6)

    C. Wisdom from God is better than a life of folly (7–10)

III. His Final Conclusions (11–12)

    A. Live by faith (11:1-6)

    B. Remember that life will end one day soon (11:7–12:7)

    C. Obey God's Word and fear Him (12:8-14)

# Introductory Notes to Ecclesiastes

## I. Name

"Ecclesiastes" comes from the Greek *ekklesia*, which in the NT is translated "church" or "assembly." It carries the idea of a preacher (or debater) speaking to an assembly of people (see 1:1-2 and 12:8-10). The Preacher here presents a practical problem and discusses it, seeking to come to a conclusion.

## II. Author

Solomon is named as the author; see 1:1-2, 12. Certainly he was known for his wisdom as well as for his wealth and enjoyment of pleasures. No king in the OT better fits the situation described in this book.

## III. Theme

The theme is given in 1:1-3, and might be expressed, "Is life really worth living?" Solomon looks at life with its seeming contradictions and mysteries, and he wonders if the "endless toil" of existence is worth it. People toil all their lives, then die, and somebody less worthy inherits their wealth and wastes it. Solomon comes to the conclusion that the best thing to do is to enjoy the blessings of God today, fear God, and keep His Word. Of course, with the added light of the NT we know that "our labor is not in vain in the Lord" (1 Cor. 15:58).

Some of the key words and phrases in Ecclesiastes are: *man* (47 times), *labor* (36 times), *under the sun* (30 times), *vanity* (37 times), *wisdom* or *wise* (52 times), and *evil* (22 times). Keep in mind that Solomon is reasoning about what he sees and knows "under the sun." If you stop with Ecclesiastes, you will stay in the shadows; you must move on to the full revelation of the NT to have the whole counsel of God. Many of the false cults quote isolated verses from this book to prove their strange doctrines.

## IV. Problems

Does Ecclesiastes teach that men die like animals, that there is no life after death? No. Read the "death" verses carefully: 2:14-16;

3:16-22; 6:1-6; 7:2-4; 9:1-4. You will note that Solomon *does* believe in life after death. In 3:17 he mentions a future judgment, and also in 11:9 and 12:14. If there is no future life after death, how can there be a future judgment? The "one thing" that happens both to man and beast in 3:19-20 is that both go to the same place—the dust. But note v. 21 where the spirit of man goes back to God; see also 12:7. Solomon did not have the full revelation of the NT concerning life, death, resurrection, and judgment, but he does not contradict NT teachings.

Does Ecclesiastes teach "eat, drink, and be merry"? No. It does, however, teach that we should receive God's blessings and enjoy them while we can. Each of the "enjoyment" passages is balanced by a "death" passage: 2:12-23 with 2:24-26; 3:16-21 with 3:12-15 and 22; 6:1-7 with 5:18-20; and 9:1-4 with 8:15-17. Solomon is saying, "In the light of the brevity of life and the certainty of death, enjoy God's blessings, the fruits of your labor, today. Use these blessings for His glory." This agrees with Paul in 1 Tim. 6:17. Solomon is not advising reckless pleasure or drunkenness. Rather, he is counseling us to appreciate life and its blessings while we can.

God's truths are not fully revealed all at once; there is a progressive unfolding of truth in the Bible. We must interpret Ecclesiastes in the light of the NT. If death ends all, then life is not worth living, and human beings are indeed miserable. But when we know Christ as Savior and Lord, life becomes a thrilling adventure of faith. And our labors are not in vain in the Lord, because one day we shall be rewarded (1 Cor. 15:51-58). Salvation and resurrection in Christ make life worth living. "He who does the will of God abides forever" (1 John 2:17, NKJV). "Their works do follow them" (Rev. 14:13). Solomon's conclusions in chapters 11–12 bear this out: live by faith, obey God, and He will take care of the rest. Enjoy His blessings now and invest your life in that which really counts.

# ECCLESIASTES

Imagine an assembly of Jewish people as they listen to King Solomon discuss an important problem. Solomon is the "Preacher" or "Debater" in this assembly (1:1-2, 12; 7:27; 12:8-10), and the topic he is discussing is this: "Is life really worth living?" Can you think of a more practical subject? And can you think of a better person to discuss it? For Solomon was the wisest of the kings, a man whose wisdom and wealth enabled him to experience a full life. In this brief section we can only touch the main points of this interesting book.

## I. The Problem Declared (1–2)

"Is life really worth living?" This is the question that Solomon is debating. In 1:1-3 he states his first conclusion: life is *not* worth living because life is full of vanity (emptiness). Then he states his reasons:

### A. Man is only a cog in a big wheel (1:4-11).

What is man compared to the vastness of the world? Everything in nature continues, century after century, but man is here for a brief space of time, then he dies. It all seems so meaningless. It is vanity. (Solomon uses this word "vanity" thirty-seven times in this book.) Since life is so short and man so insignificant, why bother to live at all?

### B. Man cannot understand it all (1:12-18).

Solomon was the wisest of men, yet when he tried to understand the meaning of life, he was baffled. How many wise philosophers have tried to explain life, only to admit their utter ignorance. Is it reasonable to live when you cannot understand what life is all about?

### C. Man's pleasures do not satisfy (2:1-11).

Solomon had plenty of money, pleasure, culture, and fame; yet he admitted that these things did not satisfy. Nor did they last. See what Jesus said about this in Luke 12:13-21.

### D. Death ends all (2:12-23).

"One event" (death) happens both to the fool and to the wise, to the rich and to the poor. A person labors all his life, then dies and leaves the wealth for another person to enjoy. Is this fair?

These four arguments seem to lead to one grand conclusion: it is not worthwhile for a human being to live. But Solomon does not draw that conclusion. In 2:24-26 he tells us that we should accept the blessings of God now, enjoy them, and benefit from them. This agrees with Paul's counsel in 1 Tim. 6:17. But even this "living for today" does not completely satisfy, because human beings want to go *beyond* today. So, Solomon backtracks in the next eight chapters (he "returns and considers"; see 4:1, 7; 9:11) and studies his arguments in a deeper way.

## II. The Problem Discussed (3–10)

### A. God has a purpose in our lives (chap. 3).

God balances life: birth-death, sorrow-joy, meeting-parting. Why does He do this? For two reasons: (1) so that we will not think we can easily explain God's works (v. 11), and (2) so that we will learn to accept and enjoy what we have (vv. 12-13). God has set "eternity" in our hearts (v. 11, where "the world" should be translated "eternity"). This means that the things of the world can never really satisfy us. Therefore, we must find God's will for our lives and let Him "mix the ingredients" according to His purpose.

### B. God gives riches according to His will (chaps. 4–6).

These chapters discuss the meaning of riches. Why is one person rich and another poor? Why is there injustice and inequality in the world? Because God has a plan for us, that we should not trust in uncertain riches but in the Lord. Do not live for riches, but use them according to God's will.

### C. God's wisdom can guide us through life (chaps. 7–10).

The word wisdom (or wise) is used over thirty times in chapters 7–12. It is true that man's wisdom cannot fathom God's plan, but God can give us wisdom to know and do His will. Simply because we cannot understand everything does not mean we should give up in despair. Trust God and do what He tells you to do.

Did you notice that in each of these sections, Solomon emphasizes the enjoyment of God's blessings and the reality of death? Read 3:12-21, 5:18–6:7, and 8:15–9:4. Since every person is going to die, we should not bother to work or save money or serve God—

is this right? "No!" says Solomon. And in chapters 11–12 he explains what he means.

## III. The Problem Decided (11–12)

Solomon has already decided that man is not a "cog in the wheel," that there is nothing wrong with enjoying riches and pleasures to God's glory, and that our inability to understand all that God is doing is no hindrance to a happy life. In 11–12, Solomon sums up the whole matter with three practical admonitions:

### A. Live by faith (11:1-6).

Circumstances are never going to be ideal in this life, but we must go ahead and obey God and trust Him for the results. If you wait for the right wind or the right day, you may miss your opportunity. You may seem to be a fool, like someone who casts bread on moving water, but God will see to it that it will come back to you.

### B. Remember that life will end (11:7–12:7).

Is this a morbid suggestion? No. It is a Christian realism. One day you will die, so make the most of the life you now have. This is not the worldly attitude, "Eat, drink, and be merry, for tomorrow we die." Rather, it is the attitude of Paul in Phil. 1:20-21 — to live is Christ, to die is gain. Note the three key words here directed especially to young people: rejoice (11:9), remove (11:10), and remember (12:1). Rejoice in God's blessings while you are young; remove from your life the sins that cause sorrow; and remember to serve God and fear Him in the days of your youth. In 12:1-7 we have a poetic description of old age and death. See if you can discover what these poetic terms refer to in the human body.

### C. Fear God and obey Him (12:8-14).

Live as those who will one day face judgment. When the fire of God tests your works, will they all burn up? (1 Cor. 3:9-17) You will want to interpret Solomon's conclusions in the light of 1 Cor. 15, the great resurrection chapter of the Bible. If death really ends all, then life is not worth living, and everything truly is "vanity" and emptiness. But 1 Cor. 15 makes it clear that death is not the end. Because Christ arose from the dead, we shall also be raised. And the glory and reward we enjoy in eternity will depend on the lives we lived here on earth. Therefore, our labor is not "in vain in the Lord" (v. 58).

From the human point of view "under the sun," it seems as if life is futile and empty; all is vanity. But when life is lived in the power of God for the glory of God, then life becomes meaningful. A person may live and labor for fifty years, and then die. Does this mean his life was wasted? Of course not. His labor is not in vain in the Lord. He will receive the rewards of his labors when Christ returns. "He who does the will of God abides forever" (1 John 2:17). The unsaved person loses all at death; so does the carnal, worldly Christian who will be "saved, yet so as by fire" (1 Cor. 3:15). But the faithful Christian who rejoices in God's blessings today and uses his life to glorify Christ, will receive abundant rewards in the life to come.

In the light of the NT, Ecclesiastes is not a "pessimistic" book that denies the joys of life. Rather, it proves that though there are many mysteries in life we cannot explain, we can live so as to enjoy God's blessings and glorify God's name.

# SONG OF SOLOMON

## A Suggested Outline of the Song of Solomon

I. The King Courts His Bride (1:1–3:5)

   A. The banquet hall fellowship (1:2–2:7)
   B. The springtime visit (2:8-17)
   C. The night quest (3:1-5)

II. The King Claims His Bride (3:6–5:1)

   A. The majestic marriage procession (3:6-11)
   B. The beauty of the bride (4:1–5:1)

III. The King Communes with His Wife (5:2–8:14)

   A. The separation from her husband (5:2-9)
   B. Her admiration of her husband (5:10-16)
   C. Their meeting in the garden (6:1-13)
   D. His admiration of his wife (7:1-9)
   E. Their satisfying communion (7:10–8:14)

Note: This is a "generic" outline that can apply to any of the interpretations suggested. Some interpreters see three main characters—Solomon, a shepherd lover, and his beloved. However, it is possible to see only Solomon and his beloved presented in the book.

# THE SONG OF SOLOMON

The title "Song of Songs" (like "holy of holies") means "the finest of all songs." Since Solomon composed over 1,000 songs (1 Kings 4:32), this must be classified as the best of them all. It is a book full of symbols and images, a book that requires maturity and spiritual discernment to appreciate and enjoy. Any student who would abuse the language and message of this priceless book is certainly revealing the carnality of his own life. We cannot examine this book in detail, but we do want to seek to understand its message from a four-fold approach.

## I. The Literal Meaning

We have here a precious love story. It involves three characters: a lovely maiden, forced to work by her family (1:5-6; 2:15); her beloved, undoubtedly a neighbor lad who has won her heart, who is also a shepherd (1:7); and King Solomon, who is known for his attraction to beautiful women (1 Kings 11:3). While on one of his trips to examine his lands, Solomon meets the lovely maiden and takes her to his palace. There she can think only of her beloved back home (1:1–2:7). She tells the women of the harem ("daughters of Jerusalem" in 2:7, 3:5, 8:4) not to try to persuade her to forsake her true love. In 2:8–3:5 she recalls her beloved and even has a dream about him. Solomon visits her (3:6–4:16) to try to win her love, but she cannot forget her beloved back home. Her beloved sees her in a dream (5:1–6:3). Again, the king tries to win her (6:4–7:9), but the maiden refuses (7:10–8:3). She is not impressed with the king's wealth, spices, lands, or flattery. Finally, true love wins out and the maiden is set free. She flees to her beloved (8:4-14) and is restored to her family again.

Of course, this interpretation does not put Solomon in a very good light. But he was not faithful when it came to marital matters, and certainly it is not wrong to see him as a type of the world, trying to woo the believer away from her true love. This will become clearer as we examine the different interpretations and applications of the story.

The Song of Solomon magnifies and sanctifies married love. God made both male and female and it was He who "invented" sex. The love of a man and wife ought to be a beautiful experience, as described in this book, but sin can destroy this beautiful gift. In

494

the Book of Proverbs, Solomon warns against sexual sins; in Song of Solomon, he extols the beauty and joy of married love.

## II. The Historical Meaning

From the earliest days, the Jews saw in this story a picture of the relationship between Jehovah God and Israel. Israel was "wedded" to the Lord at Mt. Sinai, when the nation accepted the Law. Isaiah 54 spells out this marriage relationship; see also Jer. 3 and the entire Book of Hosea. Alas, Israel was not faithful to her Divine Husband and "played the harlot" with the idolatrous nations of the world. She turned her back on her Beloved. However, there will come a day when, like the maiden in Song of Solomon, Israel will return home and be restored to her Beloved.

## III. The Typical Meaning

The marriage relationship is also used to describe the relationship between Christ and the church. See Eph. 5:23-33. This applies not only to the church collectively (all believers of this church age), but also the church locally (2 Cor. 11:2). Paul saw each local church "wedded to Christ" and in danger of being seduced into sin by Satan and the world. Just as husband and wife are "one" and belong to each other, so Christ and His church are one. We are "bone of His bone, flesh of His flesh." He is in us, we are in Him. He loved us (past tense) and showed this love by dying for us on the cross. He loves us (present tense) and shows this love by caring for us, nourishing us through the Word, and seeking to make us as beautiful spiritually as possible. In the future He will continue to love us and we will share His glory in eternity. The "marriage of the Lamb" is coming (Rev. 19:7-9). Christ shall return in glory and take His bride to heaven.

## IV. The Practical Meaning

This book presents a vivid picture of faithful love and deepening communion. The intimate terms used only illustrate the wonderful love between Christ and the Christian. Let us note how love and marriage illustrate the Christian life:

### A. Salvation.

We are "married to Christ" (Rom. 7:4). Marriage involves the whole person—mind, heart, will, body. A boy meets a girl and comes to know her with his mind. Perhaps this friendship deepens and his heart is captured. But he is not yet married to her. It is not until he says "I will" that he is married. Many people know about Christ, and even have emotional feelings that are exciting, but they have never said "I will" and trusted the Lord.

## B. Dedication.

When a man and woman are married, all that they are and all that they have belong to each other. Their bodies are not their own (1 Cor. 7:1-5); they live to please the other. So it is with the Christian life: our bodies belong to Christ (see Rom. 12:1-2), and we live to please Him, not the world. Satan and the world (like Solomon in our story) may try to tempt us from our devotion to Christ (James 4:4), but we must remain true to Him. When a man and woman love each other, no sacrifice is too great, no burden is too heavy. See 2 Cor. 11:2 for Paul's warning about "spiritual adultery."

## C. Communion.

This is perhaps the greatest lesson in Song of Solomon—the deepening communion that ought to exist between those who love each other. No matter where Solomon took the maiden, her heart was always with her beloved. She spoke of him, she dreamed of him, and when she was free, she rushed home to him. Do we have this kind of love for Christ? Do we see His beauty? (Ps. 45) Do we realize how much He loves us and longs to fellowship with us?

In Song of Solomon 5 we have an interesting picture of the believer's communion with the Lord. The maiden is asleep, but the voice of her beloved comes from outside the door. He wants her to share her love with him, but she is too lazy to get up. "I have put off my coat; I have washed my feet." It is as though she says, "Please, don't bother me. I'm too comfortable." Then she sees his hand (v. 4) and realizes her sin. Remember—his hands are pierced. She then rises, but, alas, her beloved has gone. He left some perfume at the door, but what good is the blessing without the Blesser? In trying to find her beloved, the maiden runs into trouble and discipline.

How often the Lord wants to fellowship with us during the day, but we are too busy. Like Martha (Luke 10:38-42), we are "troubled about many things." How much happier our lives would be if we would only keep our hearts open to the stirrings of His love. Just as a loving husband and wife think of each other when apart during the day, so a faithful Christian ought to think of his Savior and fellowship with Him. In 1:1-7, the maiden sees no beauty in herself, but in 1:14-17, her beloved describes her beauty in tender words. She sees herself in 2:1 as the common rose, the ordinary lily, but the beloved sees her as a beautiful apple tree, as a lily among thorns (2:2-3). (In spite of what we sing in the familiar song, it is the woman who speaks in 2:1 and not the Lord.)

### D. Glory.

The marriage has not yet taken place. We are engaged to our Lord, and the Holy Spirit is the "divine engagement ring" (Eph. 1:13-14). We have not yet seen Him, though we love Him (1 Peter 1:8). But one day the voice of the Bridegroom will be heard, and Jesus will return for His church. Then the wonderful marriage supper will take place (Rev. 19:1-9) and we shall forever be with the Lord. No wonder the maiden closes Song of Solomon by saying, "Make haste, my beloved." We can only add, "Even so come quickly, Lord Jesus."

# ISAIAH

## A Suggested Outline of Isaiah

I. Condemnation (1–39) (The defeat of Assyria)

    A. Sermons against Judah and Israel (1–12)

    B. Burdens of judgment on the other nations (13–23)

    C. Songs of future glory for the nation (24–27)

    D. Woes against the sins of the people (28–35)

    E. Historical Interlude (36–39) (King Hezekiah)

        1. His victory over Assyria (36–37)

        2. His sin with Babylon (38–39)

II. Consolation (40–66) (The remnant returns home)

    A. God's Greatness (40–48)

        The true God vs. the false gods of the heathen

        Emphasis on the Father, Jehovah God

    B. God's Grace (49–57)

        The Suffering Servant, Jesus Christ, dies for men

        Emphasis on the Son, Jesus Christ

    C. God's Glory (58–66)

        The glory of the future kingdom

        Emphasis on the Spirit (59:19, 21; 61:1; 63:10-14)

# Introductory Notes to Isaiah

## I. Name

"Isaiah" means "the salvation of Jehovah," and the word salvation is repeated many times in the book. Isaiah apparently was from a leading family, since he had access to several of the Jewish kings. He was married (8:3) and the father of at least two sons (7:3 and 8:1-3). He began his ministry near the close of the reign of King Uzziah, or about 758 B.C. He preached until the turn of the century, and tradition tells us he was sawn asunder by wicked King Manasseh (Heb. 11:37).

## II. Theme

The Book of Isaiah divides itself into two sections, chapters 1–39 and chapters 40–66. The first section warns the Jews about the impending Assyrian invasion of Judah, while the second section encourages the captives returning from the Babylonian captivity.

The main theme of the first section is God's chastening of Judah for their sins, while the main theme of the second section is God's consolation of the captives after their suffering. Isaiah experienced the events of the first thirty-nine chapters, but he prophesied the events of the last section of the book. In the first section, Assyria was the chief foe; in the last section, Babylon was the enemy.

## III. Historical Setting

You will recall that the nation divided after the death of Solomon; ten tribes in the north were organized as Israel, and two tribes in the south as Judah. The capital of Israel was Samaria; the capital of Judah was Jerusalem. Isaiah ministered in Jerusalem, but his messages touched both the Northern and the Southern Kingdoms. Isaiah lived to see Israel (the Northern Kingdom) decline and finally go into ruin under Assyria.

The political scene was threatening to Judah at that time. Assyria was the menacing power and the other nations wanted to form a coalition to fight her. However, King Ahaz of Judah would not join the league. So, Syria and Israel united to attack Judah to try to force Ahaz to cooperate. Instead of trusting the Lord for help, Ahaz turned to *Assyria* for assistance and made a secret pact. Assyria was only too glad to get her foot in the door; she defeated Israel in 721 B.C., but Judah became a vassal state to Assyria, the price Ahaz had to pay for his security. No sooner was Israel out of the way than Assyria decided to attack *Judah* and enslave the entire Jewish nation. Isaiah told the people to trust the Lord for help, but various groups told the king to turn to Egypt for aid. In chapters 36–39, Isaiah tells how God gave King Hezekiah victory over Assyria when the invading army was at the very walls of Jerusalem. However, Judah was so weakened from war, and her cities had been so overrun by the enemy, that the nation never really recovered. Assyria was defeated by the Egyptians; the Egyptians fell to the Babylonians; and in 606–587 B.C., the Babylonians took Judah into captivity. So, in the first half of his book, Isaiah counseled the nation concerning Assyria; in the last half, he comforted the remnant concerning their return from Babylon.

## IV. Christ in Isaiah

Isaiah gives a rich prophetic picture of Jesus Christ. We see His birth (7:14 with Matt. 1:23; also Isa. 9:6); the ministry of John the Baptist (40:3-6 with Matt. 3:1ff); Christ anointed by the Spirit (61:1-2 with Luke 4:17-19); Christ the Servant (42:1-4 with Matt. 12:17-21); Israel's rejection of Christ (6:9-11 with John 12:38ff, Matt. 13:10-15, and parallel references in the Gospels; also Acts 28:26-27 and Rom. 11:8); the Stone of Stumbling (8:14 and 28:16 with Rom. 9:32-33 and 10:11, 1 Peter 2:6); Christ's ministry to the Gentiles (49:6 with Luke 2:32, Acts 13:47; see also 9:1-2 with Matt. 4:15-16); Christ's suffering and death (52:13–53:12); His resurrection (55:3 with Acts 13:34; 45:23 with Phil. 2:10-11 and Rom. 14:11); and the Coming King (9:6-7, 11:1ff, 32:1-2; 59:20-21 with Rom. 11:26-27; 63:2-3 with Rev. 19:13-15).

## V. The Suffering Servant

There are seventeen references in Isaiah to "Jehovah's servant." In thirteen of these, the nation is in view (43:10; 44:1-2, 21, 26; 45:4; 48:20; 49:3, 5-7); in four, Jesus Christ is in view (42:1 and 19; 52:13–53:11). The entire section from 52:13 to 53:12 is a vivid description of the sufferings, death, and resurrection of Jesus Christ. Israel was Jehovah's servant in that the nation was used of God to bring the Word and the Savior to the world. However, Israel was a disobedient servant that had to be chastened. Jesus Christ is

501

the true Servant of Jehovah who died for the world and perfectly did His Father's will. In 41:8-9, Cyrus is the servant.

## VI. Isaiah's Two Sons

The symbolical names of his two sons (7:3 and 8:1-3) illustrate the two main messages of Isaiah's book. Shear-jashub means "a remnant shall return" and ties in with the second half of the prophecy, the return of the remnant from Babylon. Maher-shalal-hash-baz means "speed to the spoil, haste to the prey" and ties in with chapters 1–39, the defeat of Assyria.

It has been suggested that Isaiah's book is like a "Bible in miniature." Its sixty-six chapters are divided into two parts, thirty-nine chapters in the first division (like the OT) and twenty-seven chapters in the second division (like the NT). The first thirty-nine chapters emphasize judgment; the last twenty-seven emphasize mercy and comfort.

# ISAIAH 6

King Uzziah has died and the throne of Judah is empty. Like all men of faith, Isaiah turned to God for his help and comfort, and in that hour of seeming defeat, he experienced a great spiritual blessing. He saw that the throne of heaven was still occupied by Jehovah God! Note the three-fold vision God gave to Isaiah.

## I. The Upward Look—He Saw the Lord (6:1-4)

Like all devoted citizens, Isaiah had venerated King Uzziah. For fifty-two years, Uzziah had led Judah in a program of peace and prosperity. It was an era of expansion and achievement. It was unfortunate that the king had rebelled against the Word of God and died a leper (2 Kings 15:1-7; 2 Chron. 26). Isaiah realized that though the nation had prospered materially, it was in terrible condition spiritually. The economic growth and temporary peace were a veneer that covered a nation with a wicked heart. What was going to happen to Judah?

God lifted Isaiah's eyes from himself and his people to the throne of heaven. There might be confusion and unrest on earth, but there was perfect peace in heaven: God was seated in majestic power and glory. People on earth might be recalling the shame of Uzziah's death as a leper, but there was no shame or shadow of failure in heaven. Rather, the seraphim were saying, "Holy, holy, holy."

John 12:38-41 informs us that Isaiah saw Jesus Christ in His glory. He was on the throne of heaven being praised by the seraphim. His royal robe filled the heavenly temple, and the house was filled with the smoke of His anger against sin (Ps. 80:4). His angelic creatures, the seraphim ("fiery ones"), praised Him for His holiness and His glory. "The whole earth is full of His glory." Isaiah did not see much glory that day, nor do we see it today. Rather, it seems that the whole earth is "filled with violence" (Gen. 6:11). We see events from a human perspective; the angels see them from God's viewpoint. One day when Jesus reigns, the whole earth shall be full of His glory (see Num. 14:21, Ps. 72:19, and Hab. 2:14). See also Isa. 11:9.

"Lord of hosts" is Isaiah's favorite name for God; he uses it at least sixty-five times. "Lord of the armies" is what it means. The prophet also calls God "the Holy One of Israel" at least thirty times. Jehovah is the God of holy warfare, the God who opposes sin and defeats the enemy. Isaiah needed to realize this fact in a day when Judah appeared to be defeated. This is a good practical lesson for Christians today: when the day is dark, lift your eyes to heaven and see Christ on the throne. "The Lord is in His holy temple."

## II. The Inward Look—He Saw Himself (6:5-7)

A true vision of God and His holiness always makes us realize our own sinfulness and failure. Job saw God and repented (Job 42:6); Peter cried out, "I am a sinful man" when he saw Christ's power (Luke 5:8). Self-righteous rabbi Saul saw that his own righteousness was but "garbage" next to the glory of Christ (Acts 9 and Phil. 3), and he believed and became the Apostle Paul. When believers have a true experience with the Lord, it does not make them proud; rather, it humbles and breaks them.

When Isaiah confessed his sins, he mentioned especially his unclean lips. Of course, unclean lips are the products of an unclean heart. The prophet knew that he could not faithfully preach for the Lord unless he was prepared and cleansed. How different from some Christians who rush out to serve Christ before taking time to meet the Lord and be cleansed. God met the prophet's need: He sent a seraph to cleanse him with a coal from the altar. How tragic it would be to have the throne without the altar! There would be conviction of sin, but no cleansing. Note that it was more important for the seraph to equip Isaiah to be a soul-winner than to praise God. True worship ought to lead to witness and service. Too many Christians want to hold on to a "spiritual experience" with the Lord, rather than be prepared to go out to share the Lord with others.

There is a wonderful word of encouragement here: God quickly answers prayer and cleanses us (1 John 1:9). He longs to equip us to serve Him.

## III. The Outward Look—He Saw the Need (6:8-13)

Everything to this point was a preparation. Now God can call Isaiah and use him to preach His Word. The prophet is no longer wrapped up in his own needs; he wants to do the will of God. He is no longer burdened by sin; he has been cleansed. He is no longer discouraged; he knows that God is on the throne. Now he is ready to go to work.

The call is an evidence of God's grace. He is willing to use human beings to accomplish His will on earth. God certainly could have sent one of the seraphim, and it would have obeyed instantly and perfectly. But when it comes to proclaiming His Word, God must use human lips. God is still calling believers today and, alas, few are responding. In Isaiah's day, only a "remnant" would obey.

"Go and tell!" This is God's commission to us today. "You shall be witnesses to me . . . to the end of the earth" (Acts 1:8, NKJV). It was not an easy commission God gave to the prophet, for the nation was in no mood to hear his messages of sin and judgment. In chapter 1, God pictures the nation as a sick body, covered with wounds and rotting sores, and as a stubborn and rebellious animal, too ignorant to listen to his own master. In chapter 5, the nation is pictured as a beautiful vineyard that did not produce good grapes. As you read chapters 1–5, you understand the burden that God gave Isaiah. The nation was prosperous; why preach about sin? The "fashionable ladies" would not like it (3:16-26), nor would the leading rulers (5:8ff). When people are rich, full, and satisfied, they do not believe that judgment is coming.

Verses 9-10 are quoted six times in the NT: Matt. 13:13-15, Mark 4:12, Luke 8:10, John 12:40, Acts 28:25-28, Rom. 11:8; making a total of seven references in all. Is God saying that He deliberately blinds people and condemns them? No, not at all. What He is saying is that the Word of God has this hardening and blinding effect on sinners who will not listen and yield. The sun that melts the ice also hardens the clay. Note the steps downward in John 12: they *would* not believe (v. 37); therefore, they *could* not believe (v. 39); and thus they *should* not believe (v. 40) because they had sealed their own doom.

The servant of God is to proclaim God's Word regardless of how people respond. It took a great deal of faith on Isaiah's part to obey such a commission. "How long should I preach and therefore produce these tragic results?" he asks. "Until I am finished with My judgment on the land," the Lord replies. This kind of judgment is announced in 1:7-9 and 2:12-22. But the Lord will save a remnant, even though the nation will be removed far away into captivity (vv. 12-13). This prophecy applied immediately to the captivity, but it also pictures God's dealings with Israel in the last days, when a small remnant of Jews will believe during the Tribulation period. Isaiah pictures the nation as a tree cut down; the stump remains and a new shoot can grow from it. Relate this to 11:1ff, the prophecy of "the Branch—Jesus Christ."

When Isaiah walked out of the temple that day, he was no longer a mourner—he was a missionary. He was not merely a spectator; he was a participant. God had equipped him to do the job: Isaiah had seen the Lord, he had seen himself, and he had seen the need. Knowing that God was on the throne, and that God had called and commissioned him, he was ready to preach the Word and be faithful unto death. What an example for us to follow today.

# ISAIAH 7–12

There are two important principles to keep in mind as you study OT prophecy: (1) the prophets saw Christ's coming in humiliation and in glory, but did not see the period of time between these events—the church age (1 Peter 1:10-12); and (2) each prophecy grew out of a definite historical situation but looked beyond that present day to the future. We shall see these principles in the chapters before us now. The prophet is dealing with a definite crisis in Judah's history—the impending attack by Israel (the Northern Kingdom) and Syria—and he tells the nation exactly what will happen. Within these prophecies, Isaiah also announces the coming of the Messiah. Note the prophecies he gives.

## I. Judah Will Be Delivered from Her Enemies (7:1-16)

### A. The situation (vv. 1-2).

Assyria was growing stronger and threatening the other nations, so Israel and Syria joined forces to protect themselves. They wanted Judah to line up with them, but she would not. Actually, Ahaz was secretly bargaining with Assyria to protect him (2 Kings 16:1-9). The nation was frightened because Syria and Israel were about to attack and there seemed to be no way of escape.

### B. The promise (vv. 3-9).

God sent Isaiah and his son Shear-jashub ("The remnant shall return") to meet King Ahaz while the ruler was inspecting the Jerusalem water supply. Isaiah gave the king a message of hope and confidence: "Don't be afraid of Syria and Israel, for within sixty-five years they will be broken." This prophecy came true: Assyria defeated Syria (Damascus) in 732, and Israel (Ephraim, Samaria) in 721, within the allotted time given.

## C. The sign (vv. 10-16).

Ahaz acted very pious by refusing to receive a sign from God. So, the Lord turned from Ahaz and gave a sign to the entire house of David (v. 13). This sign was fulfilled ultimately in the birth of Jesus Christ (Matt. 1:23). He was born of the Virgin Mary, conceived by the Holy Spirit (Luke 1:31-35). To make the word "virgin" in v. 14 into the word "young woman" is to twist the Scriptures. His name was "Immanuel," which means "God is with us" (see 8:8 and 10). Jesus Christ is God come in human flesh, yet without sin (John 1:14). He is not merely a "good man" or a "great teacher"; He is the very Son of God. To deny this is to deny the Word of God (1 John 4:1-6).

It is possible (but not necessary) that there was some kind of an immediate fulfillment of the prophecy as a sign to the king and the nation. This does not mean a miraculous virgin birth, since only Jesus Christ could be born in that manner. But it does suggest that a Jewish virgin was wed and within the next year gave birth to a child. Before this child could reach the legal Jewish age of accountability (12 years old), the enemy nations of Israel and Syria would be defeated. If this sign was given in 735 B.C., as it probably was, then by 721 the promise would be fulfilled. As we have seen, Syria fell in 732 and Samaria in 721. It is possible that the "sign child" was born to Isaiah's wife; the record is given in 8:1-8. This would mean that the prophet's first wife (the mother of Shear-jashub, 7:3) had died, and that the prophet married the second wife shortly after uttering this prophecy. In spite of King Ahaz's unbelief and scheming (he robbed the temple to bribe Assyria—2 Chron. 28:21, 24-25), God graciously delivered Judah from her enemies. But Judah was left enslaved to Assyria, and only a divine intervention in Hezekiah's day delivered the nation (see Isa. 36–37).

## II. Israel Will Be Defeated by Assyria (7:17–10:34)

From 7:17 on, Isaiah is talking to apostate Israel and Pekah, her king. He warns the Northern Kingdom that Assyria will come upon them and completely ruin them, leaving the land in poverty and ruin instead of fullness of blessing. It was at this point that the "sign child" was born (8:1-4), and named Maher-shalal-hash-baz — "speed to the spoil, haste to the prey." His name emphasized the coming ruin of Samaria and Syria (8:4). Israel's confederacy with Syria would not protect the people (8:11-15); they needed to join with Jehovah and let Him be their stone of safety. They needed to get back to the law (8:20).

In 9:1-7 Isaiah gives a second prediction of the coming Messiah; see Matt. 4:13-16. The areas mentioned in 9:1 suffered the most when Assyria swept over Israel, but they would be the ones to see the light of Messiah. In vv. 3-5, the prophet looks down the years to the time when Israel would rejoice, when burdens would be lifted, when the weapons of warfare would be burned as fuel—the time when Jesus Christ would reign as Prince of Peace. See here the humanity of Christ ("a Child is born") and the deity of Christ ("a Son is given"). Then the prophet jumps from His humble birth to His glorious reign, when He shall rule from Jerusalem and there shall be perfect peace.

In 9:8–10:34, Isaiah continues to warn Israel of her impending doom. He also warns Assyria not to become proud of her victories, for she is but a tool in the hands of God. Her day of defeat will come too. We may see in Assyria a type of the Antichrist who will gather all nations against Jerusalem at the Battle of Armageddon. Just as God defeated Assyria with His miraculous power, so He will defeat Satan and his united armies (Rev. 19).

## III. Israel and Judah Will Unite in the Kingdom (11–12)

Note 11:12—the divided nations will one day unite and return to their land in peace. In 11:1-3 we have a picture of Jesus Christ, "the Branch." In 6:13 we saw the nation "chopped down" as a tree, with the stump remaining; now we see Christ coming from the stump to save the people. Jesus Christ is the legal descendant of David; He is "rooted" in Judah as a Jew Himself. He is called "the Branch of the Lord" in 4:2, "a righteous Branch" in Jer. 23:5; "my servant the Branch" in Zech. 3:8; and "the man whose name is the Branch" in Zech. 6:12. The Hebrew word *netzer* ("branch") ties in with the name given to Jesus in Matt. 2:23—"the Nazarene."

The four Gospels describe "the Branch" for us as follows: *Matthew*—David's righteous Branch (Jer. 23:5); *Mark*—my servant the Branch (Zech. 3:8); *Luke*—the man whose name is the Branch (Zech. 6:12); and *John*—the Branch of Jehovah (Isa. 4:2). Thus Jesus Christ will one day fulfill the OT promises God gave to the Jews and will reign over His kingdom in glory and victory (Rom. 15:8-12). We see all three Persons of the Godhead in 11:2—"The Spirit of the Lord (Jehovah) shall rest upon Him (Christ)." There is a seven-fold ministry of the Spirit here. Certainly the Holy Spirit empowered Christ in His ministry here on earth (John 3:34); and the Spirit shall also empower us today to enable us to serve Christ and glorify Him (Acts 1:8). From 11:4 on, we have a description of the glorious kingdom that Christ will establish when He returns to reign. It will be a time of honest judgment when sin will immediately be dealt with. Nature shall be restored (Rom. 8:18-25), and there will be no more curse. Violence and war will be gone. "The earth shall be full of the knowledge of the Lord" (v. 9); see Isa. 6:3 and Hab. 2:14. Please do not "spiritualize" these promises. To steal them from the Jew and apply them to the church is to twist the Scriptures. These are literal promises of a literal kingdom over which Christ shall reign one day.

In 11:10 we are told that Christ will call the Gentiles as well as the Jews. The miracle of crossing the Red Sea at the Exodus will be repeated in the last days so that Israel will be able to return to her land (11:11-16). People once laughed at these promises, but now that Israel possesses her own land and Holy City, their fulfillment seems near. Chapter 12 is the nation's song of victory. They sang this song when they were delivered from Egypt (Ex. 15:2), and also when they returned after the exile to rebuild the temple (Ps. 118:14). They will sing it again when they go back to their land in victory and glory when Jesus shall reign over a world of peace and prosperity.

# ISAIAH 40–66

Isaiah 40–66 is often called the "New Testament section" of the book. It has twenty-seven chapters in it, similar to the twenty-seven books of the NT. It begins with the ministry of John the Baptist (40:3-4 with Matt. 3:1-3) and its emphasis is Christ and salvation. At the very heart of this section is chapter 53, the greatest OT prediction of Christ's death on the cross. While Isa. 1–39 emphasizes God's judgment on His people, Isa. 40–66 sounds a note of comfort and redemption. It was written to encourage the Jewish remnant that would be delivered from the Babylonian captivity after their seventy years of captivity. Isaiah wrote this amazing prophecy over 150 years before the remnant would ever need it for their encouragement.

As you read these chapters, several major ideas will stand out.

The first is the constant emphasis, "Fear not." See 41:10, 13-14; 43:1, 5; 44:2, 8. Of what were the Jews afraid? Of the great Gentile nations that were moving in conquest across the world. Israel had been taken by Assyria; Judah had been captured by Babylon, and now a new empire—the Persians—was emerging on the scene. And all these nations worshiped idols. "If these nations are so victorious," some of the Jews argued, "then their gods must be the true gods, and Jehovah cannot be trusted." This leads to the second major idea: the greatness of God and the falseness of the heathen idols. Read carefully 40:18-20; 41:6-7, 29; 42:8, 17; 43:10-12; 44:9-20 (a scathing exposure of the stupidity of idol-worship); 45:16, 20; 46:1-2, 5-7. Please note the repeated statement that God is true and there is no other god to be compared with Him (40:18, 25; 43:10-11; 44:6, 8; 45:5-6, 14). In each of these chapters, Isaiah exposes the folly of idols and exalts the greatness of Jehovah. The Jewish remnant did not have to fear, God was great enough.

The third major idea has to do with Cyrus, King of Persia, the man God raised up to conquer Babylon and enable the Jews to return to their land (read 41:2-5, 25; 44:28–45:4; 47:11). He is the Cyrus mentioned in Ezra 1:1; he reigned from about 559 to 529 B.C. The fact that Isaiah calls him by name two centuries before he was born is another proof of the divine inspiration of the Bible. King Josiah was also named hundreds of years before his birth (1 Kings 13:2 and 2 Kings 23:15-18).

As you read these chapters, keep in mind that they have an immediate fulfillment in Cyrus and the return of the remnant from Babylon, and also an ultimate fulfillment in Jesus Christ and the redemption we have in Him. The wonderful deliverance from Babylon is a picture of the redemption Christ purchased for us on the cross. King Cyrus, though a heathen ruler, is in this sense a picture of Christ, our Redeemer (45:1-4). Isaiah 42:1-9 presents Christ as God's obedient Servant, bringing glory to the Jews and salvation to the Gentiles. Compare these verses with Matt. 12:18-20.

With this background, we may look at these chapters and see how God reveals Himself to His people and encourages them to trust Him. God reveals to them several aspects of His greatness.

## I. The Greatness of His Person (40)

This chapter contrasts the greatness of God with the feebleness of man (vv. 6-8) and the weakness of the idols (vv. 18-20). How could this feeble remnant of Jews ever return to their land and establish the nation again? God would go before them and open the way (vv. 3-5). In Matt. 3:3 this promise is applied to John preparing the way for the arrival of Christ. "Don't look at yourselves" says the prophet in vv. 9-17. "Look at your God. He is the Creator of the universe. Is He not able to strengthen you and sustain you?" Note the blessed promise in vv. 28-31.

## II. The Greatness of His Purpose (41)

Jehovah is not simply the God of the Jews; He is the Controller of the nations. He would raise up Cyrus from the east (Persia, v. 2) but bring him down from the north (after he conquered the Medes, v. 25). The nations trembled and turned to their idols, but they could not deliver them (vv. 3-7). God has a purpose in the rise and fall of the nations; Israel did not have to fear (vv. 10, 13-14) because God was with them and working out His purposes (Rom. 8:28). He would turn the "worm" into a "threshing-machine" and remove mountains! The idols had no purposes; they could not plan and control future events (vv. 21-24).

## III. The Greatness of His Pardon (42–43)

In 42:1-9 we are introduced to Jesus Christ (Matt. 12:18-20) as we see His first coming in humility and grace, and His second coming in power and judgment. Between these two events we have the present age of the church. God had permitted the Jews to be captured and exiled to chasten them for their sins (42:18-25), but their captivity would not be forever. He would come in judgment and destroy Babylon (42:10-17), using Cyrus as His tool. Chapter 43 again assures Israel, "Fear not—I am with thee." Their deliverance would make them witnesses to the world of the grace and power of God (43:10, 12). But Isaiah chides the nation for having forgotten God (43:22-27); and yet in His grace God would forgive their sins (43:25). It is possible to apply these promises of pardon to the future Jewish remnant during the Tribulation period.

## IV. The Greatness of His Promises (44–45)

Note the repeated "I will" statements in these chapters. Here God is promising the nation His help and blessing. In 44:1-8 He promises to restore them to their land, bless the land, and reign as their

King. Of course, the nation must repent of its sins before God can restore and forgive (44:21-23). In 44:9-20 the prophet again exposes the folly of the heathen idols: a man chops down a tree, uses part of it for fuel, and uses the rest of it to make himself a god. Jehovah is a God who makes and keeps His promises; the idols are but lies (44:18-20). In 44:24—45:8 we have another promise of deliverance through Cyrus. The heathen priests and sorcerers may promise defeat (44:25), but God will frustrate their lies and give Cyrus victory. Judah would be inhabited again, and Jerusalem would be rebuilt. This was fulfilled in Ezra 1. In 45:1-3, Isaiah even tells how Cyrus would capture the invincible fortress of Babylon: he would dry up one of the rivers that flowed into the city and come in under the gates. History records this feat, but prophecy announced it hundreds of years before it happened. Can anyone frustrate or oppose the promises and purposes of God? (45:5-10) No. God would raise up Cyrus to build His city (45:13); He would give Cyrus other nations as his wages for serving God (45:14). The idols would be confounded, but God would be glorified (45:16-19). Note in 45:17 that the historical blends in with the eternal: it would be everlasting salvation. Here the Prophet Isaiah looks down the centuries to the salvation we have in Christ (45:22), as well as to the future deliverance of Israel and the establishing of the kingdom.

## V. The Greatness of His Power (46–48)

These chapters describe the utter ruin of Babylon. When Isaiah spoke and wrote these words, Babylon was not yet a great world power. Some of the Jews must have wondered at his message. But Babylon did arise in power and did conquer Judah. Nevertheless, God would one day conquer Babylon, and her false gods would themselves be carried into captivity. Instead of the heathen gods carrying their people, the people would carry their gods (46:5-7). But God would carry His people (46:3-4) and bring salvation to Zion. The "ravenous bird" in 46:11 is Cyrus, of course. Read chapters 47–48 to see how God's power would destroy the great nation of Babylon.

"Fear not" is God's great promise to us as NT Christians. He is greater than Satan and this world, so we need not fear. He has a purpose for our lives, and He will fulfill it if we trust Him. He will pardon our sins and keep His promises.

# ISAIAH 53

This chapter is the very heart of Isa. 40–66, and it takes us to the cross. That these verses apply to Jesus Christ is proved by John 12:38, Matt. 8:17, Acts 8:32-35, Mark 15:28, Luke 22:37, Rom. 10:16, and 1 Peter 2:24. Isaiah 53 is quoted or referred to at least eighty-five times in the NT.

The prophecy begins with 52:13-15. Verse 13 tells of Christ's exaltation, and the rest of the section deals with His humiliation. It is this strange "contradiction" that perplexed the OT prophets, as 1 Peter 1:10-11 informs us. They did not realize that there would be a long period between Messiah's coming as the Suffering Servant to die and then returning as the Exalted Sovereign to reign. Verse 14 informs us that Christ's physical sufferings made Him look inhuman, so much so that men were astonished at Him. But when He returns the second time (v. 15), the whole world will be "startled, shocked" (the word should not be translated "sprinkle" but "startle"). See Zech. 12:9-10 and Rev. 1:7. The first time He came, He astonished a few people in Palestine; the next time He comes, He will startle the whole world. Now for the chapter before us. It traces the life and ministry of Christ.

## I. His Rejection (53:1-3)

The unbelief of Israel is now announced: they saw Him, heard Him, but would not trust Him (John 1:11; 12:37-38). There was a three-fold rejection: they rejected His words, "report," and His works, "the arm of the Lord". See John 12:37-40 especially. The prophet had been warned of this hardness of heart in 6:9-10.

The third focus of rejection was His person (v. 2). He was not born in a palace; He was born in a Bethlehem stable, and He grew up in the despised town of Nazareth (John 1:43-46). The words "tender plant" literally mean "a little bush" such as would spring from a low branch. In other words, Christ was not a great tree, but a humble bush. See Isa. 11:1. When He appeared, the nation was barren and dry spiritually. They had a form of religion, but they had no life, and because He brought life, they rejected Him. What a remarkable Man, human ("He shall grow up") yet divine. This offended the Jews who could not believe that God would come in the form of a Servant (Mark 6:1-3). His physical appearance was not unusual; there was no splendor or special human attractiveness to the human eye. Of course, to those who know Him, He is the fairest of the fair (Ps. 45:1ff). He was despised (not wanted, looked down upon), rejected (forsaken by His disciples, His nation, and His world), lightly esteemed (not valued highly, not wanted). Yet He went about doing good and helping the helpless. This only shows the wickedness of the human heart, that men would so treat the very Son of God.

## II. His Redemption (53:4-6)

Why should an innocent man such as Jesus Christ die such a terrible death on the cross? These verses explain why: He was taking the place of sinners and bearing their judgment for them. See 1 Peter 2:24 and 2 Cor. 5:21. Note the price that he paid: (1) wounded, or pierced, referring to His death on the cross, pierced by nails—John 19:37, Zech. 12:10; (2) bruised, which means "crushed" as under a burden, the weight of sin which was laid on Him; (3) chastised, or punished as though He had broken the law, in this case with stripes from the scourging.

But these physical sufferings were nothing compared to the spiritual suffering of the cross, when He bore our transgressions (vv. 5, 8), our rebellious and deliberate breaking of God's Law; our iniquities (vv. 5-6), the crookedness of our nature; and our griefs and sorrows (v. 4), our calamities and the unhappy results of our sins. We are sinners by birth ("All we like sheep have gone astray") and by choice ("we have turned every one to his own way"). See Ps. 58:3 and Rom. 5:12ff. Verse 6 begins with the "all" of condemnation, but ends with the "all" of salvation. He died for us all. These verses are the very heart of the Gospel—"Christ died for *our* sins."

## III. His Resignation (53:7-9)

He was not treated justly; He was oppressed, harassed, treated roughly. Yet He did not complain or cry out. They mocked Him and pushed Him from one place to another, yet He was silent and meek as a lamb. He was the "Lamb of God" who came to take away the world's sins (John 1:29). Verse 8 suggests that He was taken violently from prison and was not permitted to have justice. See Acts 8:33 and Matt. 27:22-31. The trial was "rigged" and the whole thing was illegal. Yet His "generation" did not protest; His disciples had forsaken Him and fled. And His death was not a glorious one; He was "cut off" like an unclean leper cast out of the city. In spite of this illegal and inhuman treatment, Jesus Christ did not protest or argue. Why? Because He had come to die for the sins of the people. Barabbas the criminal was treated with more kindness than was Jesus the Son of God.

Verse 9 should read: "And they appointed His grave with the wicked, yet He was with a rich man in His death." Were it not for Nicodemus and Joseph, the body of Jesus would have been buried in a "potter's field" or thrown on a garbage heap (John 19:38-42). God had promised His Son a "grave in the garden," and this was fulfilled. "He had done no violence, and there was no deceit in His mouth." Men were unjust, but God was just. What an example Christ is to us as He submitted completely to the will of God (1 Peter 2:18-25). When men treat us unjustly (as they will because we follow Christ), we must glorify Christ by being yielded to His will.

## VI. His Reward (53:10-12)

All of this was planned by God and His plan was a complete success. See 52:13 and 42:1-4, where we see the success of the Savior's work. These verses in chapter 53 show us the Godward side of the cross: His death "pleased the Lord." Does this mean that the Father rejoiced in His Son's suffering and death? No. But it pleased Him to see the work of salvation completed, the sacrifice accepted, and sin atoned for. Now a holy God could, in His grace, save undeserving sinners. Though Christ was slain by the evil hands of men, their deeds were overruled to accomplish the purpose of God (Acts 2:22-24). Christ's death was not a "moral example"; it was an offering for sin (v. 10). He died in our place.

What was Christ's reward, apart from the joy of having done His Father's will? He was raised from the dead ("He shall prolong His days") and given a spiritual family ("He shall see His seed"). Verse 11 presents the picture of a spiritual family, for it describes the "travail" of His soul on the cross. See Ps. 22:30 and Heb. 2:13. In Isa. 9:6 Christ is called the "Everlasting Father" and this is the reason why: His death and travail on the cross have made possible God's family of saved sinners. These are people whom He has justified, declared righteous through His grace.

Verse 12 presents another reward of the faithful Servant: an inheritance from the Father. He has conquered sin and Satan; now He divides the spoils (Eph. 4:8). When He was on earth, Christ was lightly esteemed, but now He is ranked with "the great." Kings will bow to Him (52:13, 15; Ps. 72:8-11; Rev. 19:14ff). Psalm 2 describes how Christ will one day claim His inheritance.

The closing statements take us back to the cross. Christ was numbered with transgressors—He was crucified between two thieves and treated like a criminal (Matt. 27:38). He made intercession for the transgressors, praying for them (Luke 23:34, 43). He did not speak when men cruelly reviled Him, but He did speak for the sake of lost sinners. And today He is interceding for His own (Rom. 8:34). There is no judgment upon them because He bore it all Himself. Have you trusted Him as *your own* Savior?

# ISAIAH 60–66

These chapters describe the glorious kingdom that Jesus Christ will establish when He returns to earth to reign. The word "glory" in its various forms is found twenty-three times in these chapters. There was certainly no glory in Israel or Judah when the Babylonian captivity ended and the feeble remnant returned to their land. How discouraging it must have been to return to a war-torn land, a city with walls broken down and gates burned, and a temple left in ruin. But Isaiah looked down the years and saw a glorious "holy city" with a glorious temple (60:7; see 64:11) and rebuilt walls and gates (60:10-11). Israel was the scorn of the Gentile nations, but she would be the center of the earth, the very throne of God; and the Gentiles would come to Jerusalem and worship the true God (see 60:3, 5, 11, 16; 61:6, 9; 62:2; 66:12, 19). These promises of the future glory of the nation would be a great encouragement to the Jews as they returned to their land after the Captivity. Note in these chapters four wonderful pictures of the restored nation.

## I. A Glorious Dawning (60)

### A. The new day dawns (vv. 1-9).

How dark it was for the Jews in Isaiah's day, and how much darker it would be during the Tribulation when the nation would suffer under the hands of the Antichrist and the Gentile nations. But the darkness will end with the return of Christ. The Lord Himself shall appear to the Jews—"they shall look upon Me whom they have pierced" (Zech. 12:10; Rev. 1:7). In that day Israel will share the glory of Christ as He reigns upon David's throne, and the church will reign with Him in His kingdom. Isaiah sees the Gentile nations coming to Jerusalem in peace, not war, with Israel sharing the wealth of the nations (vv. 3-9). Some apply v. 5 to the Dead Sea, for even today the Jews are extracting wealth from this body of water. Today, the nations are against Jerusalem; she has been the center of worldwide opposition. But in the day that Christ restores the glory to Israel, the Gentiles will bow down in peace.

### B. The blessings abound (vv. 10-22).

The nation will be rebuilt, and the gates will never have to be closed because of danger. The millennial kingdom (a thousand years, Rev. 20:4-5) will be a time of peace and prosperity for the whole world. It will be a "new day" for mankind when the Sun of Righteousness, Jesus Christ, returns (Mal. 4:1-3). Do not apply these promises to Christians today by spiritualizing them or turning them into symbols. They will be fulfilled literally in the land of Israel when Jesus comes again. As NT Christians, we are looking for "the Bright and Morning Star" (Rev. 22:16) that precedes the dawning; for Christ will return in the air for His church and take us to heaven before His judgments fall on the world.

## II. A Joyous Wedding (61–62)

Isaiah 61:1-2 was read by Christ in the synagogue at Nazareth (Luke 4:16-21), and He applied the words to Himself. He had come to meet the spiritual needs of the people and "to proclaim the acceptable year of the Lord." There He stopped reading, for "the day of vengeance" would not come until the Tribulation (see 63:1-4). We are living today in God's "year of acceptance," the day of grace. Of course, Isaiah is speaking here of the Lord's ministry to Israel, when He would return to convert their "funeral" into joyous "wedding." Verse 3 pictures the mourners drying their tears and putting on festive garments instead of mourning clothes. Verse 10 describes the nation rejoicing as the bride and the bridegroom.

Israel was "married" to Jehovah at Mt. Sinai, when He gave them the Law. But the nation was unfaithful and went after the gods of other nations. Because of her "spiritual adultery," the nation was sent into captivity, but even this did not cure her of her sins. Today, Israel is a "forsaken wife," but when Christ returns and the nation is cleansed, she will again be "married" to Jehovah.

Isaiah 62:4 promises that she will not be "Forsaken" or "Desolate"; rather, she will be named "Hephzibah," "My delight is in her," and "Beulah," "married." Verse 5 pictures the Lord rejoicing over His restored wife. Do not confuse this with the church, the bride of Christ (2 Cor. 11:1-2). See Hosea 2, Isa. 50:1 and 54:1.

### III. A Righteous Victory (63–64)

In 63:1-6 we have Christ pictured as the blood-stained Warrior, returning from His victory over the nations at the Battle of Armageddon (Rev. 19:11-21). His victory is pictured as a farmer pressing out the juice on the winepress. Christ's first miracle on earth was turning water into wine; His last victory before establishing His kingdom on earth will be treading out the winepress of His wrath. Why will Christ defeat the nations that try to destroy the Jews? Because of His grace and faithfulness (vv. 7-9). When Isaiah considered the goodness of God to Israel, in spite of their rebellion, he had to cry out in prayer for the cleansing of the nation (63:15–64:12). How he longed to see God work in mighty power as He had done in years past. The temple was trodden down, and the nation had possessed it but a few years (63:18). Isaiah points out their sins: uncleanness (64:5-6), unconcern (64:7), and unyieldedness (64:8). When Jesus rode into Jerusalem, He rode in peace upon a donkey. When He comes to earth the second time, He will ride in majesty on a white horse. And the nations will learn that the Prince of Peace is also a Man of War, judging sin and delivering His people.

### V. A Marvelous Birth (65–66)

God describes what He will do when the kingdom is established on the earth. He reminds the nation of her sins (65:1-7) and rebukes her by announcing His salvation for the Gentiles (Rom. 10:19-21). The OT promised salvation to the Gentiles, but it did not reveal that believing Jews and Gentiles would be made into one body, the church. The nation deserved to be destroyed, but God would preserve her (65:8). His believing remnant would inherit the land, but the unbelievers would be cut off (64:9-17). Isaiah 65:18-25 pictures the blessings of the kingdom when Jerusalem is the center of the earth. There will be long life (65:20); death will not be destroyed until after the kingdom age when Satan is finally judged (Rev. 20:7-14; 1 Cor. 15:26). People will work at their jobs in peace and happiness and see their labors fulfilled. Nature will be at peace (65:25; see Rom. 8:18-24). What a glorious day it will be. In 66:7-9 we have the miraculous birth of the new nation. "Political" Israel was born on May 14, 1948, but it is a nation in unbelief. "Righteous Israel" will be born when Jesus Christ returns and they see Him and trust Him. The Tribulation period will be the "time of Jacob's trouble" (Jer. 30:7), when the nation will "travail" in pain. It will be a time when God will purge Israel and a believing remnant will be spared to establish the kingdom. It took years of political "travail" for the present Israel to become a nation, but the restored nation will be born in a day when they see Christ. The birth is announced in 66:7-9; the joy of the birth in 66:10. But instead of the "baby" nursing on others, Israel will provide the blessings for the other nations (66:11-12). And Jehovah God will "mother" the new nation (66:13) and cause her to bring joy and blessing to the whole earth.

Note in 66:7 that *before* the "travail" of the Tribulation, the nation would give birth to Christ. See Rev. 12:1-6. There are, then, two births here: the birth of Christ, the Man-child (66:7), and the birth of the restored nation after the Tribulation (vv. 8-9). Keep in mind the order of events: (1) the rapture of the church (1 Thes. 4:13-l8); (2) the rise of Antichrist (2 Thes. 2); (3) the breaking of Antichrist's seven-year covenant with the Jews (Dan. 9:27) after three and a half years; (4) the pouring out of God's wrath on the world (Matt. 24:15-28) to judge the Gentiles and purify Israel; (5) the return of Christ with the church to the earth to defeat the nations (Rev. 19:11-21, Armageddon); and then (6) the establishing of the millennial kingdom (Rev. 20:1-6).

# JEREMIAH

## *A Suggested Outline of Jeremiah*

Introduction—The prophet's call (1)

I. National—Messages to Judah (2–33)

  A. Condemnation (2–24)
    1. The nation generally (2–20)
    2. The leaders specifically (21–24)
  B. Captivity (25–29)
  C. Restoration (30–33)

II. Personal—Jeremiah's sufferings (34–45)

  A. Before the siege of Jerusalem (34–39)
  B. After the siege, with the remnant (40–45)

III. International—Messages to the nations (46–51)

  A. Egypt (46)
  B. Philistia (47)
  C. Moab (48)
  D. Ammon (49:1-6)
  E. Edom (49:7-22)
  F. Syria, Kedar, Elam (49:23-39)
  G. Babylon (50–51) (Babylon is mentioned 168 times in Jeremiah)

Conclusion—the Prophet's captivity and release (52)

# Introductory Notes to Jeremiah

## I. The Man

The name "Jeremiah" means "whom Jehovah appoints." Apart from this appointment by God, certainly the prophet could not have continued to minister faithfully. He was of the priestly line and lived in the priests' city of Anathoth. Apparently he had some personal wealth because he was able to purchase real estate and even hire a scribe. He was called to the ministry when but "a child" (1:4-6); this was in the year 627 B.C.

## II. The Times

Jeremiah ministered during the last forty years of Judah's history, from the thirteenth year of Josiah (627 B.C.) to the destruction of Jerusalem and beyond (587 B.C.). He lists the kings during whose reigns he served (1:1-3), the last leaders of the once-prosperous kingdom of Judah. *Josiah* was a godly king; he died in 608 B.C. It was during his reign that the Law was found and the temple worship restored. *Jehoahaz* followed, but reigned only three months, so Jeremiah does not mention him. *Jehoiakim* was next (608–597 B.C.); he was a godless man and did his utmost to persecute Jeremiah. It was he who burned the scroll of Jeremiah's prophecies in Jer. 36. *Jehoiachin* was the next king, but he too reigned just three months before being taken captive to Babylon. The last king was *Zedekiah* (597–586 B.C.); he presided over the ruin of the nation and the capture of the city of Jerusalem. So, the Prophet Jeremiah lived to see his beloved nation go down into sin, war, and judgment; yet through it all he was faithful to preach God's Word throughout all the lands.

When Jeremiah began his ministry, Assyria was the leading power in the world, but Egypt and Babylon were rapidly gaining strength. In 607 B.C. the Babylonians took Nineveh and destroyed the power of Assyria. Babylon then turned to Judah, and Judah's "politicians" advised the king to ask Egypt for help. Jeremiah was always against an Egyptian alliance. He knew that Judah's only hope was the Lord, but her sins were so great, the nation had lost the blessing of God. Babylon finally did capture Judah and take Jerusalem (606–586). Jeremiah wrote Lamentations to commemorate the death of the Holy City.

## III. The Message

Jeremiah's task was not an easy one because he had to sound the death knell for his nation. The first part of his book records several of his sermons, given in Jerusalem, in which he denounces the people, priests, and princes for their sins, especially the sin of idolatry. In chapter 25 he announces that the nation will go into captivity for seventy years, and then return to reestablish the nation. In chapter 31 he prophesies a "new covenant" between Jehovah and His people, not a covenant of law and works written on stones, but a covenant of love and faith, written in the heart. In the final chapters, Jeremiah deals with the Gentile nations around Judah and tells of God's plans for them.

One of the key words in the book is "backslide" (2:19; 3:6, 8, 11-12, 14, 22; 49:4). The nation had turned her back on the Lord and was following false prophets who led them to worship idols. Eleven times the word "repent" is used by the prophet, but the nation did not repent. We read of Jeremiah weeping, so burdened was he for his fallen nation. See 9:1; 13:17; 14:17; 15:17-18; and Lam. 1:2; 2:11, 18. Because he prophesied the captivity and told the kings to surrender to Babylon, Jeremiah was called a traitor and was persecuted by his own people. No OT prophet faced more opposition from false prophets than did Jeremiah (see 2:8, 26; 4:9; 5:31; 6:14; 14:13-16; 18:18; 23:9-40; 26:8-19; 27:9-16; chaps. 28 and 29). If Judah had repented and turned to God, He would have delivered them from Babylon. Because they persisted in their sins, the nation had to be punished, but then God promised restoration "for His name's sake."

Jeremiah used many dramatic illustrations to get his messages across: fountains and cisterns (2:13); medicine (8:22); a "good-for-nothing" girdle or sash (13:1-11); a clay vessel (chaps. 18–19); yokes (chap. 27); drowning a book (51:59-64).

## IV. Jeremiah and Jesus

The similarities between Jeremiah and Jesus Christ are worth noting. Neither married (16:2), and both were rejected by their own towns (11:21 and 12:6 with Luke 4:16-30). Jeremiah ministered under the menacing shadow of Babylon, Jesus under the shadow of Rome. Both were considered traitors by their people. Jeremiah was viciously opposed by the false prophets, Jesus by the scribes and Pharisees, the false leaders of His day. Both wept over the city of

523

Jerusalem, and both predicted its ruin. Jeremiah gathered few disciples about him; Jesus had a small following. Both were arrested falsely and persecuted. Both emphasized a religion of the heart, and not merely one of outward forms and ceremonies. It was Jeremiah 7:11 that Jesus quoted when He cleansed the temple and told the priests they had made it "a den of thieves." Both emphasized the new covenant in the heart (Jer. 31:31-37; Heb. 8:7ff). In their preaching, both used striking illustrations and comparisons. Both revealed a tender, sympathetic heart that was crushed by the wickedness of a nation that should have obeyed God's Word. In the end, it seemed that both were failures in their lives and ministries, but God honored them and made their work successful.

# JEREMIAH 18–19

In chapter 18 the prophet visits the potter's house and watches him mold the clay, while in chapter 19 he takes a completed vessel and breaks it in the Valley of Hinnom. The first event pictures God's grace; the second, His judgment. As you consider the potter and the clay, you can see a picture of our lives and our relationship to God. Each object has a meaning.

## I. God Is the Potter

### A. A person.

Our lives are not in the hands of some invisible "force" or blind "fate"; they are in the hands of a Person—Almighty God. God is not just our Creator; He is our Father, and He has a personal concern for our lives. He is the Potter. See Isa. 64:8.

### B. Power.

Clay cannot mold itself; only God has the power to guide our lives. He makes it clear in 18:6-10 that He is sovereign over all people. We cannot be blessed if we argue with Him or try to tell Him what to do; see Rom. 9:20-24. Of course, this does not mean that God is to blame for the sins of men or the failures of nations.

### C. A plan.

The potter has a perfect plan for the clay; he sees the finished product in his mind. God has a perfect plan for our lives (Rom. 12:1-2; Eph. 2:10; Phil. 1:6). We cannot see the finished product, but He promises us that it is wonderful (1 Cor. 2:9).

### D. Patience.

The potter patiently works the clay, tenderly molding its shape. God patiently directs in our lives, seeking to fulfill His will. Often He uses the hands of others to help shape us—parents, teachers, fellow Christians, even those who persecute us. It takes time to make a worthwhile product, and God is willing to wait.

## II. We Are the Clay

Of course, in Jeremiah's message the clay represented the people of Judah, but we are not wrong in applying it to our lives personally.

Christians are God's vessels, molded by Him to contain the treasure of the Gospel (2 Tim. 2:19-21; 2 Cor. 4:7; Acts 9:15). Human beings are made of clay; clay is dust mixed with water. We are of the dust (Ps. 103:14), but the water of the Spirit of God has given us life through faith in Christ. Clay is of no great value in itself, but it can become something great if molded by the right hands for the right purpose. Nobody can calculate the tremendous potential in an individual's life.

The most important quality of clay is that it yields. If it fails to yield to the hands of the potter, it will be spoiled. The clay cannot mold itself; it must have the potter. There are no "self-made" Christians in the will of God. When we say "the clay cannot mold itself," we are not suggesting that people play no part in the fulfilling of God's will. We are not inactive or resigned, mere lumps of clay in God's hands. He wants us to cooperate with Him as we pray, meditate, obey His will, and yield to His tender touch.

## III. Life Is the Wheel

The wheel is spun around swiftly by the potter himself, and he alone controls its speed. Our lives as Christians are not controlled by chance or luck; they are controlled by God. He arranges the circumstances of life that mold us. It was God who arranged for young Joseph to go to Egypt where he was molded into a ruler. We may wonder about the circumstances of our lives and think that God has been unkind to us, but one day we will realize the truth of Romans 8:28 and agree that all things *did* work together for good. The most important thing about a wheel is not its size (some lives are shorter than others), but its center. If the wheel is "on center" then everything will be balanced. Christ is the center of the dedicated Christian's life (Matt. 6:33).

## IV. Disobedience Is the Marring

It would be wonderful if the clay always yielded to the potter's hands, but this is not the case. The prophet saw the vessel marred. Did the potter throw the clay away and start with a new lump? No, he made it again. This is a picture of the rebellion of man and his restoration by God's grace. Why was the clay marred? Because it wanted to have its own way (see 18:11-12). How often we as Christians mar our own lives by making our own plans outside the will of God. If only we could see the finished product that God has planned we would never disobey Him. Alas, we think we know more about life than He does.

God is gracious to forgive and to "make us again." Sometimes He must use difficult testings to get us to yield. He spent twenty years molding Jacob, who in the end became a useful vessel. After they were marred, God gave a second chance to David, Jonah, and Peter. First John 1:9 is a wonderful promise of forgiveness, but it is not an excuse for disobedience.

## V. Trials Are the Furnaces

Jeremiah does not mention the potter's furnaces, but they had to be there. No vessel is worth anything until it has gone through the furnace. The heat gives the clay strength and beauty and increases its usefulness and value. Life must have its furnaces. Job went through the furnace of pain (Job 23:10), and 1 Peter 4:12ff tells about the furnace of persecution. The three faithful Hebrew children went through that furnace and discovered that the Potter was in the fire with them (Dan. 3:19-25). God knows just how hot to make the furnace; He knows just how much trial we can bear (1 Cor. 10:13). Christians who have lived sheltered lives outside God's furnaces miss many of the blessings of His grace received by those who have been willing to suffer with and for Christ. When trials come our way, we must yield to the Potter and let Him have His way.

## VI. Breaking the Vessel Is Judgment

In 19:1-13 Jeremiah went to the Valley of the son of Hinnom, a place the Jews had dedicated to the worship of idols. Some of the worst sins in Jewish history were committed in that place; see 7:31. The name "son of Hinnom" was written "ge-Hinnom" and eventually became "Gehenna" in the Greek language, the NT word for hell. King Josiah turned this idolatrous place into Jerusalem's garbage dump (2 Kings 23:10). What an awful picture of hell—the eternal garbage dump of the universe. This time the prophet brought a finished vase, and as he held it before the elders of the land, he preached a sermon of judgment. "You have forsaken God and worshiped idols here. You have sinned against His Word. But the day will soon come when this valley will not be called 'Tophet' (burning, or filth), but 'the valley of slaughter.' Judgment is coming to Judah." Then he broke the vase—and it could never be repaired.

See vv. 10-11. A nation or an individual life can get to the "point of no return." If the clay becomes hard, it can no longer be molded. How important it is to yield to Christ early in life. Samson refused to yield, and God had to break the vessel. "There is a sin unto death" (1 John 5:16).

God wants us to be useful vessels. A vessel does not manufacture anything; it only receives, contains, and shares. We receive His blessings and share them with others. All that God asks is that we be available, clean, and empty. See 2 Tim. 2:19-21, where Paul warns us to be separated from sin. If we are too full of self, God cannot fill us, and if we are not filled, we cannot share anything with others. May the Lord help us to be vessels for honor, fit for the Master's use.

# JEREMIAH 36 and 45

Jeremiah had been preaching for more than twenty years when these events took place. Egypt had just been defeated by Babylon, so King Jehoiakim's "foreign policy" was ruined. The prophet knew that Babylon would one day take Judah captive, but he still longed to see his people repent. It takes a godly servant to continue ministering when the situation seems hopeless.

## I. The Inspiration of the Word (36:1-4)

Up to now, Jeremiah's ministry had been oral; he had preached in the temple courts and tried to awaken the backslidden nation. But God wanted Jeremiah's messages written down permanently as a part of His Word. In vv. 17-18 we see how this was done: God spoke to the prophet; Jeremiah spoke the words to his secretary, Baruch; and Baruch wrote them down. What Baruch wrote was a revelation from God, truths that no human being could have discovered for himself. The Bible is God's revelation to men and women; the truths that are in it could not have been discovered by the human mind. The Bible is the book of "Thus saith the Lord."

*Inspiration* is the word used to describe how the Bible was written. "All Scripture is given by inspiration of God" says 2 Tim. 3:16. This means that the Bible is "God-breathed"; it is not the manufactured product of the human mind. "Holy men of God spoke as they were moved by the Holy Spirit" (2 Peter 1:21, NKJV). The world speaks of great writers as being "inspired," but this is not what the Bible means by "inspiration." Shakespeare was an inspired writer in the human sense of greatness, but his writings were not inspired of God as is the Bible. The Spirit of God spoke to and through men of God to give us the Word of God. He did not bypass their personalities or make "robots" out of them; each Bible writer reveals his own individual personality in his writings. But what they wrote is the Word of God, final, complete, and authoritative. You can trust your Bible.

## II. The Proclamation of the Word (36:5-10)

By comparing v. 1 with v. 9 we get the impression that the writing of this book took at least a year. The people had asked for a special fast day, apparently to seek the help of the Lord against Babylon. The king granted this request, although later events showed that he had no respect for God or His Word. He was like many political leaders who go along with national "religious observances" yet reject Christ and the Word personally. Baruch proclaimed the Word by reading the book to the fasting people in the temple. Jeremiah was bound, but God's Word could not be bound (2 Tim. 2:9; see 2 Thes. 3:1-2). It took courage for Baruch to do this, since Jeremiah was not a popular man in the city.

God has ordained that His Word should be spread by preaching and teaching. Certainly there is a place for Bible literature and tract distribution, but it is the preaching of the Word that God especially blesses. God uses His Word to convict people of sin, lead them to honest repentance, and then bring them the assurance of salvation (see v. 3). Baruch was seeking to warn Judah to flee to God's arms of mercy because judgment was approaching. Today we are seeking to win people to Christ because the wrath of God already is on them (John 3:36).

## III. The Preservation of the Word (36:11-32)

It is interesting to see how different people respond to the Word of God. Michaiah was present when Baruch read the Word in the temple before the chamber of the scribe, Gemariah, who was Michaiah's father. Michaiah was stirred by the Word and immediately shared it with the other leaders of the nation. They sent for Baruch, who read the Word a second time. The princes were now afraid (v. 16). Somebody must tell the king.

King Jehoiakim was a godless man who received his throne only by yielding to Egypt (2 Kings 23:31–24:7). He had already killed one prophet of God, Urijah (Jer. 26:20-24); and he was certainly no friend to Jeremiah. But he consented to listen to the reading as he sat comfortably in his winter house. He should have been in the temple, humbling himself before God. How gracious God was to bring the Word to him at a time when he needed it. But as Jehudi read the scroll, the king defiantly cut it to pieces and used it as fuel for his fire. There was no fear of God before his eyes. Three of the leaders protested (v. 25), but the king would not listen. Instead of yielding to the Word, he resisted it and sought to arrest and slay Jeremiah and Baruch.

Godless people have attacked the Bible for centuries, yet it still stands. Jeremiah wrote a new copy of his book, so the king's efforts were in vain. We still have Jeremiah's prophecy, but King Jehoiakim has long since turned to dust. Men and women who love sin oppose the Bible because the Bible exposes them and warns of the wrath to come. In A.D. 303 Emperor Diocletian of Rome sought out and burned copies of God's Word, and then erected a monument that read: "Extinct is the name of Christians." Twenty years later Constantine made Christianity the official religion of Rome and put the Bible back into the hands of the people. Haters of the truth persecuted Wycliffe because he translated the Bible into English; Tyndale was burned at the stake; yet the Bible is still here. God preserves His Word. "Forever, O Lord, Your Word is settled in heaven" (Ps. 119:89, NKJV). "Heaven and earth shall pass away, but My words shall not pass away" (Matt. 24:35). The person who builds his life on the Bible builds on that which cannot be shaken.

To his new copy, Jeremiah added a special judgment for the king. Jehoiakim thought he would destroy the Word, but the Word destroyed him. He would die a miserable death and leave no heir to claim his throne (v. 30). See Jer. 22:18-19. His son Jehoiachin did take the throne when his father died, but he lasted only three months before being taken captive to Babylon (2 Kings 24:6-12). And Babylon did come to capture Judah, just as Jeremiah had prophesied. Fulfilled prophecy is one of the greatest evidences for the divine inspiration of the Bible.

## IV. The Consolation of the Word (45)

This chapter records Baruch's reactions to the events of chapter 27. Here he had shared in the writing of the Word of God, yet he had to go into hiding to save his life. Instead of being honored for his faithfulness, he was forced to suffer persecution. What a great disappointment.

No doubt some of the king's associates offered Baruch "a good job" on the king's staff, since undoubtedly he was a gifted scribe. His brother Seraiah was one of the king's officers (32:12; 51:59). Why identify yourself with a hated preacher like Jeremiah when you can be a popular secretary to the king? God knew his heart, and God spoke to Jeremiah about it. "Are you seeking great things for yourself?" God asked Baruch. "Seek them not. There is no future in this land of Judah because Babylon will come and destroy the city and the land." Had Baruch forsaken Jeremiah and the Word for an "easy place" with the king, he would have lost everything. As it was, God protected his life and used him in His service.

It is not easy to stand true to the Word in days of opposition and persecution. Paul wrote, "Demas has forsaken me, having loved this present world" (2 Tim. 4:10, NKJV). And Paul himself, like Jeremiah and Baruch, suffered persecution and trouble because of the Word (2 Tim. 2:8-9), but at the close of his life, he was able to say, "I have kept the faith."

How are *you* treating God's Word? Are you putting it on the shelf? (36:20) Are you cutting it to pieces, as do the "modern critics" of the Bible? Are you seeking to destroy it? Or are you bowing before it and obeying its truths? "All Your precepts concerning all things I consider to be right; I hate every false way" (Ps. 119:128, NKJV).

# LAMENTATIONS

We will not outline this book. It is a series of "funeral poems" marking the destruction of Jerusalem and the temple. It is written in acrostic form: each of the twenty-two verses in chapters 1, 2, 4, and 5 starts with a succeeding letter of the Hebrew alphabet; in chapter 3, there are three verses given to each letter. No book in the Bible reveals the suffering heart of God over sin as does this one. See Jer. 13:17 and Matt. 23:36-38.

# LAMENTATIONS 1–5

This is a collection of five "lamentations" or "funeral dirges" commemorating the fall of Jerusalem to the Babylonians in 586 B.C. Jeremiah was witness to this tragic event. His heart was broken as he saw Jerusalem and the temple destroyed, the people slain, and the prisoners taken off to captivity in Babylon. We can see the prophet's tears all through the book. From this book we can learn five important lessons about God and His will.

## I. The Awfulness of God's Judgments (1:1-6)

These verses compare Jerusalem to a rich princess or queen suddenly left alone and robbed of all her wealth and beauty. Once she had been full; now she is empty. Once she was honored; now she is disgraced. Her joy has been replaced by tears; her great victories are now lost in defeat. Why? Because instead of loving Jehovah, she courted many "lovers" (v. 2) and the false gods of the heathen nations. Now those heathen nations have become her enemies.

Sin always brings sorrow and tragedy. In chapter 2, Jeremiah explains that God was no longer their friend, but their enemy. Once He had fought their battles, but now it was too late. Read the sad description of the hungry eating their own children (2:20; 4:10; and see Jer. 19:9). Jerusalem not only lost her joy, wealth, and beauty, but she also lost her testimony. All the heathen laughed at her (2:15-16). Certainly this applies to the believer today: when God chastens the backslider, the experience is not an easy one. Sin always makes the sinner lose.

## II. The Righteousness of God's Wrath (1:18-22)

"We are reaping just what we have sown," the prophet is crying. The awful judgments that came were only what the city and the nation deserved. "We have rebelled against His Word." Rebellion always leads to discipline; see Heb. 12:1-14. Why did God allow His people to go into captivity? To teach them to trust Him and obey His Word. In v. 19 Jeremiah names these troublemakers: the "lovers," that is, the false gods and the pagan nations that Judah trusted when she got into trouble; and the false prophets and priests, who taught lies and gave the people a false confidence. When a nation will not listen to the truth of God's Word, there is no hope for that nation.

What can the people do? Nothing but yield to God's chastening hand and trust His mercy (1:22). Confession of sin is better than continuous rebellion against God. It was too late for God to call off the invasion, but certainly He would see the repentance of His people and begin to work on their behalf even while they were in captivity.

## III. The Truthfulness of God's Word (2:17)

"He has fulfilled His Word." For forty years, Jeremiah had warned the people that their sins would bring judgment; yet the nation would not listen. People do not want to hear the truth; they prefer the "popular messages" of the false prophets (2:14). Jerusalem laughed at Jeremiah, persecuted him, and even tried to kill him, but in the end, God honored His servant and his words came true. Read Jer. 4:5-10 for Jeremiah's message of warning. Read Jer. 5:30-31 for his description of the nation believing lies. It sounds very contemporary. In Jer. 6:13-14 he compares the false prophets to doctors who hide the symptoms but do not cure the disease. See 8:11, 21-22. In 23:9ff, Jeremiah explains what happens to a people when they reject the truth of the Word of God and believe the lies of men. Yet the truth of God's Word shall stand, just as it did in Jeremiah's day. The time has already come when people will not endure "healthy doctrine," but want instead preachers who will tickle their ears and entertain them with a message of false assurance (2 Tim. 4:1-5). God will certainly judge this world, in spite of what the false prophets say.

## IV. The Tenderness of God's Heart (1:12-16)

Jeremiah certainly reveals to us the heart of Jehovah, broken for the sins of His people. Judgment is God's "strange work" (Isa. 28:21); He does not afflict willingly. And even when He does chasten His people, He is with them in their suffering (Isa. 63:9). "Whom the Lord *loves* He chastens." Jeremiah's tears remind us that God does love His own, even if they are rebellious, and that His love for them cannot change. As the people walked by the ruins, Jeremiah asked, "Is it nothing to you, all you who pass by?" We can hear the voice of Jesus Christ here as He hung on the cross for the sins of the world. Remember how He wept over Jerusalem because He saw her day of judgment coming?

God, in love, had warned the people of their sins and His impending judgment. In fact, as far back as Moses, the Lord had warned Israel not to follow false gods (see Lev. 26 and Deut. 28). In love He had sent the prophets to warn them (2 Chron. 36:15-17), but they would not listen. Now, in love, He had to chasten them to teach them the lessons they would not learn.

## V. The Faithfulness of God's Mercy (3:18-36)

Here at the heart of this book we find one of the greatest confessions of faith found anywhere in the Bible. Jeremiah had been dwelling on his sorrows and the sorrows of his people, but then he lifted his eyes to the Lord—and this was the turning point. In the midst of sorrow and ruin he remembered the mercy of the Lord. "His compassions fail not." We have failed Him, but He cannot fail us. "Great is Your faithfulness."

The faithfulness of God is a tremendous encouragement in days when people's hearts are failing them for fear. If you build your life on people or on the things of this world, you will have no hope or security; but if you build on Christ, the Faithful One, you will be safe forever. He is *faithful to chasten* (Ps. 119:75); Lamentations itself teaches this lesson. He wants to bring us to the place of repentance and confession (Lam. 3:39-41). He is *faithful to forgive* when we do confess our sins (1 John 1:9). He is *faithful to sympathize* when we have burdens and problems (Heb. 2:17-18; 4:14-16). We never need fear that He is too busy to listen or too tired to help. He is *faithful to deliver* when we cry out for help in temptation (1 Cor. 10:13). He is *faithful to keep us* in this life and unto life eternal (1 Tim. 1:15; 1 Thes. 5:23-24). We can commit our lives and souls into the hands of the faithful Creator (1 Peter 4:19) and know that He will do all things well.

God in His mercy spared a remnant of Judah, protected and blessed them during their years of captivity, and then permitted them to return to their land once again. He enabled them to rebuild their city and temple; He protected them from heathen nations that hated the Jews. How merciful God was to His people. How merciful He is to us today.

In times of trouble we need to imitate Jeremiah who looked away from himself to the Lord, and who waited on the Lord in patience and faith (3:24-26). Too often we look at ourselves and our problems and become so discouraged that we quit. Instead, we must "look away unto Jesus" (Heb. 12:1-2) and let Him see us through. It is difficult to wait on the Lord. Our fallen nature craves activity, and usually what we do only makes matters worse. Jeremiah waited on the Lord, trusted in His mercy, and depended on His faithfulness. He knew the truth of Isa. 40:31 (NKJV), "Those who wait on the Lord shall renew their strength; they shall mount up with wings like eagles, they shall run and not be weary, they shall walk and not faint."

# EZEKIEL

## *A Suggested Outline of Ezekiel*

I. The Ordination of the Prophet (1–3)

II. The Condemnation of Judah (4–24)
- A. A disobedient nation (4–7)
- B. A departed glory (8–11)
- C. A disciplined nation (12–24)

III. The Condemnation of the Gentile Nations (25–32)

IV. The Restoration of God's People (33–48)
- A. They return to their land (33–36)
- B. They experience new life and unity (37)
- C. They are protected from their enemies (38–39)
- D. They worship the Lord acceptably (40–48)

# EZEKIEL 1–36

In the year 606 B.C., the Babylonians began the first of several deportations of the Jews; Daniel was in this group. In the second group (597 B.C.) was young Ezekiel, then about twenty-five years old. He was taken to Tel-abib near the ship canal Chebar (3:15). There he lived in his own house with his beloved wife (8:1; 24:16ff). Five years after Ezekiel came to Tel-abib, he was called to be a prophet of God, when he was thirty years old (592 B.C.). This was six years before the destruction of Jerusalem in 586, so while Jeremiah was ministering to the people back home, Ezekiel was preaching to the Jews of the captivity in Babylon. Like Jeremiah, Ezekiel was a priest called to be a prophet.

His book may also be divided into three sections, following the prophet's call in 1–3: (1) God's judgment on Jerusalem, 4–24; (2) God's judgment on the surrounding nations, 25–32; and (3) God's restoration of the Jews in the kingdom, 33–48. Chapters 1–24 were given before the siege of Jerusalem; chapters 25–32 during the siege; and chapters 33–48 after the siege. Though the prophet was in distant Babylon, he was able to see events in Jerusalem through the power of the Spirit of God. Ezekiel not only proclaimed God's message to the people, but he had to live the message before them. God commanded him to do a number of symbolic acts in order to get the attention of the people: play at war (4:1-3); lie on his side a certain number of days (4:4-17); shave his hair and beard (5:1-4); act like someone fleeing from war (12:1-16); sit and sigh (21:1-7); and, the most difficult of all, have his wife die (24:15-27). It was not easy to be a prophet.

In this section we shall concentrate on Ezekiel's visions of God's glory.

## I. The Glory Revealed (1–3)

Ezekiel ("God strengthens") was a priest in captivity (1:1), and was thus unable to exercise his ministry since he was away from the temple and the sacred altar. But God opened the heavens to him and called him to be a prophet. He had been in captivity for five years when his call came; priests began their ministry at the age of thirty (Num. 4:3). See Ps. 137 for a picture of the spiritual condition of the captives. Jeremiah had told them to settle down in Babylon for seventy years, but the false prophets told the people that God would destroy Babylon and set the captives free (read Jer. 28–29). It was Ezekiel's task to tell the people that God would destroy *Jerusalem*, not Babylon, but that there would one day be a glorious restoration of the people and a rebuilding of the temple.

The phrase "The Word of the Lord came" is used nearly fifty times in this book. How wonderful to know that God's Word is never far from God's people if they will only listen. John heard the Word when an exile on Patmos (Rev. 1:9ff), and Paul received the Word when in prison. What did Ezekiel see that day?

### A. A fiery whirlwind (1:4).

This symbolized God's judgment on Jerusalem, Babylon coming out of the north. The storm cloud with its fiery lightning meant destruction for Jerusalem.

### B. The cherubim (1:5-14).

These creatures symbolize the glory and power of God. They could see in all directions and move in all directions without turning. The four faces speak of their characteristics: the intelligence of man; the strength and boldness of the lion; the faithfulness and service of the ox; and the heavenliness of the eagle. Some see in these faces the four Gospels: Matthew (lion—king); Mark (ox—servant); Luke (man—Son of Man); John (eagle—Son of God from heaven). The creatures could move quickly to accomplish the will of God.

### C. The wheels (1:15-21).

Each creature was associated with a set of wheels, two wheels in each set. The wheels in each set were not parallel to each other, like the rim and the hub of a bicycle wheel; rather, they were at right angles to each other, like a gyroscope top. The wheels were constantly turning and, since they faced in all four directions, they could move in any way without changing motion, just like the cherubim. They were "full of eyes" (v. 18), picturing the omniscience of God as He rules His creation (Prov. 15:3), and the movements of the wheels and the cherubim coincided. All of this speaks of God's constant working in the world, His power and glory, His presence in all places, His purpose for man, His providence. The world was full of terror and change, but God was at work.

### D. The firmament (1:22-27).

This was a beautiful "platform" above the wheels and the cherubim, containing the throne of God. God is still on the throne, and His will is being accomplished in this world even if we do not always see it. The complex movements of the cherubim and the wheels reveal how intricate is God's providence in the universe; only He can understand it, only He can control it. But there is perfect harmony and order.

### E. The rainbow (1:28).

There was a rainbow in the storm. Certainly this told Ezekiel that God's mercy and God's covenant would not fail His people. See Gen. 9:11-17, where the rainbow was appointed as a sign of mercy and also Rev. 4:3 and 10:1.

Noah saw the rainbow after the storm, the Apostle John saw it before the storm, but Ezekiel saw it within the storm. This entire vision of God's glory shows God at work in the world, judging the sins of His people, but still keeping His covenant of mercy. The result of this vision was total collapse on the part of Ezekiel (1:28). But God set him up on his feet, called him to be a watchman, fed him with the Word (see Jer. 15:16; Job 23:12; Matt. 4:4; Rev. 10:9), and filled him with the Spirit. "They shall know that I am the Lord"—this phrase is found seventy times in this book; it summarizes the ministry and message of Ezekiel.

## II. The Glory Removed (8–11)

A year later, God gave Ezekiel another vision, this time of the sins of the people back in Jerusalem. The glory appeared again (8:2), and God took the prophet in vision to the holy city. There he saw a four-fold view of the sins of the people: (1) an image set up at the north gate of the temple, possibly of As-tarte, the foul Babylonian goddess, 8:5; (2) secret heathen worship in the hidden precincts of the temple, 8:6-12; (3) the Jewish women weeping for the god Adonis, who was supposed to die and be raised from the dead each spring, 8:13-14; and (4) the high priest and the twenty-four courses of priests worshiping the sun, 8:15-16. Is it any wonder God planned to destroy the city?

Of course, the glory of the Lord could not remain in such a wicked place. The glory had come to the temple, 8:4; but in 9:3 the glory moved to the threshold of the temple. The throne of glory was now empty. It would become a throne of judgment. In chapter 9 we see God's servant putting a mark of protection on the faithful remnant of believers, lest they be slain in the judgment to come. Then, in 10:4, the glory of God moved above the threshold of the house, hovering there before judgment was going to fall. In 10:18 the glory moved with the cherubim off the threshold to the eastern gate of the temple (v. 19); and finally in 11:22-23, the glory moved out of the temple to the top of the Mount of Olives. "Ichabod—the glory has departed" (1 Sam. 4:21).

Why was the glory removed? Because God cannot share His glory with another. The idols and the sins of the people had driven Him away. Their sins may have been hidden from the people, but God saw them, and God judged them. So today God will remove His glory and His blessing from our lives unless we serve Him faithfully with honest and pure hearts.

### III. The Glory Restored (43:1-12)

In chapters 40–48 the prophet sees the future restoration of Israel and her glory in the kingdom. He describes the restored city and temple, greater than anything Israel has ever known. In 43:1-6 he sees the glory of God return to the temple. Note that the glory will return by the same route it used when it departed. Of course, Jesus Christ is the glory of the Lord and He will return the glory of God to the nation of Israel. Certainly the Word given in chapters 40–48 was not fulfilled when the Jews returned to their land after the captivity, so it must have a future fulfillment when Jesus returns to earth to reign.

God is concerned with His glory. We are to glorify God in our bodies (1 Cor. 6:19-20) and magnify Him in all that we do (Phil. 1:20-21). Our good works are to glorify God (Matt. 5:16). But we can sin away the glory of God from our lives. Certainly the Spirit of God will not leave us (Eph. 1:12-14), but we may grieve the Spirit and lose the glory of God in our daily walk (Eph. 4:30). Secret sins do not remain secret very long. God sees them and, before long, others see them too.

# EZEKIEL 37–48

These closing chapters look forward to the future of Israel and Judah, to a time when God will do a new work and His glory will return to the land.

## I. The New Nation (37)

### A. Revived (vv. 1–14).

At this time, both Israel and Judah were ruined politically. Assyria had scattered Israel, and Judah had just been captured by Babylon. Both Isaiah and Jeremiah predicted a return from captivity, but Ezekiel's vision goes even farther down the years. He saw the time when the dead nation would come alive again. In the vision, he saw very many bones in the valley (literally, "battlefield"), and the bones were very dry. It was a picture of utter defeat, with the bones of the armies bleached and unburied. What a vivid description of the Jewish people! Through the power of God's Word, the bones came together and formed men, and through the power of the Spirit ("wind"), life was given to them. This does not teach a bodily resurrection, or even the salvation of the Jews. Rather, it pictures the future revival of the *nation*, when the Jews will be brought up out of the "graves" of the Gentile nations where they have been scattered. Politically, this took place May 14, 1948, when the modern nation of Israel entered the family of nations again. Of course, the nation is dead spiritually; but one day when Christ returns, the nation will be born in a day and be saved.

### B. Reunited (vv. 15–28).

The division of the nation into the Northern and Southern Kingdoms was the beginning of their downfall. One day God will reunite all the tribes under their true David, Jesus Christ. He will make a covenant of peace with them (v. 26) and bring glory to His people once again.

Is there a future for Israel? Some students say, "No, for all these OT prophecies must be applied *spiritually* to the church." We do not agree. These prophecies are too detailed to be "spiritualized" and applied to the church today. Jesus taught a future for the Jews (Luke 22:29); so did Paul (Rom. 11); and so did John (Rev. 22:1-6).

## II. The New Victory (38–39)

These chapters deal with the famous "battle of Gog and Magog." Do not confuse this war with the Battle of Armageddon described in Rev. 19:11-21, because Armageddon takes place at the end of the seven-year Tribulation period that follows the rapture of the church. Nor is it the same as the battle involving Gog and Magog mentioned in Rev. 20:7-9, for that will take place after the close of the millennial reign of Christ when Satan will again be loosed. The battle given in Ezek. 38–39 takes place at a time when the Jews are safely living in their own land (38:8, 11-12, 14) in the "latter years" (38:8). When will this be? It seems probable that this will be during the first half of the Tribulation period, when Israel will be protected from her enemies by her covenant with the head of the Roman Empire (Dan. 9:26-27).

After the church is raptured, great events will rapidly take place in the world. The old Roman Empire will be restored in Europe, headed by a strong ruler who will eventually be revealed as the Antichrist. He will agree to protect the Jews for seven years (Dan. 9:27), which is the exact length of the Tribulation period, the seventieth week of Daniel (9:25-27). The first three and a half years of the tribulation period will be relatively peaceful, and Israel will enjoy rest in her land, guarded by the Roman ruler. But Gog will want the great wealth of the land (38:12-13) and about the middle of the Tribulation period will invade Israel without warning. Then God will intervene and destroy the invading army. So great will be the defeat that it will take seven months to bury the dead (39:12), and the people will burn the abandoned war instruments for seven years (39:9-10). The Roman ruler will hasten to Israel to keep his covenant, will discover that Gog is no longer a world power, and then will set himself up in the Jewish temple as the world dictator, thus breaking his covenant with the Jews (Dan. 9:27). This will be the "Abomination of Desolation" and the signal for great tribulation to begin on the earth.

## III. The New Temple (40–46)

Certainly this temple has never been built, so it must refer to a future time. Most students take this to be the great millennial temple that will be filled with God's glory during Christ's thousand-year reign on earth. Ezekiel was told to reveal these plans to the people in order to make them ashamed of their sins and rebellions (43:10-11). It is not necessary for us to go into detail in our study. Note that the sizes are all increased, so that the entire "sacred area" is almost fifty miles square. How all of this is going to fit into the land and the city of Jerusalem, we are not told. Perhaps there will be changes in the land.

Since Christ has fulfilled the OT types (e.g., sacrifices, priest-hood), then why should they be reinstituted and practiced for a thousand years? Some believe that these practices will be to the Jew in the kingdom what the Lord's Supper is to the church today, a memorial of the work of Christ. However, it is likely that Ezekiel is using the language the people understood to convey truths about the future worship in the temple. The Passover spoke of redemption by the blood (45:21-24), and the Feast of Tabernacles spoke of God's care for His people and their joy in the kingdom (45:25). We cannot believe that saved Jews will want to exchange their close fellowship with Christ for ancient rituals that belonged to the age of the Law.

What will happen to this temple? When God creates the new heaven and earth, there will be no need for any temple (Rev. 21:1-5, 22). The New Jerusalem that John describes in Rev. 21–22 will far surpass anything Ezekiel ever saw! The entire holy city will be a temple to the glory of God.

## IV. The New Land (47–48)

### A. Refreshed (chap. 47).

The land will be refreshed by the healing waters of the river issuing from the altar of God. All of God's blessings must begin with the altar. Ezekiel is describing the healing of the land, the blessing of God upon the land that He chose for Israel. Note that there will be a new border for the land (13-21). On the west will be the Medi-terranean Sea; to the north, a line running from Tyre to Damascus; on the east, the Jordan River and the Dead Sea; and to the south, from below the Dead Sea to the River of Egypt. This means that the inheritance will all be *inside* the land, with no tribes across Jordan.

We can see in this life-giving river a beautiful picture of the Spirit of God. The source is the altar, the death of Christ (John 7:37-39). The river became deeper, so that the prophet could swim in it. Oh, that we might go deeper and deeper into the things of God and stay out of the shallow waters! The river brought healing and life; so the Spirit heals and gives life today.

### B. Redivided (chap. 48).

We have already noted the new boundaries of the land. This chapter explains how the tribes will be allotted their inheritance during the kingdom age. All of the tribes will be west of Jordan; the nation will no longer be divided. The tribes will have "belts" of land across the nation, from east to west. Seven tribes will be located at the top of the land: Dan, Asher, Naphtali, Manasseh, Ephraim, Reuben, and Judah. Then will come the huge "sacred tract" for the temple area (vv. 8-20). At the bottom of the land will be five more tribes: Benjamin, Simeon, Issachar, Zebulun, and Gad. The tribes will all be there and the Lord will be there! (v. 35) The name of the city shall be "Jehovah-Shammah": "The Lord is there!"

# DANIEL

## *A Suggested Outline of Daniel*

I. The Personal History of Daniel (1–6)

   A. Maintaining his godly walk (1)

   B. Interpreting the "image dream" (2)

   C. The golden image—Daniel not present here (3)

   D. Interpreting the "tree dream" (4)

   E. Interpreting the handwriting on the wall (5)

   F. Maintaining his godly devotion—the lions' den (6)

II. The Prophetical Ministry of Daniel (7–12)

   A. His vision of the four beasts (7)

   B. His vision of the ram and he goat (8)

   C. His prayer of confession—the seventy weeks (9)

   D. His final vision of the future (10–12)

*The Kingdoms in Daniel:* You must keep in mind that six different kingdoms are identified in the Book of Daniel. They are:

1. Babylon (606–539 B.C.)
   The head of gold (2:36-38)
   The lion with eagle's wings (7:4)

2. Media-Persia (539–330 B.C.)
   Arms and chest of silver (2:32, 39)
   Bear with three ribs (7:5)

3. Greece (330–ca. 150 B.C.)
   Thigh of brass (2:32, 39)
   Leopard with four heads (7:6)

4. Rome (ca. 150 B.C.—ca. A.D. 500)
   Legs of iron (2:33, 40)
   The "dreadful beast" (7:7)

5. Antichrist's kingdom
   Ten toes of iron and clay (2:41-43)
   Little horn (7:8)

6. Christ's kingdom
   The stone that smites the image (2:34-35, 44-45)
   The Ancient of Days (7:9-14)

Keep in mind that the Roman Empire has never been replaced by another world empire, so that it actually continues until the rise of Antichrist in the latter days. This last world dictator will establish a United States of Europe (the ten toes) after the pattern of the old Roman Empire. Note that in chapter 2 we have man's view of the nations (valuable metals), while in chapter 7 we have God's view (dangerous beasts).

# Introductory Notes to Daniel

## I. The Man

Daniel stands out as one of the greatest men in Jewish history. That he was a real person in history is proved by Ezek. 14:14 and 28:3, as well as Matt. 24:15 and Heb. 11:33. He was a teenager in the year 605 B.C. when Nebuchadnezzar came to Jerusalem and began his conquest of Judah. There were several "deportations" of Jews to Babylon, and Daniel was in the first group because he was of the princely line. It was the practice of Babylon to deport the finest of the citizens and train them for service in their own government. Daniel was still active in 539 B.C. when the kingdom was taken by Cyrus, so he lived and ministered in Babylon for over sixty years. In fact, he lived through the reigns of four rulers (Nebuchadnezzar, Belshazzar, Darius, and Cyrus) and three different kingdoms (Babylon, Media, Persia). His name means "God is my judge." He held several important positions and was promoted greatly because of his character and wisdom, and because the blessing of God was upon him. Nebuchadnezzar named him chief of the wise men and a ruler of the land (2:48), a position similar to a modern prime minister. Nebuchadnezzar's grandson, Belshazzar, called Daniel out of retirement and, because he explained the handwriting on the wall, made Daniel third ruler in the land (5:29). Darius named him leader over the whole realm (6:1-3). For at least seventy-five years, Daniel was God's faithful witness in a wicked and idolatrous kingdom.

## II. The Book

Daniel is to the OT what the Book of Revelation is to the NT; in fact, we cannot fully understand one without the other. Prophetically, Daniel deals with "the times of the Gentiles" (see Luke 21:24), that period of time that began in 606 B.C. with the captivity of Jerusalem and will end when Christ returns to earth to judge the Gentile nations and establish His kingdom. In the various visions and dreams in Daniel, we see the program of Gentile history from the rise of Babylon through the conquests of the Medes, Persians, Greeks, and Romans, and to the rule of Antichrist just before the return of Jesus Christ. This book proves that "there is a God in heaven" (2:28) and that "the Most High rules in the kingdom of men" (4:25, NKJV). Daniel makes it clear that God Almighty is sovereign in the affairs of this world; "history is His story." God can take rulers off their thrones; God can defeat the strongest nations and turn them over to their enemies. In 1:1–2:3, the writing is in Hebrew, but from 2:4 to 7:28, it is in the Chaldean language. The Hebrew sections deal primarily with the Jews.

## III. The Order of History

The Book of Daniel is not arranged in chronological order. In the first half, Daniel interprets the *dreams* of others; in the last half, he is given *visions* of his own concerning the future of his people. The historical order of the book is as follows:

| | |
|---|---|
| (1) | Captivity (605–604 B.C.) |
| (2) | Dream of the image (602 B.C.) |
| (3) | Nebuchadnezzar's image |
| (4) | Nebuchadnezzar's tree dream |
| (7) | The vision of the four beasts (556 B.C.) |
| (8) | Ram and he goat vision (554 B.C.) |
| (5) | Belshazzar's feast—Babylon falls (539 B.C.) |
| (9) | Vision of seventy weeks (538 B.C.) |
| (6) | The lions' den |
| (10–12) | Closing visions |

You can see that Daniel was a man in his eighties when cast into the lions' den.

# DANIEL 1

In the personal history of Daniel (chapters 1–6), we find three different times of difficulty: the testing of the four Hebrews when they arrived at Babylon (chap. 1); the fiery furnace (chap. 3); and the lions' den (chap. 6). In each of these experiences, Daniel and his friends won the victory, but the very first victory was the foundation for the other victories. Because these Jewish boys were faithful to God while they were yet teenagers, God was faithful to them in the years that followed.

## I. A Difficult Trial (1:1-7)

Imagine four Hebrew boys, teenagers, being snatched from their lovely homes in Jerusalem and moved to faraway Babylon. Since all of them were princes, belonging to the royal family, they were probably not accustomed to this kind of treatment. It is too bad when the youth of the land must suffer because of the sins of the parents. The Jews had refused to repent and obey the Lord, so (as Jeremiah had warned) the Babylonian army came in 606–586 B.C. and conquered the land. It was their custom to take the best of the youths to Babylon for training in the king's court. In v. 3 we see what fine specimens these four lads were: they were physically strong and handsome, socially experienced and well-liked by others, mentally keen and well-educated, and spiritually devoted to the Lord. Their lives were balanced, as we see Christ's in Luke 2:52 – perfect examples of teenagers!

But a difficult trial lay ahead of them: the king wanted to force them to conform to the ways of Babylon. He was not interested in putting good Jews to work; he wanted these Jews to be Babylonians! Christians today face the same trial: Satan wants us to become "conformed to this world" (Rom. 12:1-2). Sad to say, too many Christians give in to the world and lose their power, their joy, and their testimony. Note the changes that these young men experienced:

### A. A new home (vv. 1-2).

No longer were they surrounded by the things of God in Jerusalem, and no longer would they have the influence of their godly parents and teachers. When some Christians get away from home, they rejoice at the opportunity to "let down the bars and live it up"; but not so with Daniel and his friends.

552

### *B. New knowledge (vv. 3-4).*

The old Jewish wisdom had to go; from now on it would be the wisdom of the world, the wisdom of Babylon. They had to learn the wisdom and the language of their captors. The king hoped that this "brainwashing" would make better servants out of them. God's people often have to study things that do not agree with God's Word. Like Daniel and his friends, we should do our best but not abandon our faith.

### *C. New diets (v. 5).*

For the next three years, the four youths were supposed to eat the king's diet, which, of course, was contrary to the dietary laws of the Jews. No doubt the food was also offered to the idols of the land, and for the Hebrew youths to eat it would be blasphemy.

### *D. New names (vv. 6-7).*

The world does not like to recognize the name of God, yet each of the four boys had God's name in his own name. Daniel ("God is my judge") was changed to Belteshazzar ("Bel protect his life"). Bel was the name of a Babylonian god. Hananiah ("Jehovah is gracious") became Shadrach ("the command of the moon god"); Mishael ("Who is like God?") became Meshach ("who is like Aku," one of the heathen gods); and Azariah ("Jehovah is my helper") became Abed-nego ("the servant of Nego," another heathen god). The Babylonians hoped that these new names would help the youths forget their God and gradually become more like the heathen people with whom they were living and studying.

## II. A Daring Test (1:8-16)

The Babylonians could change Daniel's home, textbooks, menu, and name, but they could not change his heart. He and his friends purposed in their hearts that they would obey God's Word; they refused to become conformed to the world. Of course, they could have made excuses and "gone along with" the crowd. They might have said, "Everybody's doing it!" or "We had better obey the king!" or "We'll obey on the outside but keep our faith privately." But they did not compromise. They dared to believe God's Word and trust God for victory. They had surrendered their bodies and minds to the Lord, as Rom. 12:1-2 instructs, and they were willing to let God do the rest.

Daniel asked for a ten-day test, which was not very long considering that they had three years of training ahead of them; the head servant agreed with their plan. "When a man's ways please the Lord, He makes even his enemies to be at peace with him" (Prov. 16:7). See also Matt. 6:33 and Prov. 22:1. The servant was afraid to change the king's orders, lest anything happen to the youths and to himself, so Daniel's proposed test was a good solution to the problem. Of course, God honored their faith. The boys were fed vegetables (pulse) and water for ten days, thus avoiding the defiled food of the Babylonians. At the end of the test, the four lads were healthier and more handsome than the other students who ate from the king's table.

It takes faith and obedience to overcome the temptations and pressures of the world. First Corinthians 10:13 had not yet been written, but Daniel and his three friends knew its truth by experience. Note how polite and kind Daniel was to the Babylonian servant; he did not "parade" his religion or embarrass the man. This is a good example for us to follow: we may hold to our convictions without becoming cranks!

### III. Divine Triumph (1:17-21)

A test for ten days is one thing, but what about the three-year course at the University of Babylon? The answer is in v. 17: "God gave them . . ." all that they needed! He enabled them to learn their lessons better than the other students, and He added to this knowledge His own spiritual wisdom. The "magicians and astrologers" in v. 20 were the men of the kingdom who studied the stars and sought to determine what decisions the king should make. They also claimed to interpret dreams. Certainly Daniel and his friends did not believe the foolish religion and practices of the Babylonians, but they studied just the same, just as a Christian student must do when he attends a university today and is told to learn "facts" that he knows are contrary to God's Word. Daniel understood that God would use him as a witness in that godless place—and He did that for the next seventy-five years!

The king himself had to admit that the four Hebrew lads were ten times smarter than his best advisers. Of course, this kind of reputation made the astrologers envious, and it is no wonder they tried to do away with the Jews in later years. If Daniel had been worried about pleasing people and being "popular," he would have yielded to the pressures and failed the Lord. But because he lived to please the Lord, he ignored the faces and threats of people and did the thing God wanted him to do. We need Christians today who will purpose in their hearts to put Christ first in everything—in the dining room, in the classroom, and even in the throne room!

"And Daniel continued. . . ." What a testimony! Satan must have said to Daniel, "You had better follow the crowd if you want to stay around here." But Daniel obeyed the Lord—and he "stayed around" longer than anyone else. He ministered under four kings and probably lived to see the Jews return to their land at the end of the captivity. "He who does the will of God abides forever" (1 John 2:17). In fact, we today are being blessed and helped because of Daniel's faithfulness. Had he failed God when he faced tests in his youth, Daniel would never have enjoyed the victories and blessings of the later years. He was called "beloved" (10:11), an honor given in the Bible only to one other—Jesus Christ. Because he lived in the will of God, Daniel enjoyed the love of God (1 John 2:15-17). His consecration gave him courage; his faith made him faithful.

# DANIEL 2

This chapter is the outline of world history. An understanding of this chapter, and chapter 7, will assist you in your study of Revelation and other Bible prophecies. Note the chart in the Introductory Notes to Daniel.

## I. Daniel's Peril (2:1-13)

When Nebuchadnezzar first came to Jerusalem to conquer, he was not yet king; he was acting for his father, Nabopolassar, back in Babylon. This accounts for the seeming contradiction between the three years of training for Daniel in 1:5 and the "second year" of the king's reign in 2:1. Once again archaeology has proved the Bible true. The king was concerned about his future (see v. 29) and whether or not his kingdom would last. God gave him a dream describing the future, but he could not understand it. In fact, he forgot it! Christians have the Holy Spirit to teach and remind them (John 14:26). The "fake" magicians and wise men were really on the spot, for the king wanted not only an interpretation of the dream, but also a description of it! Any man could "invent" an interpretation, but it was impossible for them to describe a dream they had never seen. They tried to "stall for time" (v. 8), hoping the king would "change his mind" (v. 9). Instead, the king ordered all the wise men to be slain, and that included Daniel and his three friends. Satan is a murderer (John 8:44); he would certainly have been happy to see Daniel killed.

## II. Daniel's Prayer and Praise (2:14-23)

We must admire the courage of Daniel, for he faced the chief executioner boldly, and even went right in to see the king. "The righteous are bold as a lion" (Prov. 28:1). God overruled in these conversations (Prov. 21:1), and the king gave Daniel time, even though he had refused to give the other wise men time. Daniel and his three friends knew what to do; they spent the next hours in fervent prayer to God. "If any of you lack wisdom, let him ask of God" (James 1:5). "Ask, and it shall be given you" (Matt. 7:7). And God revealed the dream and its meaning to Daniel in the hours of the night. Read Prov. 3:32 and Ps. 25:14 to see why Daniel was given this privilege. Instead of rushing to the king, or boasting of his new wisdom, Daniel paused to praise the Lord. And you will note in vv. 25-30 that Daniel gave all the glory to God; he took none of it for himself. There is no limit to what God will do for the believer who will let God have all the glory.

## III. Daniel's Prophecy (2:24-45)

The prophet went to the chief executioner and told him not to slay the other wise men. They deserved death, of course, and it would have exalted Daniel's position had they been removed, but Daniel was not a man with hatred for his enemies. Only eternity will reveal how many lost people have been saved from physical harm by the presence and intercession of a believer. Then Daniel told the king the contents of his forgotten dream. The king had been worried about the future of his kingdom (v. 29), so God gave him a vision of the kingdoms to come. He saw a huge statue of a man: the head was of gold, the breast and arms of silver, the belly and thigh of copper or bronze (but not brass, which was not known at that time), the legs of iron, and the feet of iron and clay. He also saw a stone come down upon the feet and crush the entire image into powder. Then the stone grew and filled the whole earth like a great mountain.

Verse 28 tells us that the full meaning is for the "latter days." Each metal represented a different kingdom: Babylon was the head of gold (v. 38); it would be followed by the Medo-Persian kingdom, the breast and arms of silver; then would come Greece, the belly and thigh of bronze; Rome would follow as the two legs of iron (and the Roman Empire did divide into Eastern and Western parts). The feet of iron and clay (a brittle mixture) represented the kingdoms at the end times, a continuation of the Roman Empire divided into ten kingdoms (the ten toes). Of course, the final "human kingdom" on earth will be that of the Antichrist during the last part of the Tribulation. How will it all end? Christ, the Stone (Matt. 21:44), will suddenly appear and smite the nations of the world, setting up His own worldwide kingdom of power and glory.

This image, then, is a picture of world history. You can see that the materials in it decrease in *weight* (from gold to clay) so that the statue is top-heavy and easily pushed over. Men and women think that human civilization is so strong and enduring; really it is resting on brittle feet of clay. Note too that the *value* decreases: from gold to silver to bronze to iron to clay. Is mankind getting "better and better" as time goes on? No! Human civilization is actually getting cheaper and weaker. There is also a decrease in *beauty* and *glory* (gold is certainly more beautiful than iron mixed with clay); and there is a decrease in *strength* (from gold to clay) as we approach the end of human history. Each of the successive kingdoms had its own strengths, of course, and Rome exercised a tremendous military power, but through history civilization will become weaker and weaker. This explains why the Antichrist will be able to organize a worldwide dictatorship: nations will be so weak they will demand a dictator just to be able to survive.

Each of these kingdoms had a different form of government. Babylon was ruled by an absolute monarch, a dictator (see 5:19). The Medo-Persian empire had a king, but he worked through princes and established laws (see 6:1-3—and remember the "law of the Medes and the Persians" in Esther 1:19). Greece operated through a king and an army, and Rome was supposed to be a republic, but it was actually a rule of the military through laws. When you come to the iron and clay, you have our present governments: the iron represents law and justice, the clay represents mankind, and together they make up democracy. What is the strength of democracy? Law. What is its weakness? Human nature. We are seeing today that lawlessness comes when human nature refuses to be bound by God's order and laws.

This entire picture is not a very optimistic one. Nebuchadnezzar saw that his own kingdom would fall one day and be replaced by the Medes and Persians. This happened in 538 B.C. (Dan. 5:30-31). The Medes and Persians would be conquered by the Greeks about 330 B.C.; and Greece would give way to Rome. The Roman Empire outwardly would disappear, but its laws, philosophies, and institutions would continue until this very day, taking us down to the "feet of clay." The only hope for this world is the return of Christ. When He comes to the earth, it will be to conquer the nations (Rev. 19:11ff) and to establish His own glorious kingdom.

## IV. Daniel's Promotion (2:46-49)

The king kept his promise (v. 6) and gave honors and gifts to Daniel, who did not want to receive them since he was anxious that God alone receive the glory. Daniel was honored and promoted because he was faithful to God, and not because he compromised his convictions. He sat in the gate, which was the place of authority. Lot also sat in the gate (Gen. 19:1), but this was because he had compromised and moved out of God's will—and he lost everything! Note that Daniel did not keep the honors for himself, but asked that his three friends also share the promotion (v. 49). The more we see of this man, the more we love him for his unselfishness and humility.

We shall meet these same kingdoms again in chapter 7. There they will be pictured as wild beasts, because that is what God sees when he looks at human history. God is not impressed with gold, silver, and bronze. He sees the human heart, and he knows that the kingdoms of the world are full of violence and sin. From humanity's point of view, earthly kingdoms are like metal—durable and strong; from God's point of view, they are ferocious beasts that must be slain. Daniel had perfect confidence and peace because he knew God's plan for the future. The Christian today who knows God's Word and believes it will also have peace.

# DANIEL 3

What a dramatic story this is! Imagine three Jewish men daring to defy the ruler of the world, and daring to be different from the thousands of people in Babylon! Though this event took place over 2,000 years ago in far-off Babylon, it has lessons for us today.

## I. The Practical Lesson

There is a twenty-year interval between this chapter and the events in chapter 2. As you can see, Nebuchadnezzar's heart has not changed one bit. He admitted in 2:46-47 that Jehovah God was a great God, but this truth never really got to his heart. He praised Daniel and Daniel's God, but he did not repent of his sins and trust in Him. As a result, the king tried to force the entire empire to be idol-worshipers, which, in the long run, actually meant worshiping the king. After all, was he not the "head of gold" in the image he saw in his dream? (2:38) Then why not make an entire image of gold (probably wood covered with gold) and glorify the king even more? This is the way the human heart operates when God is not honored: man glorifies himself and tries to make everybody worship him.

Naturally, the three Jewish officers could not follow the king's orders. Romans 13 tells believers to obey rulers and laws, but Acts 5:29 and 4:19 make it clear that no Christian is to disobey the Lord by obeying the government. When the government tries to control our conscience and tell us how to worship, we obey God rather than human beings, regardless of the cost. It was not easy for Shadrach, Meshach, and Abed-nego to stand their ground as everybody else bowed down when the music played, but they refused to budge. Some of the other wise men (v. 8) took this as an opportunity to accuse the Jews, and the king was enraged when he heard that his decree had been disobeyed. Knowing that the three men were good men (and friends of Daniel), he gave them another chance, but they remained firm. They would rather burn than turn! So, into the furnace they went, bound with their own clothing. Three promises stand out in this story:

### A. The promise of persecution.

Christians should expect the furnace of persecution if they are wholly dedicated to Christ. "Think it not strange concerning the fiery trial which is to try you" (1 Peter 4:12ff). The world hates us, and Satan sees to it that the furnace gets "stoked up" seven times hotter. Of course, the three Jews could have made excuses and gone along with the crowd. Instead, they stood with one another and with the Lord, trusting God to glorify Himself either by their life or by their death. Christian, expect persecution; God promised it (Phil. 1:29; John 15:18-20).

### B. *The promise of preservation.*

God will never forsake His own when they go through the fiery trial. He may not keep us out of the furnace, but He will go with us and bring us through for His glory. Read Isa. 43:2 for God's promise to you. When the king looked into the furnace, he saw four men — and one of them was Jesus Christ. Christ walked with them; He loosed their bonds; He kept them from being harmed; in fact, they did not even smell of the fire when they came out (v. 27). The secret? Their faith — Heb. 11:30-34.

### C. *The promise of promotion.*

These men were actually better off for having gone through the fire. For one thing, it gave them opportunity to walk with Christ and suffer with Him. It is worth danger and trial to know how near the Lord can be to us. The fire set them free from their bonds, just as suffering for Christ today gives us joyful liberty from sin and the world. Their experience glorified God before others (1 Cor. 6:19-20), and the king promoted them and gave them honors. First the suffering, then the glory (see 1 Peter 5:1, 10-11).

## II. The Doctrinal Lesson

In the Bible, "Babylon" is more than a city or an empire; it represents a system. It is God's name for Satan's system in this world. Babylon started in Gen. 10:10; it was the work of Nimrod, that "mighty rebel against the Lord." Babylon stands for our rebellion against the Lord and our substitutes for what the Lord gives us. In Gen. 11 we see Babel in its rebellion against God, a human attempt at worldwide unity politically and religiously. This is what Nebuchadnezzar wanted to accomplish with his great image; he wanted to unify his kingdom under one government and one religion. But this whole scheme was man-centered; there was no place for God at all. And it centered around gold. This whole Babylonian system is Satan's counterfeit, opposing God's truth, and seeking to capture the hearts, minds, and bodies of people. Actually, the name "babel" means "the gate of God." It pretends to be the way to heaven. In truth, it is the way to hell.

We see the final development of this false system in Revelation 17–18, the material, cultural, and religious systems of the world all united in one world federation. God will permit this "one world" system to grow, and then He will destroy it once for all. It is important that you know the difference between God's truth and Satan's lies, between true Christianity and Satan's "religions." True believers are not to be a part of this worldly system (Rev. 18:4-5). Like the three Hebrew men, we must take our stand against Babylon and bear witness to the truth of God's Word.

## III. The Prophetic Lesson

We have here a picture of events in the last days. Note, first of all, that Daniel was not present when these things took place. Undoubtedly he was away on official business for the king, and the king took advantage of his absence to erect his wicked idol. This illustrates the rapture of the church: when the church is out of the world, then Satan will be able to carry out his diabolical plans for enslaving the minds and bodies of men.

Second Thessalonians 2 and Rev. 13 both make it clear that Satan will have a "heyday" after the Christians are raptured and taken to heaven. For one thing, he will raise up a world ruler, the Antichrist, who (like Nebuchadnezzar) will conquer the nations and establish a totalitarian government. The church will be gone, but there will be 144,000 Jewish believers sealed by the Lord and protected from Satan's devices (Rev. 7:1-8; 14:1-5). The Antichrist will set up his own image and force the world to worship it (see Rev. 13), but the faithful Jews will not bow down. Like the Hebrews in Babylon, the 144,000 will serve God and God will protect them. It is interesting to note that the image of King Nebuchadnezzar is identified with the number six (sixty cubits high, six cubits wide, Dan. 3:1), and the image of Antichrist is identified with his number, 666 (Rev. 13:18). It is this image that Jesus called "the abomination of desolation" in Matt. 24:15-22.

So, Dan. 3 is a prophetic forecast of Israel during the tribulation period, after the church has been raptured. Nebuchadnezzar represents the Antichrist; his image represents the image of Antichrist that he will erect; and the three Hebrews represent the believing Jews, the 144,000 who will be protected during the Tribulation. It is likely that these Jews will read Daniel 3 and understand it and know that their God will go into the furnace of tribulation with them and bring them out again for His glory.

Every day we can see our present world moving toward unification. There are hundreds of organizations and agreements that bind nations together these days. There will one day be a "United States of Europe," and the leader of that organization will become the last world dictator, the Antichrist. The stage is set. "The coming of the Lord draws nigh." Before Jesus returns, we Christians may have to go through the "furnace of fire," but we need not fear, for He is with us. And far better to go through a furnace of fire than to live in a lake of fire for all eternity.

# DANIEL 4

This chapter is an official Babylonian document, written by the king himself. It is the story of his conversion, and what a story it is. Keep in mind that it was written seven years after the experience itself, so that vv. 1-3 and 37 are Nebuchadnezzar's public testimony of what God did to him and for him. We will consider those verses at the end of our study. Now for the account of the king's dream.

## I. The Dream Received (4:4-18)

It was at a time of peace and prosperity that God sent this dream to the king, for this dream was really a divine warning to him that his sins were going to catch up with him at last. He was secure, but it was a false security, similar to the one Jesus pictured in the Parable of the Rich Farmer (Luke 12:15-21). It is when this wicked world is resting in "peace and safety" that God's judgment will fall (1 Thes. 5:3). The only true safety and rest is in Jesus Christ.

The dream was this: he saw a huge tree that overshadowed the entire earth, with the birds and animals taking refuge under it, and he heard an angelic voice say, "Cut down the tree." The tree was cut down, but the stump was left in the wet grass, with a band of iron about it, for "seven times." Needless to say, the king was greatly disturbed by this dream, especially since he had received another dream in the early years of his kingdom, and it dealt with the future of his reign.

The king summoned his wise men, but they were unable to explain the dream. Remember their boast in chapter 2: "Show us the dream and we will explain it." Well, the king did show them this dream but they could not explain it. The worldly-wise make their boast of great wisdom, but they cannot understand or explain the things of God (1 Cor. 2:14-15). The king knew that only one man could solve the problem—Daniel, the man of God. So he called Daniel to his throne and related to him the dream that had perplexed him. Nebuchadnezzar had power, riches, and glory, but he was unable to unlock the future. The poorest Christian is far richer than he, because in the Word we have God's program for the future.

## II. The Dream Revealed (4:19-27)

God used Daniel to be a "light in the darkness," for He revealed to him the meaning of the dream. But the revelation struck the prophet dumb for an hour. That must have been the longest hour of waiting in the king's history. It was plain to Daniel that the message of the dream was a sobering one. He did not take it lightly or deliver it in a careless fashion. A true prophet is always in sympathy with his message; he feels the burden of it and delivers God's Word faithfully. Many people have the idea that spiritual wisdom and knowledge always lead to joy and witness, when sometimes they lead to sorrow and silence. See Dan. 10:1-3 for Daniel's reaction to the truth about the seventy years of captivity.

The explanation is not difficult to grasp. The tree represented Nebuchadnezzar and his great kingdom (vv. 20-22). God often uses the figure of a tree to picture a kingdom; Ezek. 31 is an example, and so is Matt. 13:31-32. A tree is a good symbol of an earthly kingdom because it is rooted in the earth and depends on the earth for its food and stability. The other nations that looked to Babylon for protection and provision are pictured by the beasts and birds lodging in and under the tree. Certainly Babylon had become a great and powerful kingdom. But it was not for Nebuchadnezzar to boast, because God had given him his throne and his kingdom. That was the lesson the monarch was to learn the hard way.

"The watcher and holy one" is an angel of God, appointed to work in the kingdom of Babylon. Daniel 10:4-20 informs us that the angels are very active in the affairs of the nations of the world. The angel announced, "Cut down the tree—get King Nebuchadnezzar off the throne." What an experience the king would have! He would actually cease to live like a man and would live like a beast for seven years. The tree would be cut down, and the iron band would restrain its growth, but the judgment would not be permanent. After seven years, Nebuchadnezzar would become human again, his reason would return, and he would ascend his throne in great glory.

Why was God working this way in the king's life? To teach him humility. You will remember that in the king's "image dream" he was pictured as the head of gold; and in chapter 3, the king had made an entire image of gold to attract worship and praise to himself. God would show this proud monarch that he was actually a beast at heart. In fact, in chapter 7, Daniel will have a vision that shows that *all* the empires are nothing but wild beasts. Daniel warned the king to repent and change his ways. "Break off your sins," he begged, "and perhaps the Lord will give you forgiveness and time to serve Him." After all, God had spoken to the king on two different occasions — the dream of chapter 2 and the furnace episode of chapter 3 — and it is dangerous to turn a deaf ear to God.

## III. The Dream Realized (4:28-36)

It happened as Daniel said. God gave Nebuchadnezzar a whole year to consider the warning and turn from his sins, but the king paid no heed. In fact, he became more and more proud of his achievements. See Ecc. 8:11 and Prov. 29:1. But there came a day when judgment fell and the true beastly nature of the king was revealed for all to see. Men drove him from his palace and he lived for seven years like a beast of the field, eating grass like the oxen. When God wants to humble a proud king, He can do it quickly and thoroughly.

This did not last forever. After seven years, Nebuchadnezzar was converted. The first step (the king tells us) was, "I lifted my eyes to heaven" (v. 34, NKJV). It is too bad he had not looked to heaven long before this. "I blessed God — I praised God." That certainly sounds like a man whose life has been changed by faith in the Lord. The king had learned his lesson: he was nothing and God was everything. Read vv. 34-35 to see how much practical doctrine Nebuchadnezzar learned through this humbling experience. How tragic that the proud rulers of this present world fail to see they are nothing and God is everything. Verse 17 (NKJV) states the lesson clearly: "The Most High rules in the kingdom of men. . . ."

Now back to vv. 1-3. Here is the mighty dictator addressing all the peoples of the world and sending them *peace*. Nebuchadnezzar certainly was not known for his peaceful activities, because he was a cruel man of war. Verse 1 reads almost like a NT epistle from Peter or Paul. Note how in vv. 2-3 he gives all the glory to God and ascribes greatness to the Lord. This, again, was very unlike this heathen dictator; just seven years before he had been saying, "Is not this great Babylon that I have built?" He was boasting about *his* power and *his* majesty, with not a syllable of praise or gratitude to God. Well, all that is changed now; the king writes an official document giving personal witness to what God has done for him. Verse 37 is the grand climax: "I praise and extol and honor"—not Nebuchadnezzar—"the King of heaven" and "those that walk in pride He is able to abase." Do we not have in this chapter a foreview of what will happen to the nations in the latter days? Just about the time they will be boasting of their greatness and glory, God will send seven years of awful judgment upon them and bring them low. Then, at the end of that Tribulation period, Christ will return to earth and establish His kingdom. The nations that have trusted Him will enter into the glorious kingdom; the others will be cast out. Like Nebuchadnezzar, the believers will be converted from their pride and unbelief and will enjoy the blessing of God.

# DANIEL 5

Some twenty years pass between chapters 4 and 5. Nebuchadnezzar moved off the scene, succeeded by a son who reigned just a few years and then was assassinated by his own brother-in-law. He in turn ruled four years but was killed while in battle. The next two rulers occupied the throne a very brief time; the second of these was Nabonidus. He was actually a son-in-law to Nebuchadnezzar and was married to the widow of one of the previous kings. At this time, Nabonidus was king of the Babylonian empire and his son Belshazzar was king of the *city* of Babylon. This explains why Daniel was named third ruler (vv. 7, 29). While the events in chapter 5 are taking place, King Nabonidus has been a captive of the Medes and Persians for four months. Note the experiences of Belshazzar.

## I. Enjoying His Feast (5:1-4)

This feast was in honor of one of the great Babylonian gods, and it took place in the autumn of 539 B.C. Archaeologists have unearthed palaces at Babylon containing great halls large enough to entertain a thousand guests. They have also discovered that the walls were covered with a white chalklike substance, which explains the matter of the handwriting on the wall. The main idea in these verses is drinking wine. Wine has always been associated with Babylon and the Babylonian "system" of this world (Jer. 51:7; Rev. 14:8; 17:1-5; 18:3, 13). The king was not content to drink wine to his gods (v. 4, and see Rev. 9:20); he wanted to blaspheme the God of the Jews as well. So he had the sacred temple vessels brought in to be used at this idolatrous, blasphemous feast (see Dan. 1:2). The word "father" in 5:2 indicates "grandfather"; see also the use in vv. 11 and 13. Please keep in mind that the Medes and Persians were already outside the gates of the city when this feast was in progress. So confident was the king that his fortress city was impregnable that he laughed at the invading armies. What a picture of our world today: judgment is about to fall, yet people are making merry and worshiping their false gods. "When they say, 'Peace and safety!' then sudden destruction comes upon them" (1 Thes. 5:3, NKJV). Babylon was a strong city with walls 350 feet high and eighty-seven feet thick. The Euphrates River ran diagonally through the city, and great brass gates controlled the city entrances. How could any invading army capture such a city?

## II. Revealing His Fear (5:5-9)

The guests apparently did not immediately see the mysterious hand appear, but the king looked over their heads and saw it on the opposite wall. Imagine how shocked the guests were when they saw their king trembling, his knees knocking together. Wine could not give him courage now; he was face-to-face with a message from God. You can read v. 7, "And the king *shrieked*." He had to know the meaning of the hand and the handwriting. In fact, he offered the man who would explain it the position as third ruler of the land. (In a few hours Belshazzar would not even be alive and ruling himself.) As usual, none of the king's "experts" could explain the writing on the wall, and this made the king even more concerned. How strange that he did not know Daniel, the man who had counseled his grandfather, Nebuchadnezzar. But Belshazzar was a careless youth (he was about thirty-five years old at this time) who was more interested in power and pleasure than in spiritual matters. No wonder his city fell.

## III. Discovering His Future (5:10-29)

The Queen Mother solved the problem. It is possible that this wise woman was the widow of Nebuchadnezzar whom Belshazzar's father, Nabonidus, married in order to solidify his power in the kingdom. At any rate, she heard of the consternation in the banquet hall and came to advise the king. "O king, live forever," she said (v. 10) — and he was going to be dead before the night was over. Then she told him about Daniel and how he had advised Belshazzar's grandfather. Daniel was an old man now, and had been "retired" from public service. As an honored member of the official family, Daniel was probably invited to the feast as a guest, but he would not defile himself or compromise his testimony. Because of his separated position, Daniel was honored of God (2 Cor. 6:14-18).

The king tried to impress Daniel (vv. 13-16), but Daniel would not be impressed. He knew that the king's gifts meant nothing in comparison to the blessing of God; for that matter, Belshazzar would not be king much longer. Before explaining the handwriting, Daniel preached a sermon to the king, using the king's grandfather as his illustration. He warned the king about his pride and sin and reminded him that God judged Nebuchadnezzar severely. "And you knew all this," Daniel exclaimed, "yet you persist in living such a wicked life. Now God has sent you a message of judgment and it is too late." God gave Nebuchadnezzar a year to repent (4:28-33), but there was no year for Belshazzar to repent. He was doomed.

Now for the explanation. The words were in Chaldean. In Babylon a mina and a tekel were different weights; and the word *peres* simply means "to divide." When the Babylonian magicians saw these words on the wall, they could not understand what they meant. But God gave Daniel the interpretation: "Numbered — weighed — divided." Belshazzar's days had been numbered and time was up; he had been weighed in God's scales and found wanting; now his kingdom would be taken from him and divided by the Medes and Persians. And keep in mind that Darius was at the gates at that very hour. Did Belshazzar believe the message from God, even after all his fear and shaking? No. We find no evidence of repentance or concern. He kept his promise and made Daniel third ruler just as though his kingdom were to continue forever. The king's pride, lust, indifference, and self-satisfaction led to his downfall.

## IV. Meeting His Fate (5:30-31)

Had Belshazzar studied the Prophet Isaiah, he would have known just how the city of Babylon would be taken, and by whom it would be taken. Cyrus the Persian conqueror would defeat the Medes and then come down upon Babylon (Isa. 41:25; 45:1-4). He would dig a canal that would reroute the Euphrates River and then smuggle his army into the city *under* the gates. The Babylonians had seen the enemy digging, but they thought they were going to build a mound against the city. Actually, they were diverting the river. Why was the city taken unawares? Because most of the people were drunk. It was a great religious feast day, and the people were too involved in pleasure to think about defense. The enemy came right into the banquet hall, and the king was slain. What a warning to any nation! We have such a pleasure-mad world today that it will be easy for some enemy to take us unawares, and history will repeat itself.

Who was Darius the Mede? Isaiah had said that Cyrus would capture Babylon and set the Jews free (Isa. 44:28–45:13); see also Dan. 1:21 and 10:1. Darius is mentioned as "king" in Dan. 6:1, 6, 9, 25, 28; 9:1; 11:1. The solution is found in the word "took" in 5:31; it should be translated "received." Darius (Cyrus' military leader) received the kingdom from Cyrus, king of Persia, and ruled Babylon for him. In 6:28 we see that it was a dual kingship; Cyrus was the king of the empire, while Darius ruled Babylon and the area connected with it. Cyrus entered Babylon a mighty conqueror and proceeded to deal wisely with the people, including the exiled Jews. It was Cyrus who issued the decrees that permitted the Jews to return to their land and rebuild their temple (Ezra 1:1-4; see Isa. 44:28). So, even the rise and fall of empires is all a part of God's plan for His people.

The fall of Babylon in 539 b.c. is a picture of the future fall of Babylon (the devil's world system) as given in Rev. 17–18. And Bible-believing Christians can already see "the handwriting on the wall." But blind world rulers continue in their pride and pleasure, little realizing that the Lord is coming.

# DANIEL 6

In this chapter we spend a day in the life of the prime minister of the Medo-Persian Empire — Daniel the beloved. Remember, now, that Daniel is not a teenager in this chapter; he is a man in his eighties. This just proves that age is no barrier to serving Christ, nor is it any protection against temptation and testing. Because Daniel started young as a man of faith and prayer, he was faithful to the Lord even in his old age.

## I. A Dawn of Devotion

How did the prime minister begin each day? He prayed to the Lord. In 6:10 we are told that Daniel prayed three times a day in a special "prayer chamber" atop his house. "Evening, and morning, and at noon, will I pray," says Ps. 55:17. So, Daniel started his day with the Lord—and it's a good thing that he did. The enemy was afoot and Daniel was going to face one of the greatest tests of his life. "Watch and pray!" was our Lord's warning. Prayer was not an incidental thing in Daniel's life; it was the most essential thing. He had a special place for prayer and special times for prayer, and you can be sure that he talked to the Lord all day long. No wonder God called him "greatly beloved" (9:23; 10:11, 19), language that in the NT the Lord reserves for His own Son. It was Daniel's faithful walk and consistent prayer life that made him one of God's "beloved sons" (read John 14:21-23 carefully). How important it is to start the day with the Lord. Abraham had this habit (Gen. 19:27); so did David (Ps. 5:3) and our Lord Jesus Christ (Mark 1:35).

## II. A Morning of Deception (6:1-9)

God had honored Daniel for his faithfulness, so that he was practically the second ruler in the land. There were actually 124 persons involved in the leadership of the land: Darius the king, the three presidents (with Daniel as #1), and 120 princes. We see that Darius was so impressed with Daniel that he was planning to make him the official second ruler. The promotions of Daniel in Babylon are proof that a believer does not have to compromise to succeed (Matt. 6:33).

The other 122 leaders were not too happy about Daniel's success. For one thing, he was an alien and a Jew. Satan has always hated the Jews and done his utmost to persecute them and eliminate them. The wicked always hate the just. Certainly godly Daniel was honest and kept careful watch over the affairs of state; the other leaders were stealing from the king and covering up their thefts with false accounts. This is why Darius had reorganized the government, so that he "should have no damage" (loss). The wicked lied about God's people; they told Darius that all the presidents agreed on the plan (v. 7), when Daniel had never been consulted. How foolish Darius was to sign the decree without first consulting with his best president. But history shows that Darius was easily influenced by flattery.

## III. A Noon of Decision (6:10-13)

Daniel was one of the first ones to hear of the new decree, and he had to decide what to do. Of course, his godly character and spiritual walk had already decided for him: he would serve the Lord and pray to Jehovah just as he had always done. He could have made excuses and compromised. "Everybody was doing it." And he was an old man who had served the Lord faithfully all his life. One little compromise at the end of his life could not do too much damage. Could he not be more useful to the Lord alive than dead? No. Daniel refused to compromise. He chose rather to be eaten by lions than to miss one prayer meeting.

His enemies watched as Daniel went to his prayer chamber where the windows were always open ("Pray without ceasing"), and they could see him kneel and lift up his hands toward Jerusalem. Now they had him. But Daniel had peace in his heart. He was praying, giving thanks, and making supplication, and this is the formula for peace (Phil. 4:6-7). This was not a "crisis prayer meeting"; Daniel was used to praying and had been since he was a teenager. It is wise to start building spiritual habits when you are young.

## IV. A Sundown of Disappointment (6:14-17)

The king realized what a fool he had been, but even his power and wealth could not alter the law of the Medes and Persians. God did not want Darius to deliver Daniel; that was a privilege He was reserving for Himself. Daniel was not depending on the king either (Ps. 146:1-6). He had learned long ago to trust the living God. God did not want to save Daniel *from* the lions' den; He wanted to deliver him *out of* it.

## V. A Night of Deliverance (6:18-23)

What a contrast between Darius in his palace and Daniel in the lions' den. Darius had no peace, yet Daniel was perfectly at peace with himself, the Lord, and the lions. Daniel was in a place of perfect safety, for God was there. Darius could have been slain by some enemy right in his bedroom. Darius had labored all the previous day to save Daniel from judgment, yet he could not break his own laws. Daniel simply talked to the God of the universe and received all the power he needed. In every way, Daniel was reigning as king while Darius was a slave.

It was Daniel's faith in God that delivered him (6:23; Heb. 11:33). It is amazing that he had any faith at all, after living in that idolatrous heathen land for so many years. His daily fellowship with the Lord was the secret: he had faith, and he was faithful. See Ps. 18:17-24.

Christians today face many temptations to compromise, and it often appears that the "safest" course is to go with the crowd. But this is the most dangerous course. The only really safe place is in the will of God. Daniel knew that it was wrong to worship the king and pray to him, because Daniel knew God's Word. He would rather die obeying God's Word than live outside of God's will. Satan comes as a roaring lion (1 Peter 5:8-9) and uses our enemies to try to devour us (2 Tim. 4:17), but God can deliver us if it is for His glory. It is not always God's will to deliver His children from danger; many Christians have given their lives in the place of duty. But what a reward they receive! Read Rev. 2:10 carefully.

## VI. A Morning of Destruction (6:24-28)

Our souls revolt at the thought of whole families, including children, being thrown to hungry lions. But this was the law of the land, the same law that these wicked men had tried to use against Daniel. How tragic that their innocent children had to suffer; however, such are the awful penalties of sin. We believe that the children under the age of accountability went to be with the Lord. God always vindicates His own. "The righteous is delivered from trouble, and it comes to the wicked instead" (Prov. 11:8, NKJV). If you are going through persecution and you wonder if God cares, read Ps. 37:1-15 — and trust Him the way Daniel did.

Now we see why God permitted Daniel to go through this experience (vv. 25-27). It brought great glory to His name. Peter may have had Daniel in mind when the Spirit led him to write 1 Peter 3:10-17. When Christians overcome temptation, they always glorify the Lord, even if only the angels and demons are watching. May we, like Paul, desire that Christ might be magnified in our bodies, "whether by life or by death" (Phil. 1:20).

# DANIEL 7–8

Until now, Daniel has been interpreting the dreams of others. Now God gives him extraordinary visions of his own. These two chapters take place before chapter 5, of course, since Babylon has not yet fallen to the Medes and Persians. Remember that Belshazzar's father, Nabonidus, was actually king of Babylon (the empire) and Belshazzar was his co-regent in the city of Babylon. Nabonidus became king in 556 B.C., so we may date chapter 7 in 556 and chapter 8 in 554. Other historians prefer to date chapter 7 in 550, when Nabonidus left for Arabia and put Belshazzar officially in charge. This would put chapter 8 in the year 548. In these visions, Daniel sees the course of Gentile world history and helps us understand what will happen to the Jews in the end times.

## I. The Vision of the Four Beasts (7)

The restless sea in the Bible is a picture of the Gentile nations (Rev. 17:15; Isa. 17:12). Here it is the Great Sea, or the Mediterranean Sea, and all of the empires mentioned in this vision bordered on this sea. Daniel saw four beasts, and the angel explained what they meant. Each beast represented a kingdom (v. 17).

### A. The lion with wings (v. 4).

Here we have Babylon, corresponding to the head of gold in Nebuchadnezzar's dream of the great image (2:36-38). The winged lion was a favorite image in Babylon; you may see these figures in any museum that has a Babylonian display. The animal made to stand like a man certainly reminds us of Nebuchadnezzar's humbling experience in 4:27-37. Babylon was still ruling the world at this time, but in just a few years (as chap. 5 explains), the empire would fall. So, that takes us to the next beast.

### B. The bear with the ribs (v. 5).

Here we meet the Medo-Persian empire, known not for its swiftness or skill, but for its brute force, just like a bear. The three ribs depict the three empires already defeated (Egypt, Babylon, Libya);

and the fact that the bear stood "raised up on one side" indicates that the one half of the empire (the Persian half) was stronger and more honorable (higher) than the other half (the Medes). Medo-Persia conquered Babylon in 539 B.C., but their empire lasted only some two hundred years.

### C. The winged four-headed leopard (v. 6).

This is certainly Greece, led by Alexander the Great, who swiftly conquered the world, defeating the Persians about 331 B.C. But the great general died in 323, and his vast kingdom was divided into four parts (and thus the four heads). Four of his leading generals each took a part of the kingdom and ruled it as the monarch.

### D. The terrible beast (vv. 7-8, 17-27).

This beast startled Daniel, because nothing like it had appeared in any of the previous revelations. It seems clear that we have here the Roman Empire, corresponding to the iron in Nebuchadnezzar's image. But the picture seems to go beyond history into "the latter days," because we see ten horns on the beast, and these parallel the ten toes of the image in chapter 2, the revived Roman Empire of the last days. Verses 8 and 20 both tell us that a "little horn" (ruler) will appear and defeat three of the ten kingdoms represented by the ten horns and ten toes. This little horn will then become a world ruler, the Antichrist. His mouth will speak great things, and he will persecute the saints (believing Jews and Gentiles during the Tribulation period) for three and a half years (v. 25 — time, times, and half a time). This is the last half of the Tribulation period, the "seventieth week" that Daniel will tell us about in chapter 9. According to vv. 11-12, the three previous kingdoms (Babylon, Medo-Persia, and Greece) will be "swallowed up" and included in this last great world empire, but the Antichrist himself will finally be judged and slain. Read Rev. 13:1-2, where John describes the beast (Antichrist) and uses the very same beasts we find in Dan. 7. But notice that their order is reversed. This is because Daniel was looking ahead while John was looking back.

### E. The judgment (vv. 9-14, 26-28).

It must have shocked Daniel to see a man in heaven. He saw Jesus Christ, the glorious Son of man. Of course, God could not permit the beast to control the world. He will send His Son to judge the beast and destroy his kingdom, and then to set up His own glorious kingdom, with the saints of God reigning with Him.

This vision complements and supplements the one in chapter 2. There we have man's view of the nations (precious metals), and here we have God's view (ferocious beasts). See Ps. 49:12.

## II. The Vision of the Ram and He Goat (8)

This vision is actually an amplification of 7:6, explaining how Greece will conquer Medo-Persia. We are back to the Hebrew language in chapter 8 (to the end of the book; since 2:4, it has been in Chaldean). Chapter 8 takes place two years after chapter 7 and describes the kingdoms that will follow Babylon after it falls. God carried Daniel in a vision to the capital of Persia, the palace in Shushan (see Neh. 1:1). Why Shushan? Because Persia would be the next empire.

*The ram* (vv. 3-4) represents Medo-Persia in its conquests (v. 20); the emblem of Persia was a ram. Just about the time the ram was through "pushing," the he goat appeared from the west (v. 5) and leaped swiftly to where the ram was standing. This ram had two horns, one higher than the other, symbolizing the Medes and the Persians, with the Persians the stronger. The he goat had one great horn—Alexander the Great. Now, the he goat attacked the ram, broke the two horns, and became very great (vv. 7-8). This represents Greece's victory over Medo-Persia. But then we see the great horn broken (Alexander's death) and four horns taking its place (the four generals who divided his kingdom and ruled over it).

But here comes a "little horn" again. We met a "little horn" back in 7:8, and now we have another one. The "little horn" in 7:8 represented the Antichrist, the world ruler of the final world empire before the return of Christ to earth. But this "little horn" in 8:9 comes out from one of the four horns; that is, he is a leader who comes out of one of the four divisions of Alexander's kingdom. So, this "little horn" is not the Antichrist of the "latter days," although he has a definite connection with him. This "little horn" conquers nations to the south and east (Egypt, Persia), and then invades Palestine ("the pleasant land"). He not only attacks the Jews politically, but also religiously; for he tries to destroy their faith (v. 10) by stopping the sacrifices in the temple (vv. 11-12). Verse 13 tells us that he will set up "the transgression of desolation" in the temple and defile the temple for 2,300 days.

Who was this man? History names him: *Antiochus Epiphanes,* a wicked leader who came out of Syria, one of the four divisions of Alexander's empire. He invaded Palestine and set up a statue to Jupiter in the temple. He even went so far as to sacrifice a pig on the Jewish altar and sprinkle its blood around the courts. Imagine how the orthodox Jews felt about this. History tells us that the temple lay desolate until Dec. 25, 165 B.C., when the Jewish patriot, Judas Maccabeus, rededicated the temple and cleansed it. The total number of days between desecration and dedication was 2,300.

But this does not exhaust the vision's meaning. In vv. 17-26, the interpreting angel makes it clear that the vision reaches to the time of the end, the closing years of Jewish history. Antiochus Epiphanes is but an illustration, a foretaste, of the Man of Sin, the Antichrist, the "little horn" of 7:8. Verse 23 calls him "a king of fierce countenance." This man will make an agreement to protect the Jews for seven years (9:27), but in the middle of this period he will break his promise, invade Palestine, and set himself up as world dictator. See vv. 24-25, 2 Thes. 2:1-12, and Rev. 13. He will take away the daily sacrifices in the temple, set up his own image (this is "the abomination of desolation" of Matt. 24:15), and force the world to worship and obey him. Verse 25 tells us he will use craft and lies to accomplish his purposes. He will even stand up against Christ, the Prince of princes. But this will be a losing battle. He shall be broken "without hand" (see 2:34), defeated at the Battle of Armageddon (Rev. 19). No wonder Daniel was overwhelmed. And so ought we to be as we consider the amazing prophecies of the Word of God.

# DANIEL 9–12

These closing chapters contain some of the most detailed prophecies in the Bible, and most of them have already been fulfilled. We want to focus our attention in chapter 9, because an understanding of "Daniel's seventy weeks" is basic to Bible prophecy. This chapter deals with two different periods of time as related to the Jews.

## I. Seventy Years of Captivity (9:1-19)

### A. The prophecy (vv. 1-2)

Daniel was a student of the OT Scriptures, particularly those prophecies that related to the destiny of his people. He was now nearly ninety years old. He was reading Jer. 25:1-14, and the Lord caused him to see that his people would be in Babylon for seventy years. Note that God does not give people "visions and dreams" when He can teach them through His Word. Today His Spirit teaches us through the Word. Beware of "new revelations" that are supposed to come from dreams and visions. Daniel realized that the seventy years of captivity were about to close. Babylon invaded Palestine and began its siege in 606 B.C., and Daniel understood the prophecies in the year 539–38 B.C.; so there were but two years left in the seventy years promised by Jeremiah. What an exciting time Daniel had in his Bible study that day!

### B. The prayer (vv. 3-19).

The Word of God and prayer go together (Acts 6:4). Daniel did not go out and boast about his insight into the Word; in fact, he did not even preach a sermon. He went to his knees in prayer. This is the true attitude of the humble Bible student. It is sad to see "prophetic truth" making boasters instead of prayer warriors out of people. How strange it was for the people to see the former prime minister wearing sackcloth. Daniel's prayer is one of the greatest examples of intercession in the Bible. He confesses his own sins and the sins of his people. He reviews Bible history and confesses that the nation has been wicked and God has been righteous to judge them. He knew the warnings Moses had given (v. 13, see Lev. 26), and he knew that he and his people deserved far greater disaster than God had sent to them. It is wonderful to see Daniel identifying himself with his sinning nation, though he himself had not been guilty of these sins. After confessing his sins and the sins of the people, Daniel begins to pray for Jerusalem (vv. 16-19). No doubt he had often prayed for the holy city; in fact, this is one reason why God blessed him and made him to prosper (Ps. 122:6-9). But why pray for the prosperity of a desolate city? Because God had promised not only to end the captivity, but also to take the Jews back to their land that they might rebuild their temple. See Jer. 29:10-14 and 30:10-24. In Isa. 44:28, God promised that Cyrus would permit the Jews to rebuild the city of Jerusalem. So, Daniel was laying hold of these great promises and turning them into believing prayers. Now we will see how God answers his prayers. (Note how Daniel's prayer in Dan. 9 is similar to those in Ezra 9 and Neh. 9.)

## II. Seventy Weeks of Prophecy (9:20-27)

There was no evening sacrifice being offered in Jerusalem, but Daniel was offering himself and his prayers at the time of the evening offering (see Ps. 141:1-2), and the Angel Gabriel came to give him his answer. Daniel was concerned about Jerusalem and the holy mountain (v. 20). Would the city be restored? Would the temple be rebuilt? Would the nation ever be redeemed from sin and would righteousness ever dwell on the earth? Gabriel had all the answers for Daniel, and we find them in the famous prophecy of the "seventy weeks."

The number seven has been stamped on Israel from the beginning. They had a Sabbath of days (Ex. 23:12), setting apart the seventh day for honoring God. They also had a sabbath of years (Lev. 25:1-7); they were to let the land lie fallow on the seventh year and give it rest. Because they broke this law, the Israelites went into captivity, one year for each sabbatical year they failed to obey God (2 Chron. 36:21; Lev. 26:33-34). They also had a "sabbath of sabbaths," with every fiftieth year set apart as the Year of Jubilee (Lev. 25:8-17). But now Daniel was to be introduced to a new series of Sabbaths — seventy "weeks" (seven-year periods), making a total of 490 years of prophetic time for the Jews. (The word "weeks" in v. 24 is actually "sevens" — seventy sevens are determined, making 490 years.) Please note that this 490-year period of time has to do with Jerusalem and the Jews: "your people . . . your holy city . . ." (v. 24, NKJV). And God has specific purposes to fulfill in this period: the removing of sin and the bringing in of righteousness. The result will be the anointing of the most holy place in the temple, that is, the return of Jesus Christ to the earth to reign in glory from His temple in Jerusalem.

Now for the outline of the 490 years. Verse 25 tells us that the event that will trigger the 490 years is a decree (see Neh. 2:5) permitting the Jews to go back to Jerusalem and rebuild the city. (It is interesting that the event that will trigger the last seven years of this period will be the covenant of the Antichrist to protect the Jews. We find a decree at the beginning and at the end of the 490 years.) History tells us there were four different decrees relating to Jerusalem: Cyrus, Darius, and Artaxerxes all made decrees concerning the rebuilding of the temple (Ezra 1, 6, and 7); and Artaxerxes decreed that Nehemiah could return to rebuild the walls (Neh. 2). This was in 445 B.C., and it is the decree Dan. 9:25 is talking about; it took place nearly 100 years after Daniel received the message from God. Gabriel said that there would be a total of sixty-nine weeks, seven and sixty-two, between the giving of the decree and the arrival of Messiah, the Prince, in Jerusalem (69 x 7 = 483 years). Keep in mind that "prophetic years" in the Bible are not 365 days, but 360 days long. It has been calculated by scholars that there were 483 prophetic years between the decree in 445 B.C. and the day that Jesus rode into Jerusalem on Palm Sunday (cf. *The Coming Prince* by Sir Robert Anderson, Kregel, 1967).

But Gabriel divided these 483 years into two parts—seven weeks (7 x 7 = 49 years), and sixty-two weeks (62 x 7 = 434 years). Why? Well, it took forty-nine years to rebuild Jerusalem, and this was done (as Gabriel said) "in troublesome times." Read Nehemiah and see how difficult a task it was to restore the city. Then, 434 years later we come to Messiah, the Prince, who is "cut off" (His death on the cross) for the sins of the world. It was His death on the cross that accomplished the purposes given in v. 24. What followed His death? Did Israel accept Him and His message? No. They lied about Him, persecuted His messengers, stoned Stephen, and refused to acknowledge His kingship. What happened? Rome came and destroyed the city and wrecked the temple. The nation "cut off" Jesus Christ, so He cut them off from being a nation. Until May 14, 1948, Israel was not a free nation.

Rome is called "the people of the prince that shall come." Who is this prince? Not "Messiah the Prince," because that refers to Christ. "The prince that shall come" is Antichrist. He will be the leader of the restored Roman Empire. So, the destruction of Jerusalem in A.D. 70 was but an illustration of a future invasion and destruction to be led by Antichrist. This prince will make an agreement with the Jews to protect them from the other nations, and this agreement will be set for seven years. This final seven years is the completion of Daniel's 490-year period. Between the death of Christ and the signing of this covenant you have the entire Age of the Church, a "great parenthesis" in God's program. The 490 years are in operation only when Israel is in God's will as God's people. When Israel crucified Christ, she was set aside and the "prophetic clock" stopped ticking. But when the Antichrist signs his pact with Israel, then the last seven years of Daniel's "seventy weeks" will start being fulfilled. This seven-year period is known as the Tribulation, or the time of Jacob's trouble. It is described in Rev. 6–19.

After three and a half years, Gog and her allies will invade

Palestine (see Ezek. 38–39), and God will judge them. Antichrist will invade the land, break his covenant, and set himself up as world dictator. He will stop all worship at the Jewish temple (see 2 Thes. 2) and force the world to worship him and his image. This is the abomination of desolation (see Matt. 24:15; John 5:43; Rev. 13). How will this period end? Jesus Christ will return to earth, meet the rebel armies at Armageddon, and defeat them (Rev. 19:11-21).

## *Introductory Notes to the Minor Prophets*

The "minor prophets" are not minor in the sense of being less important than Isaiah, Jeremiah, Ezekiel, or Daniel. Their messages are very important in God's program of prophecy. The Hebrew Bible puts all twelve of these books together and simply calls them "the Twelve." Bible students call them "minor prophets" mainly because of the brevity of their writings, although Zechariah is by no means a brief — or simple — book.

In each of these books, you will usually find a three-fold lesson: (1) Historical — each of the prophets preached and wrote to meet an immediate need in the lives of the people; (2) Prophetical — each prophet illustrates or announces something about Israel's future, in judgment or in restoration; (3) Practical — the sins of the nations in that day are with us today, and there are many practical lessons for us to learn from these books. For example, in Hosea we see the backsliding of Israel, her chastening under Assyria, and her future cleansing and restoration. We also see in this book a lesson for believers today who disobey the Lord and commit "spiritual adultery" by following the world.

Here is a simple chronology of the minor prophets (and some of the major prophets) to help you keep them in their proper places historically.

| Northern Kingdom | Southern Kingdom |
|---|---|
| Jonah — 780–750 | Joel — 835–795 |
| | Amos — 765–750 |
| Isaiah — 750–680 | |
| | Hosea — 755–715 |
| Micah — 740–690 | |
| *Taken by Assyria — 721* | |
| | Nahum — 630–610 |
| | Zephaniah — 625–610 |
| | Jeremiah — 626–586 |
| | Habakkuk — 625–586 |
| | Obadiah — 586 |
| | *Taken by Babylon — 586* |

Daniel — 606–534
Ezekiel — 593–571

*Return from Exile — 536*

Haggai — 520–516
Zechariah — 520–500
Malachi — 450–400

(Note: Historians do not always agree on exact dates. This chart is designed to show the approximate relationships of the prophets to each other.)

# HOSEA

The name Hosea means "salvation." He preached in the Northern Kingdom (Israel, also called "Ephraim") during a period of national decline. When Hosea started his ministry, Jeroboam II was king, and it was a time of great prosperity. But the nation was rotting away inwardly and getting involved with foreign alliances instead of trusting God to lead and protect them. Hosea lived to see Israel taken captive by the Assyrians in 721 B.C. Read 2 Kings 15–17 for some of the historical background.

Hosea's message is to the nation of Israel, exposing their sins and warning them of coming judgment. There is also a message of hope for the future, as we shall see. But the unique thing about his message is that he had to live it himself before he could preach it to the people. The prophet had to experience deep agony in his own marriage because of the sins of his wife, but all of this was a divinely sent object lesson to him and his people.

## I. Israel's Unfaithfulness Pictured (1–3)

Hosea wanted to marry a woman named Gomer, and God permitted him to do so, but warned him that she would break his heart. God's warning came true: Gomer bore Hosea three children, then left him to live with other men. Imagine how Hosea's heart was broken over her sin. Then God commanded the prophet to go find his wayward wife, and he discovered her—being sold in the slave market! (3:1-2) He had to buy his own wife back, bring her home, and assure her of his forgiveness and love. We have every reason to believe that Gomer repented of her sins and became a faithful wife.

All of this pictured Israel's unfaithfulness to the Lord. The nation was married to the Lord (Ex. 34:14-16; Deut. 32:16; Isa. 62:5; Jer. 3:14) and should have remained faithful to Him. But Israel lusted after sin, especially the false gods of other nations, and she committed "spiritual adultery" by forsaking the true God and worshipping the idols of her enemies. They promised her many pleasures, but she discovered there was pain and sorrow as well. Like Gomer, Israel would go into slavery (captivity) because of her sins. But that is not the end of the story. Just as Hosea sought out his wife and bought her back, so the Lord would seek out His people, set them free, and restore them to His love and blessing.

You can trace the history of Israel in the names of the three children: (1) *Jezreel* (1:4) means "scattered," referring to the time when God would scatter Israel among the nations; (2) *Lo-ruhamah* (1:6) means "unpitied," meaning that God would lift His mercy from the nation and permit her to suffer for her sins; (3) *Lo-ammi* (1:9) means "not my people," indicating this present time in God's program when Israel is out of fellowship with God and its people are not His people as once they were. (In 2:1, we see there will be a time when God will call Israel "My people" and "Obtaining pity," when Christ returns and restores the nation and establishes His righteous kingdom.) In 3:3-5 we have a summary of Israel's spiritual condition.

We cannot leave these chapters without pointing out that spiritual adultery can be a sin of NT Christians as well as the OT Jew (1 John 2:15-17; Rev. 2:1-7; James 4:1-10). Christians who love the world and live for sin are false to their Savior and break His heart. Paul warned the Corinthians against this (2 Cor. 11:1-3).

## II. Israel's Sins Proclaimed (4–7)

No doubt all the neighbors talked about Gomer's sins and pointed an accusing finger at her. But now Hosea points a finger at them and reveals their sins. His message reads like today's newspaper; read 4:1-2 especially. Swearing, lying, drunkenness, murder, treachery, adultery, idolatry—these sins and many more were rampant in the nation. And to make matters worse, the nation tried to cover her sins with a shallow "religious revival" (6:1-6). Hosea is a master preacher; see how he pictures the spiritual condition of the people: (1) *a morning cloud* (6:4), here one minute, gone the next; (2) *a half-baked cake* (7:8), for their religion had not gotten deep into their lives, but was a surface thing; (3) *gray hairs* (7:9), losing their strength but ignorant of the change; (4) *a silly dove* (7:11), unstable, flitting from one political ally to another; (5) *a deceitful bow* (7:16) that you cannot depend on.

## III. Israel's Judgment Pronounced (8–10)

The backslider is always punished (Prov. 14:14), and that is what Israel was—a backslider (4:16; see also Jer. 3:6, 11). Christians who break their vows with the Lord do not lose their salvation, of course, but they do lose their joy, power, and usefulness; and they must suffer the discipline of God. Hosea could see Assyria coming to punish the nation and deliver it into slavery. He pictures this judgment as the coming of a swift eagle (8:1), the wrath of a whirlwind (8:7), and the burning of a fire (8:14). The nation is going to be scattered (8:8; 9:17), and they will reap more than they have sown (10:12-15). Sinners reap what they have sown, of course (Gal. 6:7-8); but they also reap more, because those few seeds planted multiply into a large harvest. How terrible it is to reap the harvest of sin! David sowed one seed of lust and see what a harvest of tears he reaped.

Why did God permit Israel to be judged by wicked Assyria? Because He loved His people. Love always disciplines to make the child better (Heb. 12:1-13; Prov. 3:11-12). The hand of chastening is the hand of love; it is the Father correcting a son, not a judge punishing a criminal. How grateful we ought to be for the chastening love of God—Ps. 119:71.

## IV. Israel's Restoration Promised (11–14)

Hosea does not end on a gloomy note. He sees the future glory of the nation. Just as his wife was brought back from slavery and restored to his home and heart, so the nation would one day be restored to her land and to her Lord. These closing chapters magnify the faithful love of God in contrast to the unfaithfulness of His people.

God loved Israel in Egypt (11:1), when she was a captive nation having no beauty or glory. It was His grace that redeemed her from slavery, that led her, that provided for her every need. But from the very beginning of this "marriage" between Jehovah and Israel, the people were "bent on backsliding" (11:7). God drew them with cords of love (11:4), but they tried to break those cords and go their own way. Sin is not only the breaking of God's law; it is the breaking of God's heart. Read 11:8-11 to see the yearning heart of God as He seeks to bring His unfaithful people back to the place of blessing. In chapter 12 we see the nation "talking big" and boasting of her wealth and achievements; yet God says, "They are feeding on wind—it's all hot air." The backslidden person may enjoy material wealth and physical pleasures, but this will never satisfy the heart or glorify the Lord; and in the end the backslider will be poor, wretched, blind, and naked.

Chapter 14 is God's loving appeal to His "wife" to return to His heart and blessing. He asks for sacrifices from their lips—words of confession—and not the sacrifices of animals. He promises to heal their backslidings (14:4) and restore them to His favor. He pictures the nation as a fruitful tree or vine (vv. 4-7) once the nation has turned from her idols and returned to the Lord. Of course, this will happen when Jesus Christ returns to the earth to establish His kingdom and fulfill the promises made to the fathers.

But please do not miss the personal message here: backsliders may return to the Lord, experience His forgiveness (1 John 1:9), and be restored to the place of blessing and usefulness. The closing verses present two ways: the way of the Lord, which is right, and the way of transgressors, which is wrong. Claim v. 4 for yourself and experience the healing of sins forgiven.

# JOEL

Hosea's message grew out of a personal heartbreak in his own family; Joel's message grew out of a national calamity: the invasion of a plague of locusts. Along with the locusts came a terrible drought (1:19-20), and the combination of the two brought the land to the place of famine. Joel had a message for the people of Judah, for he saw in these calamities the disciplining hand of God for their sins. But he looked beyond the locusts and saw another "army"—a literal army of Gentile nations attacking Jerusalem (3:2). In other words, Joel used the immediate judgment of God (the locusts) as an illustration of the ultimate judgment, "the day of the Lord." So, Joel's book is divided into two parts: (1) the present message about the plague of locusts, 1:1–2:27; and (2) the future message about the day of the Lord, 2:28–3:21.

Before looking at these two messages, we must understand what Joel means by "the day of the Lord." He uses the phrase five times, in 1:15; 2:1, 11, 31; and 3:14. Other prophets also use it (Isa. 2:12; 13:6-9; 14:3; Jer. 30:7-8; 46:10; and the entire Book of Zephaniah). The phrase "the day of the Lord" refers to that future time when God will pour out His wrath on the Gentile nations *because of their sins against the Jews* (see Joel 3:1-8). It will occur after the church has been taken to heaven (see 1 Thes. 1:10 and 5:9-10, and Rev. 3:10), during that period of seven years known as the Tribulation. It is described most fully in Rev. 6–19. This period will end with the Battle of Armageddon (Joel 3:9-17; Rev. 19:11-21) and Jesus Christ returning to the earth to establish His kingdom.

## I. The Day of the Lord Typified (1:1–2:27)

### A. *Proclamation (1:1-20).*

Joel addresses several different groups of people as he describes the terrible plague and its devastating results. The old men (vv. 1-4) are asked if they can remember such a tragedy from the years gone by. No, they cannot. In fact, they will tell their children and even their great-grandchildren about the awful event. In v. 4 we do not have four different insects; rather, we have the locust in four different stages of growth. There are some ninety varieties of locusts, and all of them are well able to ruin a nation. Joel next turns to the drunkards (vv. 5-7) who weep and howl because the vineyards have been ruined and their supply of drink is gone. He then turns to the worshipers (vv. 8-10) who must go to the temple empty-handed because there are no sacrifices to bring. He addresses the farmers (vv. 11-12) who are howling because their crops are all ruined. Finally, Joel turns to the priests (vv. 13-14) and tells them to fast and pray. Here we reach the heart of the matter, for it was because of sin that God was punishing the nation. So long as the people obeyed Him, He would send the rain and the harvest; but if they turned away from Him, He would make the heavens like brass and destroy their fields. See Deut. 11:10-17; 2 Chron. 7:13-14.

### B. Tribulation (2:1-11).

Joel blows the trumpet of alarm to warn the people that the destroying army of locusts is coming. Locusts do resemble tiny horsemen, and their ability to eat everything in their path has often been proved. Verse 10 suggests such great swarms that they will blot out the sun and moon.

### C. Humiliation (2:12-17).

Joel blows the trumpet the second time, this time to call an assembly to fast and pray and confess sin. This is not to be the mere outward tearing of clothes, but rather the breaking of the heart. In 1:13, Joel called only for the priests to pray; in 2:16, he summons everybody to participate in the fast. No doubt he reminded them of the promise of 2 Chron. 7:14.

### D. Restoration (2:18-27).

We have had the alarm and the assembly; now we have the answer from the Lord. What faith Joel had—"The Lord will answer." God promises to drive away the army of locusts and restore the pastures again. In fact, He will give them such "bumper crops" that they will more than make up for the years wasted by the locusts (2:25). He will do this, not because they deserve it, but that they and the heathen nations might know that He is the Lord (v. 27).

## II. The Day of the Lord Prophesied (2:28–3:21)

Now Joel moves ahead and talks about another "day of the Lord," a time of future judgment that will end in blessing for the Jews.

### A. The Spirit poured out before that day (2:28-32).

This passage is quoted by Peter on the Day of Pentecost (Acts

2:16-21), so read that quotation carefully. But notice that Peter does *not* say, "Joel's prophecy is fulfilled." Rather, he says, "This is that which was spoken." In other words, "This is that same Holy Spirit that Joel spoke about." The full prophecy of Joel, with its dramatic signs in the heavens, will not be fulfilled until the last days. By no stretch of your imagination can you find Joel's words literally fulfilled at Pentecost. No, what happened at Pentecost was but the beginning of God's blessing on Israel. Had the nation received Christ instead of arresting the apostles and killing Stephen, the promised "times of refreshing" would have come with the return of Christ and the establishment of His kingdom (Acts 3:19-26). Joel is telling us that during the last days of Israel's history, during the Tribulation period, the Spirit of God will work in mighty power in the saving of both Jews and Gentiles, and there will be mighty wonders and signs in the heavens. These are recorded in the Book of Revelation.

## B. Judgment poured out during that day (3:1-17).

Verse 1 makes it clear that the Jews will be back in their land, delivered from the captivities in Gentile nations. But all the nations will gather together to fight Jerusalem. God will bring them into the Valley of Jehoshaphat, that is, the area of the Plain of Megiddo, where the Battle of Armageddon will be fought. Verses 2-8 make it clear that this judgment will be God's punishment on the Gentiles for the way they have treated the nation of Israel and the land of Israel. Palestine has been a plundered land; many Gentile nations have robbed the Jews of wealth that is rightfully theirs. God will recompense them in the Day of the Lord. In v. 2 when God promises to "plead" with the nations, this does not mean He will beg them to repent. The word "plead" can be translated "execute judgment"; see Isa. 66:16 and Jer. 25:31. Verse 13 compares the battle to a ripe harvest of grapes; see Rev. 14:14-20, a description of the Battle of Armageddon. The "valley of decision" in v. 14 has nothing to do with "making a decision for the Lord." The word "decision" suggests threshing; the nations will be threshed, judged by the Lord. Christ will defend His land, His people, and His holy city.

## C. Blessings poured out after that day (3:18-21).

As Joel preached, the people could see the dry fields, the starving cattle, and the empty barns. They could see and hear the locusts as they ravaged the country. But Joel is picturing a time when wine, milk, and water shall flow in ceaseless measure in the land. This is, of course, the kingdom age when Jesus Christ shall sit on David's throne in Jerusalem, and when the land shall be healed and the blessing of God restored. The nation will be cleansed, and God shall dwell in Zion. This reminds us of Ezekiel's final words: "And the name of the city from that day shall be, THE LORD IS THERE."

We must not miss the personal application of Joel's message to believers today. Certainly God does send natural calamities when nations refuse to obey Him. Wars, poor crops, epidemics, earthquakes, storms—all of these can be used of God to bring people to their knees. God can even use little insects to do His will if men and women will not obey Him. Our lives personally can become dry and fruitless if we are out of God's will. How important it is to experience sincere deep repentance (2:12-13) that God might forgive us and send His blessings again.

# AMOS

It is about twenty-five years before the fall of Israel. We are visiting the city of Bethel, where King Jeroboam II has his private chapel and Amaziah is his priest. The nation is enjoying peace and prosperity; in fact, it is living in luxury. The impressive service is about to start, with Amaziah in charge, when we hear a commotion outside the chapel. "Woe to them that are at ease in Zion," cries a voice. "God will send judgment upon this wicked nation." We rush outside, and there we find a rustic "hill preacher" from Tekoa, named Amos ("burden"). He is not a prophet in the professional sense, for his father was not a prophet nor did he attend the prophetic schools (7:10-17). But he is God's man with God's message, and he is warning that judgment is coming to Israel. He uses the word "captivity" several times (5:5, 27; 6:7; 7:17). Let's pause and listen to this shepherd-farmer and seek to understand the message he is bringing.

## I. He Looks Around (1–2)

Amos begins his message by looking around at the nations and announcing eight judgments. Verse 2 makes it clear that God is roaring in wrath, like a lion leaping on his prey (see 3:8). Amos begins with *Syria* (1:3-5) and accuses them of awful cruelty in war. Then he points to *Philistia* (Gaza, 1:6-8) and condemns them for the sin of slavery. The *Phoenicians* are next (Tyrus, 1:9-10), and they are also judged for cruel slavery. Israel's old enemy *Edom* is accused of not showing pity but maintaining a constant hatred (1:11-12). *Ammon* is judged for bitter cruelty and selfish greed (1:13-15); Moab for cruelty to Edom (2:1-3); and *Judah* for rejecting the Law of God (2:4-5).

It must have pleased the Israelites at Bethel to hear Amos condemn their neighbors, but Amos did not stop. Judgment #8 was reserved for—Israel. In 2:6-16 the prophet names the sins of the people: bribery, greed, adultery, immorality, selfishness, ingratitude, drunkenness (even forcing the Nazarites to drink), and rejecting God's revelation. Amos cries, "I am pressed under this burden of sin." (The name "Amos" means "burden.") How can God ever forgive such a wicked nation? Before we condemn these nations of the past, we had better examine our own nation and our own hearts, for we may be guilty of the same sins.

## II. He Looks Within (3–6)

Having announced judgment to the nations, Amos now looks within the hearts of the people and explains why this judgment is coming. Remember that Israel was enjoying a time of peace, prosperity, and "religious revival." People were attending religious services and bringing generous offerings. But the true servants of God do not look at the outward appearance; they look at the heart. In these chapters, Amos delivers three sermons, each one prefaced by, "Hear this word" (3:1; 4:1; 5:1).

### A. A message of explanation (3:1-15).

"How can our God send judgment upon us?" the people were asking. "Are we not His chosen people?" But that was the very reason for the judgment. Where there is privilege, there must also be responsibility. Verses 1-2 make this clear. Amos is using an argument from cause and effect. If two people are walking together, they must have made an appointment (v. 3). If a lion roars, he has prey (v. 4). If a bird is in the trap, somebody set the trap (v. 5). If the trumpet sounds, calamity is near (v. 6). If the prophet is preaching, then God must have sent him (v. 7). Then Amos announces that the Assyrians are coming to destroy the nation (vv. 9-15), and the lovely services at Bethel will not hold them back. Alas, the summer houses and winter houses (what luxury!) will all be destroyed.

### B. A message of accusation (4:1-13).

The fearless prophet "starts meddling" now and begins to name sins. He calls the women living in careless luxury "fat cows of Bashan." See them telling their husbands to bring them more drinks. Amos is not impressed with the religion at Bethel; to him it is just another sin on their records. God had sent his warnings to them (vv. 6-11), but they would not listen. He had taken the best of their young men to die in war (4:10), but still the nation did not repent. God would no longer use natural calamities. Now He would come Himself (v. 12). "Prepare to meet your God."

### C. A message of lamentation (5:1–6:14).

Amos weeps as he contemplates the judgments coming to his nation. Verse 3 suggests that 90 percent of the people will die. Note the repetition of the word "seek" (5:4, 6, 8, 14). "Don't seek religious services; seek the Lord!" There were some in the nation who were saying, "The day of the Lord will come and then God will deliver us" (5:18-20). They did not realize that the Day of the Lord would be a time of judgment for *them* as well as for their enemies. They are like Christians today who "long for" the return of Christ, yet may not be prepared to meet the Lord. In 5:24 we have the key verse of the book; read "justice" instead of "judgment." Amos longed to see the nation obeying God and executing His justice in the land. In chapter 6 Amos continues to weep over the sins of the people: indifference and indulgence (vv. 1-6); injustice, immorality, and idolatry (vv. 7-14). "At ease in Zion" — what a description of some believers today!

## III. He Looks Ahead (7–9)

In the closing part of his message, Amos beholds five visions, and from these visions he discovers what God will do to the nation. (1) *Vision of Locusts* (7:1-3) — The locusts are about to destroy the crop, but Amos intercedes and the Lord stops them. (2) *Vision of Fire* (7:4-6) — An awful drought overtakes the land; the prophet prays, and God delivers the land. (3) *Vision of the Plumb line* (7:7-9) — The Lord stands beside (not "upon") the wall and tests it to see if it is straight. God is measuring Israel, and she does not conform to His Word; therefore, judgment is coming. At this point in the message, the "state priest" Amaziah could take no more, and he interrupted, "You are not patriotic! Take your soapbox and go back to the hills to preach." Amos was not afraid. He told the false priest, "God called me to preach, and I must obey. As for you, Amaziah, you will pay for your compromise and sins, because your wife will become a harlot and your family will die by the sword."

(4) *Vision of the Summer Fruit* (8:1-14) — We must take a brief lesson in Hebrew to understand this vision. The Hebrew word for "summer fruit" is *hayitz*, and the word for "end" in v. 2 is *hatz*. These words look and sound alike, and Amos used one to lead to the other. "The end is come! Israel, like summer fruit, has ripened for judgment." Again in vv. 4-14 the prophet names the sins of the people: robbing the poor of their homes (8:4); complaining about holy days interfering with business (8:5); setting excessive prices that hurt the poor (8:6). God warns that He will send His wrath upon the people, not only in natural calamities, but in a famine for the Word of God. They would not listen to the Word when they

had the opportunity; therefore, He will take His Word away from them. In that day their idols at Dan and Beersheba will do them no good (8:14).

(5) *Vision at the Altar* (9:1-10) — Now Amos sees the Lord Himself, and not some symbol. Why is God at the altar? Because judgment begins at the house of the Lord (1 Peter 4:17). The people had been outwardly religious, but they were not sincere from the heart. God orders the doorposts to be broken—and the roof caves in. Verses 8-9 summarize what God plans to do. He compares the coming judgment to the sifting of grain (see Luke 22:31-34). The good seed (true believers, the believing remnant) will be saved, but the chaff will be burned up.

Amos closes on a note of victory, for in 9:11-15 we have the promise of future restoration. Verses 11-12 are quoted in Acts 15:14-18 at the first church conference. Today God is calling out of the nations a people for His name, the church; but when the church is completed, then He will return and restore the tabernacle (house) of David and establish the Jewish kingdom. The land will become fruitful again, and the people will be blessed forever.

# OBADIAH

The time: 586 B.C.; the place: Jerusalem; the event: the destruction of Jerusalem by the Babylonian armies. We see the angry soldiers as they wreck the walls, slay the people, and burn the city. But we see something else. We see a group of neighboring citizens — the Edomites — as they stand on the other side and encourage the Babylonians to ruin the city. "Raze it! Raze it!" they are calling. "Dash their little children against the stones and wipe out the Jews!" (Ps. 137:7-9) Who are these people who desire such terrible things to happen to their neighbors? They are brethren to the Jews. The Edomites were the descendants of Esau, Jacob's older brother (Gen. 25:21-26). Esau was outwardly a much better man than scheming Jacob, yet God chose Jacob and rejected Esau. Esau moved to the mountains in the south and established the Edomite kingdom (Idumaea), but they remained enemies.

This little Book of Obadiah (the shortest in the OT) deals with these two brothers, Esau and Jacob — Edom and Israel. The prophet presents a two-fold message:

## I. God's Vengeance on Esau (vv. 1-16)

In Jer. 49:7-22, Jeremiah had already announced the doom of Edom; in fact, there are some quotations from his prophecy here in Obadiah. This is the "rumor" or "report" that Obadiah had heard: God would avenge Israel and destroy Edom. Why? Because of her sins. What were these sins?

### A. Pride (vv. 3-4).

Edom was a small nation, but she boasted of her achievements. Edom was actually cut out of the rocks; the people literally "nested" in the rocks (v. 4). Edom's chief city, Petra, was carved out of the sides of the mountains, and the fortress seemed impregnable. Compare Isa. 14:12-15.

### B. Confederacy (v. 7).

Instead of sharing the burden of their brothers in Israel, the Edomites allied with the surrounding nations to oppress Jerusalem.

### C. Violence (v. 10).

The Edomites assisted in the wrecking of Jerusalem. How? By

doing nothing to prevent it, and by encouraging those who actually did the damage. They stood "on the other side" (v. 11) and refused to stand with the Jews. This reminds us of the priest and Levite in Christ's Parable of the Good Samaritan (Luke 10:31-33). We may not actually lift a hand to hurt another, but by watching and doing nothing, we are sharing in the crime.

### D. Rejoicing (v. 12).

Edom should have been weeping over his brother's calamity, but instead he was rejoicing and jeering. See Prov. 24:17-18.

### E. Looting (v. 13).

They took advantage of the plight of the Jews and robbed the city of its wealth. This plundering was seen by God even though the thieves escaped.

### F. Hindering Jews from escaping (v. 14).

Some of the Jews tried to escape and protect their families, but the Edomites blocked the way. They even helped capture those who did escape and returned them to the Babylonians.

### G. Drunken celebration (v. 16).

The Edomites got to the wine supplies and held a great celebration. At last, their enemy was defeated.

But note v. 15 — God would treat them just the way they treated the Jews. See Ps. 137:8-9 also. They were traitors to the Jews; therefore, their own confederates would betray them (v. 7). They plundered and looted, so their nation would be robbed (vv. 5-6). Edom was violent, so they would be cut off completely (vv. 9-10). Edom wanted the Jews to be destroyed, so she would be destroyed by Babylon (vv. 10, 18). Edom would reap what she sowed. See also Isa. 34:5-15; Ezek. 25:12-14; 35:1-15; Amos 1:11-12.

## II. God's Victory for Jacob (vv. 17-21)

That little word "but" in v. 17 marks the turning point. God promises deliverance and cleansing for Mt. Zion. Yes, Israel had sinned, and the temple was destroyed because of their sins, but God would cleanse and restore "the house of Jacob" and not the house of Esau (the Edomites). Note in v. 18 that there is reunion as well as restoration, for the house of Joseph (the southern tribes) and the house of Jacob will both be as a fire against Edom. The day will come when the Jews will "possess their possessions"—their land, their temple, their city, and their kingdom. The key word in vv. 17-20 is "possess." Certainly Israel owns the land because of God's promise to Abraham. She owns her city too. But she does not fully possess them, for her land has been overrun by the Gentile nations for centuries. There is coming the day, however, when Jesus Christ will return to give Israel back her possessions that she might enjoy them and use them to the glory of God.

"And the kingdom shall be the Lord's." What a wonderful way to end this brief book! Today, the King has been rejected, and David's throne is empty in Jerusalem. The Jews are in the sad condition described in Hosea 3:4-5—without king, priest, sacrifice, or priesthood. But when Christ returns, the nation will look upon the One they pierced, they will be cleansed and forgiven, and the kingdom will be established. Daniel saw Christ, the Stone, come down and crush all the kingdoms of the world (Dan. 2:44-45). No matter what may happen to the affairs of Israel as the Gentile nations seek to control her or capture her, you may be sure that God will watch over His people and one day give them their promised kingdom.

But we must look deeper into this book if we want to get the full spiritual message, for "Esau" and "Jacob" stand for something more than two brothers and two nations. They represent two opposing forces—the flesh and the Spirit. Esau was a good-looking man, active, healthy, outgoing, athletic; Jacob was a homebody, full of deceit and selfish plans. If you were choosing one of these boys, no doubt you would have selected Esau; but God chose Jacob. Throughout the Bible, He is known as "the God of Jacob." This is God's grace. Salvation is not by merit; it is by grace and grace alone. God used Jacob to father the tribes of Israel. God gave His covenants and promises to Jacob, not to Esau.

So, Jacob represents the child of God, chosen by God's grace, often sinning and failing, but ultimately gaining his inheritance. He represents the struggle between the flesh and the Spirit (Gal. 5:16-26). Esau pictures the flesh—attractive, powerful, proud, grasping, rebellious, and always seeming to be on the winning side. Yet God has pronounced judgment on the flesh, and one day that judgment will fall. Edom was proud and rebellious; Edom laughed when Jerusalem fell. Five years later, however, Edom also fell to the Babylonians—and where is Edom today? This world boasts of the flesh, what the flesh has accomplished, how strong the flesh is; but one day all flesh will fall before the victory of Christ. Read Rev. 19:11-21, and note especially vv. 17-18 where "flesh" is mentioned repeatedly.

The struggle between Esau and Jacob, flesh and Spirit, runs all through the Bible. The Herods of the NT were Edomites. One of them killed the Jewish babies in his attempt to destroy Christ (Matt. 2:16-18). Another Herod murdered John the Baptist; another one killed James the brother of John (Acts 12). The struggle between the Israelis and the Arabs today is but a continuation of this same battle that started in Gen. 25:21-26. Flesh vs. Spirit, pride vs. submission, man's way vs. God's way: the struggle will go on until Christ returns and establishes His kingdom.

There is a law of retribution written into history: nations receive back just what they have given to others (v. 15). See Jer. 50:29. In particular, the Gentile nations will be called to account for the way they have treated the Jews. It may take years, but God's judgment will fall on all those who refuse to do His will.

# JONAH

That Jonah was an actual person in history is verified by 2 Kings 14:25, where we find his prophecy that Jeroboam II would expand his kingdom. This message certainly made him a popular preacher. But when God called Jonah to preach to the city of Nineveh, the capital of the Assyrian empire, then the prophet rebelled. History tells us that the Assyrians were a cruel and heartless people who thought nothing of burying their enemies alive, skinning them alive, or impaling them on sharp poles under the hot sun. "If the city of Nineveh is going to be overthrown, then let it be overthrown," argued Jonah. "I would rather disobey God than see my enemies saved from judgment." In the four chapters of his book, Jonah traces his experiences and the lessons that he learned.

## I. Resignation—The Lesson of God's Patience (1)

Instead of going to Nineveh, Jonah ran in the opposite direction. He fled "from the presence of the Lord," which means that he resigned his prophetic office. Jonah knew that he could not run away from God's presence (Ps. 139:7ff), but he could resign his calling and stop preaching. He became a backslidden prophet.

### A. The causes of his backsliding were many.

First, he had the wrong attitude toward God's will; he thought it was something difficult and dangerous. And he had the wrong attitude toward witnessing; he thought he could "turn his witnessing on and off" when he wanted to, and did not realize that he was witnessing either against or for the Lord no matter where he was. He also had the wrong attitude toward his enemies: he *wanted* to see them perish.

### B. The course of his backsliding was downward.

Down to Joppa, down into the ship, down into the sea, and down into the great fish. Disobedience always leads downward. But note that often things seem to "work out" even for a backslidden believer, for the ship was waiting for him and he had the money to pay the fare. He was so at peace that he was even able to go to sleep in the storm!

### C. The consequences of his backsliding were tragic.

He lost God's voice, for now God had to speak to him in a storm.

He lost his spiritual energy and went to sleep in the hold of the ship. He lost his power in prayer, and even his desire to pray. The heathen were praying, but Jonah was sleeping. He lost his testimony with the men on the ship, and he lost his influence for good, because he was the cause of the storm. He also almost lost his life. But how patient and long-suffering the Lord was with him.

## II. Repentance—The Lesson of God's Pardon (2)

Jonah was first of all chastened under the loving hand of God. Jonah admitted it was God who cast him into the sea, not the hands of the sailors (v. 3). When trials and afflictions come to us because of our sins, it is important that we acknowledge God's working (Ps. 119:67). Read Heb. 12:5-11 to see the meaning of divine chastening. Next Jonah was convicted of his sins, and this, after all, is the purpose of chastening—to bring us to the place of conviction and confession. He lost the presence of God (2:4; see Ps. 51:11); he admitted he had believed the devil's lies (v. 8); and he showed true sorrow for his sins (v. 9). In faith he asked God for His forgiveness, looking toward the temple (v. 4) as the OT Jew was taught to do (2 Chron. 6:36-39). This is equivalent to our 1 John 1:9. God cleansed Jonah and gave him another chance.

According to Heb. 12:5-11, there are several ways Christians may respond to the chastening of God: we may despise it, as Jonah did for three days, and refuse to confess; we may faint and give up; or we may endure God's chastening, confess our sins, and trust Him to work everything out for our good and His glory. To rebel against the hand of God is to ask for trouble. Jonah submitted, prayed, and trusted, and God forgave him.

## III. Revival—The Lesson of God's Power (3)

The key word in this chapter is "great." Jonah came to the great city to preach the message of God. There were nearly a million people in and around Nineveh, and the city itself had great walls and towers. It was the center of the rising empire of Assyria. But it was a sinful city (read Nahum 3) because the Assyrians were a ruthless, cruel people who had no pity for their enemies. "Violence" was their chief sin (v. 8). God gave Jonah a great commission, to preach to these Gentiles that they could escape the wrath of God and be forgiven. What a message! Jonah had to overcome his sinful prejudices to preach this message. Then, God performed a great change in the city, for from the king to the lowest citizen, there were expressions of fear and repentance. Two things contributed to this: Jonah's message and the miracle of Jonah's deliverance from the great fish, the news of which certainly reached this city. It took three days to get through Nineveh, but revival came the very first day of Jonah's ministry. The people "believed God" (v. 5), proving their faith by their works of contrition. And God forgave them. This was undoubtedly one of the greatest evangelistic harvests in history. It shows what the Lord can do with a frail human instrument willing to preach God's message.

Jesus used Nineveh to illustrate an important point (Matt. 12:38-41). He had preached to that generation for three years and had reinforced His message with His miracles, yet they would not repent and believe. The Ninevites heard *one* sermon from *one* preacher, and that sermon emphasized wrath, not love—yet they repented and were forgiven. The Jews heard the Son of God for three years, heard the message of God's forgiveness, yet refused to repent. Certainly theirs will be the greater condemnation.

## IV. Rebellion—The Lesson of God's Pity (4)

Had you been writing this last chapter, you probably would have shown Jonah in the city of Nineveh, carefully teaching the people and helping them in their spiritual decisions. But God does not write it that way. Instead of meeting a rejoicing preacher, we meet a rebellious preacher, angry at the people and angry at God. We see an adult acting like a child, a believer acting like an unbeliever. We see Jonah sitting outside the city, trying to make himself comfortable, and actually hoping that God's judgment will fall on the people. Here is an amazing thing: God sent a great awakening under the preaching of a man who did not even love the souls of the people he preached to!

This is the key lesson of the book: God's love and pity for lost souls. Jonah felt sorry for himself, and even felt sorry for the plant that sheltered him and then died, but he had no heartfelt love or pity for the multitudes in the city of Nineveh. It is possible to serve the Lord and yet not love the people. How unlike Jesus Christ he is in this chapter, for Jesus looked upon a city of lost souls and wept. God could control the wind and waves in chapter 1, the fish in chapter 2, and the gourd, worm, and wind in chapter 4, but He could not control Jonah without the prophet's surrender.

Everything in nature obeys the Word of God except human beings, and human beings have the greatest reason to obey. It would seem that Jonah did get right with God, confess his sins, and continue his ministry. And God did spare the city of Nineveh for another century and a half.

Of course, Jonah is a type of Jesus Christ (Matt. 12:39-41) in His death, burial, and resurrection. Christ was greater than Jonah in His person (He is the Son of God), His outreach (the whole world, not one city), His sacrifice (He did die to save others), and His love for those who did not deserve it. Some also see in Jonah a picture of the Jewish nation: disobedient; cast out of the land; "swallowed up" by the sea of Gentiles; preserved in spite of opposition; brought back again and given another chance.

# MICAH

The names of the kings in Micah 1:1 tell us that the prophet preached at the same time in history as Isaiah (Isa. 1:1). It is not difficult to imagine these two men ministering in Judah, encouraging each other and seeking to spread the Word of the Lord. Of the rulers, Jotham and Hezekiah were good kings who helped the nation, but Ahaz was a wicked man who sold the nation into idolatry.

This little book is composed of three "sermons" that Micah preached to the people, and each message begins with the word "hear." He deals with three very practical and important themes:

## I. Judgment Is Coming (1–2)

Micah wastes no time getting into his message. God has spoken to him and warned him that the sins of the people are so great that He must send judgment. He names the capital cities in v. 1—Jerusalem (capital of Judah, the Southern Kingdom) and Samaria (capital of Israel, the Northern Kingdom). In fact, in this first message, Micah names twelve cities and points out their sins. The sins of the cities were polluting the whole nation. That sounds very up-to-date.

What were some of the sins that God would judge? Idolatry ("high places" in 1:5) was the main sin. The people insisted on worshiping "the works of their own hands" (5:13). But people do that today. We may not carve out statues and bow before them, but we certainly live for the things we have manufactured—cars, clothes, houses, money. What we serve and sacrifice for is the thing that we worship. Micah warned that the day would come when God would destroy the idols of the people and turn them to dust (1:6-7).

In 2:1 we see the sin of covetousness: people would lie awake at night thinking up new ways to get "things," and then get up early to carry out their plans. According to Col. 3:5, covetousness *is* idolatry. Many people today have an insatiable appetite to get more things. "Take heed and beware of covetousness," warned Jesus, "for one's life does not consist in the abundance of the things he possesses" (Luke 12:15, NKJV). The people were not only covetous, but they used illegal means to get what they wanted—fraud, threats, violence (2:2). The rich took advantage of the poor, and the rulers did not obey the Law of God.

How did Micah respond to this awful message of judgment? He wept and mourned (1:8-9). Then he sent a personal message to each of the wicked cities, warning them that the day of God's wrath was just around the corner. He uses a bit of sarcasm in 1:10-16, relating each message to the name of the particular city to which it is sent. Aphrah means "dust," and they shall roll in the dust. Saphir means "beautiful," but the people shall go naked. Zaanan means "to go forth," but the citizens will be too afraid to go forth.

How did the people react to Micah's preaching? They tried to stop him. In 2:6 they say, "Stop preaching such terrible things! You know they will not happen to us. We are God's people." But Micah says, "I must preach — the Spirit of God compels me." Micah knew that the people did not want honest preaching; they preferred their drunken false prophets who lived as wickedly as the people did (2:10-11).

## II. The Deliverer Is Coming (3–5)

Not discouraged by their slanders, Micah moves now into his second message, a message of hope. First he condemns the wicked leaders of the land — the rulers, the false prophets, and the priests (3:1-7). They were devouring the people instead of helping them, and they refused to serve unless they were paid. It was the sin of covetousness again. The prophets were preaching what the people wanted to hear: "All is well — nothing will happen to us." But Micah knew that Israel would fall to Assyria (this happened in 721), and that the Babylonians would carry Judah away captive (this happened in 606–586).

Chapter 4, though, takes up a wonderful new theme: one day there will be peace on earth and righteousness will reign. Mt. Zion will become the capital of the world; all the armies will be dismissed and the weapons destroyed. How can this happen? Through the promise in chapter 5: The Deliverer will come. Micah has mentioned twelve cities, but now he mentions one more — Bethlehem, the birthplace of Jesus (5:2-3; Matt. 2:6). It is this prophecy that led the wise men to Jesus. Of course, the Jews rejected their Prince of Peace, so there has been no peace in the world. But when Christ returns to earth, He will establish His kingdom of peace and there shall be no more war.

Meanwhile, men and women can have peace in their hearts by

trusting Christ as Savior (Rom. 5:1). And this is the theme of Micah's final message, for he calls the people to make their decision to trust the Lord and obey Him.

## III. Trust the Lord Today (6–7)

The scene here is a courtroom, and God has called His people to be judged. "State your case against Me," He says. "I have a complaint against you," announces the Lord, "for I have done all I can do for you, yet you have rejected Me. I brought you out of Egypt; I led you in the wilderness; I protected you from your enemies. What more could I have done?"

In 6:6-8, the people answer: "Yes, we have sinned. How can we make up for all that we have done? We could bring sacrifices, but they can never wash away sins. All our religion can never save us. Even if we sacrificed our own children, that would not cleanse us. We know what God wants us to do: to act justly, to love mercy, and to walk humbly before our God." How true this is! God does not want extravagant gifts and sacrifices; He wants our hearts (Ps. 51:16-17; 1 Sam. 15:22; Isa. 1:10-18).

God speaks again in 6:9-16. "You must repent and obey, because judgment is on the way. Then you will discover how terrible your sins have been, your cheating and your lies. You will try to satisfy yourselves, but it will not work. You will eat but still be hungry; you will save money, but it will vanish; you will plant crops but never harvest them." What a tragic picture. Imagine seeing everything you do accomplish nothing because you are out of the will of God.

Micah the prophet speaks in 7:1-10. He laments the fact that the nation is so wicked he cannot find an honest man. Bribery, injustice, dishonesty, and greed rule the land. But Micah has faith in God (7:7-10). If God is going to punish, all Micah can do is wait patiently for Him to work. If the Lord chastens His own people for their sins, certainly He will punish the enemy for their sins also.

In 7:11-17, God makes promises to His people that He will restore them in the future. The wicked cities will be restored and cleansed, and the nation will be established in glory. But first, the Jews must go through a time of tribulation. They have been suffering for centuries, of course, but there will be a special time of trial after Christ takes the church to heaven. This is the Tribulation, or the time of Jacob's trouble.

The closing verses (7:18-20) are a wonderful confession of faith, the whole purpose of Micah's message. He wants to bring the people to faith in the Lord. God is the only One who can forgive sins (Mark 2:7; Ps. 32:5). He alone will show mercy and love to sinners; He will cast their sins into the depths of the sea. This is why Christ died, that sinners might be forgiven. Have you trusted Him and asked Him to forgive your sins? This is the theme of Micah's last message: "Trust the Lord today!"

# NAHUM

Imagine how happy the people of Judah were when they heard: "Nineveh has fallen! The Assyrian empire is no more!" (cf. 1:15) Assyria was a ruthless enemy that practiced brutality on men, women, and children. Their armies destroyed and looted; they buried their enemies alive and even skinned them alive; they impaled people on sharp poles and left them to burn in the sun. Assyria had been used of God to chasten the Northern Kingdom of Israel; that happened in 721 B.C. In 701 B.C., the Assyrians tried to conquer Judah, but God intervened and destroyed their army (Isa. 36–37). Still, Assyria was always the scourge of the nations; every nation feared her and tried to win her approval. Finally in 612 B.C., Nineveh was destroyed by the Medes and the Babylonians; and so complete was their conquest that the ruins of the city remained undiscovered until 1842.

It was concerning this future destruction of Nineveh that Nahum wrote. He wrote this little book at a time when Assyria was at the very peak of her power. Nobody would have dreamed that mighty Nineveh would fall, but God knows the future and He gave His message to Nahum to deliver to the frightened people of Judah. This was not a message of warning to Nineveh; they had heard God's warning from Jonah a century and a half before. No, there was no hope for Nineveh; God's patience had run out and His judgment would fall. Rather, this was a message of hope for Judah, to encourage them to trust God at an hour of great danger. Each of the three chapters tells us something about God and also about the fall of the city.

## I. God Is Jealous: Nineveh Will Fall (1)

The word "jealous" when applied to God does not suggest envy or selfishness. It carries the idea of being zealous for His glory and for His holiness. He burns with hatred against sin even though He loves the sinner. Just as a husband is jealous over his wife and therefore protects her, so God is jealous over His people and His law, and therefore must act in holiness and justice. He is slow to anger; in fact, He gave Nineveh 150 years of mercy. But they had gone too far in their brutality and violence, and God had to judge them.

Does God have the power to judge? Of course He does. Look at

607

His power in nature (vv. 3-6), in winds and storms, in rains and droughts, on land and sea. Who can stand before His power? Nations today seem to forget the power of Almighty God. They act as though there is no God. But you can be sure that the day of judgment will come, and in that day no nation will be able to escape.

In vv. 8-13, Nahum describes the fall of the city with two pictures: a great flood of waters that sweeps everything away; and a fire of dry thorns that burns like stubble. It is interesting to note that Nineveh did fall because of a flood of waters. The Medes and Babylonians besieged the city for many months and made little headway. Then the rainy season came and the two rivers next to Nineveh began to rise. One historian says that the Medes broke one of the dams on the river. But in any case, the swelling waters beat against the thick walls of Nineveh and broke them down. The city was literally destroyed by the flood; see also Nahum 2:6. God does not need armies; He can use tiny raindrops!

God makes two wonderful promises to His people in this chapter. In 1:7, He assures them of His goodness and tells them they will be safe so long as they trust in Him. In 1:12, He assures them that He will not afflict them again with the Assyrian armies the way Israel had been afflicted before. No matter what the difficulties may be, we can trust God to care for us and see us through.

## II. God Is Judge: Nineveh's Fall Is Great (2)

In the Hebrew text, 1:15 is actually the beginning of the second chapter. It is the joyful announcement that Nineveh has fallen. See also Isa. 52:7 for a similar announcement about the fall of Babylon; and see Paul's use of this for today in Rom. 10:15. The person who brings a message of hope and victory is a person with beautiful feet. As Christians we all ought to have beautiful feet as we carry the message of the Gospel to the lost.

Chapter 2 is a vivid picture of the invasion of the city and its ultimate fall. Assyria had emptied Israel in 721; now God was going to restore His people by punishing the enemy (vv. 1-2). The Medes wore scarlet uniforms and used scarlet shields (v. 3). The armies with their spears and lances looked like a forest of fir trees. Please do not make 2:4 a prophecy of the modern automobile. It only pictures the chariots in the streets of the city. *Huzzab* in v. 7 refers probably to the queen, being led away in great humiliation.

Note the repeated reference to lions in vv. 11-13. The lion was the symbol of the Assyrian empire, as you can see from pictures in history or archaeology books. They built huge statues of lions with the heads of men. "Where are your lions now?" Nahum asks. "Where are your rulers, your champions?"

"I am against you" (v. 13, NKJV). God brought the Medes and Babylonians against Nineveh and permitted them to spoil the city and take its wealth. For 150 years He had waited for Assyria to turn, but she refused. God is Judge among the nations; He must act.

### III. God Is Just: Nineveh Deserves to Fall (3)

Here Nahum deals with the justice of this act. Some might say, "But God used Assyria to punish the Northern Kingdom of Israel. Why punish Nineveh when once He used her as His own tool?" Or they might argue, "Look at the kingdom of Judah. She is full of sin too. Why not punish her?" Well, God would punish Judah in a few years (606–586); He would permit the Babylonians to destroy Jerusalem and take the people captive. But His purpose for Judah would be different from His purpose for Nineveh. God would chasten Judah in love to teach her a lesson; He would judge Assyria in anger to destroy her for her sins.

In 3:1 we see the great sins of Assyria listed: murders, lies, and covetousness. The Assyrians had murdered thousands of innocent people; now their own people would be slain and their bodies stacked in the streets like lumber. Nineveh had carried on a profitable commerce with the other nations and had grown rich through lies and violence. But now all their wealth would vanish in the hands of the looters. This is the justice of God. And in that day of judgment, the Assyrian soldiers (usually so brave) would act like frightened women. Every means of fortification would fail.

In vv. 15-17, Nahum compares the battle to a plague of locusts. Just as the worms eat up the crops, so the enemy would eat up the city. The Assyrian soldiers would be as strong as grasshoppers. Then in v. 18 Nahum sees the Assyrians as a slaughtered flock of sheep, their shepherds (rulers) sleeping in death.

The word "bruit" in v. 19 of the King James means "news, report." When the nations got the report of the destruction of Assyria, they clapped their hands and shouted for joy. The Lord judges the sins of nations and the sins of individuals. It is tragic to reject His warnings and persist in sin. "Be sure your sins will find you out."

# HABAKKUK

Have you ever looked out upon this world with its injustice and violence, and asked the question: "Why doesn't God do something?" It looks like the wicked are prospering and the righteous are suffering. Godly people pray, but it seems as though their prayers do no good. This is the problem faced and solved in Habakkuk. Note three acts in this personal drama as the prophet faces his doubts and finds certainty in his faith.

## I. The Prophet Wondering (1)

### A. "Why is God silent and inactive?" (vv. 1-4)

This was the first problem that puzzled the prophet. He looked out across the world of that day and saw violence (1:2-3, 9; 2:8, 17), injustice, spoiling, strife, and contention. The law was not enforced; there was no legal protection for innocent people who were sentenced as guilty. The courts were manipulated by selfish lawyers and cruel officials. The whole nation was suffering because of the evils of the government. Yet God seemed to be doing nothing about it. Along with these internal problems was the threat of the Babylonian empire as it swept across the political landscape.

God gave the prophet an answer in 5-11. "I am working a work that will amaze you," God said. "I will raise up the Chaldeans who will conquer the nations and be my instrument to chasten the people." How true it is that God is working in our world and we fail to realize it (Rom. 8:28; 2 Cor. 4:17). Paul quotes 1:5 in Acts 13:41, applying it to the spread of the Gospel among the Gentiles. God describes the Chaldean armies in these verses, and the picture is not a pretty one. They are bitter and swift; they are terrible and dreadful; they fly as eagles and swoop down for the kill. Habakkuk did not have to be told about the terror of the Chaldeans, for he knew how wicked they were.

### B. "How can God use such a sinful nation for a holy cause?" (vv. 12-17)

God's answer in vv. 5-11 only created a new problem for Habakkuk. He could not understand how a holy God could use such a wicked nation to punish His own chosen people, the Jews. "It is true that we have sinned," says Habakkuk, "and we deserve chastening; but the Chaldeans are far more wicked than we are. If anyone deserves punishment, it is the Chaldeans." Can a holy God sit and watch His own people being caught like fish or trampled like insects? (vv. 14-15) The Chaldeans will boast, "*Our* gods have given us the victory. Jehovah is not the true God."

There is nothing wrong with a believer wrestling with the problems of life and seeking to solve them. Sometimes it seems as though God does not care; it appears that He has forsaken His own and is helping the heathen. How many millions of believers have been martyred for their faith. Can we honestly worship, trust, and serve a God whose ways are so seemingly contradictory?

## II. The Prophet Watching and Waiting (2)

Instead of becoming an atheist or agnostic, Habakkuk went to his watchtower to pray, meditate, and wait on the Lord. He knew that God heard his complaint and that He would send an answer soon. God *did* answer. "I have a plan and a schedule," God said. "It will all work out in due time, so don't become impatient." Then God gave to Habakkuk three very wonderful assurances to encourage and strengthen him during those difficult days.

### A. "The just shall live by faith" (v. 4).

This is one of the most important verses in the entire Bible. It forms the text for three NT books: Romans (1:17—emphasis is on *the just*); Galatians (3:11—emphasis is on *shall live*); and Hebrews (10:38—emphasis is on *by faith*). Verse 4 describes two kinds of people: those who are "puffed up" because they trust in themselves, and those who are saved and humble because they trust in the Lord. See the Pharisee and publican in Luke 18:9-14. The Chaldeans were the ones who were puffed up by their victories, not realizing that it was God who enabled them to conquer.

### B. "The earth shall be filled with God's glory" (v. 14).

The earth in Habakkuk's day was certainly not filled with much glory, nor is it today. Look at the five "Woes" in this chapter, and you will see the sins that God hates: greedy and violent covetousness (vv. 5-11); murder for gain (v. 12); drunkenness (vv. 15-16); and idolatry (v. 19). These are the very sins that are polluting nations today. And God hates these sins today just as much as He did back in Habakkuk's day. But the promise still stands that God's glory shall one day fill this earth, for Jesus Christ shall return, put down all sin, and establish His righteous kingdom.

## C. "The Lord is in His holy temple" (v. 20).

God is still on the throne (Isa. 6). We have no need to complain or doubt, for He is ruling and overruling in the affairs of nations. Habakkuk thought that God was uninterested in the problems of life, but he discovered that God was very much concerned, and that He was working out His own plan in His own time. This is why the just live *by faith.* "For we walk by faith, not by sight" (2 Cor. 5:7; 4:18). If we look at ourselves, or at circumstances, we will be discouraged and want to quit, but if we look up to God by faith, and ahead to the glorious return of Christ, then we will be encouraged and enabled to go on in victory.

## III. The Prophet Worshiping (3)

Habakkuk is a changed man! Instead of complaining, he is praising the Lord. God turns sighing into singing if we (like Habakkuk) take time to wait before Him in prayer and listen to His Word.

First, the prophet prays (v. 2). "I see that You are working in this world," says the prophet, referring to 1:5. "Now continue that work—keep it alive and finish it." The word "revive" here has nothing to do with our modern "revival meetings." Habakkuk is simply asking the Lord to keep on working. He knows that there will be wrath and judgment, but he prays that God will remember mercy too.

Then the prophet ponders (vv. 3-16). He reviews the history of Israel and the wonderful works of the Lord. This poetic description of God's mighty power does not seem to follow any special pattern, nor does it cover all the main events in Jewish history. But Habakkuk knew that God had worked in the past, and therefore he could trust Him to work in the present and future. The mountains trembled before the Lord—and so would the Chaldeans. "Jehovah is a man of war." Israel was His people; He would care for them.

Finally, the prophet praises (vv. 17-19). These verses represent one of the greatest confessions of faith found in the Bible. "Though everything around me fail—the fields, the vineyards, the flocks, the herds—yet will I rejoice in the Lord." This is the OT version of Phil. 4:11-13. Habakkuk knew that he had no strength of his own, but that God could give him the strength he would need to go through the trials that lay ahead. "He will make me like a deer—I will jump over the mountains."

How much more this ought to mean to us. Habakkuk looked

through the fog and mist and wondered at God's program, but in Christ we *know* God's plans for this age (Eph. 1:8-10, and chap. 3). We have the entire Bible to study, and Habakkuk did not have this. We have the record of life, death, resurrection, and ascension of Jesus Christ, as well as the promise of His coming again. If any people ought to walk by faith and rejoice in the Lord, it is the Christian church today. Yet too often we doubt, complain, run ahead of God, and even criticize what God is doing.

Habakkuk shows us how to deal with life's problems: (1) admit them honestly; (2) talk to God about them; (3) wait quietly before Him in prayer and meditation on the Word; (4) when He speaks, listen and obey. Never run away from the difficulties of life, because God wants to use those difficulties to strengthen your faith. "Never doubt in the dark what God has told you in the light." The just shall live by faith.

# ZEPHANIAH

This man is no ordinary preacher. He is the great-great-grandson of King Hezekiah, one of Judah's most famous rulers. He has royal blood in his veins, but more important, he has the message of God on his lips. Strange to say, Zephaniah preached during the reign of godly King Josiah, and it was a time of religious "revival" (see 2 Kings 22–23). Josiah came to the throne at the age of eight, and at the age of sixteen he committed himself to the Lord. When he was twenty, he began a great reformation in the land, pulling down the idols and judging the false priests and prophets. He then began to rebuild the temple and led the nation in a celebration of the Passover. To all appearances, it was a time of religious concern and consecration.

But Zephaniah saw deeper; he saw the hearts of the people, and he knew that their religious zeal was not sincere. The reforms were shallow; the people got rid of the idols in their homes, but not the idols in their hearts. The rulers of the land were still greedy and disobedient, and the city of Jerusalem was the source of all kinds of wickedness in the land. Even today, many believers lack discernment and think that every "religious movement" is a genuine work of the Lord. Sometimes mere outward reformation only prepares the way for a work of the devil (Matt. 12:43-45).

We may divide Zephaniah's message into three parts, two dealing with judgment and one with mercy.

## I. God Will Judge Judah (1:1–2:3)

What a statement: "I will utterly destroy everything from off the land." Judgment is coming and nothing will escape. It will include birds, beasts, and fish; it will especially affect the idols ("stumbling blocks") of the wicked; and it will wipe out the population of the land. In v. 4 God names the trouble spots: Judah and Jerusalem. What? The people of God going through judgment? Yes. The city of God, the place where the temple stands? Yes! How can God destroy His holy people and His holy city? He does it because of their sins, and particularly the sin of idolatry (vv. 4-6). The prophet describes three kinds of sinners in these verses: those who have forsaken Jehovah and who worship only idols, vv. 4-5a; those who worship *both* Jehovah and the idols, v. 5b; and those who have forsaken the Lord openly and want nothing to do with Him, v. 6.

These same attitudes are with us today.

The coming judgment is described in vv. 7-18. He calls it "the Day of the Lord," a phrase used by several other OT writers, especially Joel. "The Day of the Lord" has a two-fold meaning: (1) locally, God's judgments on Israel and Judah in the past; (2) prophetically, that future time of judgment when God will pour out His wrath (Rev. 6–19). In this case, "the Day of the Lord" would be the Babylonian invasion in 606 B.C. and the destruction of the city and temple in 586 B.C. Zephaniah sees this invasion as a great "sacrifice"; see also Rev. 19:17-18. The noise of the invasion will start at the fish gate, the farthest gate in the city, and then travel right up to the top of Mt. Zion. But it will not be foreign soldiers doing the work; it will be God searching out the city, as with a lamp, exposing sin and punishing wickedness. Verses 14-16 use eleven different words to describe the coming day of the Lord. Rich and poor alike will suffer; no one's silver or gold will be able to save him.

In 2:1-3 the prophet turns to Jerusalem and Judah and pleads with the people to turn to the Lord and repent of their sins. "Before God's decree of judgment comes to pass, while there is still time, turn to the Lord and ask for mercy." Alas, the nation was content to be "religious"; they would not turn from their sins.

## II. God Will Judge the Nations (2:4–3:7)

The prophet names the various Gentile nations around Judah and announces that God will judge them for their sins as well. He begins with Philistia (vv. 4-7) and predicts that their populous coasts will become pastures for the flocks. Then he names Moab and Ammon (vv. 8-11), both of whom came from backslidden Lot (Gen. 19:33-38). They had mistreated God's people and proudly "magnified themselves"; therefore God would humble them. Their lands would be ruined. Their idols would prove powerless.

Egypt is next on the list (v. 12), and he promises them war that will slay their youths. Assyria and her capital city Nineveh will be so completely destroyed that their land will be a wilderness (vv. 13-15). The wild birds will dwell there with the animals. Their beautiful buildings will be buried under the sands. Nahum had also prophesied the fall of Nineveh and its complete destruction.

Again, Zephaniah closes this message with an appeal to his own people (3:1-7). If God judges the sins of the heathen, how much more will He judge the sins of Judah, the "holy nation of God"? He calls Jerusalem filthy and polluted — yet Josiah had removed all the idols. God could see their hearts, and in their hearts He saw rebellion. They had no real faith in the Lord. The princes and judges were like prowling animals, seeking someone to devour. The prophets were "light"; they lacked seriousness of thought and concern. They were also "treacherous," because they led the people astray. The priests polluted whatever they touched, including the holy sanctuary. They could see God's judgment day after day, but they did not take it to heart. They saw Him punish other nations, but they said, "It will never happen here."

Well, it did happen there. In 606 B.C. the Babylonians came and destroyed the nation, the city, and the temple. "Sin is a reproach to any people" — especially the people of God.

## III. God Will Restore His People (3:8-20)

Zephaniah closes his message with a great promise: God will one day regather His people, punish the Gentile nations, and restore Israel and Judah to their land. Verse 8 is certainly a prediction of the Battle of Armageddon, when all nations shall gather against Jerusalem in the last days (Rev. 19:11-21). But Jesus Christ will return and judge these nations, and then establish His kingdom. He will regather the scattered Jews, cleanse them of their sins, and establish His righteous kingdom, sitting upon David's throne in Jerusalem. See Zech. 12–13.

Have you noticed Zephaniah's emphasis on "the remnant"? (2:7, 9; 3:13) In his day, there was a believing remnant, a small group of people faithful to the Lord, just as there is a believing remnant today. In the last days, not every Jew will follow the Lord, but the remnant will.

What were the believing Jews to do because of Zephaniah's message? For one thing, they were to wait (3:8) and let God work out His purposes. Then, they were to sing (3:14ff) and rejoice at the goodness of the Lord. The nation would have to go through a time of trial and testing, but God would be in the midst of her (3:17) and she would not have to fear even in the time of judgment. God would love them and care for them. Then, when His wrath had been ended, He would restore the nation and rejoice over them. He would afflict those who had afflicted the Jews (3:19) and would bring the Jews back to their land. This happened after the seventy years of captivity ended.

But there is a future regathering and restoration for Israel when, according to v. 20, they will be a praise to all the earth. That has not happened. Today they are a source of international contention. But when Jesus returns, they will be the source of joy and glory in the earth, and the world will be at peace.

# HAGGAI

In order to understand the work of the last three prophets (Haggai, Zechariah, and Malachi), we must review Jewish history. In 536, Ezra took about 50,000 Jews and returned to the Holy Land. They rebuilt the altar and started the sacrifices again, and in 535 the foundation was laid for the temple. But there was considerable opposition and the work stopped. It was not until 520 that the people took up the work again; and in 515 the temple was finally completed. It was the work of four godly men that finally brought the task to completion: Zerubbabel, the governor; Joshua, the high priest; and Haggai and Zechariah, the prophets. See Ezra 5:1 and 6:14.

The purpose of Haggai's ministry was to awaken the lazy people and encourage them in finishing God's temple. It was easy to get the work started when they first arrived in the Holy Land because everyone was dedicated and enthusiastic. But after months of trial and opposition, the work lagged and finally stopped. In this little book we have four sermons from Haggai, and each one of them has a specific date. In each message, Haggai points out a particular sin that will keep us from accomplishing God's will and finishing His work.

## I. Putting Self Ahead of the Lord (1:1-15)

It was on September 1, 520, that Haggai delivered this message. Sixteen years had passed since the laying of the foundation, and the temple lay unfinished. This message was delivered to the two leaders of the nation, Zerubbabel and Joshua, the civil ruler and the religious leader. Haggai does not waste any time; he gets right to the point of his message: "The people are making excuses and neglecting God's house. But it is time to get to work and finish the house of God."

He points out their selfishness: they had built their own houses, but they said it was not time to build God's house. In other words, they were putting self ahead of the Lord. Some of the Jews even had "ceiled houses," which would be luxuries in that day. This sin is with us today, putting our own desires ahead of the will of the Lord. How easy it is to make excuses for not doing God's work! The weather is too bad to go visiting or to attend church, but not too bad for a hunting trip or a shopping spree. People will sit through a double header baseball game and never complain, yet they start to fidget if a church service runs five minutes overtime.

Haggai warns us that we really lose out when we put ourselves ahead of God. In 1:6 he tells us that our earnings vanish away and our possessions fail to last when God is left out. God held back the rain (v. 10), and for this reason the crops failed (v. 11). After all, the Jews knew God's promise that He would bless their land if they honored Him (see Deut. 28), but they did not trust His Word, so they lost the blessing. Matthew 6:33 is a great promise to claim; so is Phil. 4:19.

The message was received with real conviction (vv. 12-15), and the leaders became stirred to do God's will. "I am with you," promised the Lord. "I will be glorified." Note that the whole enterprise was a spiritual venture and not merely a work of the flesh. God's people rose up and put the Lord first in their lives.

## II. Looking Back Instead of Looking Ahead (2:1-9)

The people had been working about seven weeks when Haggai preached his second sermon on October 21, the last day of the Feast of Tabernacles (Lev. 23:34). It was supposed to be a great day of joy and praise, but instead it was a day of discouragement and complaining. Why? Because the people were looking back instead of looking ahead. When they had laid the foundation sixteen years before, the older men had wept because they remembered the glory of Solomon's temple (Ezra 3:12); and now some of the people were discouraged because the new temple lacked splendor and glory.

Of course, the plight of the people was due to their sins, but this was still no reason for looking back. In God's work, we must look ahead in faith. "Be strong and fear not!" God said to the discouraged leaders. "I am going to shake this world and one day establish my kingdom." See Heb. 12:26-29. God promises that the glory of the latter house (the temple during the millennial kingdom) will far exceed the glory of the former house (Solomon's temple). "And there I will give peace." The best is yet to come.

## III. Failing to Confess Our Sins (2:10-19)

The people expected material blessings the very day they began to work on the temple, but here it was December 24 and things were still difficult. Haggai explained why God had not yet blessed them:

they were still unclean; they had not confessed their sins. "You cannot give someone your holiness or health," he explained, "but you can give someone your uncleanness and sickness." And because the people were unclean, their work was unclean (v. 14). Read Zech. 3 in connection with this message; Zechariah had preached his message in the eighth month of the same year (Zech. 1:1), just one month before Hag. 2:10-19. God was able to cleanse the people of their sins, if only they would repent.

Once the nation had been cleansed, God promised to bless them (v. 19). It is not enough to do God's work; we must do it with clean hands and a pure heart. Unconfessed sin is one of the greatest obstacles to accomplishing the Lord's work.

## IV. Unbelief (2:20-23)

This final message, preached the same day as the third message, was directed to the governor personally. No doubt Zerubbabel needed special encouragement as he directed the work of the Lord. Satan always attacks spiritual leaders, and it is our duty to pray for them and work with them. Perhaps Zerubbabel saw the great empires around him and feared for the future of the tiny remnant of Jews. Circumstances have a way of discouraging us as we seek to build the work of the Lord.

But God encouraged the governor's faith. Unbelief always robs us of God's blessings. "I will shake the heavens and the earth," God said. "Don't be afraid of these kingdoms. I will overthrow them and destroy them. As for you, Zerubbabel, you are as a signet, a very precious jewel, to Me. I have chosen you — don't give up." How this message must have encouraged the governor and strengthened his faith.

Zerubbabel was an ancestor of Jesus Christ; his name is listed in the genealogies (see Matt. 1:12 and Luke 3:27). Zerubbabel is an OT type or illustration of Christ. Here Christ is seen as God's chosen signet, His precious seal. A signet speaks of authority and honor. God gave Zerubbabel authority to finish the temple; God gave His Son authority to save the lost and build His temple, the church (John 17:1-3).

What work is it God has called you to do before Christ returns? Have you started it but not finished it? Are you discouraged? Then beware of these sins that hinder the work of the Lord: putting self ahead of God; looking back instead of ahead; unconfessed sin; unbelief. But notice the wonderful promises God gives us: "I am with you" (1:13); "Fear not" (2:5); "I will bless you" (2:19); "I have chosen you" (2:23). Claim the promise of Phil. 1:6 and rise up and do the work of the Lord!

# ZECHARIAH

## *A Suggested Outline of Zechariah*

Introduction: A call to repentance — 1:1-6 (November, 520 B.C.)

I. Eight Visions of Encouragement (1:7–6:15) (Feb. 24, 520)

    A. The rider (1:7-17) — God has not forgotten Jerusalem

    B. The craftsmen (1:18-21) — God will destroy her enemies

    C. The surveyor (2:1-13) — Jerusalem will be restored

    D. Joshua the high priest (3:1-10) — A cleansed nation

    E. The candlestick (4:1-14) — God's power enables them

    F. The flying roll (5:1-4) — Sin will be judged in the land

    G. The woman (5:5-11) — Wickedness carried to Babylon

    H. The war chariots (6:1-8) — God controls the nations

    Crowning the Priest-King (6:9-15) — The climax of God's plan will be the crowning of Jesus Christ as Priest-King. Israel never had a priest-king, only kings and priests. This can only be a picture of Jesus Christ.

Interlude: Questions about the fasts (7–8) (Dec. 4, 518)

II. Two Oracles of Enlightenment (9–14)

    A. The first oracle (9–11)

        1. Conquest of Alexander the Great (9:1-8)

           Coming of Messiah (9:9)

        2. Victories of the Maccabees (9:11-17)

           Coming of Messiah (10)

        3. Conquest of Rome (11:1-9)

           Coming of Messiah (11:10-14)

           Coming of Antichrist (11:15-17)

    B. The second oracle (12–14)

        1. Israel in the Tribulation (12:1-9)

           Return of Christ (12:10–13:9)

        2. Battle of Armageddon (14:1-3)

           Return of Christ (14:4-7)

        3. Establishment of the Kingdom (14:8-21)

# Introductory Notes to Zechariah

## I. The Writer

Zechariah ministered with Haggai during the difficult days when 50,000 Jews had returned to Palestine to reestablish their city and their temple worship. The remnant went back in 536 B.C. and laid the foundations for the temple in 535, but opposition arose and the work stopped. In 520, the Lord raised up Haggai and Zechariah to stir up the leaders and the people, and in 525 they finished the work. Zechariah was both a prophet and a priest (see Neh. 12:4, 16), and from Zech. 2:4 we discover that he was a young man. His name means "Jehovah remembers." His father's name means "Jehovah blesses," and his grandfather's name means "His time." Put them together and you have "Jehovah remembers to bless in His time."

## II. Theme

This book ranks next to Daniel as an OT unveiling of God's plan for the Jews. The city of Jerusalem is mentioned over forty times in Zechariah. In Zech. 1:14-17 you have the key verses of the book: God is jealous for Jerusalem; He will punish the heathen for what they did to His city; and He will one day restore the city in glory and peace. The fact that God has chosen Jerusalem in His grace is often mentioned in this book (1:17; 2:12; 3:2). He will have mercy on the city (1:12) and will one day dwell in the city (8:3, 8).

## III. Interpretation

As with most OT prophecy, we must distinguish between the near and the distant meanings of what Zechariah says. In one verse he will be describing the fall of Jerusalem under the Romans, and in the next verse he will picture the coming of Messiah to reign. Zechariah's favorite name for God is "Lord of Hosts" — the Lord of the armies. He sees the Lord coming to defeat Israel's enemies and establish Jerusalem in peace and glory. To interpret these magnificent prophecies as referring to the church today is to rob this book of meaning and power. Certainly there are spiritual applications for all ages, but the basic interpretation must be for the Jewish nation and Jerusalem.

## IV. The Book

As you will see from the suggested outline, the book is divided into three parts. In chapters 1–6, the prophet describes eight visions, all of which summarize the message of the book: Jerusalem shall be delivered, cleansed, and reestablished in peace and prosperity. The section closes with the crowning of Joshua as king-priest, certainly a picture of Jesus Christ.

Chapters 7–8 are the record of a visit from some Jews to ask about their fasts in commemoration of the fall of Jerusalem. This fast was in the fifth month (2 Kings 25:8; Jer. 52:12). There is a question. If Jerusalem is going to be rebuilt, why continue the fast? Zechariah replies that their fasting ought to be from the heart and not from the calendar, and he promises that in the glorified city, their fasts will be turned into feasts.

The final section (9–14) is a description of Jerusalem and God's victory over the Gentile nations. In 9–11 we have the first "burden," and in 12–14 the second. As you can see from the outline, Zechariah deals with the invasion of Alexander the Great, the time of the Maccabees (Jewish patriots who delivered Israel from bondage for a brief time), and even the fall of Jerusalem under the Romans. Zechariah also leaps to the "latter days" to show us the Battle of Armageddon, the return of Christ to earth, and the establishing of the kingdom.

## IV. Christ

Zechariah shows us Jesus Christ in many aspects of His ministry: the King (9:9; Matt. 21:4-5); the Stone (3:9; 10:4; Rom. 9:31-33); the Slave sold for thirty pieces of silver (11:12; Matt. 27:3-10); the smitten Shepherd (13:7; Matt. 26:31); the Branch (3:8, 6:12; see Isa. 4:2, 11:1; Jer. 23:5, 33:15); the glorious Ruler (14:1-4, 9, 16-17).

# ZECHARIAH

The city of Jerusalem is frequently in the news these days, and people are asking, "What is the future of this ancient city? Can the Jews hold Jerusalem? Will it be attacked again?" The answers to these and many more questions are found in the Book of Zechariah. The city of Jerusalem is mentioned forty-two times in this book. In 1:12-17, God makes it clear that He is in control of the destiny of the city: "I will have mercy. I am jealous for Jerusalem. My house shall be built. The Lord shall yet comfort Zion and shall yet choose Jerusalem."

Zechariah prophesied at a time when Jerusalem was still in ruins. In 586 the Babylonians had destroyed the city and had taken the people captive to Babylon. In 536, after the fall of Babylon, Cyrus permitted a remnant of the Jews to return to their land, and in 535 they laid the foundation for the temple. But the work stopped, and it was not until 520 that the Jews again began to rebuild God's house. This was under the preaching of Haggai and Zechariah. But Zechariah did not see a weak nation in a ruined city; he looked down the centuries and saw the future of the city and the coming of Jerusalem's King, the Messiah. He knew the temple would be rebuilt (1:16; 4:9; 6:12-14; 8:9). Trace in Zechariah the great events related to the city of Jerusalem.

## I. Protected by the Lord (9:8)

In 9:1-8, the prophet describes the conquest of Alexander the Great, the Greek general. History tells us that Alexander destroyed many cities, but not Jerusalem. He threatened the city but never carried out his threats. Before the general arrived, the Jewish high priest had a dream which he felt was from God, and in the dream he was told to dress in his robes and meet Alexander outside the city. With him went the priests in their white robes. The scene dazzled Alexander. In fact, he claimed that he too had dreamed of this very scene. Alexander entered Jerusalem peacefully and never harmed the people or the city in any way.

## II. Visited by the Messiah (9:9)

Perhaps Zechariah saw in Alexander's visit a small foregleam of the coming of Jesus Christ to the holy city, for in the very next verse (9:9) he predicts Christ's arrival in Jerusalem. This was fulfilled on

"Palm Sunday" when Jesus rode into the city (Matt. 21:4-5; John 12:12-16). Alexander came for war; Jesus came with peace. How did they treat Him? Zechariah 13:7 tells us He was to be arrested (Matt. 26:31) and smitten. He was sold for the price of a slave (Zech. 11:12; Matt. 27:3-10). The result: He was wounded in the house of His friends (Zech. 13:6) and pierced on the cross (Zech. 12:10). What a tragedy that the "City of Peace" should reject her "Prince of Peace" and crucify Him.

### III. Destroyed by Rome (11:1-14)

The entire section is a graphic picture of the last days of Jerusalem and her destruction by the Roman armies, announced 600 years before it occurred. Zechariah sees the land spoiled; he hears the howling of the people. What caused this tragedy? The unfaithfulness of the rulers (shepherds). The religious leaders of the people rejected the truth and permitted their own Messiah to be crucified. Israel had been "God's people, the sheep of His pasture," but now they were a "flock of slaughter" (vv. 4, 7), destined to be slaughtered by Rome. Zechariah here pictures the Messiah as He uses the two staves of the shepherd (Ps. 23:4), one called *Grace* (Beauty) and the other *Union* (Bands). When Israel sold her Messiah (v. 12), then God's day of grace was about to come to an end for the nation. No longer was she united in the Lord; the nation would have to be broken. In A.D. 70 Rome invaded Israel and Jerusalem was destroyed. See Matt. 23:37-39.

### IV. Protected by Antichrist (11:15-17)

The flock of Israel rejected their true Shepherd and smote Him (13:7), but they accepted the false shepherd, the "idol shepherd"—Antichrist. Jesus predicted this in John 5:43. Daniel 9:27 tells us that after the church has been raptured, the leader of Federated Europe (the ten kingdoms of Dan. 7:7-8) will make a covenant with the Jews to protect them for seven years. Jerusalem will have three and a half years of peace, a false peace that will be the prelude to three and a half years of awful tribulation. During those first three and a half years, the two witnesses of Rev. 11:1ff will be giving God's message; and Rev. 11:4 relates them to the two olive trees of Zech. 4. In Zechariah's day, the two olive trees represented Joshua the high priest and Zerubbabel the governor, through whom the Spirit was working. But the final application is to the two witnesses in the last days.

## V. Attacked by the Gentiles (12:1-8; 14:1-3)

Jerusalem has gone through many attacks and desolations, but one more remains. During the Tribulation days (the last three and a half years), only one-third of the nation will survive to enter the kingdom (Zech. 13:8-9). Note the repetition of "in that day" at least thirteen times in Zech. 12–14, referring to the Day of the Lord. In 12:1-8 and 14:1-2, we see all the Gentile nations gathered together against Jerusalem. The Antichrist has moved into Jerusalem, broken his covenant with the Jews, and made the temple his headquarters for worldwide worship. See 2 Thes. 2 and Rev. 13. During the last half of the Tribulation, the kings of the earth will begin to assemble for that great final battle, the Battle of Armageddon (Rev. 16:12-16; 19:19-21). Note in Zech. 14:1-2 that Jerusalem does suffer terribly in this battle before the Lord returns to deliver her. Some teachers refer this passage to the Battle of Gog and Magog, Ezek. 38–39, but this does not seem consistent. Gog and Magog is in the middle of the Tribulation. The battle in Zech. 14, like Armageddon, involves all Gentile nations. Furthermore, Christ does not return after the Battle of Gog and Magog to deliver Jerusalem, as He does here in Zech. 14:4ff.

## VI. Delivered by Jesus Christ (12:9–14:11)

Just when the battle is at its worst, Jesus will return to the Mount of Olives (14:4). This will fulfill the promise of Acts 1:11-12. The glory had departed from Olivet (Ezek. 11:22-23) and will return from Olivet (Ezek. 43:2). An earthquake will change the topography of the area. See Micah 1:4, Nahum 1:5, and note Rev. 16:18-19. This change will undoubtedly make possible the new landscape required by Ezekiel's magnificent temple (Ezek. 40–48), since the present arrangement would make so large a structure impossible. The newly formed valley will also make a way to escape for the people in Jerusalem, but the final victory will be Christ's (Rev. 19:11-21).

## VII. Cleansed and Glorified by the Lord (12:10–13:1; 14:9-21)

The nation will look upon the Pierced One (12:10; John 19:37; Rev. 1:7) and will repent of her sins and mourn. God will open His gracious fountain and cleanse them of their sins. Note the specific groups of people who will repent (12:12-14): David (royalty), Nathan (the prophets), Levi (the priests). Throughout Israel's history, it has been the prophets, priests, and kings who often led the people astray.

The glorious temple will be established by the Branch (6:12-13), and Christ the King-Priest shall reign in majesty and peace. "Jerusalem shall be safely inhabited" (14:11) for the first time in history. The glorious living waters will flow out to heal the land (14:8 and Ezek. 47:1ff). The Gentile nations will worship at Jerusalem (14:16ff), and holiness will characterize the city that Zeph. 3:1 calls "filthy." The cleansing of Zech. 3 will be a reality, and there will be peace in the world. "Pray for the peace of Jerusalem" (Ps. 122:6). For when Jerusalem has peace, there will be peace among all nations.

# MALACHI

We know very little about this next to the last of the OT prophets (John the Baptist was the last—Mal. 3:1 and 4:5-6 with Matt. 11:10-15, Mark 1:2, and Luke 1:17). He ministered to the restored Jewish nation about 400 years before Christ. The sins described in this book are found in Neh. 13:10-30. Malachi directs his first message to the priests, and then he turns to the people collectively—"Like people, like priest." As the prophet delivers God's Word, the people respond by arguing. Note the repeated "Wherein?" (1:2, 6-7; 2:17; 3:7-8, 13). It is a dangerous thing when people argue with God and try to defend their sinful ways.

Malachi points out the terrible sins of the people and the priests.

## I. They Doubted His Love (1:1-5)

"I have loved you," God says to His people. "Oh?" they respond. "Wherein have You loved us? Prove it." Doubting God's love is the beginning of unbelief and disobedience. Eve doubted God's love and ate of the forbidden tree; she thought God was holding out on her. Satan wants us to feel neglected by God. "Look at your difficult circumstances," he said to the Jewish remnant. "Where are the crops? Why doesn't God take care of you?"

God proves His love to His people in two ways: (1) He graciously chose Jacob, their father, and rejected Esau, who in many ways was a much better man; and (2) He judged the Edomites (Esau's descendants) and gave to Israel the best of the lands. He promised Israel a land flowing with milk and honey, but, alas, their sins polluted the land. Even then, he graciously restored them to their land and delivered them from captivity.

## II. They Despised His Name (1:6-14)

Now God turns to the priests, who should have been the spiritual leaders of the land. The priests were not giving honor to God's name; they were taking the best for themselves. They did not value the spiritual privileges God gave them: serving at the altar, burning the incense, and eating the dedicated showbread. And they did not bring their best for the sacrifices: they brought the poorest of the animals (cf. Deut. 15:21). God gave them His very best, and He asked for their best in return, but they would not obey Him.

Verse 10 ought to read: "Who is there spiritual enough to shut the temple doors and put an end to this hypocrisy?" God would rather see the temple closed than to have the people and the priests "playing at religion" and keeping the best for themselves. The priests would not even accept a sacrifice until they had first gotten their share. It was this kind of sin that brought defeat to Israel back in Eli's day (1 Sam. 2:12-17 and 4:1-18). Verse 11 states that the "heathen Gentiles" were offering better sacrifices to the Lord than were His own people. It is too bad when unsaved people sacrifice more for their religion than do those of us who truly know the Lord.

We are priests through Christ, and we too are to bring "spiritual sacrifices" to Him (1 Peter 2:5). What are these sacrifices? Our bodies (Rom. 12:1-2); our offerings (Phil. 4:14-18); praise (Heb. 13:15); good works (Heb. 13:16); souls we have won to Christ (Rom. 15:16). Are we bringing Him our best — or only what is convenient for us?

## III. They Defiled His Covenant (2:1-17)

It was no light thing to be a priest, for this was a gracious gift of God through His covenant with Levi. Verses 5-7 describe the ideal priest: he fears the Lord and obeys Him; he receives the Word and teaches it; he lives what he teaches; he seeks to turn others from sin. But the priests in Malachi's day actually led people astray (2:8) and defiled the holy covenant.

What would God do to them? "I will curse your blessings." This ties in with 3:9 and the lack of tithes and offerings. God cursed the crops; the people were poor; they did not bring the offerings to the priests; therefore the priests went hungry. In sinning against God's covenant they were only hurting themselves. But vv. 10-16 point out another terrible sin of the priests: they divorced their Jewish wives and married heathen women. They dealt treacherously against the women and their families; see Ex. 34:10-17, Ezra 9:1-4, Neh. 13:23-31. All their weeping at the altar (2:13) could not change things; they had to put away their sins. Read v. 15 like this: "Did not the Lord make husband and wife one? Why? That you might bring forth a godly family." Actually, the nation's looseness about divorce was endangering the promise of the Seed, Christ. God hates divorce; it is the breaking of the covenant between husband and wife and between them and God.

## IV. They Disobeyed His Word (3:1-15)

In 2:17 the people had scornfully asked, "Will God punish us for our sins? Does He really care?" God answers them by promising to send His messenger (John the Baptist) who would announce the Messenger of the covenant (Jesus Christ). Jesus did come into the temple and expose its sins and purify its courts. In His ministry He revealed the sins of the religious leaders, so much so that they finally crucified Him. Of course, there is a future application here when the Day of the Lord refines Israel and separates the true from the false. Why does the Lord not simply do away with His rebellious people? Verse 6 is the answer: He changes not and must be true to His promises (Lam. 3:22).

The people had disobeyed God by robbing Him of tithes and offerings. Actually, when God's people are not faithful in their giving, they not only rob God, but they also rob themselves. God had shut off the rain and spoiled the crops because of their selfishness. Tithing, of course, is not "making a bargain with God"; but God does promise to bless and care for those who are faithful in their stewardship (Phil. 4:10-19). Certainly God is not bankrupt; He wants our tithes and offerings as expressions of our faith and love. When a believer's love for Christ grows cold, it usually shows up in the area of stewardship. If every church member would bring the Lord His due (10 percent of the income, the tithe), and then add offerings (as an expression of gratitude), our local churches would have more than enough for their ministries. And they would be able to share generously with the many other good ministries that deserve support.

Malachi closes his message with some wonderful promises to the faithful (3:16–4:6). There was that faithful remnant in this day who did not forsake God's house, but who met together for mutual blessing (3:16-18; see Heb. 10:25). "They are My jewels," says the Lord. What a beautiful picture of the faithful believer. Jewels are precious, and we are precious in His sight. He purchased us with His blood. He is polishing us with trials and testings; and one day in glory we shall shine in beauty and splendor.

Christ is pictured as the Sun of Righteousness. To the church, He is the "Bright and Morning Star" (Rev. 22:16; 2:28), for He will appear when the hour is darkest to take His church home. But to Israel, He is the Sun, bringing the "Day of the Lord," a day that will mean burning to the lost, but healing to saved Jews and Gentiles. "Elijah" in 4:5-6 refers to John the Baptist (Matt. 17:10-13; Mark 9:11-13), but it has a reference also to one of the two witnesses spoken of in Rev. 11. The last word in our English OT is "curse." At the end of the NT we read, "And there shall be no more curse" (Rev. 22:3). The difference? Jesus Christ.